THE ENCYCLOPEDIA OF THE
MOTORCAR

THE ENCYCLOPEDIA OF THE
MOTORCAR

General Editor: Phil Drackett

Foreword by Dr Ferry Porsche

Crown Publishers Inc.
New York

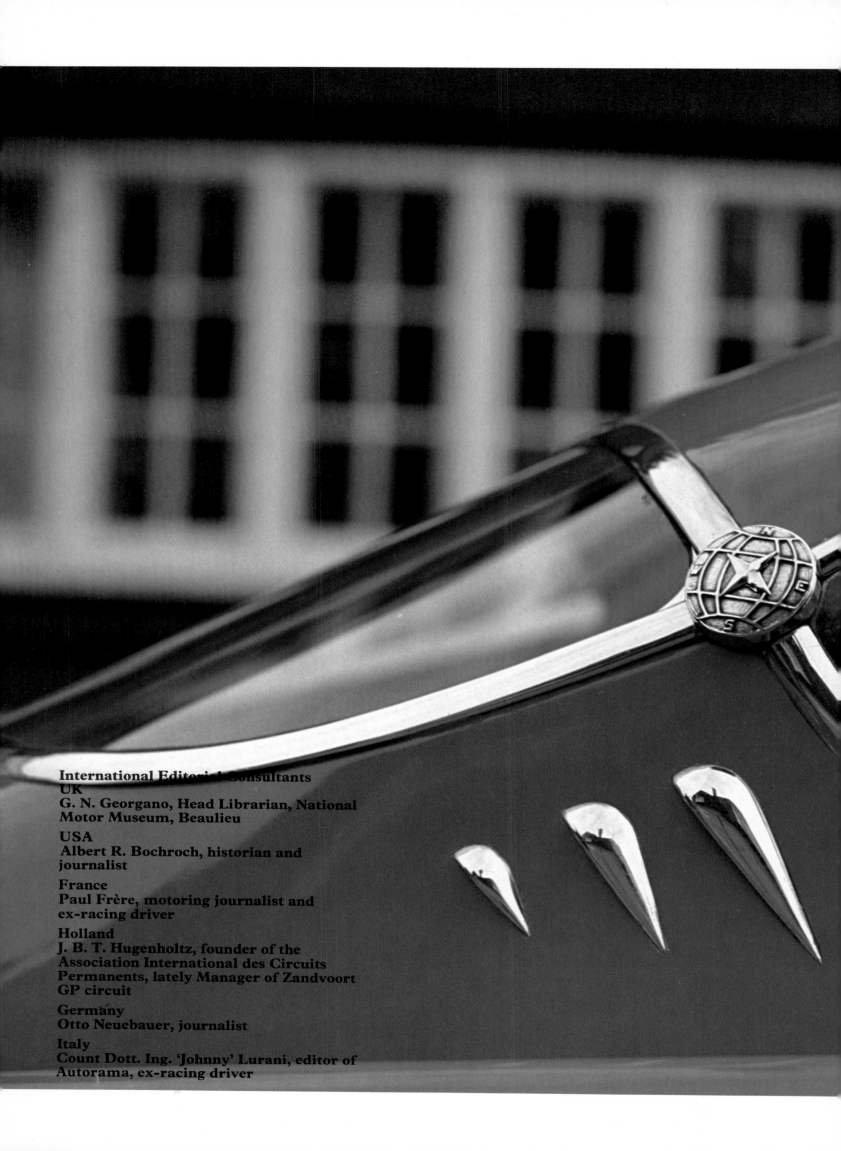

International Editorial Consultants

UK
G. N. Georgano, Head Librarian, National
Motor Museum, Beaulieu

USA
Albert R. Bochroch, historian and
journalist

France
Paul Frère, motoring journalist and
ex-racing driver

Holland
J. B. T. Hugenholtz, founder of the
Association International des Circuits
Permanents, lately Manager of Zandvoort
GP circuit

Germany
Otto Neuebauer, journalist

Italy
Count Dott. Ing. 'Johnny' Lurani, editor of
Autorama, ex-racing driver

CONTENTS

First published in the United States of
America by Crown Publishers Inc.,
One Park Avenue, New York, NY 10016

© 1979 Octopus Books Limited

Library of Congress Cataloging in Publication Data
  Main entry under title:

  Encyclopedia of the motorcar.

    1. Automobiles—Dictionaries.   I. Drackett, Phil.
II. Georgano, G. N.
TL9.E525 1979   629.22′22   79–9901
  ISBN 0–517–53833–4

Produced by Mandarin Publishers Ltd
22a Westlands Road, Quarry Bay
Hong Kong

Printed in Hong Kong

FOREWORD

Since the invention of the wheel, no technical innovation has influenced our lives in such a lasting or revolutionary manner as the motorcar. It is the most successful means of individual transport yet invented – and likely to remain so judging by present-day knowledge. The car has become so much a part of our daily life that youngsters today are more likely to recognise the name of a motorcar rather than, say, the breed of a dog or species of a tree.

I am proud of the contribution my father and I were able to make to the progress of automotive technology, an advance that today benefits millions of motorists. I also welcome this book, covering the motorcar in all its aspects, from the all-important economics of the industry to the intricacies of engineering, as well as the challenge of motor racing. Even in this age of computer-controlled testing and advanced research techniques, many famous manufacturers continue to rely on motor racing and rallying as a motivator and proving ground. For racing and rallying, while not essential to technical progress, have more often than not been found to lead to speedier and more practical solutions of important technical problems.

Today, we and all other automobile engineers are trying to find answers to tomorrow's questions. However, the simplest question to answer is that there will be cars tomorrow!

Dr. Ing. h. c. Ferdinand Porsche

THE HISTORY OF THE MOTOR INDUSTRY

There are several early designs for self-propelled vehicles, but the first to work is Cugnot's steam-driven tricycle. Daimler and Benz pioneer the first motorcar, France develops it. In the US cars are built by the Duryea brothers, Olds and Ford. The first British car is produced by Lanchester. The first motor races are held in France and the USA.

he first recorded design for a self-propelled vehicle is that of Guido da Vigevano in 1335, which provided for sails to be driven by the wind, in turn communicating their power to gear wheels and thence to the road wheels. It was never built, although a drawing exists. The vehicle was described as a fighting car or tank, and another Italian, Valturio, produced a similar design for a wind-driven tank which looks equally impractical as the sails are too small to produce enough power to turn the wheels.

Leonardo da Vinci himself, born in 1452, designed a horseless carriage – as he did a submarine and many other machines – and a working clockwork model of it does exist, though there is no record that the real thing was ever made. It was a tricycle with tiller steering to a single front wheel and it incorporated a differential, normally credited to much later inventors.

None of these very early machines appears actually to have been made or to have moved under its own power, but they crop up at intervals in history. After the Italian ones the next is credited to a Jesuit priest, Father Ferdinand Verbiest, who is said to have con-

structed a steam-driven vehicle for the Emperor Chien Lung of China about 1678. Some of his other mechanical devices exist in a museum, but there is no record of the car.

Credit for the first vehicle to move under its own power is given to Nicholas Joseph Cugnot, in 1769, but many other abortive attempts are on record. There is an Albrecht Dürer woodcut of a self-propelled carriage built for the Emperor Maximilian in 1510, but no indication of how it works, and in 1649 a Herr Hautsch of Nuremberg produced his *Triumphwagen*, driven by clockwork, with fancy decoration all over its coachwork and a dragon or sea-horse on the front. It was sold to the Crown Prince of Sweden.

Still in the very early days the Frenchman Denis Papin made a model of a steam carriage in 1698, but admitted that it was not likely to function if scaled up to a large enough size to drive a carriage. Sir Isaac Newton also mentioned the idea of a small boiler on wheels which anticipated the jet aircraft by pushing itself along by means of a jet of steam shooting out at the back. Whether it ever did so is questionable.

There were other devices which added little to man's knowledge of how to propel a carriage without horses. Prince Maurice of Nassau commissioned one Simon Stevin to construct a sand yacht in 1600. A

Frenchman, du Quet, was one of the first to toy with the idea of power-driven mechanical legs instead of wheels, and he used a form of windmill to motivate the legs. Then a Swiss, the Reverend J. H. Genevois, went a step further, using the windmill to wind up a clock spring which in turn motivated wheels, instead of legs.

It was not until two Englishmen, Thomas Newcomen and Thomas Savery, devised a steam engine in 1705, and James Watt improved it, that a sensible means of traction was available. Cugnot took advantage of it. He is sometimes called a Swiss but was a French artillery officer, born in Void, Lorraine, and the confusion arises because it was a Swiss who originally proposed the idea of a steam carriage to move artillery. Cugnot had such a device constructed by a M. Brezin.

We come to fairly firm ground with Cugnot since his *fardier*, as it was called, is still in the *Conservatoire des Arts et Métiers*, in Paris – or, at least, a later reconstruction of it. It was a tricycle with an enormous boiler in front of the single forward wheel. It could carry four people but was difficult to steer because of the great weight ahead of the wheel, and on its first outing it knocked down a wall. It was also said that unless a cannon was carried to counterbalance the weight of the boiler the gun carriage had a habit

Top: Cugnot's *fardier*, a steam tricycle.

Above left: Cowan's steam carriage of 1862, which cruised at 32 km/h (20 mph).

Above: Hancock's steam carriages, in service in London in the early 1830s.

Right: The *Zeylwagen* ('sail waggon'), a sand yacht in which Simon Stevin, who built the vehicle, conveyed Prince Maurice of Nassau, the great military leader in the war against the Spanish, along the sands from the Dutch port of Scheveningen to Petten in 1601.

Far right: A medley of steam vehicles in Whitechapel Road, London, 1830.

of tilting over on to its nose.

Cugnot built a second version in 1770 which could haul 4 tonnes and run at just over 3·22 km/h (2 mph). Although it has been generally recognized as the first proven self-propelled vehicle it was not tremendously practical and led to no immediate successors.

Scaled-down model vehicles were made by Watt and others, notably a William Murdoch, of Redruth, in Cornwall, England, whose toy steam-driven vehicle, looking like a child's tricycle with an overhead beam, was tried out one dark night and ran away, terrorizing the local vicar in the process. This was in 1784, when Murdoch was working for Watt on mining engines, and his toy was powered by a miniature replica of a beam engine.

Two years later William Symington, of Edinburgh, Scotland, produced a model steam coach looking like a stage coach with half a locomotive attached behind. Symington, however, switched his attention to boats and built Britain's first steamboat, a 7·62-metre (25-ft) 5-tonne vessel, for a Scottish landowner, Patrick Miller, of Dalswinton, near Dumfries. The vessel was tried out on Loch Dalswinton on 14 October 1788, but Symington had been anticipated by the French Marquis Claude François Dorothée de Jouffroy d'Abbans, who had tried out his steamboat near Lyons in 1783.

Meanwhile, in the United States, in 1787, Oliver Evans had obtained licences to run steam wagons in Maryland. Some say he also had licences for Delaware. He does not seem to have built any wagons but he did produce a monster called *Orukter Amphibolos* by putting wheels on to a big dredger and making it an amphibian. This is generally regarded as having made the first American journey by horseless carriage. Nathan Read, of Massachusetts, built a model steam carriage in 1788, but not much detail is known, nor whether it ran.

Steam seemed to be accepted as the motive power by all those now thinking in terms of the horseless carriage, the biggest step forward being made by a Cornish mining engineer, Richard Trevithick, who began building models in 1796 and constructed a bare chassis with boiler and steam engine in 1801.

By 1803 he had a steam road coach, capable of carrying eight passengers and running at a speed of 19·32 km/h (12 mph).

When Trevithick was out with his cousin, Andrew Vivian, on a trial run the steam coach came to an abrupt halt near the town of Camborne. They ran it into a shed and went into the inn next door, forgetting to damp out the fire under the boiler. Carriage and shed were destroyed.

It seems likely that the destroyed machine was an early design, not the 'fast road coach' which was built by Felton in London and which ran successfully until it knocked down a fence. Like so many inventors, Trevithick died in poverty in 1833.

Others were left to develop the steam carriage, among them David Gordon, in 1824; Colonel Macerone, in 1833; and Walter Hancock, from 1826–36. Hancock ran a regular service in London between Paddington and the City at a claimed 33·81 km/h (21 mph). Another who played a prominent role in the story of steam was Sir Goldsworthy Gurney. He designed a steam drag in 1830 and the vehicle was completed about 1832.

The first horseless carriage disaster came when the boiler of John Scott Russell's coach exploded after a wheel had collapsed near Paisley, Scotland, on 29 July 1834, and five passengers were killed. The railway age was dawning and the Russell disaster made wonderful propaganda for the opponents of road vehicles, prominent among whom were certain railway interests. Road tolls went up, restrictive legislation came in and for many years the development of mechanical road vehicles was held up.

One pioneer who persevered was Thomas Rickett, of Buckingham, who designed a rather solid-looking three-wheel steam carriage in 1859 and sold a similar machine to the Earl of Caithness, who succeeded in driving it from Inverness to Borrowdale over the Ord of Caithness.

Cowan, of Greenwich, built the Yarrow and Hilditch carriage shown at the London Exhibition of 1862, using a narrow track. There was as yet no differential, in spite of Leonardo da Vinci's drawings nearly 400 years earlier. Drawings of Cowan's creation show something like an ancient fire engine

with a boiler, a smoke stack sticking up at one end and top-hatted passengers seated all round.

The Englishman Roberts had, in fact, designed and constructed a carriage using a differential in 1833, but others tried driving one wheel only or driving each rear wheel independently. Some used systems of clutches, pawls or ratchets.

At this time bursting boilers were always a threat but the Summers and Ogle coach, working at 113·2 kg (250 lb) pressure in spite of the danger, achieved 51·53 km/h (32 mph) with a full load of passengers.

Walter Hancock's coaches were well established in regular service and in the same period Sir George Dance was operating between Gloucester and Cheltenham, carrying 3,000 passengers in four months. His coaches weighed 1·5 tonnes and could do as much as 16 km/h (10 mph). He also produced a light steam drag, which was hitched in front of an open carriage in place of horses.

Another outstanding performance occurred in 1833, when a coach built by Hill, of Dartford, ran from London to Hastings and back, 206 km (about 128 miles) in all. Eight years earlier, it is said, a Doctor Church operated a massive steam coach carrying 50 people between London and Birmingham, but historians doubt that Church's vehicle ever got beyond the drawing board.

One well-substantiated achievement, however, was the first mechanically-propelled vehicle in the world to run on rubber tyres, a steam carriage built to the design of R. W. Thompson by Tennants, of Leith, Scotland, in 1867. These rubber tyres were solid, though Thompson had, in fact, patented the world's first pneumatic tyres in 1846. These were fitted to horse-drawn light carriages. A section of one of them, in the Motoring Library of London's Royal Automobile Club, shows a stitched leather outer cover with a number of tubes inside.

Thompson's invention was unknown to William Dunlop when he 're-invented' the pneumatic tyre for bicycles in 1888, and many histories and accounts still credit Dunlop with what is rightly Thompson's

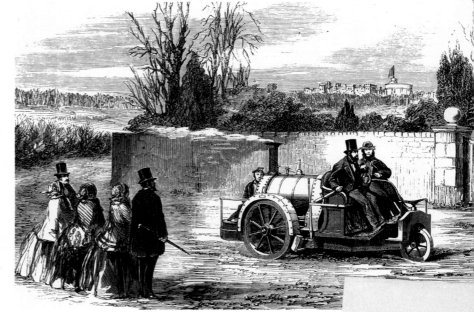

achievement.

At the steam carriage's peak no fewer than 10 companies were running coaches on scheduled routes in England. Not surprisingly this encouraged inventors in all sorts of weird and wonderful ideas. David Gordon, for example, experimented again with the 'walking legs' which had been tried so much earlier. Sir Goldsworthy Gurney also delved into this aspect of the matter, though his idea was the quite logical one that such legs could be used to assist a conventional wheeled vehicle in climbing hills. Hancock, one of the more ingenious designers, mounted his boilers not on the axle but above the springs, thus saving about one ton of unsprung weight.

Other important advances included the use of the differential and improvements in steering. As mentioned earlier, a Mr Roberts, of Manchester, England, is believed to be the first to incorporate a dif-

Left : Thompson's road steamer in Edinburgh, 1820. A contemporary newspaper report commented on the carriage's rubber tyres, which enabled it 'to pass over wet grass . . . with an incredible ease and lightness'.

Below left : A steam carriage of 1860, designed by Ricketts of the Castle Foundry, Buckingham. It carried three passengers and a firemen at an average 16 km/h (10 mph).

Below right : A 12-seater steam coach, *L'Obéissante*, built by the Frenchman Bollée in 1872–3. It weighed 4,500 kg (nearly 4½ tons).

Bottom, left to right : The Comte de Dion and Georges Bouton. Richard Dudgeon's steam car, 1857. This American vehicle was virtually a road locomotive. De Dion on a steam tricycle in 1887.

ferential, but later, in France, this was claimed to be the invention of the Marquis de Chasseloup Laubat, racing driver and world record breaker. The old steering system, which was still in general use, was to pivot the axle in the middle, carriage style, which worked at very slow speeds but was unstable at higher ones. In France a coach was run with each wheel on its own pivot (*L'Obéissante* of Amédée Bollée). This system was patented in England in 1818 by Rudolph Ackermann, a London printer, who had inherited the rights from the German George Lenkensperger, of Munich, and is universally known today as Ackermann steering.

This steering system made possible the higher speeds and manoeuvrability of all later cars and was certainly the biggest advance to date. By 1857 the last of the scheduled steam coaches had gone in England, but people had begun to build steam cars, some carrying up to eight passengers and of varying designs, some tricycles with a single front wheel and the fireman on a rear platform, as on Thomas Rickett's vehicle. Makers after that date included Yarrow and Hilditch, John Henry Knight, J. W. Boulton and Tangye. Later still came Catley and Ayres, J. L. Todd, Charles Randolph, Inshaw and Blackburn, and Loftus Perkins.

American makers of the day were Lee and Larned (1863), who built a steam fire-engine; John A. Reid; and, in 1867, Frank Curtis, of Newburyport, Massachusetts, who produced a steam buggy. In France

the company of Amédée Bollée by 1873 were producing steam carriages for private owners at Le Mans. They also made a chain-driven victoria, said to do about 40 km/h (25 mph). Léon Serpollet, a great steam pioneer, was producing tricycles with a flash boiler by the late 1880s which had a good power/weight ratio for their day.

The Comte de Dion, in France, was another contender for steam honours. The tall and stately aristocrat financed the tiny Georges Bouton in a project to make steam wagonettes, and enabled him to win the first motor race in which he was the only competitor in the class, on a course from Saint James in Paris to the bridge over the Seine at Neuilly, in his four-seater steam quadricycle. Bouton also won the next race between Neuilly and Versailles on a De Dion tricycle, beating a Serpollet steamer with a time of 30 minutes for the 20-km (12-mile) course.

In the 1890s White and Stanley, in the United States, were not yet in production, though they were experimenting with steam cars, but in England, France and Germany steam vehicles of various kinds were in production.

Internal combustion

Although steam was in the ascendancy the petrol-driven car was about to emerge and take over. Another fuel, gunpowder, had been tried as a propellant but was not controllable enough. The principle of moving a piston inside a cylinder began with the cannon in the 15th century, although the 'piston' in this case was the cannon ball, probably made of stone. One Robert Street described what appeared to be a piston engine in 1794, in England, fuelled by a mixture of some spirit, perhaps turpentine, and air, but there is no detailed drawing or record of how it was arranged.

A few years later, in 1804, in Switzerland, François Isaac de Rivaz, working quite independently of Street, produced a piston engine mounted on wheels, but his fuel was hydrogen gas, which is very combustible, as airship crews discovered to their cost much later on. The Swiss engine did not follow what we now regard as normal combustion principles; the explosion raised the piston instead of depressing it as in other applications, and its own weight provided the motive power as it fell again. De Rivaz used some form of electric ignition, while claims have been made that Street used hot-tube ignition, a method whereby a piece of tube projecting both inside and outside the cylinder is heated by a blow-pipe or other flame outside and ignites the explosive mixture inside.

History of the Motor Industry – early days

Gottlieb Daimler, who will appear later, is usually credited as the inventor of the hot-tube method, but like so many other facets of the internal combustion engine and the motorcar generally, for example Ackermann steering and the differential, it may well have been discovered, forgotten, then rediscovered later. Daimler used a platinum tube, as this was the only known metal at the time which would stand continuous heat, and with the hot-tube there was no question of timing, as with an electrical spark. The tube was kept hot continually and provided ignition at the appropriate time when a small portion of the gas-air mixture was trapped inside the open end of the tube inside the cylinder. The outer end of the tube was closed.

If Street or another inventor, Sir George Cayley, did use hot-tube ignition they were nearly 80 years ahead of their time, and Cayley certainly was in another respect, as he was building model aircraft 100 years before the Wright Brothers made the first flight in the United States. Curiously, for a man of such advanced ideas, he looked to the past for propulsion of one of his experimental engines and used gunpowder as his fuel.

The interim fuel between the death of steam – which later had a revival – and the arrival of petrol or gasolene was gas, first used in stationary engines. The Swiss, de Rivaz, was the true pioneer in this field, but even if his vehicle did move, which is uncertain, he did not continue development of his idea.

Two years before de Rivaz died in 1828 an Englishman named Samuel Brown performed a deed which should have made him famous but did not. Early in the morning of 27 May 1826 he succeeded in driving a car of his own design – powered by a crude form of combustion engine in which no actual explosion occurred, only a slow burning – up Shooters Hill, in south-east London, a feat which, contemporary accounts say, the machine accomplished with ease.

Unfortunately for Brown, steam was the fashion. Unable to produce a combustion engine that would drive a carriage as fast as steam, he dropped his idea and little more was heard of the automobile for many years.

Credit for the first practical gas engine, therefore, goes to a Frenchman, Etienne Lenoir, who in 1860 patented 'an engine dilated by the combustion of gas'. Lenoir is said to have built, in 1862, a horseless carriage of 1·5-hp which ran between Paris and Joinville. Some reports say his car ran 'several times' over the 9·66-km (6-mile) route but this cannot be confirmed. His 'car' was, in any case, a heavy wagon on which he had mounted one of his very large and heavy engines, which ran on coal gas. His engines were like a double acting steam engine in principle, with slide valves and exposed connecting rods.

In spite of the double-action principle Lenoir's engines were very inefficient and consumed 100 cubic feet of gas per horse-power. Thus a $\frac{1}{2}$-hp engine had a cylinder with a 5-inch bore and a 61-cm (24-inch) stroke. His car, which he called a 'break' (it can be translated as 'station wagon') was said to have taken three hours for the 9·66-km (6-mile) journey with the engine turning at only 100 rpm.

Some contemporary reports say that Lenoir claimed his engine could run on liquid fuel as well as coal gas, and that the break which made the Joinville runs used benzine with a surface carburettor. Certainly drawings show that he used electric ignition from a coil. This is a crucial point, for if he did use benzine his was the first petrol-driven car. The term 'petrol' was first used commercially in 1893

when motor spirit under the brand name of Standard was marketed by the British importers Carless, Capel and Leonard at 11d a gallon, but there is a reference to the word in a letter written by Eugen Langen in 1876, and the reference is clearly to motor spirit. The word is a shortened popular form of the term petroleum spirit and is derived from the two Latin words *petra* (rock) and *oleum* (oil). Benzine, which many people assume must come from the name of the pioneer Karl Benz, was in fact named after a chemistry professor at Berlin University who first produced it. The material had been known for 50 years before much use was made of it. For many years crude oil was refined only for certain products such as lamp oil, and the part which could have made motor fuel was discarded. The arrival of the motorcar changed all that.

After Lenoir, who died in poverty in 1900, the next step came from Alphonse Beau de Rochas, who worked out the four-stroke cycle – now known as the Otto cycle – of induction, compression, power, and exhaust strokes. He realized that the fault in Lenoir's system was that the charge was not compressed before firing. Rejecting the separate pumps which other engineers were working on, he arrived at the idea of using the first stroke of the piston to draw in the mixture, the next to compress it with both valves closed, the third to provide power by explosion – or, more accurately, burning of the mixture – and the fourth for exhausting the burnt gases to the atmosphere. This was in 1862.

The world was now on the verge of the arrival of the horseless carriage, but in Britain its development was crucially affected by the growing power of the railways, and Parliament was persuaded in 1865 to pass an act which restricted the use of mechanical road vehicles so severely that only slow traction engines could reasonably operate. There was a 2 mph speed limit in towns, and 4 mph one in the country, and a 'road locomotive' had to have a crew of three, one walking in front with a red flag.

Other restrictions, financial ones, were imposed by the owners of the Turnpike Roads. On the Liverpool–Preston road, for example, a four-horse coach paid four shillings toll, but a steam coach 12 times as much. Such moves held up the development of mechanically-propelled vehicles in England and,

Top : Daimler's 1885 wooden motorcycle in the Bad Cannstatt workshop where he built it.

Above left : Gottlieb Daimler.

Above centre : Karl Benz.

Above right : Charles Jarrott in a Léon Bollée tricar.

Right : A drawing of Marcus's car.

the state of the roads had the same effect slightly later in the United States. The other factor militating against the steam engine was its poor power-to-weight ratio, which called for some 440 lb (200 kg) per horse-power. It also took a long time to raise steam from cold.

Chronologically the next step after Lenoir came from Siegfried Marcus (Markus), of Mecklenburg, who constructed his first car in 1868 and showed one at the Vienna Exhibition of 1873. His first vehicle was intended as a mobile testbed for his single-cylinder engine rather than as a horseless carriage as such, and had no clutch. It was started by jacking the wheels up and spinning them, then making a more or less flying start with the engine running as the wheels were dropped back to earth.

His slightly later car, the *Strassenwagen*, which still exists in the Vienna Technical Museum, is a crude wooden-wheeled machine with iron-shod wheels and wooden blocks pressing on the rims for braking. The amidships engine produced about ¾ hp at 500 rpm and used magneto ignition. It had both a differential and a clutch and the car can still be driven under its own power. Marcus is believed to have built four cars, although his position in auto-

mobile history is disputed by some. One was broken up, one is said to have gone to Holland and another to the United States, while the fourth is the Vienna exhibit.

Nikolaus Otto worked for a company making gas engines at Dutz, in Germany, called Otto and Langen (the petrol man already mentioned). In 1876, three years after Marcus' Vienna exhibit, he patented what we still call the Otto cycle for the four-stroke engine, although it had already been discovered by Beau de Rochas. Rochas had not been specific enough in his description, which enabled Otto to take out his patent. Yet when Daimler and Benz began making engines later, in the 1880s, and Otto brought an action against French companies making their engines on the grounds that they infringed his patent, they successfully pleaded that de Rochas had anticipated Otto. This had a profound effect on the development of the automobile, as all manufacturers were now free to use the four-stroke principle.

The question of who made the first car becomes crucial in the Eighties. Cugnot rules undisputed as the man who, in 1769, made the first vehicle move under its own power. Lenoir and Marcus made

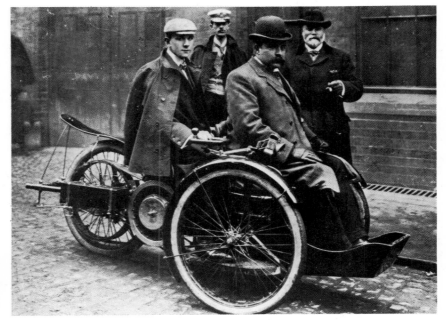

vehicles that moved but then did not persist with their manufacture and development. Gottlieb Daimler patented the first light high-speed engine in 1883. He is universally reported to have made his first vehicle in 1886, and Karl Benz is usually credited with making his first tricycle in 1885. Yet the official history issued by the modern Mercedes company, whose proper title is Daimler-Benz, credits Daimler with his 1886 invention but quotes the date 29 January 1886 as that when Benz Patent DRP 37435 'paved the way for the motor vehicle as a complete unit'. This may be politically motivated, to keep everyone happy, but Benz is generally called 'Father of the Motor Car' and supposed to have been one year ahead.

There is another contender, or to be more accurate two other contenders. Some years ago a Danish car called a Hammel appeared in England for the London–Brighton run, commemorating the emancipation of the motorist and open to cars made before 1904. The Hammel was said to have been made in 1884, and so would have pre-dated both the Germans. The Danes are convinced of this, but most historians nowadays feel that the true date of the

Above left : Daimler in his 1886 car.

Above right : Benz (in light suit) at a family picnic with one of his early vehicles, a single-cylinder car of 1895.

Right : The first Panhard et Levassor car. It used a mid-mounted Daimler engine.

Below left : Daimler's pass to the 1893 Columbia Exhibition, Chicago.

Below right : Publicity for Lawson's Great Horseless Carriage Company, 1896. The vehicle advertised is a 2-cylinder, 6-hp Daimler (Lawson had bought the Daimler rights for Britain), offered to 'the nobility and gentry'.

Hammel vehicle is perhaps 10 years later.

The other contender is the already-mentioned François Isaac de Rivaz. In 1787 he made a steam carriage which ran and is regarded by Swiss automotive historians as the first man to have made a car driven by 'explosive power'. He took his cue from an inventor, Alessandro Volta, who produced a pistol fired not by powder but by gas sparked by electricity. Swiss sources say 'the first car' was born when de Rivaz produced his car powered by the engine described earlier, and there is a modern model of it in the transport museum at Lucerne, in Switzerland. In 1807 the French government granted de Rivas a patent which can be seen in the archives of the Canton of Vallais, and which proves his claim.

There is another reconstructed model in the Milan Science Museum. De Rivaz went on to make another vehicle, 'the great mechanical carriage', which was 6 m (20 ft) long and weighed 950 kg (2,095 lb), with wheels 2 m (6 ft 6 in.) in diameter, which moved with an explosion every four seconds at a speed of 3 km/h (1·87 mph), according to Swiss sources, and was demonstrated on 18 October 1813 on the Simplon road. After a later demonstration, in 1825, it was said that the engine was dismantled and the carriage left in a barn at Vevey, from whence it eventually disappeared.

This machine, judging from the models, could not carry anyone but simply propelled itself, and so de Rivaz cannot really challenge Daimler or Benz as the first car-maker. In the years before 1904 there were 29 different Swiss car-constructors, and yet there is only one small specialist maker in that country today. There were also makers in Italy, Spain and Russia, as well as the better-known ones in France, England, Germany and the United States.

To keep a chronological order among the great names, the family Bollée – who were building successful steam carriages at Le Mans by 1873, beginning with the celebrated *L'Obéissante* (The Obedient One), made by Amédée Bollée and run with success – must come in here. A novelty was a separate engine for each rear wheel so that no differential was needed. Bollée also produced a smaller and equally successful steam machine, *La Mancelle* (1878), which had a maximum speed of 42 km/h (26·25 mph), and then, in 1881, *La Rapide*, which could do 60 km/h (37·5 mph). Amédée Bollée Jnr, the son, produced his first car, a two-seater steamer, in 1885.

By 1896 Bollée had in production a practical two-seater, petrol-engined, four-wheel car with such advanced features as a steering wheel instead of a tiller. He drove one in the Paris–Marseilles race of 1896. The company went on to make curious tricycles with a horizontal engine and belt-drive, and Léon Bollée assisted the American, Wilbur Wright, in designing an engine for his flying machine. Léon died in 1913, but many of the tricycles with the passenger in front of the driver, tandem-style, still run in old car events.

Another name to mark a milestone was that of the Frenchman, Ravel, who used liquid oil fuel in 1868 in a steam tricycle, and drove it in Paris in 1870. The machine was destroyed in the Franco-Prussian war, but Ravel did not return to the drawing board. One vehicle from this era is an American steam carriage called the Dudgeon – believed to survive still. It was a very basic machine consisting mainly of a boiler and cylinder on wheels.

Gottlieb Daimler, born 17 March 1834 in the Hollgasse in Schörndorf, Württemberg, and Karl Benz, born 25 November 1844 in Karlsruhe, were the most powerful influences upon automobile development in the pioneer years, although it is a

truism that the Germans invented the car and the French made it work. England was handicapped by restrictive laws and the United States by its vast size and lack of roads, and both countries were late developers in the automotive field.

Both Daimler and Benz began with the gas engine, which had been invented by two Italians Eugenio Barsanti and Felice Matteuchi long before in 1854. Others had experimented but the two Italians went their own way uninfluenced by other designers and demonstrated their two-cylinder free-piston engine in 1856 in Florence. Like so many others they did not persist and it was Lenoir, already noted, who made headway with his gas engine and first power-driven carriage. Daimler is known to have visited Lenoir in Paris, but decided that his engines were inefficient and too big for the power they produced. Even more to the point, they were so protected by patents that Daimler thought it best to go his own way.

Gottlieb Daimler was the second of four children of a middle-class family. His father, Johannes, was a master baker who had inherited the family business.

Gottlieb left school at 14, was apprenticed to a gunsmith called Hermann Reythal and learned about metals and how to temper them. He then moved to another gun-maker in Stuttgart, where the Daimler-Benz works is today. He moved on to the Werkzeug Maschinenfabrik and acquired a patron, Dr Ferdinand Steineis, who liked to help promising young men by sending them abroad for training and giving them financial help.

With such help Daimler moved on to the Grafenstadt Engineering Works, where he had a kind of technical scholarship, and then to the Stuttgart Polytechnic. Daimler was hot-tempered, hard-working, and liked music and singing. He went back for a second spell at Grafenstadt, during which he made his visit to Lenoir, and to England. He learned both French and English, and after several changes of job became friendly with Wilhelm Maybach, who became famous in automotive circles as Daimler's assistant.

Daimler stayed about three years in most jobs and finally found his niche at Otto and Langen's gas engine works at Deutz, where he did his most important work. Otto's engines at this time were about eight feet high, weighed nearly a ton and produced $\frac{1}{2}$ hp, and Daimler aimed at something better. He,

Otto and Maybach collaborated and in 1876 produced the 'Otto Silent Gas Engine', the world's first practical four-stroke. Daimler was not too pleased that it bore only Otto's name.

Daimler persuaded the company to buy exclusive manufacturing rights, at a reasonable price, in the American Brayton engine – which eliminated a possible competitor – and set about improving it. Then he fell out with Otto and on his return from a trip to Russia discovered moves afoot to get rid of him. He left, aged 48, and moved to Cannstatt, where Maybach joined him. They set out to design a small light engine which would run at much faster speeds than any other of the time, and on liquid fuel, to be independent of a gas supply.

Daimler's hot-tube ignition put firing speeds up from 150 to 1,000 rpm. His first powered vehicle was a crude wooden motor-cycle, ridden by his son Paul from Cannstatt to Unterturkheim and back on 10 November 1885. But the previous August Karl Benz had already driven his light tubular tricycle with a gas engine. The two men whose names are now linked in one of the world's most respected car companies worked only 60 miles apart in the Neckar valley, yet never met, one of the ironies of history.

Daimler first drove a boat with his new engine, but disguised it to look as if it were electric-powered because the public were less frightened of electricity. Then in 1886 he made his first car by putting an engine in a horseless carriage without shafts.

In fact he bought a second-hand carriage from a coachbuilder, saying it was a birthday present for his wife, then installed the engine. Daimler was showing off a splendid engine in a crude chassis while Benz had a more primitive engine in a better-designed chassis. Nevertheless the Daimler could carry four people at 10 mph, and when his old firm, Otto and Langen – in which he still had shares – turned down the offer of manufacturing rights he

set up on his own to make cars.

Benz, whose mother was a working widow, had not had the comfortable upbringing of his rival. His mother put him through university and he then set up on his own to build two-stroke engines, leaving his first job with a bridge-builder. He married in 1872 and just as Paul Daimler made the first motor-cycle ride so Frau Berta Benz made the first long car-run. She took off one night in 1888 in her husband's car, without his knowledge, and the story goes that she repaired a broken part by substituting her garter elastic but finished the run from Mannheim to Pforzheim of 100 km (62 miles) to visit her mother with the two boys, Eugen, 15, and Richard, 13, buying benzine from a chemist and getting a blacksmith to 'reline' the brakes with leather. On arrival she telegraphed her husband, who replied simply: 'Express driving chains back or I cannot leave for Munich Exhibition.'

Benz's first car was at the Paris Exhibition of 1887 and began to attract French sales. A French agent, Emile Roger, took the agency for France and called the car the Roger-Benz. Daimler too had a French agent, Edouard Sarazin, who persuaded the Paris company of Panhard et Levassor to make the German engine. When Edouard Sarazin died in 1887 his widow, Louise, kept on his work; she visited Daimler in Cannstatt and brought back one of his new engines as a pattern. Panhard-Levassor built their own car, using the Daimler engine, and also sold units to Armand Peugeot, still a solid name in French automotive manufacturing circles. Thus were the great pioneer makes linked up in the very early days.

Panhard were advertising until only recently as the world's oldest car-makers, but were absorbed by Citroën, another pioneer, and disappeared as a separate make. Emile Levassor joined René Panhard, who made wood-working machinery, to make en-

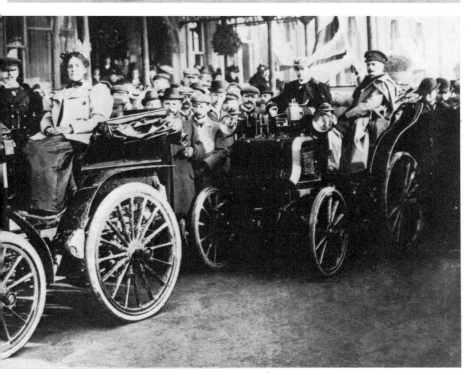

gines only. Then Sazarin's widow married Emile Levassor, cementing another international motorcar link.

In the United States things were now stirring too, and Charles Duryea, a cycle maker from Peoria, Illinois, was inspired by an exhibit at the 1886 Ohio State Fair. This was a Schank tricycle, apparently the first American motor vehicle, which was a failure.

Two years later, in August 1888, William Steinway, owner of the Steinway & Sons piano factory in New York, talked to Daimler about US manufacturing rights and signed a contract on 9 September 1888. The Daimler Motor Company was founded in Steinway Avenue, Long Island, New York. Thus, before any US makers had started up, in 1891 the Steinway company issued illustrated brochures on gas and petrol engines for tramway cars, carriages, quadricycles, fire engines, boats and industrial purposes being offered by the parent Daimler-Motoren-Gesellschaft. The first engines were made under licence in 1891 at Hartford, Connecticut and a memorial plate stating this was affixed to the wall of the building, which now belongs to the Underwood Works, in 1947. In Bowery Bay, on the Steinway Canal, there was a permanent exhibition of Daimler products.

At the Columbia Exhibition in 1893 in Chicago the company showed an electric lighting vehicle fitted with a 10-hp engine, three small 2-hp cars, a 2·5-hp car, a 6-hp fire pump, a motor boat with a 10-hp engine and 2- and 3-hp Daimler engines. In June 1893 William Steinway wrote to Daimler about the sensational success of 'these first vehicles in America', pressing him to visit Chicago to demonstrate his cars and explain their construction.

Daimler's wife had died, and he married again. He spent his honeymoon in the US, visiting Chicago, Philadelphia and New York, where he inspected industrial enterprises. Efforts to sell Daimler cars were somewhat fruitless, and William Steinway died in 1896. He had been to some extent frustrated by George Baldwin Selden, who had taken out what he called a 'master patent', hoping to control the American motor industry as Harry John Lawson had tried to do in Britain with his British Motor Syndicate in 1895.

Lawson, who had made money in bicycles, formed the Syndicate with £150,000 capital, bought the Daimler rights for England from F. R. Simms and then bought patents on all other cars – de Dion, Bollée, and so on. He also formed the Great Horseless Carriage Company, capital £750,000, and the Motor Car Club. But he failed to enforce his monopoly and eventually went broke.

Henry Ford, born in 1863 of a farming family, must rank as one of the greatest names in the history of the motorcar, though as a producer rather than as an innovator. The first American pioneers were the Duryea brothers, Charles and Frank, who had their own car running by September 1893 – some eight years after the first Daimler and Benz machines – in Springfield, Massachusetts, although there are rival claimants, notably John W. Lambert and Elwood Haynes.

Ford had his first home-made engine running in the same year, but it was 1896 before he built his first car. His contemporaries, some of whose names are still with us, were Ransom Eli Olds, who with S. L. Smith founded Oldsmobile; David Buick, a Scot whose car was not in production until 1903; and Elwood Haynes. At America's first all-car show, in Chicago in September 1900, makes shown included Duryea, Haynes-Apperson, Knox, Locomobile,

National, Packard, Pope-Hartford and Riker. Cadillac came slightly later, in production in 1903. The other great American name, Chevrolet, was not in business until 1910.

Ford originally left the farm to work for the Edison Illuminating Company and built his first two cars as a hobby pursuit. He formed the Detroit Automobile Company when he was 38 but the company died young. He then took to record-breaking and building racing cars until he formed the Henry Ford Company, which he left in 1902, before it became the Cadillac Motor Company. Ford took the world land speed record with his car called 999 in 1903 at 91·37 mph on a frozen Michigan lake, and did not found the Ford Motor Company until June 1903.

The first American car manufacturer was Duryea, although others may claim to have built a single vehicle earlier. In 1892 Frank Duryea began building an engine designed by the Pope cycle company, of Hartford, Connecticut, to fit into an existing horse buggy, but it was a failure.

Frank lost his backer, Erwin F. Markham, but

made a second car on his own, and in September 1895 he formed the Duryea Motor Wagon Company, based at Springfield, Massachusetts. He adopted the Benz engine, like so many others, and formed a British company to sell cars in the UK. Two of his cars ran in the London–Brighton Emancipation Run of 1896, and later cars were built in England. By 1917 the course of the company was run. Frank had left them two years earlier but lived until 1967, when he died aged 97. Brother Charles, with whom he had fought much of the time, died in 1938 at 76.

Ransom Eli Olds claimed to have a car running in 1886, but not many people believe this. He came from near Cleveland, Ohio, and after a family move to Lansing, Michigan, began building a copy of Otto's engine in a shed. Four years later he formed the Olds Gasoline Engine Works Incorporated and built up a successful product. He produced a steam tricycle, then a petrol-engined buggy in 1896. But production did not come about until 1899 from the Olds Motor Vehicle Company in Detroit. They carved their way into automotive history, after an early failure with a luxury vehicle, with the simple classic Curved Dash Oldsmobile with single-cylinder

engine and chain drive. It sold for $650.

Oldsmobile pioneered the idea of bought-out parts and sold 600 cars in their first real production year, 1901. The next year they were up to 2,500, in 1903 to 4,000, and to 5,000 in 1904. But in August 1904 Ransom Olds left the company and joined a new one to produce another great American make, the Reo. He undoubtedly qualifies as the first mass-producer on his side of the Atlantic, even if Duryea beat him to the draw as the first car-maker in the US. America really started some 10 years behind Europe in the motor-car story but more than made up for lost time later to become the greatest and most innovative producer of cars.

In Europe the baton had passed from Germany to France, where the pioneers were buying German Daimler and Benz engines but progressing fast with suspensions, transmissions, brakes and all other facets of development. The horseless carriage was being built in other countries, notably Italy and Switzerland, and of course Britain, but France was the forcing house where the ideas came from. Motor-racing, which was to have such an influence on early development, began in France with the 1895 Paris–

Top: An early advertisement for voiturettes.

Above left: Poster of 1899 showing a De Dion-Bouton spreading rustic alarm.

Above, centre: An 1899 Humber phaeton with a 3-hp air-cooled engine.

Above right: A De Dion-Bouton poster, of about 1902, with a pretty French girl demonstrating how easy it all was.

Bordeaux and back.

Benz and Daimler had both shown at the Paris Exhibition of 1889, which led to the connection between Daimler and Panhard et Levassor. The next year the first Peugeot appeared, also with a Daimler engine. In 1889, too, Daimler produced his twin-cylinder engine and in the following year a four-cylinder. The Benz Victoria of 1893 had Ackermann steering, and the same year saw Daimler with a jet carburettor, a big advance on the surface type.

Benz claimed his Velo of 1894 was the world's first standard production car, which can hardly be contested, but another 'first' in the Paris–Bordeaux was the appearance of the winning Panhard car with the Daimler Phoenix engine, a twin-cylinder, designed by Maybach, which could turn at 800 rpm. Two years later Daimler offered the Phoenix car, which had the twin-cylinder 1·5-litre vertical-twin engine at the front, and abandoned belt drive in favour of a four-speed gearbox in unit with the differential (what we now call a transaxle, as on the Alfa Romeo Alfetta).

The system of using a gearbox behind the engine, driven through a clutch, with chains to the rear wheels, was universally known as the Système Pan-

hard, after the maker, though Daimler had it too on his Phoenix. A refinement which used a shaft and did away with the chains was the invention of Louis Renault, and is the system most cars still use today. It is difficult to leave the two German designers for they contributed so much. The Phoenix had low-tension magneto ignition replacing the hot-tube, with an accurate timing method devised by Robert Bosch, and high-tension magneto firing arrived in 1902.

De Dion and Bouton had been steam men up to the time of the Paris Exhibition of 1889, but inspired by what they saw there they developed an air-cooled single-cylinder engine of light construction which would run twice as fast as Daimler's Phoenix – up to 1,500 rpm. Like the Germans, they sold engines to other makers and made a big impact on the European motoring scene.

A curious side-issue of the first American motor-race, oddly enough in the same year as the first proper French one, was that Frank Duryea, who won the event – there were only six starters – was so enamoured of the Benz which came second that his next car bore a curious resemblance to it. This race too was organized by a newspaper, the Chicago *Times-Herald*, another parallel.

Races and exhibitions were the life-blood of the new transport mode, and there was much international cross-pollination as ideas flowed from one country to another. The first show of all was in the Champs Elysées, Paris, in December 1894, but already both Peugeot and Panhard et Levassor had Daimler-engined cars, and Emile Roger, of course, a Roger-Benz. In England the first show was a year later, at Tunbridge Wells, where again there were Daimler-engined Peugeots and Panhards displayed. Most of the cars were imported, the only British ones being electric.

In Spain, Francisco Bonet y Dalmay, of Barcelona, had been to the Paris Exhibition and ordered Daimler engines. They had produced a car in 1889 – at least, a drawing exists, but there is no proof that the car was made. Spanish efforts do not seem to have come to much, but in Italy Fiat has been producing to this day, always moving with the times. Some lesser-known Italian inventors, such as Professor Enrico Bernardi of Padua University and Michele Lanza of Turin, produced either designs or actual cars, and Bernardi's car survives today in the Turin Museum.

In Switzerland there were many pioneer makes, the best known being Henriod and Egg. Isaac de Rivaz has already been mentioned, but there were many others. Charles Edouard Henriod and his brother Fritz had a petrol car in 1893 and another in 1896, continuing with various models up to 1910, and sold some patents to the Frenchman Darracq.

Rudolph Egg, of Zurich, had a tricycle with a de Dion motor in 1896–8, as well as later designs including a very early automatic transmission, and continued in production with various models up to 1918–19. Other early Swiss makers included Saurer, Martini, Helvetia, Popp, Rapid, Weber, Tribelhorn, Orion, Hercules, Lucia, Berna and Dufour Bellabey and SLM, the two last firms making only lorries.

But in France the industry was booming and cars were being exported to other motoring countries, though the Germans, who had started it all, were slow to buy the new-fangled machines. Armand Peugeot built the first French car in 1889, and his name is with us still on a major French make. The family had various businesses on the fringe of engineering and Armand first built a steam tricycle in collaboration with the steam pioneer Léon Serpollet, then turned to the Daimler engine being sold in France by Emile Levassor.

So his first petrol car came the following year, with its engine at the rear. He went on building and selling cars, and finished second, third and fifth in the Paris–Rouen *concours* of 1894. Sir David Salomons, who ran England's first motor show at Tunbridge Wells, in 1895, imported a Peugeot, and the following year Peugeot had their own twin-cylinder engine, still at the back. By 1900 they had moved the power unit to the front and had begun to modernize production on Mercedes lines.

But at this time Peugeot were being beaten hands-down by Panhard and Mors, the latter produced by Emile Mors in 1897. Other contestants were De Dietrich and Rochet-Schneider, the second a Peugeot copy. Renault were also on the scene before the turn of the century. Louis Renault built his first car in 1898, completing it on Christmas Eve, largely from bicycle parts, and using shaft drive and bevel pinions instead of the universal chains of the day.

The differential had been officially invented by

Onesiphore Pecqueur in 1828, in spite of earlier claims, but Renault was the first to use it. He used the engine from a de Dion-Bouton tricycle he had run earlier.

Lanchester were on the scene by 1895, when Fred Lanchester, one of three brothers, put together his first single-cylinder four-wheel car, the first British car and one of a very advanced design. The 5-hp Lanchester ran in 1896 and was followed by a twin-cylinder machine with worm-gear final drive and many ingenious features. Lanchester went on in small production of high-quality cars until they were taken over by the British Daimler Company, which had nothing to do with the German Daimler company.

Lanchester went to great trouble to avoid vibration and provide smooth running, and used a flywheel generator for his spark, avoiding the hot-tube or high-tension ignition. He had his own special and complicated valve gear, which involved the use of one valve for both inlet and exhaust, epicyclic gearing and, later, cantilever suspension. Silence was also a feature of his cars.

The other British pioneer manufacturer was Napier, inseparable from the name of S. F. Edge,

pioneer racing driver and record breaker and main publicist and salesman for the marque. The cars started out as modified Panhards but eventually Montague Napier developed his own engine and Napiers were dominant for some years.

Edge ran an 8-hp two-cylinder Napier, which was really a Panhard, in the Automobile Club of Great Britain's Thousand Miles Trial of 1900, covering much of England and Scotland and winning his class. The 16 hp four-cylinder Napier followed and then big racers of nearly 12 litres.

Napiers were made in Boston, USA, as well as London from 1906–9 and were also sold in Italy from a Genoa factory under the brand name of San Giorgio. Napier's biggest claim to fame was to be the first company to make a six-cylinder engine. This has been contested by a number of others but Napier were the first to be in successful commercial production if not the first to turn out an experimental model. Few could be unaware of this with Edge constantly in the news, one of his best stunts being a 24-hour run at Brooklands by the light of oil lamps, his average speed being approximately 106 km/h (65·9 mph).

Britain's contribution to the early history of the motor car was restricted, as already recorded, by the

Top left: Cars lined up for the Thousand Mile Trial of 1900, organized by the Automobile Club of Great Britain.

Top right: J. A. Koosen and H. Lawson in a Lutzmann, 1895.

Above left: Busey's electric landau taking part in the 1896 Emancipation Day Run from London to Brighton.

Above: The 50-hp Napier of 1901. This large, 2-ton car competed in the Paris–Bordeaux–Paris and Paris–Berlin races, achieving high speeds but retiring from both events.

crippling speed laws and the opposition of the railways and others. Some improvement began in 1878 when the man walking in front of a mechanically propelled vehicle needed to be only twenty yards ahead instead of the previously required sixty – and he was no longer required to carry a red flag.

However, there were some experimental road vehicles built in Britain in the early days of the automobile and a few deserve mention even if they were 'one offs' which did not have much influence, if any, on the motor industry.

Edward Butler showed plans for a tricycle in 1884 at the Stanley Cycle Show. He claimed that it was the first vehicle in England propelled by combustion but it was not until 1889 that the vehicle actually appeared.

Definitely a practical machine was a four-wheeler constructed in 1894 by a Walthamstow, London, builder named Frederick Bremer. This vehicle, now in the Walthamstow Museum, was restored by a band of enthusiasts in the 1960s and actually ran in the famed London to Brighton Run for veteran cars.

In 1895, John Henry Knight, of Farnham, Surrey, ran a tricycle with a gas engine adapted to use petrol. Later he converted it into a four-wheeler but he never produced more than one car.

Herbert Austin, later to become famous with a marque under his own name, was employed by the Wolseley Company at the time and, in 1896, built two experimental tricycles and then, in 1899, the first Wolseley four-wheel car in 1899.

The major breakthrough in Britain came on 14 November 1896, when the Locomotives on Highways Act put up the maximum permitted speed to 19·32 km/h (12 mph) and abolished the requirement for the vehicle to be preceded by a man on foot. The entrepreneur Harry Lawson organized the still-held Emancipation Day Run from London to Brighton and the Earl of Winchilsea ceremoniously tore up a red flag before the start – even though the legal requirement for the flag had gone eighteen years before with the earlier Act.

F. R. Simms, whose name is still in use in the industry, had purchased the Daimler rights at an exhibition in Bremen, Germany, in 1890 and formed the Daimler Motor Syndicate three years later. After the Tunbridge Wells Show a syndicate headed by Lawson bought him out, although he was to continue in the motor industry in other fields. Sometime later, Lawson and his business colleague, E. T. Hooley, went to gaol for fraud. Whilst Lawson has been dealt with over harshly in the history of the automobile there is no doubt that his confrontation with the law brought to a conclusion the undesirable monopoly he was trying to foist upon Britain, as Selden tried to in the United States. Thenceforth the British motor industry began to flourish.

Across the Continent, there were other well-known names although some did not make a significant contribution. In Germany, there was the Lutzmann car which was really a Benz and later became an Opel. In Italy, the story of the car might have been said to begin with a man named Branco who was said to have been the first person to apply a non-animal force to locomotion by turning blades with steam. This was far back in 1629 but Branco did not actually manufacture a vehicle. Three other Italians have a more practical claim for consideration. Enrico Pecori built a steam tricycle in 1891. Then there was Enrico Bernardi, who built a tricycle in 1896, 14 years after he designed an engine. And Menon built a car in 1897, front engined with tiller steering. The engine, however, was supplied by de Dion.

In France, the name is recorded of Edouard Delamarre-Debouttaville, who is said to have driven through the town of Fontaine-le-Bourg as early as 1884 in a tricycle driven by a gas engine, a claim which if true would put him ahead of Daimler and Benz.

There were other French designers with a more lasting effect on the automobile. The firm of Delahaye, although its great days were to come later with sporting success, began in 1896. Decauville produced one of the first examples of independent front suspension in 1898, did well in racing in 1899, but had disappeared by 1909. De Dion, by contrast, were to have a much longer history.

1900s

The big names in car manufacture are launched: Rolls-Royce, Renault, Fiat and General Motors. The petrol engine is modified and greatly improved and many of the features seen in the cars of today are introduced. Ford launches his immortal Model T.

Above left: The 1899 Daimler of Lionel Rothschild.

'From 1885 to 1895 men struggled to make the car go. From 1896 to 1905 they contrived to make it go properly. Between 1907 and 1915 they succeeded in making it go beautifully.' – Laurence Pomeroy Jnr.

When the bells greeted the 20th century cars were still the playthings of a few enthusiasts with the money, determination and physical endurance to cope with the problems that beset the machines. Starting the car took time, what with priming and warming up the ignition burners or installing a fresh battery, then pulling at the flywheel or winding a handle with the knowledge that a backfire could break a wrist. Journeys of any length were to be attempted only with a supply of tools, oil, grease, spare tyres and parts, pumps, puncture repair devices and an overnight bag in case dire mechanical troubles or successive punctures made it necessary to spend a night away.

Villages which had slept since the railway had killed off the stage-coach suddenly awoke to the clatter of the new motors scattering children and chickens in clouds of dust. The village smithy was invaded by strange figures in thick fur coats or white 'dusters', the men in caps and goggles, the women anonymous behind veils and masks. They wanted broken parts mended or new ones made. It is hard to say whether the cars or their occupants most frightened the horses.

Driving was an exacting task calling for continuous manipulation of a variety of controls. The engine was kept running at constant speed by a governor and the car's speed was varied by changing gear, usually moving the lever in a quadrant, one step at a time. The leather-lined cone clutches were usually fierce. Mixture was supplied to the engine by drawing air over the surface of a heated reservoir of petrol or past a petrol-soaked wick. The governor worked by holding the exhaust valve open but the accelerator pedal put it out of action. This allowed the engine to race and was therefore to be used sparingly. The modern accelerator, which controls engine speed via a butterfly valve in the carburettor, varying the amount of petrol–air mixture admitted, is something entirely different, which is why purists prefer to call it the throttle pedal.

There were drip-feed lubricants to be regulated and powdered resin to be dropped on transmission belts. Brakes were primitive, worked by hand and foot, blocks of wood or leather rubbing against the rear tyres, or, on later models, band brakes which failed to grip in wet weather. If all else failed on a hill there was a sprag to dig into the road and prevent the car running away backwards. Many cars still had solid tyres and even the early pneumatics had smooth treads, so on city streets, particularly those paved with polished wood blocks, drivers perched high above short wheelbases went in fear of the dreaded 'side-slip'. Horses still predominated on the roads. Breeding and feeding and grooming and shoeing them, making their harness, building and repairing carts and carriages, occupied hundreds of thousands of people who fiercely resented the noisy, smelly machines that scared the animals and threatened their jobs.

Gottlieb Daimler, in Cannstatt, and Karl Benz, in Mannheim, had created the petrol engines that made the motor age possible, but France, using these engines, quickly took the lead in developing the cars. By 1900 Panhard-Levassor, Peugeot, Bollée, Berliet, De Dion Bouton, Darracq, Delahaye, de Dietrich, Mors, Renault, Rochet-Schneider and many more were building cars in France.

Britain lags
Britain was straggling far behind. The notorious Locomotives on Highways Acts and the turnpike tolls had killed off the steam cars and coaches with which British engineers had led the world during the first half of the 19th century. When France was running her first motor races the British speed limit was 4 mph and drivers were still prosecuted for not having a man with a red flag walking in front of the vehicle. It has been argued that the omission of any mention of the flag from the 1878 Act made it unnecessary, but the man had to be there. Even the 1896 Act, which was celebrated by the first 'Emancipation run' from London to Brighton, merely raised the limit to 14 mph – which anti-motoring magistrates reduced to 12 mph.

Yet even in this atmosphere a few keen entrepreneurs had laid the foundations for a motor industry. F. R. Simms formed the Daimler Motor Syndicate in 1893 to exploit Daimler's patents in Britain. It was absorbed by the British Motor Syndicate, run by Harry Lawson, a company promoter of doubtful repute but extraordinary foresight who had made a fortune out of the bicycle industry and hoped, by buying up all available patents, to control the motor industry.

In 1896 Simms launched the Daimler Motor Co. Ltd. Gottlieb Daimler was a director and he took part in the London-to-Brighton run that year, but the dawn of the motor age had come too late for him to see the impact of his work on the life of mankind.

Above : Changing a tyre was a strenuous operation in *c.* 1900, requiring a great deal of physical exertion.

Right : Drivers kitted up for a drive in the early years of motoring. The riding caps, goggles and heavy overcoats were necessary protection, but gave the wearers something of the aspect of alien beings.

He died in 1900, aged 66. From then on the Daimler companies in Britain and Austria developed independently of Daimler in Germany.

But if German engines enabled France and Britain to start their motor industries, French engines were now fertilizing motor manufacture on a wider scale, thanks to the Count (later Marquis) Albert de Dion and his little engineer partner, Georges Bouton. After experimenting with steam cars for some years they turned to tricycles with single-cylinder petrol engines and then to light cars. De Dion and Bouton produced hundreds of light, efficient single-cylinder engines with battery and coil ignition and by 1900 were getting $4\frac{1}{2}$ bhp from 700 cc at 1,500 rpm.

Like most of their contemporaries these engines had automatic inlet valves worked by piston suction, which created a characteristic snorting noise. They powered large numbers of the company's own motor tricycles and light cars, and more than 50 other manufacturers bought De Dion engines for their early vehicles, among them Clément, Darracq, Delage, Gladiator, Latil (with front-wheel drive) Peugeot, Rochet and Renault in France; Ariel, Argyll and Humber in Britain; Adler in Germany; Ceirano in Italy and Peerless, Pierce Arrow in the USA

The Renaults

Louis Renault, dismissed at school as a dunce who could not spell, started teaching himself about engines in a garden shed at Billancourt, still to be seen outside the Renault administrative offices today. He bought a De Dion tricycle and converted it to four wheels, then built a little car of his own, a two-seater with a De Dion engine mounted in front. Though this was 1898 he never bothered with belts or chains. His engine drove through a cone clutch, three-speed gearbox and propeller shaft to a rear axle with a differential much as we know it today. His gearbox had a new feature – direct drive in top gear – which he patented and which brought him a nice income in royalties from other manufacturers. Demonstrated in Montmartre, the car quickly brought 25 orders and he was in business, with his elder brother Marcel looking after the office. By the end of 1900 they employed 110 people and had built 179 cars.

Several British constructors had studied Continental designs and decided they could do better. Herbert Austin, after developing sheep shearing machines in Australia for the Wolseley company, returned to England, took a share in the firm, built some experimental three-wheelers and then produced a series of cars, all with horizontal engines. Vickers took over the company and J. D. Siddeley (later Lord Kenilworth) persuaded them to make cars to his design with vertical four-cylinder engines.

Henry Royce, a skilled engineer who made electric cranes and dynamos in Manchester, decided to build a car himself after unhappy experience with a French Decauville. He completed his first car, a two-cylinder model with three-speed gearbox, in 1903. The engine had overhead inlet valves, side exhaust valves

and a three-bearing crankshaft. It ran so quietly and smoothly that the Hon. C. S. Rolls agreed to sell all of Royce's output. The Paris Salon of 1904 saw a new model with four cylinders and also a six cylinder engine. In 1905 the first V8 was built and a three-cylinder was tried. Late in 1906 the immortal 40/50 six-cylinder, later known as the Silver Ghost, was ready. It crowned an astonishing five years of achievement by a practical engineer with no previous experience of motor car design.

Royce's method was to select the best of contemporary practice, then refine and develop it until it worked superbly. Dr. F. W. Lanchester's approach was quite different. A highly qualified scientist, he tackled every problem from first principles without regard to what other people were doing. His first car had a perfectly balanced flat twin engine; each piston had two connecting rods actuating two counter-rotating crankshafts. Transmission was by a two-speed epicyclic gear and there was a low-tension magneto with magnets built into one of the flywheels – an idea later used by Henry Ford on his Model T. Lanchester even designed a disc brake, though in the end he had far less influence on the progress of the motor car than Henry Royce. The more conventional Lanchesters of later years were evolved under the management of his brother George.

In 1900 the motor car received royal approval. Just before he became King Edward VII, the Prince of Wales bought his first three Daimlers, and the company became suppliers of the royal cars before Rolls-Royce even existed, maintaining that position until after the Second World War.

Wilhelm Maybach, Daimler's associate, had taken over as technical director, and with the assistance of Daimler's son Paul he designed a new car to the re-

Top left : Louis Renault, the great French pioneer, in his first car (1899: he built the prototype in 1898). It had a 273-cc De Dion air-cooled engine.

Top right : The entry to the Renault factory at Billancourt in 1907.

reduced the need for frequent greasing and the rear wheels had internal expanding brakes. Germany had regained the initiative in car design.

But the British were moving fast. Where Daimler's cylinders were cast in pairs Napier produced a four-cylinder block in light alloy and had a six-cylinder engine in 1904 – not the first though; there was a Dutch Spyker with six cylinders in 1902.

Jellinek prevailed upon Daimler to name his new car Mercedes, after one of his daughters, and the name was retained for all future models. He later used his influence to have an Austro Daimler car named after his other daughter Maja, but her fame proved less enduring than that of the company's technical director – Ferdinand Porsche.

Enter FIAT

Italy started her motor industry even later than Britain. A few small constructors had built cars, three-wheelers or motor cycles before the end of the century – Bernardi, Lanza, Prinetti and Stucchi, Bianchi and Ceirano among them – but in 1898 a group of Piedmontese gentlemen decided to create a major motor company. The founders were Giovanni Agnelli, Count Cacherano di Bricherasio, Count Biscaretti di Ruffia, Cesare Gatti and a banker, Gustav Deslex. The cumbersome initial title of the enterprise was soon replaced by Fabbrica

Above right: The original Rolls-Royce Silver Ghost of 1906. Silver Ghosts were in production until 1925.

Above: The Prince of Wales with the Hon John Scott-Montagu (later Lord Montagu), a pioneer motorist, in the latter's 12-hp Daimler at Highcliff Castle, July 1899. The 40-mph car had a 4-cylinder engine with tube ignition.

quirements of Emile Jellinek, a wealthy financier and Austro-Hungarian consul who was their agent in Nice. Though it still had chain drive and rear wheels larger than those in front, this 35-hp model brought together many features which foreshadowed the future. Instead of wood or steel tubes, the frame had pressed-steel side members. The radiator was of a new honeycomb type so efficient that it nearly halved the amount of water needed in circulation. The water pump was driven directly from the engine and the flywheel had angled spokes which made it a cooling fan. The gate change on the gearbox quickly became universal, as it allowed the driver to select any gear instantly instead of moving step-by-step through the quadrant. Daimler patented the gate system and even Rolls-Royce paid royalties to use it. The four-cylinder engine had mechanical inlet valves, a low-tension magneto, two jet-type carburettors and a light alloy crankcase. Extensive use of ball bearings

Italiana di Automobili Torino, in turn to be abbreviated to FIAT. Giovanni Ceirano and Aristide Faccioli were engaged to design a car and it appeared in 1899, a small 3½-hp vis-à-vis four-seater with water-cooled 679-cc twin-cylinder engine at the rear, three-speed gearbox with no reverse and chain drive to the rear wheels. Front-engined models followed and in 1903 production reached 134, the first cars being exported to the USA. Another of the world's great motor manufacturers had embarked on the long road to the top.

The history of the motor industry records many excursions into blind alleys. Some were brief, like the rush to invent wheels with spring spokes when early pneumatic tyres proved unreliable, or the Gobron-Brillie and Arrol-Johnston engines with opposed pistons connected by ingenious linkages. But in the mid-decade an American named Charles Y. Knight was enticing car makers into longer (and more expensive) trips with beguiling views of a hushed and restful world along the way. Though he had no technical training he decided that car engines were too noisy and blamed the hammering of the poppet valves. This he decided to cure, and after many experiments devised an engine in which the piston worked inside two concentric steel sleeves which moved up and down inside the cylinder, opening and closing inlet and exhaust ports as they went. Poppet valves then needed frequent adjustment and grinding whereas the 'Silent Knights' were indeed quiet. Licences were taken up by Daimler in England, Daimler in Germany, Minerva in Belgium, Panhard-Levassor in France, Willys in the USA and others.

Unfortunately silence was bought at a high price in first cost and services charges. Peak power was limited because high revs could not be used, and the sleeves were difficult to cool and needed copious lubrication, which created a smoky exhaust. Daimler in England used them exclusively for about 25 years and Panhard Levassor set up new speed records with them, but the poppet valve remained the choice for high-output engines and as improved metallurgy reduced the need for frequent grinding and clearance adjustments, the Knights departed into oblivion.

A Scots engineer, Peter Burt, had a simpler idea. By using a rotating crank and ball joint instead of simple connecting rods, he moved the sleeve through an elliptical path and could therefore make do with only one sleeve. He found that a Canadian had just patented a similar idea so a deal was done and the single sleeve bore their joint name: Burt-McCollum. Argyll, the Scottish car manufacturer, bought it and demonstrated it in streamlined cars which set up many new world records.

Although the Scots have a reputation for frugality the Argyll factory was one of the most magnificent ever seen. The interior decor was inspired by the Paris Opera, the workers had excellent washrooms and there was a parquet floor in the body shop. Their chief engineer was M. Henri Perrot, and by 1911 Argyll had a car on the market with four-wheel brakes. The system became famous as the Perrot, after he bought out Rubury who had also worked on it. He was not the first, however. Cesare Isotta and Vincenzo Fraschini exhibited a car with four-wheel brakes in 1908 and had them on their cars by 1910. They were designed by Oreste Fraschini.

The inability to test cars on the road created difficulties for British car manufacturers but the situation changed with the opening of the Brooklands track in 1907. Napier now concentrated entirely on luxurious six-cylinder cars. S. F. Edge, with his flair for showmanship, staged a demonstration run at the new track, maintaining 104 km/h (65 mph) for 24 hours.

The American response

Americans depended on their railways for long distance travel. Outside the towns and cities paved roads were rare. The early motorists had to struggle through dust and sand in the summer, floods and axle-deep mud in the winter, and cars were built with the standard 4-ft 8-in track to fit the ruts created by farm wagons. There were few mile posts or signposts, no filling stations. To get about at all was a challenge – and the Americans became good at it.

Between 1902 and 1907 an American named Charles J. Glidden drove 50,000 miles in his British Napier, right across North America to Europe, Malaysia, Australia, New Zealand, Burma, China

THE FACTORY BEHIND **THE FAMOUS ARGYLL CAR.**

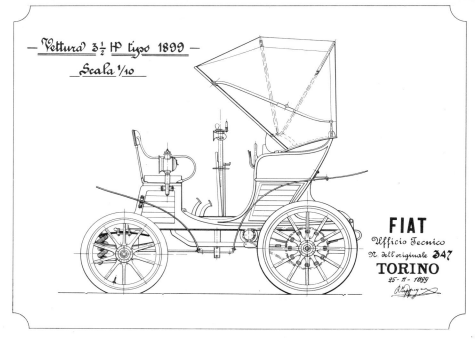

— Vettura 3½ HP tipo 1899 —
Scala 1/10

FIAT
Ufficio Tecnico
N. dell'originale **347**
TORINO
25-11-1899

Twelve Months of Meteoric Progress

4 cylinders
20 H. P.
Sliding gears
Bosch magneto

Hupmobile

$750
(F.O.B. Detroit)
Including three oil
lamps, horn and tools

Hundreds of people were undoubtedly impressed a year ago by the mere smartness of the Hupmobile its beauty, its generous size, the obvious strength of its construction, the clean-cut appearance of the power plant, the very evident use of the best materials.

It took very little motor judgment or experience to see that $750 had never bought such value before.

But in the year that has elapsed since the Hupmobile made its bow, this first judgment has been supplemented and confirmed by a series of performances which are remarkable.

The Hupmobile in contests of speed and endurance, has repeatedly proved itself to be the peer of cars of twice its power and even four and five times its price.

Early in the year it won cups and perfect scores, for instance, in the Baltimore and Detroit reliability and endurance runs.

It carried off the palm in the Buffalo fuel economy contest.

At San Francisco it made the fastest time and a perfect score in the 200-mile annual mud plug.

In its class it won the six-hour race at Brighton Beach; and on the Los Angeles motordrome turned the mile in 58 seconds.

Crossing the desert in the Phoenix-Los Angeles race the Hupmobile took its place among the larger competing cars.

It climbed to 9,000 foot elevations in the Colorado mountains; topped the peaks of the Adirondacks; it was the first car ever to negotiate Georgia's famous Stone Mountain, under its own power, and the second to ascend Mount Greylock, Massachusetts.

In the dead of winter — through the season's deepest snows and severest cold — three Hupmobiles were driven from Detroit to New York; while in the West a tour, under conditions equally severe, was made for 800 miles from North Dakota into Canada.

The Hupmobile is today without an equal in its class, as it was the day the first Hupmobile left the factory at Detroit.

It is prized alike by the man who owns but one car — the Hupmobile — and the man whose private garage houses the costliest types of American and foreign manufacture.

It has made possible the joys of motoring to hundreds who, of necessity, awaited the coming of such a car as the Hupmobile.

Your ideals of motor car construction may be high; but you will find them realized in the Hupmobile.

If you have the engineer's love for fine machinery — the expert's admiration for skillful workmanship you will take your hat off to the Hupmobile.

It remains the most remarkable car the industry has produced.

HUPP MOTOR CAR COMPANY, Desk 24, DETROIT, Michigan

Introducing the Studebaker "Suburban"

THE ADAPTABLE CAR

AS A SMART RUNABOUT

COMBINATION PASSENGER AND BAGGAGE CAR

AS A LIGHT FOUR PASSENGER CAR

WHEN EQUIPPED with regular rear seat, a light four-passenger touring car; rear seat removed (can be done in a moment) and rumble seat substituted, a smart runabout; without rear or rumble seat, a combination passenger and baggage car.

A necessary adjunct to every suburban or country home

The Studebaker "Suburban" is adaptable to numerous uses that will readily suggest themselves.

For instance: When your home is located at a distance from the railway station and you have a visitor arriving on a late train, you can remove the rear seat and, if you wish, bring home your visitor and his baggage in one trip; or, if there is a party you can send your man back to the station for their baggage.

Your baggage can be carried to the beach in your "Suburban."

It is just the car for a hunting, fishing or other outing trip, for running out to the golf or country club as a light four-passenger touring car or as a smart runabout.

The Studebaker "Suburban" is a car you will use every day in half a dozen different ways — it is literally the *adaptable* car.

The Studebaker "Suburban" chassis is identical with that of the regular Studebaker "30" touring car, which is a sufficient guarantee that from a mechanical standpoint the car will give satisfactory service.

Write for full description of the Studebaker "Suburban" and other gasoline and electric models.

Studebaker Automobile Co., Main Factory South Bend, Ind.   General Office Cleveland, O.

BRANCHES

Top left : An Argyll car in front of the factory at Alexandria, near Glasgow. This was the frontispiece of the company's catalogue for 1908.

Centre left : The brothers Studebaker, founders of the famous American company, pictured in *c.* 1875.

Bottom left : A drawing of the first Fiat, the 3½-hp of 1899.

Above : A 1910 poster advertising the 20-hp Hupmobile.

Above right : Publicity in 1908 for the Studebaker Suburban – probably not the kind of name that would be chosen for a car model today.

and Japan. In 1903 H. Nelson Jackson drove a two-cylinder Winton across North America in 63 days. In 1908 a Thomas Flyer won the New York–Paris race via San Francisco, Alaska, Japan and Siberia, serving notice on the world that America could build tough, durable cars. Soon they were cheap, too.

The Duryea Brothers were cycle makers who became the first to sell practical motor vehicles, and in 1895 Frank Duryea won America's first motor race, from Chicago to Evanston and back. Contemporary photographs show the cars covered in mud. Until the roads were improved most journeys were short, and for some time steam and electric cars outnumbered those with petrol engines.

While Europe was divided by national frontiers the United States offered a single enormous potential market and there was already a basis of large-scale production for the car makers to use. Bicycles, sewing machines, stoves, revolvers and agricultural machinery were being mass produced. Before the automobile was heard of the Studebaker brothers were building 75,000 horse-drawn wagons a year at South Bend, Indiana, and it has been estimated that about 150,000 carriages a year emerged from Flint, Michigan. There were machine shops, forges and foundries ready to produce parts in great quantities for the car-makers. Wheels, springs and axles were readily available, and soon engine manufacturers appeared, ready to do for the American industry what De Dion Bouton had done for manufacturers in Europe.

Ransom E. Olds started making steam and petrol engines with his father in 1890. His little curved-dash Oldsmobile had two cylinders, two seats and

axles mounted on the ends of half-elliptic springs running the full length of the tubular frame. It became the first car in real quantity production. There were rows of machines in the machine shop, each set up to do one operation continuously. Engine assembly was organized on a smooth flowing basis, leading to the test bed. In 1901 Olds built 600 cars, in 1904, 5,000. He recruited young and talented engineers, Roy D. Chapin and Howard E. Coffin, who later started Hudson, and Robert C. Hupp who with his brother Louis created the Hupmobile, but his backers hankered to build big luxurious cars so he sold out and started REO. The backers went their way and lost control of the company to the predatory William Crapo Durant.

Riches for the tough

It was a period of frenetic activity when enormous fortunes could be made by unsentimental men with strong nerves and sound judgment. Durant was the wealthy son of a successful carriage maker and had no need to work, but he could not resist the challenge and excitement of the new motor industry and he moved among the struggling new manufacturers like a shark in a shoal of herring. One of these was a young Scotsman, David Dunbar Buick. He sold his successful bathroom fittings business, started making engines and in 1903 built his first car. While other people were content with side valves or T heads, Buick adopted overhead valves and Buicks have never had anything else. The need to expand forced him to sell control to a wagon maker, who in turn ran short of cash and sold out to Durant. Eventually, with no stake left in his own enterprise, Buick de-

parted, leaving Durant with the Buick name and company. Durant's ambition was to assemble a complete range of cars that would dominate the market and in 1908 he created General Motors, putting in Buick, then adding Cadillac, Oldsmobile and Oakland.

Cadillac was named after a French officer who had founded a fur trading post on the site of Detroit in 1701. The company was originally started by William H. Murphy to make cars designed by young Henry Ford, but Ford left after one of those policy disagreements in which single-minded characters are often involved. Murphy therefore bought his single-cylinder engines from a company run by Henry Martyn Leland, who eventually merged his company with Cadillac and became its president. He was a toolmaker and gunsmith who had learned his trade making Colt revolvers, and he established the Cadillac tradition of precision engineering which made it possible to mass-produce high quality cars.

Assembling a car had usually involved some hand finishing, fitting and filing, and the implications of Leland's precision methods were dramatically demonstrated in Britain at the instance of F. S. Bennet, the Cadillac importer. RAC officials selected three new cars at random from stock. Their performance was checked at Brooklands, then all three were

Above left : Cadillac single-cylinder of 1905.

Above right : An early Hupmobile, 1909: a light roadster with a 4-cylinder water-cooled engine.

Left : A 1908 Auburn Model G, a touring car with a 2-cylinder 24-hp engine.

Right : The Italian Marchand bicycle and sewing machine company built cars from 1898 to 1909. This poster dates from between 1900 and 1906.

stripped down, the components vigorously jumbled and some more added from stock. Three new cars were then assembled from the collection of bits under the watchful eyes of RAC observers and tested again. One went on to win its class in the RAC 2,000 Miles Trial and Cadillac were awarded the Dewar Trophy for the year's greatest contribution to motoring.

Durant kept up the breathless pace of his empire building until he had acquired about 20 companies. Then he made a bad mistake, spending $7 million on a company which owned some worthless patents on electric lamps. In 1910 he lost control of General Motors to a syndicate of bankers who made two inspired choices, installing Charles W. Nash as President and Walter P. Chrysler as manager of Buick. But Durant was not finished.

The rise of Henry Ford

With General Motors launched on its way to become the world's greatest car manufacturing group, let us look at the beginnings of number two. Henry Ford was already 45 when the immortal Model T was launched in October 1908. It had been a hard struggle. His first job had been with Edison on electric lighting, but in his spare time he had built himself a simple little car – as so many hopeful American mechanics were doing at the time. It had bicycle wheels and no brakes. Then he built another which looked good enough to justify going into business as the Detroit Automobile Company, but it failed and at the age of 38, with a wife and small son, he decided to attract attention to his cars through motor racing. He made people in Detroit take notice when he beat the pioneer car constructor Alexander Winton in a match race, though he afterwards admitted he had been frightened to death. He found backers for a new venture, the Henry Ford Company, but disagreed on policy and left the firm, which was ultimately reconstituted as the Cadillac Automobile Company.

Ford went back to racing again with his 999 – it had a big four-cylinder engine and handlebar steer-

ing – and another car, known as the Arrow. To drive them he engaged a champion cyclist, Barney Oldfield, who was to become one of America's greatest racing drivers. To people around Detroit Henry Ford was known mainly as a motor racing man, but in 1903 two historic events took place, few people appreciating their significance at the time. At Kitty Hawk, South Carolina, the Wright Brothers got their first aeroplane off the ground and in Detroit the Ford Motor Company was formed.

Ford, like practically every motor-maker in those days, started with an assembly operation, buying parts from outside specialists. He gave John and

Horace Dodge, two brothers in the bicycle and engine business, an order for 650 chassis at $250 each and Model A, with two cylinders and chain drive, was launched at $850. The backers wanted something more expensive and luxurious, with a higher profit per unit, so Model B was produced. But with Model C Ford went back to the low-price market where he, like Olds, believed the future must lie. The basic conflicts which had afflicted the Henry Ford Company arose again between those who wanted to build a few high-priced cars and Ford, who wanted to build large numbers at the lowest possible price. But from now on Ford would stay; those who disagreed with him must go. At one time he had talks with Durant which might have led to Ford becoming part of General Motors, but the story goes that Ford insisted on cash, not shares, and the deal fell through.

Model K was a six-cylinder selling at $2,500 but Ford was not interested. It was Model N, a four-cylinder four-seater, which provided the experience leading to the launch of the Model T. By ploughing back profits Ford was preparing to make more of the car himself. The bodies were still bought out and the body builder quoted $152. Charles Sorensen, one of Ford's aides, had one built in the works and costed it in detail. Confronted with the evidence, the body builder agreed to supply them for $72.

Sorensen joined Ford at the age of 24 as a pattern maker earning $3 a day. He stayed nearly 40 years, became executive vice president of the corporation and had a vital role in the production of 30 million cars. But on the financial and sales side the success of the company up to the First World War was largely due to the tight control exercised by James Couzens.

The patent time-bomb

A dark cloud now lay over the future of the motor industry – the Selden case. George E. Selden was a patent attorney who foresaw the future of the motor industry as early as 1879. Long before Harry Lawson he planned to dominate it by establishing patent rights. He had seen an engine produced by an inventor called Brayton and incorporated its principles in his patent specification, adding water cooling, a clutch, gear change, steering and brakes in stages until he had a portmanteau patent for a complete vehicle. His problem was that the industry was developing slowly and his patent might run out before he could collect royalties. But he knew the law and earned himself the title of 'Prince of Procrastinators' by delaying issue of the patent for 16 years.

Selden's application lay in the files like a time bomb under the infant motor industry until it was issued in 1895. W. C. Whitney, the lawyer and financier, acquired an interest in the patents and started to sue car manufacturers, importers and dealers for infringement. Ten manufacturers, including Cadillac and Packard, formed the Association of Licensed Automobile Manufacturers, to buy Whitney off with a royalty of $1\frac{1}{4}$ per cent on every car they built, but Ford flatly refused to join and was sued.

It was the supreme test of Ford's nerve, but while the case was pending he went ahead with plans for the Model T and the great new plant where it was to be built. In 1909 he lost the case but he appealed and in 1911 he won. The Selden bubble was burst by a technicality: the engine specified was based on Brayton's system, whereas all cars in production operated on the four-stroke cycle as defined by Otto. Ford had set the motor industry free. The case was still going on when the Model T was announced in October 1908 and followed the Model N into production at the Piquette Avenue plant. The great revolution in mass production was planned there but came later. In 1909, when production began, prices started at $850 and 18,664 cars were built. In 1910 prices came down to $780 and 34,528 were built.

Like Olds and others, Ford decided that a gearbox with sliding pinions, which needed double-declutching to achieve quiet changes, was quite beyond new drivers with no mechanical aptitude, so the Model T had a two-speed epicyclic transmission. There were three pedals. The one on the left was pressed

Top left : The Model N of 1906 – the first Ford to sell in large numbers in Britain. It was a 4-cylinder, 15-hp runabout, the immediate forerunner of the Model T.

Top right : The immortal Model T on a testing American road in the second decade of this century.

Right : Poster advertising the Ford 'stars' of the 1905 New York show: the $950 Model C, developed from the original A, and the $2,000 Model B, the first Ford 4-cylinder.

Far right : The first Ford plant at Detroit.

right down to move away in low gear and fully released for top. Halfway was a neutral position which could be held by pulling on the handbrake, though sometimes the car would start creeping when the engine was started. The centre pedal engaged reverse and the right-hand one a band brake on the transmission. The handbrake worked tiny drum brakes on the rear wheels. There was no accelerator pedal; levers for hand throttle and ignition control were on the steering column. The starting handle had to be wound briskly to get the flywheel magneto to generate the required current, hard work if the contacts in the timer on the engine had not been kept clean, while if one forgot to retard the ignition there was a fair chance of a damaged wrist from a backfire. But the price was unbeatable, the car stood up to endless abuse and soon a Ford owner could find spare parts and service all over America, Europe and many other parts of the world.

1910s

In the USA the world's first great mass production plant is built by Ford. In Europe the car factories start producing arms. Rolls-Royce of Britain turn to making aero-engines as do BMW of Germany. Renault produce lightweight tanks, and everywhere motor power is enlisted to help fight the war.

Left : Rubbing down with felt and pulverized pumice stone at the Fisher body plant, Detroit. This company supplied bodies to General Motors.

Below left : The end of the process at Ford's Highland Park factory, where mass production began in 1914: vehicles emerging from final assembly.

By 1910 oily struggles beneath the car and wrestling matches with punctured tyres had become less frequent. The best cars had reached a high pitch of reliability and refinement and there were various ways of dealing with punctures. Michelin had proved the removable rim in racing, but when Napier tried to enter a car with Rudge Whitworth quick-change wheels in the French Grand Prix of 1908 the entry was refused. The idea, changing the whole wheel when you had a puncture, soon caught on.

Most manufacturers still confined themselves to building chassis. On low-priced cars they fitted standardized bodies bought from outside specialists. Those who could afford more expensive cars bought the chassis and commissioned a coachbuilder to build a body on it. With the wait for the chassis and the wait while the body was built, many months could pass between placing the order and taking delivery of the car. The horse carriage makers had turned to producing bodies for cars and offered a bewildering choice: torpedo, coupé, phaeton, spider, skiff, limousine or landaulet.

In the United States Ford was swamped with orders for his Model T but the real mass production miracle did not take place until the new Highland Park started up in January 1914. It was not simply the moving assembly line on the ground floor, with bodies dropped on to the chassis from a marshalling area on the first floor. Operations throughout the plant were synchronized so that each part arrived at the assembly line by conveyor at the right moment. A complete press shop had been bought from another company and installed. It was a plant in continual evolution as new ways were found to save time or cut material costs. There were no precedents to work from. They made it up as they went along.

But the wonder of the world's first great mass production plant was completely overshadowed by an announcement Ford had made a few days earlier. Minimum daily wages were to go up immediately from $2 to $5 a day. The news made Henry Ford world-famous overnight and thousands of workers flooded into Detroit looking for jobs. Output soared, overheads per unit dwindled and prices were cut until the workers themselves could afford cars. A torrent of dollars poured in and in 1916 the company made $60 million.

Ford under attack

Henry Ford was already planning the great River Rouge plant to raise output to 10,000 cars a day and he announced a limitation on dividends to help finance it. The Dodge brothers, always ready for a fight, decided to sue and Ford was ordered to pay out $19 million. Much of the money would go back into his own pocket, but he decided to buy out all the shareholders. He leaked word that he was thinking of using his tractor company, Henry Ford and Son, to build a new car, better than the Model T (he had used a similar ploy to rid himself of a shareholder who had opposed the Model T). The price of shares dropped and he got them at a bargain price. But the rate of appreciation remained fantastic. For an original investment of $10,000, the Dodge brothers collected $25 million. The sister of James Couzens, the company's financial and sales wizard, had invested a modest $100 16 years earlier. Now she collected over $262,000 and the shareholders had already shared $30 million in dividends.

John and Horace Dodge had seen how Ford was becoming more and more self-sufficient and as major

Below : Assembling the Ford Model T chassis.

Below right : Painting and varnishing at the Fisher body plant, 1918.

Bottom : Pictured with the first Chevrolet, 1912, are Louis Chevrolet (standing hatless on the left), William C. Durant, with derby, on far right, and Durant's son, Cliff, at the wheel with his wife beside him.

suppliers they felt vulnerable, so they had started their own motor company, making an open four-cylinder car. It had an all-steel body, using the techniques developed by Edward Gowen Budd, of Philadelphia, the specialist in steel pressing and welding techniques who was to be a powerful influence in mass-production body-building. Many other people would be using wooden body frames for another 20 years.

Ford now owned the business, but a new threat to his supremacy was in the making. After losing control of General Motors Durant had turned to two brothers, Louis and Arthur Chevrolet, sons of a Swiss clockmaker, who had been drivers at Buick. Louis was a clever mechanic and a successful racing driver, and with him Durant formed the Chevrolet Motor Company. Working with a designer named Etienne Planche, Chevrolet had the first prototype of a new car, a four-seater touring car with T-head six-cylinder engine, ready for production in 1911. But while Chevrolet was away Durant brought in other people. Chevrolet, furious, resigned, and apparently threw away the chance of a great fortune by selling his shares to Durant, who once again cheaply acquired the rights to another man's name

and fame. He built up Chevrolet, making profits while General Motors were stagnating, and quietly did share exchange deals with dissatisfied GM shareholders until one day he was able to tell the GM board that he controlled their company once more. Chevrolet, incorporated into GM, went from strength to strength, overtook Ford and became the world's top-selling make, but it brought neither joy nor profit to Louis Chevrolet.

Louis and Arthur now started building racing cars and their machines won the Indianapolis 500 Miles race in 1920 and 1921 (the third brother, Gaston, was killed racing). They set up one of the earliest tuning houses, selling thousands of Frontenac OHV conversions and other performance parts for the Model T. Their ultimate achievement was a conversion with twin overhead crankshafts and sixteen valves but they seem to have imposed stresses on the engine that Ford's designers had not allowed for. 'Sammy' Davis once recalled how he had nearly lost his feet while testing a 'Fronty Ford' when the flywheel magneto disintegrated like an exploding grenade.

From 1914 Europe was engaged in the bloodiest war in history, but the United States was still at

peace, roads were being surfaced and the gilded youth of America was acquiring a taste for sports cars. Fierce rivalry developed between the Mercer Raceabout and the Stutz Bearcat. They looked somewhat alike, with low bonnet, two seats in the open and a cylindrical fuel tank across the back, but the Mercer had a most distinctive feature – the famous monocle windscreen.

Competition was keen in the luxury class too. In 1912 Cadillac adopted a complete electrical system including lights and a self-starter evolved at Delco under the great Charles F. Kettering. It was not the first starter. Several makes had used compressed air, and in France Delaunay Belleville offered a compressed-air starter which would also pump up the tyres and act as an emergency brake on hills. However, the RAC considered the electric starter worthy of a second Dewar Trophy. One of the consequences of the innovation was that it led to a rapid increase in the number of women motorists.

For 1915, Cadillac introduced a V8 engine of 3,150 cc and have been building V8s ever since. Packard left everyone gasping with a side-valve V12 of 6,950 cc.

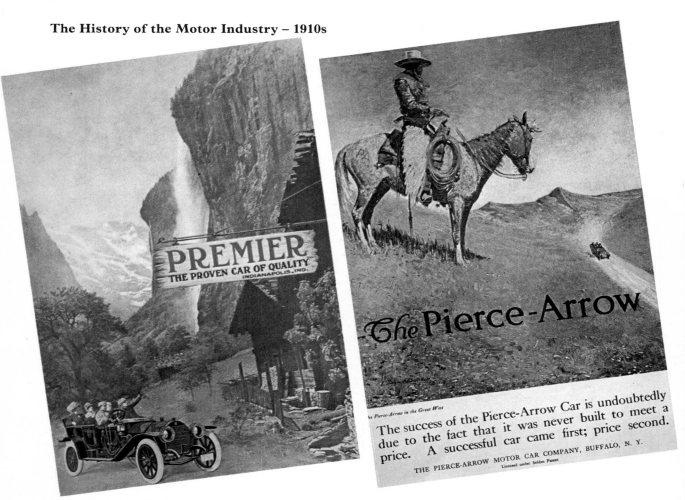

PREMIER
THE PROVEN CAR OF QUALITY
INDIANAPOLIS, IND.

The Pierce-Arrow

The Pierce-Arrow in the Great West

The success of the Pierce-Arrow Car is undoubtedly due to the fact that it was never built to meet a price. A successful car came first; price second.

THE PIERCE-ARROW MOTOR CAR COMPANY, BUFFALO, N. Y.
Licensed under Selden Patent

The First World War

The First World War started in a motor car, the Graf & Stift in which the Archduke Franz Ferdinand was assassinated at Sarajevo, but when the armies mobilized for the greatest confrontation in history their transport still relied largely on horses. The German invasion of France and Belgium was led by cavalry. Attempts had been made to awaken military minds rooted in the past to the fact that motor vehicles would play a vital part in future warfare. Austro Daimler built an armoured car with four-wheel drive and machine gun turret in 1904, and it was demonstrated before the Austro-Hungarian Emperor. It frightened the horse of one of the assembled generals, which threw its illustrious rider, and no more was heard of armoured cars. The German General staff took note of what was happening and from 1908 people who bought trucks designated as suitable for army use received a subsidy of about 25 per cent of the price to keep them available for requisition in the event of war. The same system is used in Switzerland today. In England the Automobile Association staged a demonstration to show how quickly detachments of Guards could be moved into action by motor vehicles, but little came of this far-sighted act. The full impact of the mechanized age on warfare had yet to arrive.

On 7 September 1914 Paris was threatened by the German advance. The government moved out and General Gallieni was appointed military governor. General Manoury's army was in retreat, but if a flank attack could be mounted quickly Von Kluck's army might be encircled. The railways could not move all the men in time so Gallieni commandeered more than 600 Paris taxis, and in two trips each they moved 6,000 men to the front. They were the AG 1 Renault cabs with two-cylinder 1,205-cc engines, henceforth immortalized as the *Taxis de la Marne*. It was an example of improvised mobile warfare that was soon forgotten in the years of bloody attrition in the trenches.

Arms instead of cars

The consumption of bullets and shells soon exceeded anything that had been dreamed of; the factories of the motor industry on both sides were set to work producing shells for the artillery. Louis Renault speeded up production by making the cases for 75 mm artillery shells in two pieces screwed together instead of one. Premature explosions rose alarmingly, wrecking guns and killing crews, but the problem was solved and shells were sent to the guns in millions.

One who went into business making shells and other war supplies was André Citroën. Of Dutch origin, he had acquired the rights to a method of manufacturing double helical gears during a visit to relatives in Warsaw and had built up a business making them in Paris. Another relative introduced him to the management of Mors, who were still making cars, one at a time, by an obsolete method. Citroën began to reorganize the business and introduced a new sports model with a Belgian Minerva-Knight sleeve-valve engine just before the war. When the war ended he was a rich man, with a modern factory on the Quai de Javel ready to produce his own cars bearing the double chevron emblem inspired by the tooth formation of the gears which had started his career.

The lessons of motor racing were applied to producing light, powerful engines for aviation. The Mercedes engines with steel water jackets and overhead camshafts used in German aircraft had much in common with the winning engine in the 1914 French Grand Prix, or the one that Ralph DePalma had meant to run at Indianapolis in 1914 and which apparently influenced Packard's Col. Vincent as he designed the Liberty engine. In Munich the pressure of war production led to the fusion in 1917 of the Bayerische Flugzugwerke AG, who made aircraft, and the Rapp Motorenwerke, who made aero-engines, to form BMW Gmbh. Soon after the war they established a world altitude record with a BMW aero-engine.

Above, far left : The great outdoors utilized to sell the Premier, manufactured from 1903 to 1925 in Indianapolis.

Above left : A Pierce-Arrow doing what a car has to do in this publicity for a prestigious American make.

Above right : A 1914 Ford Model T Speedster in the wide, open spaces of America.

Right : The American Mercer Model 22–72, a seven-seater touring car of 1916.

While Germany was mobilizing Ettore Bugatti, an Italian citizen, was helped by his friend Graf Zeppelin, the aircraft designer, to cross into Switzerland, whence he went to Italy and then to Paris. In a hotel room he designed an eight-cylinder aero-engine which was bought by Delaunay Belleville, of France and Diatto, of Italy. He then put two eight-cylinder units side by side and geared them to a common output shaft – sixteen cylinders producing 500 hp. The design was seen by an American mission and the Bugatti team were shipped to the United States, where the engine was put into production at the Duesenberg works. Zeppelin's friendly intervention had created new problems for his fellow German fliers!

On both sides some of the best cars continued in production as staff cars or ambulances. Daimler-Foster tractors hauled the British howitzers and when the first tanks were built they were driven by 105-hp Daimler six-cylinder engines.

The Rolls-Royce 40/50 was a much coveted staff car and the chassis was also used for an armoured car with a machine gun turret. This was used in France, East and West Africa, Egypt and, with Col. T. E. Lawrence, against the Turks in Arabia. But Rolls-Royce had now embarked on the course that was to reduce the car division to a small appendage of one of the world's greatest aero-engine manufacturers. Their Eagles powered both fighters and bombers and were used by Alcock and Brown for the first direct air crossing of the Atlantic in 1919.

Italy came into the war in 1915 and Isotta Fraschini switched to military vehicles and aero engines, Cattaneo designing the V4B of 250 hp and the handsome 500-hp V12 with overhead camshafts.

In Austria Porsche was designing artillery tractors, culminating in the gigantic petrol-electric 'C-Zug' which hauled the devastating Skoda 42 cm mortar over the Alpine passes.

Eventually the French, like the British, decided that they needed tanks to break the stalemate on the Western front. Renault, true to the principles which had worked so well in motor racing, argued for a light, manoeuvrable machine. His first project weighed only four tons but went up to seven tons by the time the military were satisfied. It needed a crew of only two, one to drive and one to fire the 35-mm cannon, and it was powered by a 35-hp truck engine. Large numbers were made and some remained in service until the Second World War.

Top left : Archduke Franz Ferdinand and the Duchess Sophie leaving Sarajevo Town Hall on 28 June 1914. The car in which they were to meet their fate is an Austrian Gräf & Stift.

Above left : FT light tanks in production at the Renault factory in the First World War.

Above right : Renault AG1 cab, the type that in 1914 won renown as improvised military transport, the *Taxi de la Marne.*

Right : Marne taxis leaving for the front.

1920s

The post war period brings a new generation of car manufacturers: Citroën in France, the Anglo-French combine of Sunbeam, Talbot and Darracq, AC, Alvis and Leyland in Britain. In the USA two men make their names: Chrysler and Cord. The Austin 7 becomes Britain's answer to the Model T. And the Model T is finally replaced by the Model A.

The war consumed large numbers of the men of a whole European generation and changed the structures of society irrevocably. The horrors had been too great to contemplate indefinitely and the need to forget produced the frivolity and frantic pursuit of pleasure now recalled as characteristic of The Twenties.

Some people had done well out of the war and had money to spend, creating a new market for high-grade expensive cars, as long as the money lasted. Thousands of people had learned to drive in the armed forces but had little money to spend and wanted cheap transport.

Production capacity had been increased enormously to feed the war machines and some factories were converted to civilian car production in a few months. Technical advances made in aviation were incorporated into car design. Among the finest of the new crop was the 37·2-hp six-cylinder Hispano Suiza, with an overhead camshaft engine clearly influenced by the company's aero-engine work and four-wheel brakes assisted by a mechanical servo on the gearbox – this long before most competitors had plucked up courage to tackle the problem involved.

Two French plane-makers – Maurice Farman and Gabriel Voisin – started building cars. The latter took over a 3·5-litre four-cylinder engine with sleeve valves from his friend André Citroën, who had decided, with a dedication akin to Henry Ford's, to concentrate entirely on making cheap cars in large numbers. Citroën's first car, the Type A, was a 10-hp tourer. It was launched at 7,950 francs, but post-war inflation pushed this up to 12,500 francs within months. Soon it was joined by the first great Citroën success, the little yellow duck-tail two-seater that later grew a third central rear seat, an arrangement from which the designation 'Cloverleaf' was derived. Opel, who had made Darracqs under licence ten years before, brought out a close copy of the Citroën. It was painted green and acquired the nickname of 'Laubfrosch' (tree frog). Citroën was one of the new generation. While others still sold chassis to be delivered to coachbuilders of the buyer's choice or bought their bodies from outside specialists he made the whole car and sold it fully equipped.

Renault expands

While Citroën knew how to raise money and put it to work Renault was the opposite. He paid his bills promptly, less a discount for cash, and had a horror of getting into debt. He had extended his factories over much of Billancourt – by the time-honoured method of making life unbearable for freeholders who refused to sell out – and he owned 98 per cent of the shares. He was now extending on to the Isle of Seguin, once a pleasant retreat for young Parisians at week-ends but to end up completely built over, the Renault factory windows looking out like the portholes of a vast ship moored in the Seine. He was not one to put all his eggs in one basket; the Renault range included the durable two-cylinder model related to the Paris taxis, two four-cylinder cars and two sixes, one of these the fabulous 9-litre 40 CV Torpedo used – on hire for 1,500 francs a month – by the President of the Republic as well as film stars and other beautiful people. In 1925 it set up 17 international speed records at France's new race track and proving ground at Montlhéry, south of Paris, includ-

Top left : Type As at the Citroën factory, Paris, *c.* 1920. Citroën was the first European manufacturer to apply American mass-production methods.

Above left : Amilcar 4CGS (S), 1926/7, the racing two-seater that helped build the reputation of this French make.

ing 12 hours at 161 km/h (100·45 mph).

Immediately after the war there was a brief boom in cyclecars, spartan devices with features like wire-and-bobbin steering, belt drive and tandem seats, the driver sometimes sitting in the rear, as on the Bédélia. In France there was a tax advantage if the vehicle's weight was under 350 kg (770 lb), and over 300 makes appeared, most of them very briefly. Amilcar, Salmson and Sénéchal survived to become manufacturers of small sports cars. In England the two proprietors of the successful GN parted when the market collapsed, eventually to produce their own sports cars, Godfrey building the HRG and Archie Frazer Nash the Frazer Nash, using multi-chain transmission with dog engagement as on the GN.

Peugeot abandoned the pre-war Bébé designed by Bugatti and produced the Quadrilette, first with tandem and later with staggered seats, a 667-cc four-cylinder engine and a two-speed gearbox on a rear axle with no differential. It did well in fuel-economy contests and is said to have achieved 90 mph. It grew up into the 172 and 190, which appeared in great variety from sports cars to four-seater saloons.

Hotchkiss were not just emerging from a temporary period of arms production during 1914–18; the business had been started by an American making

guns in Paris for Napoleon III during the Franco-Prussian war. Now they concentrated on cars, producing durable if unexciting vehicles which kept them in business after some more glamorous names had faded away.

Panhard, embarking on a successful period with their sleeve valve cars which was to take them up to the Second World War, produced a striking car called the Dynamic. It had three seats in front, with the driver in the centre, behind a curved three-pane windscreen that was known as the Panoramique.

Sunbeam–Talbot–Darracq

In 1919–20 came the creation of an ambitious Anglo-French combine which anticipated the international operations since achieved by the Americans, but was unfortunately not very successful. It united Sunbeam, Talbot and Darracq under the STD banner. Talbot had French origins, having been formed with backing from Lord Shrewsbury and Talbot to make the cars of Adolphe Clément in England. Clément was the hard-headed operator who had built Clément and Clément-Bayard cars. The English cars were originally called Clement Talbots but later the Clement was dropped.

Alexandre Darracq made a fortune out of the cycle industry, then went into cars and in 1902 produced the two-cylinder model which much later became internationally famous as 'Genevieve' in the film of that name. A variety of four-cylinder models followed, but Darracq retired in 1913, leaving the management of the company to others.

The combine brought new tasks for the ubiquitous Louis Coatalen. As a young French designer he had started at Humber in 1901 and in 1902 had produced a four-cylinder car with electric and tube ignition and limousine bodywork, a rarity in those days. He then moved to Hillman and married one of Mr. Hillman's daughters, but in 1909 joined Sunbeam, where he designed the series of Sunbeam racing cars which won the 1912 *Coupe de L'Auto* and were so successful in the 1920s. In 1922 Coatalen produced the Talbot 8/18, an unusually quick little car, following up with the roomier 10/23.

Vauxhall, which had grown out of the Vauxhall Iron Works, making marine engines, and had moved to Luton in 1906, introduced the overhead-valve version of the prewar 30/98 sports tourer, developed from the 'Prince Henry', and in 1925 were just starting production of a new model with single-sleeve

Above right : The 7·5-hp Citroën two-seater with 'Cloverleaf' bodywork, 1924.

Right : The Panhard Dynamic of 1937. As well as an eccentrically styled body it had a central driving position.

valves when General Motors took over the company.

Napier had an impressive six-cylinder 40/50, a designation which emphasized their desire to compete with Rolls-Royce. It had a better engine than the Rolls, but was inferior in chassis design and refinement. S. F. Edge, Napier's driving force, had retired before the war and Napier, wishing to concentrate on aero engines, stopped car production in 1925.

There was still the Rover 8, with air-cooled V-twin engine, and the Jowett, with water-cooled flat twin, which found faithful buyers in its native Yorkshire up until 1939. In 1977 one of them was auctioned for £5,000. Van and estate car 'twins' continued until 1953.

But few could compete in the British popular car market against the two new pace-setting models, the Morris Cowley and the Austin Seven. William Morris, champion cyclist and cycle maker, started selling his Morris Oxford in 1913. Like Henry Ford he was a mechanic, but not an engineer; like Ford he soon quarelled with his backers and made himself sole owner of the enterprise; like Ford he started with an assembly operation, buying parts from outsiders at keen prices. White and Poppe designed a

Above left : The Austin Seven, introduced in 1922. It ranks among the greatest of all small cars.

Above right : The 1923 10·8-hp Clyno, an example of a short-lived make from Wolverhampton.

Left : One of the great names of the British car industry began with this Morris Oxford two-seater of 1913.

special four-cylinder engine of 1,018 cc for the car and supplied it with gearbox for £50. The car was priced at £175, a two-seater with three-speed gearbox, torque tube drive and a worm drive rear axle.

A four-seater Cowley was to come next, but Morris could see no hope of competing against the Ford Model T assembled at Trafford Park unless he could get components at American prices, so in 1914 he visited the United States twice. On the second trip he took Landstad, chief designer of White and Poppe, and they worked out the design of the Cowley on the boat. Then they ordered parts for 3,000 cars: 1,495 cc Continental U-type 'Red Seal' engines, which had proved too small for the US market, at £17 14s. 2d.; gearboxes at £8 2s. 6d.; axles and steering gear for £16 5s. 2d. The car was launched in 1915 and though a U-boat sank half the engines and local body supplies dried up, over 1,100 Cowleys were built during the war.

Austin, the British Ford

There was now 33⅓ per cent import duty on cars and components, and Continental had ceased making the engine, but H. M. Ainsworth, who then ran the Coventry Hotchkiss factory (and later controlled the Paris plant), provided a copy of the Continental engine with slightly longer stroke to give 1,548 cc.

By 1920 the easy money had been spent and the post-war boom was collapsing. Stocks of unsold cars were mounting so Morris took the decision that made his fortune. In two stages the price of the Cowley four-seater was slashed from £525 to £341, with corresponding reductions in other models. Sales doubled and in 1923 the price came down again to £255. That year Morris passed Ford – who was hit by a new tax of £1 per hp – to become Britain's biggest car manufacturer with an output of over 20,000. Two years later he made 54,000.

Yet the car which can most properly be regarded as England's Model T was the Austin Seven, introduced in 1922. Herbert Austin was offering a minimal practical motor car for people who had previously

had nothing better than a motor bike and sidecar. It was a proper car, not a cyclecar. Its four-cylinder side-valve engine of 696 cc, soon increased to 747 cc, had an aluminium crankcase and a two-bearing crankshaft in ball and roller bearings. Top speed, initially 67 km/h (42 mph), soon went up to more than 80 km/h (50 mph) and there were four-wheel brakes, the front worked by the handbrake, the rear by the pedal. With torque tube drive to an axle on quarter elliptic springs it suffered from roll oversteer, which made the steering twitchy, but it introduced a whole generation to motoring and started a cult. Many coachbuilders produced special bodies for the Seven – including a Blackpool sidecar-maker named William Lyons who thus took a first step forward to the creation of Jaguar Cars.

Enthusiasm for the little car spread round the world and pumped life into other peoples' industries. Made under licence in France as the *Rosengart*, it started a chain of events that led to the Simca. In Germany the Seven was built by the old-established Fahrzeugfabrik Eisenach as the *Dixi*, and when they were taken over by BMW it became BMW's first car. In Japan it was the car that launched Datsun on their way, and in the United States it became the Bantam, launching the company that created the Jeep for the Second World War. The Austin Seven was introduced at £225 but within a year the price had come down to £165.

For a time two other companies seemed to keep pace with Morris and Austin. Singer survived to become part of the Rootes Group; Clyno did not. Clyno built low-priced popular cars with Coventry Simplex engines. Instead of strict cost accounting they seem to have worked on a principle of following Morris prices, even to trying to sell at the magic figure of £100. As the story was told by a Morris man, Clyno had a contact at the printers who produced Morris's catalogues and so had advance information on price movements – until Morris sent the printers a catalogue with fictitious prices. Whatever the cause, Clyno died in the crash of 1929–30.

Top left: A 1921 Leyland Eight: a limousine version of this splendid and expensive car with bodywork by Vanden Plas. The designer, J. G. Parry Thomas, developed his first two Thomas Specials, famous at Brooklands from 1924 to 1926, from this car.

Left above: The Leyland Eight engine, 1921. It was a 7,266-cc straight eight, producing 145 bhp.

Left: A Bentley 6½-litre coupé of *c.* 1928 with coachwork by Weymann. This model made no great impact, but was the basis of the renowned Speed Six.

Top right: The 1929 Bentley Speed Six two-seater – the luxury sports tourer at its best.

The growth of steel bodies

As saloon bodies became more popular the cost of presses and tooling to produce steel panels and the weight of steel bodies raised serious problems, but a Frenchman, Charles Weymann, devised a new kind of body which gave many manufacturers a reprieve. It was a fabric covering on a wooden framework. Weymann's patents embodied a system of joints and mountings which avoided squeaks and rattles, but many other bodies were built without benefit of his inventions.

The American industry was irrevocably committed to steel bodies and after a visit there in 1925 W. R. Morris came to an agreement with the Budd company, which held the main patents, and started the Pressed Steel Company in Oxford. To sell bodies to other manufacturers he soon found it necessary to sever the Budd connection and the firms separated only to reunite under the British Motor Holdings banner in 1966.

Morris had already bought the British Hotchkiss company to guarantee his supply of engines, and Lord Thomas, who was invited to join Morris after writing a description of one of his cars as a reporter on *The Motor*, recalls the total concentration that Morris gave to important business. The day he went to settle terms for the Hotchkiss purchase he complained repeatedly about the heat and insisted on having the windows open during the discussion. It emerged later that he had been so preoccupied with the deal that morning that he had forgotten to take his pyjamas off and wore them under this suit at the meeting.

Early Leyland

The desire of Leyland, the truck manufacturers, to enter car-making after the War led them into two sharply contrasting projects. Their chief designer, J. G. Parry Thomas, was given a free hand to produce the finest car possible, and he evolved the magnificent Leyland Eight, with a straight-eight ohc engine of 7,266 cc producing 145 bhp. The car was full of interesting ideas – vacuum-operated brakes, combined torsion bar and leaf spring rear suspension, automatic chassis lubrication and a starter operated by the gear lever. Yet only a few were made and Thomas left by agreement to devote himself to full-time racing. Thomas's assistant was Reid Railton, who later designed the car with which John Cobb

broke the World Land Speed record three times, as well as the Railton Terraplane sports car, based on a Hudson chassis, in the late 1930s.

Leyland had a longer run with something utterly different: Leslie Hounsfield's quaint little Trojan, which they built under licence. This was just about the simplest practicable economy car. The engine, under the front passenger's seat, was a square-four two-stroke with the cylinders in two pairs, each sharing a common combustion chamber. One cylinder had the inlet port and its twin had the exhaust. The engine ran up to only about 1,500 rpm and gave a modest 11 bhp. Top speed was well under 64 km/h (40 mph) but the car was a strong, if leisurely, hill-climber. A two-speed epicyclic transmission was found adequate, with drive by a single chain to a solid axle. The long cantilever springs were so flexible that the cars ran for years on solid tyres and would do up to 160,000 km (100,000 miles) without major engine overhauls. After some years Trojan took over manufacture themselves, and Leyland withdrew from the car business.

A rich crop of new British sports cars distinguished themselves in the Twenties. W. O. Bentley's new 3-litre set the lap record in the first Le Mans 24-hour race in 1923 with rear wheels brakes only, won the 1924 event with four-wheel brakes, then ran into trouble for two years while the Lorraine Dietrich, successor to the great pre-war De Dietrich, scored. The 3-litre was victorious again in 1927 after a crash at the White House put the new 4½-litre out of the race (the 4½-litre duly won in 1928). A 6½-litre six-cylinder model had appeared in 1925, able to carry spacious and luxurious bodywork, and in 1929 came the Speed Six, with higher compression and twin carburettors to deliver 180 bhp at 3,500 rpm and another Le Mans victory. The 4½-litre models were second, third and fourth. In 1930 another Speed Six victory ended Bentley's historic domination of this exacting race. The 220-bhp 8-litre was launched with a new chassis but, hit by the depression, the company did not reap the rewards of its successes. For several years Bentley had had financial problems. Napier were rumoured to be thinking of buying it to stage a comeback in the car business when Rolls-Royce stepped in in 1931, acquiring the Bentley name but dropping all the cars. Of the Bentleys built up to that time many survive and are carefully preserved.

AC's eternal engine

AC built their first real car in 1919. The engine, designed by John Weller, was a six-cylinder of 1,991 cc in light alloy with wet liners and a chain-driven overhead camshaft. It remained in production for 44 years, improvements and developments raising its power output from 40 to 105 bhp. This must be a record life for any car engine, though it was nearly equalled by the 42 years of Jowett's side-valve flat twin, which continued in their cars into the 1950s and was running with overhead inlet valves in prototype two-cylinder cars when the company closed down. AC's transmission was through a three-speed gearbox in a light alloy casing that formed a unit with the worm-drive rear axle. In 1921 the aggressive S. F. Edge joined the AC board and the company's founders left, though sales were boosted by a successful competition programme.

In 1924 an AC completed 24 hours at Montlhéry at 132·76 km/h (82·58 mph), beating Edge's Brooklands record of 1907. In 1926 ACs driven by the Hon. Victor Bruce and W. J. Brunell won the Monte Carlo Rally and set up a new 24,140-km (15,000-mile) record in 10 days at Montlhéry.

Alvis, formed by T. G. John – formerly with Siddeley-Dessy – won friends with their fast and strongly built 12/50 1½-litre four-cylinder pushrod model before embarking on a racing programme with front-wheel drive models designed by G. T. Smith-Clarke and W. M. Dunn, their technical director and chief designer. The first was a 1½-litre straight-eight with Roots superchargers. In 1928 Alvis sports models with four and eight cylinders were produced, but they proved tricky to handle and expensive to repair and the company reverted to rear-drive models not a moment too soon.

Lea Francis had built cars in pre-war years, but first made a hit with their 1½-litre four-cylinder push-rod model which in its supercharged Hyper form won the 1928 Tourist Trophy on the Ards circuit outside Belfast, driven by Kaye Don. Like Lagonda, Invicta, and (on some models) Frazer Nash, Lea Francis bought their engines from Henry Meadows Ltd, but for a car assembled from bought-out parts the 'Leaf' had a lot of character.

Bentley were already established when Sunbeam revealed their 3-litre six in 1925. It had a smoother engine than Bentley's four-cylinder and was possibly the first production model with two overhead camshafts to be offered to the public. With a maximum speed of over 145 km/h (90 mph) it was faster than the Bentley, but its cantilever rear springs gave inferior road-holding. Sunbeam produced touring cars in bewildering variety in the Twenties; pre-war engines were converted with overhead-valve detachable heads. The six-cylinder 4½-litre 24/60, a

Top left : The Rolls-Royce New Phantom (later called the Phantom I) of 1925. At this period, Rolls-Royce manufactured in Springfield, Mass., as well as Derby.

Above left : A 1934 Talbot 105 sports saloon with coachwork by Young of Bromley. Talbot 105s had considerable competition success.

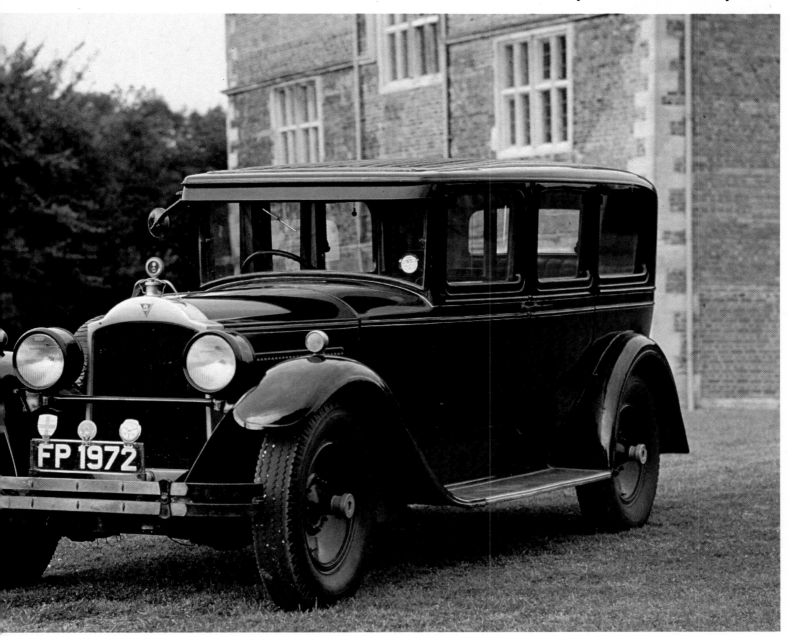

Above : The 1924 Packard straight six. This design was in production for most of the 1920s.

high-geared car capable of relaxed high-speed cruising, was perhaps the most highly praised of the Sunbeam tourers.

The Riley family created a new market for themselves with the Riley Nine. Its four-cylinder 1,089-cc engine, with two camshafts, high in the block, operating inclined valves in hemispherical heads via short pushrods, was a rewarding one for tuners. A low build, good brakes, a four-speed gearbox with constant mesh third and the racy lines of the Monaco fabric saloon combined to create a winner. The Brooklands short-chassis two-seater with dropped frame led to the Imp, and then came a six-cylinder engine of 1,498 cc to the same basic design that went into the MPH two-seater. This car, much modified, started Mike Hawthorn on his racing career and provided the inspiration for the ERA racing single-seaters.

Rolls-Royce started manufacturing the Ghost in the United States to avoid prohibitive import duties. To broaden their British market in difficult post-war conditions the Twenty arrived in 1922 with 3·1-litre six-cylinder pushrod engine and semi-elliptic springing. It was a nice car with precise controls but with its heavy luxurious bodywork it would barely reach 96 km/h (60 mph). In 1925 the Ghost was superseded by the 'New Phantom' which had a similar chassis powered by an overhead-valve engine of

7,668 cc, and in 1929 the Twenty gave place to the 20/25, equipped with a larger engine which eventually went into the new Rolls-designed Bentleys.

Royal Daimler

Daimler, with the prestige of royal patronage, staked a strong claim to be seen as producers of Britain's supreme motor car with the 1927 Double-Six, a limousine 17 ft 8 in. long propelled in silence by a V12 sleeve-valve engine of 7,136 cc. It had dual ignition with a separate magneto to each bank of cylinders. The King's current cars were converted with the new engine and a new car was ordered. Like all Daimlers by now, it had transmission by fluid coupling and a pre-selective Wilson epicyclic gearbox.

The Coatalen-designed Talbot 8/18, which grew up into the 10/23, had been a popular small quality car, but by 1925 Talbot's Barlby Road plant was faltering badly and Coatalen gave the Swiss designer Georges Roesch a free hand. He scrapped the existing range and concentrated on one new model of distinctive and original design, the 14/45, which brought Talbot new prestige and success in Britain. The engine was a small six of only 1,665 cc producing 45 bhp. It looked small for the comfortable saloon body, but its very light pushrod valve gear let it rev freely.

The radiator was attached to the engine, eliminating the need for flexible hoses, and the engine shared its oil with the gearbox. Steering joints needed no greasing as they were supplied with oil stored inside the track rods. Routine maintenance was cut to a minimum, though more serious attention was for experts and involved extensive dismantling, which depressed the price in the used-car market.

Big brakes and a strong, rigid chassis encouraged a demand for more power which was set by the 2,276-cc '75', then the 3-litre '95' and '105' and finally the 3,378-cc '110' delivering 120 bhp. Handsome tourers with tapered tails became a familiar sight on the race tracks (second and third and Index of Performance at Le Mans). Not only were they fast; they were invariably the quietest cars on the circuits, expressing the British (and Swiss) tradition of achievement without ostentation.

Thanks to the efforts of Austin, Morris and their imitators Britain soon had Europe's highest ratio of cars to population. Those early small cars were remarkably durable, and cheap used models brought motoring within the reach of millions. By the early Thirties one could buy a well-used Austin Seven in good running order for £5. It was simple and easy to repair and spare parts for it could be bought from car breakers for a few shillings.

In Germany and Italy motoring for the millions came much later. Runaway inflation and six million unemployed put car ownership out of reach of most Germans. Those who had work to go to went by bus or bike. Five years after the war Germany had a little over 100,000 cars, or one to every 590 people. Most manufacturers preferred to play safe by building fairly high-priced cars rather than chase a mass market, but a few did try to provide cheap, popular machines. Opel's copy of the Citroën duck-back two-seater was followed by the 1,016-cc 4/14 four-

seater. Opel, like Mercedes, combined taxable and brake horsepower in the model code. The tax on engine size did, as in Britain, force firms to design more efficient engines, producing more power from a given size, but the German system did not lead to the extremes of small bores and long strokes seen in England.

The ugly breakthrough

The comedians' favourite was the little Hanomag, a two-seater with a single cylinder 499-cc engine at the back. If it had not been so ugly more people might have noted that it was a breakthrough in body design. It had no separate wings or running boards but an all-enveloping shape putting the full width to practical use, which some manufacturers had not achieved twenty years later.

Two interesting small cars of the period came from Austria and the newly-formed Czechoslovakia. Hans Ledwinka, who had worked on big cars at Steyr, moved to Czechoslovakia in 1921 and in 1923 produced the revolutionary Tatra Type 11 of which developments remained in production until 1938. It had a 1,056-cc air-cooled flat twin engine on the front of a central-tube chassis with independent rear suspension and a rigid front axle with a transverse leaf spring. At the rear he used swing axles, a simple idea later adopted by Porsche for the Volkswagen. From the Type 11, which the Austrians named the 'tin dachshund' Ledwinka developed in 1931 the T57, a small saloon with independent suspension all round and a shape which broadly anticipated that of the VW Beetle. The engine was an air-cooled flat four of 1,200 cc.

Porsche was still at Austro-Daimler. He designed the Sascha 1,100-cc sports car at the suggestion of Graf Sascha Kolowrat, a film magnate, who raced one successfully. They won their class in the 1922

Top left: The 7·1-litre, 6-cylinder Mercedes-Benz Tourenwagen of 1928. It was one of a range of sports models that achieved notable racing success.

Above left: The rear-engined, 2-litre, 6-cylinder Benz Tropfenwagen. An advanced design intended for Grand Prix honours, it ran only in one big race, the *Grand Prix de l'Europe*.

Top right: Hanomag 499-cc, two-seater coupé introduced by the Hanover firm in 1924. It was dubbed the Kommisbrot ('army issue loaf') because of its square shape.

from the carburettor and compressing it, the more usual arrangement. The carburettor therefore had to be adapted to work either with compressed air or at atmospheric pressure.

Daimler and Benz merged in 1926 and the Mercedes star was set inside the Benz laurel wreath to form the basis of today's Mercedes-Benz emblem. Porsche did not achieve happy relations with the new management so he returned to Austria, this time as technical director of Steyr, and was replaced by Hans Nibel, the Benz designer. Unfortunately for Porsche, Steyr was soon swept into an amalgamation with Austro Daimler. This confronted him with the bankers with whom he had already crossed swords, so he returned to Stuttgart, this time to set up his own independent consultancy. It would lead to the most widely sold car in history, the VW Beetle.

Streamlining

Rapid wartime developments in aviation had stimulated an interest in streamlining, and a few designers tried to apply it to car design though with little success. These were, in Britain the North-Lucas, a graceful long-tailed coupé by Farman in France, and in Germany the revolutionary Rumpler.

Dr Edmund Rumpler, designer of the Taube

Above : One of the classics of the history of automobile design: the 12-bhp Tatra Type 11, introduced by the Czech company in 1925.

Above right : Rear-engined 2·6-litre Rumpler saloon of 1921. This was a pioneering design, mechanically as well as in appearance.

Targa Florio. Designs for new large cars flowed from his bureau, but his personality was as spiky as his moustache and after a furious disagreement with the company's financial backers he moved to Mercedes at Stuttgart where he succeeded Daimler's son, Paul, as technical director.

Daimler had started experimenting with superchargers to boost the performance of road-going production cars, and Porsche continued the policy enthusiastically. The supercharger was clutched in by pressure on the throttle pedal beyond full throttle position. Immediately a fearful howl spread terror among bystanders. The noise alone made it unsuitable for elegant limousines, but the company persevered with it until the Second World War. Its most apt application was on the great 7·1-litre sports cars, the SS and SSK, where the noise matched the general impression of stark brute force. The superchargers were Roots type, and as they were to be used only intermittently they fed compressed air into the carburettor instead of sucking petrol-air mixture

aeroplane, was no stranger to car design. He had taken out patents on swing-axle suspension before the war and now produced a car far ahead of its time, a four-seater saloon of teardrop shape with mid-mounted engine in a sheet steel punt chassis. The engine, mounted ahead of the rear axle, was water-cooled and had six cylinders arranged in three pairs in broad-arrow formation to keep length to the minimum. In front was a rigid axle on long cantilever springs, but the rear end had independent suspension by swing axles. This reversal of normal springing priorities appeared later on the ADR Austro Daimlers built during the regime of Karl Rabe, Porsche's protégé at Austro Daimler, and on cars designed by Porsche himself at Steyr.

The Blitzen Benz single-seater, reaching 228 km/h (142 mph) in 1912 had demonstrated the advantages of a smooth shape and low frontal area, and in 1922 Benz employed Rumpler's techniques to produce a low-built mid-engined two-seater racing car of teardrop shape with mid-mounted six-cylinder twin ohc

Above left : The 1925 Loco-mobile 6-cylinder tourer. Of high quality, it was one of the most expensive cars then on the American market.

Above right : Handsome American : the first Cord, the front-wheel drive L29, introduced in 1929, seen here in convertible cabriolet form.

Right : At the lower end of the American price range was the Essex Four saloon of 1929. (Hudson executives picked the name from the map of England thinking 'Essex' had something to do with six – *pace* the East Saxons! – and six cylinders were only achieved later.)

engine and swing-axle rear suspension. Twelve years later the shape and the layout were reproduced in Porsche's Auto Union single-seaters.

Already it was becoming clear that true stream-lining must enclose the wheels, and at the French Grand Prix at Tours, in 1923, both Voisin and Bugatti ran cars with all-enveloping faired bodywork. They were straight-sided, like a slice cut from an aeroplane wing. The Bugattis had a very short wheel-base, proved difficult to handle, and crashed, which, with hindsight, is not really surprising for the shape seems likely to have produced a good deal of lift at the rear end.

Italy's Monza race track was completed in 1922, but Fiat ensured early testing of production cars by building their new Lingotto plant with a banked test track on the roof (half a century later it was featured in the film 'The Italian Job'). Fiat moved steadily towards mass production with two small cars which became well known for finish and relia-bility. The Type 501 was a 1½-litre four-cylinder of which some 45,000 were made. The 509 had an over-head camshaft engine of only 990 cc. Designed to climb Alps, they felt a bit low-geared on the level but had good brakes and nice road manners.

By far the most significant new model was the Lancia Lambda, which went into production in 1923. Vincenzo Lancia had worked with Ceirano and had stayed on when their workshops were taken over by Fiat, becoming one of Fiat's top team drivers. He retired from racing in 1906 and started his own company, producing some sound and solid cars, including the eight-cylinder Trikappa.

The Lambda brought a fresh and original ap-proach. Instead of a chassis it had a sheet steel unit structure extending right up to the waistline. As the passengers sat in it, not on it, the car was extremely low built for those days. Independent front suspen-sion of the sliding pillar type was not new – Decau-ville and Sizaire Naudin had used it in conjunction with transverse leaf springs, and Morgan three-wheelers had it with coil springs – but Lancia's arrangement was the most refined so far. The stub axle was attached to a tubular kingpin which moved in vertical guides above and below and bore against coil springs at the upper end. Filled with oil and the necessary valves, the kingpin was a telescope

damper and the light tubular frame supporting it all spread the loads into the main structure at widely separated points.

There is a problem with this type of suspension. Because the front wheels remain strictly parallel the track varies as they rise and fall. This really calls for a telescopic track rod, but as that is not acceptable the wheels tend to flap, causing a characteristic shake of the steering wheel. It can be reduced if suspension travel is kept quite small. Anyone who has followed a Morgan over rough country will have observed that some riding comfort is obtained by flexing the chassis. Lancia, on the other hand, had devised a structure of great torsional stiffness, and it is a tribute to the clever designers (Falchetto and Zeppegno worked on it with Lancia) that the car maintained a legendary reputation for ride, road-holding and steering precision through nine series, during which the size of the narrow V4 engine was increased from 2,120 to 2,570 cc and maximum speed rose to over 128 km/h (80 mph). Block and sump were in light alloy with iron liners; carburettor and exhaust pipe were attached to the rear of this very compact engine.

Ford's autcornucopia

Meanwhile the United States was racing ahead, producing cars at a rate and at prices almost un-believable to most Europeans. Freed of the obliga-tion to pay dividends to shareholders, Ford poured money into the new River Rouge plant at Detroit, the greatest and most fully integrated car plant the world had ever seen. It had its own berths for ships bringing coal, ore and limestone, its own railway sidings, a network of access roads and car parks for the employees who had become the aristocrats of American labour. There were two blast furnaces (later three) a forge and a foundry. They did not waste time or fuel making pig iron. Molten iron went straight from the smelters to holding furnaces in the foundry where its composition was checked and corrected before pouring the castings.

Ford was now so wealthy that he could authorize colossal expenditure with a casual 'What are we waiting for?'. Nothing must check the smooth flow of cars. If suppliers failed to deliver through poor organization or labour troubles Ford men tried to

help. If that failed they moved into the business. The Rouge acquired its own glass works, producing glass in a continuous ribbon. Ford designed and made the machinery. They installed their own rolling mill for sheet steel. The time lag between arrival of raw materials and their emergence in the finished car was cut from more than 20 days to four days, an enormous saving in storage space and idle capital.

Between October 1908 and May 1927 Ford made 15,007,033 Model Ts. The car and its maker were world famous, but people had outgrown it. Sorensen wrote later: 'Henry Ford made a car for the common man, but the common man was getting some uncommon ideas.' William H. Knudsen, whom Ford had fired, was running Chevrolet and catching up fast. As the Rouge neared its target of 10,000 units a day Ford cars began accumulating on dealers' parking lots. On 26 May 1927 the Rouge shut down and

gaged a new design team and built the prototype of the first Chrysler car. With its high-compression six-cylinder engine and hydraulic brakes it was good enough to raise the finance needed.

In 1925 Chrysler bought the company, killed off the Maxwells and started production, but he needed more space, so in 1928 he acquired Dodge by a share exchange and launched the Plymouth. He already had enough confidence in the Chrysler to match it against Europe's best at Le Mans, where his cars came in third and fourth.

Durant had run into further financial trouble and the bankers bailed out GM on condition that he resign. Alfred P. Sloan then took charge and created the organization and corporate policies which were to turn GM into the most powerful corporation in the world, with an annual budget greater than those of many sovereign states. He decentralized, giving each division management the freedom to run its

Below left : A 1924 example of the 1½-litre Fiat Tipo 501, an Italian family car with a name for longevity.

Below : Aerial view of the Ford plant, Rouge, in 1931.

Bottom : The vehicle test track at Fiat's Lingotto plant, 1925.

remained shut for nine months. It would be impossible to contemplate now, and it would not have been necessary if Henry Ford had allowed his son Edsel to bring forward a replacement in time, but he seems to have been in a state of shock, unable to believe that his creation had reached the end of the road. Many dealers deserted to Chevrolet. Production of the Model A began in 1928. Against opposition from Henry Ford it had what he called a 'crunch' gearbox with three speeds. It also had a laminated safety glass windscreen. It emerged just before the Great Depression. In 1930 1,155,162 were built, in 1931 541,615.

At General Motors Durant continued his acquisitions. One of the best was the Fisher Body Corporation, formed by seven brothers who stayed with it and made an important contribution to the success of the corporation. But others were failures and in 1920 Walter Chrysler, exasperated, resigned – one man who got away from Durant without leaving his name behind. He reorganized Willys Overland at a salary reputed to be $1,000,000 a year, then breathed new life into the ailing Maxwell Chalmers. He en-

own business within broad policy lines laid down by the main board. Consultants engaged to examine the ailing Chevrolet division concluded it had no future and recommended it should be closed down, but Sloan gave Knudsen the job of reviving it and he made it the top-selling make in the USA and the world.

Dramatic Auburn

Another young man now made a bid to build up a new corporation. Errett Lobban Cord had made his fortune before he was 30 and was invited into Auburn when it was almost dead. He became President in 1926, bought Lycoming, who made the engines, and the company which made the bodies and created new models of dramatic beauty which unfortunately concealed indifferent engineering. Count Alexis de Sakhnoffsky was engaged to design the body for the two-seater Auburn Speedster, which sold in supercharged form – with a guarantee of 160 km/h (100 mph) – at a fraction of the price of a Stutz. Duesenberg was taken over and the two brothers, August and Fred, designed the Model J. The supercharged

Right : A 1928/9 Lancia Lambda tourer. Lambdas were in production, in nine series, from 1923 to 1931.

Below right : Inside Ford's Rouge plant.

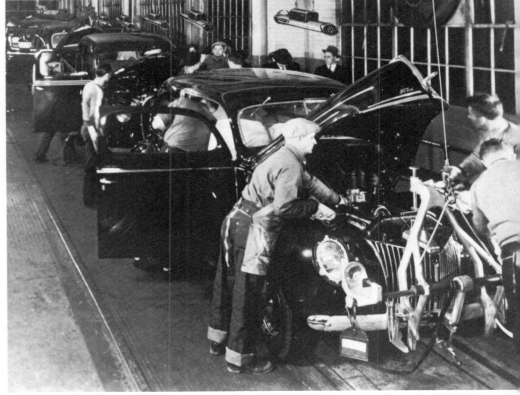

chassis alone cost $15,750 at a time when a complete Ford Model A could be bought for $385. In 1929 came the first Cord, the L 29, designed by Carl van Ranst, who had worked with Harry Miller on racing cars at Indianapolis. It had front-wheel drive with a De Dion front axle on four quarter-elliptic springs. It was handsome, but it was also too heavy. This was not a good range with which to face a depression and Cord needed all his agility to survive.

By 1929 most people were enjoying an improved standard of living and car ownership was increasing rapidly, but in the United States the boom created a mood of euphoria and wild speculation. Car sales floated up on the tide of easy money until the fatal morning in 1929 when the selling started on Wall Street. As the bottom dropped out of the market panic spread. Millions of shares were jettisoned, millionaires and small punters were ruined, the crash set off a chain reaction worldwide. It was the dividing point, chronologically and psychologically, between the Twenties and the Thirties. Some car makers went under; others emerged seriously weakened.

IN A CLASS BY ITSELF

1930s

The Wall Street crash halves production in the US car industry, although it revives in the mid-thirties. Motoring is made easier with simpler gears and better suspension. Cars take on a more streamlined appearance. Front-wheel-drive cars are mass-produced by Citroën. Hitler commissions Ferdinand Porsche to design a people's car – the Volkswagen.

The effect of the Wall Street crash on the American motor industry was devastating. In 1929 4,587,800 cars were built. In 1930 only 2,784,700 rolled out and 130,000 car workers lost their jobs. By 1932 the year's production was down to 1,135,500 and about 12,000 car dealers had gone out of business. It was not until four or five years later that rising car sales signalled that the country was emerging from the Great Depression.

Henry Ford had largely withdrawn from day-to-day control of his empire. Confronted with Franklin D. Roosevelt, the New Deal and demands for a union closed shop, the arch exponent of free enterprise refused to take part in negotiations, assigning the job to a security man and former boxer, Harry Bennett. Bennett came to exert a sinister influence within the company and seems to have contributed to the growing estrangement between Ford and his son, Edsel.

In 1932 the Model A was replaced by the Model B. The basic engine was a four-cylinder, but this was soon forgotten in the rush to buy the alternative V8, which cost only a few dollars more. Ford refused to consider a six, as Chevrolet used them, and he even built an experimental five-cylinder but finally decided to produce the world's cheapest V8. The foundry was re-equipped and highly automated to make blocks and crankcase in a single casting and cast crankcases in pairs. With very good acceleration and a top speed of about 128 km/h (80 mph) the V8 set new standards of performance for cheap cars, though the rod-operated brakes on early models caused some anxious moments.

At Lincoln Edsel Ford produced a big new V12 to supplement the V8 which had been so popular with both gangsters and those whose job it was to pursue them, and in 1935 the techniques of the Ford V8 were applied to the new low-priced Lincoln Zephyr V12. All previous Lincolns had been fitted with bodies by specialist coachbuilders, but the Zephyr had a shapely body of semi-unit construction based on a project for a rear-engined show car designed by John Tjaarda. An immediate success,

Left : The Wall Street crash was responsible for this car being offered for $100.

Below left : Lincoln Zephyr, a 4·4 litre V12, shown here in its 1937 coupé form.

Below right : An American classic: the 1931 Cadillac V16.

Bottom left : A 1931 Duesenberg 6·9-litre, 8-cylinder Model J. Introduced in 1928, it was the biggest, fastest and most expensive American car of its day.

Bottom right : The first Silver Arrow, by Pierce Arrow, seen here at a 1958 meet.

its influence was seen later in another American classic, the first Lincoln Continental. Ford had bought Lincoln when the Lelands ran into financial difficulties. They stayed with the company for a time but left after disagreements on policy. Ford also launched Mercury to plug a gap in the range, but the group could not match the array of talent and managerial skill in GM's many divisions and by the time the Second World War started GM had 50 per cent of the US market.

Making motoring easier

The American public were showing the resistance to radical change which characterizes them, but there were new ideas to make driving easier – free wheels for simpler gear-changing, a two-speed axle with vacuum control to combine fast acceleration with economical cruising, and in 1939, from Oldsmobile, the first Hydra-Matic, with fluid coupling and a hydraulic control system that was a miracle of complexity.

Independent front suspension really took hold in 1934, with 'knee action' coil springs and wishbones on Buick and Dubonnet on the top-priced Chevrolets. By the end of the decade Buick and Oldsmobile were using coil springs at the rear too, though with a rigid axle. In 1935 Fisher introduced the 'turret top' on GM cars, a one-piece steel roof without the

fabric insert which had been used up to that time.

In 1934 Buick got a new general manager, Harlow Curtice, a future president of GM, who worked closely with Harley Earl, GM's head of styling, to give Buick a new and brighter image. Earl had started at Cadillac, and his flair for showmanship really established the importance of car styling as a selling factor during the years of annual changes and 'planned obsolescence' which Sloan devised to encourage people to trade their cars in every year. His successor at Cadillac was a young man named Bill Mitchell, who eventually followed him into the top job and retired only in 1977.

Cadillac introduced their first V8 in 1915 and it has remained their basic engine ever since, but in 1931 they apparently detected enough people who had avoided ruin in the Depression to offer one of the great American cars of all time: the 7·4-litre V16 with engine designed by Ernest Seaholm. It was a narrow 45-degree unit with overhead valves quietened by hydraulic tappets. The two exhaust systems and the updraught carburettors with exhaust-heated hotspots were on the outside of the blocks. In the centre was a single ignition distributor. Power output was 165 bhp at 3,400 rpm. Seven years later they did an extraordinary thing, replacing this splendid engine with a cheaper side-valve one.

E. L. Cord also found enough clients with money in the bank to survive the crash. Just before the market crashed Duesenberg had introduced the superb Model J, with a special straight-eight Lycoming engine which had twin overhead camshafts operating four valves per cylinder. A small pump forced oil to all chassis lubrication points at regular intervals and monitor lights showed when to change the engine oil and top up the battery.

On this machine the leading coachbuilders on both sides of the Atlantic produced some of the most beautiful bodies ever seen for clients who included King Alphonso of Spain, other royalty and leading film stars. To follow up this success came the SJ, with centrifugal supercharger, said to do about 210 km/h (130 mph).

Next came a new Cord 810, an inspired creation by Gordon Buehrig with perfectly proportioned, uncluttered lines and retractable headlamps that still look modern 40 years later. Sadly, mechanical problems slowed down production, especially of the easy-change transmission. A tiny lever in a gate on the steering column selected the gear; a clutch pedal with rather long travel then actuated electro magnets and vacuum servos to free the clutch and change gear. The single bearing in each hub also seems to have been heavily loaded in this powerful front-drive car. The end came in 1937 and Cord departed for fresh fields and pastures new.

The Pierce Arrow, one of the old-established American prestige cars, had been taken over by Studebaker, which did not improve its image, and when a new V12 engine was announced, a new syndicate bought its independence, but failed to prolong its life for long despite the appearance of Silver Arrow, an advanced styling study, at the Chicago World Fair. Headlamps and front wings were merged smoothly into the sides and the spare wheel was carried in a front wing, an idea still used by Bristol.

It was a much more elegant car than the Chrysler Airflow, introduced in 1934, which was said to offer gains in speed and fuel economy but retained conventional wings and running boards and seemed to offer maximum ugliness for minimal aerodynamic advantage.

Chrysler had made a more valuable contribution to the development of the automobile two years earlier with 'floating power', mounting the engine-gearbox unit on rubber at three carefully calculated points. It opened the way for rubber in suspension, the mountings of screen wipers and at any point where it could prevent noise and vibration being transmitted into the body.

Ventilation, another aspect of comfort, was advanced by 'no draft' ventilation from Fisher, using pivoted 'ventipanes' to take in or extract air. Like many other simple ideas it must have earned GM large sums in royalties.

Buying into Europe

As the prospect of selling their big, thirsty cars to highly taxed Europeans melted away the American corporations moved swiftly and established local companies to make cars better adapted to local markets. GM had taken over Vauxhall in 1926, Opel in 1929. Ford moved British production to their Dagenham plant, the only one in Britain with its own blast furnace, in 1929, and opened their Cologne plant in 1931.

The Vauxhall image was changed gently from that of fairly exclusive low-production models to popular low-priced ones via a series of cheap sixes (including the 1933 Cadet, with Britain's first synchromesh gearbox) to the little four-cylinder 1,203-cc Ten, of 1938, with Dubonnet front suspension incorporating torsion bar springs. Opel, already well established in the small car market, created a new range with up-to-date styling including headlamps recessed in the front and Dubonnet independent suspension. In the late Thirties they were exported to Britain at prices that sharply undercut those of Vauxhall and other local products despite the $33\frac{1}{3}$ per cent import duty, producing shrill protests from the British industry. There was a feeling at the time that GM, unable to get profits out of Nazi Germany, must be taking cars out instead.

Ford plants in England and Germany produced the Model A and B with small 2-litre engines, then local versions of a joint small car, the Model Y, with 933-cc side-valve engine, known in Britain as the Eight and later developed into the Popular. The British version bore a strong resemblance to the 1933 V8 in the US. They came out of the same studio, and it is said the baby car provided the inspiration for the big car.

The Ford V8, with the full-size USA engine of 3,622 cc delivering 85 bhp, was built in Britain and Germany, and there was a smaller V8 of 2,228 cc, 60 bhp, which was also used in the French Matford, built in the former Mathis factory.

Having bought Wolseley in 1927, Morris had acquired a design department familiar with overhead camshaft engines as a result of war-time experience in building Hispano aero-engines. Their new small ohc four went into the Morris Minor, which was produced to meet the challenge of the Austin Seven.

But this engine's camshaft was driven through the armature shaft of a vertically mounted dynamo. Oil could seep from the valve gear into the dynamo, so on grounds of serviceability and cost a side-valve engine was substituted.

MG, mighty midget

The engine fired the imagination of Cecil Kimber, who ran the Morris Garages in Oxford. He had built an experimental sports car on the basis of a bull-nose Oxford chassis and sold some handsome aluminium-bodied sports tourers on the later version with rectangular radiator. He produced a delightful little sports two-seater on the new Minor chassis with a fabric body which he bought in quantity for £6 10s. Thus the M-type MG Midget was born, first of a line that was to engage in thrilling battle with the sports Austins and Singers and to establish Britain as supreme producer of low-priced sports cars.

Kimber's next model, the J2, produced a cautionary tale for car manufacturers. Road-tested by Sammy Davis, of *The Autocar*, it reached a maximum 128 km/h (80 mph), sensational for such a small car. But owners complained that their production models fell well short of the magic figure and it cost a lot of money to pacify them. However, MG went on from strength to strength – the Magna, the Magnettes, the supercharged K3 that Nuvolari drove, the streamlined record-breakers. Kimber had those rarely combined precious gifts, a sense of style and an eye for detail. They enabled him to design cheap cars that looked desirable and expensive. But in one of the erratic moods which deprived him of all his best executives, Morris fired Kimber. MGs were never the same again.

Britain had no roads on which high speeds could be sustained for long periods so cars were low-

Top left: Luxury, elegance and power, European-style: a 1934 French Hispano Suiza.

Top right: Luxury, elegance and power, American-style: a 1933 Auburn sedan.

Above left: The Chrysler Airflow of 1934, an unlovely essay in streamlining.

geared, with widely spaced gearbox ratios to give good top gear performance and an emergency low ratio for steep hills. When British owners ventured on to the new motorways in Italy and Germany they often added the clatter of failed bearings to the tinkle of cowbells and Glockenspiel. Even Rolls-Royce felt it wise to circularize owners, advising them not to drive flat out for long periods on the treacherous foreign highways. British roads were so narrow and sinuous that they made it unnecessary to design for sustained high speeds, but they were also so smooth that they encouraged decadence in suspension design. The situation aroused some enthusiasts to such fury that they concluded few post-1930 cars were worth a damn and formed the still-flourishing Vintage Sports Car Club.

The type of car these purists objected to was exemplified by the Wolseley Hornet, which had a small six-cylinder engine of the same basic design as the four in the Minor, whose body it borrowed. Soon there was a flock of sports bodies for the Hornet chassis, many complete with aero-screens and

Above right : Packard 1601 straight eight convertible of 1938.

Right : A Citroën 7CV Traction Avant in 1938. The design, another milestone in automobile history, was introduced in 1934 and lasted more than two decades.

stoneguards on lamps and radiators to suggest that they were just back from racing at Le Mans. William Lyons produced one of the best-looking while on his way to more serious things. There were several other baby sixes, mostly awful.

Lagonda, Rolls, Daimler

One man who understood the problem was W. O. Bentley, who joined Lagonda as technical director in 1935, the year a Meadows-engined 4½-litre won the Le Mans race. He designed a new chassis with independent front suspension by torsion bars and transformed it into a quieter more comfortable car with lighter controls. He then designed a V12 engine with single overhead camshafts to produce a silent, luxurious car which could cruise at 160 km/h (100 mph) for long periods.

Rolls-Royce also ended the period with a V12 engine, a 7·3-litre pushrod unit in the Phantom III, which was unfortunately not developed to its full potential when war stopped production. It still had a four-speed gearbox with right-hand change, mounted separately from the engine, but Daimler had advanced along the road to easier driving on

65

their own cars and those of Lanchester, which they had taken over, by using a fluid coupling in conjunction with the Wilson preselector gearbox (which was used without the fluid coupling by several other manufacturers). The fluid coupling lacked the third element necessary to multiply torque, but it enabled the car to be stopped and restarted by using only brake and accelerator, the left-hand pedal having the sole function of engaging the gear preselected on the steering column.

In 1934 the STD group was broken up. Rootes acquired the British assets and the Sunbeam and Talbot names and Anthony Lago took over the French factory and the Talbot-Darracq names. Georges Roesch, called upon to design cars of a type foreign to his nature, departed, leaving Sunbeam and Talbot to become elements in Rootes badge engineering, though they gained prestige for the group in events like the Monte Carlo Rally.

William and Reginald Rootes took control of their father's business in bicycle manufacture and car sales after the First World War and built it up into one of Britain's biggest car-making groups. In 1927 they began their acquisitions, progressively taking over Hillman, Sunbeam, Talbot and Karrier commercial vehicles and adding Singer and the coachbuilders Thrupp and Maberly later. In 1932 the Hillman Minx was launched. It was destined to be one of the longest-lived models in British production. With Rootes, Ford, Vauxhall and Standard in mass production Austin and Morris had lost their dominant position on the British market. But car production was still far from being a fully integrated operation. Briggs, Pressed Steel, Fisher and Ludlow and other smaller specialists still supplied the bodies.

By 1933 Morris's market share had dropped to 33 per cent and he brought in Leonard Lord, who had reorganized Wolseley. Lord was a tough, ruthless individual capable of numbing rudeness, but he was probably the best car production man in Britain, driving men and machines to their utmost capacity. He increased profits and market-share for Morris but left after a row about his own share and joined Austin, whose approaches to Morris for a merger had been rejected and who was now prepared to make a fight of it. By 1937 Britain was second only

Top left: S.S. Jaguar 100, the 3½-litre sports car that first appeared in 1938. The model name 'Jaguar' was not applied to the make as a whole until 1947.

Top right: MG Mark I 18/80s leaving the factory for Carbodies of Coventry, 1929.

Above: Famous baby: a 5-hp Fiat Topolino four-seater, 1939.

Left: Volkswagen 30 prototype, 1937.

to the USA as a car producer. In that year Japan built precisely 1,819 cars.

Citroën's end

Louis Renault's empire now included the whole of the Isle of Seguin, in the Seine, which was covered with factory buildings. He invited his rival, Citroën, to see it but said afterwards, 'The only bad trick I ever played on Citroën was to show him the Isle Seguin.' Impressed by his rival's plant, the master of Javel ran up huge debts to compete. His revolutionary new front-wheel-drive car could have saved him, but, pressed by his creditors, he was forced to announce it before it was ready, even before all the equipment to make it had arrived from the United States. Michelin, the biggest creditor, moved in to take control and cut costs. Announced in May 1934, the car created a sensation, but its engine was too small and many other changes were needed. At the Paris Salon in 1935, the Traction was shown in its production form with engines of 1,628 and 1,911 cc. But André Citroën did not live to see it. A broken man, he had died of cancer three months earlier.

With its low-built body-chassis designed in collaboration with Budd, its torsion bar suspension (independent in front) and its engine-differential-gearbox unit attached to the front of the shell by four prongs, it was far ahead of most contemporaries. A six-cylinder model followed, with enlarged body, and with a gap during the war years the Traction remained in production until 1957.

Interest in front-wheel drive was also increasing in Germany. The DKW (first built with rear-wheel-drive in 1927) now appeared as a fast car first with a fabric body and two-cylinder two-stroke engine of 490 cc, later with handsome steel saloon and cabriolet bodies and larger engines. The engines were mounted transversely but, when after the war a three-cylinder was added, it was placed fore and aft. In 1932 DKW linked up with Audi, Horch and Wanderer to form Auto Union.

But the rear engine idea was spreading through several drawing offices. Even Mercedes-Benz were affected. In 1933 they unveiled the 130H saloon with 1·3-litre in-line engine overhung at the rear end of a tubular chassis. To make matters worse it had

swing axles at the rear, though for many years no one seems to have realized what a lethal combination a rear engine and swing axles could be. Stuttgart persisted with a bigger model, the 170H, but hedged their bets by producing a front-engined 170V with the same engine and suspension.

One company which had no such hesitation was BMW. Starting with the Dixi version of the Austin Seven, they quickly evolved a larger model with independent front suspension of a very simple kind, then launched a series of small six-cylinder cars of modern design which soon attracted attention. Greatest of all – and still much coveted 40 years later – were the handsome 327 2-litre coupé and convertible and the 328 sports two-seater, with its vertical and cross-over pushrods working inclined valves in hemispherical combustion chambers. It was the most versatile sports car of its day, winning rallies and muddy trials and running away from single-seaters on the race tracks, still carrying full touring trim of lamps, wings and windscreen. Beside it Jaguar's 3½-litre SS 100, with its non-independent suspension, looked like a relic of the vintage era.

People's Beetle and Little Mouse

The story of how the Volkswagen project developed through the Thirties has been told many times: how Porsche crystallized his concept through prototypes built for Zündapp and NSU; how Hitler, exasperated by German industry's failure to produce the cheap 'peoples' car' ('Volkswagen') he wanted, commissioned Porsche to design one with state backing. Industry's resistance to the idea is easily explained. The cheapest DKW cost 1,680 marks. Porsche calculated that the minimum price for his design would be 1,550 marks. Opel thought they could sell their new small car for 1,450. Hitler wanted a car selling for 900 marks, later raised to 990. By the Second World War the first three prototypes had completed the required 48,800 km (30,000-mile) endurance test, the first 60 pre-production prototypes to the final design had been built by Daimler-Benz and the vast plant at Wolfsburg had been completed.

As Italy was drawn towards war on the Axis side, IRI, the state financed organization, had to rescue Alfa Romeo, which had found fine cars and racing success no substitute for money in the bank. But Fiat were strong and full of ideas with a fast, stylish pillarless 1100 four-door saloon, the Balilla Coppa d'Oro sports car (like a miniature Alfa Romeo) and their own peoples' car, the 'Topolino', ('little mouse') a cheeky baby with forward-mounted four-cylinder engine, independent front suspension, hydraulic brakes and road holding that set a new standard.

Experimental work on streamlining continued in Europe, producing some striking results in speed and fuel economy. Sir Denniston Burney's rear-engined cars had no commercial success and Ledwinka's V8 Tatras, to the same basic layout, combined the natural instability of an oversteering rear-engined swing axle design with aerodynamic instability due to the centre of gravity being far behind the centre of pressure. V8 Tatras commandeered by the Germans invading Czechoslovakia were said to have featured in such disastrous accidents that they became known as the Czech secret weapon.

Professor Kamm made the most useful discovery, demonstrating that a car with a well-shaped front part can obtain good results without a long tapering tail. The Kamm form, with its sharply cut off tail, put an end to the futile pursuit of the 'teardrop' and paved the way for today's practical drag reduction techniques.

BUGATTI

AUTOMOBILES

EB BUGATTI

1940s

Once again the motor industry turns to war production: tanks, Jeeps, armoured cars and amphibians, and, of course, aero-engines. After the war two aircraft manufacturers, SAAB and Bristol, start producing cars. The post-war car is inexpensive and functional as typified by the Morris Minor and the 2CV Citroën.

Cristalli SECURIT

LA NUOVA BALILLA

1940's SMARTEST
DESCRIBES THE BRILLIANT PLYMOUTH "SPORTSMEN"

FIAT 1500

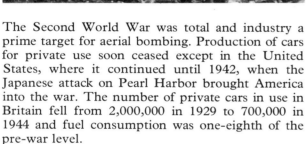

The Second World War was total and industry a prime target for aerial bombing. Production of cars for private use soon ceased except in the United States, where it continued until 1942, when the Japanese attack on Pearl Harbor brought America into the war. The number of private cars in use in Britain fell from 2,000,000 in 1929 to 700,000 in 1944 and fuel consumption was one-eighth of the pre-war level.

The British government had enrolled the motor industry in its pre-war Shadow Plan to boost output of aero-engines in an emergency. The factories were built and equipped and the car manufacturers were given a free hand to run them. Daimler, Rover, Standard and Rootes produced parts while Austin and the Bristol Aeroplane Company were to assemble the engines.

After the fall of France, when invasion was expected daily, there were fewer than 100 tanks in the hands of the forces in Britain and more were desparately needed. In one year Vauxhall-Bedford designed the 38-tonne Churchill, built prototypes, erected a new factory, established sources of supply for materials, installed the machine tools and started production. The new engine was designed and running in 89 days.

It used to be thought that the Nazis had planned the VW plant as a war factory from the start, but this seems to have been disproved. Permission to produce the military 'Kübelwagen' and amphibian designed by the Porsche organization was delayed, allegedly because established manufacturers, turning out their own cars for war use, were in a position to sidetrack it, and much of the plant was taken up with a jumble of other activities. In the whole war only about 55,000 kübelwagens and 15,000 amphibians were produced.

On the Allied side the one really new car was the Jeep. Built by Willys and Ford in vast numbers to designs by the Bantam organization, it was a nimble and efficient four-wheel-drive cross-country vehicle, but had a great thirst for fuel. Humber produced a large number of four-wheel-drive staff cars, Daimler the 4 WD Scout armoured car and Chevrolet the twin-engined Staghound armoured car with Hydramatic transmission.

There was great devastation from bombing on both sides but experience showed that heavy presses suffered little damage from anything short of a direct hit. The Mercedes-Benz body works was reconstructed by cleaning up the big presses in the open and using them to straighten mangled girders and roof trusses. Improvisation and hard work got production going again all over Europe in a surprisingly short time.

The fate of Louis Renault

In France the Liberation was followed by a bitter witch-hunt against those alleged to have collaborated with the Germans during the occupation. Some accusations were in good faith, others were to settle personal scores. Louis Renault, who had made enemies in his battles with the trades unions before the war, was vilified in the Communist press and accused of collaboration. He was arrested and taken to Fresnes prison. What happened after that not many people care to recall, but the author Saint Loup, admitting little initial sympathy with Renault, interviewed many witnesses for his book *Renault de Billancourt*. In two weeks the man who had entered prison fit and athletic was reduced to a physical wreck whimpering about maltreatment during the night. His wife, frantically rushing from one office to another for permission to visit him, was refused admission to his cell by armed civilians who warned her not to make a fuss or her son would suffer. When she did see him Renault was a dying man, suffering atrocious convulsions. Before he was buried she managed to have an X-ray photograph taken through the coffin. Verdict of the radiologist: fracture of a vertebra in the neck.

Renault was accused of putting his factory at the service of an enemy who would have taken it anyway.

Top, far left : The Churchill, British infantry support tank of the Second World War, put into production in miraculously short time by Vauxhall-Bedford.

Top left : Louis Renault in 1944, shortly after his arrest on a charge of collaborating with the Nazis.

Top centre : A pre-war German V8, the Horch Type 830 of 1938.

Top right : A 1938 Bugatti Type 57, 3·3-litre drophead coupé.

Above : Porsche 356 speedster, 1955.

He repaired the factory after it had been badly damaged by a British air raid in May 1942. The workers asked him to do so, for if the plant stopped production they would be sent as slave labourers to Germany. Renault was also said to have been late in delivering supplies to the French forces before the war but delivering promptly to the Germans during occupation. De Gaulle signed the decree nationalizing the company and confiscating all Renault's assets in it.

Later the figures were compiled. On a programme of 41,909 vehicles set by the Germans deliveries were 7,677 short but 1,792 vehicles had found their way to French buyers who had no permits. Renault was vindicated – but he was also dead. He had been a great industrialist but one fatally indifferent to politics and public relations.

Billancourt was wanted for a plant to build a French Volkswagen, for which Renault had built a prototype in secret during the war. After a spell in prison at Baden Baden Dr Porsche was taken to Paris to look at it. He said afterwards that he did little to change it apart from making suggestions to im-

prove its weight distribution. Early in 1947 Porsche and his son-in-law Dr Piech were moved to Dijon and imprisoned there, but the following year they were released on payment of a 500,000-franc bail each which Ferry Porsche raised by designing a Grand Prix racing car for Cisitalia.

Fortunately France found a giant of a man to run the nationalized Regie Renault, a man universally respected and with the character and authority to close ranks and set the company on a new course. Pierre Lefaucheux was a doctor of law with a degree in engineering. He had been railway engineer, construction engineer and administrator of an arms plant. As a major commanding resistance forces in the Paris region he had been denounced to the Gestapo and put in the Mauthausen concentration camp, but his wife contrived his escape by an amazing feat of nerve and courage just as the allied invasion of Germany was beginning.

Lefaucheux accepted the provisional government's invitation to take charge at Renault on condition that he had a hand in framing the company's new constitution. After a long, hard battle he achieved a charter guaranteeing Renault freedom from interference by politicians and civil servants. He realized that Renault must be free in order to compete effectively in world markets and summed up his philosophy like this: 'The State must not manage things itself. It must delegate powers without reservation. It must reign but not govern. . . . Nationalization does not necessarily imply State control.'

When the fighting was over and the British and Americans had withdrawn to the agreed frontiers much of Germany's mineral and industrial wealth had disappeared within the Russian zone. Included were the Auto Union plants at Zwickau and the BMW car factory at Eisenach. The new frontier was drawn just east of the VW plant at Wolfsburg (VW executives smile wanly when visitors who were not born at the time ask why it was built so near the frontier!). Later the proximity of the frontier, with the barbed wire, minefields and watch towers on the other side, presented certain advantages to the company. Many VW workers in these years were refugees from across the border and they were now so pleased to have secured their freedom that they worked with tremendous enthusiasm.

VW, 'not worth a damn . . .'

With hindsight scorn has been heaped on the delegation under Henry Ford II which dismissed the VW and its plant as 'not worth a damn' and the British technical mission which saw no commercial future in it, but the first model, on which they had to pass judgment, was a crude and noisy car. By the time it had passed the Model T Ford as the best selling car of all time, it had been so developed and redesigned that not a single original part remained. It started with a non-syncromesh gearbox, very little luggage space, a single instrument, no fuel gauge and cable brakes (the German authorities would not pay the high royalties demanded by Lockheed). It had the tricky oversteer that comes from a combination of rear engine and swing axles and needed constant gear changing in traffic. Its advantages were a lightly loaded engine which proved very durable (until attempts were made to increase power) and high gearing, which meant it could be driven flat-out indefinitely without trouble. It also gave a good ride over poor roads.

Production was started by the British army to provide themselves with vehicles. Later exports began to earn foreign currency which would lighten the British taxpayer's cost of administering the UK zone of Germany. One secret of VW success was the insistence on setting up spare parts stocks before cars were delivered. The British officer in charge, Major Hirst, did this after war-time experience of having to cannibalize new trucks when no spare parts were available. He claims he stopped the first export consignment of cars, bound for Holland, because the dealer had not fulfilled his agreement to set up a stock of spares.

There is irony here. While the British government was driving its own motor industry to export anything and everything, regardless of service and spares back-up – a policy to cause lasting harm to the reputation of British cars – a British officer was ensuring the future success of German exports by doing exactly the opposite.

Many fine pre-war cars had gone for good – the Rolls-Royce Phantom III, the Lagonda V12, the

Bugatti 57 series and the Royale (Bugatti died in 1947), the Horch, the Mercedes-Benz 540K and Grosser Mercedes, all the BMWs and the supercharged Alfa Romeo 8C two-seater.

Many less costly models, more suitable for post-war conditions, with fuel rationed and of low quality, were revived, but 1947–8 saw the real post-war designs emerging.

Two aircraft manufacturers started building cars. SAAB, in Sweden, combined a two-cylinder two-stroke and front-wheel drive with a streamlined shape. Bristol, in Britain, profited from the free use of ex-enemy patents to use a copy of BMW's 328 engine in a platform chassis with transverse leaf spring front suspension and a rear axle on torsion bars. The body was formed of 28 small pressings welded together and fitted on to a wooden frame.

Frazer Nash, using a Bristol engine, were able to advance ahead of the 328 chassis design with their new cars thanks to the presence of Dr Fiedler, from BMW, but he returned to Germany when BMW resumed production at Munich.

The war and the loss of all their tooling had apparently disorientated BMW management. Starting up in Munich in 1954 they built two vehicles, both out of character: a little Isetta mini car under Italian licence and a big, expensive V8 car. It was not until 1961 that Paul Hahnemann became famous by setting them to work that they should have been

Top left : A 1951 Standard Vanguard 1, a car introduced in 1947. Of generally modern appearance, its rear-end design did not meet with universal approval.

Above left : The 1949 Jowett Javelin from Yorkshire. This was an advanced design that in various guises had impressive competition results.

New Studebaker for 19...

Above right : The American industry was quickly into its post-war stride, with Studebaker often an innovator in styling: a 1950 advertisement.

Centre right : Advertisement for a 1947 Studebaker: new for that season was the revolutionary wrap-around rear window.

Below right : A 1949 Studebaker, glamorously portrayed.

doing all the time, building a sporting saloon (this time a four-door one) with a splendid new overhead camshaft four-cylinder engine. BMW enthusiasts instantly recognized it as the real thing and the company has never looked back. Engines lighter and more efficient than those of their main competitors have played a major part in BMW success, a situation for which Alex von Falkenhausen was responsible until his recent retirement. In the immediate post-war period he built and raced Veritas two-seaters based on the 328.

Back in 1936 Daimler-Benz had stolen a march on the industry with the 260D, their first diesel car. They built it in small numbers but by 1949 they were ready to go ahead with real series production of a new model, the 170D, using the same X-form tubular chassis as the petrol-engined 170. For nearly 30 years since they have developed and popularized diesel cars, passing the million mark in production.

Among the newcomers in Germany were two of whom more would be heard: Porsche and Borgward. Porsche had built a streamlined VW coupé for the projected Berlin–Rome race of 1940 that never took place, but a streamlined coupé, the 356, now went into production with a VW engine reduced to 1,089 cc, using two carburettors and special cylinder heads to raise power from 28 to 40 bhp. The shape was scientifically slippery and the car swiftly gained a reputation for high speed with very low fuel con-

The New Studebakers for 194...

sumption. Carl Borgward, of Bremen, evolved the Hansa saloon with pushrod engine and backbone chassis employing swing axle rear suspension.

Post-war UK

British manufacturers had been left in no doubt that their raw materials supplies depended on their success in exporting. Sales on the home market were severely restricted. As the USA, undamaged by the war and free of economic restrictions, seemed the most promising market, British car-makers adopted bench-type front seats and horrible, complex and costly steering column gear-changes which the Americans were said to demand. This deplorable fashion even infected Ferrari, who put a steering column shift on some of his Type 166 2-litre V12 cars.

Three early post-war designs from Britain were the Standard Vanguard, Jowett Javelin and Morris Minor. The Vanguard had a flush-sided body of modern shape, independent front suspension and a four-cylinder pushrod engine of 1,849 cc with a fairly short stroke. (This had grown to 2·1 litres by the time the car went into production.) Length was kept below 14 ft so that the car would fit into the average British suburban garage, but the wheelbase, six inches shorter than that of the old Twelve, seemed unnecessarily short. Apparently Sir John Black, who ran Standard, had a theory that the production cost of a car was directly related to the length of its wheelbase.

The Javelin was that *rara avis*, a car designed entirely by one man. Gerald Palmer, a young draughtsman from MG, produced an original design with 1½-litre flat-four pushrod engine (made from light alloy die castings), a unit structure built by Briggs and suspension by torsion bars, independent in front. It was an instant success, winning its class in the 1949 Monte Carlo rally and 24 Hours race at Spa.

The post-war Morris Minor, first major model from Alec Issigonis, was originally planned with a flat-four engine but started life with a 919-cc side-valve unit off the shelf, and despite several subsequent engine changes retained its popularity and its reputation for reliability. The headlamps, located

on the front grille of the original design were soon raised to comply with US regulations.

Lord Austin was dead, leaving Leonard Lord to launch a vigorous export drive in the USA with the A40, a new small saloon with a 1,200-cc side-valve engine and coil spring front suspension. It was unveiled in New York before the British press had even heard of it.

Among performance cars the most significant by far was the Jaguar XK 120. Exhibited at London's first post-war Motor Show in 1948, it attracted such worldwide attention that the intention to build a small series with aluminium bodies was abandoned and tooling for steel pressings started. Prewar SS cars, predecessors of the Jaguar, had engines based on Standard units with pushrods and cylinder heads by Weslake, but the XK 120 was the first to have Jaguar's new 3·4-litre engine with twin overhead camshafts. As usual William Lyons devised the body lines. Chief engineer William Heynes, chief designer

Top left : Alfa Romeo 8C 2900 B Corto.

Above left : Renault 4CV in 1955, when more than half a million of this rear-engined car had been built.

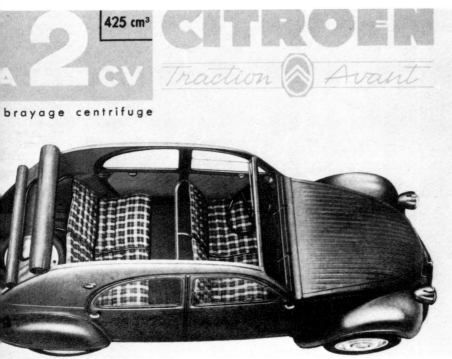

slow extinction by tax collectors who regarded them as exterior signs of wealth and so increased assessments accordingly. The most important new models were therefore small cars like Peugeot's durable 203, with an unusually advanced engine which had inclined valves in hemispherical heads operated by pushrods, and the nimble Dyna Panhard, using a light alloy air-cooled flat-twin engine with torsion bar valve springs to drive the front wheels. But the one destined to become most familiar was Renault's new baby, the rear-engined 4 CV. Nearly 1½ ft shorter than the VW, it had a water-cooled in-line engine of 760 cc, unit body structure and coil spring suspension, with simple swing axles at the rear. It had only three speeds and though it weighed 135 kg (300 lb) less than the VW it was geared to do 21 km/h (13·5 mph) per 1,000 rpm in top against 33 (21) for the VW. Nevertheless *The Motor* said it had 'general characteristics far more in line with popular requirements than those of the Volkswagen.'

America's love affair with the automobile was to raise the number of cars in use from 24 million to 61 million in ten years. A new manufacturer appeared, Henry F. Kaiser, who had shaken up the shipbuilding business by mass-producing Liberty ships. With Joe Frazer, an ex-Willys man, he set up the Kaiser Frazer Corporation in the former Graham plant in Detroit, building a big car with a body designed by Howard Darrin, and later a small car, the Henry J.

The search for style
The war marked a watershed in the outward form of the motor car. Separate wings and running boards were replaced by a smooth all-enveloping shape. It was a difficult transition and some designers never managed it successfully. The 1948 Earls Court show revealed some excruciating confections which showed that the great British coachbuilding houses no longer had anything to contribute to the evolution of style.

France did little better and the lead passed to the Italians, who have held it ever since. Pinin Farina showed his sure touch in his Cisitalia coupé, which for a time was an exhibit in the New York Museum of Modern Art. Carrozzeria Touring also produced some beautiful designs in a transitional style recalling the 1940 Packard Clipper. Unfortunately when Packard moved on to the full 'pontoon' form the result was dull and heavy; the best of America's postwar crop were the Studebakers credited to Raymond Loewy, although Virgil Exner is said to have had a hand in them.

In matters of style, Citroën are perhaps the most baffling of all manufacturers. They can produce designs of great originality and charm, like the first Traction or the DS 19, but in between come apparitions of mind-numbing ugliness like the 2 CV or the Ami-6. First new model after the war, the 2 CV was a highly original attempt to produce the minimum acceptable motor (the brief spoke of 'four wheels and an umbrella'). It had no radiator, ignition, distribution or door hinges. Simple interlocking flanges took the place of hinges and the wings could be removed in seconds, using the wheelbrace. Yet it had four doors, a sun roof and seats that could be lifted out for picnics, or to make space for bulky loads. The suspension, interconnected between front and rear, gave a soft pitch-free ride, and the flat twin air-cooled engine driving the front wheels seemed happy to be driven flat-out indefinitely. The 2 CV soon became a cult, and probably no other car has penetrated to so many remote places on the earth, from Africa to Asia, from Alaska to Tierra del Fuego.

Top right : Final inspection of cars at the Morris works, Cowley, Oxford, in 1946.

Above right : Citroën 2CV Traction Avant of 1954, twenty years after its introduction.

Claude Baily and engine specialist Walter Hassan did the rest. Victory in the TT, three successive Coupes des Alpes and countless other successes quickly established Jaguar as a major manufacturer of high-performance cars.

The Lagonda V12 had become a war casualty but W. O. Bentley set a fresh course, designing a new 2½-litre six-cylinder engine with twin overhead camshafts for a chassis which had independent suspension all round, coil springs in front and torsion bars at the rear.

Donald Healey was quick off the mark with his new sports car, using a Riley 2·5-litre engine. The chassis, on which A. C. Sampietro collaborated, had coil spring suspension. In front were two trailing arms, the lower one in light alloy on needle roller bearings. The Silverstone two-seater had a distinguished competition career.

In France the surviving Grandes Routières – Hotchkiss, Delahaye and Talbot – were doomed to

1950s

Cars in the USA become increasingly flamboyant with ostentatiously styled tail fins and wrapround windscreens plus a huge engine. Citroën's DS19 makes a technological breakthrough with hydro-pneumatic suspension. Issigonis designs the Mini, the most successful small car to date.

By 1950 the ravages of war had been largely repaired and vast sums were being invested to increase car production. At the war's end the world had some 45 million cars in use; by 1956 there were 100 million and the figure has been rising ever since. But increasing competition was forcing the industry to concentrate into larger, more powerful units.

In 1952 Austin and Nuffield merged to form the British Motor Corporation. In effect this was a take-over by Sir Leonard Lord, who was in command of Austin and was settling the old score of his abrupt departure from Cowley years earlier. Morris, now Lord Nuffield, had quarrelled with everyone who was of sufficient stature to succeed him, and seemed to have lost interest in the business, devoting his time to charitable work. But while he gave away millions to alleviate suffering and improve the lot of mankind the business which provided the money languished, without proving ground, research laboratories or modern design facilities, and he proclaimed his personal indifference to the product by continuing to run an old pre-war Wolseley Eight.

From now on his empire would be run from the forbidding administration block at Longbridge – known to staff as 'the Kremlin' – but true integration would never be achieved within BMC. Instead the era of 'badge engineering' was at hand. Austin engaged Pinin Farina to design the little A40 with A35 mechanical parts and he made it one of the best-looking British cars since the war. His next job was

Above left : American with a European flavour : the rear-engined Chevrolet Corvair, a compact car with an air-cooled flat six unit.

Above right : A British-built American : the Nash Metropolitan, which had an Austin A40 engine and was manufactured at Longbridge.

Left : Lord Nuffield in 1947, content with a pre-war Wolseley Eight.

a new saloon body shell which was used for Wolseley, Austin, MG Magnette, Morris Oxford, and Riley. Incidentally it was some time later that Pinin Farina changed his name to Pininfarina. There had already been another company, Stabilimenti Farina, run by his brother, and when his nephew, Giuseppe Farina, the racing driver, announced his intention of setting up as a coachbuilder, Pinin thought it was time to change his own name to avoid confusion.

In America, Nash and Hudson came together to form American Motors, and when his dreams of becoming a major car-maker faded, Henry Kaiser's company was absorbed by Willys. Nash and Austin devised a unique example of transatlantic cooperation in the little Nash Metropolitan. Typically American in style, but built at Longbridge with A40 mechanical parts for the American market. Tooling costs were probably a quarter of what they would have been in the USA, and the Metropolitan was followed by a limited-production sports car, the Nash Healey.

A glitter of chrome – and fins

Studebaker started the period brilliantly with the Starlite coupé, one of the most beautiful American cars ever seen, but it was soon encrusted with the usual chromium barnacles, first a three-pointed star (quickly removed under pressure from lawyers acting for Daimler-Benz), then irrelevant brightwork by the square foot which destroyed it entirely. It was a foretaste of the excesses which were to mark the Fifties. Soon the stylists were revelling in wrap-round windscreens and giant tail fins which, like the steering column gearshift and bench-type front seat, were slavishly followed in Europe by people who should have known better. The wrap-round screen distorted vision in the corners (which could not be wiped) and took the main part of the glass so far away that dead flies and raindrops came into focus. It demanded a heavily cranked and reinforced pillar, which painfully struck the kneecaps of people getting in and out. The tail fins reached grotesque proportions while doing nothing for directional stability that could not have been done better by proper chassis engineering. And some chassis improvements were urgently needed to cope with the sudden increase of power demanded by the publicity departments.

For the great horsepower race had started. Com-

pression ratios went up to 10-to-1 on the big V8 engines. Packard announced 275 bhp from 5·7 litres. Chrysler introduced their hemispherical-head 5·4-litre with 300 bhp and the race was on. Cadillac announced 325, and so it went on until an Eldorado was credited with 400 bhp, an output that would have transported the occupants comfortably in a private plane. In fact the figures were meaningless, for they were obtained by current SAE standards on the test bed, without power-consuming auxiliaries like dynamo, power steering pump or air conditioning compressor and without standard inlet or exhaust systems. Much less power reached the wheels, but the tyres fitted, the vague steering and the drum brakes still in general American use would ensure that any attempt to use the full performance, especially on a wet road, would lead straight to the graveyard.

Ford had an immediate success with the compact and sporty Thunderbird, announced in 1953, but in 1957 they bit the dust with the Edsel, probably the greatest flop in the history of the American industry. Hailed in a colossal advertising campaign as a new kind of car, it turned out to be the old kind, notable only for front-end styling which sparked off some blue jokes and press-button selection for the gears, a bad idea because it meant that the driver had to take his eyes off the road. Its market image was not clear either, as it entered two price classes, one above Mercury and one below.

The public had had enough. They turned to smaller and more practical cars in what *Automobile Year* called 'The reaction of reason against the infatuation with excessive size and power which no longer has any practical value. . . With broadening horizons the ubiquitous automobile is losing its status as a success symbol.'

The tail fin era was the high point of the stylist's ascendancy over the engineer, and styling became a dirty word. The people who shape today's cars prefer to call themselves designers. They are specialists who understand the economic and industrial consequences of every line they draw. Their activities are circumscribed by books full of international regulations and their creations must earn favourable verdicts from the computer, the wind tunnel and the public at secret pre-release 'clinics'.

But there was one more disaster in the pipeline. In 1959 Chevrolet revealed the Corvair. Designed to

cater for that very trend to smaller cars, it weighed 545 kg (1,200 lb) less than an Impala but had almost the same passenger space. Its styling had an immediate impact worldwide – but its engineering created impacts of another sort. Its flat-six air-cooled engine was overhung at the rear and the early examples, with swing axle rear suspension, suffered vicious oversteer. GM engineers seemed to have taken the worst features of the VW and exaggerated them. After extensive modification it was phased out in 1969 (it had also proved costly to make), but by then consumerist Ralph Nader and his 'Raiders' were in full cry and a legislative strait-jacket was being fashioned for car designers throughout the world in the name of safety.

Piston engines challenged

The Fifties brought two possible alternatives to the piston engine. In 1950 Rover revealed their first experimental gas turbine car. Fiat and Renault showed their designs and Chrysler built 50 gas turbine Plymouths for long-term evaluation. Since then progress has been made in reducing the lag in throttle response as the rotor speeds up to 20,000 rpm or more and in producing heat-exchangers to put the waste heat in the exhaust to use. The gas turbine's clean exhaust and smooth flow of power are attractive, but fuel consumption remains fairly heavy and the cost of tooling for mass production would be very high.

The other new power unit was the Wankel engine. After many years of experimental work NSU released details. In 1963 a rear-engined Prinz was put on the market, followed by the excellent NSU RO80 saloon with twin-rotor engine driving the front wheels. Neither achieved large sales, but in Japan Toyo Kogyo manufactured their millionth Wankel engine early in 1978. Early sealing problems appear to have been overcome and fuel consumption comparable with good piston engines is being obtained on experimental Audi units. Compact, light and delightfully smooth, the Wankel is a most attractive power unit, though it is now being challenged by exhaust-driven superchargers which can dramatically increase the power-to-weight ratio of existing piston engines and offer very good fuel economy at a fraction of the Wankel's price.

In February 1955 Renault was plunged into mourning. On the way to a conference in his Frégate, Pierre Lefaucheux skidded on an early morning patch of ice. The car rolled over but was little damaged in a perfectly survivable accident. But Lefaucheux's suitcase hit him and broke his neck. He died a disillusioned man. His high hopes of making Renault a model of efficiency among nationalized industries and a model employer had been obstructed by Communists using the unions for political warfare, he believed. He wrote in the works magazine of professional agitators who treated Renault as a war machine and believed that 'the Regie must be hampered in every possible way and as often as possible in order to place it in a difficult financial position, to cause it if possible to go bankrupt and . . . prevent it from giving the staff the material advantages that can be granted only if the concern is flourishing.'

In the same year Heinrich Nordhoff invited thousands of guests to Wolfsburg for an immense jamboree to celebrate the production of the one-millionth Volkswagen. He had no labour problems. Too many of his workers had escaped from the other side of the Iron Curtain and knew what it was like.

Nasser's 1956 seizure of the Suez Canal brought a new crisis. With the Canal blocked Europe's oil supplies from the Middle East had to go via the Cape, greatly increasing costs.

Rolls-Royce introduced their Silver Cloud and abandoned manual gearboxes, but buyers who were concerned about rising petrol prices had the most interesting choice of small cars in a long time. Renault's Dauphine, launched in 1956, was a logical step up from the 4 CV, with a remarkably good luggage boot for a rear-engined car. It gave a very lively performance and excellent economy from its

Top left : Bentley R series Continental of 1953.

Above left : The Edsel, a Ford line that lasted for only two seasons. In this instance, costly market research proved unsound.

Above right : A 1951 Studebaker.

Right : American luxury: the large Packard Caribbean convertible of 1953. The company merged with Studebaker the following year.

845-cc pushrod engine, thanks to resolute weight reduction. British engineers examining it found body panels and glass of lighter gauge than any available in Britain, and on dynamo, starter, door handles – everywhere – weight had been saved.

Fiat also returned to the rear engine with their 600. Designer Dante Giacosa had built prototypes of other configurations but the rear-engined model turned out the smallest for given interior space, and as material costs represented 50 per cent of total production cost this was a strong argument, coupled with the fact that expensive constant-velocity joints were not required in the transmission. Admitting that oversteer was a problem, he dealt with it by a simple and ingenious idea. The transverse leaf spring at the front was clamped at two points but free in the middle. In corners it acted as an anti-roll bar, helping to promote a countervailing understeer.

Harry Webster adopted the conventional front-engine rear-drive layout in designing the Triumph Herald, and gave it a separate backbone chassis. Triumph bought some of their panels out, so the body was made of small pressings bolted together. This was exploited by producing saloon, coupé and station wagon, all with the same panels below the waistline.

The magnificent Mini

But the design which has outlasted them all is the Mini. It was the brilliantly successful result of an intuitive approach by one man, Alec Issigonis. He spent no time studying market research or examining possible alternatives, with the exception of the power unit. An opposed piston two-stroke and a vertical twin four-stroke were tried before he settled for the production A-type four-cylinder reduced to 850 cc. Explaining his highly personal approach to design, he said, 'We built parts and prototypes quickly from rough sketches and diagrams, then tried them out on the test bed or test track before handing them over into the intellectual atmosphere of the drawing office.' Ten-inch wheels, with special tyres produced by Dunlop, were an essential element in this brilliant space-saving design, and Moulton suspension, using rubber partly in compression and partly in shear, gave results not possible with steel springs.

The Mini has profoundly influenced design in all major car-producing countries. Even the United States is now building cars with transverse engines and front-wheel drive. But though more than four million Minis have been built they seem to have made little profit for the company.

Two brave moves by small car-makers deserve mention here. In 1958 the Van Doorne brothers, successful truck manufacturers in Holland, decided to enter the highly competitive small-car market. They had something unique to offer – a simple stepless, continuously variable, automatic transmission using rubber belts – and it succeeded. The first little car had a light alloy flat-twin engine of 590 cc, air-cooled, and front suspension was by transverse leaf spring with telescopic dampers acting as struts. Later models used Renault engines and a De Dion rear axle replaced the independent layout. DAF continued bravely into the 1970s, when the car side was taken over by Volvo.

Top left : Citroën provided originality of design once more in 1956 with the DS 19; shown here is the 1961 model.

Above left : The Fiat 600, an advanced rear-engined design of 1955.

In Britain Colin Chapman built a special place for Lotus in the sports car market by highly original engineering. With the Elite he produced the first unit body-chassis structure in resin-bonded glass fibre. Plastic bodies had been made before; the Chevrolet Corvette body was produced by advanced methods that greatly reduced the time required to produce the mouldings, and in Britain the Jensen 541 S had a plastic body. But the Elite was unique. Though the hard discipline of racing revealed weaknesses, and for subsequent models Chapman reverted to a separate chassis, he continues to use moulded bodies.

But the technical breakthrough of the decade was revealed at the Paris Salon of 1956. Citroën announced a car which stands as a landmark in technical progress, the DS 19. With independent hydro-pneumatic suspension, self-levelling to cope with load variations, it set new standards in riding comfort. It was the first production saloon to have disc brakes (mounted inboard in front) and braking effort between front and rear was varied according to load distribution. Clutch and gear-change were hydraulically operated and steering was power assisted.

Top right : The Renault 4CV – a 1957 model, a decade after the car's introduction.

Above right : The 1956 Renault Dauphine, with rear-mounted 845-cc engine: the first French model of which two million examples were sold.

Right : On 6 August 1955, one million Volkswagens had been produced since the Second World War and Wolfsburg spelled it out in suitable fashion.

1960-70s

Mergers and alliances between big companies take place in Britain and Europe. New designs of the sixties range widely from the Ford Cortina to the Jaguar E-type. Safety becomes a burning issue. The motor industry is hit by OPEC's increase in the price of oil. Japan takes second place in the league of car-producing nations.

A DODGE
HAT SPECIAL?

1969 POLARA

most people want.

Then cut the price.
And give it a name . . .
DODGE WHITE HAT SPECIAL POLARA.
The Dodge Polara White Hat Special comes in a 2-door or 4-door hardtop—with the features listed below—at a special low package price.
• Vinyl roof in black, white, tan, green or standard top • Front, rear bumper guards • Fender-mounted turn signals • Outside, remote-control rearview mirror • Whitewall tires • Deep-dish wheel covers • Bright trim package.
Look for the special "White Hat" sticker.
It's your ticket to a money-saving deal.

It's your move. Get
DODGE fever

LANCIA-ITALIA

CINTUF
PIRE
vin
1972
RALLYE M

1974 is a beautiful time for Mo

Monaco. A country so thrilling and beautiful there's a magic to its name. That's Monaco, the country. But there's another Monaco.
Dodge Monaco. Unmistakably new for 1974. Outside, it's a car styled with elegance and flair. While inside awaits a quiet world of luxury and comfort. Exterior styling and interior luxury, however, do not tell the entire story of the 1974 Dodge Monaco. Throughout, there are a host of Ch advances . . . torsion-bar su famous Electro Dodge Mo ably new. Unmis This year, unmis

The History of the Motor Industry – 1960–70s

In the Sixties the weaknesses which had been developing for years – loss of export markets, poor productivity and low returns on capital – wrought far reaching changes in the British motor industry. Daimler, which had been producing dreary, uninteresting cars, was swallowed up by Jaguar, providing them with much-needed extra production capacity at a favourable price. The famous Daimler radiator grille was put on some Jaguar saloons and an impressive new limousine was developed with Jaguar engine and suspension and a Vanden Plas body.

Standard Triumph became rather small and vulnerable when they sold the Ferguson tractor business to Massey Harris, and the Herald was an attempt to enlarge their product line quickly. Teething troubles proved expensive and in 1961 they were saved from collapse by a Leyland take-over.

In 1965 Alvis were taken over by Rover, who in turn were scooped into the Leyland net two years later. Meanwhile BMC had taken over Jaguar, but Sir William Lyons found he had jumped on to a sinking ship. With profits falling sharply the new combination, now called British Motor Holdings,

fell easy prey to Leyland and Sir Donald Stokes (later Lord Stokes) took command. Unfortunately events were to show that, as the Expenditure Committee of the House of Commons expressed it, Leyland had neither the financial nor the management resources to make a success of the merger.

Like Renault in France and Alfa Romeo in Italy, British manufacturers became increasingly the targets for damaging strikes. One such, at a press shop in Acton, closed down the whole Rootes Group for three months in 1961. Lord Rootes stuck it out but the company, heavily extended in financing the Linwood plant to build the Imp, was mortally wounded. Difficulties with a labour force new to the motor industry and troubles with porous castings in the light alloy engine and the pneumatic throttle control delayed deliveries of the Imp and it never achieved the hoped-for market share. Two years of losses forced Rootes to seek help from Chrysler, who took complete control in 1974.

Apart from serious industrial disputes, the British motor industry has suffered ever since the war from attempts by governments to use it as a means of regulating the economy. Taxes and credit regulations have changed incessantly in attempts to enforce short-term changes in demand, with a frivolous disregard for the effect on long-term planning. Lord

Top left : A 1962 Triumph Herald 1200 saloon.

Top right : A 1962 Pontiac Tempest sedan.

Above left : The Jaguar E-type 4·2-litre sports car started on its successful career in 1961.

Above : The long-running Ford Cortina, a 1969 model.

Left : Morris Minor 1000. This model dates from 1961, when a million Minors had been sold.

Stokes pointed out that during the Sixties alone the industry had to contend with 17 changes in taxation or credit arrangements. Other European motor industries were able to plan their investment and model policies in a stable environment, and so to operate more efficiently.

VW goes public

In 1960 VW were relieved of one element of uncertainty – who owned the company? In 1949 the British authorized the West German Federal government to dispose of the firm. They delegated control to the state government of Lower Saxony. But more than 80,000 savers had been buying stamps before the war and sticking them in books which the Nazis assured them could one day be exchanged for a new People's Car. Lengthy litigation was settled with the offer to these savers of cash or a discount off a new car. Then the company was floated on the stock market, the Federal and State governments each taking 20 per cent of the shares, the public the rest. In 1965 VW celebrated the production of their ten-millionth car.

A sharp downturn in the American market in 1960 had some disastrous results. The new compact cars had handsomely succeeded in their main purpose of choking off the imports and they took 25 per cent of the market, but it was a very anaemic market. In France, Germany and Britain production was cut and thousands of men were laid off. Renault had to make heavy sacrifices to move 60,000 cars which were rotting in the open in the US. Only VW rode out the storm unharmed, thanks to their hand-picked and tightly controlled dealer network. They sold 177,000 cars in the US in that year and advanced steadily to a record 400,000 by 1966. By 1961 US production had dropped 26 per cent and it was estimated that there were a million unsold cars in stock. British exports dropped 50 per cent and, true to form, the British government decided that if the motor industry could not sell its cars abroad it must not be permitted to sell them at home either. Purchase Tax was increased to 55 per cent. Fuel tax, annual licence and profits tax were increased and credit was restricted. Finally, a specially vindictive punishment was devised for Rolls-Royce, Aston Martin, Jensen and any other make which might be trying to preserve Britain's standing in the prestige car market:

a top limit of £2,000 was placed on tax deductible expenditure on cars for business use. Yet 15 years later, when the British industry had been brought down to ruin, plenty of politicians were ready to criticize it for failing to plan and invest.

The American compacts had a number of interesting features including a light alloy six-cylinder engine from American Motors and a light alloy V8 from Buick which was later sold to Rover and, in developed form, powers the Range Rover, the 3500 and the Morgan Plus 8. Most unusual was the Pontiac Tempest, with a big 3,185-cc four-cylinder engine connected to a rear-mounted clutch, gearbox and differential by a long flexible propeller-shaft which sagged in the middle to permit a low floor level.

A German victim of the recession was Carl Borgward. His Borgward, Goliath and Lloyd range covered a broad spectrum from baby cars with two-stroke engines to well-equipped middle-range cars with air suspension. He was clever at improvising but lacked the resources to weather a severe storm. Lancia were in trouble too, partly as a result of an expensive racing programme, and Vincenzo's son lost control to Carlo Pesenti, who had made a fortune out of cement. He installed Dr Fessia as technical director and the first result was the Flavia, with flat-four engine and front-wheel drive, drawing on Fessia's experience with the stillborn Cemsa Caproni project.

Jaguar launched the E-type, another instant success, and Triumph unveiled the Spitfire sports car, with a body designed by Michelotti, who also did the Herald. Then Ford scored two big hits. From Dagenham came the Cortina, a product of market research and analysis by product-planner Terry Beckett, who had spotted a need for a lively, economical car with more body and boot space than anything then to be had in its class. Its success propelled Beckett on his way to the Chairman's desk at Ford of England.

Over in the States Lee Iacocca had devised another winner, a compact and sporty car called the Mustang with body lines by Gene Bordinat. It swept the newly affluent youth market and became the best-selling car in the whole Ford range, helping its creator towards the Ford Presidency.

In 1963 sales recovered as the economic brakes applied during the Suez crisis were released. The

Morris 1100, with Hydrolastic suspension inter-connected between front and rear, turned out to be another successful Issigonis design. Ford of Germany got a new Taunus but were to regret it. Originally designed in Detroit as the Cardinal, it embodied eccentricities like steering and front suspension wobbling about with the engine.

The creative mid-Sixties

A fine crop of new designs came in 1964–5; Rover's 2000, with telescopic De Dion axle and girder frame covered with unstressed body panels; the majestic Mercedes-Benz 600, with air suspension and hydraulic assistance for brakes, steering, seat adjustment and central locking; the first V12 Lamborghini, from a tractor manufacturer who had decided he could make better cars than Ferrari; Oldsmobile's Tornado, a new American essay in front-wheel drive, with silent chain connecting the V8 engine to a Hydramatic transmission alongside; Renault's 16, a trend-setting five-door front-drive hatchback with versatile seating arrangements so far ahead of French taste it took some time to get established; the Audi 100, designed by Daimler Benz engineers after they had bought the company, with 11·2-to-1 compression and Heron heads; and Peugeot's 204, with transverse light-alloy ohc engine driving the front wheels. And in 1966 came the Fiat 124, one of Europe's most successful family cars, forming the basis for the Russian Lada and Jensen's FF with permanent four-wheel drive and Maxaret anti-lock braking.

Citroën was causing concern to Michelin, who controlled it. The secretive management under Pierre Bercot produced occasional brilliant ideas but lacked marketing skill and showed scant regard for profit. At the end of 1964 they formed a company with Peugeot to work together on new projects, but in two years Peugeot decided it would not work. Pierre Dreyfus, Renault's new chief, had been watching uneasily, realizing that a Peugeot-Citroën fusion could create a formidable competitor.

Renault had now got the rear-engine bug out of its system. The front-drive R4 utility hatchback was a success and under the technical leadership of Yves George a complete switch to front-wheel-drive was under way. Dreyfus initiated talks with Peugeot and was soon able to announce a Peugeot-Renault agree-

ment covering cooperation on technical and industrial problems, rationalization of investment and improvement of production methods.

Citroën had taken over Panhard and extinguished it, and in 1968 they moved in on Maserati, who were given the job of producing a new V6 engine for Citroën's prestige SM, a splendid but space-wasting coupé which had the technical features of the DS plus new ones like power steering whose assistance varied inversely with the speed. Bercot also had an agreement with NSU for joint production of Wankel engines in the Comotor plant, in Luxembourg, but this led to nothing more than a few high-priced GS saloons with Wankel engines. With the situation deteriorating, Bercot turned to Giovanni Agnelli and worked out an agreement for a Fiat–Citroën collaboration, but it was soon clear that Fiat expected control; Citroën would not concede this so Fiat withdrew.

By 1975 Citroën's situation was desperate and the French government stepped in. Citroën's Berliet truck subsidiary was pressed upon a reluctant Renault and the car business was placed under the wing of an

Top left : Fiat's wind tunnel.

Above left : Mercedes-Benz 600, a 6·3-litre Pullman limousine, introduced in 1964.

was acquired from Daimler-Benz and NSU were taken over, with them a new model which became the VW K 70. It had not been designed for mass production so a year was lost in redesigning it, and after it came out more time was needed to cure noise and poor performance, but it served notice that VW were no longer tied to rear engines and air cooling. The losses began mounting alarmingly and the trades unions did not like Lotz, so he was sacrificed by the government interests and Rudolf Leiding was brought in.

With his chief designer, Ludwig Kraus, from Audi, Leiding embarked on the swiftest and most comprehensive new model programme ever seen. Working, as he put it, 'a 25-hour day', they drove themselves and their staffs to create an entirely new range of cars with new bodies, engines, transmission, suspension. When Kraus had to retire because of injuries received in a car crash Dr. Ernst Fiala took charge. And out they came – Audi 80, Passat, Scirocco, Golf, Audi 50 and Polo; two-doors, four doors, hatchbacks, station wagons, all with overhead camshafts and front-wheel drive, every one an immediate success. The pace was maintained with the five-cylinder Audi 100, the Golf diesel and the Audi

Top right : Fiat crash test. From the mid-1960s, legislators and manufacturers became increasingly concerned with improving safety standards.

Above : The Rover 2000, an advanced design from a highly regarded British company, 1964.

Above right : Fitting the wheels in the Volkswagen works, Wolfsburg.

equally reluctant Peugeot, which got substantial state aid for its trouble. The nightmare of Pierre Dreyfus had now come true. He was faced with a French competitor of his own size. The collaboration on engines via the Peugeot–Renault–Volvo agreement continued. The Renault 14, first Renault to have a transverse engine, used a Peugeot power unit. But they no longer shared so many secrets.

By 1970 Lancia was facing collapse. They had never been able to use their expensive new plant at Chivasso to the full and could not finance the new model programme they needed. Fiat did not need Lancia but had to rescue them to avoid serious unemployment in Turin, or a possible foreign takeover. Ing. Montabone was installed to bring out the new Beta range, based on Fiat mechanical parts, buying time while more distinctively Lancia models like the Gamma could be created.

Heinrich Nordhoff died in 1968. Like Henry Ford he had found it hard to believe that 15 million owners could be wrong, that people could lose interest in the car that was a familiar sight all over the world. His successor, Kurt Lotz, had to move fast. Audi

Avant hatchback – and still the Beetle poured out of overseas plants on its way to a 20-million total, though no longer made in Europe. In two years VW had sustained crippling financial losses; now the money started rolling in again. But not soon enough to save Leiding, who had been replaced by Toni Schmucker.

Selling safety

Many in the industry believed that trying to sell safety features implied that motoring was dangerous and was bad for business. In 1956 Ford tried it in America and got a good response from the public, but the word went out that 'Ford sold safety and Chevy sold cars.' The argument was an excuse for inaction until 1965, when Ralph Nader's book *Unsafe at Any Speed* made car safety a burning topic. Nader had an easy target in the Corvair, with its lethal combination of rear engine and swing axles, but he cited other examples too – tyres too small for the load, brakes that failed, suppression of information about dangerous faults. The American industry was superbly equipped with proving grounds,

laboratories and instrumentation to analyse every aspect of car performance, yet no great benefit was discernible in the products. Though Michelin and Pirelli were making radial ply tyres in quantity by the mid-Fifties and disc brakes started appearing on British and French cars in 1956, these important safety features did not come into general use in the USA until nearly 20 years later.

Before Nader started his campaign Volvo was providing padded instrument panels, safety belts, attachments for head restraints and disc brakes as standard equipment. In 1951 Mercedes-Benz had taken out a patent for a rigid passenger compartment with deformable impact-absorbing ends and had been running a big programme of crash tests to develop it in production form. Now much of the industry's scientific manpower was switched to full-time work on the twin subjects of safety and pollution. The American authorities put out contracts for the first Experimental Safety Vehicles, then other governments joined in and for years ESVs showing an increasingly cost-effective approach were exhibited at international conferences. Now hundreds of cars and many dummy passengers are sacrificed in crash tests each year to ensure that new models meet increasingly stringent regulations.

This imposes heavy burdens on small manufacturers with limited resources and on specialist coachbuilders. The leading Italian houses, Bertone and Pininfarina, are not seriously affected for they saw in the Fifties that they must become industrialized to survive, and they equipped themselves not only to design and build prototypes but to produce complete cars in quantity for the big manufacturers. Karmann, in Germany, took the same course. Gaetano Ponzoni and Bianchi Anderloni, of Touring Superleggera, tried to do the same. They built a beautifully equipped factory, but failed to get enough contracts and had to close down, ending a distinguished career.

Italdesign has a different policy. Its design chief, Giugiaro, is world famous, but around him he has a group of specialists who can cost a new design, work out the best ways of making it and even design

Top left : Lamborghini's Miura P.400 of 1966, with transverse 4-litre V12 unit, was capable of over 170 mph.

Top right : The first Lamborghini car, 1963, had a 3½-litre V12 engine developing 360 bhp.

Above : The Renault 16, introduced in 1965: revolutionary body configuration and 63 bhp.

Left : Citroën 2CV in cabriolet form, 1961.

the tooling to produce it in quantity; an attractive package for manufacturers not big enough to keep a complete design staff fully occupied or for those who are temporarily overloaded.

Pininfarina built what was then the best full-scale wind tunnel in Europe, now an essential tool for the body designer where he can try out ways of reducing fuel-consumption, improving stability and ventilation or diverting mud from windows and lamps. Ford, Fiat, VW, Volvo and the British industry at MIRA now have large tunnels, some climatized to run cars in Arctic or tropical conditions. They have revolutionized the approach to 'streamlining' by showing that small changes in the shapes of conventional cars can bring appreciable gains in fuel economy and stability.

1970s

The Seventies began well, with production and sales building up to where most manufacturers set new production records in 1973. There was, of course, a spectacular failure in 1971 when Rolls-Royce, ruined by heavy losses on the RB211 engine for the Lockheed Trident aircraft, had to be rescued by the British government and nationalized. Whitehall was not interested in the Car Division, which represented only about 5 per cent of turnover, so after an agonizing period of suspense under the management of a receiver it was reorganized as Rolls-Royce Motors and launched as a new public company. Since then, under the shrewd management of David Plastow, it has become the most consistently successful British motor company, supplementing a healthy profit on cars with diesel engines, piston aero-engines and other special products.

The euphoria of 1973 was short-lived. Sheikh Yamani managed to weld the Organization of Petroleum Exporting Countries (OPEC) into a power bloc strong enough to dictate terms to the industrialized West. Oil prices quickly quadrupled. The shock started a worldwide recession. Wild thoughts of another Suez, with the West going to war to secure its fuel supplies, quickly subsided and the oil-consuming countries quietly acquiesced in an unparalleled transfer of wealth from the West to the Middle East.

Higher taxes, fuel rationing, speed limits and credit restrictions hit the motor industry and production plummeted as motorists travelled less and, more slowly, decided to make do with their existing cars

instead of buying new. In 1973 the United States built 9,667,571 cars; in 1975 it was 6,717,043. West Germany dropped from 3,648,681 to 2,907,819. France from 3,202,391 to 2,952,824, the UK from 1,747,316 to 1,267,696. The only European manufacturers who managed to keep going at full capacity were BMW and Mercedes-Benz.

But to the dismay of European producers the rise of the Japanese continued almost unchecked. In 1973 they built 4,470,550 cars, in 1975, 4,567,854. They had started modestly after the Second World War, building Austins, Hillmans and Renaults under licence to gain experience of modern production methods, and had then created new models of their own. They began exporting to Far Eastern and other preferring countries which did not have motor industries, then swept into Australia.

The Americans realized the extent of the Japanese threat and decided to buy a piece of the action. GM acquired shares in Isuzu, Ford in Toyo Kogyo (Mazda), Chrysler in Mitsubishi. Japanese cars were imported into the USA and sold under American names. When the rise in the deutschmark made imports from Germany too expensive, GM introduced Japanese Opels, and when deliveries of Avengers from Britain became erratic Chrysler substituted Colts from Japan. As Americans lost interest in the Beetle, which had hit a peak of about half a million sales a year, the Japanese consolidated their position. In 1977 they sold about 1,380,000 cars in the USA – three times as many as West Germany and twice as many as the rest of the world combined.

Ironically their invasion of Europe was largely financed with British Leyland money. To gain control of its European sales network, Leyland spent millions of pounds buying out its importers and Belgian assembly plant, only to see the money invested in setting up sales and networks for Japanese cars. The invasion first established footholds in Belgium and Switzerland, but, seeing the British industry so crippled that it could not meet home demand, the Japanese moved into the UK and quickly took up to 11 per cent of the market, provoking protests which have led to some easing of the subtle non-tariff barriers with which the Japanese discourage car imports into their country. There has been some voluntary restriction of Japanese imports into the UK, but with Ford, Chrysler and GM, and even British Leyland, importing cars built in Europe to make up for the deficiencies in their UK

output the total market share of the imports has been as high as 46 per cent.

Leyland – paralysed giant

Lord Stokes, wrestling with a group that had too many factories, too many models, too many workers and not enough output, had been unable to halt the decline of British Leyland, and early in 1975 the government had to move in to avert complete collapse, acquiring about 95 per cent of the shares. Lord Ryder, a publishing and paper-making entrepreneur, was given the job of devising a new structure for the corporation. It proved unworkable, and Ryder's production and export targets proved far too optimistic. Hundreds of millions of pounds of the taxpayers' money were swallowed up and there was little to show for it. To try to correct the widespread impression that British Leyland had become an organization for creating jobs, not motor cars, another change was made in 1977. Alex Park, who had succeeded Lord Stokes, was discarded and Michael Edwardes, from the Chloride group, moved in to start yet another reorganization.

Only a few months after the Leyland rescue, Chrysler, heavily hit by the collapse of the American market, announced their desire to abandon their strife-ridden UK interests. They even offered Chrysler UK to the British government as a free gift

but it was not accepted. Instead, after a week in which John Riccardo crossed the Atlantic daily in his executive jet, he was persuaded to keep Chrysler UK going and integrate it with his other European operations, Simca, in France, and Barreiros, in Spain, in exchange for a government promise to compensate him for the losses involved. The taxpayers who had paid exorbitant taxes when buying and using their cars now found themselves paying more taxes to build cars in utterly uneconomic conditions.

GM did better with Vauxhall, installing Bob Price, who had hoisted their ailing South African subsidiary to No. 1 position. He inspired the workforce to improve quality, created the hatchback Chevette, which was adopted as the T car, GM's first car for worldwide production, and strengthened the range with an Opel-based Cavalier imported from Belgium.

Having set up Ford of Europe in 1968, Ford led the way in international integration, culminating in the establishment of the new plant in Spain, where Fiat had previously enjoyed a comfortable lead through their 40-per-cent holding in SEAT. The prospect was attractive enough for the Spanish government to change the law. Previously car manufacturers wishing to set up in Spain had to guarantee 95 per cent local content. Ford wished to import engines from the UK and Germany and trans-

Top left: Car production in Japan, now placed second after the United States in the world table.

Top right: The highly commended Rover 3500, 1976.

ing a much improved Fiat 127 to compete.

Giovanni Agnelli and Henry Ford II have much in common. Both were brought in after the untimely deaths of their fathers, to control vast enterprises founded by their grandfathers. Agnelli's father had died in an air crash, Ford's from cancer. Both exercise power more freely than any chairman of General Motors; neither can be forced to retire at a fixed age by any company rule. Both have been obliged to move far ahead of the politicians in setting up practical international collaboration and Agnelli has not always concealed his contempt for the limited intellects dredged up by political processes. The contrast between their results and those of nationalized industries is sharply illustrated in Italy, where Fiat-Lancia-Autobianchi-Ferrari holds more than 80 per cent of the market despite the investment of large sums of government money in Alfa Romeo. The Alfasud plant, near Naples, planned for 280,000 units a year, does not produce half as many and makes a heavy loss on every car sold.

In recent years Ford have very cleverly changed their corporate image. Previously associated with the cheapest cars – the Model T, the Popular, the Anglia – they now offer the young a sporty image based on more than 100 Grand Prix victories with

Above : Japanese cars lined up for export.

Above right : The 1977 Fiat 127. This transverse-engined 900-cc car was introduced in 1971.

missions from France, so a guarantee to export two-thirds of output and restrict sales in Spain to 10 per cent of the market was accepted instead.

The Fiesta saga

Ford set up in Spain to build the Fiesta, and the story of that car's lengthy gestation has already filled one book. Ford could no longer ignore a market which had become the most fiercely competitive of all, where profits were notoriously small and the most successful models were front-wheel-drive cars intrinsically expensive to make. The Mini, Fiat 127 and Renault 5 were firmly established and the VW Polo was on the way. In the early stages the Fiat was seen as the car to beat and the first mechanical assemblies were run in Fiat body shells. The years of design and redesign, of cost-cutting, of secret clinics where the public passed judgment between nameless prototypes and their competitors, plus the building of the vast plant at Valencia – all made this the costliest single project in the history of the industry and by far the biggest gamble Ford had ever taken. Needless to say, Agnelli lost no time in launch-

Ford Cosworth engines and innumerable international successes with Escorts. Basically an utterly orthodox cheap saloon, to compete with the Opel Kadett and Vauxhall Viva, the Escort was viewed with scorn by Ford of Germany, who thought it too crude to appeal to sophisticated German buyers. They were proved utterly wrong, possibly with the aid of works rally teams equipped with twin-cam sixteen-valve engines. The image-building started with the four consecutive Ford victories at Le Mans in 1966–9 and was continued with Formula Ford low-priced single-seater racing. Ford bought Ghia, the Italian coachwork designers, which gave them the use of a prestige name and emblem to put on top models and also brought into the fold a successful young designer, Tom Tjaarda, son of the man who had designed the body for the Lincoln Zephyr.

From 1969 the new Ford image was boosted by the Capri. Using stock engines and other parts, it was not a sports car – indeed the word 'sports' was not mentioned, in case the insurance companies should impose prohibitive premiums – but a four-seater for the young family with a sporty image. It was a runaway success. Mastermind behind the operation was Walter Hayes, Ford's Director of Public Affairs. In the later stages he found a powerful ally in Bob Lutz, former jet pilot and sales director of BMW, who helped transform the Taunus-Cortina and the Granada of 1976–7 into cars which could be regarded as serious alternatives to BMWs.

BMW themselves had an image problem during the revulsion from speed that followed the fuel crisis. The word 'Turbo' in reverse on the front air-dam of the turbo-blown 2002 was denounced in the German press as a demand for other drivers, reading it in their driving mirrors, to make way, and BMW were branded as dangerous aggressors by the older generation, who sailed along in Mercedes. BMW switched the emphasis to comfort and refinement while making sure that standards of performance and road-holding were maintained, and the crisis passed. When their new plant at Dingolfing was running at full capacity they were selling more petrol-engined cars than Mercedes-Benz, who kept their overall lead only because of their position as top producers of diesel cars.

Things to come

As the motor industry moves into the Eighties the general pattern is of the strong becoming stronger and the weak becoming weaker, leading to further concentration into fewer units. The trend can be resisted by first-class management and an inspired product policy, as BMW has shown, and voluntary cooperation could help to preserve individual identities. Through PRV, Renault, Peugeot and Volvo share the costs of engine design, development and production. Renault and British Leyland are examining ways of working together on transmissions. Fiat, Alfa Romeo and Renault Saviem have developed a range of light diesel engines together. VW and Daimler-Benz have an informal arrangement for technical collaboration, while VW engines are to be bought on a short-term basis by Chrysler.

But if management and control are concentrated into fewer and larger units, car manufacture is being dispersed into more and more distant units as markets in the developed countries near saturation and their people become less keen to work on assembly lines. An army of workers anxious to build cars and a home market capable of great expansion led Ford to set up the great Fiesta plant in Spain. Renault has started to build a motor industry in Portugal. Fiat is challenging VW's domination in Brazil and has set the pace in providing know-how and technical collaboration to develop motor industries in communist bloc countries, although there are signs that here Fiat may have created new competitors for themselves on world markets.

Chrysler UK helped to set up an Iranian motor industry, assembling Hillman Hunters. The industry is being expanded under the technical guidance of an Englishman, George Turnbull, who set up the South Korean motor industry, and Peugeot are now involved, providing parts of their 305 model. In Turkey Anadol build cars with Ford mechanical parts and glass fibre bodies designed in England by Ogle, using production techniques developed by Reliant. The smaller the market, the more unlikely are the partners who are drawn together to maintain a foothold: VW assembling Japanese cars in Australia or making Jeeps in South Africa after having built all the Volvos out there.

In the world car production league General Motors appears quite unassailable, producing up to five million cars a year in the USA alone. Ford is

second, producing more than two million, but Chrysler US, with about 1·3 million cars a year, has dropped to fifth place, behind Toyota (1·8 million) and Nissan (1·7 million), whose swift rise has hoisted Japan into second place among the car producing nations. Taking cars only and ignoring the Jeeps, American Motors has dropped to 29th in the world table, behind BMW, SEAT and Audi.

Sixth in the world output table is Fiat, in Italy, while VW and Renault closely contest seventh place. But the success of VW, Daimler-Benz and BMW backed by the very successful American subsidiaries, GM Opel with over 900,000 cars a year and Ford of Germany with about 800,000 puts West Germany solidly in third place among car producing countries. France is fourth, thanks to Renault and Peugeot-Citroën who in 1976 made more cars than Renault. Italy holds fifth place, thanks to Fiat but with little help from Alfa Romeo which, held back by chronic labour troubles, is not even among the top 30 companies.

The UK has dropped to sixth place, British Leyland never approaching its potential output of over one million cars a year and unable even to keep pace with Opel or Ford of Germany, while American

Top left : Vauxhall Chevette L, 1975.

Top right : Mazda RX3, 1974 – a limited number were put out when the Toyo Kogyo company celebrated the production of their 500,000th rotary-engined vehicle.

Above left : Ford Fiesta, 1976.

Above right : Cadillacs ready for shipping from Detroit.

Right : The 43-bhp Renault 5, French challenger for the small car market.

companies in Britain import cars to make up deficiencies in their British output. A point often overlooked is the large output from countries not normally regarded as car manufacturers. Canada and Belgium each turn out more than a million cars a year, mainly from American subsidiaries, though British Leyland relies increasingly on its Belgian plant, at Seneffe, where it has been achieving uninterrupted production and good quality.

The possibility that the supply of oil will run out soon after the end of the century has led to some gloomy views of the future for the motor industry, but an industry giving employment to millions of people and which has been the pacemaker and stimulant for economic activity throughout the world cannot be lightly written off. Between now and the end of the century lighter, more efficient cars will appear, using a fraction of the fuel needed today. A reduction of 30 per cent, giving up to 60 mpg, is already a possibility. And if the oil ever does run out cars will run on hydrogen or alcohol, or on oil extracted from coal or some other fuel, for it is readily apparent that people will not easily relinquish the mobility and the freedom that only the car can provide.

PETROLEUM

Petroleum

etroleum or crude oil is the source of most of the fuels and lubricating oils used in internal combustion engines, including those in motorcars. It is a complex mixture of hydrocarbons (compounds whose molecules contain only hydrogen and carbon atoms) and was formed naturally at a much earlier stage in the world's evolution following the overlaying of vegetation through seismic activity.

The use of petroleum dates back to the earliest civilizations. In various places, it has seeped to the surface and been used, among other functions to provide fuel for lights and pitch for the caulking of ships. However, the natural occurrence of petroleum on the surface is not widespread, and the modern exploitation of the product dates from the first known instances of drilling for oil in North America in the mid-nineteenth century. There are varying claims as to who first 'struck oil'. The principal argument is between the United States and Canada. According to the US version, Edwin L. Drake became the first man to strike oil on 27 August 1859. Drake was a train conductor on the

New York and New Haven railroad, his only material possessions being some stock in a company called the Pennsylvania Rock Oil Company. This concern owned a farm near Titusville, Pennsylvania, which was the site of some oil springs.

Drake was taken ill and lost his job. Another stockholder, James Townsend, asked him to visit the farm and make a report. On the strength of that report, Townsend took over the farm and formed another company called Seneca Oil. Drake was made general agent at a thousand dollars a year and instructed to drill for oil. With Uncle Billy Smith, a local blacksmith, he drove an iron pipe 10 m (32 ft) through quicksands and clay until they reached bedrock. Then they started drilling.

On Saturday afternoon, 27 August 1859, just as they were about to stop work for the day, the drill dropped into a crevice at 20·7 m (69 ft) and slipped down 15 cm (6 in). The men pulled out the tools and went home.

On Sunday afternoon, Uncle Billy, out for a stroll with his sixteen-year-old son, Sammy, stopped by the well and peered down. Floating on top of the pipe was a dark, glimmering liquid – oil. Western Pennsylvania became boom territory, towns sprang up and disappeared again, fortunes were made and lost overnight. Ironically, Drake and Uncle Billy had hit on the only spot for many miles around where

there was any oil at that shallow depth of 20·70 m (69 ft).

The above version of the first drilling of oil has been generally accepted by historians but Canadians disagree. According to the Canadian version, the world's first oil well was drilled in Ontario.

A family named Rouse settled at a place called Black Creek in Ontario in 1837. On their property they found a black, gummy substance which presumably gave the place its grim-sounding name. Then in 1851 two brothers named Tripp mined and distilled it and produced asphalt. For this they received an award at the 1855 Paris Exhibition, an award which clearly proves, says Canada, that the Tripp brothers were the first men to develop petroleum commercially. Financial difficulties caused Charles Tripp to sell most of his holdings to one, James Miller Williams. He grew tired of wresting asphalt from the gum beds and thought some form of lighting would give a better reward. Instead of chopping and boiling, he dug – and at 4·20 m (14 ft) he struck oil. The year was 1858, a year before Drake's discovery. Around the site grew the boom town of Oil Springs which flourished until even more oil was found at Petrolia, eight miles away. Today Oil Springs is the site of a modern Oil Museum.

The Americans claim more documentary evidence

Top left : Oil derricks at Oil Creek, Pennsylvania, in 1865, a few years after the first drillings for oil had started the serious exploitation of petroleum.

Above left and centre : Edwin L. Drake and Billy Smith, believed by the Americans to be the first men to 'strike oil'.

Above right : Drilling for oil in the difficult conditions of the North Sea has entailed the construction of enormous platform rigs.

Top right : Men at work on a land-based oil rig in the United States.

Right : Early equipment is already of interest as industrial archaeology. This old oil rig was photographed in the United States.

than the Canadians. The Canadians, on the other hand, can produce newspaper reports of 1858 which refer to oil being barrelled up and transported to Hamilton, Ontario.

Whatever the answer to the rival claims, that time was undoubtedly the period in which serious oil production got under way and set in motion the processes which led to the modern motorcar.

Since that time, fields have been opened-up in many different parts of the world; according to The British Petroleum Co. Ltd, probably at least 1,500 fields are currently in production, and there could well be a similar number of additional discoveries that have not yet been worth developing.

The petroleum fields usually lie well below the earth's surface, whether they be under land or water. They are tapped by drilling and, because the liquid is generally under considerable pressure, extraction is a matter of controlling rather than encouraging the flow. In the case of under-land fields,

the practice today is to pump the crude through pipelines to the refinery or oil terminal port; from the latter, huge tankers – often 200,000 tonnes or more – transport the oil to the overseas refineries.

For sub-aqueous fields the problems of drilling and extraction are obviously more complex. Deep-water drilling, as in the North Sea, requires huge platform rigs. Loading the petroleum directly into tankers is technically easier than the alternative of a sea-floor pipeline but it involves very costly vessels that have to make alternate journeys unladen. On the other hand, laying a pipeline over a long distance and an irregular sea bed is a mammoth undertaking, and the risk of pollution through any failure is greater, but the operating economics are much better than for tankers. The choice of solution therefore depends on the individual circumstances.

Nature of petroleum

Petroleum's unique character stems from its being not one substance but a range of them, having a wide span of boiling points and densities. Consequently they can be separated by fractional distillation – that is, passed through a tower which is hotter at the bottom than the top, so the various fractions can be drawn off at different levels. The resulting spectrum, starting from the lowest boiling point, comprises petroleum gases, liquid fuels of decreasing volatility, and residual products from which lubricating oils, heavy fuel oils and bitumen can be extracted. Those liquid fuels in turn consist of three main groups which are gasoline or petrol, kerosene or paraffin, and gas oils which include diesel fuel and light fuel oils.

The discovery of petroleum and the isolation of its lighter fractions as liquid fuel made the internal-combustion engine practicable for road vehicles and subsequently aircraft. Without such a convenient fuel it is quite possible that those late-19th-century engine pioneers would not have bothered with the transport side, maybe concentrating instead on improving the industrial gas engine which had already been in existence for some years.

This is not the place for a long dissertation on the chemistry of petroleum, but a brief outline of its constitution is desirable. The actual analysis varies from field to field – even from well to well – but in general terms the major elements of a crude oil are the carbon (85–90 per cent) and hydrogen (10–14

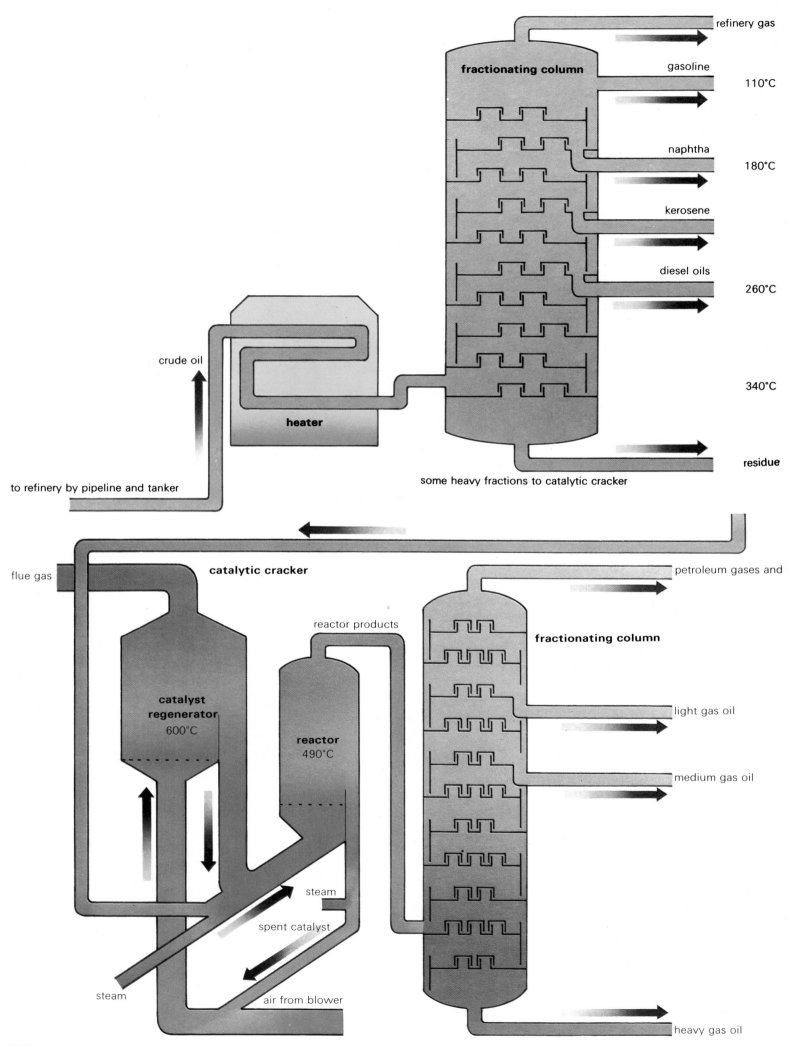

refinery gas

gasoline

110°C

fractionating column

naphtha

180°C

kerosene

diesel oils

260°C

crude oil

340°C

heater

residue

some heavy fractions to catalytic cracker

to refinery by pipeline and tanker

flue gas

catalytic cracker

petroleum gases and

reactor products

fractionating column

catalyst regenerator
600°C

reactor
490°C

light gas oil

medium gas oil

steam

spent catalyst

steam

air from blower

heavy gas oil

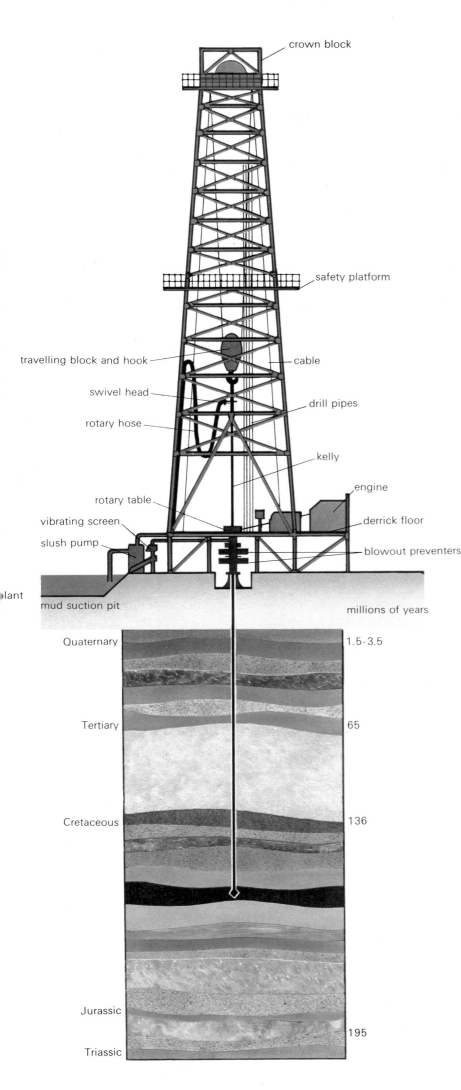

crown block

safety platform

travelling block and hook

cable

swivel head

drill pipes

rotary hose

kelly

engine

rotary table

derrick floor

vibrating screen

slush pump

blowout preventers

plant

mud suction pit

millions of years

Quaternary — 1.5-3.5

Tertiary — 65

Cretaceous — 136

Jurassic — 195

Triassic

per cent) of the hydrocarbon content, plus small amounts of sulphur, nitrogen and oxygen, and usually traces of other elements including nickel and vanadium.

Three principal types of hydrocarbon – paraffinic, naphthenic and aromatic – are found in petroleum. Each comprises a range of compounds having the same basic molecular structure but a different number of carbon and hydrogen atoms in the molecule and hence different molecular weights; the lighter the distilled fraction the larger its proportion of compounds of low molecular weight. The differences between the basic molecular structures of the paraffins, naphthenes and aromatics results in different chemical and physical properties; since the relative proportions of the three groups varies from one crude to another, the distillates clearly have corresponding variations. Consequently, one crude may be fundamentally best suited to the production of high-grade gasoline, for instance, and another to the production of diesel fuel or even lubricating oil. However, refinery techniques now enable so many changes to be rung that the actual composition of a particular crude is no longer of great importance.

Improving petrol's knock resistance
For the first two decades of this century, normal fractional distillation – although it gave more low-grade than high-grade gasoline – met the market requirements. The less good fuel was acceptable to the not very energetic road-vehicle engines of those days, while the other's use was virtually confined to racing and aircraft units (sometimes with the admixture of benzol, a hydrocarbon produced during the coking of coal).

The principal advantage of the lighter gasoline fraction was that it allowed an engine to have a higher compression ratio without detonation or knock (explosive ignition instead of normal burning of the fuel/air mixture). However, one of the major objectives for engine progress after World War 1 was to achieve more power by raising the compression ratio; since knock can be destructive, the demand for the higher-grade fuel rapidly increased.

To meet this demand merely by increasing refinery production would have meant surpluses of other fractions – an economically unacceptable situation. What was urgently needed, therefore, was something to give the lower-grade gasoline the same resistance to knock as the higher-grade variety.

The answer was found by US chemists in 1920. It was tetraethyl lead (TEL for short), only a few cubic centimetres of which in a gallon of petrol were enough to allow the knock-limited compression ratio to be raised by 50 per cent or more. Not only did TEL upgrade the heavier fraction as required but it also enabled more power to be extracted from engines already on a high-grade diet. Hardly surprisingly, 'leaded' fuels quickly came on to the US market, and were available in Europe too just a few years later.

It is appropriate to mention at this stage that the knock resistance of a gasoline is indicated by its 'octane number' or 'octane rating'. This is determined in the laboratory, using a special single-cylinder research engine with a variable compression ratio. The engine is run under specific conditions, first on the test fuel and then on a series of reference fuels to find one that gives the same knock intensity as the test fuel.

These reference fuels contain only iso-octane and heptane, which are paraffinic hydrocarbons chosen because they have respectively a high and a low

resistance to knock. The reference fuels all have different proportions of the two ingredients, and the test fuel's octane number is the percentage of iso-octane in the matching reference grade. For evaluating test fuels of over 100 octane rating, as available for some engines of very high performance, special reference fuels are used: they consist of iso-octane with the addition of very precisely measured quantities of TEL.

At the time of writing, four grades of petrol – designated two-star, three-star, four-star and five-star – were available for motorists from garage pumps in Britain. The corresponding *minimum* octane numbers of these grades are 90, 94, 97 and 100 respectively.

Refinery advances

Going back into the past again, TEL on its own ceased to be sufficient by about 1930 because the demand for high-grade gasoline had expanded so much in relation to that for the heavier petroleum fractions. Hence the refineries had to find ways of increasing the crude's yield of the lighter products. The first process to be adopted for that purpose was 'cracking' – breaking-down the heavier hydrocarbon molecules (those with more carbon and hydrogen atoms in them) into a larger number of lighter molecules more suitable for motor fuels.

Cracking was soon followed by 'reforming', a somewhat similar process in which low-grade gasoline was improved in quality by rearranging some of the molecules to form different compounds with superior anti-knock properties. Initially, cracking and reforming were effected thermally, by the application of great heat and pressure, but catalytic

cracking – more efficient and versatile – was introduced around 1935 and soon became popular.

The next step forward was the adoption during the Second World War of the catalytic version of the reforming process, to enable enough high-octane fuel to be produced for the powerful piston engines of military aircraft. Post-war progress has brought in several additional processes, all aimed at increasing the percentage yield of high-octane petrol. Two of these processes – polymerisation and alkylation – are noteworthy since they work the other way from cracking: molecules of petroleum gases, the lightest hydrocarbons, are made to combine to form liquids of higher molecular weight.

Little need be said about the light gas oil burnt in automotive diesel engines, partly because such engines are still very much in the minority for cars and partly because this fuel has involved much less technology through the years. However, it has been improved significantly by the introduction of methods of reducing the content oil suphur and aromatic hydrocarbons; sulphur is undesirable in any petroleum fuel because of its corrosive and pollutional potential, while the aromatics, though valuable in a gasoline engine for their knock resistance, adversely affect the burning properties of a diesel fuel.

Lubricating oils

Mineral oils for engine and transmission lubrication are produced by the vacuum distillation of the residue of the crude after the removal of the gasoline, kerosene and gas oil fractions. The distillates are then purified in stages by the removal of waxes, aromatics (undesirable also in a lubricant) and

Above: This 35 cm (12 in) marine pipeline was floated from Lutong to the Shell Main Oil Pump Station in Seria. In the picture, the plastic floats are being removed, the pipeline having reached dry land.

Top : The trans-Alaskan oil pipeline winding across a characteristic landscape. It is seen variously as a technological triumph or an environmental hazard.

Above : This throng of French cars illustrates the besetting and often conflicting problem of conserving world energy resources and reducing pollution.

being topped-up. The late 1930s therefore saw the dawning of the 'age of the additive'.

First on the scene were metallic compounds that not only gave greater resistance to metal-to-metal wear in conditions of marginal lubrication but also had an anti-oxidant effect. Their use reduced the need to use a thicker oil when an engine was made to give more power, or to change the lubricant more frequently where the consumption was reduced.

Then, shortly after the Second World War, engine oils having dispersant/detergent additives began to appear. These kept combustion and oxidation products in fine suspension so that they could not settle out in oilways or on piston and ring surfaces. In conjunction with more effective anti-oxidants they effected a big improvement in engine cleanliness and performance retention over long periods.

The third major type of oil additive, which arrived shortly after the dispersant/detergent variety, was the viscosity-index improver. It consists of a 'long-chain polymer' which converts an ordinary single-grade oil into a multi-grade – one that has the cold viscosity of a light oil but the hot viscosity of a considerably heavier one. Multi-grade oils are given a two-figure designation: a typical one, SAE 20W–40, has the cold viscosity (and hence gives the easy starting) of a quite thin, SAE 20W lubricant yet the viscosity of a quite thick, SAE 40 one at its working temperature. Because of their superior characteristics, these multi-grade oils are now widely used in car engines despite higher cost.

Conservation and pollution

During recent years mankind has come to realize that, thanks to the internal-combustion engine – in the motorcar in particular – the world's reserves of petroleum are rapidly being exhausted. A lot more fields may yet be discovered but few experts believe that these reserves will see us far into the 21st century. Because of the inestimable but considerable time necessary to harness alternative sources of energy – a subject in itself – it is clear that increasingly strict measures will be introduced to limit the consumption of hydrocarbon fuels.

It looks as though this objective will be sought by a combination of means. The use of public transport in place of private cars will be encouraged and speed limits will tend to become stricter, while engine capacity and perhaps performance could be restricted, as could vehicle dimensions and weight, both of which have a bearing on fuel consumption. Vehicle manufacturers are already having to quote official consumption figures, and their engine specialists will undoubtedly be encouraged to improve the efficiency of their products – by intensive research into combustion or the diesel principle.

Unfortunately, that other vehicular preoccupation of the world's legislators – the reduction of atmospheric pollution – does not run easily in harness with fuel conservation. No one can deny that, until a few years ago, the motor vehicle was making a big contribution to poisoning our planet. However, the photochemical smog in the Los Angeles basin – nasty as it was – hardly justifies the USA's imposition of progressively more draconian laws that, by 1977, were causing the motor manufacturers an enormous amount of trouble in producing *legal* engines of notably feeble performance, higher fuel consumption and high cost. The impartial observer cannot help feeling that a more modest anti-pollution target and a tougher economy one would have been more appropriate to the times.

unstable materials which could result in undue corrosion or sludge deposition.

A primary characteristic of the resulting oils is that their viscosity or thickness varies considerably with temperature. The extent of the thinning-off with heating varies somewhat with the crude and with the treatment given to the oil after the distillation stage.

In addition, the strength and hence the 'lubricity' of the oil film on rubbing surfaces depends largely on the viscosity. In the days when engine power outputs were low, so also were bearing loadings and temperatures; consequently, a 'straight' oil of the type so far discussed could be thin enough for reasonably easy cold starting, and good initial lubrication thereafter, while retaining adequate film strength at its normal running temperature.

As engine outputs increased, though, and operating conditions toughened, even the refinery-made improvements to the viscosity index (the rate of viscosity change with temperature) became insufficient to avoid the need of oils that were unduly thick when cold. Also, design and manufacturing improvements were markedly reducing engines' oil consumption, so the inevitable deterioration of the lubricant through oxidation became more of a problem than when the system was frequently

HOW CARS WORK

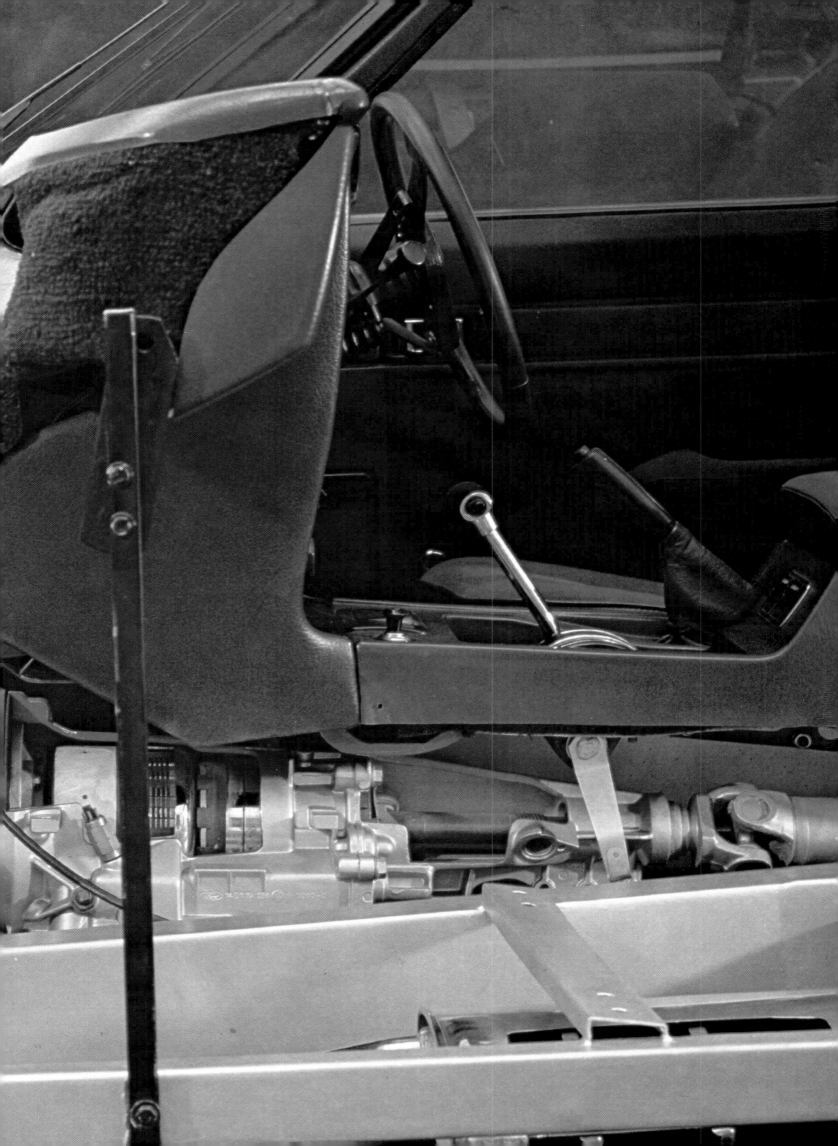

The motor car became possible in 1862, when Beau de Rochas patented the four-stroke cycle for internal combustion engines. His invention, used to this day, opened the way towards engines which were lighter and more economical than any previously known. Heavy steam vehicles were already in use on roads as well as on railways, but suddenly much lighter, simpler and livelier horseless carriages became a possibility. In 1885–86 Gottlieb Daimler and Karl Benz applied simple internal combustion engines to road vehicles which were far lighter than contemporary steam wagons. By 1891 the Societé Panhard et Levassor had evolved a car layout which is still recognizable in many popular models.

A motor car may be quite a simple mechanism in its bare essentials. It has wheels to run on, an engine for propulsion, a clutch to let the engine be coupled to the wheels, change-speed gearing to suit varied gradients and speeds, brakes to slow or stop the car when necessary, a frame to hold all the components together, and some sort of springing to protect the whole assembly from road bumps. Beyond that list, most extra items are desirable refinements rather than elements essential for the car to work.

Panhard et Levassor cars from 1891 onwards featured a multi-cylinder internal combustion engine mounted at the front, with its crankshaft fore-and-aft along the centreline of a four-wheeled vehicle. Directly behind the engine was a friction clutch, then change-speed gearing with four different ratios, and bevel gears to turn the drive through a right-angle to the rear wheels. The only two fundamental differences from a modern car layout were that reverse gear was given by a separate bevel gear rather than by extra pinions in the change-speed mechanism, and that flexible transmission of power to the sprung rear wheels was by chains rather than by jointed shafts.

A few years after the first front-engined Panhard et Levassor vehicles were built, some remarkably good cars were on the road and a speed record of more than 145 km/h (90 mph) had been set by Henry Ford. In the long period since 1903, cars have been made more comfortable in all weathers, quieter, easier and safer to drive, more reliable yet less demanding of skilled maintenance, and capable of sustaining whatever speeds the law permits. Above all, cars and the factories which build them have been evolved together to permit mass production by available numbers of craftsmen and other less-skilled workers.

Mainstream development of cars from the layout of 1891 has continued, but two important diversions to substantially different car layouts must be recorded. One enjoyed a period of great popularity and then lost favour, whereas the other has gained so much favour in recent decades that in many countries it has become the new orthodoxy.

Karl Benz built his first car in 1885 with the engine between the two rear wheels. Virtually without exception, car-makers have judged that a vehicle should be steered by its front wheels and the simplest mechanical arrangement is certainly to transmit power to the un-steered (rear) wheels. Dr Ferdinand Porsche's Volkswagen design of the 1930s was based on an appreciation that the lightest, simplest and cheapest way in which to build a car was with the engine and gearbox immediately adjacent to the driven rear wheels.

Rear-engined cars were at their most popular in the 1950s and 1960s, fore-and-aft engines being mounted just behind the rear wheels with the clutch and gearbox in front of the engine. Power came out of the gearbox at the same end by which it had entered, but through a second shaft parallel to the input shaft, and bevel gears then took power 'round a corner' to the rear wheel drive shafts.

There is a wider clear space between a car's rear wheels than between the front wheels, which must swivel to steer the car. So, a short but wide engine makes especially good use of available space. Volkswagen had 'horizontally opposed' cylinders, set in pairs at each side of a short crankshaft, whereas most other small car engines have cylinders arranged in one line above a longer crankshaft. Because they were initially planned to be as simple and light in weight as possible, many rear-engined cars had finned cylinders cooled directly by air blown over them, instead of cylinders cooled by water which (although better able to get heat away from critical areas) must itself be cooled in turn by a separate radiator.

Small rear-engined cars gave very good service, but the tail-heaviness of a car with most of its mechanism at the back posed dynamic stability problems. Instability on corners or in emergency swerves was eventually overcome on the best rear-engined models, but it proved more difficult to make a tail-heavy car run really straight when a gusty cross-wind was blowing. Rear-engined cars have lost favour, but the layout has not been totally abandoned, and new design ideas or changed economic conditions could revive its popularity.

Front-wheel-driven cars existed from an early stage in motoring history and became quite important commercially in the late 1930s. In return for the extra complexity of transmitting power to steered front wheels, it was hoped that pulling rather than pushing the car along the road would enhance stability. Certainly concentrating all mechanism at the front of the car, rather than having an under-floor gearbox and a drive shaft to the rear axle, let a car be built with a lower floor and so a lower roof.

Citroën have an important place in history as early mass-producers of front-wheel-driven cars. A major vogue for fwd began when the Morris Mini-Minor was introduced in 1959. Transverse rather than fore-and-aft placing of the four-cylinder engine, with the gearbox below the engine which was right between the car's front wheels, saved a lot of space. To get a lot of passenger room within compact overall dimensions, much larger cars have been built with layouts rather similar to the Mini. A front-wheel-driven car's nose-heavy weight distribution tends to make the steering heavier to operate, but it certainly helps a designer to make his car dynamically stable, and to achieve good traction on muddy or snow-covered roads. In many parts of the world, front-wheel drive is now very popular indeed.

From the first very simple vehicles, cars developed to be much more complex and better equipped. Protection of the driver and passengers against bad weather evolved gradually through partial to complete enclosure. This made ventilation necessary, then controlled heating for cold weather, and for very hot countries, refrigerated air conditioning. Electric starters which eliminated the need to crank engines by hand were a major advance. Pneumatic tyres, putting an air cushion between the wheels and the ground, proved vital for fast and smooth travel over imperfect road surfaces. Powerful lights, to permit fast travel at night, needed subtle control so that oncoming drivers were not dazzled. First for front windscreens and later for other glazing, means were evolved for getting rid of raindrops, condensation, mud and ice.

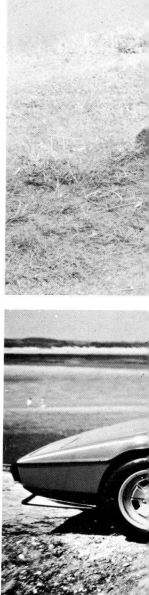

Top : Model-A Cadillac of 1903. Similar in many respects to the early Fords, it had a single-cylinder 1½-litre engine.
Above : Lotus Esprit Mark II.

Cars changed in their proportions, partly to suit operation at high speeds and partly at the dictate of fashion. Lower build, which reduces air resistance and enhances stability, requires extra length to accommodate the passengers' outstretched legs. Increasing width let the improved cornering grip of modern tyes be used without risk of overturning.

Engineers have commented, with considerable truth, that development is more important than design. Within the range of reasonable alternatives, major changes of layout may do less to create a better or a worse car than will attention to (or neglect of) countless trivial-looking details. Engineering theory can guide a designer, but practical experience of a particular design or of closely similar predecessors provides more exact knowledge of how strong or rigid each part should be, about the best combinations of materials and surface finishes for parts which must work together, and about the best clearances to allow between moving parts. When a bold new design is introduced, a lot of new lessons may have to be learned before detailed perfection is achieved.

So, the more radically new a design is, the more it may cost for modifying prototypes before the product is even as good as the preceding design. New mass-production equipment may have to be developed to build the radically new product faultlessly and reliably. Finally, people all over the world must be trained to maintain or repair the new design and provided with spare parts stocks.

Accordingly, major developments in car design have come to take longer to reach the market because engineers must think in terms of producing millions of examples. Progress does continue, but much of it has in recent years been directed compulsorily towards reducing air pollution and making collisions less injurious. If conspicuous design changes are rare, there is still a continuous process of refined designs evolving to take advantage of new materials, new manufacturing techniques or newly-available components which either make cars perform better or make them better value for money.

How Cars Work – general arrangement

Very early in the history of motoring, engineers evolved a car layout of which many features are still considered orthodox.

Compare the Panhard et Levassor of the 19th century (right) with the General Motors Chevette of the late 20th century (below). Both cars are four-wheeled, and have driven rear wheels which are held parallel to each other by a rigid axle. Each has an engine working on the four-stroke 'Otto' cycle placed at the front of the car, with the crankshaft aligned fore-and-aft. Each has a friction clutch behind the engine, taking power to change-speed gearing in which different pairs of toothed wheels rotating on parallel shafts can be brought into use as required. Bevel gearing is used in both designs to turn the power flow through a 90° angle to the rear wheels.

Supported at each corner on flexible steel springs, the car of 1891, like that of the late 1970s, has 'Ackermann' steering of the front wheels, and friction braking.

Within this unchanged general layout, tremendous increases in speed, safety and refinement have been achieved by evolutionary progress. The modern car is longer and lower, carrying four people within its steel 'hull' rather than two people on top of a chassis. An engine with twice as many cylinders is started electrically rather than by hand; mechanical parts such as the gearbox and brakes are enclosed; tyres are pneumatic and steering is by a wheel rather than a tiller.

Other arrangements of a car's main components have been tried, some of them achieving great popularity. Nevertheless, a layout evolved in motoring's pioneer days still remains highly competitive.

Front engined, rear wheel driven (General Motors Chevett

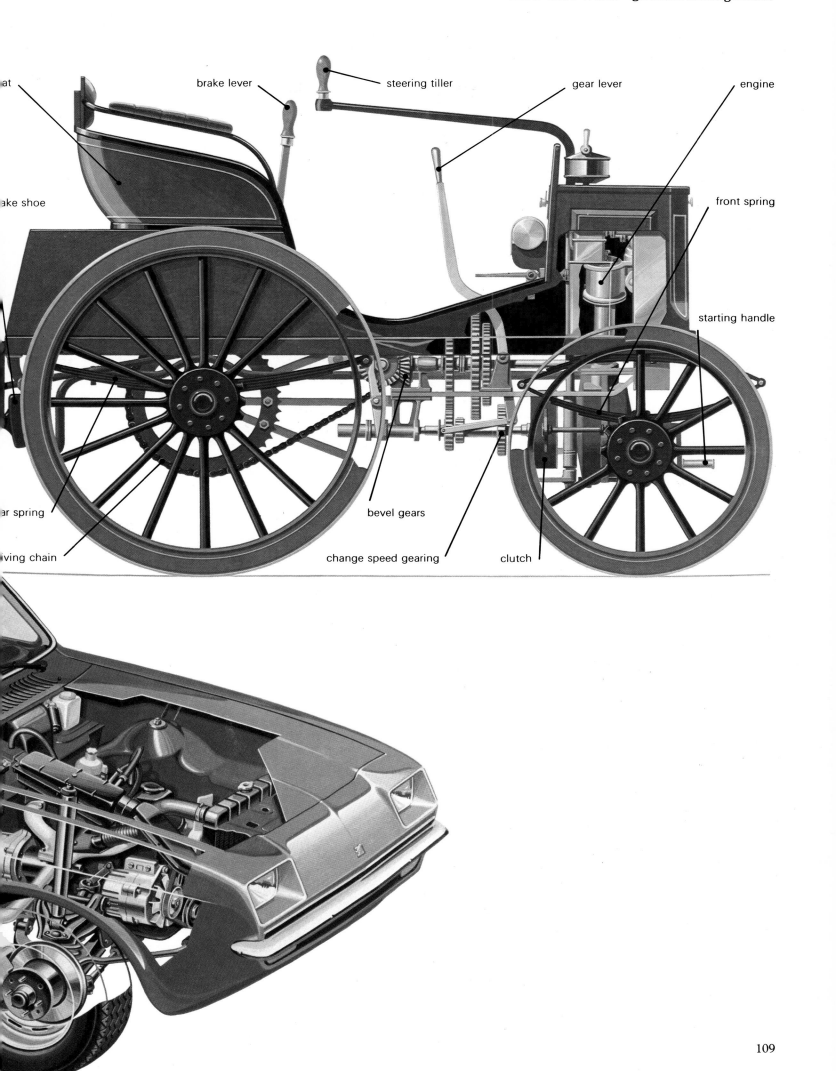

at

brake lever

steering tiller

gear lever

engine

ake shoe

front spring

starting handle

ar spring

bevel gears

iving chain

change speed gearing

clutch

Valve Gear

Internal combustion engines develop power by burning fuel in air, actually inside their cylinders. Combustion heat expands the air, which exerts pressures, and with more of the air-plus-fuel mixture acting on a crank to rotate a shaft. The phrase 'internal combustion' distinguishes this sort of engine from others which burn the fuel externally, for example under the boiler of a steam engine.

An internal combustion engine can operate at pressures close to atmospheric, as exemplified by some early gas engines. Invention of the four-stroke cycle let the 'internal combustion' happen at higher pressures, and with more of the air-plus-fuel mixture compressed into the combustion chamber, the power obtainable from a working cylinder of any particular size was multiplied. Instead of being a bulky unit for static use, an internal combustion engine on Otto principles can be made compact and light enough to propel a car.

Two revolutions of an engine's crankshaft, with two downward and two upward strokes of each piston, form a four-stroke working cycle. The first downward stroke draws into the cylinder air with which a suitable amount of fuel has usually been pre-mixed. An upward piston stroke then compresses the air/fuel mixture into a relatively small space at the closed end of the cylinder. Around the end of this compression stroke, the fuel/air mixture is ignited, combustion heat raising the pressure so that the piston is forced downwards on its third working stroke. Finally, on the upward fourth stroke of the piston, burnt and expanded mixture is pushed out of the cylinder to make room for a fresh, combustible charge.

In this cycle, power is developed only during the third of the four piston strokes. During the other three strokes, the engine must be kept turning in spite of friction and other resistances, by the momentum of a heavy flywheel, or by power from other differently-phased pistons if the engine has multiple cylinders, or by a mixture of these two. Single cylinder engines power the simplest motor cycles, but multiple cylinders make an engine run more smoothly, car engines normally having between four and twelve cylinders.

Three fundamental factors determine how much power an engine can develop: First, cylinder size determines the volume of air/fuel mixture that can be handled in each working cycle; secondly, the speed at which working cycles are completed; thirdly, the average pressures generated by combustion and not wasted in frictional or other losses. (Such effective pressures depend on how completely each cylinder fills with air/fuel mixture, on how much this mixture is compressed before ignition and expanded afterwards, and on how effectively the fuel is burned to generate maximum heat at precisely the right instant.)

Although car engines normally have multiple cylinders, each cylinder is an exact replica of the others. When engineers want to perfect the details of a new design, they sometimes start by building a model engine with just one cylinder. This allows for simpler and cheaper experiments with the effects of varying details of their design.

An engine's cylinder is simply a straight tube, usually of iron, with its inner surface machined smooth to let a piston slide up and down. Some steam engines are 'double-acting' with steam pressure applied alternately to each side of the piston but internal combustion engines are normally single-acting, with combustion pressures above the piston

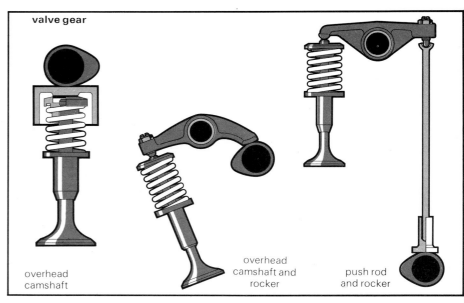

valve gear

overhead camshaft

overhead camshaft and rocker

push rod and rocker

and lubricated mechanism at about atmospheric pressure below the piston. Each cylinder's 'working' end is closed off by a cylinder head and a space called the combustion chamber is left between this and the piston when the latter has reached to top of its stroke.

Within the cylinder head there must be provision for admitting the petrol/air mixture to the cylinder, for igniting this mixture, and for letting the burnt mixture out again. In other words, there must be an inlet valve, a sparking plug and an exhaust valve, any or all of these being occasionally duplicated.

Many types of valve have been tried in engines, and to the regret of engineers, rotating valves have not proved as good as simpler designs akin to slamming doors. During a working cycle, pressures in an engine's cyclinders vary from rather below atmospheric to many times above atmospheric, and temperatures also fluctuate rapidly. It has proved impractical to produce a reliable rotary valve which, at reasonable cost, is pressure-tight in both directions, rotates freely without rapid wear, and does not let its lubricant enter the cylinders.

What does work remarkably well, in spite of its apparent crudity, is the poppet valve. Looking rather like a mushroom, this valve has a head which closes onto a conical seating, and can be lifted to open a way into or out of the cylinder. Slight flexibility of the valve head, which is forced tightly onto its seating by combustion pressure, can ensure that pressure does not leak away. A spring which pulls the valve shut prevents spent exhaust gas being sucked back into the cylinder during the period when the other valve is admitting fresh petrol/air mixture.

Poppet valves in engines are opened by cams on one or more rotating shafts. More than half of each cam is circular, but one part of the cam comprises a lobe of carefully chosen profile which indirectly at the right moments operates on the stem of the 'mushtoom' to open the valve, then releases the pressure and thereby lets the spring pull the valve onto its seating.

Each valve should be wide open during precisely one stroke of the piston, no more and no less. There are however mechanical limits to how quickly a valve can be opened or closed. A compromise must be struck between not having the valves wide open for long enough, and having them slightly open before and after the ends of the piston stroke: slight reversal of gas flow at low engine speeds is accepted as the price of adequate gas flow at high engine speeds.

Poppet valves in an engine are normally set directly above the pistons to give easy flow of mixture into, and of exhaust gas out of, the cylinder. Each valve is held closed on a conical seating in the cylinder head, except when a rotating cam opens it temporarily. If the camshaft is low down at one side of the engine (right) push-rods and pivoted rockers can be interposed between cam and valve. Locating the camshaft or camshafts on the cylinder head eliminates the need for push-rods, at the expense of requiring a longer chain, belt or gear-train to link the camshaft to the crankshaft. In the 'overhead camshaft' engines which have become popular, valves may be operated almost directly from the cams (left), often with a piston to resist side-thrust, inside which shims of varying thickness may be inserted to compensate for wear. Other designs retain rocker-arms (centre) to reduce engine height or to allow two lines of valves to be operated from cams on a single shaft.

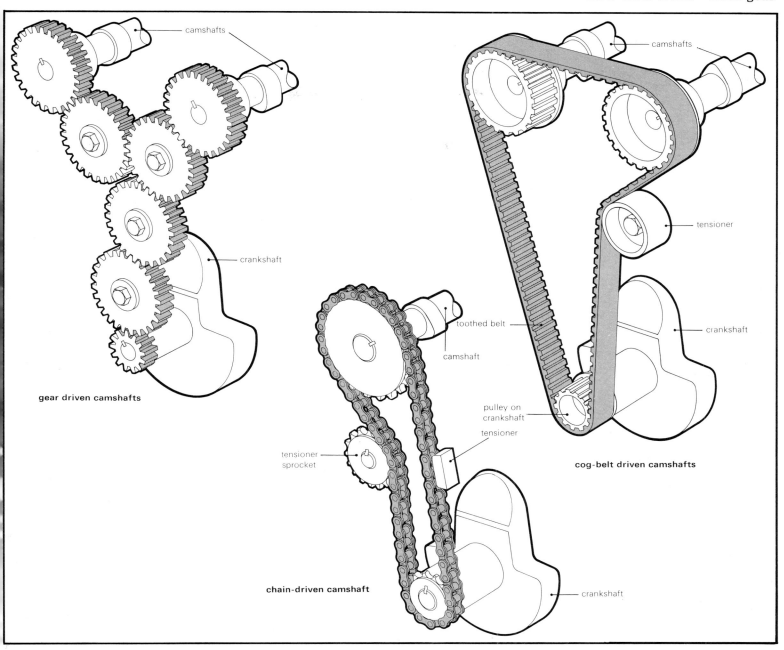

gear driven camshafts

chain-driven camshaft

cog-belt driven camshafts

Four-cycle car engines have one or more camshafts to open and close valves at the right times. Gear drive (top left) is strong and precise, but apt to be noisy. Chain drive (centre), with some device to maintain tension, is simpler and quieter, so has enjoyed a long period of popularity. Drive by a flexible belt (top right), with hidden reinforcement to prevent stretch and moulded teeth to mesh with 'cog' pulleys, has gained favour more recently as it operates quietly and does not need any lubrication.

Because valves should be opened and closed as quickly as possible, but without intolerable clatter, or mechanical stresses so great as to cause breakage, moving parts are made as light as possible. To ensure that valves can seat perfectly even when heat expands engine components to varying extents, a small clearance must usually be left between cam and valve. There will be provision for adjustment of this clearance by a mechanic or automatically when wear takes place.

Until the 1950s, many engines were built with 'side valves' located alongside the cylinders. This was a convenient mechanical layout, for a camshaft quite close alongside the crankshaft and driven by a pair of gears or a short chain could operate the valves directly. However, this mechanically neat system produced a combustion chamber of large area and shallow height, extending over the tops of the inlet and exhaust valves as well as over the piston. When engine speeds were increased to achieve greater power, flow of mixture from the inlet valves to the cylinders was apt to be restricted, and combustion in the shallow space was not always sufficiently rapid.

Modern car engines have 'overhead valves' located more or less directly above the cylinders, so that fresh mixture flows easily from the inlet valve into the cylinder, and the combustion space is compact enough for all the petrol/air mixture to burn quickly when fired by an electric spark. Sometimes the overhead valves are still operated from a camshaft placed quite low down beside the crankshaft, the cams actuating long push-rods and pivoted rockers reversing an upward pushrod movement into a downward push on the valve stem. Such a system involves extra weight moving to and fro with each valve, but it keeps the drive from the crankshaft to the camshaft short, and lets the cylinder head be removed for internal cleaning or other maintenance work without the camshaft being disturbed.

Gradually however it has become more usual to operate overhead valves by means of an 'overhead camshaft' on the cylinder head. This restores lightweight moving parts at the cost of requiring rather a long drive from the crankshaft to the camshaft. Trains of gears have been used to drive camshafts on racing engines and their derivatives, for strength and maximum precision of valve timing regardless of cost or noise. Chain drive is much more common, although a long chain subject to fluctuating tension needs a spring or hydraulic tensioner to prevent it thrashing about. Most recently, flexible belts with internal teeth have become popular for camshaft drives.

rear-engined car (VW 'Beetle')

Lighter, simpler and cheaper probably than any other car layout is that with the engine just behind driven rear wheels, exemplified above by the VW 'Beetle' which enjoyed a very long period of popularity. There is no propeller shaft taking power from one end of the car to the other; the passenger compartment 'amidships' can be unobstructed and structurally simple and, unlike those in more nose-heavy types of car, the front wheel brakes are not required to do much more work than the rear brakes.

As higher standards of performance and refinement came to be demanded of quite inexpensive cars, the rear-engine layout became less attractive in spite of increasingly sophisticated design details. Tail-heavy weight distribution made it difficult to achieve stability, in cross-winds as well as around corners, together with good steering response. Controllable interior heating to keep passengers comfortable made lightweight air-cooled engines less attractive than those from which hot water could be drawn to warm the car. Luggage capacity at the front of the car was judged inadequate by many buyers. Eventually, Volkswagen and Renault, both companies which had built rear-engined cars in very large numbers, switched their allegiance to front wheel drive for all new car designs.

Front wheel drive from a transverse engine has become tremendously popular with car designers all over the world, since the Morris Mini-Minor, designed by Sir Alec Issigonis, was introduced in 1959. A best-seller which typifies more recent developments of the same theme is the Ford Fiesta illustrated below.

Placing an in-line four-cylinder engine across the front of a car, just ahead of the wheels which it drives, leaves maximum space for passengers within the wheelbase, and is compatible with excellent capacity for luggage at the rear of the body. Concentration of heavy mechanism at the front of a car provides dynamic stability, and the driven front wheels have good traction on slippery surfaces.

Because the front wheels of the car are steered, four-wheel-drive cannot be as simple a layout as other systems. Sophisticated forms of universal joint are needed to transmit power smoothly to wheels. The power unit must be short, to fit into a space left by wheels turned to full steering lock, and this requires some extra complexity of gearing.

Cars with transverse engines and front wheel drive have proved so attractive to buyers, that much effort has been put into design details which minimize the cost of manufacture, and simplify access to components for maintenance or repair. Major companies in Europe, America and Asia have now almost entirely adopted this layout rank as the 'orthodox' one for a modern small or medium-sized car.

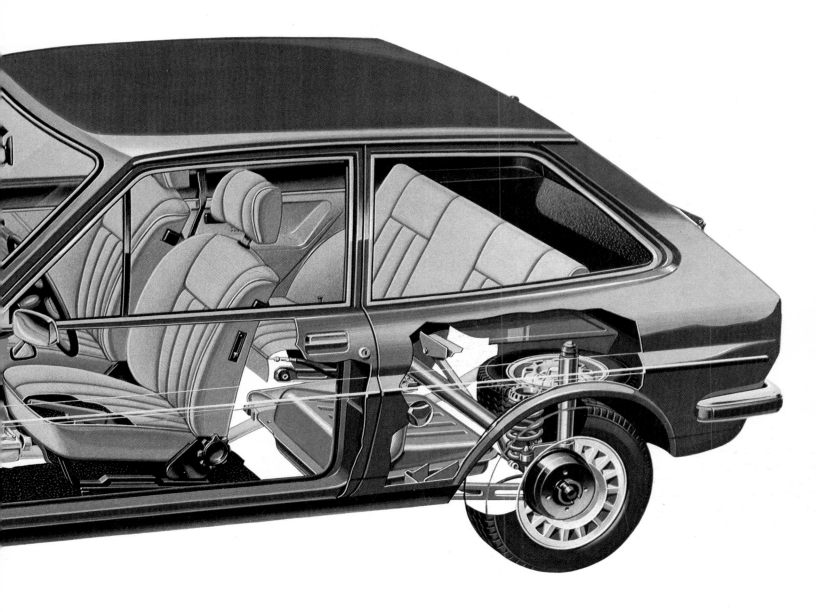

ansverse-engine, front wheel drive car (Ford Fiesta)

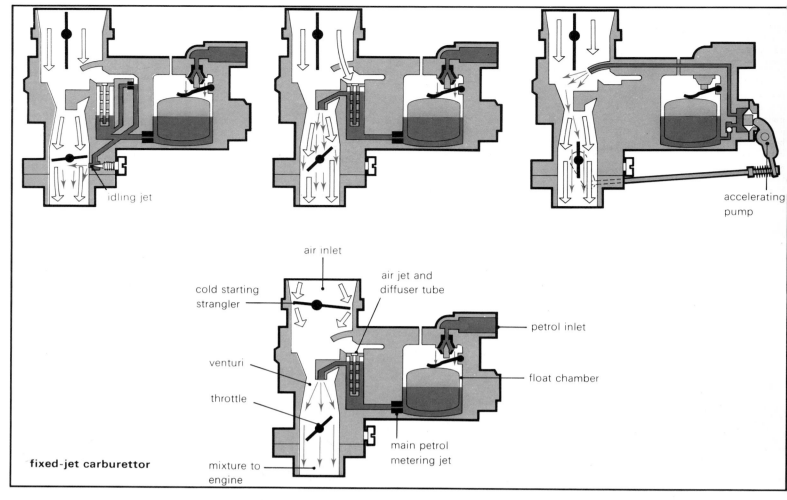

fixed-jet carburettor

Labels: idling jet, accelerating pump, air inlet, cold starting strangler, air jet and diffuser tube, petrol inlet, venturi, float chamber, throttle, main petrol metering jet, mixture to engine

Carburettors

Comparable in importance with the cylinders in which fuel burns is the system which continuously feeds a readily combustible mixture of petrol and air to these cylinders.

Petrol, which has proved the best all-round car fuel, is a mixture of different hydrocarbon chemicals, plus traces of chemical additives which improve its combustion and other characteristics. For complete combustion of all its hydrogen and carbon to steam and carbon dioxide, 1 kg of petrol needs about 15 kg of air.

In practice, for a car engine to give utmost economy of fuel, it should be fed with about 10 per cent less than the 'chemically correct' quantity of petrol for the air entering its cylinders. This ensures that virtually all the fuel finds oxygen molecules with which to burn completely. Reducing the fuel supply much further will diminish power output to a disproportionate extent, because combustion will become unduly slow, or it may cause mis-firing and allow unburnt fuel to go to waste through the exhaust valve.

For a car engine to develop maximum power, however, it is best fed with about 10 per cent more than the chemically correct quantity of fuel. This modest excess of fuel ensures that, even with imperfect mixing, all the air in the cylinders is used to generate heat, and so to produce power. If much more fuel than this is supplied, however, power output will diminish gradually, as surplus petrol vapour crowds out air. There is in fact a 'rich' limit beyond which too much petrol in too little air will not ignite at all.

Modern legal controls on air pollution by cars which limit emissions of carbon monoxide (formed when excess fuel is not completely burned), of hydrocarbons (which reach the exhaust pipe if a cylinder-

full of petrol/air mixture fails to burn) and of oxides of nitrogen (formed at very high combustion temperatures) have made accurate fuel metering more important than ever before. Exact fuel metering requirements vary, however, according to whether extra-clean combustion inside the engine is being sought, or impurities are being burned up with excess air in a special exhaust system.

Fuel metering and mixing the fuel with air entering the cylinders are tasks performed, on most car engines, by a carburettor. Rather as an incidental, the carburettor incorporates the throttle valve which, by restricting air flow to the cylinders when it is partially closed, lets engine power output be reduced as required by traffic conditions.

Carburettors are normally based on the simple principle that when air flows through a narrow passage, the extra energy needed to make it move faster is obtained from a reduction in pressure. In popular parlance, the faster the air flows through a narrowed passage in the carburettor, the greater the 'suction' developed at the throat of the so-called 'choke tube'. This suction can be used to draw from a reservoir an amount of fuel appropriate to the rate at which air is flowing into the engine's cylinders.

For a suction carburettor to perform consistently, it must draw fuel from a constant-level supply, and not directly from a tank in which the level will fall gradually. The float chamber in a carburettor contains a float-operated valve (akin on a smaller scale to the ball cock in a domestic water cistern) which admits just enough fuel from a pump to keep the liquid level just below the jet which discharges fuel into the air system.

Because the flow characteristics of air and of liquid petrol differ, a simple petrol outlet jet of calibrated size placed where air flow through the carburettor is fastest will not produce a consistent mixture of petrol

Phases in the operation of a 'fixed choke' carburettor are illustrated above. When the engine is idling (top left) fuel from a constant-level float chamber is mixed with air as it passes the edge of an almost-closed throttle. With a partly open throttle (top centre) the main fuel outlet has come into action, delivering fuel into air flowing quickly through the narrowest throat of the venturi. When the throttle is opened quickly, extra fuel is pumped into the air stream momentarily (top right) to improve acceleration. To help an engine start from cold, an air strangler can be closed across the carburettor air intake (lower diagram) so that extra fuel is drawn out of the metering jets.

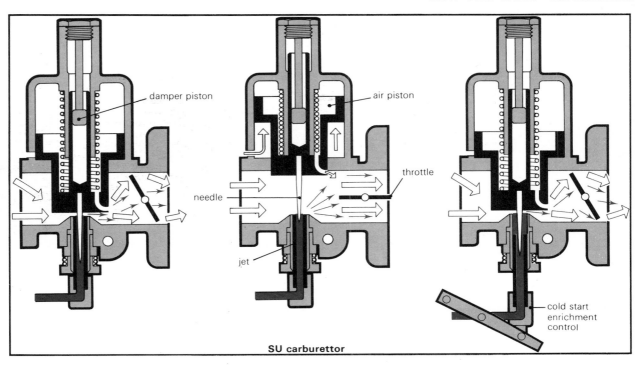

SU carburettor

Labels in diagram: damper piston, air piston, throttle, needle, jet, cold start enrichment control

In a constant-depression carburettor, the size of the venturi air passage is adjusted automatically to maintain constant air speed past the fuel jet. A tapered needle adjusts the size of the fuel jet in proportion to the area of the air passage, maintaining the correct fuel/air ratio at any condition between idling with an almost-closed throttle (left) and full-power operation (centre diagram). For cold starting, a richer fuel/air ratio is obtained by moving the petrol jet down, away from the taper needle. Air passage size is controlled by a simple pneumatic piston. If air speed through the carburettor increases, extra suction beyond the 'throat' is transferred through an air duct to the top of the pneumatic piston, which rises to open up the 'throat' in which a constant air speed is consequently obtained. A simple oil-filled damper in the piston rod prevents too-rapid upward movement of the air piston, and has the effect of giving a slightly richer fuel/air mixture during acceleration.

and air. It will deliver too little fuel at low air speeds and too much at high air speeds, unless correction is applied.

Rival carburettor-makers have their own more or less complex correction systems of extra fuel jets or air bleeds. There may be a compensating jet which delivers extra petrol at modest air flow rates, but is arranged so that its output hardly increases at higher air flows when the 'main jet' is providing ample fuel. There may be air bleeds which, besides limiting the suction applied to the main petrol jet, help to break up the fuel with air bubbles so that it mixes better with the air flowing through the carburettor.

When an engine is idling with its throttle almost closed, air flow through the choke tube is too slow, and the resulting suction is too slight, to provide accurate control over the very small fuel flow. So a tiny extra fuel jet is placed near the edge of the closed throttle, where a sort of miniature carburettor is formed when the engine is idling. Once the throttle is opened, this idling jet is virtually inoperative. As an aid to quick engine acceleration when the throttle is opened suddenly, most modern carburettors incorporate a small pump operated mechanically from

the throttle that gives a squirt of extra fuel in anticipation of the engine's needs.

A very different looking type of carburettor is based on constant vacuum or constant depression pattern. In this sort of carburettor, the effective area provided for air flow through the choke tube is variable and self-regulating to maintain a constant air speed. A spring-loaded piston is lifted by suction in the choke tube, until the suction is only just enough to support the piston which, as it rises, increases the area for air flow. As extra flow makes the piston rise higher, a tapered needle is lifted further out of the petrol jet to let an appropriate extra quantity of fuel be fed into the increased flow of air.

Because a fundamental problem of carburettor design is how to cope with widely varied rates of air flow, some carburettors are built with two parallel choke tubes. There will only be airflow through one choke tube when the engine is operating on light load, the second throttle only opening when the driver presses quite hard on the accelerator pedal.

Instead of having a carburettor, an engine can be equipped with a fuel injection system which pumps an appropriate amount of fuel to each cylinder under pressure. Systems which inject petrol directly into the cylinders have been used, but to avoid exposing spray nozzles to combustion heat and pressure it is more usual to spray fuel into the air shortly before it reaches the inlet valve of the cylinder. Some systems of fuel injection offer at least 10 per cent more engine power, because they do not restrict the air flow into the cylinders with a choke tube. Other systems have as their main advantage extra precision in metering the right amount of fuel to each individual cylinder of an engine.

Extremely varied systems of fuel injection are competing on the market, and whilst it appears probable that designs featuring electronic control of fuel flow will become dominant, design is at present in a state of flux. Actual injection of fuel in all pioneer systems (and some current ones) was by plunger pumps with their effective stroke length controlled in various ways. In many recent systems there is a constant high-pressure supply of fuel provided by an electric pump and injection nozzles are opened electro-magnetically to deliver the right quantity of fuel to each cylinder at the correct instant.

Fuel injection systems spray petrol into the air intakes of individual cylinders, eliminating the need for restriction of air flow by a carburettor. Early forms of this system depended on varying the effective stroke of a piston-type injection pump. Most recent systems have the injection nozzle opened electro-magnetically for varying brief periods to admit the right amount of fuel from a high-pressure supply pump.

fuel injection

Labels in diagram: injection nozzle, inlet valve, inlet port

All early fuel injection systems dispensed with the choke tube, as do some present ones, making the engine act as its own air flow meter. The amount of fuel injected per induction stroke is regulated primarily according to throttle opening or to the resulting inlet pipe air pressure, with fine adjustments to match other variables such as atmospheric temperature and pressure. Considerable sophistication is needed to match fuel flow to air flow accurately, in part because 'organ pipe' resonances in the pipes to individual cylinders result in much more complete filling at some engine speeds than at others.

In seeking extreme precision of fuel metering, which under American clean air laws must be checked at intervals during an 80,000 km (50,000 mile) endurance test, engines have been found less than ideally consistent as air flow meters. Various changes such as wear or the accumulation of deposits can alter their characteristics sufficiently to put some types of petrol injection equipment significantly out of tune. So designers have in some instances gone back to measuring air flow at the engine's intake and using this measurement to control the injection system. A moving air valve which is opened against a spring by air flow is being used, and though this valve pivots rather than slides, it is akin in principle to the moving piston in a constant-depression carburettor.

Engines

Although the basic functioning of a car engine can be considered in terms of just one piston, car engines usually have four or more cylinders. As has been indicated, a piston only develops power during one stroke in every four, and despite provision of a flywheel, a single cylinder engine would tend to propel a car with a series of pulses rather than with a smooth, steady push. Also, the inertia forces which result from a piston moving rapidly up and down a cylinder in a straight line cannot be balanced out completely with simple weights on the rotating crankshaft. Only with at least one other piston moving to-and-fro in an opposite direction can balance of the moving parts be obtained and unpleasant (or even destructive) vibration in a car avoided.

Multiple cylinders can be arranged in many different ways, though only a few have proved popular with car designers. In addition to seeking smooth operation, an engine designer considers such factors as ease of manufacture and maintenance, weight, compactness in relation to an intended car

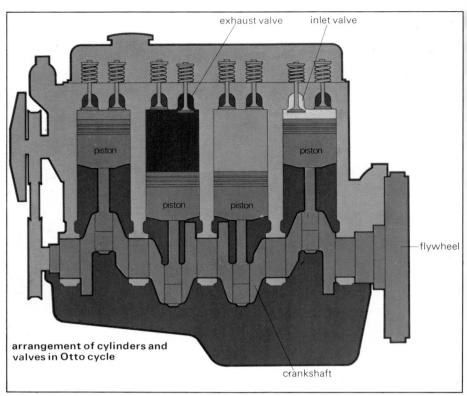

arrangement of cylinders and valves in Otto cycle

layout, ease of distributing petrol/air mixture evenly to all cylinders, simplicity of operating valves and of lubricating the total mechanism. Cylinders can be set in a line above the crankshaft, or in two lines at varied angles, or in a ring around the crankshaft, or above two crankshafts coupled together by gears.

In a great many countries, engines with four cylinders outnumber all others as the favourite compromise providing reasonably smooth operation at reasonable cost. Most four-cylinder engines are arranged with the cylinders in a line above the crankshaft – not necessarily vertical, as a sideways tilt often lets the engine fit more neatly into the car. Crankshaft design is such that the front and rear pistons of a four-cylinder engine are moving down when the pair between them are moving up.

Mechanical balance of the four-in-line engine is not quite perfect. Because of the angularity of connecting rods which link pistons to the crankshaft, each piston reverses direction rather more suddenly at the top than at the bottom of its stroke, creating greater inertia forces for a shorter period. Resulting 'secondary' vibration, at double engine frequency, can usually be concealed fairly well by mounting the engine on rubber blocks of carefully tuned flexibility.

Stages in the four-stroke 'Otto cycle' in a one engine cylinder (below). Petrol-air mixture is drawn in through the inlet valve, compressed into a compact combustion chamber, ignited by a spark, allowed to expand and finally pumped out via the exhaust valve. Above, the phasing of these processes in a 4-cylinder engine, with similar colour-coding, and with (from left to right) a 1-2-4-3 'firing order'.

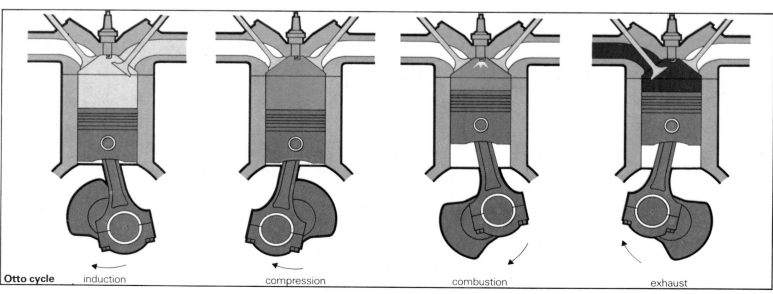

Otto cycle   induction   compression   combustion   exhaust

Four cylinders do not provide completely smooth torque either, because power is delivered in the central part of each working stroke but not at the extreme start and finish of the stroke. Thus there is a double incentive for designers to plan engines with more than four cylinders, when space and cost permit.

Usually a six-cylinder engine is significantly smoother than a four, because power flow is virtually continuous and even secondary unbalance of the reciprocating pistons can be eliminated. However, the relatively long and narrow shape of an in-line six-cylinder engine can sometimes be inconvenient to fit into a car. Another problem is that a relatively

long 'six throw' crankshaft is not very rigid, and torsional vibration can pose problems as power impulses and piston inertia forces act successively at different points along the shaft's length.

In larger sizes of car, engines with eight cylinders have become popular, two lines of cylinders being set side-by-side above one crankshaft, with a 90° angle between groups of cylinders. Connecting rods from two pistons work side-by-side on each throw of the crankshaft, which can be shorter and simpler than the crankshaft of an in-line six-cylinder engine. Whilst the V8 may not be a smoother engine than the six it is sturdy and quite light in weight for the power it develops. Its short, wide shape fits quite

Because each cylinder of an 'Otto cycle' engine develops power on only one stroke in every four, car engines are usually built with at least four cylinders to ensure reasonably smooth running. Illustrated is a typical Ford engine for small cars, with four cylinders set in a line

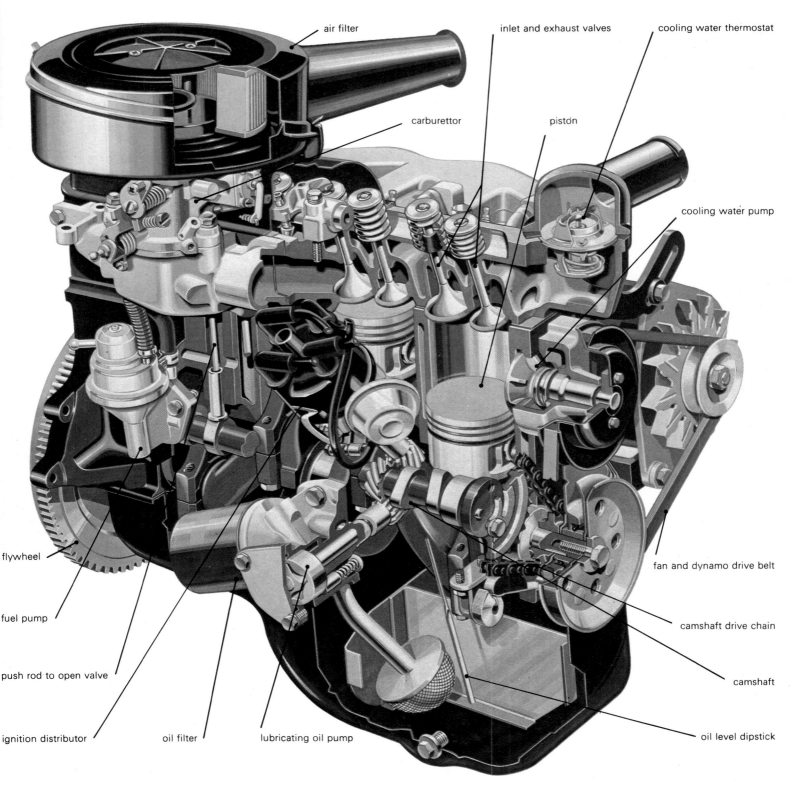

air filter

inlet and exhaust valves

cooling water thermostat

carburettor

piston

cooling water pump

flywheel

fan and dynamo drive belt

fuel pump

camshaft drive chain

push rod to open valve

camshaft

ignition distributor   oil filter   lubricating oil pump

oil level dipstick

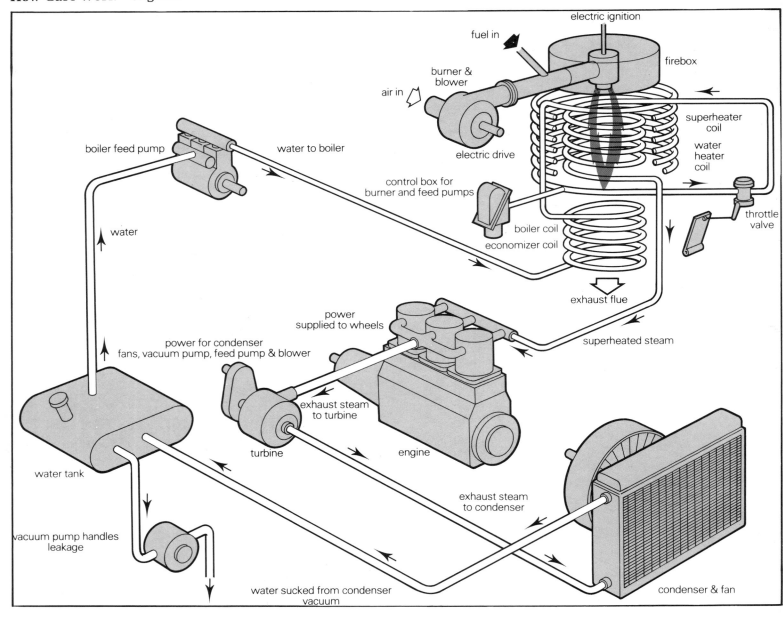

electric ignition

fuel in

air in

burner &
blower

firebox

electric drive

superheater
coil

water
heater
coil

boiler feed pump

water to boiler

control box for
burner and feed pumps

throttle
valve

water

boiler coil

economizer coil

exhaust flue

superheated steam

power for condenser
fans, vacuum pump, feed pump & blower

power
supplied to wheels

exhaust steam
to turbine

turbine

engine

water tank

exhaust steam
to condenser

vacuum pump handles
leakage

water sucked from condenser
vacuum

condenser & fan

successfully into the layout of many of today's cars.

Engines with more than eight cylinders are normally confined to the top of the luxury or high performance car markets. The smaller the individual cylinders of an engine are, and the shorter the to-and-fro distance which pistons travel, the higher the speed to which the engine can be run without mechanical stresses becoming excessive. So, for extreme performance, V12 engines are built in modest numbers. For luxury cars also, it does seem that a V12 engine can be smoother than a V8.

Structurally, the main element of a modern car engine is the cylinder block, which is a single sturdy casting whether the engine has its cylinders in line or in a V. Bearings in which the crankshaft rotates are at the base of this casting, to the top of which is bolted a removable cylinder head casting (or, for a V engine, castings). Most often the cylinder block is of iron, in which can be machined durable cylinder bores. Quite a popular alternative is to make the block of lighter aluminium alloy and to insert sleeves of a harder material for the wearing surfaces of the cylinders. A few engines have aluminium cylinder blocks without liners, ways having been found to let the pistons slide directly on a specially treated aluminium surface.

Pistons are invariably of a light alloy, for minimum weight and inertia stress. Ferrous metal is used for three or more outwardly-sprung piston rings which,

by sealing the working clearance between piston and cylinder, keep combustion pressure confined above them and lubricating oil below them. Pistons are of much more sophisticated design than is apparent at a glance. They must resist high mechanical and thermal stresses, and subtle techniques are used to control or direct their expansion when they are exposed to combustion heat.

Although piston engines have served well for so many decades, engineers have always wished that they could eliminate reciprocating parts and use simple rotary motion. Much the most successful effort in this direction has been the Wankel engine. This design is based on the familiar four-stroke Otto cycle of induction, compression, combustion and exhaust, but petrol/air mixture goes through the cycle as it is moved around a chamber by an approximately triangular rotor.

The Wankel engine has an inconspicuous crankshaft, but instead of a connecting rod and piston there is a rotor on each crank throw. Gearing compels this rotor to turn around its own axis, at one-third of the speed at which the crankshaft is rotating and in the same direction. A flat-ended chamber of dumbell shape exactly matches the path followed by the three tips of the rotor as it turns on an axis which is itself moving at a lower speed.

Diagrams show how, in each of the three spaces between the rotor and the chamber enclosing it, the processes of the four-stroke cycle can take place.

Steam power is periodically reconsidered as an alternative to the internal combustion engine, and the diagram above shows the fundamentals of a typical system. Fuel is burned inside a spiral of boiler and superheater tube (top right), from which it is piped to a much more compact engine. Exhaust steam drives a turbine to provide power for pumps and other auxiliaries, before going to a radiator-like condenser and, as liquid, back to the water tank. A feed pump then forces water into the boiler ready to go through the cycle afresh.

Continuous burning of fuel makes the Stirling-cycle hot air engine potentially 'cleaner' than Otto-cycle engines, and quiet in operation. A 'displacer piston' above the working piston moves air or gas to and fro through heater and cooler units. The resulting alternate expansion and contraction of the sealed-in air or gas moves the working piston to develop power.

Wankel engines are very smooth running at high speeds and have been sold in large numbers. Developing the Wankel engine to be competitive with piston engines in cost of manufacture, durability, ability to operate at widely varying speeds and economy of fuel has been very costly indeed – but ever-improving piston engines have not been superseded.

It has, for example, proved difficult in a Wankel engine to separate working chambers completely with the equivalent of just one piston ring, which must operate virtually without oil, and must slide along a somewhat switch-back surface without rapid mechanical wear. Each sparking plug in a Wankel engine does three times as much work as it would in a normal engine, and is exposed to much more continuous heat. Burning of petrol/air mixture in rather long and narrow spaces between rotor and case has not always been as quick or complete as might be wished. Many such problems have required fresh know-how to replace the knowledge which piston engine designers had been accumulating since the 19th century.

To use poppet valves in a Wankel engine would add a lot of extra moving parts and destroy the smoothness of a rotary engine. Instead, ports cut in the casing, where the rotor uncovers them and covers them again at appropriate stages in the working cycle, admit fresh mixture and release exhaust gas. Early Wankel engines had all these ports in the periphery of the casing, but this unavoidably gave rather long periods of inlet port opening which was excellent for power at high speeds but did not provide adequate behaviour at low rates of revolution. More recent designs have inlet ports in the sides of the chamber, where they can be designed for rather shorter opening periods. Best engine performance is then moved down the speed range, away from the rather critical maximum safe operating speed beyond which engine wear becomes very rapid.

After vast sums had been spent on learning about the Wankel principle, the problems needing to be overcome were compounded by new exhaust gas purity laws and by increasing emphasis on fuel economy. Engines with reciprocating pistons and poppet valves still dominate the scene.

Clean air regulations have encouraged engineers to look afresh at external combustion engines which, instead of burning fuel very hurriedly inside the cylinders, burn it continuously outside the cylinders. Steam engines have been studied and tested, and so have hot-air engines. Gas turbines also have the merit of burning fuel continuously, even though they are technically internal combustion engines working on a form of four-stroke Otto cycle. As yet, though, it does not look as if any rival is going to match the piston engine's efficiency as a power unit for cars.

Steam power is often thought about in terms of railway locomotives which required handling by two skilled men, consumed huge quantities of water and emitted steam, smoke and soot in vast quantities. To be controlled simply by an accelerator pedal, to condense all its water for re-use and to burn its fuel in a clean way, the steam engine needs tremendous elaboration of detail. To be immune from freezing worries, it must replace water with some other liquid, contained within a system from which it cannot escape by either leakage or evaporation. Other alternative power unit types pose comparable problems.

Stirling engine cycle

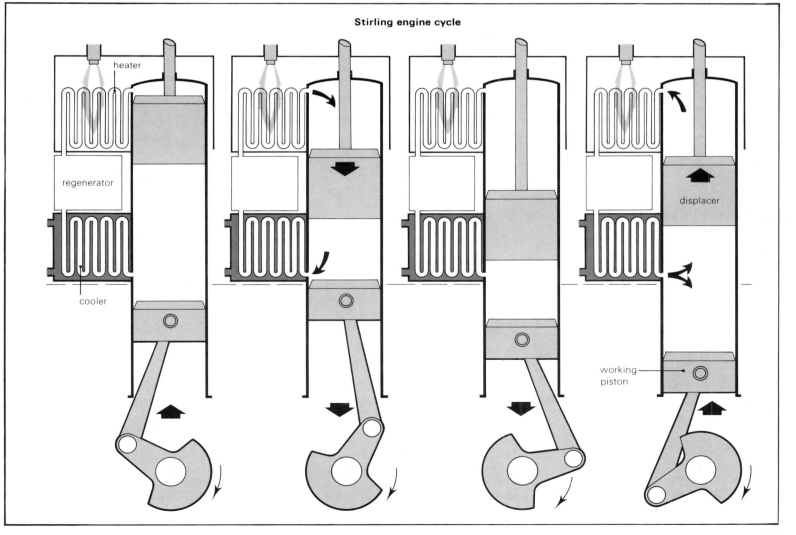

heater

regenerator

cooler

displacer

working piston

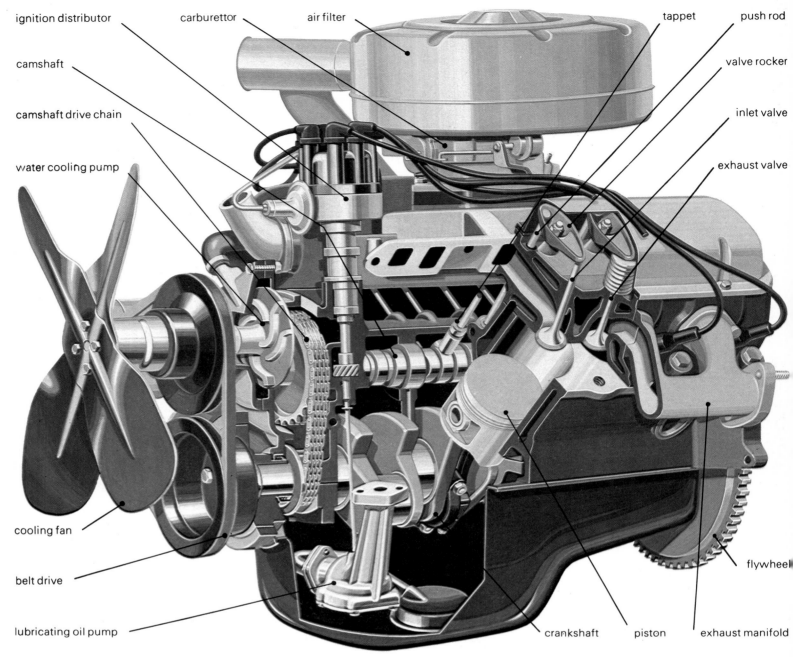

ignition distributor
camshaft
camshaft drive chain
water cooling pump
cooling fan
belt drive
lubricating oil pump

carburettor
air filter
tappet
push rod
valve rocker
inlet valve
exhaust valve
flywheel
crankshaft
piston
exhaust manifold

V-8 engine

Above : Large and sophisticated cars are often equipped with V-8 engines (above). These can provide a high power output relative to their bulk, and are smooth in operation. With two cylinder blocks set apart at a 90° angle, a four-throw crankshaft with two connecting rod bearings side-by-side on each crankpin can provide four evenly-spaced power impulses per revolution. One central camshaft driven by a short chain can operate all the engine's 16 valves through pushrods and rocker-arms. Usually one carburettor (often with multiple throats alongside each other) is placed above the centre of the engine, and each group of four cylinders has its own exhaust system on the side of the engine.

Opposite : Rotary power without to-and-fro movement of pistons, long a dream of inventors, became a reality in the Wankel engine. The diagrams below show how rotation of an approximately triangular rotor, on a crankpin which itself rotates at one-third of rotor speed, takes place within a shaped, flat-ended chamber. In each of three spaces between the rotor and the casting, fuel/air mixture goes through the familiar stages of the 'Otto' four-stroke working cycle. The large perspective drawing shows how the principle is built into a two-rotor car engine. In place of poppet-type inlet and exhaust valves, there are ports located, respectively, in the side and the periphery of each chamber, positioned so that the rotor uncovers them at appropriate stages in each working cycle.

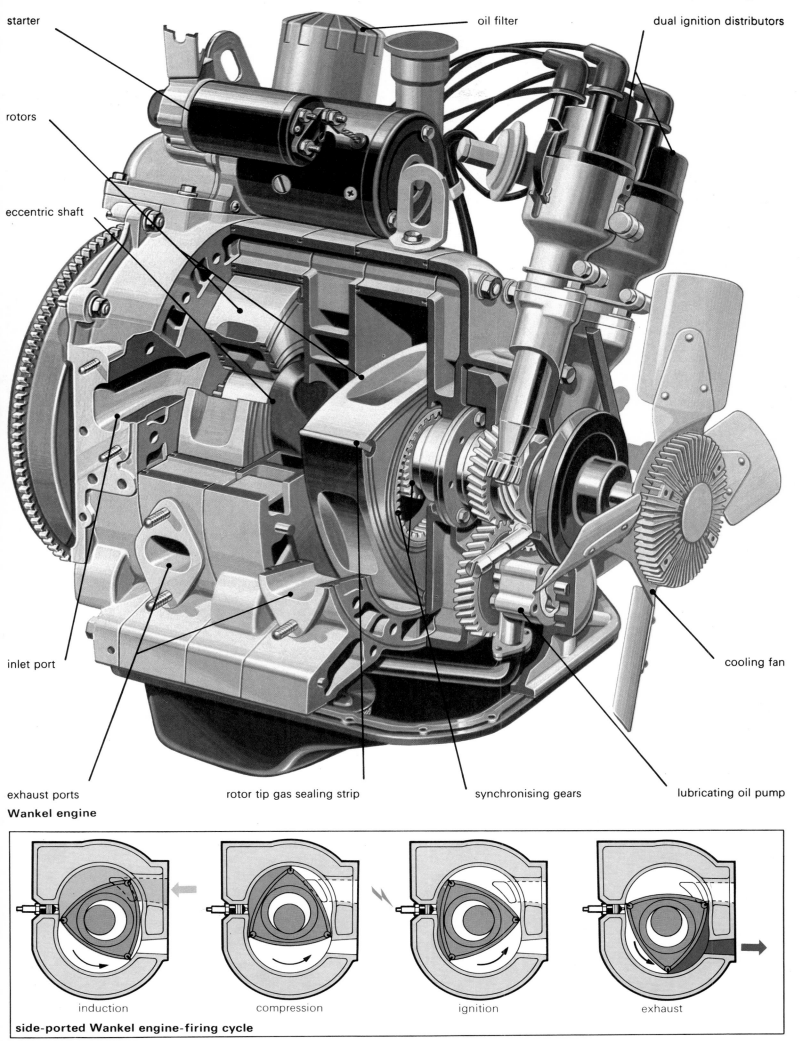

starter

rotors

eccentric shaft

inlet port

oil filter

dual ignition distributors

cooling fan

exhaust ports

rotor tip gas sealing strip

synchronising gears

lubricating oil pump

Wankel engine

induction

compression

ignition

exhaust

side-ported Wankel engine-firing cycle

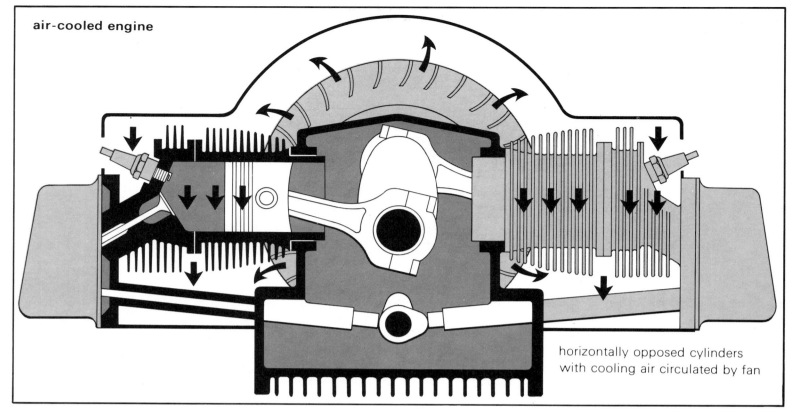

air-cooled engine

horizontally opposed cylinders
with cooling air circulated by fan

Cooling systems

Heat liberated by burning fuel is the internal combustion engine's power source but there are limits to how much heat the mechanism can withstand. Cooling of some parts is essential for reliability and will, incidentally, let an engine develop more power because a cool petrol/air charge in the cylinders is heavier than a hot one of similar volume.

Blowing air over the exterior of the cylinders is the simplest way to cool an engine. The amount of cooling obtainable in this way is increased if the engine is built of a light aluminium alloy that conducts heat readily, iron or steel being used only for inserts at points where hard wearing surfaces are essential. Fins on the exterior of the cylinders, which provide more surface area onto which air can blow, also help to dissipate heat.

More often today, a car engine is cooled by a jacket of water (usually containing additives to prevent freezing and corrosion) around its cylinder heads and at least the upper parts of the cylinders. Initially water cooling was preferred because it could get more heat away from critical areas around sparking plugs and exhaust valve seatings. More recently, it has become important that cooling water provides a reasonably consistent supply of 'waste heat' from the engine which can be used to warm the car interior when required. With an appreciable weight of water in a system, the heat available for the car interior does not fluctuate so quickly when conditions vary.

Today's typical cooling system comprises jackets around the engine through which a pump circulates the coolant; a radiator with a large surface area for transferring heat from the coolant to the atmosphere, and a fan to blow air over the radiator surfaces. A thermostat valve will usually by-pass coolant from the engine outlet back to the inlet, without passing through the radiator, if it is below a chosen running temperature. A separate miniature fan and radiator system inside the car provides warmth for passengers.

Nowadays a liquid cooling system is usually sealed off with a spring-loaded filler cap which, opening only under considerable pressure, lets the water/anti-freeze mixture reach a higher temperature before it boils. Also there is likely to be an overflow tank. Any water that is forced out of the main coolant circuit as the engine warms up is sucked back again from the overflow tank when the engine is stopped and cools down. Ethylene glycol is commonly mixed with cooling water to prevent freezing, this being a much less volatile alternative to alcohol.

Ignition

Infallible and accurately-timed ignition of the petrol/air mixture in the cylinders is vital to an internal combustion engine's efficiency. If combustion starts too soon, rising pressure will resist the piston's upward movement to the end of the compression stroke and power will be lost. If combustion starts too late, pressure will not rise until the piston has moved part way down on its working stroke and the engine's full potential power will not be developed. Plenty of engines run up to a speed of 6,000 revolutions per minute, at which speed there is only 1/100 second for the whole of a compression stroke, burning of the compressed fuel, and an expansion stroke by the piston. For utmost mechanical work to be extracted from the fuel's chemical energy during a piston stroke lasting 1/200 second, quick combustion of fuel must be initiated at a precisely timed instant.

A high-voltage spark provides the ignition in petrol engines. Rapid though burning of the petrol/air mixture must be, it is not an instantaneous, explosive process. To allow the necessary burning time, an ignition spark needs to be timed slightly ahead of the top dead centre stage in piston movement. Optimum spark advance is a compromise, balancing the back-pressure caused by early ignition against the loss due to late development of pressure.

The number of degrees of crankshaft rotation before the piston attains top dead centre position depends on many factors. Optimum spark advance is different for every design of engine and to a lesser extent for every individual example of one design because of manufacturing variations. Spark timing should vary with engine speed, with throttle opening, and ideally even with air temperature and barometric

Internal combustion engines need to be cooled, so that neither components nor lubricating oil reach harmful temperatures, and so that the fuel does not ignite spontaneously. Many cars have been built with direct air cooling, typified by the VW 'Beetle' engine with its two pairs of horizontal cylinders. A fan combined with the flywheel blows air downwards past the cylinders, which are finned to provide extra surface area, and enclosed by ducts which keep the cooling air close to them. A lubricating oil cooler was also provided, and a thermostatic control of the air outlet aperture kept engine temperature reasonably constant in varied driving conditions.

pressure. Spark timing other than that which would give maximum power must sometimes be used in order to make an engine run more smoothly and quietly or to help it to comply with exhaust gas purity regulations.

Ignition sparks are arranged to occur between two electrodes of a sparking plug screwed into each combustion chamber. A sparking plug has a narrow gap between an insulated central electrode and one or more electrodes on its body. Careful experiment goes into selection of sparking plugs, with just the right degree of cooling for a particular type of engine. Incandescent surfaces must not ignite the fuel before the spark occurs, yet the insulator surface must get hot enough to burn off any sooty deposits that might shirt-circuit the vital spark gap. Each manufacturer has a range of sparking plugs to meet varying requirements.

It is possible to obtain the pulse of high-voltage electricity which 'fires' a sparking plug as a discharge of stored energy from a condenser. Normally however an induction coil is used to produce the necessary high-voltage current from a batter-and-generator system operating at a modest 12 volts. On a magnetic core, two coils of insulated wire are wound: a low-tension coil with relatively few turns of quite thick wire, and a high-tension coil with many more turns of quite fine wire. When a 12-volt current flowing through the low-tension coil is interrupted, the suddenly changed magnetic field induces a pulse of high-voltage electricity in the secondary coil, and this is what fires the sparking plug.

It is possible to have one ignition coil for every cylinder of an engine, or to have a coil with two secondary windings serving a pair of cylinders – an unwanted spark at the end of an exhaust stroke does no harm. Much more usually one ignition coil will serve up to eight cylinders and a distributor that rotates at half engine speed directs each spark to the cylinder in which it is required. A voltage high enough to produce a spark in a cylinder where petrol/air mixture is highly compressed is readily able to jump another small air gap between rotor and fixed contacts in the ignition distributor.

Spark timing is determined by the instant at which 12-volt current flow through the ignition coil is interrupted. Traditionally a mechanical contact breaker provides this interruption of current flow, and for convenience the contact breaker is combined in the same casing as the distributor. Two contact-breaker points are pressed together by spring pressure, and a mechanical cam moves one of the points away from the other to induce each spark.

Because electro-magnetic induction in the ignition coil is a two-way process, some unwanted sparking takes place between the contact breaker points as they move apart. This is doubly undesirable as it blurs the spark at the plug electrodes and causes erosion of one half of the contact breaker with a pimple building up on the other point. Such unwanted sparking is minimized with the aid of a small condenser that is able momentarily to store the pulse of electrical energy which otherwise would cause sparking.

To an increasing extent, electronic devices are now being used either to reduce the current flowing through the contact breaker so that its life is extended, or to eliminate the contact breaker completely. A transistor circuit can now interrupt the primary current to the ignition coil in response to a much smaller electrical signal. Transistor-assisted contact-breaker systems pass a much reduced current through the traditional points so that sparking across them is prevented.

Liquid cooling, as illustrated diagrammatically below, is now used on the great majority of car engines. Cylinders and combustion chambers are surrounded with liquid, usually water plus anti-corrosion and anti-freezing additives. A pump circulates this water around the engine, at a rate controlled by a temperature-regulating thermostat. Hot water from the engine goes to a radiator over which cooling air is blown by a fan or, in cold weather, to a smaller radiator-and-fan system which heats the car interior.

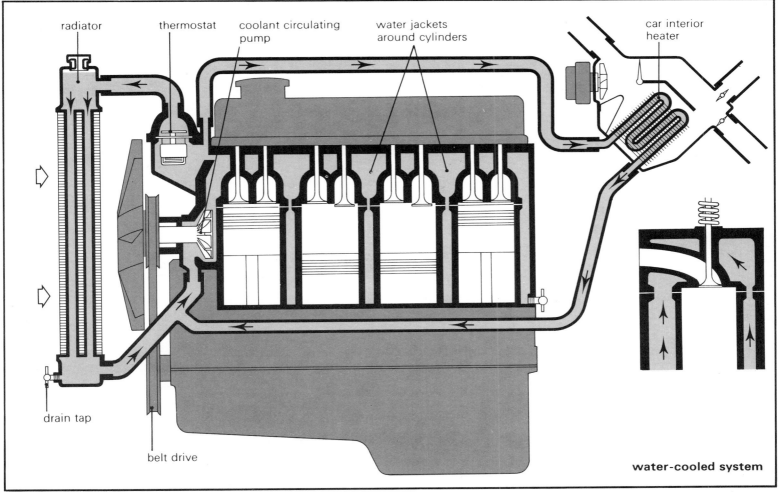

radiator   thermostat   coolant circulating pump   water jackets around cylinders   car interior heater

drain tap

belt drive

water-cooled system

Other forms of triggering to make a power transistor interrupt current flow to the ignition coil dispense altogether with the contact breaker. The small voltage change needed to control the transistor can be induced in a small pick-up coil on the side of the distributor when a magnet mounted on the rotor moves past. Alternatively a photocell can respond to light from a durable low-temperature electric lamp filament when this light shines through a slot in the rotor.

Electronically-triggered ignition systems still employ the mechanical systems for adjusting spark timing that were evolved for use with contact breakers. On the drive shaft to the contact breaker cam or to the triggering device, there is a system of centrifugal weights which when they move outwards against the resistance of springs at increasing engine speeds, advance the phasing of the spark relative to the crankshaft. On the casing of the distributor, a flexible diaphragm sensitive to suction in the carburetter moves the fixed part of the triggering system to advance spark timing when the engine is running on part throttle. As part of a clean air combustion control system, another diaphragm device may retard the ignition when the driver releases the accelerator pedal completely.

Exhaust

When the engine's exhaust valve opens, with the piston about 85 per cent of the way down the cylinder towards the end of its working stroke, burnt gas suddenly starts to emerge from the cylinder under quite high pressure, very hot if not still burning. This hot gas must be piped away to a convenient outlet, usually at the back of the car. On its way to the outlet, noisy pressure pulsations must be damped down to leave very little noise, or failing that, a noise that is at least acceptable. To meet increasingly strict clean air laws, impurities may need to be removed from spent combustion products whilst they are in the exhaust system.

Quietening and purification of the exhaust should as far as possible be done without imposing back pressure which, resisting upward piston movement, would reduce power output. Rather, the momentary low pressure left behind as exhaust gas from a cylinder goes to the silencer should, if possible, be used to help empty the cylinder completely without gas flowing back to refill a space that fresh petrol/air mixture should occupy.

To achieve the best extractor effect, exhaust pipes from various cylinders can be paired together in subtle ways, to separate for as long as possible overlapping flows of gas from cylinders which fire in close succession. Individual pipe lengths can be tuned like organ pipes to assist engine performance at a chosen speed.

Silencing each sudden rush of pulsating exhaust gas can be attempted in various ways, and more than one will be used on the same engine. Expansion chambers in the exhaust system help; a perforated pipe which lets pressure escape to an outer chamber can be encircled with glass fibre or steel wool to absorb noise; and a system of perforated pipes can be arranged so that as gases follow routes of varied lengths through the silencer, pressure pulses cancel each other out. Design of a silencing system to suppress noise can involve both science and trial-and-error.

For many countries, the exhaust system must help the car comply with clean air laws. There is very, very little time for petrol/air mixture to burn in an engine's cylinders, and to get sufficiently complete

ignition

sparking plugs

storage battery

key-ope
switch

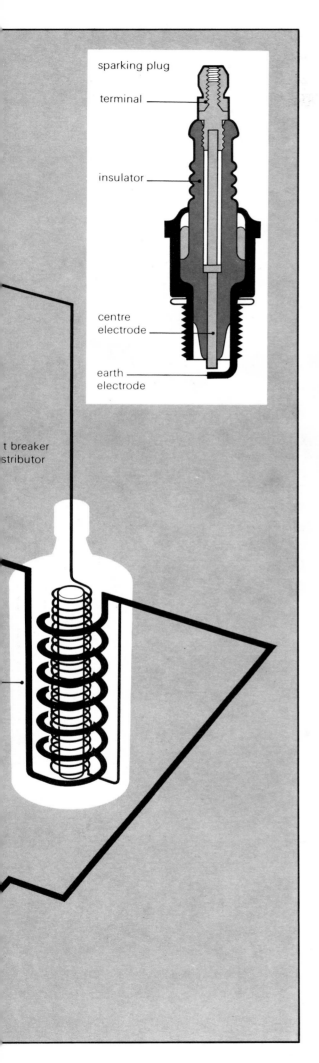

sparking plug

terminal

insulator

centre
electrode

earth
electrode

t breaker
stributor

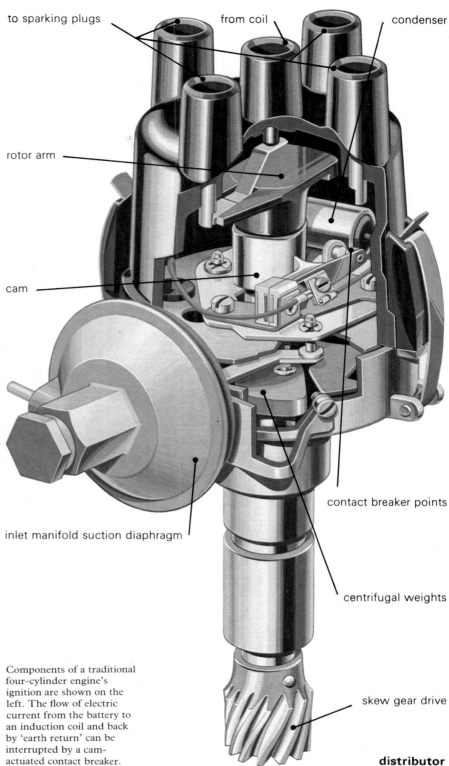

to sparking plugs

from coil

condenser

rotor arm

cam

inlet manifold suction diaphragm

contact breaker points

centrifugal weights

skew gear drive

distributor

Components of a traditional four-cylinder engine's ignition are shown on the left. The flow of electric current from the battery to an induction coil and back by 'earth return' can be interrupted by a cam-actuated contact breaker. These interruptions of low-voltage current induce pulses of high-voltage electricity from the coil, which are directed by the distributor rotor to the appropriate sparking plug, creating a spark at the air gap inside an engine cylinder which ignites the fuel/air mixture. On the right is a typical grouping of the contact breaker and distributor into one compact unit, with two separate mechanisms which can adjust the spark timing to suit varying engine speeds and loads. Progressively, replacement of such mechanism by electronic devices is now altering many ignition systems.

combustion of hydrocarbon fuel to carbon dioxide and steam, it may be necessary to complete the burning process in a suitably designed exhaust system.

Thermal reactors provide the simplest method of after burning. Exhaust gas from the engine is kept as hot as possible by being led through ports isolated from engine coolant to the heart of a reactor chamber, which is kept hot by being surrounded with the still-hot gas from its own outlet. Air may be injected to the engine's exhaust ports to assist the burning up of any residual hydrocarbons or carbon monoxide. With air injection, the engine may deliberately be fed excess fuel with the wasteful object of ensuring that its exhaust gas will burn well.

Catalytic reactors are a more sophisticated form of after burner for exhaust gas. Compounds of platinum and other substances have a surface action on gases passing over them when they are very hot

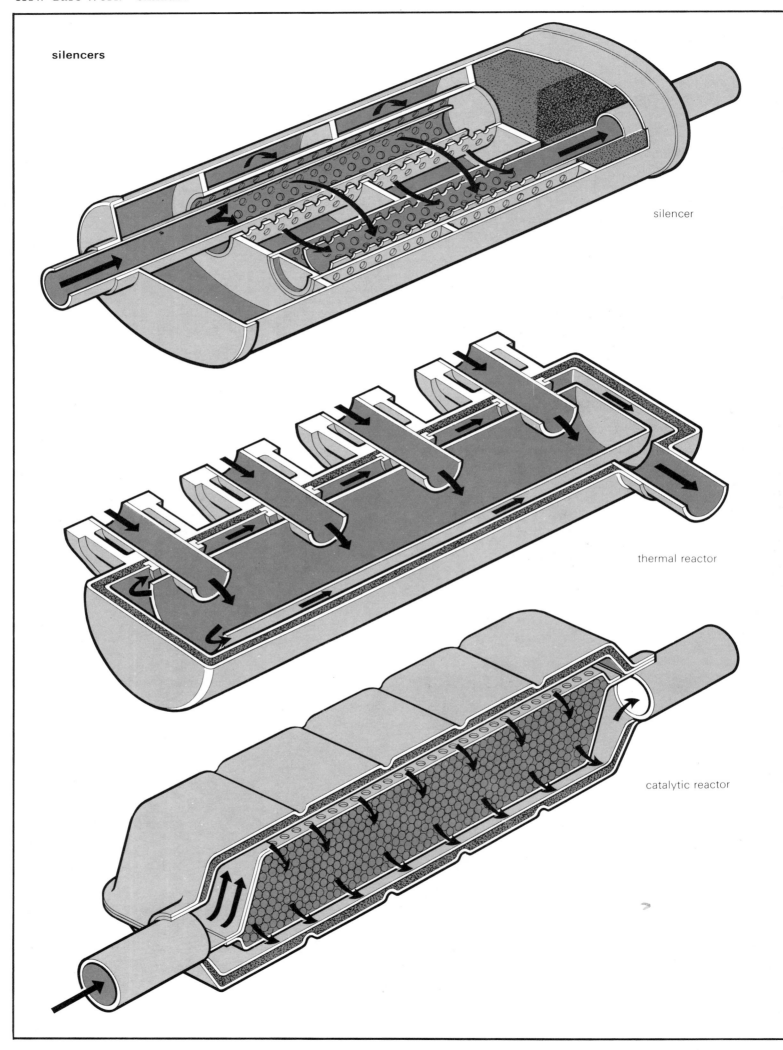

silencers

silencer

thermal reactor

catalytic reactor

Pulses of exhaust gas leaving an engine create much noise, unless rapid fluctuations of pressure are smoothed out in a silencer such as that shown in the top drawing. One or more simple expansion chambers between the engine and the outlet to the atmosphere may help reduce noise. Other silencing methods include passing the gas through holes of restricted size, and lining the expansion chamber with materials such as glass fibre or steel wool.

Since regulations concerning air pollution by cars were introduced in various countries, exhaust systems have sometimes been re-designed so that they burn up impurities in what, ideally, should be a mixture of nitrogen, carbon dioxide and steam.

The central diagram shows a thermal converter, designed to keep exhaust gas hot by expanding it first into a chamber surrounded by other exhaust gas. If air is injected to the engine's exhaust valves, any unburnt hydrocarbons or partly-burnt carbon monoxide which leave the cylinders (because of a misfire or an over-rich fuel/air mixture) should burn up in the converter.

The bottom picture shows one layout for a catalytic converter, which can burn up impurities even more effectively. Hot exhaust gas has to filter through a honeycomb or other porous block, the surfaces of which are coated with a catalytic material to encourage the desired chemical reaction.

which is more thorough than simple burning in a hot chamber. Other catalysts can break down the oxides of nitrogen that are formed at very high combustion temperatures, from the nitrogen and oxygen in air.

A catalytic reactor passes the exhaust gas over very large areas of catalyst-coated surface. Problems of strength at sometimes extreme temperatures have been tackled by such methods as fusing catalyst-coated ceramic granules together to form a porous block through which exhaust gas is passed.

Whereas great heat is a problem at one end of an exhaust system, low temperatures can cause trouble nearer to the outlet. Steam is the combustion product of the hydrogen in petrol, and for a while after an engine has been started from cold this steam will condense in the exhaust system. Especially when cars are used for short trips that do not get the whole exhaust system really hot, acid moisture will collect at any low point towards the outlet of the system after the engine has been stopped. If a manufacturer does not spend enough on corrosion-resistant material, rust from the inside will eventually cause a hole in the pipe or silencer.

Exhaust pipes are usually hung flexibly under a car to allow for movement of an engine on its own flexible rubber mountings and to reduce noise transmission into the passenger compartment. Most of an engine's movement on its flexible mountings consist of oscillation around the crankshaft axis. When the engine is transversely mounted this can be hard on an exhaust system extending at right angles to the crankshaft rather than parallel to it. Either the system must be made very strong or a sort of ball-and-socket joint must be used to permit harmless flexing.

Efforts to reduce air pollution by cars have tended to increase the amount of waste heat radiated from the exhaust system. This can result from the completion of the combustion process following the injection of extra air. Also, if the throttle is kept partially open when the car is slowing down, heavily delayed ignition prevents the development of much unwanted power.

Transmission

Whereas some types of electric and steam engine can start up under load, an internal combustion engine will only operate effectively between fairly well defined minimum and maximum speeds. Power cannot be transmitted to the car's wheels until the engine has been started and brought within its useful range of operating speeds, so some sort of progressive clutch (mechanical, electrical or hydraulic) is required between engine and wheels.

Again, there are types of electric and steam engine that can develop much more effort at low speeds than at high speeds, which enables them to deliver their horsepower equally effectively either uphill or on the level. An internal combustion engine's tractive effort, however, varies only to a modest extent over the speed range and diminishes below about 50 per cent of maximum operating speed. Cars therefore need some sort of change-speed gearing, also between the engine and the wheels, which lets available engine horsepower be used as a large tractive force at low road speeds uphill, or as a smaller tractive force at high speeds on level road.

Refined almost beyond recognition, the transmission layout originated by Panhard et Levassor in 1891 is still common today. A friction clutch combined with the flywheel that an internal combustion engine needs can be engaged to start the car from rest. Mechanical change-speed gearing by toothed cog-wheels lets any of several ratios be engaged, the clutch being disengaged during any change from one gear ratio to another.

It has become most usual to provide a car with four forward gear ratios, plus a single reverse gear for short-distance movements at restricted speeds. The lowest gear ratio is chosen to let a laden car be started from rest up a steep hill, and the highest gear ratio is chosen to let the car reach its maximum speed (determined by air and other resistances absorbing all the available horsepower) without over-speeding of the engine. Two other intermediate ratios are usually judged to give the car versatile performance over a range of speeds, but three-speed gearing may be used in a car which has a big reserve of engine power or, conversely, which is being built down to a minimum cost. Some cars are provided with five gear ratios, mainly so that an extra-high top gear which reduces engine speed can provide quieter and more economical running on high-speed roads.

A modern friction clutch is normally held in engagement by springs that grip a flat driven plate between the engine flywheel and a pressure plate. The driver can release spring pressure and disengage the clutch by pressing a pedal which, through a thrust bearing, moves a ring of levers on the rotating part of the clutch. In the past, cone clutches were quite popular, the spring force needed to transmit power being less than with a flat clutch plate if two conical elements were pressed into frictional contact.

Deceptively simple looking, a single dry plate clutch is nowadays a very refined device. Friction material on the driven disc may be mounted in such a way that initial contact with the flywheel is gradual rather than sudden. Springs around the centre of the plate provide carefully tuned torsional flexibility, further to smooth out the processes of starting from rest or re-engaging the drive after a change of gear ratio.

For many years change-speed gearing used to involve sliding the actual gear wheels along splined shafts to mesh whichever pair of toothed wheels provided the required gear ratio. As cars became more refined, gear wheels with 'helical' teeth cut at an angle came into favour. Noise was reduced because each gear tooth rolled into mesh progressively. With angled teeth, the gear wheels themselves could not readily be slid into engagement so constant mesh gear wheels were adopted, one wheel of each pair being free to rotate on its shaft until a separate dog clutch was engaged.

Quite soon after constant-mesh gearing became popular, synchromesh was introduced to make it easier to engage ratios without unpleasant noisy clashing. Spring-loaded metal friction cones were arranged to contact each other before the dog clutch engaged a ratio, the object being to synchronize the rotational speeds of the parts to be meshed together. As a later refinement, blocker devices were evolved to delay engagement of the dog clutch until the synchronizing friction cones had completed their job.

Improvements in driver-controlled clutches and gearboxes did not eclipse interest in automatic systems, however. Engineers designed various mechanisms that allowed a car to be driven simply by means of the accelerator and brake pedals, there being no clutch pedal. There was no need to use a gear lever except for selecting forward or reverse drive. Quite varied systems have been developed and marketed, but variations on a single principle far outsell all rivals.

In most automatic transmissions the friction

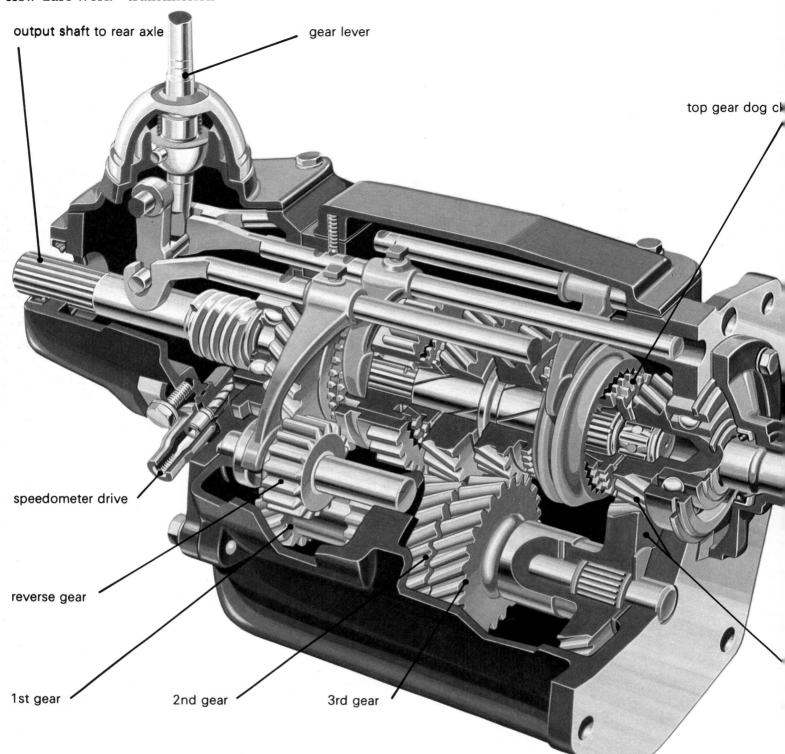

output shaft to rear axle

gear lever

top gear dog cl

speedometer drive

reverse gear

1st gear

2nd gear

3rd gear

This modern four-speed synchromesh gearbox could be regarded as a direct descendant of exposed gearing on the 1891 Panhard et Levassor. Fully enclosed and lubricated, it has helical gear teeth which roll into contact with each other much more quietly than did the straight teeth of the older-style gearbox. These gears are continuously in mesh, those for a desired ratio being engaged to the shafts by dog clutches, friction devices preventing engagement of the dog clutches until speeds have been correctly sychronized. Shafts rotate on roller and ball bearings, so that very little power is wasted, and oil seals on shaft ends prevent any leakage. At the rear of this gearbox, a skew gear is provided to drive the car's speedometer and distance recorder, the splined output shaft allowing for varying propeller shaft length as the car's road springs deflect on bumpy roads.

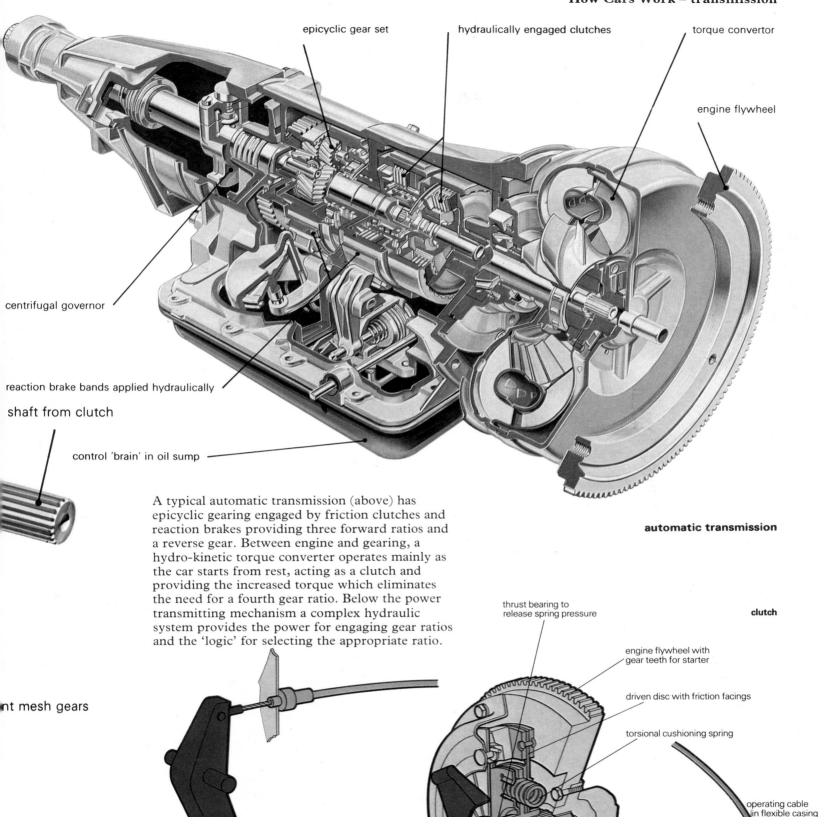

epicyclic gear set

hydraulically engaged clutches

torque convertor

engine flywheel

centrifugal governor

reaction brake bands applied hydraulically

shaft from clutch

control 'brain' in oil sump

automatic transmission

A typical automatic transmission (above) has epicyclic gearing engaged by friction clutches and reaction brakes providing three forward ratios and a reverse gear. Between engine and gearing, a hydro-kinetic torque converter operates mainly as the car starts from rest, acting as a clutch and providing the increased torque which eliminates the need for a fourth gear ratio. Below the power transmitting mechanism a complex hydraulic system provides the power for engaging gear ratios and the 'logic' for selecting the appropriate ratio.

thrust bearing to release spring pressure

clutch

engine flywheel with gear teeth for starter

driven disc with friction facings

torsional cushioning spring

operating cable in flexible casing

diaphragm spring

nt mesh gears

clutch pedal

For starts from rest and for changes of ratio, a car with a gearbox of the type shown opposite needs a friction clutch which can be engaged and disengaged gradually. Springs keep the clutch engaged, unless the pedal is pressed to take the clamping load off a friction disc. In the example on the right, a diaphragm spring holds the clutch engaged.

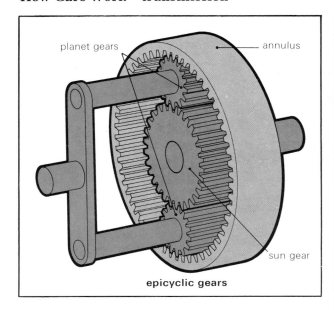

epicyclic gears

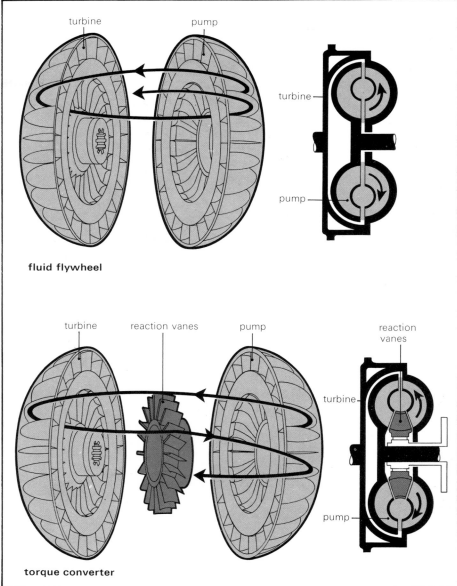

fluid flywheel

torque converter

clutch is replaced by a hydro-kinetic torque converter, which does two jobs smoothly and automatically. When the engine is accelerated the car will move away from rest as if a clutch was being engaged very gently. At low car speeds the hydraulic system provides the torque-increasing, speed-reducing effect of a pair of gears.

In conjunction with the torque converter, a type of change-speed gearing which lets ratios be changed without de-clutching usually provides three forward gears and a reverse gear. Engagement of ratios is controlled by a brain mechanism which responds to car speed and to how hard the driver is pressing on the throttle pedal.

Torque converters evolved from the fluid flywheel which simply comprised a centrifugal oil pump driving a turbine that was almost a mirror-image of the pump. At low engine speeds, oil was circulated quite slowly by the pump and did not create enough effort in the turbine to propel the car. When the engine was speeded up, faster oil circulation from the centrifugal pump produced sufficient torque from the turbine to set the car moving and eventually to propel the car with no more than about 5 per cent slip in the fluid drive system.

A fluid flywheel was purely a clutch, which could slip or give almost complete engagement but could not generate more output effort than the engine was putting into it. By adding a set of reaction vanes anchored to the casting, however, it does become possible to get torque multiplication from this sort of fluid drive when the output shaft is turning more slowly than the input shaft. And by mounting the reaction vanes on a one-way jamming-roller clutch, they can do their job of approximately doubling engine torque when the car is starting from rest, but will rotate forwards without interfering with fluid circulation once the car has gained speed.

The type of mechanical gearing most usually combined with a torque converter is epicyclic gearing in which are combined an internally toothed ring gear or annulus, a central sun gear, and planet gears in the intermediate space. This system can be used and elaborated in various ways. It lends itself to use of either a friction brake which prevents rotation of a reaction element in the system, or a friction clutch to engage a gear ratio smoothly yet positively, without any possibility of clashing or any need for the accelerator pedal to be released during changes of ratio. Mechanical gearing of this kind usually provides for the equivalents of top, third and second ratios in a driver-operated synchromesh gearbox,

the torque converter providing extra tractive effort at low speeds equivalent to what first ratio in a manual gearbox would give.

An automatic gearbox is unable to look ahead and anticipate road conditions, as a skilled human driver can. It is able, however, to respond promptly to changed conditions by engaging a suitable ratio, without becoming tired or lazy. Primarily, automatic gear selection depends on car speed, as measured by some sort of centrifugal governor. Also, ratio engagement is influenced by accelerator pedal position. The automatic brain assumes that if only light pressure is put on the pedal a high gear will be suitable, but that when the driver presses hard on the accelerator he wants a lower gear if this will produce more acceleration. Actual engagement of ratios is usually by a complex hydraulic mechanism, but the 'logic' that controls ratio selection may be either hydraulic or electronic.

Other forms of automatic transmission also exist because engineers would like to find less expensive designs to satisfy the motorist, yet they would prefer to have smooth progression through an infinite range of gear ratios rather than steps between a few ratios. Automatically controlled clutches and synchromesh gearboxes have been tried, almost inevitably with an automatic device to close the throttle during changes of ratio. Friction drive systems, which let the gear ratio be varied progressively by alteration of their geometry, have shown more promise.

Epicyclic gear trains of the type illustrated (top left) are used in a majority of automatic transmissions, in quite varied and subtle combinations. Derived from the simpler 'fluid flywheel' (top), the hydro-kinetic torque converter (above) has also become the norm. Between a centrifugal pump and a driven turbine, a set of reaction vanes mounted on a one-way roller clutch provides increased output torque when the output shaft is stopped or turning slowly.

shaft from
engine

vee belts

forward and reverse
bevel gears

Daf belt drive

Friction drive with variable geometry is an alternative basis for an automatic transmission. The ingenious DAF system, illustrated (above and right) in an early form, automated the much older idea of belt drive with expanding pulleys. By making one pulley wider and the other narrower, a V-belt operates at changed radii, and an infinite variety of gear ratios (within a finite range) is obtained. A clutch and reverse gear complete the system.

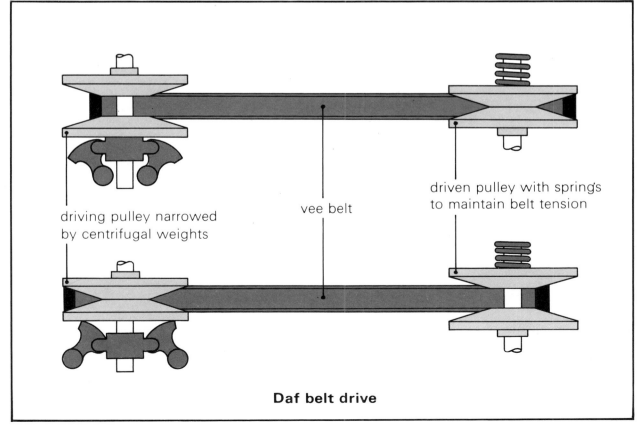

driving pulley narrowed
by centrifugal weights

vee belt

driven pulley with springs
to maintain belt tension

Daf belt drive

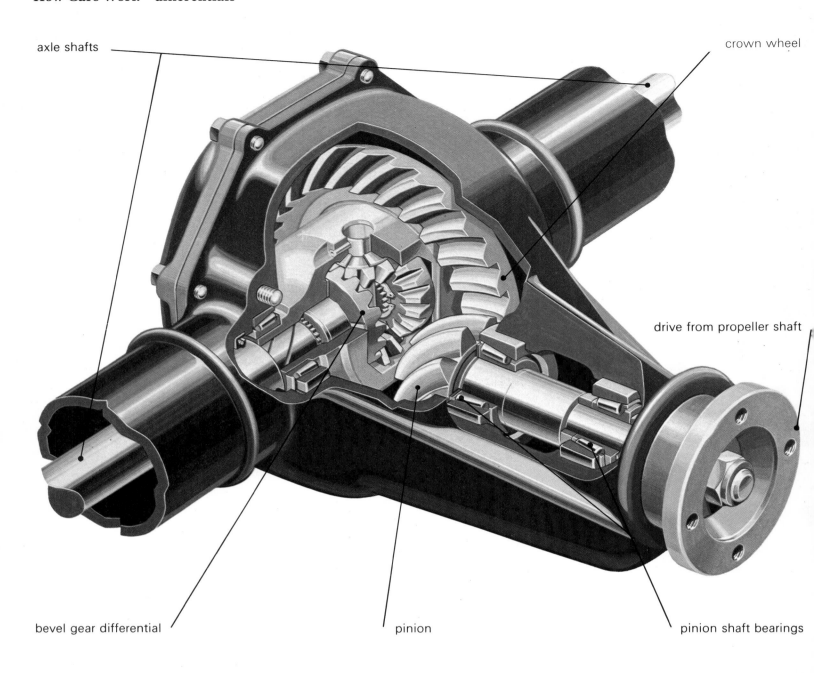

axle shafts

crown wheel

drive from propeller shaft

bevel gear differential

pinion

pinion shaft bearings

Differentials

Two wheels, which may be either the front or the rear pair, are used to propel the vast majority of cars. One driving wheel alone might lack adequate grip on many occasions, and unsymmetrical thrust might impair car stability. Considerable extra cost and weight is involved in transmitting power to all four of a car's wheels and has not usually been thought worthwhile, except for vehicles specially designed so that they can operate away from hard-surfaced roads.

A car must be able to negotiate sharp corners as well as travel along straight roads, and when cornering the outer wheels have to roll a longer distance than do the inner wheels. Very early in motoring history it was necessary to invent a device that would let two driven wheels rotate at unequal speeds while transmitting engine power to the road.

In the so-called differential gear, balance beam principles are applied, though by toothed gear wheels which can provide an unlimited range of movement. There are two output gear wheels in a differential, each linked to a road wheel of the car. Aside from the effects of friction in the mechanism, exactly half the effort available from the engine is applied to each output gear wheel. This equality of

tractive effort remains true even if one driven wheel is not rotating at all, the balance gearing then doubling the speed of the other driven wheel.

In this extreme case, the differential is seen as a necessary evil. It does indeed let a car go around corners, without engine power being wasted on scrubbing rubber off the tyres. If, however, one driven wheel encounters a slippery surface with perhaps mud or loose sand at the edge of a road, the wheel on the firm surface will not receive any more tractive effort than the one which spins easily.

To lessen this nuisance, engineers have evolved what are often called spin-limiting differentials. In most instances the name is inexact because it remains possible to have 100 per cent slip with one wheel rotating at double speed and the other motionless. Extra friction is deliberately built into the mechanism, however, so that the non-rotating or slow-turning wheel can receive more tractive effort than the spinning wheel. This deliberately-introduced friction may come from end thrust on bevel gear wheels deliberately angled steeply for the purpose, there being little friction when driving normally but more when the driver accelerates hard.

When a car has its engine mounted fore-and-aft, power has to be transmitted around a right-angle

Centrepiece of a modern car's driven rear axle (above) is the differential. This mechanism allows left- and right-hand wheels to turn at different speeds when the car goes around a corner, while transmitting equal shares of tractive power from the engine to both wheels. Similar in principle to a balancer beam, the differential uses toothed gear wheels to provide unrestricted ranges of movement.

Transmitting power around a 90° corner is essential in all save transverse-engined cars, and this has been done in various ways.

Bevel gears (top right) were used on pioneer cars, being strong and reasonably easy to make on standard workshop equipment. Subsequently, the gear teeth were cut at an angle, the more gradual load transfer from one tooth to the next in a 'spiral bevel' producing quieter operation.

Worm gearing (lower drawing) was also applied to some early cars and has retained a small following since. It can be quiet, but is best suited to rather large speed reductions.

Normal today is the hypoid bevel gear (top left) which, with the pinion shaft several centimetres below the axis of the gear which it drives, is something of a hybrid between the spiral bevel and the worm gear. Efficiency can be quite high despite some sliding between gear teeth, and the lower line of the shaft from engine to rear axle allows the floor to be set closer to the ground.

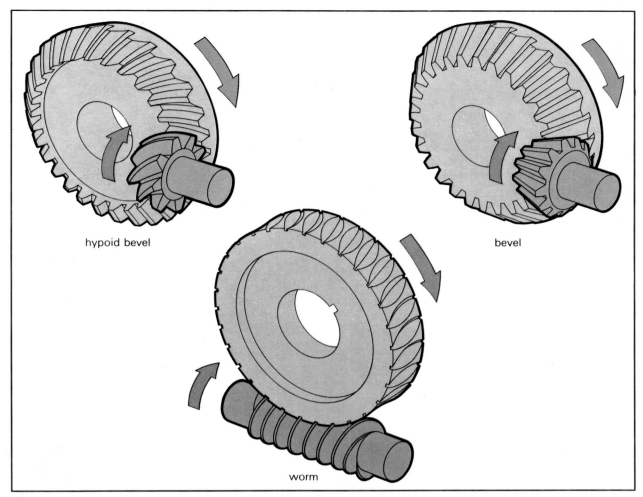

hypoid bevel

bevel

worm

corner to reach the road wheels. Most often this right-angle drive is by a bevel gear, which in a car of very early date would have straight-cut teeth, though these gave way to 'spiral bevel' gearing with teeth angled to roll into mesh more quietly.

An early alternative to bevel gearing was the worm gear, in which a worm wheel with teeth in very much the form of a screw thread meshes with the periphery of a driven gear wheel. This sort of gearing can be very quiet, but it involves the car's propeller shaft being considerably above or below axle shaft height, and sometimes it imposes practical restraints on what gear ratios can be provided.

Extremely common today is the hypoid bevel gear, which may be regarded as something of a compromise between the spiral-tooth bevel gear and the worm gear. Hypoid gearing locates the driving pinion a few centimetres below the centreline of the driven gear, its subtly curved teeth having a mixture of rolling and sliding contact and developing some end thrust – although neither the sliding nor the end thrust are as great as in a worm gear.

A lot of modern front-wheel-driven cars and a few rear-engined models have transverse rather than fore-and-aft engines. With a transverse engine, either spur gears (with helical teeth for quietness) or chains can be used to transmit power from the engine to the differential gear. Often there are two stages of gearing, one from a clutch on the engine's flywheel to the gearbox beneath the engine, and a second from the gearbox to the differential. In other models, a compact engine and gearbox are mounted in line across the car, with gear or chain drive from the gearbox output shaft to the differential.

Rear-wheel-driven cars often have the differential mounted at the centre of an axle in which rigid shafts transmit power to the rear wheels. As the axle must be able to move up and down over road bumps, flexibility is necessary in the drive shaft from the engine-clutch-gearbox assembly to the rear axle. This will usually involve one or more universal joints which, actually or in principle, consist of two hinge joints set at right angles to each other so that the joint can bend yet still transmit torque from the engine. Often a so-called propeller shaft incorporates a telescopic joint to permit slight length variations, sliding splines transmitting the torque.

Universal joints of the simplest type do not transmit power at precisely constant speed when they are operating at a significant angle. If two similar joints working at equal angularity can be used in the drive to a rear axle or rear wheel, suitably phased, the speed fluctuations that each produces twice per shaft revolution can almost balance each other out. When the steered front wheels of a car are driven, however, the outer universal joint in each wheel driving shaft will often have to work at a much greater angle than the inner universal joint, and objectionable pulsations in the flow of power could result. Almost always with front wheel drive, and often also in other applications nowadays, universal joints of sophisticated constant velocity types are used. Some such joints, which transmit power by means of balls sliding in curved grooves, can absorb axial displacements without need for separate telescopic joints.

For use away from hard surfaces, cars with four wheel drive are built. Just as the inner wheels of a car roll a shorter distance than the outer wheels when a corner is negotiated, so the rear wheels roll a slightly shorter distance than those at the front. To prevent power and tyre rubber being wasted, four-wheel-driven cars usually have either an extra differential gear between their front and rear propeller shafts, or else a lever which lets the front wheel drive be disconnected when the car is being used on hard-surfaced roads.

Brakes

Even in the days when propulsion was by a horse, a road vehicle needed a brake with which it could be slowed down, stopped or prevented from rolling away. Horse-drawn vehicles had a shoe that could be put under one wheel and locked when a steep hill had to be descended. They also often had brake blocks that could be pressed against one or more iron-tyred road wheel rims by means of a pedal or lever within the driver's reach. And even an old leather-soled boot or shoe used occasionally to improve the friction between brake block and wheel rim.

Motor cars soon began to travel much faster than horse-drawn vehicles had been able to, and once rubber tyres were introduced it was found best to provide a rotating surface other than a tyre for the brake to rub against. When a circular brake drum was provided, on one or two rear wheels or somewhere on the drive line to those wheels, it was found that tightening a strap around the drum provided more retardation for less effort by the driver than did pressing a simple shoe against the drum. Slightly flexible metal brake bands came into use, surfaced with leather or other materials which provided good frictional characteristics.

Water can drastically reduce the effectiveness of a friction brake, and the working surface of a band brake was exposed to rain or splashes from wet road surfaces. It became possible to produce better all-weather brakes by expanding friction material against the sheltered inner surface of a drum, rather than by contracting a band around the outer surface, and this also let cooling air have free access to the outside of the brake drum. By careful choice of pivot locations, internal brake shoes could be made quite effective. Lining materials based on asbestos were evolved and gave good friction and did not burn out when they got hot on the way down a long hill.

A great deal of effort went into refining drum brakes. The doubling of car speeds required a fourfold ability to dissipate kinetic energy as heat. Water was excluded more effectively, cooling fins were provided and materials more resistant to heat were employed. Stretch of the drums away from the shoes due to heat and internal pressure was controlled, and techniques to prevent brakes squealing were learned. Designs were adopted which used frictional drag to help apply the shoes to an extent safely short of jamming the brake.

Internal expanding drum brakes still do a very useful job, mainly on the rear wheels of cars. From aircraft landing wheel systems, however, there came the idea that a brake with greater ability to dissipate heat could be made by squeezing a flat, rotating disc between two pads of friction material. Expansion due to heat does not put this sort of brake out of adjustment as it can a drum brake, and with most of the disc surface exposed to the air quite effective cooling is obtained. Because of centrifugal action, and because brake pads of small area work under high pressure which squeezes out water, disc brakes need surprisingly little protection against rain.

A modern car tends to carry rather more than half of its weight on the front wheels. When the brakes are applied, further loading is flung forwards from the rear to the front tyres. Therefore, to make full use of available tyre grip on the road surface, much more than half of the braking should be done by a car's front wheels. It has become common practice to equip cars with disc front brakes but to retain internal expanding drum brakes at the rear where much less heat is generated. As an important practical detail, it has proved easier to make a mechanical parking brake work effectively in a drum than on a disc, perhaps because a drum becomes slightly oval under pressure from the brake shoes and in this way helps to hold a car motionless.

In contrast to the modern practice of making front-wheel brakes do most of the work, it was normal until the 1920s to build cars without front-wheel brakes. Until then, cars were not built with their heavy engines in such a far-forward position as is now usual, and because they operated mainly at lower speeds on less crowded roads rear-wheel braking was acceptable. It was not practicable to install powerful front-wheel brakes until springing and steering systems were able to cope with the resulting stresses, or until operating mechanisms were refined enough to ensure that one-sided braking would not pull the steering to one side or the other.

Early brake operating systems were of course mechanical. In a drum brake, a sort of cam would press the ends of two hinged brake shoes apart when it was rotated. Operation of the cam at each wheel was by tension rods or cables from the brake pedal or lever, rotating cross-shafts taking effort from one side of the car to the other. Systems incorporating balance beams to equalize braking effort between pairs of wheels were evolved, although there was some worry that a breakage at one point in the mechanism might put two or even four brakes out of action. Flexible cable systems were designed to transmit brake application forces to steered and sprung front wheels, using a tension wire inside a casing which could bend into a curve but would not shorten under compression.

Mechanical systems for applying brakes on sprung and steered wheels reached a high standard in the 1950s with roller-bearing wedges replacing cams as brake shoe expanders. However, by that time hydraulic brake operating systems had become very reliable and quite inexpensive after some 20 years of development, and mechanical operation is now confined to the parking brake on most cars.

In a simple hydraulic brake operating system the driver's pedal moves a piston in a cylinder, creating pressure in a suitable non-freezing fluid. This pressure is piped to other cylinders in the brakes on the car's four wheels where it moves slave pistons to apply the brakes. Operating pressure is equal throughout the hydraulic system. Desired proportioning of braking effort between front and rear wheels is achieved from appropriate slave cylinder and brake dimensions. To allow fluid lost by leakage to be replaced and for follow up of any brake lining wear, the pedal-actuated master cylinder has a hole in its side so that when the brake is released any extra fluid needed to keep the cylinder full can enter from a small reservoir. Hydraulic brake fluid must resist boiling up to a very high temperature, and should not readily absorb atmospheric moisture.

A truly balanced brake operating system is liable to be put out of action if a failure occurs at any one point. In a mechanical linkage this risk can be reduced by restricting the movement range of balancer devices. A hydraulic brake operating system can also be divided so that no failure can put all four brakes out of action.

In most instances brake hydraulic systems are now split between the front and rear of a car, although a failure which leaves only the rear brakes working might reduce stopping power to only about one-third of normal. Some cars with steering designed especially so that unsymmetrical braking will not pull it sideways, have the left front and right rear

Shown here is the layout of a typical brake operating system, with one pedal operating brakes on all four wheels and a handbrake lever arranged to keep two brakes applied when the car is parked.

To ensure that the correct share of braking effort is applied to each wheel, regardless of road bumps and without inconsistent friction, a hydraulic system is used to transmit and share-out pedal effort. Fluid pressure, generated by a piston linked to the brake pedal, and sometimes multiplied by a power assistance system, is directed to operating pistons on individual wheel brakes through rigid and flexible pipes.

Power assitance is usually pneumatic, taking advantage of the fact that brakes are normally applied only when the engine's throttle is closed, and when inlet manifold pressure is far below atmospheric. Control valves ensure that output effort from the vacuum servo is a constant multiple of whatever effort the driver is applying to the pedal.

In a simple hydraulic system the failure of one pipe or of a piston's fluid seal could release all operating pressure. Modern systems are divided in various ways, valves closing if there is an unequal flow of fluid to one part of the system, to cut off the leaking area and leave at least two of the car's brakes in operation. The most sophisticated systems have duplicated hydraulic systems on each wheel, so that failure cannot leave any wheel completely un-braked. Fluids used in hydraulic systems need to be non-corrosive, immune from freezing even at very low temperatures, yet with boiling points high enough to remain free from vapour in close proximity to red-hot brake discs. In a vented system they should not absorb moisture from the atmosphere, as this would lower their boiling point. Hydraulic pipes are mainly of metal, with flexible links to allow for any deflections. These flexible pipes need to stretch as little as possible under high internal fluid pressures, as any stretch wastes brake pedal movement.

Parking brake application is usually mechanical, with a ratchet on the control lever to keep the brake applied when the car is parked. Not normally applied when the car is moving, the parking brake need not be so perfectly balanced in action, and tension cables may be run through flexible casings to the wheel.

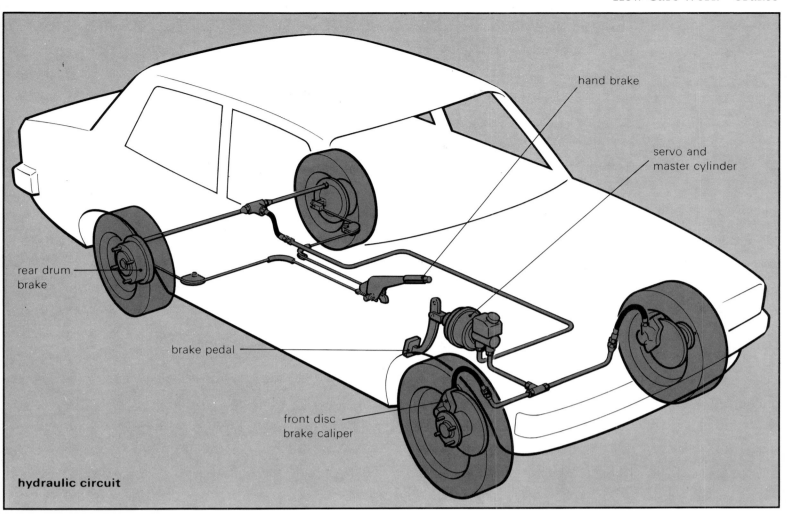

hand brake

servo and
master cylinder

rear drum
brake

brake pedal

front disc
brake caliper

hydraulic circuit

For simplicity, parking brakes are usually confined to un-steered rear wheels. A few front-wheel-driven cars have parking brakes which act on the front wheels, and because nose-heavy weight distribution is emphasized by forward weight transfer during braking, a handbrake working on the front wheels can be much more effective as an emergency brake. A great many cars are designed with disc front brakes and drum rear brakes as illustrated. It has proved simpler to make an effective parking brake of drum than of disc type, and the extra heat-dissipating capacity of disc brakes is often needed only at the front of a car.

brakes operated by one half of the hydraulic system, the right front and left rear brakes operated by the other half. This arrangement should guarantee at least 50 per cent of normal braking power after any failure. At greater cost, some cars have two separate hydraulic operating systems in each front brake. These are served by their own flexible pipes so that no single hydraulic failure could leave the driver without front wheel braking.

The friction material in a brake is what really does the work. Often based on heat-resistant asbestos fibre impregnated with various resins, it may on occasion incorporate strands of fine wire. A brake lining must grip consistently over a range of temperatures from below freezing up to red heat. It should take a long time to wear away, should not damage the metal it rubs against, and should provide at least reasonable friction when wet. No ideal brake lining material has yet been found for those with most grip tend to behave differently when hot, and those that can work at the highest temperatures tend to behave less well when cold.

Brake lining materials that are durable and consistent in their behaviour do not have such high coefficients of friction as car designers might wish. Disc brakes today are not made with the self-wrapping characteristic that sometimes magnified the power of drum brakes, partly because such self servo also magnifies the effect of any change in friction characteristics of the lining. Instead it has become usual to provide even small and light cars with servo power braking systems, which multiply up whatever effort the driver applies to the brake pedal.

A driver normally closes the engine's throttle before applying the brakes, and this leads to powerful suction in the engine's inlet pipe which can be

used to assist braking. Atmospheric pressure on one side of a sliding piston or flexible diaphragm of quite large size, and suction on the other side, produce a force which can be applied to the far smaller hydraulic master cylinder of the braking system. A spring loaded valve responsibe to brake pedal effort controls admission of air to one side of the servo device, ensuring that whilst output effort may be double or treble that exerted by the driver, the servo will not lock the car's wheels by applying brake pressure out of proportion to the driver's effort.

A pneumatic tyre grips the road surface best when it is rolling along but provides rather less grip if a locked wheel is sliding along without rotating. So for utmost retardation in an emergency and to enable the driver to retain steering control, it is best to avoid any situation where a car's wheels become locked by the brakes.

Because weight is thrown forward to an increasing extent as braking effort is increased, rear brakes can usefully do a greater share of the work when a car is being slowed down gently (as on a wet or icy surface). It has become common to equip cars with devices that limit rear brake operating hydraulic pressure, either to a designed maximum or in more advanced systems to a maximum that varies with the load of passengers and luggage being carried.

At a much higher cost, true anti-lock brake control systems exist. These sense any tendency for one or more wheels to lock under excessive braking effort. Then ease off the brakes momentarily and re-apply them within a fraction of a second so that the wheels keep turning and the tyres provide utmost grip as well as directional stability. Goods vehicles, which are subject to very wide variations in rear axle or trailer load, are proving the most rewarding applications for anti-lock brake control devices.

135

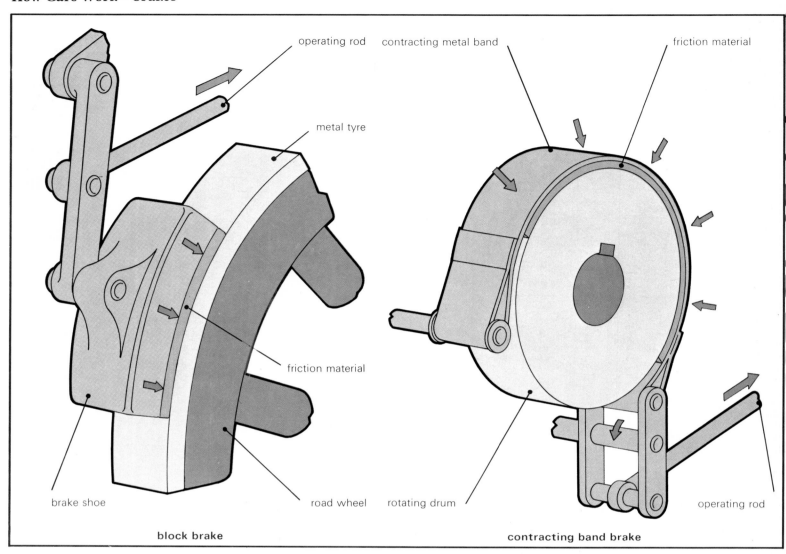

operating rod

metal tyre

friction material

brake shoe

road wheel

block brake

contracting metal band

friction material

rotating drum

operating rod

contracting band brake

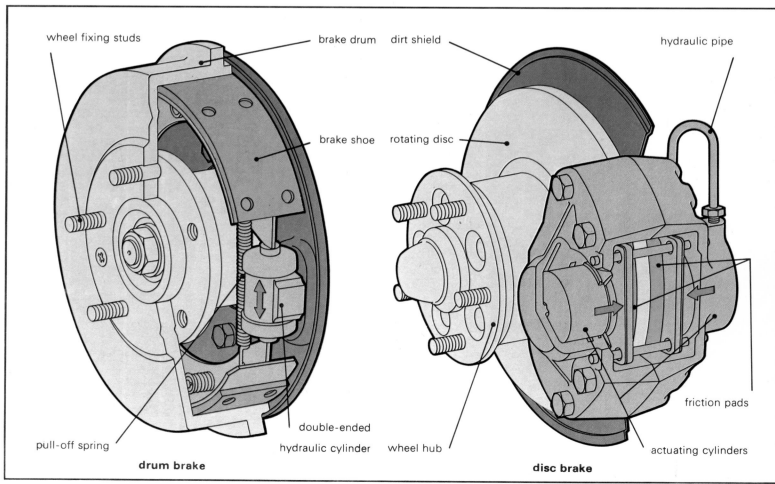

wheel fixing studs

brake drum

brake shoe

pull-off spring

double-ended
hydraulic cylinder

drum brake

dirt shield

hydraulic pipe

rotating disc

friction pads

wheel hub

actuating cylinders

disc brake

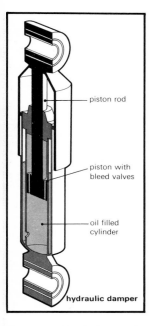

piston rod

piston with
bleed valves

oil filled
cylinder

hydraulic damper

Telescopic 'shock absorbers'
(above) are widely used to
check persistent bouncing of
car springs by forcing oil
through restrictions.

Opposite : Brakes on some of
the earliest cars were
patterned after those of
horse-drawn carriages (top
left), a leather-faced shoe
being pressed against a road
wheel's solid tyre. When
more powerful brakes were
needed, special brake drums
were provided (top right)
around which a brake band
could be tightened.
Protection of brake friction
surfaces against wet weather
was much improved when
internal expanding drum
brakes (lower left) were
introduced. Illustrated is an
example with a hydraulic
piston and cylinder to press
a pair of brake shoes
outwards. To provide
greater ability to dissipate
energy as heat, disc brakes
(lower right) were later
introduced. Squeezing the
metal discs between two
friction pads eliminated
problems which had arisen
of thermal expansion moving
brake drum surfaces away
from the brake shoes.

Suspension

Roads are never completely smooth, so for a car to
be comfortable and durable, it must have flexible
springs to smooth its passage over road bumps. In
fact, two stages of springing have proved necessary.
Directly in contact with the road, the pneumatic
tyre with its flexible tread of rubber absorbs small
road surface irregularities and rounds off the corners
of sharp bumps. Between its pneumatic tyred wheels
and the main structure, a car needs springs with
greater movement ranges, plus so-called shock-
absorbers which in reality prevent persisting bounce
of the car on its springs.

Very varied forms of car spring are in use. Like
horse drawn carriages of the 19th century, early
cars were usually supported on steel leaf springs.
Several fairly thin spring leaves clamped together
would bend to let the axles move up and down when
crossing bumps, but were stiff enough in other directions to hold an axle in reasonably accurate alignment. Modernized only in material quality and in
detail, such leaf springs remain in use today on some
cars and on many trucks.

A coil spring, also made of steel, is lighter in
weight than a leaf spring of similar flexibility and
load capacity. Alone, however, a coil spring is unstable and liable to wobble sideways, so when used
to support a car, it must be accompanied by some
sort of linkage to keep the wheels in alignment. A
drawing shows a typical linkage used with coil
springs to control a car's rear axle, letting one or both
wheels move up and down over bumps, but not
letting the axle rotate under drive or braking torque,
nor letting it move or turn sideways.

Torsion bar springs, straight steel rods twisted by
levers at their ends, fit conveniently into some car
designs. It is also possible to use the deformability
of rubber in various ways, to support a car flexibly.
Another form of springing used by certain car
makers involves compressing an enclosed pocket of
air or of inert nitrogen gas.

It is commonplace to find on a car two types of
auxiliary to the main springs. So that neither over-
loading nor extra-severe bumps cause metal-to-
metal impact between axle and body, it is usual to
provide rubber buffers which act only when the
normal load-supporting springs are deflected to an
abnormal extent. Quite often also, to prevent a softly
sprung car leaning sideways to an undue extent when
going around a corner, one or two torsion bar springs
are placed across the car, pivoted so that rise and fall
of the axles is not resisted, but twisted if body roll
shifts weight from one side of the car to the other.

A car which behaved like a trampoline would not
be comfortable or safe, so bounce of the springs has
to be damped. When internal friction in leaf springs
proved inadequate, separate devices misnamed
shock absorbers were produced, resisting spring
movement by means of friction between hardwood
discs and metal. More progressive control of bounce
is now obtained hydraulically, there being a piston
in an oil-filled cylinder at each corner of the car.
Bleed holes and valves let the resistance to oil flow
from one end of the cylinder to the other be adjusted
so that bounce is controlled without desirable spring
deflections being unduly resisted.

Springing systems which use an axle to link two
wheels together are simple to visualize, but are not
used on all cars. For comfort and good grip of the
road, a vehicle should have as little unsprung weight
as possible moving up and down with its wheels when
imperfect roads are traversed. Unsprung weight can
be reduced by mounting the differential gear on the
sprung part of the car, taking power to each wheel
through a universally jointed shaft, instead of building this unit into an axle. Early de Dion cars separated the differential from the axle, and their rear
axle layout is still occasionally used. More often
though, if the differential is sprung, an independent
linkage is used to control alignment of each wheel
without there being an axle beam.

Whilst the rigid rear axle remains deservedly
popular on many types of car, the rigid front axle is
now a rarity on private vehicles. For a variety of
reasons, independent wheel suspension linkages
have become the norm for cars, although front axles
are retained for many trucks and buses.

A fundamental difference between the two ends
of a car is that the front wheels are steered. A rapidly
rotating wheel, brake and tyre has some of the characteristics of a gyroscopic spinning top, and if tilted
sideways as one end of an axle meets a bump, the
wheel tries to pivot around its steering axis. Very
large forces can be developed, producing unpleasant
reactions in the steering. Contrastingly, rear wheels
mounted rigidly on axle shafts without steering
swivels do not pose this problem.

As has been mentioned also, front brakes are
usually required to do twice as much work as rear
brakes, and forces which they generate are not easily
absorbed in the simplest leaf-spring and rigid-axle
systems. As a further complication, it has been found
preferable to have rather softer and slower-acting
springs at the front of a car than at the back, so that
as wheels meet a bump one after the other, any
persisting movement by the springs gets into step
rather than getting out of phase and making the car
pitch uncomfortably.

Fashion encouraged car designers to overcome
problems such as these by adopting independent
front wheel springing linkages, rather than by producing more sophisticated rigid-axle layouts. A
separate linkage to control each wheel's rise and fall
can certainly reduce or eliminate many gyroscopic
effects, permitting use of taut, low-friction steering
mechanisms.

What may nowadays be called the classic form of
independent front wheel springing uses two transverse links to locate each wheel, the links being
roughly triangular in shape (they are often called
wishbones because of this) so that they can resist
braking forces. Commonly, a ball-and-socket joint
at the outer end of each link serves a dual purpose,
letting the wheel carrier be steered as well as providing for vertical deflections of the springing system.
This front suspension layout may be used with any
type of spring; a coil is the most widely used form,
but in some designs a torsion bar extends rearwards
from the lower wishbone.

An alternative which has become extremely
popular is the Macpherson strut suspension. This
has some similarity to the systems with two transverse
links per wheel but instead of an upper wishbone
there is a sturdy telescopic strut on which the coil
spring is often mounted. On paper, this system
appears over-simplified, in that wheel inclination and
lateral position change as the spring is compressed.
In practice, sturdy simplicity lets it work extremely
well, and there are some significant practical advantages. Absence of upper wishbones means that
extra space is available around the engine; wide
spacing between mounting points means that use of
rubber to keep road noise out of the car has very
little ill effect on steering accuracy.

Originally the famous Volkswagen had two trailing links to locate each front wheel, a special short-

rear suspensions

axle with leaf springs

axle with coil springs
and locating radius arms

independent suspension
linkage with coil springs

front axle with transverse
leaf springs

Macpherson telescopic
struts and coil springs

transverse links
and coil springs

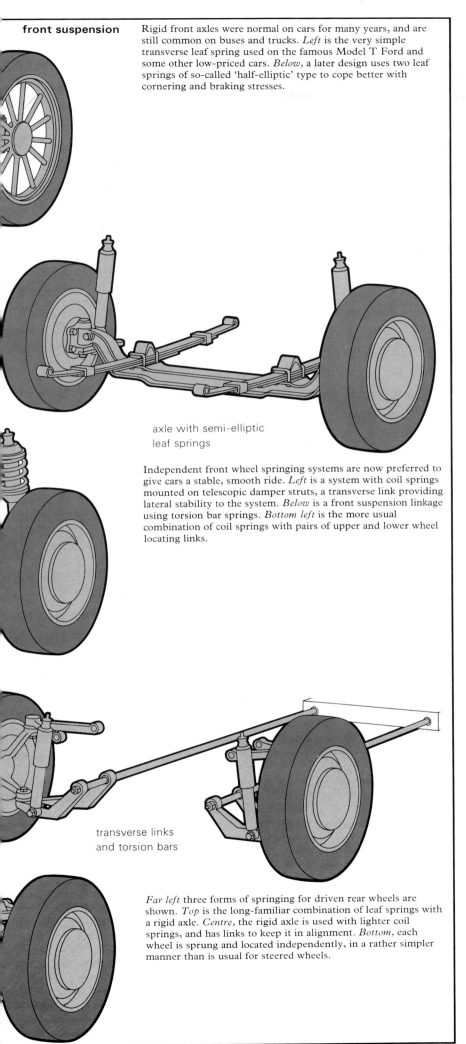

front suspension Rigid front axles were normal on cars for many years, and are still common on buses and trucks. *Left* is the very simple transverse leaf spring used on the famous Model T Ford and some other low-priced cars. *Below*, a later design uses two leaf springs of so-called 'half-elliptic' type to cope better with cornering and braking stresses.

axle with semi-elliptic
leaf springs

Independent front wheel springing systems are now preferred to give cars a stable, smooth ride. *Left* is a system with coil springs mounted on telescopic damper struts, a transverse link providing lateral stability to the system. *Below* is a front suspension linkage using torsion bar springs. *Bottom left* is the more usual combination of coil springs with pairs of upper and lower wheel locating links.

transverse links
and torsion bars

Far left three forms of springing for driven rear wheels are shown. *Top* is the long-familiar combination of leaf springs with a rigid axle. *Centre*, the rigid axle is used with lighter coil springs, and has links to keep it in alignment. *Bottom*, each wheel is sprung and located independently, in a rather simpler manner than is usual for steered wheels.

and-thick type of laminated torsion bar spring being mounted transversely. On paper this system gave excellent geometry, but when more flexible springs with a longer range of movement were wanted, correspondingly longer links would not have been rigid enough laterally to resist cornering stresses, so strut suspension was adopted in its place.

For the occupants of a car to be mentally as well as physically comfortable, it is important that they should enjoy a quiet ride as well as a smooth one. Various sorts of thud from individual bumps and roars from textured road surfaces are apt to enter a car as it rolls along the road. Thick floor covering can minimize noise, but some sort of barrier to the transmission of noise through the structure is desirable. Designers try to interpose rubber between the springing system and the body, in places where it will not let the wheels get out of alignment. Sometimes the independent springing systems for the two wheels at one end of a car are mounted on a cross-beam or frame, which holds them in alignment and is itself insulated from the rest of the car with rubber mounts spaced apart very widely.

Load variations pose another problem for designers of car springing systems. When a full complement of passengers and luggage is being carried, springs are compressed much further than when the driver is alone in the car, most of the extra load being in most instances carried by the rear springs. With simple designs, springs tend to be either too-stiff under a light load or else too-flexible under a heavy load. When empty, a car rides high on its springs, whereas when laden it sinks down until the springs have little movement range left to absorb big bumps. There are types of spring which stiffen up when they are deflected by a heavy load, but these alone offer only a partial solution to the problem. Some of the mote refibed cars how have self-levelling springs, either for the rear or for all wheels. An automatic system jacks up the car on its springs to a normal ride height after any load change, hydraulic power to do this coming either from an engine-driven pump, or from a pump combined with one of the shock absorbers.

Tyres
Engineers would probably have found ways to build acceptable cars if the pneumatic tyre had never been invented, yet it is undeniable that pneumatic tyres play a vital part in making cars comfortable, controllable, safe and quiet in very varied conditions.

Tyres provide cushioning against shock from the sharper irregularities in road surfaces, by putting flexibility right at the road surface, with next to no inertia to prevent the rubber flexing instantly to wrap itself over a pebble. They provide grip on all sorts of surfaces, so that the car can be propelled, steered and stopped quickly if the driver wishes. And, so far from making a car feel as if it was supported on four wobbly rubber air cushions, tyres let cars be steered with remarkable accuracy.

Compressed air in a flexible container provides the cushion under each of a car's wheels. During much of motoring history, the compressed air was contained by a separate inner tube within the visible tyre casing. Then it was found that, solid wheel rims having replaced those with spoke holes, air pressure could hold the tyre so tightly against the wheel rim that the inner tube had become unnecessary.

Although the visible part of a tyre is made of vulcanized rubber (either natural, synthetic or a blend of the two) its strength comes mainly from other materials beneath the weather-resistant black

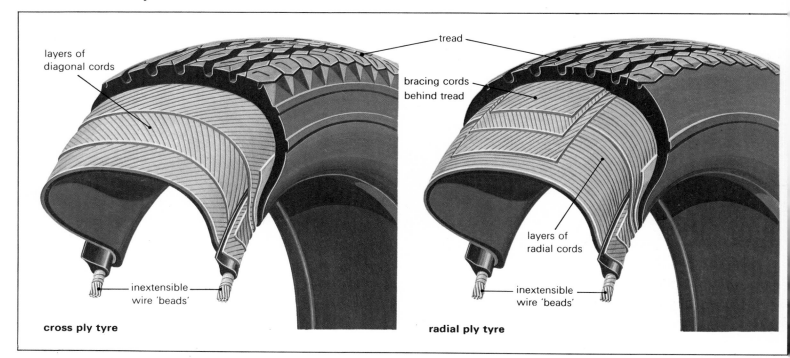

layers of diagonal cords

tread

bracing cords behind tread

layers of radial cords

inextensible wire 'beads'

inextensible wire 'beads'

cross ply tyre

radial ply tyre

skin. There is a so-called bead at each edge of the tyre, a ring of virtually inextensible wire to keep the rubber tyre a secure fit on the metal wheel rim. Giant truck wheels may be made in sections, to let the tyres with their inextensible edges be installed. A car wheel is made with a one-piece rim in which a central well is formed, and when the inextensible tyre edge is slid into the well at one side of the whole, the other side of the tyre edge will just reach over the lip which subsequently holds the tyre secure on the wheel.

To provide strength for resisting internal air pressure, yet sufficient flexibility to absorb bumps, tyres are built on a basis of special fabric. Woven fabric did not give the right blend of flexibility with resistance to stretching, so layers of parallel threads (always referred to as cords) are used instead, held together mainly by being coated with rubber. Often car tyres were built with four layers of cords, alternate layers criss-crossing their neighbours as they ran diagonally from the wheel rim to the periphery of the tyre and on to the other edge of the tyre. This so called cross ply tyre construction, still used to a certain extent, can be applied with more or fewer than four layers or plys of cords.

Present-day car tyres are more often of what is called radial ply construction, with the internal cords running almost radially rather than diagonally. This produces a more flexible casing, in which additional bracing is used directly behind the tyre tread, the part of the tyre which actually comes into contact with the ground. Precisely controlled tread flexibility, to let the car be kept directionally stable whilst letting road surface irregularities be absorbed is provided by backing the rubber tread with extra layers of cords, which may be of steel, nylon, rayon or glass fibre.

Whereas most of a tyre has only a protective skin of rubber over the fabric, the tread which actually rolls along the road is a ring of thick rubber, bonded onto the rest of the tyre during manufacture. Its thickness allows for inevitable wear, and lets a pattern of grooves be used to improve grip on many sorts of surface. In dry weather, a completely smooth rubber tyre tread can grip excellently on a hard road surface, smooth tyres being used on racing cars in suitable weather. When it rains however, a film of water can persist between a smooth-treaded tyre

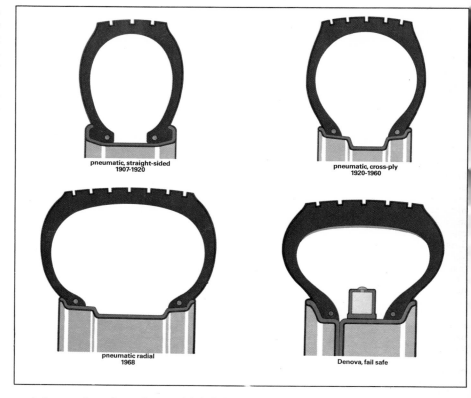

pneumatic, straight-sided 1907-1920

pneumatic, cross-ply 1920-1960

pneumatic radial 1968

Denova, fail safe

and the road surface along which it is rolling, and if that happens, there will be next to no grip to let the car be steered or braked safely.

Grooves in tyre treads can serve two purposes, besides identifying the product of a particular company. Their edges wipe moisture off a smooth road surface, so that the rubber can grip properly. Grooves also act as drainage channels along which water can escape from under the rolling tyre. Often a combination of narrow slits and wider grooves is used, in a slightly irregular pattern to break up sound pulses as the car rolls along the road.

Over a long period of motoring history, car wheels have gradually tended to become smaller in diameter, as lighter and more compact tyres became able to cope with required speeds and loads. Tyres for these shrinking wheels grew wider in cross-section, and were run at lower inflation pressures, as engineers sought better grip and smoother riding. In recent years, tubeless tyres have gradually departed from

Pneumatic tyres need the reinforcement of inextensible 'cords' within their rubber exterior. Top left is a 'cross ply' tyre with layers of cords criss-crossing diagonally. Top right is the more modern 'radial ply' design, with extra layers of tread bracing to compensate for more flexible side walls. Above are four stages in the evolution of pneumatic tyres, from high-pressure tyres of narrow section to a modern wide 'low profile' design and a self-sealer against punctures.

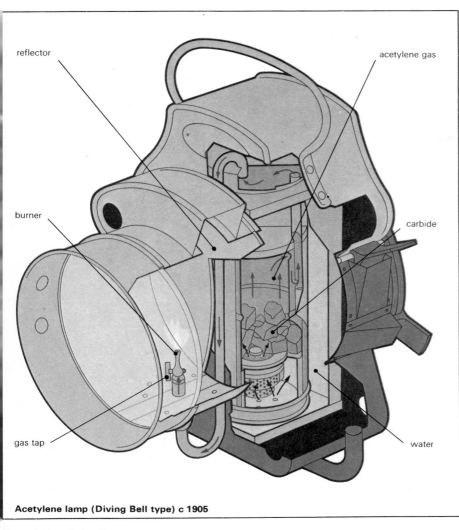

reflector

burner

gas tap

acetylene gas

carbide

water

Acetylene lamp (Diving Bell type) c 1905

the almost circular cross-section which suited an inner tube, becoming wider in the tread and fitting onto wider wheel rims, but with a reduced height from the road up to the wheel rim.

Flexing as they rotate under load, tyres become heated by internal friction when a car is driven briskly. Too much heat can weaken the materials, and special high-speed tyres are made for very fast cars. To make them cool-running, such tyres have extra-strong casings and extra-hard grades of tread rubber, so they tend to give a harsher ride and to have rather less grip on wet roads than do less-expensive tyres suitable only for more moderate speeds.

Lights

Motorists expect to be able to use their cars at any hour of the day or night in almost any weather. Their cars need lights as a warning to other road users of their presence, and to let the driver see the way ahead. A car's presence on the road is indicated by low-powered lights near to its four corners, red at the back and white (or in some countries amber) at the front. To meet legal requirements, illumination of the registration number on the back of the car is usually provided whenever any lights are switched on.

To let the driver see where he is going at night, cars are equipped with headlamps, normally in pairs so that a failure of one won't produce sudden and complete black-out. Headlight systems provide alternative types of beam, which the driver selects with a two-way switch, a main beam which gives maximum vision when the road ahead is free from other traffic, and a dipped or passing beam which provides a shorter range of forward vision and does not dazzle other road users.

Powerful headlights for car drivers began with the acetylene type, in which burning gas was generated when water dripped onto calcium carbide (top). Trouble-free lighting came with electricity, the drawings (right) showing all-glass or (far right) metal-and-glass units of combined reflector and lens. Inserted bulbs have two filaments to provide main or dipped beams, the narrower 'quartz iodine' bulb, which contains traces of iodine, operates more efficiently at a higher filament temperature.

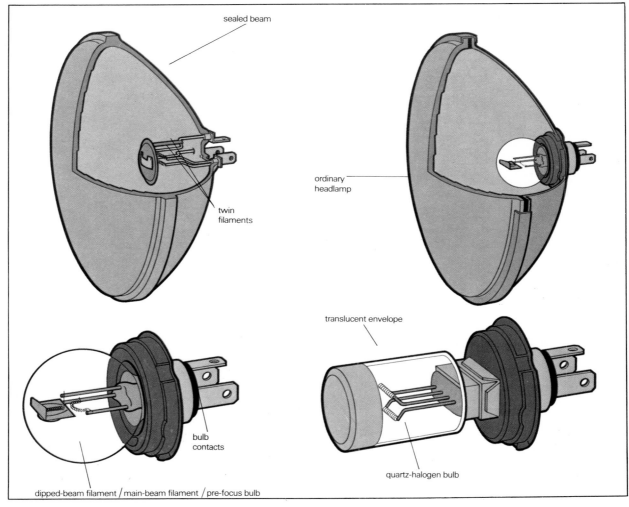

sealed beam

twin filaments

ordinary headlamp

bulb contacts

dipped-beam filament / main-beam filament / pre-focus bulb

translucent envelope

quartz-halogen bulb

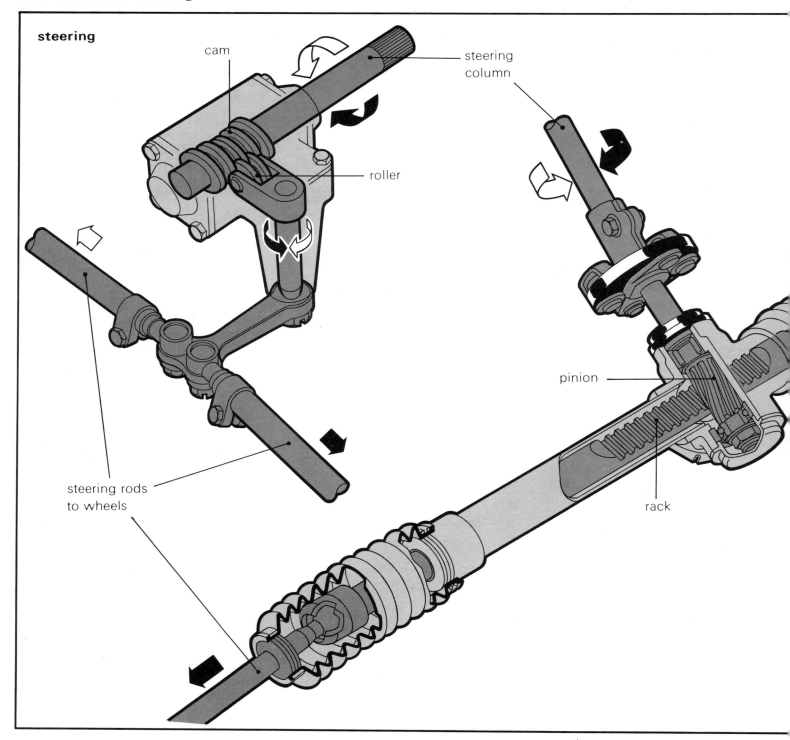

steering

cam

steering
column

roller

pinion

steering rods
to wheels

rack

Early cars had oil lamps, or gas lamps burning acetylene generated by dripping water onto calcium carbide. For a long time now, the convenient light source has been an incandescent, electrically-heated filament of tungsten. Light from a filament is concentrated into a forward beam by a parabolic reflector, the lamp glass which keeps this reflector clean having prism shapes moulded into it to spread the beam laterally over the width of the road. The dipped beam is designed to shine downwards at a slight angle, and a screen around part of the filament is often used to cut off that part of its light output which might cause dazzle. When a car has only two headlamps, each lamp will incorporate two filaments, one positioned to provide the main beam and the other used to provide the dipped beam. Cars which have four headlamps get the dipped beam and part of the main beam from one lamp at each side of the car, additional long-range lamps being switched on as part of the main beam only.

Traditionally the electric light filament worked

within a compact glass bulb, a vacuum or a filling of inert gas preventing quick burning up of the filament. In the 'sealed beam' alternative, the whole reflector and front glass of a headlamp may serve as in effect the bulb, this system being efficient but tending to increase replacement costs.

How much light an electric filament can produce, for a given input of electrical energy and output of heat, depends on how high a temperature the filament can be run at, without burning away rapidly. In the quartz-halogen bulb, special quartz glass surrounds the tungsten filament very closely, and there is iodine in the bulb: chemical reactions between the tungsten filament, the iodine and the very hot glass keep the filament intact at exceptionally high temperatures. In car headlamps, quartz-halogen bulbs give brighter, whiter light than do other possible light sources.

In addition to headlights for normal after-dark travel, cars are sometimes equipped with more specialized auxiliary lamps. Foglamps with very low

Mechanisms designed to provide smoothly accurate steering fall mainly into two groups. *Top left* is a steering gear using a worm-like cam to move a roller. Below it is a rack-and-pinion mechanism of a type that has become especially popular for small cars.

beams and hardly any upward light output will illuminate the road for some distance ahead, causing much less back-glare from water droplets in the atmosphere than would normal headlamps. Long range lamps with very concentrated beams permit faster travel on straight roads free from other traffic. Driving lamps giving a broad beam which is not shallow like a foglamp beam can be helpful along very winding lanes.

Steering

Directional control of a car is invariably by steering the front wheels in the desired direction – rear wheel steering involves difficulty in getting away from a kerb, and problems of instability at high speeds. Always, the front wheels are steered separately, as swivelling of a complete axle (as was done on some horse-drawn vehicles) wastes space and reduces the vehicle's stability when a sharp corner is being negotiated.

Space inside a car's front wheel is often quite crowded, with bearings for the wheel to rotate on, brake mechanism, and often a universal joint for driving the wheel. Often the steering swivel can only be accommodated somewhat inboard of the wheel's

A car's two front wheels need to be steered simultaneously if the car is to roll easily along the road without tyres being forced to slide sideways, but they do not need to be steered through precisely equal angles. When a car is rounding a sharp corner, its inside front wheel needs to be steered through a greater angle than the outside front wheel, as shown in a diagram. This Ackermann effect, named after the man who introduced it on horse drawn vehicles, is obtained by suitably angled linkage between the wheels. Because tyres have some lateral flexibility, and the outer tyres carry the greater load when a car is rounding a corner, the optimum difference between steering angles of two front wheels is in practice rather smaller than the geometrical diagram suggests.

When cars first began to travel fast, kick-back from bumpy roads to the wheel or tiller with which the driver was steering the car posed problems. A deliberately heavy tiller handle or steering wheel rim to absorb the shock was one palliative, but designers soon evolved steering gears which were, to a greater or lesser extent, irreversible. Forms of gearing which use screw or worm-and-wheel principles work much more efficiently to transmit effort

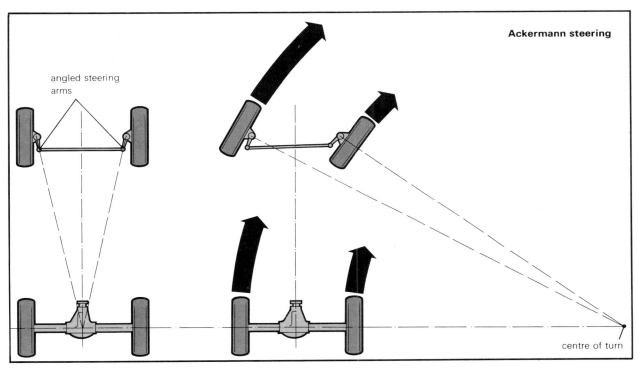

Ackermann steering

angled steering arms

centre of turn

First used on horse-drawn carriages, Ackermann steering geometry steers the inside front wheel through a greater angle than the outside front wheel. This effect is achieved simply by use of non-parallel steering arms as shown in the left hand sketch. Because flexible pneumatic tyres do not always roll in exactly the direction to which they are pointed, cars do not always follow Ackermann principles precisely.

centre, although this involves a possibility that any drag force from a road bump or from the brake will try to turn the wheel outwards around its steering swivel.

To overcome this problem, most cars have their steering swivels inclined sideways, so that they point towards the contact patch of the tyre on the road. Drag forces act at ground level, so this arrangement prevents them trying to deflect the steering. With such inclined swivels, a car's front wheels will lean outwards as they are steered to go around a sharp corner, but this only happens at quite low speeds and seems to cause no problems.

In the days of rigid front axles, the steering axis for each wheel used to be a so-called king pin. Modern suspension systems usually replace this component with two ball-and-socket or other joints spaced quite widely apart one above the other, which define the axis around which the front wheel can be steered. Wide spacing reduces stress and permits the use of bearings which need little lubrication.

in one direction than in the other – the driver can steer the car by rotating the screw or worm without much hindrance by friction, whereas reaction back to his hands from the road meets much more resistance. The principle is the same as the one which dictates that a screw can be turned easily with a screwdriver, but not with a hammer!

Steering gears based on these principles are still in use, but refinements in car design have greatly reduced the need for resistance to kickback. Good design of the front suspension and steering swivels can greatly reduce unwanted reaction from bad roads or from unbalanced brakes, and a freely reversible mechanism lets a car's steering self centre in a convenient manner. Pneumatic tyres have an inherent tendency to run straight, and this can be emphasized by locating the steering swivel axis slightly ahead of the tyre's centre.

Especially for cars of low weight but sometimes on heavier models also, an extremely simple and 'reversible' steering mechanism, the rack and pinion, has now become very popular. A rod with gear teeth cut along it is mounted across the front of the car, so that it can slide to and fro, its ends being linked to steering arms on the two front wheels. A small gear wheel on the bottom of the steering column moves the rack to the left or the right when rotated. Cutting of the gear teeth at an angle, and use of a spring-loaded friction pad to press the rack into close mesh with the pinion, provides some slight damping of road shock in a simple, mechanically precise steering gear.

When a big and heavy car is supported on broad tyres, steering it can be hard work, especially at low speeds. Rather than gear the steering so that very large wheel movements are needed, car makers now provide large and expensive models with power-assisted steering. A hydraulic pump driven by the engine provides fluid at high pressure to a sort of hydraulic jack, which can help turn the front wheels of the car to the left or the right. A small and very vital spring-loaded control valve senses what effort the driver is applying to the steering wheel, and directs enough high-pressure fluid into the jack to multiply that effect by a designed factor.

Interiors

Inside a modern car, comfort at least equal to that expected at home is combined with the requirements of brisk travel. Seating is designed to complement the car's springing system without being bouncy on rough roads, and to provide support during acceleration, cornering, braking or even in a crash, without being unduly bulky. Often seats are designed to fold in one or more ways, to form a simple bed or to make room for extra luggage.

In most countries, car buyers want interior heating, usually by waste heat from the engine but occasionally with special petrol-burning heaters which have automatic ignition and control. Generally the heat is applied to fresh air entering the car, slight pressure from a front-facing intake (helped when necessary by an electric fan) preventing draughts entering the car elsewhere. A progressive tap controlling water flow through the heater is the simplest form of regulation, but mixing heated and unheated air to achieve just the right amount of warmth permits more consistent control of temperature in varied driving.

For hot countries, air conditioning systems which can refrigerate the interior of a car are available. Such systems can enhance comfort in humid conditions even when the weather is not uncomfortably hot, as refrigeration extracts moisture from the air in a car which can then be re-warmed by the heater system. All heating systems make some provision for blowing warmed air onto the interior of the windscreen and perhaps of other windows also, to prevent vision being impaired by condensation or by hoar frost.

Every car must by law have a speedometer, so that a driver who exceeds speed limits cannot plead ignorance as an excuse! An odometer recording distance run is readily combined with the speedometer, using the same drive from the transmission or from one wheel. A gauge indicating how much fuel is in a car's tank has come to be regarded as virtually essential. According to what a car maker thinks will please potential buyers of any particular model, other instruments and tell-tale lamps may be provided.

Often a tachometer or rev counter indicates engine speed separately from car speed, electrical types which in effect count ignition system impulses needing only a simple wire to link them to the engine. A thermometer for the engine's coolant is common, and on occasion a second thermometer for the lubricant is provided. There may be an engine oil pressure gauge to reassure the driver about lubricant circulation, an ammeter to show what electrical energy is flowing into or out of the battery or a voltmeter to confirm that the battery is adequately charged.

Replacing or complementing instruments, coloured tell-tale lamps can be arranged to light up as a warning that something is amiss, as confirmation that something is in order, or simply to let the driver know which headlamp beam in in use. Sometimes it is sensible to have both a tell-tale and a gauge, one catching the driver's eye when it lights up and the other giving more detailed information about, say, an unusually high coolant temperature or an unusually low engine oil pressure.

Chassis and Bodywork

All the dynamic elements which enable a car to go, stop and be steered, and to ride smoothly over varied surfaces, have to be held together. The structure which does this is an important element in the design, with great influence on the car's behaviour.

Early cars were naturally influenced very strongly by the horse-drawn vehicles which had preceded them. Carts were often built on a foundation of two wooden beams, running from front to back at each side, and early car chassis frames also tended to be based on two beams. Engineers who produced vehicles with engines thought mainly in terms of metal, but they often used wood reinforcement.

In the pioneer days, as to a diminishing extent after the 1930s and to a very small extent indeed today, a chassis was planned as an engineering structure onto which any required accommodation for passengers or other loads could be superimposed. It was quite late in motoring history that bodywork designed primarily to enclose the passengers was given the extra reinforcement which let it be self-supporting, the separate chassis being eliminated.

Early car frames were designed simply to support the weights of power unit, passengers and luggage within the span between a front and a rear axle. In the manner of bridge girders, side members were designed so that they did not break or sag unduly under the load.

As cars became faster and better sprung, various sorts of unpleasant vibration were encountered, and the need for resistance to twisting between the two ends of a car became increasingly evident. This was at a time when chassis were being curved downwards between the axles, a design which provided lower floor and seating heights but tended to reduce rigidity. As one measure to restore and increase torsional stiffness, tubular cross-members were used in place of open channel sections, to inter-connect the side members. Channel-section side members were turned into closed box-sections of much greater torsional rigidity, by having additional pressings welded to their open sides. X-bracing was introduced, linking diagonally opposite corners of a chassis to make it much more resistant to twisting, a few designers making the 'X' their chassis and virtually eliminating side members.

Early car bodies were usually built with wooden frames. Metal panels were often used to keep the weather out, but to suit far-from-rigid chassis frames, some bodies were clad in tightly-stretched, deliberately flexible fabric. As larger numbers of examples of individual body designs came to be produced

Essentials of a car driving compartment, such as a wheel for steering, pedals for acceleration and braking, were standardized quite soon after the motor car was invented, and remain with us today.

Simplicity was the rule in 1918, the only instrument in the top illustration being a speedometer. With the fuel tank above the driver's feet, it was easy to remove the filler cap and see whether refuelling was due.

Frequently the provision of a small glass peep-hole enabled the driver to check that the engine oil was circulating properly.

By 1930, a sports car instrument panel gave the driver much more information. The speedometer was matched by a tachometer indicating the engine's speed of rotation, there was a lubricating oil pressure gauge, and probably other dials showing the fuel contents and the engine water temperature. Controls on the steering wheel hub permitted 'fine tuning' of carburetter mixture strength and of spark timing.

An air-conditioned car of the late 1970s may have digital indication of car and engine speed. Other instruments will have electrical operation, so that noise cannot be transmitted from the mechanism to the sound-insulated car interior. Warning lamps of various colours draw the driver's attention to any malfunction, or to such matters as need to release the parking brake or secure safety belts. The whole area in front of the driver and passengers will have been designed to have as few projections as possible, and to be crushable so that personal injuries in a crash will be minimized.

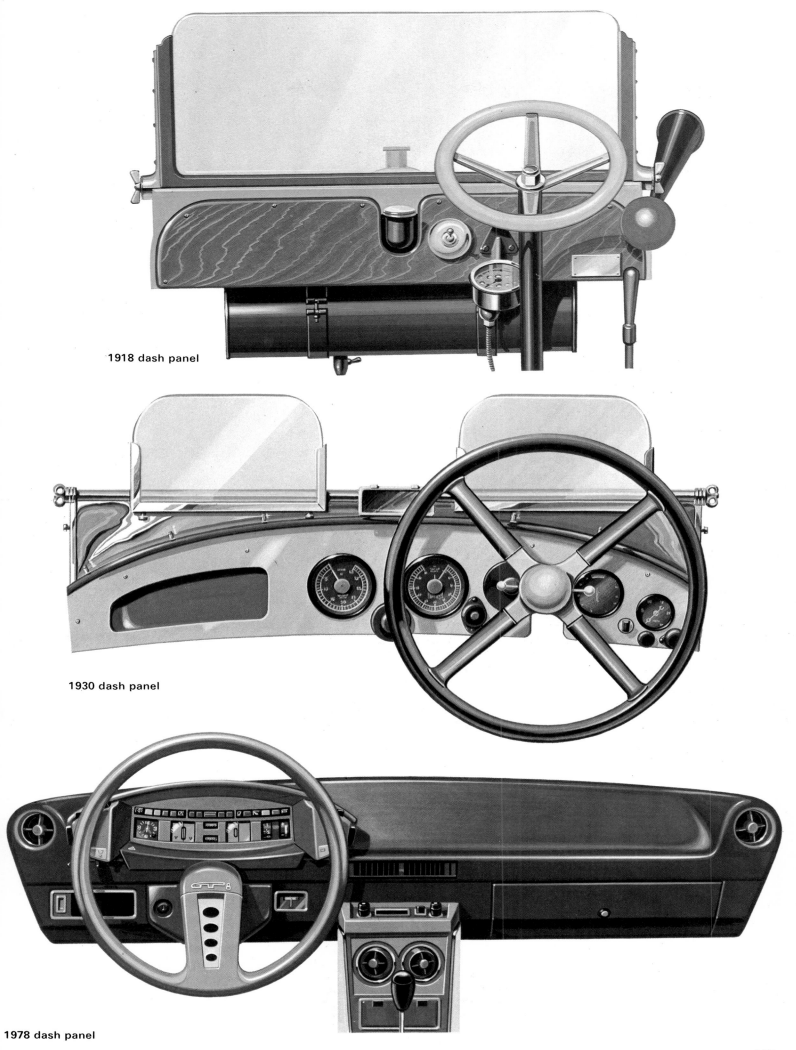

1918 dash panel

1930 dash panel

1978 dash panel

however, it became economic to stamp out steel body panels which, when welded together, formed a body strong enough to do without wooden framing.

All steel car bodies, made from quite thin sheet metal, tended to have a 'cheap and nasty' reputation at first, because all sorts of noises tended to resonate more loudly inside a 'tin box' than in wood-framed bodywork. A lot of hard work on details gradually brought internal noise under control, and eventually Rolls-Royces with pressed steel bodies arrived on the scene!

Noise sources can often be isolated from a potentially resonant body by means of flexible rubber. Drumming of panels can be minimized by stiffening them, either with pressed-in corrugations or with added reinforcement members. Noise can be absorbed or its emission reduced by covering panels with felt or other soft materials.

A steel car body is likely to be about ten times as deep vertically, from roof to floor, as is the side member of a chassis. Big apertures for doors and windows do not enhance strength, but with careful design a body can be made extremely sturdy, even when quite slender windscreen pillars are used to link the roof with the underframe. Passengers can be given considerable protection against crash injuries, especially if the engine compartment and rear luggage locker are designed to crumple first and cushion any impacts.

Parts for steel car bodies are pressed from quite thin sheet steel, and overlap is provided where panels need to be joined together. At the overlap, panels are stitched together by 'spot-welds' spaced a few centimetres apart, the panels being nipped between electrodes and a very heavy electric current passed through their contact area momentarily, heat and pressure fusing them together. When a joint between panels needs to be weatherproof, a sealing compound is used, there being gaps between individual welds.

Whereas the old-fashioned chassis gained its strength from fairly small areas of quite thick steel, the modern car without a chassis depends for its strength on much larger areas of quite thin sheet steel. Far greater surface areas are vulnerable to corrosion, yet a much smaller depth of pitting will penetrate right through the metal. When salt came into widespread use for keeping roads clear of ice, corrosion of steel car bodies became a major worry.

Car makers are reluctant to build bodies from stainless steel, which would be more costly to buy and press into the desired shapes. They have become more careful to avoid providing nooks and crannies in which salty road dirt can collect, and are using more thorough processes to clean and prime bodies before painting them. Enclosed spaces are being treated with wax or other anti-rust substances. To a substantial extent though, car makers lack confidence that they can justify great expenditure on rust proofing treatment, which is invisible to the buyer, when fashion changes will reduce a car's value even if it does not wear out.

Making a vehicle work was the pre-occupation of early car designers, and passengers were accommodated whenever there was room for them. Now, designers virtually start by planning an elegant shape which will accommodate passengers and luggage, and will move easily through the air, leaving engineers to fit necessary mechanisms into any available corner. The space in a four wheeled car which is least useful and accessible is the narrow one between front wheels which are swivelled to steer the car – and often the whole power unit is packed into

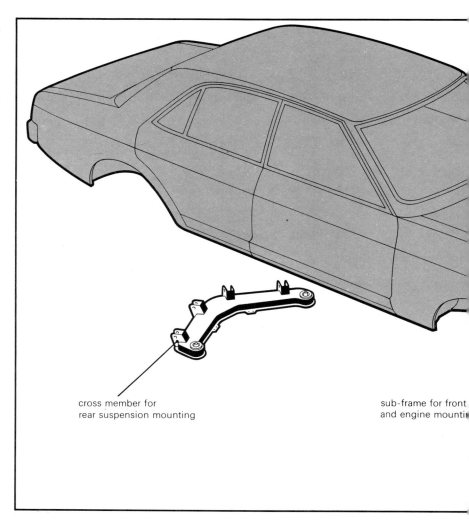

cross member for
rear suspension mounting

sub-frame for front
and engine mounti

that modest space.

How a car body is shaped is important, functionally as well as because good-looking cars are easier to sell. Air has to be pushed aside as a car travels along the road, and the effort needed to do this quadruples each time the car's speed is doubled. By the time a speed of about 65 km/h (40 mph) has been reached, an average car is using about as much power to overcome air resistance as to overcome friction in tyres and wheel bearings. At about 110 km/h (70 mph), air resistance is likely to be absorbing about 75 per cent of the power.

When a boat moves through water, the turbulent white wake behind it, and the waves spreading out to each side, are visible evidence of where the power has gone. In wet or dusty conditions, the turbulent air wake behind a fast-moving car is to some extent visible also but the three-dimensional whirling of the air is confusing. Whereas an aeroplane operates with plenty of free air space around it, a car is close to the road surface and passes close to other vehicles, these factors making it harder to ensure smooth air flow around a body.

Air resistance depends on the size of a car. Mainly it is frontal area which matters, determining the size of hole which must be punched through the air, but length can have some effect on air friction also. Shape matters in respect of how smoothly a car's frontal shape cleaves the air, of how many projections create additional air turbulence, and of how effectively rear end shaping lets air re-fill the space behind the moving car.

Whereas a boat's sharp prow is needed to cut through almost incompressible water, a moving car sends a pressure wave ahead of it through compressible air, and quite a rounded front can be efficient. Smooth shaping of details is important, especially

Structurally the modern car's steel body is usually so strong and rigid that it does not need to be mounted on a separate chassis. Sub-frames are sometimes used at the front and rear to provide mounting points for the power unit and the springing systems, and controlled flexibility at the mountings of sub-frames in the body preventing the passage of vibration or noise. Use of large panels of fairly thin steel to form car structures, and widespread application of de-icing salt to roads, have made the rust-proofing of car bodies extremely important. Body shape is important, to minimize wind resistance and noise at open-road speeds.

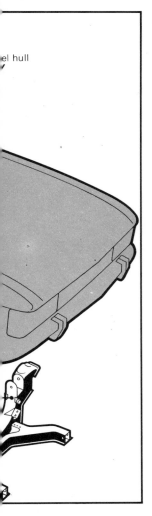

Car chassis frames in the 1920s often took the form shown at the top of this page, two side members of channel-section steel being strong but not very resistant to twisting. Later designs with box-section sides and cruciform bracing provided a much more rigid foundation for draught-proof bodywork and for precise steering mechanisms. Sports cars are in many instances still built on chassis frames, the deep cruciform example in the bottom drawing providing a sturdy basis for moulded bodywork of fibreglass-reinforced plastic.

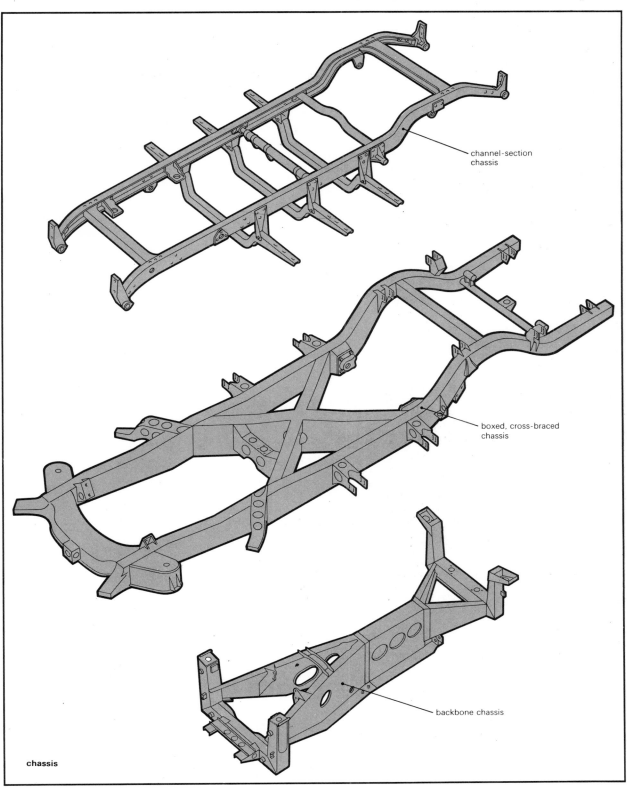

channel-section chassis

boxed, cross-braced chassis

backbone chassis

chassis

at corners around which air is flowing most quickly, such as at windscreen pillars on which rain water guttering can cause eddies. An ideally streamlined car should probably have a long, tapering tail like an aeroplane fuselage, but this would be impractically bulky, and quite a square-cut rear shape can be more efficient than an over-steep taper. Sometimes, designers find that less-than-ideal streamlining minimizes wind noise inside a car by keeping the fast-flowing air slightly away from the windows!

Racing car designers found that they could get a lot of extra tyre grip for high speed cornering by using inverted aerofoils to create downthrust. Production car designers then found that at speeds used on public highways, aerodynamic forces had significant vertical components, some elusive problems of instability having resulted in part from weight being lifted off the wheels. Air dams to deflect the flow around a car rather than under its nose, and rear spoilers to direct air flow upwards, are not always merely fashionable decorations.

Road vehicles have to operate in cross winds which create lateral forces, at times suddenly when the shelter of buildings is left behind. When adjusting suspension and steering characteristics to make a car stable as it goes round corners, engineers are dealing with sideways forces which act at the car's centre of gravity. Sideways forces due to cross winds act at an aerodynamic centre of pressure which may be quite remote from the centre of gravity, and are accordingly more apt to make a car unstable. Wind forces acting far ahead of the centre of gravity pose an especial problem for tail-heavy cars, such as those with rear engines.

MANUFACTURING

Manufacturing – concept stage

Though a new motor car design still needs the boardroom's go-ahead it is no longer the managing director's exclusive brain-child, as once it was, but is the joint product of thousands of specialists.

Nor is it possible any longer to go to a single place and see a car being made, for the component parts are produced in many different places and brought together for assembly.

We chose one of the Ford plants in Britain, because Ford manufacture a bigger proportion of the car than other firms do – though this is still only some 40 per cent, the remaining 60 per cent being made elsewhere.

First step towards the production of a new car is the 'political decision' on what kind of car the company wishes to produce. After this the car exists on a piece of paper, a letter from one office to another setting out what it is proposed to build. More cars are now sold outside of the USA than within it, and the Western European market is only some half-million units behind the domestic American one. This affects the thinking of the big American companies that still dominate production. They must take account of world conditions.

The decision on what to build is not taken lightly, for hundreds of millions of pounds in tooling and development will be involved during the four or five years that normally elapse between conception and production. The Ford Fiesta was a case in point. Those in favour of the project wanted to make a smaller car than the company had made before, to compete with small cars from Fiat, SEAT, Renault and the Japanese on world markets. Opponents said: 'You may broaden your market share but make no more money, because, generally speaking, the bigger the car the bigger the profit.'

This stage is known as Strategy Direction or Concept Approval and happens about four years before production, when the company has accepted one set of business arguments for future production. Then what is called Coordinated Product Planning begins in the product development organization. The car engineering department will process the idea through to the finished vehicle in three sections: Package Engineering, which controls size, seating and major component installation; Advanced Vehicle Engineering, which takes over the package and brings it through management approval and release to the production engineers; and Surface Layout, which produces master layouts to work from.

Decisions must first be made about which end the engine will be, which wheels will be driven, whether it will be a completely new engine or a 'carry-over' model, what sort of suspension will be used, and so on. Anything from four to 100 choices will be sketched and estimates will be made of the cost of new installations to build a new car. Changes to the track on which cars are built are fairly straightforward, as are changes in welding lines, but altering the transfer lines on which machining is done is very expensive, so comparative studies must be made.

Comparative evaluation may take six months, then clay models will be made of one of the recommended alternatives and the decision 'notchback or hatchback' must be taken. Sometimes a market research clinic is used and members of the public are asked to choose, without knowing what make of car they are looking at, between a full-size model of the new design and existing competitors.

Meanwhile engineers are working out how many parts are new in the various designs, how many modified and the cost of machining the new parts.

Some 40 or 50 designers, 200 engineers and hundreds of people in the manufacturing groups will be involved, all co-ordinated by three product engineers. Even now the chosen model may prove to be too costly to make and have to be reconsidered.

Go With One

Eventually the stage of Go With One is reached. This is when a particular design has passed all the tests and Programme Approval is given to commit people to deliver certain articles or components in certain volumes at a certain time and at a certain price. No big investment has yet been made, but it would now be possible to build the car. In fact it is two years away from production and the machine tools have not been bought. When that stage comes – purchase of land, machine tools and production facilities, launching money – costs will be astronomical. In the case of the Fiesta, for instance, Ford spent $80 million, including the cost of a new plant.

The car is now beginning to take shape and a concept study will begin. This means covering a large drawing board with a sheet of film on which the chosen car is shown in the company of secondary choices and the team choose the 'best ball package', the one giving the best headroom, kneeroom and luggage space combined with other desired features. Clearances may have to be changed to accommodate the desired instrument panel, heater or radio, or suspension compliance may be altered for comfort – at the cost of luggage space in the boot. This is known as 'trading objections', a process in which the product planner, who is in charge, will protect styling features from the engineers, who have different objectives.

Each team will be asked to compromise so as to produce what is, in effect, the greatest good for the greatest number. The climate of emphasis in these matters changes. Whereas in 1973 the accent was on fuel-economy it will now be something else. When there is final agreement a number of models will be built in Royalite, a thick plastic sheet that can be formed in the shape of the car's panels which clip together. A computer will calculate stresses.

Two sets of figures have been kept throughout – the Green Book, which shows how much can be spent, and the Red Book, which shows the cost of each piece of the car. Though there are still two years before production, when Programme Approval is given the machine tools must be ordered and the team committed to timing and production volumes. Orders are also released for transfer line presses from the USA and Germany, as well as Britain, and contracts for any new buildings are signed at this stage.

Drawings are now released to engineering, who must start issuing tooling drawings, making production samples and running tests. Some parts cannot be made with the existing tools and must be hand-made. When a car is put together it is tested on the track, and any parts that consistently fail have to be changed, either in design or in manufacturing method. For example, a forging, which is stronger, may have to replace a casting, which is cheaper. Or a plastic sun roof panel may have to become steel if it is unsatisfactory.

Continual changes arise from the knowledge gained by testing. As details are finalized a toolmaker works on final drawings. Making the tools may take 18 months, and the final following six months are spent scheduling the control exercise for manufacturing. The plants, if there are new ones, have been built and the machines are coming in. The components from outside are also arriving.

Overleaf: The blast furnace at Ford Motor Co, recently closed, turned out 850 tonnes of pig iron a day.

Above: The jetty at the Ford Motor plant, Dagenham.

Centre right: Changes are often made to a car at the cost of luggage space. In the Ford Fiesta, load space with the rear seats folded is 42·6 cu ft (1·205 m³) and the tail gate provides bumper level access – two of the factors which led to the 1978 Design Council award.

Below right: View of the Fiesta's well-designed engine compartment showing accessibility to those components which need regular attention, such as the battery, the air filter, etc.

Far right: Ford prototypes of cars that never were. The Bobcat was the code name for what eventually became the Fiesta.

1970 European Prototype

1970 European Prototype

1972 Mini Mite

1972 de Tomaso Mini

1973 Ghia Wolf

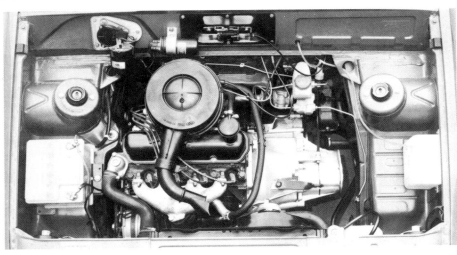

1973 Bobcat II
(Dunton)

151

engine assembly

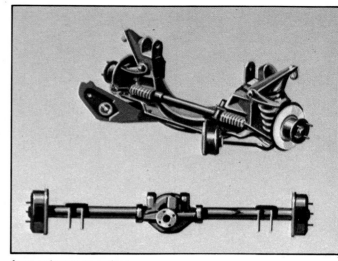
front and rear suspensions

construction of a Ford 2 litre Ghia

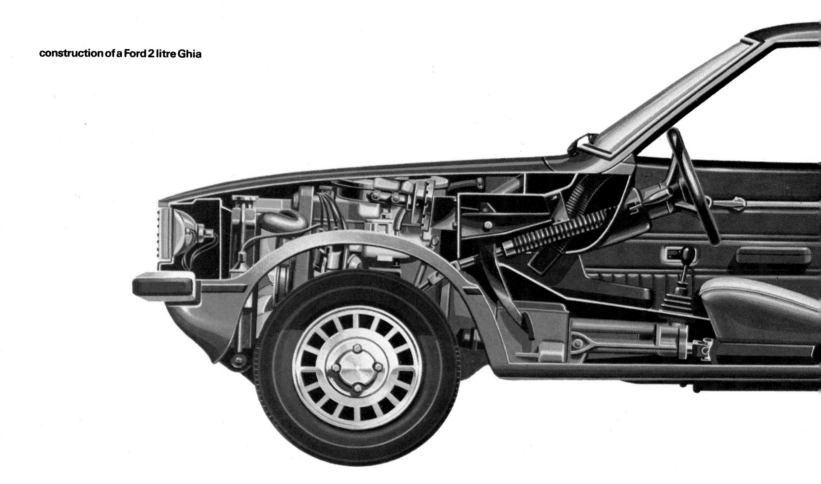

main assembly (shell onto components)

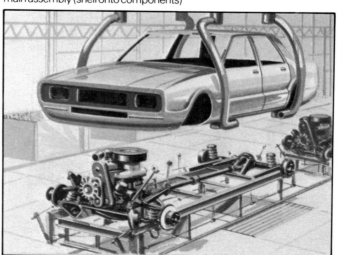

installation of seats

bodyshell welding

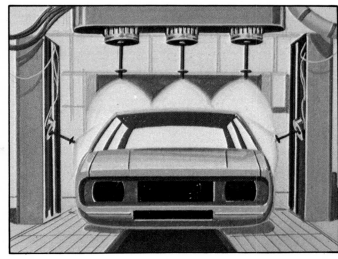

paint spraying

final assembly (i.e. wheels etc.)

Manufacturing – components

Prototypes of the car are hand-built in the engineering department and then comes the 'pilot build', the first car to be made off the tools, six months before Job 1, the first actual production car. Ten or twenty hand-built examples are made for evaluation. There may be 4,000 parts in the car, 60 per cent of them new and untried. It may take six or seven weeks to prove the pilot-built samples, then specific instructions for building each part must be issued on the lines of: 'Join strut to body, insert bush, tighten four bolts, load floor-pan into jig, weld.'

These instructions are being written by Process Engineering during the pilot build to make up a book of process charts. The engineers have not yet signed the vehicle off for production and may still be trying to solve ride, handling or noise problems. Pilot parts may become obsolete because of essential changes.

The next stage is the function building of 100 to 200 vehicles – 'pre-production samples' – in the volume plant that will eventually make the car, using multi-welding machines. There may be rejects, and no more than 90 per cent are likely to be what engineers call OK samples. Finally the engineers will sign off the samples on ride, handling and NVH (Noise, Vibration and Harshness) and promise no more changes with perhaps 10 per cent of parts still to be approved.

Cars go out

Early cars now go out to the Press for the launch and to dealers as demonstrators, and there will be meetings of sales representatives and dealers in all countries. The Service Department will have been involved already but will now make test appraisals to see if there are any special problems from their point of view. After the first build there will be a rest period of six weeks during which the 10 per cent of NOK (not-approved) parts must be cleared for production and the plant move into STB, or 'start training build'.

During the first build, which has already taken place, the production line is not run at the normal speed of 50 or 60 jobs an hour, or whatever the rate may be, but more slowly. During STB it runs at full speed. STB goes on for four or five months up to the full production period, the daily rate building up as everything settles down.

Meanwhile salesmen have been taking orders and the programme is scheduled five months ahead. Each car is built for a particular customer according to his wishes, and a monthly schedule is produced to tell the line what to make. This is the climax of the earlier programme, which was broken down into three stages: Evaluation of preferred alternatives; Selection of preferred alternatives, or Strategy Approval; Programme Approval, leading up to manufacture.

When we come to actual manufacture we find the company, as we have seen, making only some 40 per cent of the car. Many components must be ordered from outside suppliers and those like wheels and tyres – from several suppliers – will be ordered by computer on a daily basis. Coils of steel up to 2·5 m (about 8 ft) wide will be coming in to be cut up and fed to the body presses. Also coming in will be glass, paint and the raw material for the foundry – iron ore, from which will be made iron for casting engine blocks, crankshafts, camshafts and transmission casings.

All metal body parts will be pressed on the premises and moulded plastic parts like glove-box lids, sun visors and armrests will be produced. Trim

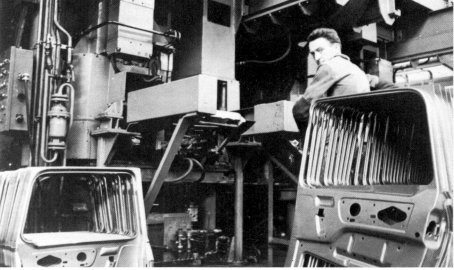

panels will be fabricated in the plant, bonded together from vinyl and cardboard in a special press.

Foam rubber is 'bought out' but is used in the seats – made in the Paint, Trim and Assembly section of the plant – by women workers who sew the covering and foam on to springs and frames. The company make their own carburettors, instrument clusters, sparking plugs and distributors, but not in the same factory; they come in from other parts of the Ford empire.

Some electrical components, like starters and alternators, are brought from specialist manufacturers, but engines, transmissions, all radiators (other than some for the truck range) and wiper motors are 'home made'. Radio sets come from Canada, but window winders and seat tracks are home-produced. The computer calculates the daily rate at which parts are needed.

In the first stage of body production 100 pressings are spot-welded together with welds in 1,500 places in sub-lines, the main items being the floor group, the body-sides group, the rear end and the dash and cowl structure, the cowl being the section in front of the windscreen behind the bonnet and running down to the sides behind the front wheels.

The key process

Some of the automatic welding machines work on a circular track known as the merry-go-round, and parts assembled there are next loaded on to a key process called the framing lines, where the floor-pan is joined to the sides and roof in an operation called

Top left : Producing axle shafts at Ford's: the raw castings, piled in front, are heated and then passed onto a conveyor belt.

Above left : Blanks are fed into an automatic press to make car doors at the Renault factory.

Above right : Inspections are carried out at the foundry's mould line before the mould is closed. These Vee block moulds and light car blocks then move onto the pouring station.

Right : Every day the Dagenham coke ovens convert 1,000 tonnes of coal into coke for the blast furnace and foundry.

154

the 'butterfly', the sides coming down together from above to join the floor-pan, then the roof, cowl and back.

The rough-looking products of the foundry bear little resemblance to engine blocks or transmission casings until they have been cleaned up and machined. The castings move into the assembly plant either on a track or a fork-lift, according to the layout. In some cases engines are built in a separate factory and brought in complete for installation in the car, but in the present case we see them being made alongside the other components.

It is difficult to follow the construction of a complete car without dashing about from one building to another, but in the modern manner the body shell is welded together after the various sub-assemblies have themselves been joined up, then the rest, including the mechanical parts, is added.

When the sub-assemblies have been welded up they join the major part, consisting of the biggest piece of steel, the floor-pan, which is moving on what is called a body skid. As already described the sides drop from above and are clamped to the floor-pan in jigs that hold them together and check the door openings with brass dummy doors.

While steel fingers hold the pieces together other automatic fingers grip the assembly at various points, switching on the electric current that makes the spot-welds. These automatic welding machines can work in very awkward corners, but hand welding is also used for certain operations. Once it is all electrically stitched together the body-shell travels, suspended from overhead hooks, while the power train – engine, propeller shaft, gearbox and suspension – is installed from below. This is called 'decking from below' and differs from US practice. Because American cars have chassis frames, unlike the monocoque British and European cars, 'decking', or power train installation, is done from above. In Italy and Sweden there are departures from both systems, and these will be examined later in the story.

Dagenham, on which this account is based, is one of Ford's 19 British assembly plants. It is sited on the river Thames, near London, which helps with its water problem, for some 83 million gallons go through the plant daily, some returned. Limestone for the furnaces comes in from South Wales, Devon and Cornwall. Engines are made at the rate of 6,500 a day in one building while complete cars are assembled in another. The company has been using 300,000 tonnes of steel a year, plus 250,000 tonnes of coal, 400,000 tonnes of iron ore and 100,000 tonnes of limestone. It buys from 2,000 suppliers of production parts and 5,000 suppliers of facilities and raw materials.

any of the bought-out parts.

The sheet steel that is the basic raw material of the car comes from Wales, Holland, USA and Germany, and there may be as much as 1·6 km (1 mile) of metal in the ribbon rolled up in stores. It is in various widths of up to 1·65 metres (65 in) and is cut to the right size by giant guillotines before being fed to the 150 presses, all working at pressures from 200 to 2,000 tonnes per square inch of surface.

The machines cut up to 250 pieces for each body-shell from rolls weighing up to 18 tonnes each, and there are 5,000 spot welds in each car, including the 1,500 in the sub-assemblies already listed. The press forces the metal against a die, and the cost of these dies is one of the major items in car-building. Usually a machine runs for 72 hours on a continuous three-shift cycle making the same body panel; then the dies are changed and the press makes something else while its previous production is stored in a high bay warehouse.

Thus the various components of the car cannot all be made at once, but must be pressed in sequence according to the orders of the computer, then stored

The recently closed (1978) blast furnace turned out in its time 850 tonnes of pig iron a day, consuming 2,200 tonnes of iron ore, limestone, coke and ballast. Its by-product of 300 tonnes of slag was sold for road-making. Nothing is wasted in the plant. Swarf from the metal-cutting machines goes back to be melted down. Aluminium swarf is sold back to the producers.

Car-building operates on the principle of producing parts for stock, these to be drawn on as they are needed for assembly. As we have noted, each car is a particular one, ordered by a particular customer, in the colour he wants, with the engine he wants and in his choice of tyres, seats and trim colour, plus other extras or special requirements.

Made to measure

If we could follow the manufacture of one car – difficult because of the methods described, with some components coming from stores and others from distant factories – it would take some 22 hours, comprising 10 hours stamping and welding, six hours painting and six hours in assembly. This does not include the time taken for the manufacture of the engine, transmission and other components or of

Top : Nothing in the plant is wasted: the slag from this blast furnace, now closed, was sold for road-mending.

Above left : A powered grinding wheel is used to smooth and finish welded joints on the Fiesta at Dagenham.

Above centre : Welding part of the body shell for Fiesta cars at the Ford plant, Valencia, Spain.

Below left : The Fiesta being paint-sprayed – the top three coats are applied manually and the final one has to be baked for about an hour.

until that particular model is being made. The pressings called for are carried by fork-lift truck to the pre-production line workshops and the smaller sub-assemblies are joined by spot welding. These are then fitted into jigs, which hold the pieces as they are fed into the automatic welders. So the super-structure – the top part of the car – and the floor-pan assembly come out in one piece.

Finally the superstructure, floor-pan and wings come together and are welded into one unit. At one stage in production the whole car is turned upside down in a jig while stitch-welding is done. This part of the process takes about an hour; then doors, bonnet and boot lid come in by overhead monorail and join the parent car. Meanwhile major panel joints are gas welded, to give greater strength and, para-doxically, greater flexibility when the car is under stress on rough roads.

Computer talking
At each stage the computer spells its instructions out through telex machines to the operator on the spot in the factory, and each car carries a card, its 'passport', describing its own particular specification, so that the operative can see that it has the right engine,

seats, tyres and so on. Complete assembly of the bodyshell will have taken a further five hours on average.

Inspectors take a detailed look at the car at each stage and rectification of minor faults can be carried out along the line. But anything serious means that the car is sidelined off the main assembly track and rectified by experts before resuming its journey through the factory.

Now that the shell is in one piece it moves on to the paint section, where it is first degreased by high-pressure sprays of solvent, then phosphated to give good anti-corrosion and paint-adhesion surfaces. Then, suspended from above, it is 'baptized' by complete immersion in a tank of grey electrocoat which adheres electrically to the metal shell. The primer seeps into every nook and cranny and pro-tects the car for life, including box sections which could not be reached by a manual spray.

After its paint bath the shell moves on, still drip-ping, for the surplus paint to be rinsed off. Then comes the drying process, in this case in a gas-fired oven, where the car is stoved. Outer joints are now sealed and the shell goes on to an electrostatic paint sprayer which automatically applies another grey primer sealing coat, again stoved. Special undercoat-ing goes beneath the body to protect it from rusting, chipping by stones and other hazards to parts close to the road.

Next the shell is sanded, and then comes another bath, this time in demineralized water, and a final drying before the beauty treatment.

The top three coats of paint, in the chosen colour, are applied manually by men with spray guns work-ing in long booths, and the last process is stoving in a steam-heated oven. Any blemishes in the paint will not be dealt with at this time; the complete car can be pulled out of line for rectification by special squads who do this work all the time.

Before being painted the shell is inspected and, if necessary, rectified by men known as dingers, discers and buffers, who respectively hammer out dents, sand down blemishes and buff up the metal where necessary. Joins between metal pressings are filled with lead to give a clean finish, then sanded flush – except on Fiestas, which are solderless-jointed. In its six hours in the paint shop the car has acquired three grey undercoats and three top coats in addition to all the washing and cleansing which should ensure a perfect finish without the 'orange peel' which disfigures so many modern cars.

Eighteen different spray guns are used to reach odd corners and the undercoat has 40 minutes' baking, the final coat one hour. Finally the paint is cooled slowly with cold air blasts. Cars pulled out for finish faults are resprayed as necessary and sent round the circuit again, but obviously if they have come off the line complete they have to be dealt with by hand; they cannot go back into the mechanical painting process with their wheels, tyres, engines and transmissions in place. Adding parts to the engine assembly is called 'dressing'.

The completed bodyshell now keeps on moving along the track to the trim shops, where the tele-printed instructions are noted on the 'passport'. This will tell the assemblers such information as the type of seats to install – whether they are to be reclin-ing or standard. At this stage the front grille, elec-trical harness, lights, head lining, door windows and windscreen are fitted – the last by means of a clever trick with a piece of string. A further six and a half hours have elapsed while the bodyshell has been prettied up with all its interior fittings.

In the next hour or so the horns, battery, brake fluid reservoirs, steering column, radiator and water hoses, brake lines and all under-bonnet parts are fixed into place and the shell is beginning to look more like a car, though it still has no mechanical parts, power unit or wheels. The instrument panel is fitted with protruding wires for joining up to the engine and elsewhere, and the door fittings and catches make the outside shape more familiar.

Up to this point the car has been moving at floor level most of the time so that the operatives can reach it easily to do their work. They work in two shifts on week-days but there is normally no assembly work at weekends. While the assembly men carry on, specialists stand by to repair machines in the event of breakdown, and the company are very happy if these men have little to do. They are electricians, tool-makers, repairmen and other specialists.

Change in level

At this point the embryo car is lifted from above and hovers over the waist-high track where the men with the running gear – engine, transmission, suspension and so on – are waiting to mount their units in the bodyshell. Already attached to the engine are the carburettors, exhaust manifold, generator and fan. It then joins the clutch/gearbox unit and is put into a jig, where it is joined by the propeller shaft (if a rear-driven car), rear axle, front and rear suspensions with hubs and brakes, and the whole lot is coupled up and bolted in place.

The right body unit for this engine will have been directed to its appointed rendezvous by the computer, and the two are married on the raised track. Our shell is now nearly a car, and as it goes along the raised line items like the rear-view mirror, wipers and interior trim are fitted. The radiator is filled with anti-freeze and the brake system with hydraulic fluid. Oil, petrol and brake pipes are linked up underneath and steering, pedals and gear lever are added. Carpets and mats almost finish the trim side.

The computer, via the telex, will now send down

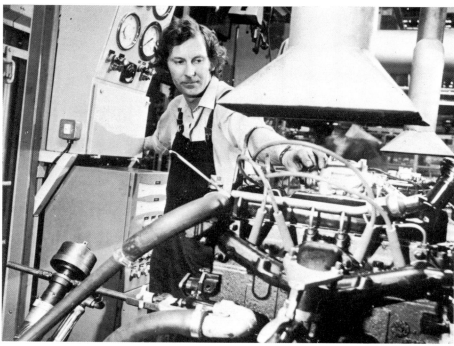

in the front and rear mirrors of the tent and runs the machine up through the gears on a rolling road to test engine, transmission and brakes. After leaving the line the car is driven on to a conveyor belt that runs through a water test, where jets working at 20 psi squirt the car for four minutes to search out leaks in the water-proofing, between windows and seals for example.

Once past this test the machine is ready for the road and is driven out to be dried down, given a final check and parked ready for the transporter to take it to the dealer.

Before the wheels and tyres were fitted they had been balanced and checked by computer, both statically and dynamically, so that there would be no steering problem from out-of-balance forces. As the tyre-and-wheel assembly spins on a rig an arrow indicates the spot where any extra balancing weight should be added.

The engine has been checked in engine assembly, clearances of valves and points have been set, valve and ignition timing have been checked and the carburettor set up. Now there should be nothing to stop the car being driven away.

In engine assembly

While the car was being assembled along the line, production of other parts – engine, transmission, seats, steering boxes and so on – was continuing elsewhere, either in other buildings on the same site or in other factories.

Engine blocks come in from the foundry and go through all the necessary machining operations on transfer lines. These operations include drilling and honing the bores, facing top and bottom for cylinder head and sump, and drilling for camshaft, oil holes and accessory fittings like distributor drive, and induction and exhaust manifolds. As one operation is completed the machine passes the block on for the next.

These transfer machines work to fine limits. They achieve higher standards of accuracy than do the old hand-working methods and they are checked regularly to ensure that their operations are within permissible tolerances.

At the same time the raw crankshafts are being ground, so that the journals are ready to receive main and big-end bearings, and balanced by drilling surplus metal out of their webs.

Crankshafts are fitted into the block by machine, though an operator makes a final check on the bearing caps with a torque wrench. Piston rings are also machine-fitted, as are the pistons into the bores, so there is little handwork on the engines. When an engine is assembled completely to its 'passport' specifications it is set up by a skilled engine tuner who does no other work. He sets clearances, timing and carburettor before signing the unit off as fit to be installed.

Camshafts are also produced automatically, checked for precision and then fitted into the block. Any errors, machine or human, will be picked up by one of the various inspection processes that are carried out before the final running check. If the line stops for any reason the man in charge of the section in question jumps to it at the sight of the red signal lights and gets things moving again as fast as he can.

The men on the line can take a 10-minute break every two hours, for it has been found that a tired man produces less than one who has rested. Workers can be identified by the collars of their working coats. A brown collar indicates an engineer, blue is an inspector, yellow identifies a material handler. The

Top left : Golf models on the overhead conveyor belt at the Volkswagen works, Wolfsburg, Germany.

Centre left : Rust-inhibiting material is injected into truck doors at General Motors.

Below left : Operators at Ford's Dagenham plant use a mini-computer to assist them in making precise adjustments of engine speed and ignition timing.

Top right : Automatic wheel/ tyre assembly and balancing machine at Ford's assembly plant.

Above : Part of the Ford engine plant where crankshafts are machined.

the appropriate wheels, fitted with the tyres the customer has ordered. The tyres will have been fitted to the wheels by an ingenious machine which slips the tyre casing over the wheel with the aid of soap, then inflates it, not through the valve but through the circumference of the wheel over the rim. Pressures are automatically set to the right figures for the type and size of tyre.

The brakes are bled when the propshaft and other parts are fitted underneath, a gallon of fuel is put in the tank and the car is ready, for the first time, to move under its own power and on its own wheels – once they have been fitted. It moves along the 'dragline', as it is called, with a venting pipe hitched to the exhaust to take the fumes outside. Adjustments to the engine are checked as it idles and then the car goes to the tracking station – rather like a high tent with mirrors at front and rear – where suspension and steering settings are checked and adjusted if necessary.

The driver also tests all controls, checks the lights

ordinary operatives do not have coloured collars but are supplied with overalls.

No one wastes time, for each department has to be self-supporting and sell its goods to the appropriate next one. Foremen ride about inside the plant on bicycles and managers on electric buggies, all to save time. Stocks of all parts are held to allow time for tool changes on the machines.

An ingenious circular store feeds raw pistons to the machines by lifting them and allowing them to fall to the appropriate station by gravity.

Paint and trim

In the section where seats are made 160 women, the only female workers, machine-cut seat coverings from material and stitch them together. A section of Body Engineering is a Body Materials Laboratory, where new styles in dyed textiles, coated fabrics, laminates, carpets and plastics are rigorously tested for durability, safety, resistance to abrasion, colour-fastness and other qualities. This research has led textile manufacturers to produce high-standard materials known as 'automotive quality'.

All trim materials must meet minimum standards of performance and durability that include satisfactory service in all climatic conditions for at least four years without deterioration in appearance or aesthetic quality. Temperatures of more than 110°C (230°F) have been recorded on the vinyl seats of cars parked in hot sunshine, which is why cloth seats are fitted in most models.

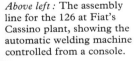

Above left: The assembly line for the 126 at Fiat's Cassino plant, showing the automatic welding machine controlled from a console.

Below left: The Fiat ROBOGATE assembly line at the Rivalta factory – a new automated car production system.

Above right: Cars being tested in Pininfarina's wind tunnel. The car is placed on a turntable and strain gauges measure the effects of wind speeds blowing through the tunnel.

Top right: At the Volvo plant, a car is being tested on a 'shake rig' which simulates driving on bad roads. A few days of concentrated testing corresponds to the lifetime of the car.

Quality of materials and the quality control of manufacture are major headaches for car-makers, and in Japan, whose cars have a high reputation for reliability, the industry has a much larger number of inspectors in proportion to productive workers. Also for quality reasons, for the first 90 days of normal production of a new model responsibility for the whole programme remains with engineering, not production, so that all of the engineering and design changes – inevitable with a new model – can be scrutinized during that period.

This is a follow-on from engineering involvement in the design concept, when the model is designed round what are called 'hardpoints', aspects of the structural design requiring long-term tooling and so having to be fixed early in the design cycle. In Ford's case there are normally 14 hardpoints ranging from windscreen surface and periphery to underbody assembly. Once the hardpoints are fixed Body Engineering can start preliminary production exercises 26 months ahead of Job 1, the first production car.

At this stage the plastic replicas of intended body panels (mentioned earlier) are made in order to check their suitability for manufacture in terms of cost and feasibility. As the trim and fascia panels are developed the hardware – the heater parts and other interior metal – and instrument panel controls are installed in the wooden seating buck and checked for location and reach. When the car goes into production, engineering follows through to make sure

that what worked on the buck is still valid for series production.

Hardpoint Approval to go ahead is normally given 30 months ahead of Job 1 and approval of the full-size clay model of the intended car 27 months ahead, or three months after Hardpoint Approval. First studies begin 45 months ahead and concern future economic conditions, personal incomes, spending habits of prospective buyers, legal requirements – increasingly complex with Common Market and clean air laws – styling and performance trends and variants on the basic design needed in the programme.

A complete car can have more than 4,000 components and can be some four years gestating. Also it must pass European Acceptance Standards, as well as rig and road tests, before getting approval. Some idea of all this can be gained from the experience of Ford's Granada range. It cost $100 million (£50 million) to develop and involved 1,500 people directly and 3,000 more as time went on towards production. After testing on proving grounds in Britain and Belgium, and road tests from the Arctic to the tropics, 100 pilot-build cars were loaned to company marketing, sales and service people for further road evaluation.

The Italian way

Italy's giant Fiat company have introduced a new automated car production system which they claim will make conventional production line methods obsolete. Called ROBOGATE, it uses many robot machines and enables different bodyshells to be made consecutively down a single automated production line without altering tooling or capital equipment.

The system, developed by COMAU, a group company specializing in machine tools and welding systems, is used at Fiat's Rivalta and Cassino factories, where it enables the costs of capital equipment to be amortized over different models and offers production flexibility.

ROBOGATE is a development of the system used at the Mirafiori, Turin, plant to make the Fiat 131, which has no fixed production line but uses trolleys guided by magnetic under-floor cables (as at Kalmar) to take the bodyshell from station to station, some with robot welders and some conventional. Each trolley can be programmed to either of two vehicle types.

161

The trolley is loaded with a jig which carries references to a particular body type. The floor-pan, body sides and roof are assembled automatically in succession on the jig, as in a normal plant. Sensors ensure that the right parts are chosen. The carrier then travels round the robot welding stations, electronically triggering the welders to carry out the relevant operations. At Rivalta and Cassino two body types are run on each line, but more types could be produced.

A computer runs the whole system, choosing components and trolleys, and finally making quality-control checks. If there is a change in the market and buyers want, say, estate cars instead of saloons, then at the turn of a switch the production system can accommodate itself to the market without stopping or slowing the line and without laying workers off because the demand for a particular model has dropped.

Some 70 per cent of the ROBOGATE system's capital cost is attributable to the fixed components, only 30 per cent to the aspects concerning mixed-model output capacity. Thus costs, as mentioned above, can be amortized over a whole range of models instead of just one, as in the conventional system of production.

Many factories already run mixed-model lines, but not with this degree of automation and cost-cutting. Robot welders are now widely used and there is increasing automation of production. Renault of France, for instance, have a machine that supplants the worker lying on his back in the car to stick on the adhesive roof or head lining. It can pick up the one-piece lining with sucker cups, transfer it in through the space where the windscreen is to go and press it to the roof until the adhesive takes.

The march of automation to be seen in most car factories contrasts with the Kalmar system, which is effectively an attempt to turn the clock back, to eliminate the soulless atmosphere of the big factory by restoring workshop intimacy. Whether this could be made to work in the big plants that turn out thousands of cars a day is yet to be seen.

A different method

All car-makers follow the same basic production pattern, with variations in nomenclature and detail procedure. But Volvo, of Sweden, who produce a small number of cars by comparison with giants like Ford and GM, have tried out a different production system in a specially built plant at Kalmar. It is a system that has aroused much comment and interest.

Volvo claim that the Kalmar layout is unique, 'an assembly plant with the human being at the centre'. In fact they have reverted to a system, used in Britain in the 1920s by Bentley and others, in which a team of workers drew the parts for a car from stores and built the whole car, for which they were responsible. A big difference, though, is that in the 1920s the car body was made as a separate enterprise; the car was considered mechanically complete when it was a running chassis, its body to be added later by the coach-builder.

Nowadays, as we have seen, the body is built first and the mechanicals are hung on it. At Kalmar production has been arranged to make it easier for the workers to find sense and satisfaction in their work, 'job satisfaction', as industrial psychologists call it. Volvo say that their Kalmar workers can work in groups, communicate freely, change jobs in rotation, vary their work-rate, 'relate' to the product, feel responsible for quality and influence their working environment.

Does the system work? Production under it started in 1974, with teams of 20-odd men and women, each team with its own workshop and entrance, changing room and coffee room. Each team performs one function – assembling the electrical system, for instance – and is responsible for quality.

Heavy lifting has been eliminated from the production process and moving platforms have replaced conveyor belts to make work easier. The car is turned so that the workers can get at it easily without stooping, bending or other contortions. There are two ways of working: 'straight assembly', in which the work is done with the car on stationary platforms, or 'dock assembly', in which the team is sub-divided into groups of three or so and they do all the tasks of the team on a platform docked beside the track.

Either way the people can work for 20 or 30 minutes on one operation, then switch. They may also make use of a buffer zone where cars may be stored at the beginning and end of each team area, and may take a break when the zone is full. There are differences between the assembly techniques and those on a conventional track as the bodyshell is already painted when it reaches Kalmar, but basically what Volvo call a chassis – actually an underbody – is assembled at the same time as the bodyshell moves in and the two are married together just as elsewhere. The whole process is computer-controlled.

The aim at Kalmar is to create the atmosphere of a small workshop in a large plant. The assembly areas are light and airy and are located on the outer walls of the polygonal plant. Large windows let in the sun and the noise level is only 65 decibels. The plant covers 250,000 square metres (300,000 square yards) but only some 600-plus people work there. It was designed to produce 30,000 cars a year on one-shift working, but was turning out only 24,000 two years after opening.

Production teams at Kalmar – about 30 in all – are divided between body assembly, chassis assembly and final assembly. The car-carriers run on magnetic tracks in the floor or can be moved manually. Normally they are governed by the computer.

Top left: Fitting front fenders and grille on a saloon at the General Motors' plant.

Top right: The Volvo technical centre at Gothenburg has a total floor space of 108,000 metres covering offices, workshops, ultra-modern laboratories, safety centre and climatic plant – and a work force of 1,200 people.

Centre: At the Volvo plant at Kalmar, a car is produced by a team of workers working together and exchanging jobs. Here a body shell is being lowered onto its mechanical components.

Teams with a spread of ages seem to work best and those including at least two women are more stable and cooperative. There are no grades or hierarchy within teams but they may choose a team leader who acts as spokesman, receives and transmits information and shows recruits how to work. Team leaders are appointed by the company after consultation with the trade union.

In some teams job-switching is determined by a schedule drawn up by the team members. In others it is determined by pressure of work, men and women switching to those jobs that most need doing. People do not like being switched from one team to another because newcomers tend to get the simplest and most boring tasks. Task-times are worked out in agreement with the trade unions, and teams that work faster are said to be 'working ahead' and can take longer breaks.

The buffer zone system – having cars finished by one team and awaiting the attention of the next – has not worked out. Some teams use them to cover hold-ups, others make up time by working ahead and

Centre right : Fitting a fuel tank at Volvo is made easier by turning the car on its side.

Right : At Volvo's climatic plant cars are tested under a variety of conditions, including high wind speeds and very hot and cold temperatures.

Volvo's investigations show Kalmar to be as efficient as conventional plants, though no more so. In some ways it is a disappointment. Kalmar's workers like the system but the quality of their products is no higher than in other plants. They turn out cars at the same rate as elsewhere but with more 'indirect time', the time spent irrespective of volume output. While Kalmar cost 10 per cent more to build than a conventional plant the introduction of a new model there would be simpler and cheaper.

there is competition between the two demands. Those who do get ahead can take an extra 4-minute break for every 16 to 20-minute work cycle. The computer keeps the cars moving at a uniform pace from station to station regardless of working rates. Some teams reject the idea of working ahead and keep to a steady pace. Others like to get ahead, feeling secure at being up to the norm.

Within a fixed framework of quantity and quality the teams may decide on their own immediate work. They can influence their work directly by changing job distribution (some people work faster than others), organization of materials and work methods, and by agreement on whether to 'work ahead' or not.

The system of feedback of quality faults from the computer has also been less successful than had been hoped. Workers prefer to be told personally what is wrong, not by an electronic device. It was hoped that there would be less need for rectification of cars after manufacture at Kalmar than elsewhere, but this has not been realized. Three-quarters of the workers are satisfied with the environment, though some complain of too little room between cars in places, making work difficult.

Absenteeism runs at 14 per cent at Kalmar, compared with a rate of 19·2 at Torslanda and Gothenburg. Workers complain that the constant stream of visitors to their novel plant is irritating and holds up their work.

HISTORY OF MOTOR SPORT

Motor racing is almost as old as the horseless carriage itself. While some historians see the Paris–Rouen event of 1894 as the world's first car race, certainly by the following year motor racing appeared in a recognizable form. This was only nine years after Karl Benz and Gottlieb Daimler triggered the first real motoring impetus with their petrol-engined vehicles. As early as 1878 there had been a steam wagon race in the United States, covering 323 km (201 miles) from Green Bay, Wisconsin, to Madison in the same state. Six entries were faced with an 18-day schedule and special tests including a ploughing competition. Only two wagons actually started and one, an Oshkosh, reached the finish.

In France, too, the first competitions involved steam vehicles. The Comte de Dion, his partner Georges Bouton and Léon Serpollet were foremost in driving and demonstrating various vehicles of this kind.

But in the early 1890s the petrol-engined products of Panhard et Levassor, Peugeot and Benz began to appear on the roads of Europe and gallant pioneer motorists ranged far and wide. Serpollet, still faithful to steam, piloted his own car from Paris to Lyons in 1890.

Paris–Rouen 1894

Because the public did not appreciate the possibilities of these 'revolutionary' means of transport, Pierre Giffard, of the newspaper *Le Petit Journal* decided to organize a competition to demonstrate their potential.

Giffard had previously organized a Paris–Brest–

Top left : The Paris–Rouen, 1894. De Dion is shown with Bouton at his side on their steamer. The vehicle had articulated carriage. Although first to reach Rouen, De Dion and Bouton were placed second overall.

Top right : Engraving of the scene before the start of the Paris–Rouen event, 1894.

Left : Acclamation from the crowd for Emile Levassor in the 2·4-litre Panhard et Levassor. He was first home in the 1895 Paris–Bordeaux–Paris race, and averaged more than 25 km/h (15 mph) in a drive of over 48 hours.

Paris cycle race. Now, in *Le Petit Journal* of 19 December 1893, writing under his pen name, Jean sans Terre, he announced a competition for *voitures sans chevaux*. The next day rules were published for a trial to be conducted along the Seine valley from Paris to Rouen. They required that vehicles should be able to move under their own power and should complete a preliminary trial. In the contest a panel of judges would travel the course on the competing vehicles, changing from one to another along the way (the Mobil Economy Runs, some 60 years on, were to use a similar method). The judges would choose the winner on a basis of vehicles being 'without danger, easily handled and of low running costs'.

The preliminary trial required entrants to cover 50 km (32 miles) in three hours. It is now thought that Giffard, advised by Emile Levassor, confused maximum speed with average speed. It is possible that the organizers thought 16 km/h (10 mph) too dangerous a speed. However, the time limit was later extended to a more sedate four hours.

The competition was fixed for 1 June 1894. There were no fewer than 102 entries, with motive power ranging through steam, petrol, compressed air, electric and 'automatic' to such optimistic devices as pedals, a system of levers, 'weight of passengers', an arrangement of pendulums and 'gravity'. Most failed to materialize for the eliminating trials and finally only 21 starters took part in the run. It was twice postponed: first to enable M. Marinoni, proprietor of the sponsoring newspaper, to attend, the second time because most of the entrants were not ready.

At last, on 22 July 1894, the competitors set off from the Boulevard Maillot at 30-second intervals. They were allowed breaks of 1 hour 40 minutes en route.

The first vehicle to arrive at the Champ de Mars in Rouen was the Comte de Dion's steam tractor, 10 hours 47 minutes after leaving Paris. Immediately a great debate ensued. De Dion's vehicle towed its passengers in a conventional horse carriage from

which the front axle had been removed and replaced by a towing eye. The judges refused to recognize the hybrid as a true *automobile* and awarded the first prize of 5,000 francs (about £200) jointly to the Peugeot brothers and Emile Levassor, whose vehicles both employed 'the petrol motor invented by Herr Daimler of Württemberg'.

Giffard, mindful of the importance and influence of de Dion, persuaded the judges to award second prize to the Count. Regulations apart, many motoring histories still record de Dion as winner of the world's first motor race. Others deny that Paris–Rouen was a race at all.

De Dion may well have thought this way himself. Certainly he and others formed a committee to plan a far more serious test of cars and drivers, a 'no-holds-barred' long-distance race. *Le Petit Journal* greeted the plan with horror and refused sponsorship, fearing that some dreadful accident might rebound on the newspaper.

Paris–Bordeaux 1895

The Comte de Dion and his committee pressed on with their plans and soon amassed a prize fund of some 70,000 francs (£2,800). The race, from Paris to Bordeaux and back, was scheduled for 11–14 June 1895. The Committee covered themselves against charges of recklessness by ruling that the fastest cars of the time, two-seaters, would be ineligible for the first prize.

Meanwhile things were happening elsewhere. While preparations for the ambitious Paris–Bordeaux event went ahead in France some amateur sportsmen in Italy were planning a motor race, although of a humbler status. It took place on 29 May 1895. The course ran from Turin to Asti and back, a distance of 100 km (62 miles), and there were five starters: a Benz motor car, a Daimler omnibus, a steamer named *Staffette* and two Hildebrand-und-Wolfmuller motorcycles. The road to Asti was steep and tortuous; the steamer expired, the Benz retired after the first leg and Simone Federmann won in the Daimler, having averaged 15·5 km/h (9·6 mph) to beat the two motorcycles.

Twelve days later the great Paris–Bordeaux–Paris race was flagged away from the Place d'Armes at Versailles. Twenty-two starters actually set out on the daunting 1,178 km (732 mile) course and fifth away was 52-year-old Emile Levassor on a new Panhard with a Daimler-designed Phoenix engine. He stayed at the tiller throughout and created an epic of long-distance driving skill.

Levassor travelled so quickly that he reached his scheduled driver-changing depot three hours early only to find that his replacement had not yet arrived. Refusing to let his riding mechanic take the controls, he pressed on, tearing through the night towards Bordeaux. After a mere eight-minute rest there he set off on the return journey to Paris. Driving through the second night, with only a dim glow from the car's oil lamps, he fell asleep, and was awakened abruptly when the Panhard charged a roadside bank. Damage was minimal and Levassor's furious drive continued. A jammed governor control affecting the exhaust valve prevented the car from increasing speed and cost Levassor 22 minutes, but after 48 hours 48 minutes on the road he arrived at the Porte Maillot, in Paris, almost six hours ahead of Rigoulot's Peugeot. He had averaged 24·25 km/h (15·07 mph) in his epic drive. But the Panhard was a two-seater, and so, under the regulations, Rigoulot's four-seater Peugeot collected first prize. Yet the public hailed Levassor's incredible feat; at last the motorcar was recognized as a genuine substitute for the horse.

The growth of city-to-city racing

Cycle racing had been established on a city-to-city basis and now motor racing was to follow the same pattern. In these pioneer years most major events were held in France and started and finished in the capital, Paris. The big event of 1896 was from Paris to Marseilles and back over a daunting 1,709 km (1,062 miles). The roads in 1896, were poor by today's standards, weather equipment on the cars was minimal and the reactions of the rural peasants were uncertain, few of them having ever seen a horseless carriage before. To add to the drivers' difficulties the 1896 race was partly run in savage gales and rain storms. The winner was Mayade, in a Panhard, at 25·26 km/h (15·2 mph).

Levassor, in a similar car to the winner's, met with disaster. There are differing versions of what happened. Some say he was suddenly confronted by a stray dog, swerved to avoid it, lost control of the tricky tiller steering and overturned the Panhard. Others say that Levassor simply fell asleep – as he had done before.

Accounts differ also on what happened afterwards. It is said that Levassor suffered head injuries from which he later died. Many motoring historians do not accept this. He walked away from the accident virtually unscathed, caught the train to Paris the same evening and was there to greet his team-mate at the finish. Certainly in 1897 his health was good enough for him to follow, driving his own car, the Marseilles–Nice–La Turbie race, which was open only to amateurs. He died on 14 April 1897 of an embolism.

Whatever the causes, direct or indirect, of Levassor's death, he was a great loss to the infant cause of motoring and his tremendous drive of 1895 will never be forgotten.

As city-to-city racing gained momentum in Europe the sport began to take hold in the United States. America's first race, sponsored by the *Chicago Times-Herald*, took place in 1895, and the following year *Cosmopolitan Magazine* sponsored a race in New York State. Meanwhile city-to-city races developed in Europe. Experience gained in the Paris–Bordeaux–Paris event led organizers to introduce overnight stops, passage controls and neutralized sections in major events to protect both competitors and spectators. The late 1890s saw the advent of high-built, spindly-wheeled and predominantly solid-tyred vehicles.

Competition between individual makes of vehicles was intense, as was the rivalry between advocates of different kinds of propulsion. The petrol engine rapidly established its ascendancy, although the famous steam omnibus *La Nouvelle* had contested the Paris–Bordeaux–Paris. Nor were these city-to-city races confined to four-wheel cars; all manner of tricycles and motorcycles were to be seen.

Such intense rivalry in a booming motoring market gave the incentive for rapid technical development, and as the pace of technology grew speeds increased and riding crews began to adopt special protective clothing. Thick furs, mackintosh capes and coats, strap-on helmets, mica goggles and often leather face masks became common. Dust, flying pebbles and low tree branches could be very dangerous.

The eight years from 1895 saw the Panhards dominate at first and their engines grew larger while

Right: Entrants for the 1899 Tour de France organized by the French Automobile Club (ACF).

Below: Artist's impression of the winner, Charron, in a Panhard, about to overtake a racing Bollée in the Paris–Amsterdam–Paris, the major event of 1898.

Far right, above: André Michelin's entry for the 1898 Paris–Bordeaux–Paris, a pneumatic-tyred Peugeot.

Far right, below: Le Petit Journal's illustrated supplement covering the Paris–Rouen trials it organized in 1894 for 'horseless carriages'.

their bodywork became lighter. In 1897, there were no major events and only three short races of just over 160 km (100 miles) took place. Panhard had to give way temporarily to other makes. The Marseilles–Nice–La Turbie event, which Levassor followed in the unaccustomed role of spectator, was won by the Comte de Chasseloup-Laubat in a big de Dion and Jamin, in a tiny Bollée voiturette, won both the Paris–Dieppe and the Paris–Trouville. Then, and for some years to come, the Bollées were among the fastest motorcars in the world.

By 1898 the competition calendar was fairly full. The Achères speed meeting was held and the first World Land Speed Record established – at 63·14 km/h (39·24 mph).

The major race of the year was the first capital-to-capital event. Run from Paris to Amsterdam and back, it was the first motor race to cross national frontiers. Charron won the 1,430 km (889 miles) contest on one of the big, fast Panhards, not yet specialized racers but heading that way.

That 1898 season also saw the first French race to be run on a circuit of roads. The *Course de Périgueux*

PARIS–BORDEAUX 1895   1ʳᵉˢ VOITURE sur PNEUS MICHELIN

Le Petit Journal
SUPPLÉMENT ILLUSTRÉ

Concours du « Petit Journal »
LES VOITURES SANS CHEVAUX

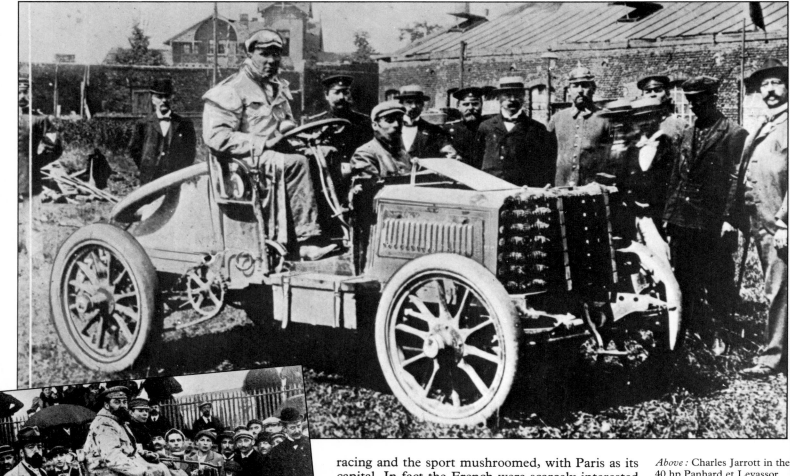

racing and the sport mushroomed, with Paris as its capital. In fact the French were scarcely interested in racing in other countries. The 1899 season saw events from Paris to Bordeaux, St Malo, Ostend, Boulogne and Bayonne, and the great 2,317 km (1,440 mile) Tour de France was run in several stages round an enormous loop of public road, rather ineffectively closed for the occasion. It was won by the famous *Chevalier* René de Knyff, a director of Panhard and a leading figure in the French Automobile Club who, driving his Panhard racer, was able to see road racing from both sides, as organizer and as driver. He became something of a national celebrity at this time, together with less aristocratic Panhard drivers like Charron and Girardot. These two, with another driver named Voigt, later founded their own marque under the CGV initials. Mors cars also did well at this time, notably at the hands of 'Antony' and 'Levegh', pseudonyms covering the identities of Debraye and Velghe.

Entries for most races continued to be all-embracing, as in the Paris–Trouville of 1899, which had classes for racing cars, motorcyclists, cyclists, horsemen and pedestrians. 'Antony' won this for Mors.

As the new century dawned, Mors cars began to challenge Panhard's more fiercely for the honour of being Europe's most potent racers, while smaller and lighter vehicles from Renault and the new German Mercedes (née Daimler) made their presence felt.

Motor racing becomes international

It was in 1900, at the height of the city-to-city era, that truly international competition was introduced. The pioneer was an American, James Gordon Bennett, who had arrived in Paris in 1887 to establish a European version of his father's *New York Herald*. Bennett was a remarkable man – he had sent Stanley in search of Livingstone – and was to sponsor a variety of events, including motor boat

Above: Charles Jarrott in the 40 hp Panhard et Levassor he drove to 10th place in the 687-mile Paris–Berlin race of 1901.

Left: The winner of the 1898 Paris–Bordeaux–Paris in a Panhard. Note the tiller steering.

Right above: Marcel Renault in his light car in the 1902 Paris–Vienna. He won his class at an average 63·09 km/h (39·2 mph).

Right below: Renault 8 hp single-cylinder racing voiturettes of 1901.

substituted a roughly circular loop of public roadway for the out-and-back or point-to-point formula of other events. Just one lap had to be covered, measuring 144 km (90 miles), and a gentleman named Leys won, driving the inevitable Panhard and beating Osmont's de Dion motorcycle.

Sadly this race produced motor sport's first immediately fatal accident. The Marquis de Montaignac, driving a heavy Landry, was in pursuit of de Montariol's little Benz, *Parisienne*. At Bayroux he caught up and passed the Benz, and in doing so, it is said he turned to wave to his opponent. The tiller steering of those days was notoriously unforgiving and the Landry swerved into the path of the Benz. The cars collided, the Benz capsized and the Landry left the road, somersaulting down a bank. The Marquis died within three hours, his hapless mechanic shortly afterwards. A passenger in the Benz was badly hurt.

The accident cast a pall over the hitherto carefree racing fraternity. It also ended tiller steering. The widespread adoption of the geared steering wheel system improved performance and greatly reduced accidents thereafter.

More and more manufacturers supported motor

racing and ballooning. Ironically, although these events were much more successful than his venture into motor racing, it is by the latter that he is best remembered.

Bennett had been present at the Paris–Rouen trial of 1894 and he is said to have inaugurated the race series which was to bear his name after hearing the American manufacturer, Alexander Winton, issuing a rather vague challenge to the great Fernand Charron. He offered a trophy for an international motor race series, to be contested by teams of no more than three cars each, representing the manufacturers of their own countries. The Automobile Club of France (ACF) was to organize the first competition in 1900 with a race from Paris to Lyons. Each national team would be chosen by qualifying trials. The trophy was itself to be held by the winning national authority, which then had the right to organize the following year's Cup race on its own soil.

Shortly before the advent of Gordon Bennett an accident in the Paris–Roubaix race had resulted in the wife of a French parliamentary deputy being injured and every competitor held on criminal charges. The future of motor racing seemed to be

in jeopardy. But at the last moment the new series was allowed to go ahead. The sport survived.

Bennett's rules had overlooked a glaring fact – that only the French motor industry was strong enough in sporting interest to select representatives. The inaugural event was total chaos. Only the French had run a proper selection process. Even then dissatisfaction with the final choice caused deep rifts within the ACF itself.

The French fielded three Panhards to face a Belgian Bolide and an American Winton. Two of the Panhards were the only finishers, Charron winning from Girardot.

The ACF had won the right to organize another event in 1901, but such was their low opinion of the Trophy's importance that they ran the race simply as a class within the Paris–Bordeaux. The result was another fiasco, for Girardot's Panhard was the only team car to finish and it was only tenth in the overall race result. Fournier's Mors, winner of the big race, was nearly 26 km/h (16 mph) faster than Girardot's Panhard, winner of the Gordon Bennett.

If, in 1902, the French had won the Trophy for the third time they might have locked it in the display cabinet at the Place de la Concorde ACF offices and conveniently lost the key. But the French industry lost its team cars on the Paris–Innsbruck cup-qualifying section of the Paris–Vienna race and the trophy fell to an Englishman, Selwyn F. Edge, in his Napier, the sole surviving team entry.

Thus perpetuated, the Gordon Bennett was next run over a road course at Ballyshannon, in Ireland,

Top left : Léon Théry in a Richard-Brasier in the 1905 Gordon Bennett Cup race, which he won at 77·89 km/h (48·4 mph). Behind is C. S. Rolls in a Wolseley.

Above : Charles Jarrott at the wheel of a 1904 Wolseley.

Left : Camille Jenatzy and the 16 hp Mors he drove in the 1899 Tour de France.

Top right : S. F. Edge in the 1901 50 hp Napier, and the winner's plaque he received after gaining the Gordon Bennett Cup for Britain in 1902.

Below right : One of the many accidents that marred the 1903 Paris–Madrid race.

the British Government refusing to close roads on the mainland. At Ballyshannon the Belgian 'Red Devil', Camille Jenatzy won the Trophy in a German Mercedes, so for 1904 Germany had the honour of organizing the race. It took place over a closed-circuit public road loop in the Taunus Hills.

There the admirable Léon Théry seized the trophy for France in his Richard-Brasier, and repeated the performance in 1905, when, as host nation, the French chose a serpentine circuit round the Auvergne Mountains, just outside Clermont-Ferrand.

The French were delighted to have shown the way not only to the upstart Americans but also the Germans and British. But they took another look at the rules of the Gordon Bennett competition and decided that they were irksome. In particular they objected to the limit on the number of cars entered by each nation. They felt that as France had the most motor manufacturers France should be allowed a proportionately larger team than other nations. The ACF therefore decided to stage its own international motor race and the Gordon Bennett was allowed to lapse.

The end of city-to-city racing

In 1900 the *Course du Catalogue* had been run over two laps of a triangular 72 km (45 mile) public road circuit near Melun. An extension of the *Course de Périgueux* idea, it was a preview of the way in which motor racing was to develop, being the first time that a racing field had passed the same way, in the same direction, more than once. Léonce Girardot set fastest time to win this first true circuit race and the modern concept of reconnaissance and practice

laps became possible.

One week later a more important circuit race, the *Course du Sud-Ouest*, was run at the southern city of Pau and was won by de Knyff. But it was not until 31 July 1902 that the first true circuit race, with no intervening neutral zones, was held. It was the *Circuit des Ardennes*, over six laps of an 83·5 km (53 mile) circuit, centred on Bastogne, in Belgium. Britain's Charles Jarrott, in a Panhard, won, averaging an heroic 85·9 km/h (54 mph) over the 512-km (318-mile) course.

By this time there were city-to-city races from Paris to Berlin and Paris to Vienna, round the whole of France, and, in a two-day, two-stage loop, round the northern part of the country, over a gruelling 864 km (537 miles).

Some opposition to public road racing had grown and a crop of accidents contributed to questions being asked in the French Parliament which led to a total ban a few days after the 1901 Paris–Berlin race. But the Automobile Club's titled committee wielded considerable influence and, as they had no desire to organize more than one major event a year, the ban became less than total and city-to-city authorization could still be arranged if the right people were asked in the right way.

This state of affairs, with important races being run in Belgium and Italy, persisted into 1903, when the ACF decided to run its major event as a 1,200-km (764-mile) race from Paris to Madrid. Authorization was withheld and prospects looked bleak as first the

Pau Week and then the projected Nice–Salon–Nice race were refused permits. Then King Alfonso of Spain granted authority to run the section from Irun, at the Franco-Spanish border, to Madrid. Soon after this the French authorities relented and gave permission for the event.

The race was run on 24 May 1903, but it was stopped abruptly at the Bordeaux stage control after a series of horrifying accidents. It was also the end of the 'heroic age' of city-to-city racing.

The Paris–Bordeaux stage was very fast and many of the machines taking part were demonstrably too speedy for the roads and the uncontrolable crowds spilling on to them. Louis Renault had been the third man to start from Versailles, but entering the stage at Rambouillet, 32 km (20 miles) from the start, his light car took the lead. On the straight, tree-lined section from Bonneval to Chateaudun, he estimated his speed as 145 km/h (90 mph).

Behind him some gruesome accidents took their toll, and at Couhé-Verac, a small town between Poitiers and Ruffec, Marcel Renault, Louis's brother, was killed when his 30-hp car overturned. As remaining members of the Renault team arrived at the scene they retired, but out in front Louis thundered on, unaware, the first competitor to reach Bordeaux.

While Renault had enjoyed a clear road, free of other competitors and their dust, one man behind him was even faster. Fernand Gabriel, on the giant 70-hp streamlined Mors, had drawn 168th place at the start, had battled his way through dust, flying stones and debris, had picked his way through a litter of crashed cars and the crush of wayward spectators and was still the third to arrive at Bordeaux. He had covered the distance at 105 km/h (65·3 mph), a time of 5 hours, 14 minutes. Salleron, in another Mors, was placed second and the English driver, Charles Jarrott, on a De Dietrich, was third.

In the winners' wake a trail of crashed and abandoned cars spread over 217 km (135 miles). Two drivers, three mechanics and at least one spectator had been killed. The authorities stepped in, the race was called off at Bordeaux and the surviving vehicles were impounded and freighted ignominiously back to Paris by rail.

Small cars and the growth of circuit racing

The tragic outcome of the Paris–Madrid ended city-to-city racing. Much shorter public road circuits – though still enormous by today's standards – became the norm. They were relatively easy to police and gate money could be taken, so the way was clear to establish motor racing as a paying spectator sport. While the monstrously heavy cars of the time took most of the honours their lighter rivals were now a growing threat.

The turn of the century had seen heavy cars the size of the 10-litre Mors, while the largest voiturettes, or small-capacity cars, used engines of about 1·4 litres. For 1901 the ACF had introduced four classes based on weight: the over-650 kg (1,433·5 lb) heavy cars; 400–650 kg (882–1,433·5 lb) light cars; 250–400 kg (551·25–882 lb) voiturettes; and, last and least, a cyclecar class below 250 kg (551·25 lb). In practice, and certainly in the public mind, the voiturette and light cars were virtually synonymous.

The Renault brothers were prominent amongst voiturette and light car manufacturers, their machines having grown from a single-cylinder vehicle of 49 cc in 1900, through a 3·7-litre in which Marcel Renault won the Paris–Vienna in 1902, to a 6·3-litre (still below 650 kg) for Paris–Madrid. Since for that event Mercedes were running 12·5-litre engines, Panhard 13·5 and Mors 12 litres, the Renaults were still small cars by the standards of the time. Even so their speed constituted a serious challenge to the heavy car establishment. In some quarters the light construction of these very fast machines was viewed with suspicion and Paris–Madrid nearly brought about the demise of the class which had first shown its potential with Jamin's late nineteenth century Bollée. Although the light cars

Top left: Marcel Renault driving his 30 hp Renault through Tours in the 1903 Paris–Madrid race.

Above left: Marcel Renault's fatal crash at Couhé-Vérac in the 1903 Paris–Madrid event.

Above : Louis Renault, also in a 30 hp Renault, was the first of the light car class to arrive at Bordeaux, where the 1903 Paris–Madrid was stopped. He had averaged 99·4 km/h (61·76 mph).

and voiturettes did survive 'the Race to Death' that disaster brought about one major change: the ACF decided that in future tricycles must be separated from cars. Nevertheless, during 1904–5, only the *Circuit des Ardennes* offered a class for light cars, most people regarding them as being capable of tackling the heavier machines on level terms.

There were more serious problems. The Prime Minister of France, M. Combes, promised the nation in 1904 that road racing was finished.

The Automobile Club de France, however, was still influential. By special dispensation a 93·6-km (58·2-mile) road circuit in the sparsely populated Argonne was closed to allow that year's Gordon Bennett eliminating trial to be held to choose the French team.

The British, denied the use of public roads for racing on their mainland, ran their eliminating trial around the Isle of Man.

In Belgium, the Ardennes race fell to Heath's Panhard after Teste's sister car lost the lead because the driver insisted upon strapping ruined, useless tyres back on to its tail before continuing after a wheel change.

In Italy, the Sicilian *Cav.* Vincenzo Florio inaugurated his *Coppa Florio* race on a circuit from Brescia via Cremona and Mantua and back to

Brescia. Vincenzo Lancia won for FIAT, averaging a staggering 115·8 km/h (72 mph) for the two lap, 372 km (231·25 miles). Teste's Panhard was actually faster still but the luckless driver was penalized three minutes for refuelling in the Mantua control.

During the Salon at the end of 1904 a group of prominent French manufacturers had asked that a race be organized to replace the Gordon Bennett, one in which every firm capable of building a racing car would have equal entry opportunities. The ACF adopted this memorandum, which asked that the Gordon Bennett be scrapped unless its rules could be liberalized.

Grand Prix

The ACF organized a Grand Prix race, as it was christened, to be run on the Auvergne circuit in 1905, incorporating the Gordon Bennett. They ruled that the first 15 cars in the French eliminating trial should represent their nation in the Grand Prix while the fastest three would form the Gordon Bennett team. Germany and Britain were allowed six entries each in proportion to the size of their industries – while Austria, Italy, Switzerland, America and Belgium had three each.

The journal *L'Auto* offered 100,000 francs (£4,000) to the winner of the Grand Prix. When

news of the combined race was released in the foreign press a storm of international abuse rained about the ACF. The objectors pointed out that running so many cars on the twisty Auvergne course would court a repetition of the Paris–Madrid disasters. The ACT relented, saying that they would run the Trophy and Grand Prix races separately. Later they postponed their Grand Prix project for a year and stated that whatever the outcome of the Gordon Bennett they would abstain from contesting the Trophy in future and would support only their own Grand Prix race in its place. It was the end for James Gordon Bennett's race series.

All major manufacturers looked towards 1906, which opened with races at Daytona Beach, USA, and in Cuba. On 9 May the first Targa Florio (Florio Plate) race was run in Sicily over three laps of a staggering 150-km (93-mile) circuit climbing and diving over 343 metres (1,130 ft) in the coastal Madonie mountains east of Palermo. The Italas of Alessandro Cagno and Graziani finished first and second from ten starters, and the winning average of 48·8 km/h (29·1 mph) was a telling commentary on the course. The redoubtable Mme Le Blon acted as riding mechanic in her husband's Hotchkiss, and

Above : Szisz, the Renault test driver, wins the first Grand Prix 2-day race at Le Mans, 1906.

Left : A decorative commemoration of Lautenschlager's win for Mercedes, and Germany, in the 1908 Dieppe Grand Prix.

Above right : Léon Théry and his mechanic after victory in the 1905 Gordon Bennett Cup.

they were fifth amongst the six finishers.

Already expensive preparations were being made for the inaugural *Grand Prix de l'Automobile Club de France*. The ACF committee chose a truly grand challenge and had prepared a 103·18-km (64·12-mile) closed public road circuit on the outskirts of Le Mans. This triangular *Circuit de la Sarthe* lay to the east of the city extending to the villages of La Ferté Bernard to the north-east and down to St Calais in the south-east. St Calais itself was bypassed by a planked artificial roadway, elaborate stands were erected facing the replenishment depots and a tunnel connected the two beneath the track. Some 65,000 metres (more than 40 miles) of palisade fencing was erected to control the crowds. Tuesday and Wednesday, 26–27 June 1906 were to be race days, with the field covering six laps of the great circuit on both days and being locked overnight in a *parc fermé*.

Beneath a blistering sun, on rough roads and reaching speeds towards 100 mph on the longest, 32-km (20-mile) straight, it was a race of tyre life. Only drivers and their riding mechanics were allowed to replace worn and punctured covers, and Renault, Itala and Fiat adopted the new Michelin detachable wheel rims to assist. This system allowed the old tyre to be removed complete with its rim simply by releasing eight bolts. The new tyre, ready inflated on its rim, could then be bolted into place. While other teams exhausted themselves and lost time in slashing away worn tyres with knives, then levering into place and laboriously inflating new tyres, the detachable rim teams ran clear.

A Hungarian works Renault test driver named Ferenc Szisz – he had ridden with Louis Renault in the Paris–Madrid – handled one of the big 13-litre 90 hp Renaults and took the lead on lap three of the first day's racing, holding it to the finish despite breaking a rear spring on the second day. He won from the Italian Felice Nazzaro in a 16·3-litre 100 hp Fiat, averaging 101·195 km/h (62·88 mph) overall. Fastest race lap fell to Paul Baras' big Brasier at 52 mins 25·4 secs, 117·94 km/h (73·3 mph).

The race was seen more as a dull two-horse battle between Renault and Fiat than a meaningful struggle between nations, and one writer observed that 'the feeling of sport was almost entirely absent'.

However, while the heavy machines contested this first Grand Prix, interest in the voiturette classes

had revived. *L'Auto* had established a cup competition to be contested 'not by mere racing cars' but by roadworthy vehicles limited by weight as in the past but also restricted in engine size to less than one litre. This engine-size restriction was revolutionary, as formerly the weight regulations had simply encouraged constructors to fit the biggest engine they could into the flimsiest chassis. Although interest in what was to become the *Coupe de l'Auto* competition was minimal the newspaper went ahead and the event they ran that November as a reliability trial was a complete fiasco. However, in 1906, *L'Auto* promoted a true race at Rambouillet, won by Georges Sizaire's Sizaire-Naudin. That year's regulations fixed a maximum weight of 700 kg (1,543 lb) compared with the Grand Prix top limit of 1,000 kg (2,205 lb), while the old one-litre restriction was waived in favour of a cylinder bore restriction of 120 mm for single cylinder engines and 90 mm for twins. The winning Sizaire-Naudin was a single-cylinder design of 1,357 cc, delivering 18 hp and with shaft drive, as against the much larger, mainly chain-drive heavy cars seen in the Grand Prix. This voiturette class was to have far-reaching influence on the development of Grand Prix racing through the years.

Rules and regulations

Every year the ACF strengthened its position as leading world authority in motor sport and every year it announced new regulations for its mighty Grand Prix race, the annual event which was to become the ultimate test of cars and drivers. From 1906 to 1914 the Grand Prix regulations were as follows:

1906 Weight limitation of 1,000 kg (2,205 lb)

1907 Fuel consumption allowance of 30 litres (6·6 Imp galls) per 100 km (62 miles) of race distance, approximately 9·4 mpg

1908 Piston area of engines restricted to 117 square inches, equivalent to 155 mm bore diameter for 4-cylinder, 127 mm for 6-cylinder

1909–11 Grand Prix racing abandoned for four years due to trade depression

1912 Grand Prix racing revived without weight and engine-size restrictions

1913 Fuel consumption allowance reintroduced, this time 20 litres (4·4 Imp galls) per 100 km (62

miles) of race distance, approximately 14 mpg.
Weight restricted to between 800–1,100 kg (1,764–
2,425·5 lb)

1914 Capacity limitation introduced at 4½ litres,
weight limited to 1,100 kg (2,425·5 lb)

Thus, with enclosed circuits, strict regulations or
'Formulae', an established top level of international
motor racing and a revived minor class, the sport
itself was set to develop into the form we know today.
Those who say that it has now developed into 'big
business' are wrong. It was always big business,
right from the beginning.

Racing towards the war
Through 1907–8 the Grand Prix established itself
firmly as the world's premier motor race, and 12
litres became an average engine size as engines grew
during the years of weight limitations. The 1906
Panhard '130' actually displaced 18·2 litres, and at
one stage Dufaux built a fantastic 26·4-litre 4-
cylinder for sprint and record work. The largest-
engined true GP car was the 19-litre Christie of
1907. A middling power output for a typical GP car
of the period would be 140 bhp at around 1,800 rpm.
Some constructors adopted dropped chassis frames
to lower their cars while scuttles and cockpit sides
began to grow to enclose the crews. Racing techniques themselves developed, with pressure refuelling and national racing colours in use in 1907.
The Grand Prix that year was run over a 76·9 km
(47·8-mile) circuit near Dieppe and Nazzaro's overhead-valve Fiat outpaced Szisz's side-valve Renault
to reverse the 1906 result. Even worse in French
eyes was their defeat by the German Mercedes team

at Dieppe in 1908, when Christian Lautenschlager
won what was his very first motor race, and two
German Benz cars came second and third. The best
French machine – Rigal's Clément-Bayard – was
fourth, followed by three more Germans: Mercedes,
Opel and Benz.

This crushing defeat stunned the French industrial establishment and, since they were beset by a
worldwide trade depression and building already
very highly specialized Grand Prix cars was pro-
hibitively expensive, the *Grand Prix de l'ACF* was
allowed to lapse.

The established French manufacturers signed an
agreement banning Grand Prix competition but
making no mention of voiturette racing. Here a new
generation of smaller, lighter and more nimble
racing cars found its role. Had it not been for the
exploits of such voiturette-makers as Delage, Sizaire-
Naudin and Peugeot the long tradition of effective
French motor racing might have been broken there
and then.

As it was, Vincenzo Florio founded the Sicilian
Cup voiturette race to precede his Targa Florio in
1907. It comprised two laps of the mighty Grand
Madonie circuit and Georges Naudin won, at 38
km/h (23·7 mph) in a Florio-owned Sizaire-Naudin,
with Florio himself second in a de Dion-Bouton.
Naudin also won the *Coupe de l'Auto* for his marque's second consecutive success at Rambouillet
later that year, and in 1908 completed Sizaire-
Naudin's hat-trick by winning the Coupe yet again,
at Compiègne.

While the voiturettes battled it out in France,
Belgium, Spain, Italy and Sicily, some major devel-

Above : Felice Nazzaro in his
Fiat in the 1907 French
Grand Prix. He won at
113·64 km/h (70·61 mph).

Top right : Szisz in his
Renault in the 1907 French
Grand Prix, in which he
came 2nd.

Centre right : Triumphant
Mercedes 12½-litre,
4-cylinder cars in the 1908
French Grand Prix. Left to
right: W. Poege's car (5th);
Lautenschlager's (1st); and
Salzer's, in which he led for
the first and fastest lap.

Far right : The first Brooklands meeting was held in
1907. Here F. Newton is
shown in a 60 hp Napier
car.

Bottom right : Albert Guyot
victorious in the voiturette
class of the French Grand
Prix, 1908.

opments had occurred in Britain. The first Tourist Trophy (TT) had been run in the Isle of Man in 1905, yielding valuable lessons from its rather dull and restrictive touring car entry. A Scots-built Arrol-Johnston won the inaugural event, Rolls-Royce were victorious in 1906 and in 1907 a Rover won. The TT attracted little international interest and an open event held in 1908 fell to a Hutton, a 4-cylinder car made by Napier but given a different name as Napiers were so indelibly associated with 6-cylinder cars.

Britain's performance motoring development had been sadly retarded. A few sprints and hillclimbs had been held on short stretches of public road where a local magistrate or squire was sympathetic to the cause. Britain's feeble European showing reflected her lack of a serious industry test course, and during 1906 a Weybridge landowner, H. F. Locke King, began to build one. This remarkably philanthropic act cost him some £150,000 of his own money, and in 1907 his Brooklands Motor Course was opened. It was a kidney-shaped 4·42 km (2·75-mile) concrete speed bowl with banked curves at

either end. Spectators could watch cars run nearly all the way round and before its closure in 1939 Brooklands witnessed a long string of record runs and race meetings. The track also became the home of the British aviation industry, and in many ways aviation profited more from Locke King's generosity than did motor racing.

In its early years Brooklands' effect was marked. It forced the development of streamlining so that the shape of racing cars changed accordingly, notably to adopt long-pointed tail cowls. Brooklands was the first of many speed bowls, notably Indianapolis in the USA, Monza in Italy, Sitges in Spain, Montlhéry in France and eventually Avus in Berlin. Circuits in Argentina and Maroubra and the Melbourne Motordrome in Australia also developed on the Brooklands speedway theme, vastly different from the established major race concept of closed public roads.

France was still the seat of international motor racing, and in 1909 a Grand Prix was arranged to be run at Anjou, but when only nine entries were received instead of the prudently-stated minimum of 40 the event was cancelled. In 1911 the *Automobile Club de la Sarthe* organized a free formula *Grand Prix de France* around a section of the 1906 Le Mans circuit. Victor Hémery won it in a tuned 10-litre touring Fiat at 91·25 km/h (56·71 mph) while of greater note was Friederich's tiny Bugatti in second place. The race was a modest success and sparked the ACF into organizing a true Grand Prix at Dieppe in 1912. While the 1911 Le Mans race had been interesting, that year's *Coupe de l'Auto* voiturette race at Boulogne was one of the most exciting events yet seen. Paul Bablot's Delage beat Georges Boillot's Lion-Peugeot by just 71 seconds after seven hours' racing. The ACF chose to insure themselves against a poor Grand Prix entry for 1912 and ran it concurrently with the *Coupe de l'Auto*.

Peugeot ran in what was now the 3-litre voiturette class as well as the GP, which they tackled with a new 7·6-litre shaft-drive car and Fiat represented the old order with their 14-litre chain-drive mon-

sters. The result was a triumph of new over old, with Boillot's revolutionary twin overhead camshaft, 4-valve-per-cylinder Peugeot winning from Louis Wagner's ageing Fiat. Third overall, and leading home sister cars to score 1-2-3 in the *Coupe de l'Auto*, was Victor Rigal's Brooklands-developed long-tailed Sunbeam.

Such foreign innovation was expressly forbidden by the 1913 Grand Prix regulations. Peugeot won again and dominated the season.

Then, in 1914, Grand Prix racing attained a height which in many respects it has never reached since. The Grand Prix that year was run over 20 laps of a hilly 37·631-km (23·38-mile) circuit at Lyon-Givors and full teams were entered by now fewer than 14 manufacturers, all gambling huge sums to secure the commercial success which victory in the prestigious Grand Prix could bring. The race crushed French morale as Boillot's Peugeot broke down in his attempts to beat off the team of five Mercedes from Germany. Two of them also broke down, but the survivors finished with Lautenschlager, the 1908 victor leading their 1-2-3 finish. Within a month France and Germany were plunged into war, and both Peugeot and Mercedes found a racing refuge in America.

Racing resumed

Twenty years of peace between world wars saw motor racing survive the great depression and reach a frenetic climax during the 'thirties as the most powerful Grand Prix cars ever constructed made a deep impression on all who saw them. European racing restarted quickly in 1919 in Sicily, where the Targa Florio fell to André Boillot (younger brother of Georges) and his Peugeot. A newcomer from Italy, Antonio Ascari, proved faster round the first part of the Madonie course before crashing his Grand Prix Fiat over a precipice.

Now the dominance of the reliable and simple 4-cylinder engine was to be ended. Wartime aero engineering had promoted the multi-cylinder cause

Top left: Bablot in a Delage (No. 10) narrowly defeated Boillot's Lion-Peugeot (No. 4) in the 1911 *Coupe de l'Auto* at Boulogne.

Top right: French Grand Prix, 1913, at Moreuil showing Georges Boillot, the winner, in his Peugeot.

Above left: The Ballot-Wagner team at Le Mans in the French Grand Prix of 1921.

Above right: Georges Boillot's Peugeot at speed in the 1913 *Coupe de l'Auto*, Boulogne.

Right: Georges Boillot in a 4½-litre Peugeot competing in the 1914 French Grand Prix at Lyon.

and inline 8-cyclinder engines appeared in 1919 from Ballot in France and Duesenberg in the USA. When the *GP de l'ACF* was revived on a new 17·262-km (10·726-mile) Le Mans course for 1921 the Club borrowed the 3-litre Indianapolis Formula and the Ballots were beaten by an American team of Duesenbergs featuring hydraulic braking systems and the vivid driving of Jimmy Murphy.

That same year Italy staged her very first Grand Prix race at Brescia, where two 8-cylinder Ballots defeated the Turin-built straight-eight Fiats. In 1922 the Italians had completed their Monza speedway, in the former Royal park just outside Milan, and that became the home of Italian GP. The British TT race was revived and by 1924 a Spanish premier-league race was added – although not acknowledged as a *Grand Epreuve* – at San Sebastian. In 1925 the Belgian GP was added to the calendar and in 1926 the first British and German GPs were run.

The Grand Prix Formulae of this period – applying to more than just one unique race – were more

stable than those before the war and may be summarized as follows:

1921 3-litre capacity limit, minimum weight of 800 kg (1,764 lb)

1922–4 2-litre capacity limit, minimum weight of 650 kg (1,433·25 lb)

1925 As above but riding mechanics finally banned, wide two-seat body styles still obligatory, rearview mirrors demanded

1926 1½-litre capacity limit, minimum weight of 600 kg (1,323 lb), single seats allowed but wide bodies still mandatory

1927 1½-litre capacity limit, minimum weight of 700 kg (1,543·5 lb)

1928 Engines free, minimum weight on sliding scale between 550 kg (1,212·75 lb) and 750 kg (1,653·75 lb) related to engine size. Race distance minimum of 600 km (362 miles)

1929 Commercial petrol mandatory, with a consumption limit of approximately 14·5 mpg.

1930 As above but permission given to add 30 per cent benzole to commercial fuel

1931 Free formula – races to last a minimum 10 hours

1932 Free formula – races to last 5–10 hours

1933 Free formula – race distance of 500 km (312 miles) minimum

The effects of the great depression of 1929–33 are clearly seen here, but in the early 'twenties at least top-class racing proved fiercely competitive. Fiat dominated 1922 and avenged their Brescia defeat by Ballot in winning not only the inaugural Italian GP at Monza but also the French race at Strasbourg. There Felice Nazzaro – winner of the 1907 Grand Prix – won again for Fiat averaging 127·67 km/h (79·33 mph) over the 802·8-km (498·85-mile) distance. The Strasbourg course was not only very fast but also, by existing standards, very short for a public road venue at only 13·38 km (8·3 miles) to the lap. The race saw the first massed start replacing the old 'despatch at intervals' system, and it was also the last Grand Prix in which spare wheels were carried on the car. The decreasing lap length, improving tyres and the organizers' desire to stimulate tyre development contributed to this change.

The victorious Fiat Tipo 904s were brilliantly engineered little 6-cylinder models and Sunbeam faithfully copied them to win the 1923 French GP

at Tours. There the new supercharged 8-cylinder Fiat 805s proved shatteringly fast but their supercharger intake system ingested dust and debris, costing Italy the race. Major H. O. D. Segrave was left to win in his Sunbeam 'Fiat in green paint'. On their home ground at Monza, however, the new Fiats were not to be denied and their unmatchable pace made supercharging vital for racing success.

Ironically Alfa Romeo, the rival Italian marque based in Milan, promptly lured away Fiat's leading engineers and appeared with their own supercharged straight-eight design for 1924, the P2. The Alfas and the Fiats clashed at Lyons in the French Grand Prix and the 'pirates' won. Campari, driving an Alfa, was the victor and once again Fiat were beaten, in effect, by their own designs because the 1923 Sunbeams had been designed by former Fiat men, Bertarione and Becchia, and the 1924 Alfas by yet another Fiat drawing-board genius, Vittorio Jano. Giovanni Agnelli, Fiat's boss, declared he had had enough of creating engineers who would take Fiat drawings to rival concerns. He was going to withdraw his company and cars from motor racing. He kept his word and the French Grand Prix remained the only battle between the similar Alfa Romeos and Fiats.

Although top class races were then much longer than they are today and Grand Prix racing was very much the province of high-quality established

manufacturers, the modern pattern was emerging, with proper pits – named after the replenishment trenches provided at Dieppe in 1908 – team direction signals and proper practice and reconnaissance sessions.

Besides supercharging, the Grand Prix at Tours featured V12-cylinder engines, all-enveloping streamlined bodywork from Bugatti and Voisin and, also from the latter aviation-minded company, 'chassisless' monocoque construction. Both Fiat and Talbot-Darracq, now grouped with the British Sunbeam concern, produced 1½-litre voiturettes in this period, employing half their 1921 3-litre, 8-cylinder engines. The 4-cylinder Fiats generally stayed at home, ruling Italian racing, while the French Suresnes-built Talbots dominated elsewhere in Europe and won everything they tackled from 1921–1926. They gained the name 'The Invincibles', and their record was typified by the 200 Miles Race at Brooklands from 1921 which Talbots won five times. When Fiat's management decided to attempt the race in 1923 Talbots were entered for a Spanish event. The Fiats were forced to retire and Alvis went on to win for Britain.

The birth of sports car racing

Immediately after the Great War interest grew in forms of competition which did not demand pure-bred racing cars. Prewar interest in promoting a

Top : Fiats at the 1924 French Grand Prix, Strasbourg – from the left, Biagio Nazzaro (Felice's nephew, killed in this race); Felice Nazzaro, who won for Fiat; and Pietro Bordino.

Above left : De Viscaya's Bugatti at the pits during the 1922 Italian Grand Prix, Monza.

Above : H. O. D. Segrave at the 1921 French Grand Prix, Le Mans.

Top right : The start of the 1929 Ulster TT. Boris Ivanowski is in No. 32, Giuseppe Campari in No. 35. To the right are 3-litre cars not yet released.

Right : Antonio Ascari led the field in his Alfa Romeo P2 until two laps from the finish of the 1924 French Grand Prix. The photo shows him pushing his car after it had broken down.

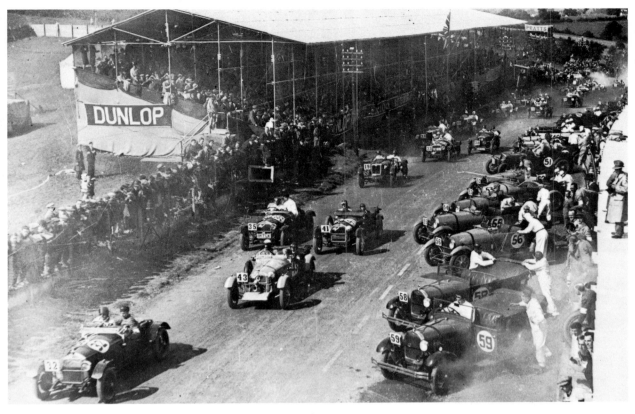

practical high-performance road car had been mirrored in the Tourist Trophy, although that event was perhaps too staid in conception. Of greater note were the Herkomer and Prince Henry Trials held in Germany from 1905–11. The International Touring Car Competition for the Herkomer Trophy comprised a road test of around 800 km (500 miles) from Frankfurt to Innsbruck, then a hillclimb at Semmering and a brief speed trial.

Professor Hubert von Herkomer RA, a professional portrait painter, devised the idea and the first event, in 1905, was contested by standard heavy touring cars. In 1906, however, the rules were liberalized and competitors took advantage by using sketchy, lightweight bodies and some very advanced engineering beneath the engine covers. An enthusiastic Herkomer competitor was Prince Henry of Prussia, the Kaiser's younger brother. When the last Herkomer Trial was completed in 1907 the Prince launched his own trophy for a touring car event for four-seaters with a bore restriction of 146 mm for 4-cylinder engines and 120 mm for 6-cylinders. Though trade entrants were excluded the inaugural event of 1908 was notable for the presence of several recognized drivers in some very exotic machinery. It was won by Fritz Erle's 50-hp Benz, wearing the flared wings and streamlined scuttle of what came to be recognized as a 'sports car'. The 1909 event was mediocre but in 1910 it was won by the *Prinz Heinrich* Austro-Daimler, designed and driven by Dr Ferdinand Porsche. The British Prince Henry Vauxhall, production-based but light, powerful and very fast, also made its debut in this event.

The Austrian Alpine Trial took over the Prince Henry mantle in 1911, although already well-established by that time. These were essentially carefully regulated long-distance drives but they provided a stimulating challenge for the promotion-minded manufacturers of the time who sought competitive success with what were basically production models and in them the classical 'sports car' was developed.

After the war a Parisian entrepreneur named Eugène Mauve brought 24-hour racing, which had proved popular in the pioneer days in America, to Europe. His first *Bol d'Or* was run with a minimum of organizational efficiency at St Germain in 1922 and fell to André Morel's 1,100 cc Amilcar at an average of 60·4 km/h (37·54 mph). This was the forerunner of a far more significant event launched in 1923 by the Le Mans club; the world famous Le Mans 24-Hours *Grand Prix d'Endurance*. Like the British TT it was intended originally for touring cars. It was launched on 26–27 May 1923, when Lagache and Leonard drove their 3-litre Chenard et Walcker a distance of 2,209 km (1,372·9 miles) in the 24 hours to average 92 km/h (57·2 mph). Only three of the 33 starters failed to finish despite bad

weather and a poorly surfaced 17·26-km (10·726-mile) circuit, this time to the south of the industrial city. A shortened version of that course is the one surviving today.

Le Mans quickly attracted an increasingly potent and rugged type of sports car of which the legendary 3-, 4½- and 6½-litre Bentleys, which won five times in 1924 and from 1927–30, are typical. In Italy Count Franco Mazzotti, Ing. Giovanni Canestrine, Comm. Renzo Castagneto and Count Aymo Maggi revived the fearsome challenge of city-to-city racing in 1927 when they launched the Mille Miglia, starting in Brescia, looping literally 1,000 miles around Italy and returning to Brescia via Rome. Alfa Romeo generally dominated the event with their sophisticated Grand Prix-bred twin-cam cars. In Britain the TT had died after 1922 but was revived on Ulster's Ards circuit in 1928 when Kaye Don won in a 1½-litre Lea-Francis. In 1929 the great German driver Rudolf Caracciola won there in a 7-litre Mercedes-Benz, while 1930 saw Alfa Romeo victorious with Tazio Nuvolari – perhaps the greatest all-round

driver of them all – leading a Milanese 1-2-3. After 1930 the British RAC introduced a handicapping system which reflected its Brooklands background with that institution's Edwardian reliance on horse racing practice. The TT thereafter fell from International significance with its time-cum-distance allowances for the hordes of small-engined MGs, Rileys, Austins and so on which entered.

During the great depression, when private owners took the place of the factories in all levels of racing, they were virtually free to race what they liked. Sports cars were muddled in with true racers in many events, even running without mudguards and lights in Grand Prix events while sometimes purebred GP cars made the reverse transition and adopted fenders and lights for the Mille Miglia, or fenders for the Targa Florio. When the protectionist French found their racing authority threatened – particularly by a re-emergent Germany in the 'thirties – they promptly demoted their great Grand Prix to sportscar status merely to give the home product some chance of winning it . . .

turned to the $1\frac{1}{2}$-litre voiturette class where they dominated the ERAs and Maseratis. Then, at Tripoli in 1939, Mercedes-Benz made a one-time appearance with a special $1\frac{1}{2}$-litre supercharged V8 voiturettes which defeated the Italians, two of these W165 cars leading home one surviving Alfa Romeo by more than four minutes!

During 1939 the 3-litre German Grand Prix cars featured twin-stage supercharging in which one compressor fed a further compressor before the aggregate boost of both was blasted into the engine. These units produced close on 500 hp and Hermann Lang, a one time team mechanic, dominated the year for Mercedes, while the great Nuvolari, driving for Auto Union since late-1938, won the very last race of this period at Belgrade on the day war erupted.

That ended the interwar period of motor racing in which circuits had grown shorter, paying crowds larger and cars unimaginably faster and more sophisticated, establishing the sport not only as an instrument of commercial promotion but also as a weapon of political prestige. As Italy remained neutral into 1940 her voiturette class continued with Alfa Romeo fighting off Maserati. Two streamlined BMWs did nothing to cement German-Italian relations when they beat all the Alfas in the year's closed-course Mille Miglia – and then Italy too went to war. Vehicle development was in an advanced state at Mercedes, Auto Union and Alfa Romeo for the $1\frac{1}{2}$-litre supercharged Formula which had been expected to start in 1941 – but by that time their industrial duties lay elsewhere.

Postwar revival

Europe was shattered by six years of war but everywhere its peoples were hungry for sporting spectacle. By its nature motor racing was less likely to be revived early than almost any other major sport, but the enthusiasm of its followers quickly set the wheels rolling. In different circumstances France would have been celebrating the 50th anniversary of that first great Paris–Bordeaux–Paris race, but just one week after the Japanese surrender was signed they ran the first postwar circuit race – in the Bois de Boulogne on 9 September 1945.

Three races featured at this *Coupe de Paris* meeting, the first falling to Franco-Italian engineer Amedée Gordini in his Simca-Fiat special. Henri Louveau won the *Coupe de la Liberation* in a Maserati and then the twice pre-war Le Mans winner, Jean-Pierre Wimille, averaged over 112 km/h to win the *Coupe des Prisoniers* feature event in his 4·7-litre *Monoplace* Bugatti.

In Italy work was revived on the potent Maserati

Top right : Mercedes cars at the 1937 AVUS Grand Prix.

Upper right : Rosemeyer in an Auto Union chasing Lang's Mercedes in the Donington Park Grand Prix, 1937.

Centre right : Von Brauchitsch in a Mercedes at the Nürburgring.

On the right is the British driver, Richard Seaman, after he won the German Grand Prix in 1938.

and Alfa Romeo voiturettes which had raced so effectively prewar and right at the close of the year a minor hillclimb was run at Naples. During 1946, Europe's first full postwar racing season, there were 17 major meetings. Most were run on town circuits easily accessible to a public starved of petrol and private transport. Paris, Marseilles, Nice, Perpignan, Nantes, Dijon and Lille all had their motor racing, while the Belgians packed into Brussels' Bois de la Cambre or went to Chimay, where Englishman Leslie Brooks won in his ERA. The Italians walked or boarded trams to attend races in the Valentino and Sempione Parks in Turin and Milan. The Spaniards flocked to Barcelona for the Penya Rhin GP and the Swiss to Geneva for the *GP des Nations* in the grounds of the so-called Peace Palace.

All the winning cars and drivers bore famous prewar names. The 16-valve Maserati voiturettes which had shone prewar were winning along with the 3-litre Grand Prix Alfa Romeo 308 and the Belgium airfield experiment was important. The Royal Automobile Club took note, and were soon to have their own permanent airfield-based Grand Prix circuit to replace the Donington Park and Crystal Palace road courses lost to them during the war.

The Isle of Man and Ulster, however, fell outside these restrictions, and Britain's first postwar road race was organized by the Ulster Automobile Club on 10 August 1946 at Ballyclare. There the Anglicized Siamese Prince 'Bira' beat Parnell by one second in his ERA. As in continental Europe the races were run to a free formula. If it had wheels and an engine it could race – and did.

During 1947 this happy-go-lucky type of racing continued while the Swiss, Belgian and Italian GPs were revived at Berne's magnificent Bremgarten course, at Spa-Francorchamps and in Milan, where

repair work still had to begin on war-damaged Monza. The *Alfetta* was all-conquering, notably when driven by Wimille, and it was announced that the sport's reconstituted international governing body, the *Fédération Internationale de l'Automobile* (FIA), would enforce a formal GP Formula from 1948. It was logical to base their choice on existing cars and experience. The prewar 3-litre supercharged GP cars were mostly locked away in ruined Germany or hidden in what had now become Iron Curtain countries. There was no shortage of $4\frac{1}{2}$-litre unsupercharged GP cars, nor of $1\frac{1}{2}$-litre supercharged voiturettes, so these limits were chosen as the postwar Formula.

The larger disparity between $4\frac{1}{2}$ litres unsupercharged and $1\frac{1}{2}$ litres supercharged was to prove much better balanced than had been the 1938–9 Formula. The unblown cars were reliable and could cover a 500 km (312 mile) GP distance non-stop, while the blown $1\frac{1}{2}$s were very much faster but more highly-stressed and they required at least one, and maybe two, refuelling stops to go the distance. This provided some close and exciting tortoise-and-hare contests, but never so close as to shake the Alfa Romeo works team's stranglehold.

Alfa, Maserati, the new Ferrari *equipe* and the ancient British ERAs turned out to represent the supercharged class while Talbot-Lago relied on the ponderous economy of their $4\frac{1}{2}$-litre unblown 6-cylinder engines. With Louis Chiron and Louis Rosier driving the big blue Lagos were good enough to win – unless Alfa Romeo were running.

Then, during the winter of 1948–9, Trossi died in a Milan cancer clinic and Wimille crashed fatally while practising a little Simca-Gordini in the Argentine. Their loss, added to the death of Varzi the preceding summer at Berne, left Alfa Romeo with-

Above: Alfa Romeo drivers at Silverstone, August 1950 – Fangio (seated) and Farina.

Right, from top to bottom: Farina's Alfa Romeo catches fire at the 1951 British Grand Prix, Silverstone, but swift action is taken.

Ascari in a $4\frac{1}{2}$-litre Ferrari in the 1951 French Grand Prix at Reims.

Parnell in a BRM at the 1951 British Grand Prix, Silverstone.

out drivers. The Portello management announced that they would withdraw from GP competition for the 1949 season.

Ferrari and the new star Alberto Ascari, son of Alfa Romeo's 'twenties driver, Antonio Ascari, dominated the Alfa-less season with new V12-engined cars; when they failed the ageing and by now grievously overstressed Maserati 4-cylinder, 16-valve machines took the honours.

The World Championships

For 1950 the FIA instituted for the first time their World Championship for drivers. There was a constructors' championship too, but it was the new driver competition which captured the public imagination. The cult of personality swept motor racing, and as the years passed the major manufacturers slipped away from Grand Prix racing, realizing that it was now the name of the man, not the machine, that stole headlines. They turned instead towards endurance racing with the Le Mans 24 Hours, revived postwar in 1949, as the most prestigious prize of all – and to rallying, in which the Monte Carlo Rally was the big promotional bonanza where success was rewarded by massive publicity and increased sales.

The first World Championship GP was the British event, held on the RAC's Silverstone airfield circuit on 13 May 1950 and won by Dr 'Nino' Farina in an Alfa Romeo Tipo 158. British interest in motor racing at all levels was beginning to grow, and Raymond Mays and Peter Berthon launched a national industry-sponsored GP project named BRM (British Racing Motor). This frighteningly ambitious project was based upon a 1½-litre 16-cylinder engine with Rolls-Royce aviation-style centrifugal supercharging. It was to prove the most powerful racing engine for its size ever built, though it suffered problems which BRM's organization found insuperable. BRM failed, but the enormous publicity it enjoyed between 1945–51 put motor racing on the map in Britain, and that was to prove significant.

Meanwhile the GP Formula which had existed since 1948 had continued to run through 1953, but after Ferrari's unsupercharged 4½-litre V12 cars finally gained the ascendancy over Alfa Romeo's ageing 158/159 series cars in 1951 the historic Italian marque withdrew – with the first two World Championships to their drivers Farina and the Argentinian Juan Manuel Fangio. BRM could not guarantee to start their troublesome V16, and Formula 1, as the GP class was now known failed, largely because Ferrari had no serious competitors.

Right : Leslie Johnson in a 5-litre ERA in the 1948 British Empire Trophy race.

Far right : Alberto Ascari (right) and Giuseppe Farina.

Since 1948 an unsupercharged 2-litre voiturette class had been established, known initially as Formula B at which time GP events catered for 'Formula A', later to be popularly retitled Formula 2. When the GP class died at the end of 1951 the FIA allowed World Championship GP organizers to open their entry lists to F2 cars. The result was two years of World Championship Formula 2 racing in 1952–3, both totally dominated by Ferrari, for whom Ascari took two consecutive world titles.

The new Formula 1 announced for 1954–7 then catered for 2½-litre unsupercharged cars or for only 650 cc supercharged. Weight was free and the regulations attracted the might of Mercedes-Benz plus the Italian Lancia concern, a horde of British outfits and the inevitable Ferrari and Maserati establishment. The Italian concerns had played the lead and a very good second fiddle during the Formula 2 years. Meanwhile, however, the growth of British interest – and of sports and production car racing in Britain – should be examined.

Britain and the growth of motor racing

Prewar there had probably been fewer than three dozen purpose-built racing cars in the British Isles, but postwar British interest in motor racing was immense and dynamic. From 1946 a vigorous 500 cc racing movement grew from the Bristol area of England, using motorcycle engines mid-mounted in sketchy four-wheeled chassis and driving by chain to the rear axle. The Cooper Car Company, headed by former mechanic Charles Cooper and his driver son John, came to dominate the class and Britain suddenly found herself with the most effective driver training school in the world. Stirling Moss and Peter Collins were two 500 cc graduates who assumed world class. Other small concerns sprang up and, tackling Formula 2 racing before it gained great prominence, then found themselves in the Grand Prix arena virtually by accident. HWM and Connaught were two such teams, and Cooper went on to build front-engined cars using Bristol power for Formula 2. One of these cars started Mike Hawthorn on the way to world fame and to a GP-winning place in the Ferrari works team.

Britain was not alone in developing a schoolroom class of single-seater racing but the 500 cc movement was by far the most vigorous and best-supported of those that sprang up. Eventually, with cars being built in France, Germany, Sweden and Italy, the 500 cc division won international recognition as Formula 3. Other purely national Formulae gained acceptance in individual countries – like the 1,100 cc 'circus' promoted by the Cisitalia concern in Italy immediately after the war – they attained little international significance.

Sports car racing

Apart from the specialized single-seater classes, sports car racing flourished and increasing attention was paid to racing production cars. Most of the interwar speedways had seen races and trials for production touring cars, while between 1922–5 the French Touring Car Grand Prix accompanied the *GP de l'ACF* as a supporting event. Classes catered for two-, four- or five-seat cars, ballasted to represent the weight of passengers. A fuel consumption Formula was enforced and though the class was nominally for standard cars such specials appeared as the 1924 Peugeots with retractable headlamps and faired rear wheels. Streamlining was common and as the Le Mans 24 Hours gained in stature the Touring Car GP was allowed to die. Similar events at Monza,

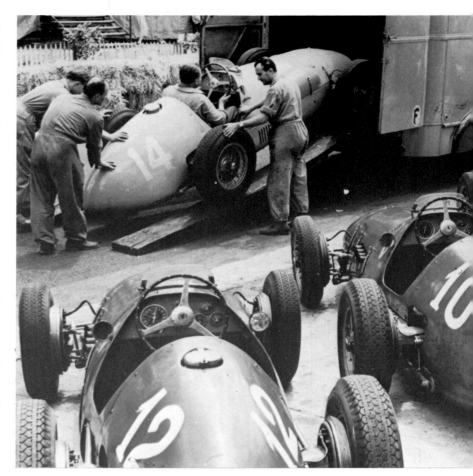

San Sebastian and Spa also died or, like Le Mans, evolved into sports car events. The 1930s, in fact, had been virtually devoid of competition for standard family cars.

When Le Mans was revived in 1949 with a prototype class 'to encourage the return of normality' the door opened to very specialized cars which were virtually GP designs with enclosed wheels, offset driving positions and lighting sets. When a World Sports Car Championship was instituted in 1953 such racing giants as Ferrari, Jaguar, Lancia, Aston Martin, Mercedes-Benz and Maserati competed for the prestige title keenly. Sports cars entered the 1950s as open cockpit roadsters which could be driven to and from the circuits. They ended the decade as purebred racers impractical for normal road use.

British production car racing was revived at Silverstone in 1949, when the British Racing Drivers Club (BRDC) and the *Daily Express* newspaper combined to run a one-hour race for the type. Jaguar domi-

Top: The Ferrari team cars lined up before the start of the 1952 French Grand Prix at Rouen.

Above: The HWM team at the pits in the 1950 Swiss Grand Prix (Formula 2) at Berne.

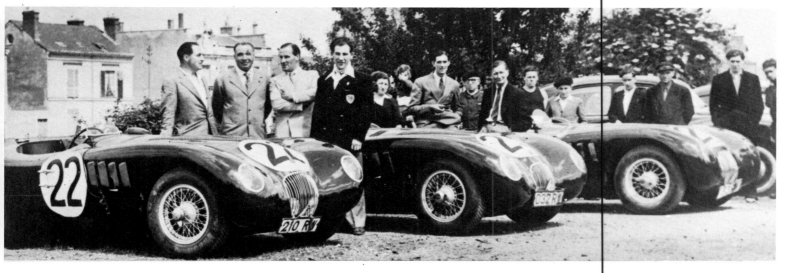

Top: Major P. K. Braid's 500 cc Cooper came to rest on the roof of a military guardroom after a freak crash in the 1949 Blandford Road Race, Dorset.

Above: The Jaguar XK120C line-up for the 1951 Le Mans 24-Hour. Stirling Moss is fourth from the left.

nated the event with three new XK120 roadsters, but the huge Silverstone crowd loved the antics of the overdriven standard saloon cars chasing the Jaguars. Thereafter production car racing became a popular feature of major international meetings in Britain and gained prominence at club racing level, where meetings on airfield circuits and new permanent road racing tracks, such as Brands Hatch, Kent, proliferated. On the Continent enthusiasts who had been hillclimbing progressed to circuit racing, sometimes on airfields but more often on shortish public road loops which could still – and *can* still – be closed for racing.

In the early 1960s an extremely complex European Touring Car Challenge series was initiated, subdivided by engine capacity and producing a European touring car champion driver rather than a manufacturer. This was progressively modified into the European Touring Car Championship for manufacturers in which notably Alfa Romeo, Ford (Cologne) and BMW (Munich) became locked in

battle. Qualifying races included the Six Hours Race at the Nürburgring and a revived 24 Hours at Spa, and for a brief period in the early 1970s major manufacturers invested a great deal of money trying to win this now prestigious title.

Another European championship which blossomed forth, then faded, was the Mountain Championship for hillclimb cars. Using classic long-distance point-to-point mountain climbs, established mostly in the interwar years, this series became a battleground between Porsche and Ferrari during the 'sixties. In recent years however, this particular competition has lost all of its inter-marque significance and become instead a private owner's hunting ground.

Grand Prix Racing, 1954–65

The highest level of motoring competition underwent extreme change in these 11 years. The international single-seater Formulae applied were as follows:

1954–7 Capacity limit of 2½ litres unsupercharged or 750 cc supercharged, weight optional. Races to last minimum 3 hours or 500 km (312 miles). Formula 2 suspended.

1958–60 Capacity restrictions continued, racing fuels barred, use of 100-30-octane aviation grade 'AvGas' compulsory. Race distance cut to 300 km (180 miles) or minimum 2 hours. New unsupercharged 1½-litre Formula 2 introduced.

1959 Production-based single-seater Formula Junior introduced, 1,100 cc push-rod engines, weight minima 360 kg (793 lb) with 1-litre engine or 400 kg (882 lb) with 1,100 cc.

1961–5 New 1½-litre unsupercharged Formula 1 replaced old 2½-litre class. Commercial fuel. Minimum weight 450 kg (990 lb). Enveloping bodies banned. Onboard starters and roll-over driver-protection obligatory. Formula 2 suspended, Formula Junior continued until 1963.

1964–6 New 1-litre Formulae 2 and 3 introduced, replacing Junior. F2 allowed free design racing engines while F3 demanded only production-based push-rod units, subsequently extended into 1971.

When the new Formula 1 took effect in 1954 Ferrari, Maserati and Lancia were all prepared to maintain Italy's dominance in Grand Prix racing, but halfway through that season Mercedes-Benz entered the field, and after winning on their debut in the French GP at Rheims they proved their fuel-injected 8-cylinder W196 cars to be superior. Juan Fangio took the World Championship, having started the season with Maserati, but taking up a lucrative Mercedes contract midseason with victory at Rheims.

During 1955 Mercedes-Benz were virtually untouchable, Fangio notching his third GP title in five years and their GP-based 300SLR sports cars also took that World Championship to Germany. Stirling Moss proved capable of keeping the Argentinian master in sight in the GP cars, and was far more effective in Mercedes' sports car outings, where he won the Mille Miglia, the RAC TT and the Targa

Florio. At Le Mans that season a 300SLR driven by the Frenchman Pierre Bouillin, under the pseudonym 'Levegh', crashed into the crowd, killing himself and 86 spectators and injuring many more. This calamity had a far-reaching effect as circuit safety standards were intensely scrutinized. Many events were cancelled and the Swiss Government promptly placed a total and irrevocable ban on circuit racing in their country.

Having proved their technical dominance, Mercedes-Benz withdrew at the end of 1955 and the last non-Championship race of that season, at Syracuse in Sicily, saw the Maserati works team humbled by Tony Brooks' British-built Connaught. It was the first all-British victory in a European GP race since Segrave's Sunbeam had won at San Sebastian in 1924. The British were encouraged, and while Fangio won 'his' World Championship yet again in 1956 (driving Ferrari) the British Vanwall team became competitive. They enjoyed the technological skills of the Vandervell Products bearing company and in 1957, with Moss, Brooks and another 500 cc graduate named Stuart Lewis-Evans driving for them, they began to win Championship GP events. In 1958, Fangio took his last Championship, for Maserati, before retiring, but Vanwall's men fought furiously with the Ferraris, driven notably by Mike Hawthorn. Into the last race at Casablanca the Championship lay between Hawthorn and Moss in the Vanwall. The result gave Ferrari's Hawthorn the Drivers' Championship, while Vanwall's Moss missed the personal title by one point but gave his team the prestigious Constructors Championship. Tragically Lewis-Evans was burned to death in this race and Vanwall withdrew from competition that winter.

These 1958 cars were the ultimate expression of the classic front-engined GP design idea. In Britain the Cooper Car Company had developed 2-litre Formula 2 versions of their sweepingly successful mid-engined F3s in which the power unit was mounted between the driver's cockpit and the rear

Top left: Works Connaughts at the 1956 International Trophy meeting, Silverstone.

Top right: Fangio's Mercedes in the 1954 Spanish Grand Prix.

Above left: Mike Hawthorn in the 1958 French Grand Prix.

Above right: Stirling Moss in a Lotus-Climax leads Richie Ginther in a Ferrari at Monaco, 1961.

Right: Moss driving a Vanwall to victory in the 1957 Italian Grand Prix at Monza.

axle. Tackling their first few F1 events in 1957–8 they found the chassis nimble and speedy. All they lacked was competitive power from their proprietary Coventry-Climax engines.

When the AvGas fuel restriction and shorter races were decreed for 1958 the small lightweight Coopers could run nonstop with no fuel capacity handicap. When full 2½-litre Climax 4-cylinder engines became available to Cooper they put the front-engined cars to flight. Australian team leader Jack Brabham won the 1959 Championship for Cooper Cars and repeated the feat in 1960, when BRM, Lotus and even conservative Ferrari introduced their own mid-engined cars.

Within three short seasons Grand Prix dominance had swung from Italy to Britain, where specialist chassis-buiiding teams were using engines and transmissions built on a proprietary basis by outside concerns. BRM were struggling on with their own engines and transmissions, but now Maserati were out of racing and while Ferrari built every major part of the cars they raced they did not see which way the British went. Italy had also lost all its great drivers. Ascari was killed in 1955, Castellotti in 1957 and the last of their champions, Luigi Musso, in 1958. English-speaking drivers like Moss, Brooks,

Hawthorn, Brabham and the Americans Phil Hill and Dan Gurney were the new aces.

That final season of 2½-litre racing in 1960 had been run under a bitter political cloud, for the newly successful British were upset about the forthcoming 1½-litre Formula for 1961. Ferrari had a potent V6-cylinder F2 design running reliably and it was now outpacing the modest 4-cylinder Climax F2 cars which had dominated the class in the days when Cooper's tenets of practical simplicity had triumphed over science and sophistication.

But 1961 was to see Ferrari triumph in the World Championship, which Phil Hill won after his rival team-mate, Wolfgang von Trips, was killed in the deciding GP at Monza. The British had tried to prolong 2½-litre racing with an Intercontinental Formula which was to die after one mediocre season. The production of new 1½-litre F1 engines by Coventry-Climax and BRM invigorated the new style of Grand Prix 'special builders', Lotus displacing Cooper at their head.

Graham Hill and Jim Clark fought a season-long battle through 1962 for BRM and Lotus-Climax

respectively. In the last race of the season, at East London, South Africa, Hill and BRM gained the titles. In 1963 it was Clark's turn and in 1964 Hill/ BRM, Clark/Lotus and John Surtees/Ferrari stood to win the Championships in the last race of the season at Mexico City and the British ex-motorcycle champion and his Italian team did so. The final season, 1965, saw Clark and Lotus win the concluding 1½-litre World Championships again.

The tracks

As seen by mention of the South African and Mexican GPs, the Formula 1 World Championship had spread far beyond its European origins, and the 'world' title had become more meaningful.

At the start of the 2½-litre Formula in 1954 there had been eight Championship-qualifying GPs, half of them run on artificial circuits. The series began in the Argentine, then progressed through Belgium, France, Germany, Britain, Switzerland and Italy to Spain. The Buenos Aires circuit was laid out in one of the city's sports parks; Britain's venue was the famous airfield perimetre track at Silverstone; Germany used the unbelievable 22-km (14-mile) artifi-

cial course at Nürburg, in the Eifel Mountains and, of course, the Italian GP was based at Monza.

The other four circuits were closed public roadways, in the grand old tradition but far shorter and more modest in conception. Belgium's Circuit National de Spa-Francorchamps comprised a very fast triangle of undulating roadways high in the Ardennes hills and measuring 14 km (8·76 miles) to the lap. The Champagne circuit of France, at Rheims-Guex, was flatter, straighter and faster. It formed another classic triangle, with a lap of 8·3 km (5·16 miles), and the 1950s saw intense rivalry between the French and their Belgian neighbours as each side fought to make their circuit faster than the other's. In 1954 Fangio's Mercedes won at Rheims, averaging 186·5 km/h (115·9 mph) for the 506-km race as against his Maserati average over the same distance at Spa of 186·32 km/h (115·8 mph). While his Spa fastest lap had been accomplished at 191·5 km/h (119 mph), Mercedes-Benz team-mate Hans Herrmann took the honours at Rheims with a blistering 195·33 km/h (121·4 mph). By comparison the supposedly superfast Monza track and road circuit outside Milan yielded Fangio a race average of

Above left : Jim Clark on a victory lap in his Lotus-Climax after winning the 1964 British European Auto Racing Grand Prix at Brands Hatch at an average 151·5 km/h (94·14 mph). Graham Hill (BRM) was 2nd, John Surtees (Ferrari) was 3rd.

Above : Stirling Moss in a Lotus challenging Ginther in the 1961 Dutch Grand Prix at Zandvoort.

Top: Hill and his Lotus beside the track as Clark rushes by in the 1962 Rand Grand Prix. 'The engine just stopped', was Hill's laconic explanation.

Top right: Jack Brabham won the World Championship with Cooper cars in 1959 and 1960, and with his own Brabham Repco in 1966.

180 km/h (111·9 mph) and Gonzalez took fastest lap for Ferrari at 187·6 km/h (116·6 mph). These men were faster on the public road . . .

The Nürburgring was a unique circuit. Built during the mid-'twenties depression in Germany and intended as a measure to bring employment to a deeply deprived area of the nation, its two circuits, the 22-km (14-mile) *Nordschleife* and a much more modest *Südschleife*, looped around the Eifel mountain tops in a more dramatic manner than its near neighbour across the Belgian border at Spa.

The total combined distance of the two Nürburgring courses was 28·3 km (17·58 miles) and the whole circuit had been used for the first German GP – second of the national series – held there in 1927. From 1931 only the *Nordschleife* was used for the GP races until in 1960 the *Südschleife* was revived for a one-off Formula 2 GP designed to give the Porsche team a win on their home soil.

For many years the Nürburgring and Monaco were to remain yardsticks of prewar and postwar Grand Prix performance until the safety campaigns of the 'seventies first modified the Ring almost beyond recognition and finally saw it banned for Formula 1 use. The process was more an insight into the motor racing politics than a commentary on the circuit itself. As it was, in 1954 the Nürburgring fastest lap fell to Mercedes-Benz driver Karl Kling at 137·9 km/h (85·7 mph).

Slowest circuit of the Grand Prix series for many years was the 'jewel of the Mediterranean', Monte Carlo, where round-the-houses circuit racing had started in 1929. This tight 3·145-km (1·95-mile) circuit saw some truly classic Monaco Grand Prix races from 1929–36, then in revived form in 1948 and 1950 and from 1955 to date. During the 'fifties the Monaco course provided another pre- and post-war measure of comparison, but in the 'seventies it too has changed, although its essentially slow speed and glamorous nature keep it acceptable to the motor sport's powers-that-be.

On its 2½-litre Grand Prix debut in 1955 the Monaco course was lapped at 110·5 km/h (68·7 mph) by Fangio's Mercedes-Benz, and his figure compared with Rudolf Caracciola's prewar lap record, set in a 1937 Mercedes, at 107·48 km/h (66·79 mph).

In 1957 the Nürburgring saw a rivetting race between Fangio's lone Maserati and the two young Englishmen, Hawthorn and Collins, in their Ferraris. Fangio left the lap record at 147·2 km/h (91·5 mph) which compared with the prewar figure of 137·8 km/h (85·62 mph) established by Rosemeyer's 6-litre Auto Union in 1937, the advantage of ten more cylinders and 3½ more litres having been offset by 20 years' tyre and chassis development.

By the end of the 2½-litre Formula in 1960 McLaren's Cooper established the Monte Carlo lap record at 117·6 km/h (73·1 mph), and the final 2½-litre Nürburgring record had been set in 1958 by Moss's Vanwall at 149·5 km/h (92·9 mph).

The 1½-litre Grand Prix cars, their British critics vigorously claimed, would provide only the saddest shadow of their 2½-litre counterparts' performances, but in 1961 this premise looked shaky as Moss's obsolete 4-cylinder Lotus and Ginther's new V6 Ferrari lapped Monaco in 1 min 36·3 sec, compared with McLaren's 2½-litre record time of 1 min 36·2 sec. At the Nürburgring Phil Hill, for Ferrari, demonstrated how potent the new mid-engined 1½-litre cars could be as against a three-year-old front-engined record. His fastest lap was 152·7 km/h (94·9 mph). Hill's 8 min 57·8 sec simply shamed Moss's 9 min 9·2 sec.

Enormous strides in tyre development and suspension design contributed much to such improvement, and by the end of the 1½-litre Formula in 1965 the Monaco lap record was down to 1 min 37·7 sec, 123·6 km/h (76·8 mph) and stood to Graham Hill's credit in the BRM, while at the Nürburgring Jim Clark's Lotus had taken the record down to 8 min 24·1 sec, 162·8 km/h (101·2 mph). Only a year before a 100-mph lap of the Nürburgring would have been considered unlikely. The introduction of broader tread 'doughnut' racing tyres had made this giant stride possible.

The World Sports Car Championship

From its inception in 1953 the World Sports Car Championship embraced the calendar's endurance races. In original form it had begun with a twelve-

hour race around the perimeter, track and runways of the Sebring airfields, in Florida, USA, and had included the Mille Miglia – last of the city to city races – the Nürburgring 1,000-km, the 1,303-km (810-mile) handicap TT in Ulster, 24-hour races at Le Mans and Spa and the remarkable Carrera Panamerica in Mexico. This was even more of a throwback than the Mille Miglia, for it was purely a stage-by-stage, point-to-point from one end of Mexico to the other. That 1953 Championship saw Ferrari win in Italy, Belgium and Germany; Jaguar taking Le Mans; Aston Martin the TT; Lancia the Carrera and the American Cunningham team their own Sebring 12 Hours.

Sports cars with top drivers ran in many minor non-championship events and most major international meetings offered supporting events which included sports cars and often production-car racing.

Ferrari dominated the 1954 Championship, were humbled by Mercedes in 1955, then reigned supreme from 1956–8. Aston Martin, aided by Moss's superlative skill, took the title in 1959, by which time Jaguar had five prestigious Le Mans victories to their credit, Maserati no longer fielded works teams and the Mille Miglia and the Carrera had come to an unfortunate end.

Piero Taruffi won the last Mille Miglia round Italy in his Ferrari in 1957, when the Marquis de Portago's sister works car crashed, killing driver, co-driver and several spectators.

The Portago accident proved the high speeds of modern machines had now made this splendid but too dangerous race an impossibility.

Italian roads were far too busy to be easily closed or, once closed, adequately policed and protected. There were demands from many quarters for the Mille Miglia to be discontinued and the authorities had no alternative but to agree.

Even people like Count 'Johnny' Lurani, who had started in nine Mille Miglia races and finished in seven, winning his class three times and finishing second in his class three times, had to agree that the great race had had its day. The Carrera, too, fell victim to the march of time.

Quite apart from the top-ranking sports cars at the top of the Championship league, many of which – like the 4·5-litre V8 cylinder Maserati 450S for example – offered Grand Prix-grade performance, many manufacturers made their bread and butter by producing smaller capacity sports racers. This was how the Lotus company was launched in Britain, and as club level racing bloomed in Europe and across the western world many specialist concerns grew to supply raceworthy cars for the vast and growing demand.

From 1958 a 3-litre capacity limit was applied by the FIA on Championship sports cars but the breed of open-cockpit two-seat cars was dying as the title chase became a Ferrari-dominated bore. In 1962 the FIA switched their competition and split it into a bewildering series of capacity classes, offering a GT Championship for the type of roofed-in sports car which was rapidly developing.

At Le Mans the organizing *Automobile Club de l'Ouest* were not to take this change easily, and they led the Sebring, Targa Florio and Nürburgring 1,000-km organizers in establishing the *Challenge Mondial de Vitesse*, open to 'prototype' sports racing cars. In this way the exciting-looking open cockpit specials were perpetuated at top international level, and the 1962 Le Mans 24 Hours saw Phil Hill/Oliver Gendebien winning respectively their third and fourth *GP d'Endurance* and notching up the last major victory for a front-engined Ferrari, a 4·4-litre V12 'prototype'.

Ferrari developed open mid-engined cars from 1961–3 which, with sketchily roofed-in cockpits, became GT cars for 1964 so far as the firm was concerned. The FIA disagreed and refused to recognize, or 'homologate' them as such and a fearsome disagreement resulted between the governing body and the autocrat of Maranello, Enzo Ferrari himself. His temper was not improved by the American Ford V8-powered Cobra coupes winning the GT Championship in 1964, and when Ford (Detroit) entered Le Mans with their extremely sophisticated and well-promoted GT40s the stage was set for a bitter Ford-versus-Ferrari battle which characterized the classic endurance events of the mid-'sixties.

Ford succeeded at Le Mans at their third attempt, in 1966, using very powerful and reliable 7-litre production based V8-cylinder engines. Ferrari could run them close but not beat them with their 4·4-litre V12 racing-engined cars, and when Ford won Le Mans again in 1967 and the Texas Chaparral-Chevrolet won the BOAC Six Hours, ending the Championship at Brands Hatch, the Stars and Stripes flew high in Europe. While Ford won much

Top left : The winning Ferrari, Le Mans, 1963.

Top right : Porsche 917, victor at Le Mans, 1971.

Above left : Porsche 917/10 Turbolader.

Above right : Night scene at Le Mans, 1978.

Right : Porsche 908, introduced in 1968.

of the modern 'sports car' prestige at Le Mans, the Championship battle lay between Ferrari and the German Porsche company, who had contested every round. Porsche had developed from contesting the endurance race 2-litre classes year after year into producing progressively larger teams of larger-engined cars and they only lost the 1967 'International Championship for Makes' in that last race to Ferrari.

At Le Mans that year the winning Dan Gurney/A. J. Foyt 7-litre Ford Mk IV had averaged 217·9 km/h (135·48 mph) for the 24 Hours. The executive sporting body of the FIA, known as the *Commission Sportive Internationale* (CSI), hastily limited prototype sports cars to a 3-litre capacity, while so-called production sports cars, of which 50 minimum had to be built, were allowed a 5-litre limit. Ferrari abandoned sports car endurance racing in 1968, leaving a clear field for Porsche and the Gulf Oil-backed JW team Ford GT40s. Porsche lost Le Mans to the Fords and, determining to win this great prestige event, built on their overall Championship success of 1968 with their 3-litre *Typ* 908 cars. As the CSI

cut its 5-litre production requirement to 25 cars in 1969, the Stuttgart company developed a 4·5-litre flat-12 cylinder engine from proven components of their 3-litre flat-8 cylinder *Typ* 908. This fearsome power unit appeared in 25 extremely expensive and staggeringly potent streamlined 917 coupes. The CSI had set their 5-litre and 3-litre limits to equalize production-based and pure racing engines. Now Porsche had built and sold sufficient pure racing engines to qualify as a production design, and there was to be no holding them.

In 1970–71 the Porsche 917s did most of the endurance race winning while the determined German concern produced special lightweight 3-litre *Typ* 908/3 'roller skates' for use on the tighter circuits like the Targa Florio course and Nürburgring. Ferrari was back in the fray with a 5-litre V12 Tipo 512 and picked up some success, while the 3-litre racing-engined cars were GP designs in disguise from Gulf-Mirage and Alfa Romeo. When a sports Alfa Romeo won the Brands Hatch 1,000-km event in 1971 it was that company's first major Championship race victory since their great Grand Prix days in 1951.

Porsche won 'their' Championship and came to win Le Mans as well. The speeds of which the CSI

had always been so wary had spiralled alarmingly.

In 1971 Pedro Rodriguez/Jackie Oliver won the Spa 1,000 km in a Gulf-Porsche 917 (now run by the ex-Ford (John Wyer team) at an average of 248·9 km/h (154·7 mph)) and their equally brave and skilled Swiss team-mate, Jo Siffert, set fastest race lap in another 917 at 260·79 km/h (162·08 mph) – remember, on a loop of public roads! At Le Mans Rodriguez set fastest lap at 244·26 km/h (151·81 mph).

Thereafter the 5-litre class was dropped, a strict 3-litre capacity limit was applied and Championship sports racers became literally GP cars in enveloping bodies. Ferrari, Alfa Romeo and Matra-Simca, in France, built the main contenders and when Ferrari pulled out to concentrate on Formula 1 after 1973 and Matra-Simca retired in 1974, top class sports car racing was in the doldrums. The European 2-litre sports car Championship had flared into healthy and essentially private-owner-orientated life in 1970 but lacked spectator attraction. By 1975 that Championship had staggered into a string of cancellations and only a couple of actual races. Escalating costs killed off the American Can Am sports car series, whose free-formula unlimited capacity antecedents in 1964–5 had proved faster than 1½-litre Formula 1 cars on some circuits, and the advent of super-expensive turbocharged Porsches in its European counterpart, the InterSerie, killed that too.

During 1975 Alfa Romeo's privately-run sports car team was left to win an unhindered Championship of Makes. The supposedly dangerous Targa Florio (in which five fatalities had occurred since 1906 compared with nearly 60 over the years at the younger Indianapolis 500 Miles track race) was dropped from the Championship after 1973 and many of the traditional 1,000-km races were also to be cut back.

Ignoring representations from the major sports car manufacturers, the CSI chose to promote a two-tier championship in 1976. One was for 'Group 6' sports racers, the other for 'Group 5' or 'Silhouette' class production cars. Turbochargers were allowed in both series, and while Alpine-Renault had ups and downs – they were beaten by Porsche and particularly Alfa Romeo in Group 6 – Porsche and BMW ran strongly in Group 5 with the former concern winning most of the races. Public interest in the class was now minimal. Meanwhile Le Mans had again trodden its own non-Championship path, with the autocratic ACO choosing a generally balanced and successful mix of both Groups which saved their 24 Hours classic from the regulation-bound extinc-

tion which had demolished the once great sports car Championship as a whole.

The 3-litre Grand Prix era

After the diminution of engine and car size and of races in general during the 1½-litre years, the CSI relented and established a 3-litre Formula 1 capacity limit for 1966–72. This Formula in much amended form has been with us ever since. It is the longest-lived GP Formula in history by far. It has witnessed the development of the most all-embracing set of regulations in history, the most basic change in the face of the sport and some of the best-supported, most competitive and fastest Grand Prix racing ever seen.

Whereas it was common for the Formula 1 field of the 1950s to comprise perhaps a dozen cars, setting off on a 500-km (312-mile) Grand Prix, the 3-litre era has seen as many as 35 cars attempting to qualify for up to 32 grid places in a race of only 250 km (155 miles) or some 90 minutes' duration. This recipe as packaged and sold in the countries of Europe, North America, South America, South Africa and recently in Japan, has proved very successful, though many die-hard enthusiasts decry the passing of what they see as 'proper' Grand Prix racing. From there being nine World Championship races in 1966, first year of the Formula, the class developed to support no fewer than 17 in 1977.

The highly enjoyable but insignificant non-Championship Formula 1 races had declined because of the extremely commercialized interests of the predominantly British-based teams involved in the circus. Most of these concerns turned to the Ford-initiated Cosworth DFV V8 engine for power, and the introduction of this unit in 1967 for exclusive use by Team Lotus, and its subsequent release for general F1 sale in 1968, caused near uniformity of performance, and therefore extreme competitiveness, in the sport. A fierce tyre war between Dunlop, Firestone and Goodyear, which had started in 1964, flared anew in the early years of the 3-litre Formula. Dunlop surrendered after 1970 and Firestone at the end of 1974, leaving Goodyear with a monopoly which lasted until Michelin entered the circus in 1978. The technological competition during this period, however, led to developments which shattered all speed records.

Jack Brabham's own team stole the honours in the first years of the Formula, when superior designs were being developed and his practical and simple Repco-Brabhams excelled. Thereafter Cosworth engines were predominant, Lotus and the cars which

Top left : Jack Brabham, who raced with great success in the late 1950s and 1960s. This photograph shows him in 1969.

Above : Emerson Fittipaldi on his way to victory in a Lotus in the 1972 Belgian Grand Prix at Spa-Francorchamps.

Above right : A Formula Ford race getting under way at Brands Hatch, 1977.

Right : Jody Scheckter in a Wolf Ford in the 1977 Monaco Grand Prix. His win marked the 100th World Championship victory for the Ford DFV engine.

Left : Jackie Stewart in his Matra Ford MS 80 after the start of the 1969 Dutch Grand Prix, Zandvoort, which he went on to win.

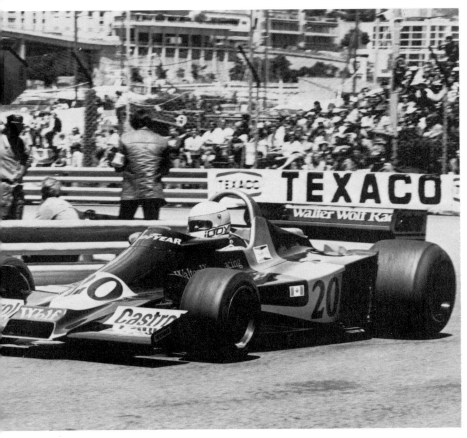

Jackie Stewart drove being ascendant, until Ferrari became the top team under the influence of their Austrian driver, Niki Lauda, from 1974–7.

Today Formula 1 racing is a healthy entirely self-supporting type of motor racing. Grand Prix racing has come a long way since 1906.

Other Formulae, 1964–77

When Formula Junior (devised by Count 'Johnny' Lurani) ended its competitive and desperately rough-and-tumble five-year career with the close of 1963 the two 1-litre Formulae (2 and 3) replaced it. The senior of the two catered for true specially designed racing engines, while the other was for production-based units allowed limited modification and was the logical successor to Formula Junior. Both were to become well supported in Europe, with British Cosworth-produced, Ford-derived engines dominating in British-built chassis. When a new

1·6-litre Formula 2 was introduced from 1967 the British-dominated *status quo* persisted. The 1-litre Formula 3 class – which had proved extremely successful and had provided close racing, and a searching school for budding drivers – continued until, in 1972, both 'rungs of the ladder' were modified once more. Then a 2-litre F2 class was instituted while a new 1·6-litre production-engined F3 came into being. The latter was far too restrictive in character and in 1975 was uprated to 2-litre capacity, though with more restrictive engine specification than 2-litre F2 and running on narrower tyres, by that time the great arbiter of racing car performance. In 1976 Formula 2 itself was liberalized and specially designed racing engines were admitted for the first time since the 1964–6 period.

Essentially F3 had formed the traditional bottom rung of the International single-seater racing ladder up which those with sufficient talent – or backing – could logically progress to Formula 2 and then – hopefully – into Formula 1. Until 1971 Formula 2 races were typified by the presence of star Formula 1 Grand Prix drivers, giving newcomers a chance to pit their skills directly against the established aces. In recent years the increasing pressures of the World Championship F1 calendar, and the growing reluctance of GP drivers to employ their expensive talents elsewhere, has taken much of the value and interest from F2 racing, now a province governed largely by French and German engines, often in British chassis.

MOTOR SPORT AROUND THE WORLD

Motor Sport Around The World – international colours

Between the two World Wars, the sport had been largely confined to Grand Prix racing, voiturette or light car racing, sports car racing (including dramatic battles on the open road like the Targa Florio and the Mille Miglia) and racing on closed tracks, built for the purpose, such as Brooklands (England), Montlhéry (France) and Indianapolis (USA). Rallies were rather more genteel than they were to become after the Second World War and, apart from the long established Monte Carlo Rally, attracted little public attention. It is probably true to say that in Europe, at least, hill climbs and reliability trials came next in popularity to racing. In the United States of America, racing was much more varied and a large number of spectators were attracted to the dirt tracks and midget car stadiums.

When the Second World War ended it naturally took some time for motor sport – requiring as it did not only men but machines, fuel and circuits – to resume. Formula Libre (open to any type of car) was frequently the form taken by motor racing.

Moss, reckoned to be the best man never to win the World Championship for Drivers.

Coopers too went on to greater things. The first international class records to be set in Great Britain after the Second World War fell to Wing Commander Freddie Sowery, driving a Cooper, and the marque eventually developed into a highly successful Grand Prix venture, with Australian world champion Jack Brabham and New Zealand's Bruce McLaren as their most famous drivers.

The comparatively affluent society which followed in later decades brought the introduction of many motor sport variations. Grand Prix/Formula One remained the headliner but rallying soared to new popularity and hot rods, drag racing, stock cars, buggy racing and a host of others, contributed to a very motor sport conscious world.

The following sections on motor sport deal with the main forms of competition prevalent on the Continent of Europe and in Great Britain and the Commonwealth, other than Formula One racing, and motor sport in the United States, Australia and New Zealand is covered in the Grand Prix chapter.

A significant development at this time was the introduction of 500-cc – or Half-Litre – racing. This was the brainchild of a man named Dick Caesar and some friends from Bristol (England). They constructed what were in the first place little homemade racing cars, usually using engines from motorcycles.

From the beginning in 1945, the '500' movement spread rapidly through the British Isles and on through France, Belgium, Germany, Italy (not surprising since Count 'Johnny' Lurani had been the first man to clock more than 100 mph in a 500-cc car), Switzerland, Scandinavia, Holland, Czechoslovakia and even to Australasia, South Africa and Singapore.

Cooper Cars, evolved by father and son, Charles and John Cooper, powered with JAP engines, were the backbone of the class although there were scores of other makes.

It is not putting too high a value on 500-cc racing to say that it saved motor sport from extinction in many countries. In time it developed into International Formula Three but, more importantly, it developed many drivers who were to make their names in higher realms of competition, the most prominent of them being the English driver, Stirling

International racing colours

Argentina	Blue, Yellow and Black
Austria	Blue, with silver stripe
Belgium	Yellow
Brazil	Pale Yellow and Green
Canada	Red, with a white stripe
Chile	Blue, Red and White
Cuba	Yellow and Black
Czechoslovakia	Blue, White and Red
Germany	Silver
Denmark	Silver Grey
Egypt	Pale Violet
Finland	White, with blue Latin cross
France	Blue
Great Britain	Green
Greece	Very Pale Blue, with two white stripes
Holland	Orange
Hungary	Red, White and Green
Ireland	Green, with orange band
Italy	Red
Japan	Ivory White, with red disc
Jordan	Brown
Luxembourg	White, with red, white and blue stripe

Overleaf: A Porsche Turbo 935, driven by Jost, Wollek and Barth in the 1978 Le Mans 24 Hours Race, at the bottom of the Mulsanne straight.

Top: A. F. Ashby was one of the leading drivers at Brooklands from 1927 onwards, the year that marked his first win. Here in 1930, because his car lost its oil pressure, he did not finish first.

Above left : Count Giovanni ('Johnny') Lurani in an MG Magnette, co-winner with G. E. T. Eyston of the 1100-cc class of the 1933 Italian Mille Miglia.

Above centre : John Cooper in 1948 driving one of the renowned 500-cc cars he designed and built in conjunction with his father, Charles. They then went on to build championship-winning GP cars.

Mexico	Gold, with blue cross
Monaco	White, with red band
Poland	White and Red
Portugal	Red and White
South Africa	Gold and Green
Spain	Yellow and Red
Sweden	Yellow and Blue, with three blue bands
Switzerland	White and Red
Thailand	Pale Blue and Yellow, with yellow band
Uruguay	Pale Blue, with red band
USA	White and Blue

Note : With the growth of sponsorship in motor sport, many cars, especially at international level, race in the colours of sponsoring organizations and, if they carry the national colours at all, it is usually in the form of a band on the bonnet, a stripe on the body or the national flag in sticker form.

International flag signals

RED: Complete and immediate stop

YELLOW (waved): Great danger – prepare to stop

YELLOW (motionless): Take care – danger

YELLOW with vertical RED stripes: Take care – oil has been spilled somewhere on the road

BLUE (waved): Another competitor is trying to overtake you

BLUE (motionless): Another competitor is following you very closely

WHITE: An ambulance or service car is on the circuit

BLACK (with competitor's number): Signal for the competitor to stop on the next lap

BLACK and WHITE diagonally divided (with competitor's number): Last warning to driver in connection with unsportsmanlike behaviour

BLACK/BLACK and WHITE chequered (shown together): No contest

BLACK and WHITE chequered: Signal for the winner and end of the race.

Light signals will be used for starting races.

Classification of cars (as at 1979)

The cars which compete in events under the regulations of the FIA (International Automobile Federation) are distributed in the following categories and groups:

Category A

Recognized production cars (numbers in brackets are those of the required minimum production in 12 consecutive months, except in Group 4 where the period of production is 24 consecutive months)

Group 1: Series production touring cars (5,000)

Group 2: Touring cars (1,000)

Group 3: Series production Grand Touring cars (1,000)

Group 4: Grand Touring Cars (400)

Group 5: Special production cars deriving from Groups 1 to 4

Category B

Group 6: Two-seater racing cars

Group 7: International formula racing cars

Group 8: Formula Libre racing cars

Grading of drivers

Since 1972, the FIA has graded racing drivers in two categories:

Grand Prix graded drivers (GP)

These comprise the World Champions of the previous five years; drivers who at least twice in a year finished in the first six of World Championship races (taking into account the previous two years); the winner of the Indianapolis 500 the previous year; the winner of the European Championship for Formula Two cars the previous year (providing he has had at least three first places in that Championship); and drivers who have finished once in the first six of a race counting for the World Championship of Drivers and once in the first three of an event counting for the World Championship of Makes (previous two years taken into consideration).

Drivers in this category in 1979 were:

Mario Andretti (USA), Vittorio Brambilla (Italy), Patrick Depailler (France), Emerson Fittipaldi (Brazil), Bruno Giacomelli (Italy), James Hunt (Great Britain), Jean-Pierre Jarier (France), Alan Jones (Australia), Jacques Laffite (France), Niki Lauda (Austria), Jochen Mass (Germany), Riccardo Patrese (Italy), Didier Pironi (France), Clay Regazzoni (Switzerland), Carlos Reutemann (Argentina), Jody Scheckter (South Africa), Hans Stuck (Germany), Patrick Tambay (France), Bobby Unser (USA), Gilles Villeneuve (Canada), John Watson (Great Britain).

Long distance graded drivers (LD)

These are drivers who, in one and the same year, have been classified at least twice amongst the first three in events counting for the World Championship of Makes (taking into account the previous two years).

Since in these events cars have more than one driver, grading qualification can only be earned by teams of not more than two drivers and that for the whole duration of the event.

Drivers in this category in 1978 included Brambilla, Jarier and Mass of the Grand Prix graded drivers plus the following:

Eddie Cheever Jnr (USA), Spartaco Dini (Italy), Egon Evertz (Germany), John Fitzpatrick (Great Britain), Giorgio Francia (Italy), Hans Heyer (Germany), Jacky Ickx (Belgium), Leo Kinnunen (Finland), Arturo Merzario (Italy), Dieter Quester (Austria), Manfred Schurti (Liechtenstein), Marc Surer (Czechoslovakia), Tom Walkinshaw (Great Britain) and Bob Wollek (France).

The 15 nations represented in the lists of graded drivers show the international nature of the sport.

Formula Two racing

Outside Formula One, Formula Two racing is generally regarded in Europe as providing the best and most exciting racing. This Formula has seen some great days: the time when Formula One foundered and Formula Two took over the Grand Prix series, for example; and great drivers: Britain's Mike Hawthorn, who became World Champion, and Austria's Jochen Rindt, only man to have been awarded the Championship posthumously, can be said to have been products of Formula Two racing. The pattern continues with most of the recruits to Grand Prix racing teams passing through the ranks of Formula Two drivers on their way to the top grade.

During the Seventies, the French have dominated the formula, partly due to the backing given to French drivers and cars by the giant Elf oil company. The 1977 European Champion was René Arnoux, driving an Elf-backed Martini-Renault. He won outright four of the 13 races in the series to clinch a title he had missed by just one point the season before.

Competing cars, under a formula due to be revised

at the end of 1978, are limited to 2,000 cc and super-chargers are not permitted. It provides truly international competition – of the 1977 championship rounds, four were held in Italy, three apiece in England and France, two in Germany and one in Portugal – and drivers of six nationalities shared the top ten places, thus slightly loosening the dominance of the French. Perhaps the most pleasing feature of the competition was that entries always exceeded the available number of starting places, thus ensuring a high-grade field in every race.

When any international motor racing formula draws towards the end of its prescribed life there is a tendency for manufacturers to draw in their horns for there is little point in spending large sums of money on development work on cars which may run only one season before being rendered useless by new formulae.

Despite this Formula Two seems, for a long time to come, to be sure of prospering and continuing as the No. 1 nursery for Grand Prix drivers besides being a first-class attraction in its own right. The 1978 schedule listed two more European Championship rounds for a total of 15, the circuits staging these events being Thruxton, Hockenheim, Nürburgring, Pau, Mugello, Vallelunga, Rouen, Donington, Nogaro, Pergusa, Misano, Magny-Cours,

Top and *Above left:* Formula 2 racing at Thruxton, Andover, in 1978.

Above centre: Ricardo Patrese at Monaco, 1978, in a Formula 1 Arrows with a Cosworth V-8 engine.

Above right: Kart racing at Silverstone in 1978.

Left: Mechanics working in the pits on the engine of a Formula 3 racer.

Zolder, Hockenheim again and, finally, Estoril.

Although the presence of Grand Prix drivers in Formula Two races undoubtedly helps the gate and gives lesser drivers something to aim at, the FIA make sure that the Formula continues to encourage up-and-coming pilots by limiting the number of Grand Prix (Category A) drivers in any one round to six, and by running a scheme giving priority of entry to Category B drivers. In this way it is hoped that the supply of Hawthorns and Rindts to Grand Prix racing will long continue.

Formula Three racing

The international Formula Three is also due for revision at the end of 1978. It caters for cars limited to 4 cylinders and with a maximum cylinder capacity of 2,000 cc. The main point is that the engine must be derived from a car model of which at least 5,000 have been produced in the past 12 months. Various performance restrictions are imposed on the engine in addition to the cylinder capacity. Wankel rotary engines are also permitted in this class of racing. Restrictions are imposed on the drivers too and

he hardly distinguished himself. But the late Carlos Pace, No. 1 driver for the Brabham team, began that way and so did some other Grade A drivers.

The 1975 and 1976 European Formula Three Champions, Australia's Larry Perkins and Ricardo Patrese have since raced in Formula One and two other stars of the formula in 1976, the Italian Bruno Giacomelli and Britain's Rupert Keegan, have also moved up the scale. The 1977 Champion, Piercarlo Ghinzani (Allegrini March 773) is another to watch for the future, as is the runner-up, Sweden's Anders Olofsson (Ralt RT1), both men being in their mid-20s.

Demonstrating also that single-seat racing has a sensible line of development – from karting to Formula 3, 2 and then Grand Prix racing – is the fact that three of the brightest young stars in Formula Three have come straight from the ranks of kartists. These are Nelson Piquet, Brazilian kart and Formula Vee champion, who finished third in the 1977 European Championship; Guiseppe Gabbiani (Italy) who won his second ever motor race, the

graded A and B drivers are not allowed to take part, thus leaving the field clear for the driver with his way to make in international racing.

The formula has had a somewhat chequered career inasmuch as in some countries other types of racing have gained a firm hold, often because of the availability of certain types of machine. For example, Formula Ford has played a great part in bringing along young British drivers as has Formula Vee (based upon the Volkswagen) in Germany and the Scandinavian countries and Formula Renault and Formula 2CV in France. Nevertheless, Formula Three has survived, has produced some good drivers and its importance to the scheme of things has been recognized by the FIA creating an official *European Championship*.

There is, indeed, every sign of a boom in this branch of the sport. Although competing has become a highly expensive business, the number of entries in 1977 reached an all-time high – more than 60 cars being entered for some of the 14 Championship rounds. The number of rounds increased with Belgium, Austria, Spain and Great Britain all holding events for the first time.

There are a number of modern Grand Prix drivers who never competed in Formula Three and although double World Champion Niki Lauda did so,

opening round of the championship; and Elio de Angelis (Italy), who won first time out at Monza.

But while Formula Three attracts the drivers and the entries, there must remain a question mark against it since, on its own, it has singularly failed to attract the paying public and seems only able to survive as a supporting event.

Karting

The sport of karting is said to have been born in California, USA, in 1956 where it was known as go-karting. When it was introduced to Great Britain three years later, it was found that there were certain contractual and copyright difficulties about the nomenclature 'go-kart' and so the controlling body of motor sport in Britain and the Commonwealth, the RAC, decided to describe it simply as karting. Under this name, the sport spread worldwide, even penetrating behind the Iron Curtain. By 1978, some 56 nations were said to be actively involved.

There are those who sneered at karting with remarks about 'children and toys' but the FIA and its constituent sporting bodies said that karting was undeniably a form of automobile competition since the vehicle used complies perfectly with the definition in the International Sporting Code of a land vehicle propelled by means of its own, running on at least four unaligned wheels, always touching the ground, of which at least two are used for steering, and at least two for propulsion.

But, said the FIA, the problems raised by karting, while being similar to the ones raised by normal motorcar competition, nonetheless appeared in a different light. So, in 1962, the FIA created the CIK, or International Karting Commission, to direct the sport. At the time of writing, 19 nations are represented on this commission: Federal Germany, Belgium, France, Great Britain, Greece, Japan, Italy, Monaco, the Netherlands, Sweden, Norway, Finland, Denmark, Poland, Portugal, Switzerland, Czechoslovakia and the USSR.

Karting has been described by some as 'poor man's motor racing' but certainly in recent years it has produced some drivers who have gone on to do well in more advanced forms of single-seater racing. It does, however, enable people to take part in motor sport at a relatively low cost. In Britain alone, 4,000 of the 32,000 competition licences issued annually are for karting and it is estimated that scores of thousands more take part in 'fun karting' in private grounds or on unlicensed tracks. The small size of the kart enables it to be easily stored (it can even hang on the garage wall) and easily transported (in a car boot – large version – or on a very small trailer or in a light van). Nor is a team of mechanics required since the engines weigh only between 4·5 kg (10 lb) and 29·5 kg (65 lb).

Karts are divided into different classes, some of which vary considerably from country to country. At the bottom of the tree are the promotional classes, those designed to provide an introduction to the sport at the lowest possible cost. In Britain this class is known as Class Britain (with Junior Britain for those drivers under 16 years of age); in France it is Classe Bleu (after the French racing colours); in Germany Klasse Silber (for similar reason); in Italy Classe Cadetti; and so on.

The middle area includes a variety of National classes aiming to provide full competition racing but with very expensive equipment barred. It is in the lower and middle categories that the countries involved differ most although a Formula Europe has been introduced which may eventually be adopted by all.

At the top level in all participating countries are the classes designed to provide the best possible competition between karts of given engine capacity and it is in these *International* classes that all the big championships, including the World and European events are held.

Both in national and international classes, engines run from 100 cc to 250 cc and in the international classes it is only at the lowest and upper limits that there are further restrictions. International 100-cc machines must have engines costing not more than 1,400 Swiss francs (£265) whilst the 250-cc engines are limited to 2,000 Swiss francs (£380). Engines of 100 cc are also restricted to one cylinder and a minimum weight of 120 kg (268·8 lb); 250 cc to two cylinders with a maximum of 28 mm per cylinder for twins and a minimum weight of 170 kg (369·6 lb).

Whereas when the sport began industrial engines were used – lawn mower engines for the lower classes – specialized engine production now takes place. By the same token, frames once of mild steel are now made of the best quality aircraft tubing.

The lower-powered karts do not normally have gearboxes but at the top end of the scale they have five-speed gearboxes which enable the engines to be tuned (and driven) like conventional racing cars.

Grand Touring, Touring, Saloon and Sports Car racing

Many devotees swear that racing in these groups is far more exciting than single-seater Formula racing. Certainly it can look far more exciting, with the cars closely bunched, heeling over as they go through the bends and altogether looking far less as if they are glued to the track or running on rails than the somewhat anonymous Grand Prix cars of modern times. Some of them are even faster than Grand Prix cars as times down the straight at Le Mans will testify.

However, constant changes in the rules and classifications have bedevilled the sport in these categories and a classic instance is the World Championship of Makes, Group 5 (special production cars deriving from Groups 1 to 4) being introduced as a World Championship category in 1976. In theory this meant even better racing with the Championship open to Groups 1–5 in two divisions: up to 2-litres and above 2-litres. Races run from 6 to 12 hours or one or two 6 hour heats entirely run in daytime (except for events already in existence and organized over a period exceeding 12 hours). The total of points obtained during the year is made up for each make per division, the highest total in one or other division being champion. There are restrictions on the amount of work which may be done in the pits and the parts which can be replaced. Three drivers per car may be nominated and drivers entered by the same competitor may act as substitutes for one another.

In practice, 1976 became a two-horse race between the German teams of Porsche and BMW and when the latter reduced their participation, the 1977 series became a Porsche procession. Ironically, with most of the cars in this category coming from Germany, the German National Championship was more hotly contested than the world title.

Nor has the world series brought about truly inter-Continental confrontation. For example, only one European car, Porsche, went to the United States for the Watkins Glen round of the championship in 1977. It won.

For 1978, the Championship embraced a 12-race series taking in Daytona, Mugello, Dijon, Spa, Silverstone, Nürburgring, Österreichring, Watkins Glen, Mosport, Vallelunga, Estoril and Hockenheim. With Porsche continuing to dominate (20 cars

Top : At the beginning of th Nürburgring Rally, 1974: Hans Stuck in a BMW 30C SL behind a Ford Capri RS 3100.

Above centre : A Group 1 Escort at Spa in Belgium.

Above right : Ronnie Peterson in a turbo-charged BMW at Silverstone, 1978.

Right : Two Group 5 Porsche Turbos at Silverstone in 1978.

out of a total entry of 37 in one race), hope for the future rested with possible participation of the Japanese Toyota, a revival of interest by BMW and public excitement at the participation of the 3·2 litre turbocharged Porsche.

The Championship has also suffered from a lack of name drivers, a situation which looked like righting itself with the emergence of exciting pilots like the Frenchman Bob Wollek and the Italian Ricardo Patrese to join the ranks of drivers like Jacky Ickx (Belgium), Jochen Mass (Germany), Henri Pescarolo (France) and Derek Bell and John Fitzpatrick (Great Britain) who have made a speciality of this type of race.

The World Championship for Sports Cars has had somewhat similar difficulties. In 1977 there were no competitors outside Europe so for 1978 it reverted to the *European Championship for Sports Cars*.

Open to Group 5 and Group 6 cars, divided into two categories according to size and type of engine, races have to be a minimum of 250 km or 2 hours. The championship goes to the driver with the highest number of points in either category.

The series was dominated in 1977 by Alfa Romeo, the red Italian cars winning all eight races. It was the second 'recent' world title for Alfa as a German-entered team had taken the championship in 1975.

For the public, the main thrill in 1977 resulted from the fact that Alfa, safe in the knowledge of victory, permitted their two top drivers, Arturo Merzario and Vittorio Brambilla, to fight it out between themselves as to who won. In the sequel, they emerged with four victories each but the spectators had enjoyed some thrilling racing in the clashes between the two Italian stars.

The secondary struggle was between the 2-litre entries, mostly from Italy and Great Britain. In fact, cynical comment was made that so far from being a world championship, the series was basically a European 2-litre championship.

The other main championship in this type of racing is the *European Championship for Touring Cars*, reserved for makes, with its accompanying *European Cup* for drivers.

This series is open to Group 2 touring cars with no upper limit on cylinder capacity but events are

divided into classes according to cylinder capacity. Races must last for at least $3\frac{1}{2}$ hours or have a minimum length of 500 km. Two drivers must share the wheel. As with the World Championship for Makes there are restrictions on the work which may be undertaken at the pits and the parts which may be replaced.

The 1977 series, a 12-rounder, was noteworthy for the reappearance of Jaguar, once the most famous name in saloon and sports car racing. But the British Leyland cars lacked reliability and in seven races managed only a second and fourth place.

The title went to an outstanding exponent of the art, the Austrian Dieter Quester (BMW) with a remarkable five wins, a second and a fourth, thus finishing in the first four in seven of the 12 races.

There were 13 qualifying events in 1978: Brands Hatch, Monza, Salzburgring, Mugello, Jarama, Estoril, Österreichring, Brno, Nürburgring, Zandvoort, Silverstone, Zolder, Paul Ricard, with two circuits in reserve – Pergusa and Donington.

Touring car (or saloon, the names are synonymous) races are often tremendously exciting, the cars going round 'door handle to door handle'. Most of the leading motor sport countries hold National Championships.

Le Mans 24 hours

There is a handful of motor sport events which transcend all groups and classifications. The names of these events have become household words, names known to the general public and meaning something even to those who take little or no interest in motor sport. This select little company includes the Indianapolis 500 Miles Race in the United States, the Monte Carlo Rally and Les 24 Heures du Mans, otherwise known as the Grand Prix d'Endurance.

As with the Monte Carlo Rally, Le Mans has sometimes been in the doldrums in the Sixties and Seventies yet it remains a race which has a strange fascination world-wide.

There are two myths about the event: it is *not* a Grand Prix, being open to production cars and prototypes (Grand Prix cars are, in fact, banned); nor was the first race held in 1921 and won by the American, Jimmy Murphy, in a Duesenberg. Murphy's victory was in the French Grand Prix which was held that year at Le Mans but it was this race which encouraged Georges Durand and Charles Faroux to organize the first Le Mans 24 Hours in 1923.

There were no final placings in that first event but 30 of the 33 starters finished, two Chenard et Walcker cars driven by Lagache and Léonard, Raoul Bachmann and Dauvergne, covering the greatest distance, 2,207·5 km (1,372 miles) in the case of Lagache. The fastest lap was put up by the lone British entry, a Bentley, driven by Duff and Clement, which clocked 108 km/h (67 mph).

The following year, the same Bentley was pitted against 39 French cars and this time it emerged triumphant. It was, perhaps, an omen for the pre-Second World War history of Le Mans was very much bound up with the Bentley marque, despite the fact that Ettore Bugatti is alleged to have once described them as 'the fastest lorries in the world'.

Le Mans went from strength to strength, the racing being only part of what would be called to-day 'a show business spectacular'. Crowds of half-a-million or more were and are attracted to this pastoral rendezvous, 320 km (200 miles) south-west of Paris where, once a year, the quiet country calm is blasted by the roar of mighty engines, 'les routes nationales' are closed to ordinary traffic and all the fun of the fair, sideshows, roundabouts and the like, spring up in the fields surrounding the circuit.

If Le Mans has been a Mecca for the French 'amateur' driver it has also been a happy hunting ground for the British, especially so in the years when British cars and drivers had not attained their recent pre-eminence in Grand Prix racing.

The legends of Le Mans are many. The vintage year of 1929 when the Bentley of Captain Woolf

'Babe' Barnato and Sir Henry 'Tim' Birkin led three stable companions across the finishing line, a 1–2–3–4 victory which did not eclipse the magic of the win scored two years previously by 'Sammy' Davis and Dr Benjafield when Davis extricated his Bentley from a six car pile-up at the White House and went on to victory.

The British drivers became famous as 'The Bentley Boys' and a colourful assortment they were in those halcyon days of the late Twenties: Davis was a journalist, Benjafield a medical specialist, George Duller a jockey, Jack Dundee a theatrical impresario – all amateur drivers but backed by the millions of 'Babe' Barnato and the Hon. Dorothy Paget.

Barnato and Rubin were the victors in 1928 but only after a tremendous struggle with the Chryslers who, with the Stutz team, had entered the lists on behalf of the USA.

In 1930, Bentleys faced the challenge of the illustrious Rudolf Caracciola in a huge 7-litre Mercedes but they won for the fourth successive year, Barnato and the ill-fated Glen Kidston being first and Watney and Clement second. It was a unique personal triumph for Barnato who had been at the wheel of the winning Bentley three years in a row.

The Bentley's day was done and although British drivers were to win again in 1931 – Birkin and Lord Howe – they were driving an Italian Alfa-Romeo. Alfa were to receive more laurels through Chinetti and his French co-driver, Etancelin, but there was a last flourish from Great Britain in 1935 when a Lagonda won in the hands of Luis Fontes and J. S. Hindmarsh. With war on the horizon it was to be 16 years before a British car won again – the Jaguar of Peter Whitehead and Peter Walker.

The race had been revived in 1949 and in 1950, war-torn France received a much needed boost when the Rosiers, father and son, piloted a Talbot to the chequered flag.

Above: Several of the cars competing in the 1978 Le Mans 24 Hours Race. The team of drivers for WMP 76 was Dacremont, Hoepner and Debais, No 3, a Renault Alpine, was driven by Jarier and Bell. The team driving No 20, a Cheetah, was Plastina, Luini and Grandjean. The No 7 Porsche, of the several Porsches entered for the race, was driven by Mass and Hayward.

Below right : The 1956 Le Mans was won by the Scottish racing team, Flockhart and Sanderson, in their Jaguar – the marque that won several times at Le Mans during that period.

The following year introduced many of the characters who were to play leading parts in the Le Mans story during the next decade or so. Apart from resulting in the first of a string of Jaguar wins, the race saw the advent of a team of Chrysler-engined Cunninghams, led by Briggs Cunningham; and there were no less than seven Ferraris, one driven by twice-successful Chinetti, another by Belgian bandleader Johnny Claes and two by women, Mme Simon, of France, and Betty Haig, of Britain. Moss, Fangio, Rolt, Hamilton and Macklin were other drivers with major roles still to play.

In 1952 there could well have been another French win for Talbot had not Pierre Levegh obstinately insisted on trying to complete the 24 hours single-handed. Instead the chagrined French, after leading their own race for 95 per cent of the distance, watched two German Mercedes, a British Nash-Healey, an American Cunningham and two Italian Lancias fill the first six positions.

Levegh's desire to win without a relief driver was to have further consequences. But first came another Jaguar success, Tony Rolt and Duncan Hamilton becoming the first men to win Le Mans at more than 100 mph. The Moss–Walker Jaguar was second and the Whitehead–Stewart car fourth, a 1–2–3 for the British marque being prevented by the American Cunningham of Fitch and Walters. Sadly Anglo-American, Tom Cole, was killed when his Ferrari somersaulted.

Rolt and Hamilton came within 4·8 km (3 miles) of winning again in 1954 but the honours went to a Ferrari driven by the burly Argentinian, Froilan Gonzales and his French team-mate, Maurice Trintignant, truly an international victory.

Unfortunately, 1955 was to bring about the greatest disaster in the history of motor racing, a disaster which could have so easily spelled the end of Le Mans just as de Portago's crash in the Mille Miglia sounded the death knell of that classic road race.

There was a tremendous entry. Jaguars had a team which included Rolt, Hamilton and the young Grand Prix star, Mike Hawthorn. Ferrari still had the French champion, Trintignant and a sensational young Italian, Castellotti. There were Aston Mar-

tins and Maseratis and Gordinis and a lone Lagonda. There was, above all, the Mercedes team, fresh from Moss's triumph in the Mille Miglia, and with their best drivers, Fangio and Moss, regarded everywhere as No. 1 and No. 2 in the world. Mercedes, impressed by Levegh's dogged efforts at Le Mans, also included the French veteran in their team.

For some 2½ hours it was a great race. Then Lance Macklin (Austin-Healey) was signalled into his pit. Behind him, Hawthorn, also bound for a pit stop, pulled out around Macklin before braking and, behind Hawthorn, Levegh came up at 240 km/h (150 mph). Levegh braked, lifted his hand in what many interpreted as a warning signal to those behind and collided with Macklin. There was an explosion. Levegh was hurled through the air, the engine of his car ploughed into the crowd. Scores were left dead, dying or critically injured.

Many there were not to know the full extent of the disaster until they read their newspapers next day. The race went on. Hours after the crash, the word came from Stuttgart to withdraw the two remaining Mercedes. The Jaguar of Hawthorn and Peter Collins continued to circulate smoothly for what in any other circumstances would have been hailed as a magnificent victory. It was blotted out by the memory of nearly 100 dead.

Le Mans, however, survived the disaster and the arguments which followed in which accusations were levelled at all and sundry.

Every year the crowds are still attracted to the Circuit de la Sarthe. Every year some of the world's most exotic racing machinery is forced to the limits of speed and endurance – aided these days by turbochargers. There is perhaps not so much national and team rivalry as once there was. The 1977 race was won by a Belgian, the former Grand Prix star, Jacky Ickx, in partnership with a German, Jürgen Barth and an American, Hurley Haywood. They were driving a Porsche. Second was a Mirage-Renault, driven by an Australian and a Frenchman.

In the Sixties and Seventies it has sometimes seemed that the drivers most prominent have been those who have never quite made the topmost rung of Grand Prix racing, or have been on the way down: the New Zealander Chris Amon, the American Masten Gregory, the afore-mentioned Jacky Ickx and the veteran Graham Hill, after a terrible crash in the United States Grand Prix. The more likely

Ray Allen was the first race winner in the category but the first real star to emanate from the Formula was the lanky Australian, Tim Schenken. Many others have followed, not least Formula One aces James Hunt, Jody Scheckter, Emerson Fittipaldi and the late Ronnie Peterson.

Less than a year after its innovation, Formula Ford made its debut in Austria and before long racing was taking place in some 20 countries and across four continents.

It is estimated that there are at least 250 Formula Ford cars in racing trim and events for them are taking place every weekend in some part of the world. The latest recruits are India and Malaysia. So popular is the class that 146 Formula Ford cars entered at the 1978 International Trophy meeting at Silverstone (England), so many that they had to be split into three groups for practice. The fastest 30 were then accepted and the next fastest 36 had to take part in a qualifying race to find six more cars to complete the field in the race proper. It is doubtful if there is such intense competition in any other branch of motor sport.

Formula Renault evolved from Formula France in 1969 when the giant Elf oil company, newly formed, decided to base a young and dynamic image on motor sport. Not surprisingly, Elf turned to France's biggest car manufacturer, Renault. Race meetings all over the country sprouted events for Renault 8s and then 12s and in short order the Formula became Formula Renault Europe as other countries displayed interest.

The Formula has been responsible for producing most of the leading French drivers of modern times, amongst them Laffite, Jarier, Arnoux, Tambay, Pironi and Prost.

The Renault 8 proved itself wonderfully adaptable for motor racing – it was the first mass produced car to be fitted with disc brakes in 1962 – and the Cup Gordini became a sought after prize.

When Renault turned their attention to Formula One racing with a car powered by a turbo compressed Gordini V6 engine, they looked no further than Formula Renault for their driver, Jean-Pierre Jabouille, who had made his racing debut in a Renault 8 Gordini in 1966. He was three times runner up in the French Formula Three Championship (1968, 1969 and 1971) and in 1976 became the European Formula Two Champion, winning at Rome, Mugello and Hockenheim.

Thirty-five years of age in 1978, Jabouille was not old for a Grand Prix driver (witness Fangio) but to Renault his biggest asset was that he had proved himself a driver who understood his car and could advise the technicians on what was going wrong and what was going right, tremendously important especially when a car is in its formative period.

Formula Vee (later followed by Super Vee) has also been a good proving ground for stars of the future. Apart from its native Germany, the formula has been very popular in the Scandinavian countries, especially Sweden where the Volkswagen has proved itself a handy car on snow and ice.

Formula Vee has been popular too in countries such as Brazil where it has helped the development of some Brazilian drivers who have 'emigrated' to Europe in recent years.

A comparative newcomer to the nursery grades is the Alfasud Trophy. The Alfasud, offspring of Alfa Romeo, is known as the family car that wins races.

At first it was the customers who took part in automobile events at the wheel of an Alfasud. The idea of a Trophy for appropriately modified Alfasuds

Above : Racing for the Alfasud Trophy. The first event took place in Austria in 1975, since which time there have been Alfasud Trophies awarded in France, Italy and Germany as well.

Left : Jean-Pierre Jabouille at Monaco 1978. His car marked the advent of turbocharged cars in Grand Prix racing.

answer is the Le Mans 24 Hours Race requires different qualities from a driver than the Formula One Grand Prix.

The Nursery grades

Karting apart, it is arguable that in post-Second World War circuit racing, three limited Formulas have played the most prominent part in acting as nursery schools for racing drivers. These are Formula Ford, Formula Renault and Formula Vee (for Volkswagens).

Ford was 'born' at the English circuit of Brands Hatch in 1967. The racing driver school, Motor Racing Stables, tired of novices blowing up expensive engines, fitted a standard Ford Cortina engine in a Formula Three car. This was so successful that the Ford Motor Company was approached for approval and help in setting up Formula Ford races. Jim Russell, head of the other main racing driver school in the United Kingdom, joined in and the Formula was under way. It remains popular and continues to be a proving ground for would be world champions.

was born in 1975 and tried out in Austria on the initiative of a former race driver, Hans Ortner. By 1977, there were Alfasud Trophies in Austria, France, Italy and Germany as well as the Alfasud Europa Cup.

Alfasud has brought a crop of new drivers into the limelight, amongst them Filippo Niccolini (Italy), Baronio (Italy), Michel Lemetayer (France), Georg Weber (Germany) and Hans Meier (Austria).

Ice racing

Ice racing, for obvious reasons, is not a worldwide activity but is extremely popular in Scandinavia, the USSR and other countries of Eastern Europe and in the New World, where film star Paul Newman became a 'convert'. It is probably true to say that this branch of the sport has produced more top rally rather than race drivers, nearly all the top Swedes and Finns of international rallying having experience of ice racing. About 30 cars take part in each race and as they pile into the first bend, neither spectators nor drivers can see much through a curtain of snow and ice. When accidents do happen it is usually because one or more cars have slid into the snow walls surrounding the track or have turned over on their roof.

The best tracks permit speeds of about 160–170 km/h (99–105 mph) and on ice that means that drivers must judge their speed into the next bend with split-second precision. On occasions when the snow walls have been frozen to ice, the drivers try to use them bobsleigh-fashion to pass their rivals. The tracks are usually about 1,500 metres in length with a straight of about 500 metres and three right-hand bends and two left. There is usually a small circular rink where the cars can be warmed up.

A great variety of cars is permitted – standard, GT and sports, all in different classes. At one time race and Formula cars also featured but lack of entries of this type caused their abandonment, at least in Sweden.

There is little in the way of special equipment on the cars – other than spiked tyres.

Hill climbs

Hill climbing is one of the oldest forms of motor sport in existence (hill climbs were featured in the Automobile Club of Great Britain's Thousand Miles Trial of 1900 and 1903) and between the wars many of the stars of international Grand Prix racing also took part in hill climbs. The French innovator, J. A. Grégoire; the Auto-Union ace, Hans Stuck Snr; and Rudolf Caracciola, the Mercedes star; all these and many more took part in the leading Continental events. Stuck, who lived to see his son, Hans Jnr, also become a Grand Prix driver, died in 1978. From 1924 to 1963, he had driven a great variety of cars, both in racing and hill climbs. He drove an Auto-Union to many pre-war hill climb victories and a BMW in post-war events. He won more than 400 victories in his long and illustrious career and was said to have turned down an offer from the USSR to set up a racing drivers' school there. (Twenty-seven Auto-Unions allegedly found their way to the USSR after the Second World War.)

In England, Shelsley Walsh was, and is, the most famous hill climb venue where once Brooklands track stars like Raymond Mays competed; in Scotland there was the equally famous 'Rest And Be Thankful' under the watchful eye of that most notable of motoring club officials, A. K. Stevenson, of the Royal Scottish Automobile Club. Hill climbing has been a regular feature of motor sport in the

USA also, where the Pike's Peak Hill Climb wound 14,110 feet up a mountain in Colorado.

In modern times, although hill climbs continue to be held, the advent of other forms of motor sport, some of them with more visual spectator appeal, has tended to overshadow the older form of competition.

In Great Britain, it remains a very healthy arm of motor sport with something like 100 drivers or more in contention at a dozen or so venues ranging from the famed Shelsley Walsh to the almost equally famed Prescott; Bouley Bay and Val des Terres in the Channel Islands; and Craigantlet in Northern Ireland.

There is an officially recognized FIA European Hill Climb Championship for Drivers, competitors being divided into two categories:
(A) Production Cars (Touring and Grand Touring) and
(B) Competition Cars (Special Production Cars and Racing Two Seaters).

The minimum average upward gradient of a hill climb course has to be 5 per cent and the minimum distance covered by each competitor 10 km (6 miles). If the course is less than 10 km then competitors must make two climbs.

At the end of the season, the top driver in Category A becomes Production Car Champion and the leading man in Category B, Competition Car Champion.

There is also an FIA Hill Climb Challenge Trophy which goes to the winner in the division of Category A from which the Production Car Champion did not come. In other words, if the outright Category A winner should be a touring car driver then the Challenge Trophy goes to the top man in the grand touring division, and vice versa.

The European Mountain Championship, as it was then termed, was instituted in 1930 when the racing category was won by Stuck in an Austro-Daimler and the sports class by Caracciola in a Mercedes-Benz. The last pre-war winner was Hermann Lang (Mercedes-Benz) in 1939 and the Championship was not revived until 1957.

One European champion could also claim the unofficial championship of the world. Edgar Barth was the winner in 1959 when, for the only time in its history, the Championship included the American Pike's Peak as one of the qualifying events.

Hill climbing is inherently safer than many other forms of motor sport but there have occasionally been fatalities, usually caused by cars overturning. Amongst those who have been killed in hill climbs are the only Italian champion, Ludovico Scarfiotti, who was also a prominent Grand Prix driver. Scarfiotti was European Hill Climb Champion in 1962 and 1965 but was killed at the Rossfeld Hill Climb in 1968. The worst accident in the history of hill climbs occurred at Château Thierry, France, in 1935, when

Top left: Hans Stuck Snr was one of the greatest hill-climbing exponents. Here he is seen in his 6-litre Auto Union on the Grossglockner hill climb in 1938.

Top centre: A 1930 double-12-type MG at the Northern Car Club Trials at Buxton.

Top right : Dennis Poore, in an Alfa Romeo, making BTD (best time of the day) at the Scottish hill climb, 'Rest and Be Thankful', in 1951.

Above : John Cobb in his Brooklands record-breaking Napier Railton at the Brighton Speed Trials during the period between the wars.

Cattaneo's Bugatti spun, skidded off the course and killed eight spectators.

The European hill climb season runs from April to September and there are 15 qualifying events in the Championship. Probably the most famous of all the current venues is Freiburg, scene of many great triumphs, but there is a glamorous ring about most of them and if the reader thinks some sound more like mountains than hills, he is right. Ampus Draguignan starts off the current season and is followed by Col Saint-Pierre, Alpl, Montseny, Sierra da Estrela, Freiburg, Coppa Sila, Trento Bondone, Dobratsch, Chamrousse, Coppa Bruno Carotti, Mont Dore, Chambon du Lac, St Ursanne Les Rangiers, Los Montes de Malaga and Cefalu Gibilmanna.

All these climbs are difficult, but some very high speeds are reached. The Swiss St Ursanne climb is the speediest at the present time, Markus Hotz (March BMW F2) holding the record with a speed of 154·68 km/h (96·11 mph). And this, mark you, whilst climbing to a height of 780 m (2,599 ft).

The slowest is the Italian Trento Bondone course. Not surprisingly since it covers 17·3 km (10·75 miles) and climbs to a height of 1,610 m (5,282 ft). Present record holder is Mauro Nesti (Lola BMW) at 95·77 km/h (59·50 mph).

Speed Trials, Sprints and Drag racing

A companion to hill climbs in the speed events category is the *Sprint* or, in other words, a hill climb without the hill, cars being timed over a measured distance, the fastest being the winner.

One of the oldest motor sport events still in being, the annual Brighton Speed Trials, is probably the most famous survivor of this type of event. The Trials were first held in July 1905, just a month before the first hill climb at Shelsley Walsh, which makes them, apart from the RAC Tourist Trophy motor race, the oldest motor sport event still being held.

The trials take place on the Madeira Drive section of the promenade at the English seaside resort, a venue also famous as the finishing straight of the RAC London to Brighton Run for Veteran Cars, the Pioneer Motor Cycle Run and the Historic Commercial Vehicle Run.

All sorts of machinery takes part, ranging from motor cycles to Grand Prix cars.

The Brighton Speed Trials were not, however, the first of their kind. The famous Nice Speed Trials began in 1899 when LeMaitre's 20 horse-power Peugeot set a speed of 60·34 km/h (37·5 mph). Brighton was not even the first in England, neighbouring Bexhill holding trials in May, 1902, when Léon Serpollet in his famous steam car clocked 87·4 km/h (54·3 mph) with the aid of a ramp.

The first Irish speed trials were held in Phoenix Park, Dublin, later to be the venue of the Irish Grand Prix, in July 1903. Baron de Forest (Mors) defeated Gabriel (Mors) and Charles Rolls (Panhard) over the flying kilometre.

Cooper Cars, later to become Grand Prix champions, scored their first competition success when the Brighton Speed Trials were revived in 1946 after the Second World War. John Cooper won the 850 cc class but the fastest time of the day was put up by Raymond Mays in a 2-litre ERA with a fantastic 146·98 km/h (91·03 mph) from a standing start. Woman driver Patsy Burt, later to become the first official British Sprint Champion, shattered this in 1968 when, driving a McLaren Oldsmobile she clocked 178·08 km/h (110·69 mph) for the standing kilometre which did not, however, surpass the 186·66 km/h (115·97 mph) registered by George Brown in 1963, riding a Vincent motor-cycle.

Speeds like this demonstrate that although sprints are not nearly so dangerous as motor racing itself,

213

they are not a form of competition suitable for people incapable of handling the fastest machinery.

Speed trials and sprints have long been surpassed in the United States by a refinement of the sport known as Drag Racing, which now has a hold on the Continent of Europe and in Great Britain too where the Santa Pod Raceway is the leading venue.

In Drag Racing, the same principle exists as in Sprints, the cars and drivers being pitted against the clock rather than against each other. Usually two cars are timed simultaneously over a 402 m (quarter-mile) course from a standing start.

Terminal velocity and elapsed time are recorded, terminal velocity being the speed attained at the end of the run and elapsed time being the time taken for the run.

Cars, usually long spindly specials these days, can be piston-engined or rocket or jet-engined.

The world record for piston engines over two runs was set in 1972 by British driver Dennis Priddle driving his 6,424-cc supercharged Chrysler, using nitromethane and methanol, at Elvington, North

Yorkshire, with 216·18 km/h (134·28 mph) an elapsed time of 6·70 seconds. But in a jet-engined dragster, Craig Breedlove has recorded 607·93 km/h (377·75 mph).

With dragsters capable of reaching speeds such as this from a standing start it is not surprising that braking systems are not always up to coping with the situation and most of the fastest dragsters are equipped with parachutes which blossom out behind them at the end of the run and by creating wind resistance assist in bringing them to a safe halt.

Rallying

Rallying, in essence, began almost with the invention of the motor car itself. Long distance trials were held before the turn of the century and the very first Brighton Run in 1896, although little more than an organized procession, might be described as a rally of sorts. But the true progenitor of the rally was the reliability trial. These events took place in the pioneering days in Great Britain, the rest of Europe and the United States. In Britain, the Thousand Miles Trial of 1900, the brainchild of newspaper magnate Alfred Harmsworth, later Lord Northcliffe, is an historic milestone. Not only was it a practical

demonstration of the possibilities of the new fangled horseless carriage but it also foreshadowed the special stages which were to feature in many rallies 60 years later. Various tests, including hill climbs, were set the drivers as they motored around the British Isles.

The Thousand Miles Trial of 1903 went several steps nearer the modern rally with road sections and timed hill climbs, noise and dust-raising checks. The dust tests have disappeared but noise checks are still with the sport. Motoring historians, however, tend to give credit to Germany for staging the first proper rally in 1904 with the first Herkomer Trial, which was repeated in 1906 and 1907 and followed for four more consecutive years by the Prince Henry Trials. Then, in 1911, the first Monte Carlo Rally was held. It was to become the most famous rally of them all, although its importance has recently slipped.

Twenty-two cars started in the first Monte: ten from Paris, four from Brussels, two apiece from Vienna and Geneva, one from Boulogne and three from Berlin, these last three having the longest

Top : Jean-Luc Therier and M. Callewaert in an Alpine Renault at the 1971 Monte Carlo Rally.

Above left : Gas and Trevoux, winners of the Monte Carlo Rally in 1934, with their 3½-litre Hotchkiss.

Above right : Timo Mäkinen and Geoff Mabbs during the 1963 Liège-Sofia-Liège Rally, waiting while a check is made on their Austin Healey 3000 – the outstanding rally car of that period, although on this occasion it gave way to Böhringer's 230L Mercedes.

Left : Henri Rougier's winning Turcat-Méry at Monte Carlo in 1911.

distance to cover. Sixteen reached the finish, the winner being Henri Rougier, driving a Turcat Mery, who had started from Paris.

The following year 78 cars started – one of them from Russia – Julius Beutler (Berliet) being the winner. War clouds were gathering over Europe and the next Monte would not be held until 1924.

The original meaning of 'rally' was 'a gathering at a specified point' and in the early Montes all that was required of competitors was that they should motor from one of a number of distant starting points to Monte Carlo within a specified time limit. In those days the condition of the roads, especially in the depths of winter, made the journey a difficult one and it was a great achievement to arrive at Monte Carlo without losing marks. To most of the world, the Monte was the one and only rally between the wars. Certainly, it was the only international event of its kind of any significance and although most of the drivers were amateurs, the Monte was always fiercely contested before ending in a whirl of champagne, lovely ladies and the casino in the Principality.

In Great Britain, rallies tended to be tours of the countryside with a number of driving tests (*Auto-*

tests as they were later called) at various points along the route. It was not until 1932 that the first RAC Rally of Great Britain was held and this followed the traditional pattern culminating in driving tests at Torquay after a route covering some 1,600 km (1,000 miles).

There were dramatic changes after the Second World War. First of all, the Ordnance Survey and the Grid System were employed in British rallies, making them a test of navigational skill, and rallying rapidly increased in popularity. As many as 400 cars were entered for a single event. Internationally, there were to be even more far reaching innovations, of which more later.

Thus today, there are seven main types of rally. As defined by top British official, Les Needham, they are:

Night Rally : The basic type of rally, with numerous controls which the cars must pass through, there being penalties for late (and sometimes early) arrival. The controls are usually defined by means of Grid References or other simple types of plotting using an Ordance Survey map.

Day Rally : Occasionally of the same pattern as a Night Rally but more often day events tend to be special stage events.

Special Stage Rally : These often incorporate road sections with controls, as in the Night Rally, but the most important part of the event consists of driving over closed private roads, usually in forests, army ranges, airfields and 'stately homes', in a bid to achieve a target time. Navigation as such plays a much smaller part in the results of these events (indeed many of them use a system of directional arrows, the most popular being the 'tulip' system). This type of rally can be held day or night and, indeed, the modern RAC Rally, now rated one of the world's top two or three rallies, takes this form.

Hunt the Marshal Rally : A specialized form of the sport, not so popular as once it was, where competitors have to locate marshals in hiding off the road. The driver is almost incidental in this form of rallying since the marshals' hiding places can only be found by navigational accuracy of the highest order.

Treasure Hunt : A not very serious branch of rallying, the type usually indulged in by works, social and tennis clubs and the like. Even maps are not always used, the competitors being given clues instead.

Continental Rally : In Europe, due to the type of roads available, rallies do not often rely on complicated navigation to cause competitors to lose time but just set very high average speeds on difficult roads. In effect they are similar to British special stage events but the roads are not necessarily closed to other traffic nor are they on private property.

American Rallies : In the USA, the road laws are such that speeds are severely restricted with the result that most of the events are *Regularity Rallies* although there are a few special stage events. In regularity rallies a set average speed has to be maintained constantly with penalties for deviations (either early or late) at any of many secret checks. Timing is usually to fractions of a minute. This type of event is not popular in Europe.

Most regularly held events, all over the world, fall into one of the categories above but in addition in modern times has come an event which is a throwback to the early days of motoring when the pioneers took part in such odysseys as Peking to Paris and the transcontinental events in the United States.

These are the long distance marathons to Mexico and Australia, drives which take competitors halfway round the world. To understand how all this has

come about it is necessary to look at the whole pattern of international rallying since the end of the Second World War.

The first international rallies when peace came followed the traditional pattern. The Monte still held pride of place and so many British crews entered that the RAC of Great Britain had to form a special selection committee because even when the Monaco authorities allocated Britain a quota of 300 or more, there were still entries surplus to requirements. Other rallies which featured prominently were the Dutch Tulip Rally, the Alpine, Liège–Sofia–Liège, and in Canada, the Shell event.

At this time in rallying history, the Liège–Sofia–Liège was generally regarded as the toughest. Originally the Liège–Rome–Liège, the Marathon de la Route, its severity can be judged by the fact that in 1961, for example, only 8 out of 85 starters finished the 5,470 km (3,400 mile) journey.

About this time the pattern began to change. The Greek Acropolis Rally came into contention. No snow and ice there, but a grind through dust and heat with temperatures often soaring to 49°C (120°F) in the forbidding Greek mountains. This event really hit the headlines when the 1960 European Champions, the Germans, Schock and Moll, brought their Mercedes into Athens after 62 hours of driving without incurring a single penalty mark. Schock underlined a brilliant performance by setting a record for the mountain trial which concluded the rally. He traversed the 10 km (6 mile) route along the 2,500 m (8,200 ft) high Parnassus in 7 min 48 sec.

In Britain, where the international event was known as 'The Rally of the Tests' because the only way it could be made competitive in the face of restrictive highway laws, was to hold a series of tests on race circuits and seaside promenades, there were changes which were to alter the whole face of the sport.

At a stroke, organizer Jack Kemsley converted it to 'The Rally of the Forests' with fast and furious special stages on forestry land. Kemsley was not the inventor of forest stages – there had been one or two in the RAC Rally years before – but he was the first

to build an entire rally around them. As a result, the British event attracted far more foreign competitors, especially from Sweden. The Rally itself established a reputation as one of the toughest in the world.

And on the other side of the globe, the RAC's rival to that distinction was also making news. The East African Safari, which began life as the Coronation Safari, was talked about wherever rallyists foregathered. The Safari brought another dimension to the rallying scene. More blunt in its aims than other events, it simply demanded high speeds over atrocious terrain. All the organizers had to do was to sit back and wait for the cars to break up. And most of them did.

Amongst the developments brought about by the Safari are many in the realm of tyres. Tyres have had to be designed which will stand 1,000 km (620 miles) of boulder-strewn corrugated murran, a great test of strength, and also cope with speeds of 195 km/h (120 mph) in temperatures approaching 30°C (86°F) along main tarmac highways. The Dunlop Company built two layers of steel into the side-

Left : A Daihatsu driven by a local driver on the East African Safari Rally of 1978.

Below left : A competitor traversing the sands of the Nevada desert during the Desert Auto Race.

Below right : Walter Rohrl in his Fiat, winner of the 1978 Greek Acropolis Rally.

Bottom left : Arne Hertz and Stig Blomqvist in a Saab during the 1973 *Daily Mirror* RAC Rally.

Bottom centre : Finnish driver, H. Valtaharju, in his Ascona, taking part in the 1977 Arctic Race in which he finished 9th.

Bottom right : Triumph TR7 in the Lombard RAC Rally of 1977.

walls of their 1978 Safari tyres in order to prevent punctures. The end result has justified the effort. When Sweden's Björn Waldegård won the 1977 event in a 'works' Ford, it was the eleventh time in 14 years that the winning car had been shod by Dunlop.

Some of the difficulties posed by the Safari may have helped to inspire a revival of the old time long distance events, the World Cup Rally from London to Mexico, coinciding with the 1970 World Cup Football Finals; and the London to Sydney Marathons. The World Cup Rally introduced special stages, or primes, as long as 900 km (560 miles).

Like motor racing, rallying has become much more commercial and although the rewards for drivers are not so great as in Grand Prix racing, the leading men like Waldegård, Roger Clark, Timo Mäkinen, Rauno Aaltonen and company, make a good income from the sport.

Over the years, the championships contested have varied although there has usually been some form of European Championship.

At the time of writing there is a World Championship for Makes, won in 1977 by Fiat, which also carries FIA awards for drivers and co-drivers. Eligible cars are Groups 1–4, in other words, series production touring cars, touring cars, series produc-tion grand touring cars and grand touring cars. World Championship Rallies are scheduled to admit cars in these groups until at least the end of 1980, three years notice being given of any change. Four wheel drive cars and cars not recognized are not permitted in World Championship Rallies. Eleven events currently qualify for the world title: Monte Carlo, Swedish, Safari, Portugal, Acropolis, Rally of the South Pacific, Thousand Lakes, Criterium du Quebec, San Remo, Rallye de France/Tour de Corse and the RAC.

The European Rally Championship for Drivers is open to both men and women and is decided on the basis of each individual's best eight results. Many more events are qualifying rounds for this championship than for the world title but they do not all earn the same number of points per placing for the competitors. The rallies are graded with coefficients from 1–4, 4 being the best, and drivers scores are multiplied by the coefficient of the event in which he (or she) is taking part. Thus points scored in the Arctic Rally are multiplied by four; in the Snow Rally only by two.

In addition to the Arctic, the other rallies graded 4 are the Rallye du Pologne and the Royal Scottish Automobile Club's event. There are four events graded 3 – Costa Brava, Elba, Alpin and the Circuit of Ireland. Six are graded 2 – Galway, Snow, Sachs Winterrallye, Sicily, Lugano and Criterium Lucien Bianchi (commemorating the racing driver); and 35 events are coefficient 1. The rallies in the two top grades must be inspected each year if they are to retain their status but organizers of events in the lower grades may apply to be inspected with a view to being upgraded. Thus the list of European Championship events is liable to change.

The top driver naturally becomes European Champion but there is also a Cup for the highest placed driver not on the FIA seeded list; another for the highest placed co-driver (based on the same scoring methods as for drivers); and a third – the Ladies Cup – reserved for exclusively female teams and which goes to the highest placed lady driver.

There is also an FIA Cup for Rally Drivers. Qualifying events for this fall into three categories. A: all rallies counting for the World Cup Championship of Makes; B: all events counting for the European Rally Championship for Drivers with a coefficient of 4 (although the coefficient will not be used to multiply marks); and C: a maximum of five very

well known rallies which do not qualify for one of the above. The 1978 list of these included the Rally of South Africa, Rallye du Bandama, the Southern Cross Rally and the Giro d'Italia.

Other international rally competitions are the West Europe Cup and the Triple Crown Championship for the Bruce Trophy. This latter is competed for between England, Wales, Scotland and Ireland. The 1977 winners were England, represented by Andy Dawson, Russell Brookes, Chris Sclater and Roger Clark.

Rally drivers are also seeded by the FIA and these drivers (in whatever order decided by the organizers) must precede the others at the start of international events. This can be of great importance, especially on special stage rallies, since without a seeding system the better drivers would often be baulked by slower and less capable competitors.

Drivers included in the list must have fulfilled one of the following: (1) been amongst the first three in a World Championship event the year before; (2) have won a World Championship event in one of the three previous years; (3) have been in the first five in the previous year's European Championship; (4) have won the European Championship in one of the three previous years; (5) have been on the FIA graded lists of Grand Prix or Long Distance drivers.

Autocross and Rallycross

Autocross and Rallycross have developed from the production and reliability trials and from rallies. Both sports owe their origin to the British who, in the immediate post-war years, started racing cars around fields for a little fun and excitement. No one is sure who first put autocross on a proper basis, controlled by officials and timekeepers, but certainly both the now defunct East Anglia Club and the Hagley & District Light Car Club were amongst the pioneers of this sort of event. Oddly enough, the very similar rallycross originated quite independently. Television producer Robert Reed, doing a programme on the RAC International Rally of Great Britain, realized that the event consisted of very thrilling stages plus boring interludes when the cars drove from one special stage to another. He reasoned: why not televise an event which just has special stages? And so rallycross was born.

In essence, in Great Britain at least, autocross has remained largely amateur and of late with the advent of commercial sponsors, semi-professional, while rallycross, backed by television, has attracted the works entries and professional drivers like Peter Harper, formerly one of the world's top rally drivers.

Despite their parochial origins, both autocross and rallycross are now internationally recognized and there is a European Championship for Drivers in both events.

Twelve events count towards the Autocross Championship with the cars being divided into four divisions: Group 1 and 4 cars under 1,600 cc and over 1,600 cc, buggies, and special autocross cars.

Rallycross is confined to Group 5 rigidly closed cars with no class divisions, all cars running in the unlimited category. There are nine rounds scheduled for the 1978 European championship, one of them being at the English circuit of Lydden, the sport's first permanent home.

Autocross is basically what it has always been – a race around a field. Because of the limitations of certain courses, cars sometimes set off singly although it is more usual to start in pairs and, in some cases, they are started four abreast. Depending on the length of the course, a second and third pair can

be despatched while the first pair are still on the course. The official definition of autocross is one of the simplest in the book of regulations: *A race or speed event on a grass or unsealed surface.*

Rallycross is more glamourized and the terrain is deliberately made more awkward, forcing drivers to combat grass, tarmac and mud with humps and inclines to add to the fun. The definition is: *A race or speed event which takes place on a combination of a sealed and unsealed surface as part of a permanent circuit.* The cars start four abreast.

The growth of auto and rallycross is now worldwide. Austria, Germany, Holland and Italy were amongst the first countries to realize the potential of the latter and Australia and New Zealand soon followed. With European Championships already held in both events. a World Championship seems a probability.

In 1978 came the introduction of yet another refinement to the sport originating from rallying – rallysprint. This takes rallying to the ultimate in TV sport with competitors taking part in just one stage.

Sporting car and Production car trials

An exciting but not internationally popular form of motor sport are the trials often referred to as 'mudplugging'. Under sporting car regulations, little specials with a crew of driver and passenger hurl themselves at muddy gradients and with the passenger bouncing vigorously up and down or leaning out on one side or the other to aid in getting a grip, endeavour to get as far up the greasy slope as possible. The climbs are marked out in stages and marks are won or lost according to how far the car travels. A typical National Championship event would have, say, three rounds of nine hills each.

Short circuit racing

Short circuit racing is a title which can cover a tremendous variety of racing on stadium, hard tracks, dirt tracks and on grass, with machinery ranging from the scruffiest old banger to a sleek single-seater.

Racing on dirt tracks and speedway ovals, includ-

going to the roughest, toughest survivor of them all. But in other races, the machinery is tended with the loving care given to Grand Prix cars and some thrilling racing results.

Stock car racing is not recognized by the FIA and at one time the sport was a very ragtail business but better organization has been introduced, professional promoters with a vested interest in keeping the sport on sound lines have come in, there is an exchange of views, cars and drivers between countries and some National Stock Car Boards of Control have been formed.

Motor Racing and Rallying in Australia and New Zealand

The development of motor sports in Australia has been rather overshadowed in the past by events on the other side of the world. With very little in the way of locally built cars and engines in Australia until the Fifties, and in New Zealand even today, enthusiasts have often been forced to rely heavily on imported machinery. However, this has not hindered a vigorous array of activities that have

Top : The starter drops the Australian flag to start the 99-mile International Gold Star motor race, 1963. This was the second international meet to be staged at the Lakeside circuit, Brisbane, and was won by the English driver, John Surtees.

Above : Bruce McLaren roars across the finish line at Lakeside in 1964 to take third place – and win the Tasman Cup series with the best overall score. Jack Brabham won the Lakeside event, but finished second to McLaren in the points table.

Above right : Jack Brabham, winner of the Australian Grand Prix for the third time at Sandown Park, 1964, has his cup filled with champagne.

Left : Second to Brabham at Sandown Park was the Melbourne driver, Bib Stilwell, in his Repco-Brabham car.

ing midget cars, has always been popular in the USA but attempts to introduce this type of sport in Great Britain and on the Continent of Europe have rarely caught on.

What has caught on in the Old World in modern times is stock car racing, not to be confused with what the Americans call stock car racing – known as production car racing to the rest of the world. Stock cars, European version, are generally stripped down and reinforced saloons: and there is a great deal of 'coming together'.

This is, perhaps, an oversimplification. This sort of racing as practised in Europe divides, roughly, into four classes:

Hot rods : Should not be confused with drag racers whatever Hollywood films depict. Hot rods are usually hotted up saloons capable of some quite remarkable performances.

Superstox : Usually look more like racing cars – if you can imagine racing cars with the driver enclosed in a hutch and the front of the car sprouting iron girders.

Stock cars : Usually recognizable as family saloons even if most of the comforts have been removed.

Bangers : Ditto but more battered and bent.

There are other variations, such as speedcars, bombers, super rods, and so on.

Some of this racing is very primitive and in some events contact is the name of the game, the honours

taken in single-seater and saloon car racing, hill-climbing, rallycross, sprints, trials, grass track racing and, increasingly in recent years, the exciting spectacle of special stage rallying.

Today the sport is booming and, with many Australian built cars now available and a number of very competitive Japanese imports, the nature of competition is rapidly changing. No longer do the Australians and New Zealanders need to rely so strongly on British and European trends and, with this change, has come a new inner strength. In Australia the sporting activities are governed by the Confederation of Australian Motor Sports (CAMS), while across the Tasman, the New Zealand administration is by the Motorsport Association of New Zealand (MANZ). In the past the two countries have cooperated closely, although in recent years there has been a distinct parting of the ways, especially in regard to the annual Tasman series of motor races that did so much to popularize the Australasian motorsporting concept abroad.

After the First World War the sport resumed in both countries largely through hillclimbs and trials, but then came the era of the street circuits and eventually the permanent race track. The first Australian Grand Prix had been held at the picturesque Phillip Island Circuit in Victoria in 1928. It was won by an Englishman, Captain A. C. Waite, in an Austin Seven.

The race remained at Phillip Island until 1935. Since then it has had various venues including the Victoria Park in Melbourne and more recently it is staged at Sandown Park in the same city, where it runs alongside a horse racing circuit. Gradually new circuits sprang up all over Australia. In Tasmania there was a superb road circuit at Longford, on the outskirts of Sydney the splendid Warwick Farm track and, in the Blue Mountains behind the city, the Katoomba track. Also in Victoria there is the Calder circuit while in Queensland came the Surfers Paradise and Lakeside circuits. Sadly in the early Seventies, the pretty Warwick Farm circuit, scene of some great Australian races, closed down and the Katoomba circuit also finished. In their place a new modern track was built at Oran Park. There is also a modern raceway in Adelaide.

One of the earliest New Zealand circuits was at Ardmore near Auckland, which was in operation from 1954 until 1962. Another popular track, adjoining the horse racing course at Levin, survived until just a few years ago. Now the important tracks are Pukekohe, on the outskirts of Auckland, Bay Park near Tauranga, the new Manfeild Circuit near Feilding, Ruapauna, in Christchurch, and Teretonga, which is on the outskirts of Invercargill and is the world's southernmost race track. The airfield Wigram circuit in Christchurch is used only once a year, for the international series each January.

The championship that brought many of these circuits world renown, and did more to enhance Australasian motorsports than anything else, was undoubtedly the Tasman Championship. The series began in 1964 and was a logical development of the individual international races which promoters had been organizing in both Australia and New Zealand since 1960. At its height the Tasman Cup series involved four or five races in each country in January and February every year, when the world's top drivers were keen to take part. The works teams from Europe were able to take over modified Formula One cars for the short season.

The first Tasman title, in 1964, went to Bruce McLaren in a Cooper. Former World Champion, Jim Clark, won the series three times (1965, 1967 and 1968) for Lotus and a whole string of big name drivers took part over the years. Jackie Stewart

won the title in a BRM in 1966 and Chris Amon took victory in a 2·4-litre V6 Ferrari in 1969. The following year, Kiwi driver Graeme Lawrence became the first resident Tasman Champion when he wrapped up the championship in the same ex-works Ferrari.

However, commercialization of the sport and the swelling international calendar abroad brought about the end for top class overseas participation. No longer could Formula One drivers afford to be away for so long and soaring costs also took their toll.

The promoters decided to switch the formula and, after much thought, opted for the American Formula 5000. The 5-litre V8 formula was a controversial choice but, for the next five years, it carried the promoters through and the combined series continued. Lawrence actually beat the F5000 cars to win the series in 1970 and then countryman Graham McRae came along with a McLaren F5000 to dominate the Tasman for several years. McRae won the series for three years in a row, first in a McLaren and then in his own-built car. It wasn't until 1974 that Englishman Peter Gethin ended his run by snatching overall honours in a Chevron.

Australian driver Warwick Brown won the title in a Lola in 1975 and then the trans-Tasman co-operation ended. With F5000 fading out, both in England and America, the New Zealanders opted for Formula Atlantic, which they adopted as their national formula and called Formula Pacific. International championships held for Formula Pacific cars in 1977 and 1978 attracted reasonably good overseas support and both years the championship fell to the Finnish driver, Keijo Rosberg in his Chevron.

Meanwhile, in Australia, the promoters stuck with F5000. Vern Schuppan won a shortened series in 1976 and then Brown triumphed in the two following years. Today, the two countries have decided to continue following their separate paths, the New Zealanders with Formula Pacific, which has been chosen as a national formula by a number of other countries in South East Asia, and the Australians retaining F5000.

All other racing has been rather over-shadowed by the strength of these premier single seater categories, which has been a pity because both countries

saloon car racing, or 'tin tops' as they are referred to there. The locally-built General Motors cars and the Ford of Australia models battle it out in the national touring car championship and there is intense rivalry between the current Holden Toranas and Ford Falcons. In the smaller classes competitions between imports such as Alfa Romeos, Triumph Dolomites, Mazdas, BMWs, Datsuns and Toyotas provide arguably some of the best motor racing in the country. The leading drivers – Allan Moffat, Colin Bond, Pete Geoghegan, John Goss and Peter Brock – are household names and the culmination of each year's racing is the annual confrontation at Bathurst. This long distance touring car event is staged at the breathtaking Mount Panorama circuit in New South Wales and, as far as the public and the motor industry is concerned, is the most important event on the calendar. It is a classic Ford-versus-Holden battle and, in the last couple of years, top-line international drivers of the calibre of Jacky Ickx, Johnny Rutherford, Derek Bell and even Stirling Moss, have taken part. The annual 1,000-km (620-mile) race round the 6·1-km (3·8-mile) circuit of public roads provides a spectacular occasion.

Top : The first London-to-Sydney marathon took place at the end of 1968. The 72 cars still in the race set out from Perth on the gruelling last leg in which they were allowed 66 hours to cover 3,000 miles across Australia.

Above left : Australian police inspect the cars for roadworthiness.

Above centre : Unloading cars from the liner *Chusan*.

Above right : Andrew Cowan, winner of the London–Sydney marathon in 1968, drives his Mercedes through the welcoming crowd as he takes first place in the 1977 marathon.

Left : Cars on the grid on the major Australian race circuit, Warwick Farm, Sydney. Car No 3 is a Repco-Matich, whose driver is being congratulated (far left).

have flourishing lesser formulae and, in recent years, these have produced a number of talented young drivers to follow in the steps of Brabham, McLaren, Hulme and Amon overseas. In both countries there is Formula Ford, indeed one of the best prospects to emerge from that formula in Australia in recent years has been young Geoff Brabham, son of the former World Champion. The Australians also have their own brand of Formula Two, based on a 1·6-litre single overhead camshaft engine, and in both countries there are other well-supported single seater classes like Formula Vee. However, it is in the premier classes that reputations are made and in Australia the leading local drivers over the years have included familiar names like Bib Stilwell, Lex Davison, driver-turned-constructor Frank Matich and the Geoghegan brothers, Leo and Ian.

In New Zealand the ranks have also included some colourful characters. McRae and Lawrence immediately spring to mind, yet there have been other enthusiastic supporters like David Oxton and Kenny Smith in recent years while Howden Ganley made his name overseas in Formula One.

In both countries, although particularly in Australia, there has always been tremendous support for

New Zealanders are also staunch supporters of saloon car racing and they too have their annual classic, which is staged at the Pukekohe Circuit near Auckland. The leading local is the Timaru driver, Leo Leonard. In both countries there are also plenty of other saloon car categories, including one make classes. There is also a continuing interest in modified saloon cars which is a hang over from the days when the countries had to rely solely on tuning imported cars to go racing. The New Zealanders have retained their 'all-comers' classes and enthusiasts have built some fearsome V8-engined hybrids.

Although New Zealand does not have its own locally-built car, the country assembles models from Australia and overseas. The Australians have a growing local industry in racing and there are several prominent companies like Repco, the engine building concern that built Jack Brabham's world championship winning engines, and Garrie Cooper's Elfin car factory. Veteran driver Frank Matich builds his own F5000 chassis and there are plenty of smaller constructors. In New Zealand the leading constructor in the last decade has been George Begg.

Rallying is a sport that has only emerged onto the international scene with any real impact since the

late Sixties. Both countries have keenly contested national championships and stage rallying has today taken over from the earlier trials and navigation events. Each country has one premier event. In Australia it is the annual Southern Cross Rally, which now attracts a representative overseas entry including occasional works teams, usually from companies like Ford of Britain and the Japanese manufacturers.

In New Zealand the ambitious rally organizers stage an annual event that alternates each year between the two main islands and, it too attracts a number of overseas names. The man who stands out amongst the overseas drivers in both countries is Scotsman Andrew Cowan who has won both the top New Zealand event and the Southern Cross Rally. And, of course, he also won both the London to Sydney Marathons! The New Zealanders managed to have their International event included in the World Rally Championship in 1977 and the tough five day rally saw a bitter struggle between the works cars from Fiat and Ford. However, the event was dropped by the FIA from the 1978 championship.

Today racing and rallying in Australia is very different from what it was even five years ago. No longer must the increasingly independent countries rely so heavily on what is happening in overseas motorsports and the level of local participation has climbed steeply. Formula Pacific has given New Zealand a more realistic national category to pursue and, in Australia, F5000 will see the country through until the Eighties.

The World Land Speed Record

Officially there was no such thing as a World Land Speed Record until 1964. Car records are divided into sections, known as International Class Records, covering nearly all engine sizes, distances and durations. To establish the record two attempts must be made, one trip in each direction, in order that no undue advantage can be taken of following winds or downhill gradients. The average speed of the two runs is then taken. This has not always been the case; the early record runs were in one direction only.

The story began in 1898, at Achères, in France, when the Comte de Chasseloup-Laubat covered the kilometre one way at the then staggering speed of

63·14 km/h (39·24 mph) in an electric car.

Soon afterwards, at the same venue, the Belgian racing driver Camille Jenatzy attacked the record with an electric car of his own design, *La Jamais Contente*, which he was said to have named after his wife. He was successful but the Comte returned to the attack and the title passed backwards and forwards until Jenatzy finally emerged triumphant in 1899, the first man to clock more than 100 km/h.

Steam took over three years later when Léon Serpollet, in a steam-car of his own manufacture, beat Jenatzy's figures and became the first man to pass 75 mph. The internal-combustion engine made its first impact on the record scene in the same year when American millionaire W. K. Vanderbilt Jnr, driving a Mercedes-Simplex, equalled Jenatzy's record but failed to pass Serpollet's recently-established figures. Undeterred, the American had another go with one of the Paris–Vienna type Mors, and this time, at Ablis, near Chartres, he succeeded. He did not hold the record for long. First Fournier, then Augières, also driving Mors, beat his record.

Steam's last stand

The year 1906 dawned with the record held for France by Victor Hémery (Darracq) who took his car across to Daytona Beach, USA, for some international speed trials. It was there, at Daytona, later to be the scene of many record attempts, that steam made its last great stand. Frank Marriott, driving a steam-propelled Stanley, became the first man on earth to travel at more than two miles a minute.

Marriott's record withstood all attempts on it for nearly four years until Hémery, driving a giant Benz, regained the title on the British track, Brooklands. Hémery was the last man to set the record by travelling in one direction only, and after his fine run the ruling of a drive both ways was introduced.

It was not until 1914 that L. G. Hornsted (Benz) became the first man to establish the record with the average of two runs, also at Brooklands.

During the period 1904–20 a number of record attempts were made in the United States and although some of these were successful they were never officially recognized, since they were timed by the Automobile Club of America, not then internationally recognized.

Top left: Both Sir Malcolm Campbell and his son, Donald, set world speed records. Here they are back in 1926, the son in a pedal car, the father in his Bluebird.

Top right: The Bluebird speedboat of 1939 is seen here with its owner before its trial run at Lake Coniston in England's Lake District.

and the American Ray Keech briefly took the record in 1928 in the giant White Triplex which subsequently killed Lee Bible.

After Segrave's death, Campbell became the undisputed 'King of Speed', taking the record more times than any other man. In 1935 he broke the record for the eighth time – the last time it would fall at Daytona – and, dissatisfied with the surface, went next to the Bonneville Salt Flats in Utah, USA, where he became the first man to surpass 300 mph. Knighted like Segrave, he turned his attention to the water.

Then began a battle between two more Britishers, John Cobb and George Eyston. Eyston broke Campbell's record in 1937 and improved on his own figures in 1938. In the same year Cobb took the title, only to have Eyston regain it. In 1939, Cobb broke the record again – and then came the war. In 1947, Cobb, driving the same car, became the first man past 400 mph but only in one direction.

Although Cobb, too, was killed in a water speed record attempt it was to be 17 years before his record was officially broken by Donald Campbell, son of Sir Malcolm.

Before Campbell the Younger had established his record a young American named Craig Breedlove

Above : Craig Breedlove in 1965 when he broke the World Land Speed Record with 600·601 mph in his jet-propelled 4-wheeler, Spirit of America Sonic I.

Above right : George Eyston in his supercharged MG Midget at Brooklands in 1931 (top). One of the record-breakers, J. G. Parry Thomas, in 1925, driving at full speed at Brooklands in his Leyland Thomas Special (below).

In 1922, a Sunbeam became the first British car officially to establish the record, driven by Kenelm Lee Guinness. It was to be the last world record at the Brooklands track.

The struggle to become the 'world's fastest' on land was now to reach new proportions. Waiting in the wings were names like Campbell, Segrave and Parry Thomas.

Malcolm Campbell, already a well-known racing motorist, bought Guinness's car, considerably modified it and in 1925, on the Pendine Sands, first broke the record. Then, on another attempt, he became the first man to beat 150 mph.

For the next five years – until Segrave's death in attempting the world water speed record – the world land speed record was largely a two-man contest between him and Campbell, although the ill-fated Parry Thomas twice claimed the honours in 1926

had clocked even better figures, although his record, in a three-wheeled jet, was not to be ratified by the authorities.

In the same year that Campbell established the new wheel-driven record Green in Walt Arfons' car and Art Arfons in his own creation both beat Campbell's figures. The world had to recognize that no conventional motor car could match the new projectiles for speed. Indeed by 1965, when the Summers brothers managed to beat Campbell's record with a wheel-driven car, Breedlove had pushed the unlimited record to over 600 mph, and in 1970 Gabelich became the first man to break the 1,000 km/h barrier.

The FIA had long accepted the situation. It created separate categories for wheel-driven vehicles and others in 1964, officially acknowledging the World Land Speed Record for the first time.

B oth the Philadelphia Centennial Exposition of 1876 and the 1892 Chicago Fair had exhibited internal combustion gasoline engines. Made in Germany by the pioneer builder Nikolaus Otto and in Michigan by Clark Sintz, they were designed primarily as power sources for industrial and marine use.

It was inevitable that the mechanically enterprising in Europe and the United States would soon install them in wagons and carriages. Two of America's first builders, the Duryea brothers and Elwood Haynes, had internal combustion prototypes running by the spring of 1894.

Informal racing probably took place the instant the first two self-propelled vehicles crossed paths. By 1895, with steam-, electric- and petrol-driven horseless carriages to choose from, American racing was ready for its official beginnings.

Herman Kohlsaat was not to become the owner-publisher of the *Chicago Times-Herald* until April 1895, but when he was in Paris he was intrigued to learn that *Le Petit Journal* had sponsored the Paris–Rouen race and that other Paris newspapers had also made much of the event.

When Frederick Upham Adams, a mechanical engineer and dedicated automotive evangelist, approached 'Judge' Kohlsaat with the idea of having the *Times-Herald* sponsor a motor race, he received a surprisingly warm reception. After Kohlsaat had overcome strong staff objections to supporting a race for horseless carriages Adams laid out the route, scheduling the 'motorcycle' races for 2 November 1895.

The term 'motorcycle' was short-lived. Unhappy with 'horseless carriage' and critical of 'automobile' as being too 'Frenchified', the *Times-Herald* sponsored a national contest for a new name. Motorcycle earned the 500-dollar first prize, but it never caught on and soon it vanished.

Many of Chicago's 85 entrants had more enthusiasm than practical plans, and only two machines were ready as race day approached. Concerned lest the event and its sponsor lose credibility, the race judges, a distinguished group of engineers and scientists, postponed the race until Thanksgiving Day, 28 November.

However, so as not to disappoint those who might have missed the news of the postponement an exhibi-

tion run was staged on 2 November. Two cars, a Mueller-Benz driven by Oscar Mueller, the owner's son, and a Duryea in the hands of J. Frank Duryea, accompanied by his brother Charles, started the 148-km (92-mile) run from Chicago to Waukeegan and back. Forced into a ditch by a farm wagon, the Duryea was unable to finish. Averaging 15·6 km/h (9·7 mph), the Benz collected 500 dollars as sole finisher.

Eleven entrants had promised to be ready the day before, but only six made it to the starting line on 28 November. Two were electrics, three of the four petrol-powered machines had Benz origins, while the single-cylinder, 4 hp Duryea Motor Wagon completed the field.

The Mueller Benz, considerably modified by its American owner, had been built in Germany. The R. H. Macy Benz and the De La Vergne Refrigerating Co Benz were made under licence by Roger, of Paris, and were brought to the USA by the R. H. Macy department store after they had raced in Paris–Bordeaux the June before.

Chicago weather that Thanksgiving Day would have taxed even modern machines. Over a foot of snow had fallen and the area's primitive roads were a mass of ice and slush.

First off at 8:55 am were J. Frank Duryea and his umpire. The De La Vergne Benz that followed was unable to complete the preliminary leg from Jackson Park to the official 55th Street start. Jerry O'Connor, driving the Macy Benz, had the first of his three accidents when, within minutes of the start, he slid into a horse-drawn streetcar. The Sturgis and Morris and Salom electrics left shortly after 9 o'clock, but both battery-powered competitors failed to complete the course. Sixth and last to leave was the Mueller Benz, which had been delayed for an hour en route to the start by problems with new belts installed the day before.

The good-natured crowd lining the streets was quick to help errant cars out of snow-banks as the Chicago police hurried ahead of the racers to clear the route. At the half-way point the R. H. Macy Benz was 2 minutes in front of the Duryea and 45 minutes ahead of the Mueller Benz. Horse-drawn carriages became a major obstacle and each driver's umpire made careful reports of the reasons, mechanical as well as human, for delay.

Overleaf: Raymond Beadle's *Blue Max* dragster on its way down the quarter-mile.

Top left: The winning Duryea being pushed up a hill during the 1896 race sponsored by *Cosmopolitan Magazine.*

Top right: The Sturgis Electric in need of help while taking part in the 1895 *Chicago Times-Herald* Race.

Above centre: Lining up for the start of an automobile race in the early days.

Right: The first organized race in America was the *Chicago Times-Herald* contest of 28 November 1895. J. Frank Duryea is sitting behind the tiller of his winning car.

Motor Sport in the USA – the first races

Among the notes of the distinguished industrialist Charles Brady King, who was umpire on the Mueller Benz, are found the following:

1/2 minute stop, blocked by Cottage Grove cars . . . 12:31 stopped 3/4 minute, frightened horse . . . Right chain off 12:50 1/4, 1/2 minute stop . . . 1:48 stopped 1/2 minute to oil machinery. One pint of gasoline removed from carburator and thrown away . . . 3:03 stopped to bend clutch second time, 8 minutes delay (clutch worked perfectly after this adjustment) . . . 6 gallons (scant) gasoline consumed. 6 pails broken ice. 3 pails snow.

When darkness fell and temperatures dropped the crowd became unruly. Youngsters snow-balled the police and routed them. Only a handful of spectators remained to see the Duryea chug into Jackson Park at 7:18 pm, the winner of America's first motor race with an average speed of 10·71 km/h (6·6 mph).

Twenty-four minutes running time behind the Duryea came the Benz, now driven by Charles B. King, its umpire. Oscar Mueller had collapsed from exposure.

It was King who first drove an automobile on the

streets of Detroit and on 1 November 1895 was one of those responsible for establishing the American Motor League, the first of all automobile clubs. Twelve days later the Automobile Club of France was founded in Paris, to be followed by Great Britain's Self-Propelled Traffic Association, organized by Sir David Solomons at the Cannon St Hotel, London, on 10 December 1895. Only the French club survives today.

'For best performance in the road race, for range of speed and pull with compactness of design', the Duryea won 2,000 dollars. Then, to the consternation of the two finishers, the judges awarded the *Chicago Times-Herald* Gold Medal 'for the best showing in the official tests, ease of control, absence of noise or vibration, cleanliness and general excellence of design' to the Morris & Salom Electrobat.

Another publication, *Cosmopolitan Magazine*, sponsored America's second race, a 20-mile run up the Hudson River from New York to Irvington. Although the organizers received 30 entries only six started, Frank Duryea earning the 3,000-dollar purse as the only finisher.

Motor Sport in the USA – Vanderbilt Cup

America's third event – the Narragansett Park, Rhode Island State Fair races of September 1896 – had a great influence on the future of American racing.

Narragansett Park was a one-mile dirt track built for horse racing. It had enormous grandstands and was completely enclosed. It was not to happen overnight, but American promoters moved to staging automobile races at fairgrounds and other horse racing tracks. Here they could collect admission charges from all spectators, not only those occupying the start/finish area grandstands, and they would be rid of the growing nuisance of crowd control.

As late as 1915 ten of that year's AAA national championships were held on road courses. By the end of the First World War, however, road racing had all but disappeared from the American scene.

Willie K. and the Vanderbilt Cup

Although he had raced on the beach and in hill climbs around his Newport home while still an undergraduate, in April 1902 Wm. K. Vanderbilt Jr made motoring history when his Mercedes reached 105·85 km/h (65·79 mph) on the Achères Road, near Paris – the first time a gasoline-powered car had held the mile mark. Later that year Vanderbilt pushed a giant 80 hp Mors to an official 122·41 km/h (76·08 mph). In 1902 he also competed in Paris–Belfort and the Circuit des Ardennes and, in 1903, Paris–Madrid.

At Ormond Beach on 27 January 1904 Vanderbilt

Left : Poster advertising Locomobile cars using a picture of the winning Locomobile at the finish of the 1908 Vanderbilt Cup Race.

Below left : Vanderbilt (front right) at Ormond Beach where he beat Ford's land speed record in 1904.

Below right : All eyes fix on George Robertson, winner of the 1908 Vanderbilt Cup Race staged at Long Island.

overshadowed the 147 km/h (91·4 mph) AAA mile record set by Henry Ford just 15 days earlier over the frozen ice of Lake St Clair. Mr and Mrs Ford, who had come to Florida to soak up sun and accolades saw him do it.

Vanderbilt and his Long Island friends gave Ormond-Daytona a lift socially as well. Not only were the Florida beaches a good spot for rapid motoring but the curious could also see many of America's Society names at play.

Vanderbilt also lent his considerable political influence to the 'Good Roads Movement' and he wrote several of the earliest books on motor travel. But it is not of these, nor as a driver, that he is remembered, for in 1904 he brought America into the mainstream of international racing when he established the Vanderbilt Cup.

Eleven Vanderbilt Cup races were held between their New York beginnings in October 1904 and the final Cup race of the original series at Santa Monica on the shores of the Pacific in November 1916. (There was a short-lived revival in the 'thirties but Willie K. had nothing to do with it.)

Using a 45·76-km (28·44-mile) combination of suburban New York streets and adjacent Long Island roads, the first Vanderbilt attracted a strong field of six French, five German, two Italian and five American cars. The race was won by the Panhard of Long Island-born George Heath with a 84 km/h (52·2 mph) race average. Heath completed 457·6 km (284·4 miles) of racing, less than two minutes ahead of young Albert Clément's Clément-Bayard.

An almost uncontrollable crowd of 50,000 thrilled to the sight of legendary stars such as De Dietrich driver Fernand Gabriel, who was forced to hide from

his admirers. The American veteran Herb Lytle's Pope-Toledo finished third, the trim Packard Gray Wolf, smallest of the 18 entries, was fourth and the French champion, Georges Teste recorded a blistering 114·1 km/h (70·9 mph) fastest lap.

Except for the problem of crowd control the first Vanderbilt Cup was considered a success. One year later 14 of Europe's best drivers, including Victor Hémery, whose Darracq won, joined Vincenzo Lancia, Ferenc Szisz, Felice Nazzaro, Arthur Duray, Camille Jenatzy and Louis Wagner to defeat the American entries that included Walter Christie's FWD monster, two Pope-Toledos, a White Steamer known as *Whistling Billy* and Joe Tracy, the best-placed American, whose Locomobile finished third. The crowd had grown to over 200,000 and, ominously, lack of crowd control had increased proportionately. Desperate for additional police, the organizers had turned, in vain, to the state of New York.

When Louis Wagner's Darracq won the Cup in 1906, he told reporters it had been a miracle that he had avoided hitting any of the hundreds of spectators milling about the circuit. New York police estimated the 1906 crowd at more than 300,000 as the metropolitan press took up the cry for greater safety.

An unsuccessful attempt was made to shift the 1907 Vanderbilt Cup to New Jersey. The governor of New York was asked, and again refused, to supply troops to help patrol the course. Reluctantly Willie K. cancelled the 1907 race and began construction of the Long Island Motor Parkway, a private toll road. Nine miles of the new parkway were completed in time for the 1908 race. Adding it to 14 miles of the old course resulted in a 23·46 mile circuit that would be covered 11 times.

It was a momentous year for the Americans as young George Robertson finished 1 min 48 sec in front of Herb Lytle's Isotta to give an American car its first international victory.

American Grand Prix races

One month after the 1908 Vanderbilt Cup Savannah, Georgia, a sleepy town in the deep South, staged the first American Grand Prize. Lacking everything needed to hold an international motor race except enthusiasm, the local automobile club used convict labour to build a wide, hard-packed, 40-km (25-mile) palm-lined course, then acquired the Georgia state militia to guard it.

After discharging their passengers transatlantic liners remained in the harbour to become floating hotels. Long trains of sleeping cars were chartered to bring spectators from the Midwest and North, and they too stayed over to house part of the crowd.

Southern hospitality nearly overwhelmed the European drivers. The French ace, Louis Wagner, whose Fiat was to win the first American Grand Prize, said he had never seen such kindness and that he and his fellow drivers could not wait to return. Drivers and crews were taken on hunting and fishing trips, and some of the Europeans became life-long friends of their Georgia hosts.

Constant bickering between the broadly-based American Automobile Association and the more elite Automobile Club of America, then recognized by European Auto Clubs as the official American racing body, had resulted in the American Grand Prize races going to Savannah. From 1909 until the final races were held in California in 1916 the Vanderbilt Cup was overshadowed by the newer series.

The New York area retained the Vanderbilt Cup

for two more years. New regulations permitting stripped chassis production cars saw foreign participation limited to Lewis Strang's Fiat, Spencer Wishart's Mercedes and Joe Seymour's Isotta. Louis Chevrolet's Buick, the early leader, set a 122·75 km/h (76·3 mph) fastest lap, but the 1909 victory went to Harry Grant's Alco-6.

Thirty race cars, all American but four entered by Benz, started the 1910 Cup. Harry Grant won in the same Alco that had triumphed the year before, but the smallest car in the race, a Marmon driven by Joe Dawson, finished only 25 seconds behind. Once again Louis Chevrolet built up a substantial lead before crashing at the half-way point.

In 1911 the Vanderbilt Cup moved to Savannah where it ran on 27 November as a preliminary to the Grand Prize held on 30 November. Although limited to 14 machines, several Americans, such as Ralph Mulford, Ralph DePalma, Bob Burman and David Bruce-Brown, who had captured the Grand Prize for Benz the year before, were among those favoured to win the GP. After a race-long struggle with DePalma's Mercedes, Mulford's Lozier captured the 468-km (291-mile) Vanderbilt Cup.

With Mulford entered in the same white Lozier for the Grand Prize, American fans began dreaming of a double victory. Mulford didn't win, although it was close. Running second to David Bruce-Brown's Fiat with one lap to go, Mulford took the railroad overpass too fast, flew into the air for 20 feet and broke his driveshaft on landing.

It was young Bruce-Brown's second Grand Prize. Never one to mince words, the usually testy Victor Hémery, on being beaten by the New Yorker by 1·42 sec the year before, had said, 'It is hard luck to lose by just one second, but I have been beaten by a master.'

So ended the Savannah races. They had seen the world's best, but the burden of maintaining the course – there was also pressure to sell part of the land – and the almost overwhelming expense incurred by the race backers, forced them to decline any further commitments. Milwaukee, Wisconsin,

Winner Grand Prize   DAVID BRUCE-BROWN

staged the eighth Vanderbilt Cup and the third Grand Prize in October 1912. DePalma's Mercedes won the Cup race over Hughie Hughes' Mercer, as only eight machines, of which three were Mercedes, took the starter's flag.

Three days later, on 5 October 1912, 24-year-old David Bruce-Brown and his mechanic were killed when a tyre failed while he was practising for the GP. His Fiat team-mate, Caleb Bragg, won the race, followed by Ervin Bergdoll's Benz, Gil Anderson's Stutz and Barney Oldfield's Fiat.

Unable to find a home in 1913, the following year both events were held at Santa Monica, California, where DePalma's Mercedes and Oldfield's Mercer played a cat-and-mouse game that saw them slip into the first two places after Eddie Pullen's Mercer crashed while leading. Having seen a pre-arranged (and deliberately misleading) signal that DePalma was about to come in for tyres, Oldfield roared into his own pit for a tyre change only to look up and see Ralph laughing as he accelerated away.

It was sweet revenge for DePalma, who recently had quit as Mercer's team captain when they had hired Oldfield without his approval. Three days later Mercer had its revenge when Pullen's Mercer beat a star-studded field that included DePalma's Mercedes and a Sunbeam-60, the latter a great rarity as British cars of the era normally ignored American racing.

The meeting was held on a 6·18-km (3·84-mile)

Top left: David Bruce-Brown in his Fiat was the winner of the 1911 American Grand Prize – the last of the races to be held at Savannah.

Top right: Barney Oldfield in his Fiat at the 1912 Grand Prize, Milwaukee, where he was placed fourth.

Centre: 'Death Curve' on the Santa Monica course was where the wheel of Pullen's Mercer came off during the 1914 Cup.

Left: The tyre change which cost Oldfield the 1914 Cup race.

Far left: Barney Oldfield, one of the top racing stars before the First World War.

Motor Sport in the USA – New York to Paris

circuit at the grounds of San Francisco's Panama-Pacific Exposition. Torrential rain caused the 1915 Grand Prize to be run before the Cup race. Using the AAA's new 450-cu in. (7,374 cc) formula, the events attracted 31- and 30-car starting fields, most entrants running in both events. Dario Resta, an enigmatic, Italian-born Englishman, drove his works Peugeot to victory in both the 644-km (400-mile) Grand Prize and the 483-km (300-mile) Vanderbilt Cup, as Howie Wilcox's Stutz finished second in both events.

Returning to Santa Monica's seaside course in 1916, Peugeots dominated both races as Resta repeated his Vanderbilt Cup win, Johnny Aitken winning the final Grand Prize. Unhappy in his relationship with the AAA and what he considered their cavalier treatment of the Cup series, Willie K. withdrew his support after the 1916 Vanderbilt Cup. But it is unlikely that the Cup or Grand Prize would have been held the following year, when America joined the Allies.

Coast to Coast, New York to Paris and the Glidden Tours

The car manufacturers who depended on racing to publicize their products and the gentry who embraced fast motoring as a sport, became American motor sport's biggest promotors. America's railroads were its biggest enemies.

When turn-of-the-century motorists tried to improve on the frightful condition of American highways they met a stone wall of railroad-inspired resistance. 'Horseless carriages may be practical in Europe, where everything is close together,' preached the rail lobby, 'but there are 3,000 miles of mud and mountains between our shores. Pave the city streets, if you must, but long-haul traffic is the railroad's job.'

The railroads did more than talk. They bribed state legislators and a shameful number of US congressmen. Fortunately the ever-growing motoring public persuaded a few politicians to see things differently.

Attempts to drive across the United States began almost as soon as Americans discovered the automobile. In July 1899 a Mr and Mrs John D Davis began a journey from New York to San Francisco. Leaving Detroit on 19 August, neither the Davises nor their machine were ever seen again.

The first successful continental crossing was made during the summer of 1905 by Dr Horatio Jackson and Sewell Croker. The doctor's Winton took 63 days to get from San Francisco to New York. Even before the Winton arrived in New York, a Packard that was to cut three days from the Winton's time had left San Francisco.

By 1906 transcontinental trips were being made in 15 days, but no one, until the New York–Paris race of 1908, had dared a winter crossing. *Le Matin*, the Paris newspaper that staged the 1907 race from Peking to Paris, then joined with the *New York Times* in sponsoring a contest even more arduous and bizarre, a race from New York to Paris via the Pacific Ocean and Asia.

More than 250,000 New Yorkers jammed Times Square on the cold, clear morning of 12 February 1908 as six machines – a German Protos, an Italian Zust (the marque that captured Paris–Peking), three French makes (De Dion, Motobloc and Sizaire-Naudin) and the American Thomas Flyer – awaited the start.

Each entrant carried firearms as well as sails, skis, shovels, spare parts and food. Totally lacking protec-

tion, for neither windscreens nor tops were yet accepted, the crews, bundled in furs and blankets, waved their national colours and drank champagne as they waited for the start.

Fortunately for motoring history, several journalists and authors-to-be, including young Antonio Scarfolio, son of a prominent Italian newspaper publisher, and George Schuster, driver of the winning Thomas Flyer, have left us memorable accounts of their adventures.

Originally the New York–Paris route called for crossing the United States to San Francisco; taking a ship to Valdez, Alaska; driving 300 miles over river ice and coastal bays; crossing the frozen (in theory) Bering Sea to Vladivostok; driving across trackless Siberia; then on to France, via St Petersburg and Berlin. Obviously, most of the route was untried.

Using railroad lines and Indian guides, as well as several parcels of spare parts that fortuitously reached them en route, the Thomas was in the lead when it reached San Francisco, having covered 6,115 km (3,800 miles) in 41 days.

Arriving in Valdez, Alaska, ahead of the pack, they found snow so deep that the Thomas could not even leave the dock. Telegraphing race headquarters for instructions, they were advised to return to Seattle and take a boat to Japan. As the only car to make the Arctic junket, the Thomas was awarded a 15-day bonus.

Four machines got as far as Siberia, but only the Protos and the Thomas tried to cross the Asian continent. Showing amazing resource and endurance, both crews made it. After covering 21,470 km (13,341 miles) in 169 days the Thomas arrived in Paris on 30 July, the winner by 16 days.

Above left: The Thomas Flyer driven by George Schuster on its journey round the world to finish first in the race from New York to Paris via Asia held during the winter of 1908.

Above right: The winning Thomas Flyer surrounded by admirers on its arrival in Paris 1908.

Left: Ralph De Palma pushing his car over the finishing line at Indianapolis in 1912.

Below left: Ray Harroun in his Marmon Wasp – winner of the Indianapolis 500 in 1911.

Looking back on their experience many participants reported that the most difficult part of their journey had not turned out to be the burning deserts and soaring peaks of the American West. Nor was it roadless Japan or the trackless wastes of Siberia with its deadly quicksand swamps, mile-wide bridgeless rivers and raging torrents. No, wrote those who chronicled the historic event, the conditions encountered within hours of the start, in upstate New York, proved to be most difficult of all.

When the United States Office of Public Roads celebrated the 100th anniversary of Lewis and Clark's opening of the American Northwest by holding a convention in Portland, Oregon, in June 1905, two Curved Dash Oldsmobiles, Old Steady and Old Scout, made the 7,081-km (4,400-mile) trek from New York to Portland in 44 days.

Still another strong influence for better American highways were the Glidden Tours. As a young newspaper reporter in Boston, Charles Glidden had had the foresight to invest in Alexander Bell's new telephone company. In 1903, with Mrs Glidden as a passenger, he drove his Napier beyond the Arctic Circle and began a carefully documented and photographed journey that was to cover 50,000 miles and take him around the world.

In 1904 Glidden donated a touring trophy for American Automobile Association members who won tours of 1,000 miles or more. Bitterly contested by the automotive industry, Glidden reliability runs became big business, the winners widely advertised and well rewarded. Inactive for many years, Glidden tours were revived in 1954 and are again annual events, only now for antique cars.

Early Indianapolis

Although American cars and drivers – Ray Harroun's Marmon and Joe Dawson's National – won the first two 500s, from 1913 through 1919 (except when racing was suspended in 1917–18) it had been largely an overseas show of foreign makes: Jules Goux, Peugeot; René Thomas, Delage; DePalma, Mercedes; Resta's two Peugeot wins; then, in 1919, Howdy Wilcox's Peugeot (which was Speedway owned) became the last foreign car to take Indianapolis until Wilbur Shaw's Maserati achieved back-to-back wins in 1939–40.

Carl Fisher, whose Indianapolis-based company was a major automotive supplier, began planning the Speedway after witnessing the success of the 1904 Vanderbilt Cup and the 1905 Gordon Bennett races in France. Joining Fisher were James Allison, who was to sell his engine company to General Motors; Arthur Newby, whose National would win the 1912 Indy, and carburettor manufacturer Frank Wheeler.

Opening in 1909 with a mixed card, it was not until 1911, when the 4-km (2·5-mile) track was resurfaced with over three million bricks and the first 500-miler was held, that Indy became an American racing fixture.

Former racing driver, First World War flying ace and successful industrialist Eddie Rickenbacker bought the Speedway in 1927, beginning a series of rule-changes intended to encourage the country's manufacturers to return to racing. Riding mechanics were again required but the so-called 'Junk' formula was no match for the Millers, Duesenbergs and Offenhauser-powered specials.

During the Second World War Rickenbacker allowed Indianapolis to fall into disrepair. Only in 1946, after Speedway manager Wilbur Shaw convinced Tony Hulman that he should buy the track, did it return to its former glory.

The drivers

The emphasis in early American racing had been on showmanship. Pioneer racers like the Duryeas, A. L. Riker, Winton and Ford had turned from the steering wheel, or tiller, to concentrate on manufacturing automobiles. Joining the gentlemen drivers were America's first professionals, many of them former bicycle racers and mechanics, such as Barney Oldfield, Ralph DePalma and Louis Chevrolet.

Oldfield specialized in barnstorming tours that featured arranged finishes with the cigar-chomping Oldfield winning in the final seconds. Driving Henry Ford's 999 in October 1902, he had beaten reigning champion Alexander Winton. It was his first race and he was promptly hired by Winton. Oldfield soon moved on to Peerless, then to the radical FWD Christie. Driving a Benz in 1910, he ran a 131·724-mph record mile at Daytona. As a member of William Durant's Buick team he set several sprint records at the 1909 opening meet at Indianapolis. But when the first 500 was held in 1911 Oldfield was under AAA suspension and could not participate.

Oldfield's widely publicized rivalry with the gentlemanly Ralph DePalma made good headlines, and the story of their 1-2 finish at Santa Monica became an auto racing classic. When Oldfield retired in 1917 he was a wealthy man with a flourishing tyre business. He was a casualty of the crash of 1929, but was able to bounce back as an automotive consultant. Remembered largely for his showmanship, Barney Oldfield's flamboyant life-style obscured his considerable talent as a driver.

Italian-born Ralph DePalma's gracious manners did nothing to slow him down on the race track. Among the 2,000 races he won during his 25-year career were two Vanderbilt Cups, the American Grand Prize, the Indianapolis 500 and the Elgin Trophy. DePalma drove seven different makes at Indianapolis alone – Simplex, Mercedes, Mercer, Packard, Ballot, Duesenberg and Miller – and his record 613 leading laps at Indy stood for many years.

DePalma's torpedo-shaped Packard 12 raised the mile mark to 241·149 km (149·875 mph) at Daytona in 1919 and in 1921 his Ballot finished second to Jimmy Murphy's Duesenberg in the French Grand Prix. Peter DePaolo, DePalma's talented nephew, began his career as riding mechanic for his uncle. Recalling how DePalma's refusal to use Oldfield tyres was costing them victories, young Peter told his uncle, 'If you don't change to Barney's tyres, I'm going to leave you.' Leave he did, and DePaolo's own distinguished record is highlighted by his being the first to win Indianapolis with better than a 100-mph race average.

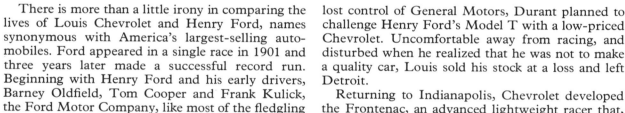

There is more than a little irony in comparing the lives of Louis Chevrolet and Henry Ford, names synonymous with America's largest-selling automobiles. Ford appeared in a single race in 1901 and three years later made a successful record run. Beginning with Henry Ford and his early drivers, Barney Oldfield, Tom Cooper and Frank Kulick, the Ford Motor Company, like most of the fledgling car industry, leaned heavily on racing success stories to sell cars. It is likely that Ford, from its earliest days to the present, has supported auto racing far more than any other car manufacturer. The past decade alone has seen Fords or Ford engines in victory lane at Indianapolis, in Grand Prix racing, at Le Mans and in stock cars.

Louis Chevrolet was born in Switzerland, his younger brothers, Arthur and Gaston, in France. After serving apprenticeships with several European car-makers, Louis migrated to Montreal in 1905 and briefly worked there for De Dion Bouton. Moving to New York, he joined Fiat, and in 1905 drove one of the firm's 90s to a double victory at Morris Park, on the outskirts of New York, beating Barney Oldfield and Walter Christie in the 3-mile feature event.

By 1906 Louis was working for Walter Christie, helping the Philadelphia innovator build the Darracq-powered record car which Chevrolet, Victor Hémery and Demogeot drove in the Daytona 'Tournament of Speed.' Although Demogeot was to record a shattering 197·020 km/h (122·449-mph) average over 3·2 km (2 miles), the Darracq-Christie feat was overshadowed by a Stanley Steamer's even faster run.

General Motors president William Durant invited Louis to join the prestigious 15-car, 40-man Buick racing team in 1909. He did well immediately, but Louis Chevrolet was also a gifted mechanic, and in 1911 Durant asked him to design and lend his name to a new line of passenger cars. Having temporarily

lost control of General Motors, Durant planned to challenge Henry Ford's Model T with a low-priced Chevrolet. Uncomfortable away from racing, and disturbed when he realized that he was not to make a quality car, Louis sold his stock at a loss and left Detroit.

Returning to Indianapolis, Chevrolet developed the Frontenac, an advanced lightweight racer that, as a Monroe Special, won the 1920 Indianapolis 500 with brother Gaston at the wheel. Six months later Gaston was killed on the boards of the Beverly Hills Speedway. Arthur Chevrolet had been injured at Indianapolis earlier that year and Louis never raced again.

In 1921, Tommy Milton earned the first of his two Indianapolis 500 victories in a Chevrolet-built Frontenac-8, and until 1931 Fronty-Fords ran regularly at the Speedway. But this was the age of the all-conquering Duesenbergs and Millers. The Chevrolet brothers' future now lay in their remarkably popular Fronty-Ford Model T conversion heads that dominated dirt-track racing for many years.

Louis Chevrolet also made an early start in the aircraft industry, but he was plagued by poor business judgement and died penniless in 1941. Arthur, who had been working as a boat mechanic, took his own life in 1946.

The Duesenberg Brothers and Henry Miller

Fred and Augie Duesenberg's first victory at the Speedway in 1922 was a somewhat hollow one, as Indianapolis winner Jimmy Murphy had installed a Miller engine in the chassis of his Duesenberg. Although Murphy won the 1921 French GP in the same machine, using a Duesenberg engine, he was to use Miller engines for most of the remaining races in his tragically brief career.

Frequent winners during the 1920s, the peak of America's board track era, the Duesenberg brothers also built Tommy Milton's successful Land Speed

Top left: Tommy Milton in his Frontenac in 1921 – the first of his two Indianapolis 500 victories.

Top right: Jimmy Murphy in his Murphy Special – winner of the Indianapolis 500 in 1922.

Motor Sport in the USA – land speed records

Leon Duray took two Packard Cable Specials – Miller 91s – to Europe in 1929 establishing records at Montlhéry and breaking the lap record at Monza. It was Duray's two *traction avant* Millers, acquired by Ettore Bugatti in exchange for three Bugatti passenger cars, that inspired Molsheim's twin OHC type 50. Beginning in 1928, Millers captured seven consecutive Indianapolis 500s and were to win again in 1936 and 1938.

It was a by-product of Harry Miller's, a 4-cylinder marine engine based on half of a Miller-8, that was to rule American oval track racing for more than 30 years. First used at Indianapolis in 1930, the Miller-Goosen engine became known as the Offenhauser when Miller's old foreman bought the Miller plant in 1934. Supercharged, normally aspirated or turbocharged, the 'Offy' dominated American oval track racing until 1965, when Jim Clark's Lotus-powered-by-Ford interrupted the long reign. Winners as late as 1975, it was not until 1977 that Drake Engineering developed a completely new Offenhauser engine.

One of the shortest and brightest careers of the 1920s was that of Frank Lockhart. In 1926 he led an almost solid parade of 14 Millers over the line on his

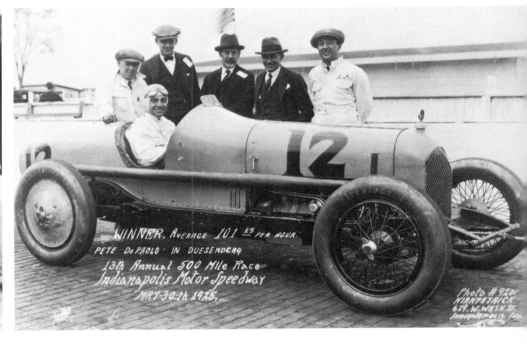

Above centre : Frank Lockhart took first place in his Miller Special at Indianapolis in 1926.

Above right : Peter DePaolo, nephew of Ralph DePalma, who won the 1925 Indianapolis 500 in a Duesenberg.

Record car. However, it is luxury touring cars, particularly the models J and SJ, that the Duesenberg reputation has come to depend on.

Harry Miller, a self-taught Wisconsin machinist, arrived in Indianapolis in 1911, the year of the first 500. His first engine was built in 1914 as a rush job for Bob Burman when the young star could not get a Peugeot replacement from France. Miller built a similar engine for Barney Oldfield's record-breaking *Golden Submarine*, and in 1920 made the first Miller straight-8 when the AAA formula was reduced from 300 cu in (4,916 cc) to 183 cu in (2,999 cc).

Miller's career was aided considerably by his employing brilliant Leo Goosens as his designer and by having Fred Offenhauser as a shop foreman. When the AAA further reduced engine displacements to 122 cu in (1,999 cc), Miller straight-8s dominated the 1923 Indy, won by Tommy Milton in the HCS-Miller Special. Making both FWD and rear-engined cars, Miller shifted to the 91 cu in (1,491 cc) 1926 formula by producing the elegant pencil-slim supercharged Miller 91, believed by many to be the handsomest of all race cars.

very first visit to the Speedway. Working with Stutz president Frank Moskovics, Lockhart built the handsome twin-Miller-powered Stutz Black Hawk Special in which he lost his life at Daytona in April 1928 when a tyre failed at over 200 mph.

Florida's sands and wooden bowls

Although capricious tides and ever-increasing crowds forced the Land Speed Record runs to leave Ormond-Daytona in the mid-1930s, racing on the Florida beaches remained a motor sport fixture until 1959, when Bill France shifted Speed Week to his newly-opened Daytona Speedway.

Speed Week began in 1902 as a publicity stunt for the Ormond Beach Hotel, when Alexander Winton and Ransom Olds first raced on the beach, each conveniently reporting identical 92-km/h (57-mph) times for the measured mile. Both Ormond and Daytona Beach, 11·25 km (7 miles) to the south, vied for this new attraction, as both shared the same 152-metre (500-ft) wide arrow-straight 24-km (15-mile) stretch of hard-packed sand.

Daytona Beach built a clubhouse for the racers.

Ormond Beach retaliated late in 1905 with a large garage. Both towns received substantial support from local businessmen. Beginning in 1905, the Sir Thomas Dewar Trophy, whose winner was crowned 'Speed King of the World', assured Ormond-Daytona of international recognition.

It was in 1905 that the rule-bending dual-engined Mercedes of Boston's H. L. Bowden and the Napier of England's Arthur Macdonald exceeded 100 mph and both received credit for breaking the record. The Dewar Cup, however, prophetically went to the strange little *Wogglebug*, a Stanley Steamer driven by Louis Ross.

Top European professionals like Victor Hémery in a Darracq and Vincenzo Lancia's Fiat were expected to sweep the 1906 meet. But another Stanley Steamer made the headlines when Fred Marriott, a Stanley shop foreman, averaged an awesome 205·033 km/h (127·659 mph) for the mile and 173·8 km/h (108 mph) for five miles in winning the Dewar Cup.

Returning in 1907, with beach conditions far from ideal, Marriott roared towards the traps at 257·5 km/h (160 mph) when he hit a rough spot in the sand, became airborne and crashed. Fred Marriott survived, but the deeply disturbed Stanley brothers, after years of success in hillclimbs and races, never competed again.

The beach races of 1910 received world-wide attention when Barney Oldfield announced his intention of setting new marks. Racing the Benz used by Hémery at Brooklands in the Frenchman's unsuccessful attempt to better Marriott's time, Oldfield called his new machine the Lightning Benz (Blitzen came later). Making good on his boast, Barney bettered Marriott's four-year-old mark with a 211·94 km/h (131·72-mph) mile run. Reading a cable of congratulations from the Emperor of Germany, he bragged to the press that no one would ever go faster.

He was proved wrong one year later when the Benz-owner Ernst Moross retained Bob Burman, who celebrated his 27th birthday by going through

These posters advertising motor oil show Castrol using the land speed records to advantage.

The events illustrated are as follows:
1927 Major Henry Segrave sets the record at 203·792 mph, although the poster uses his one-way speed of 207 mph to attract attention.
1928 Captain Malcolm Campbell breaks the record at 206·95 mph.
1929 At Daytona Beach again, Segrave reaches the record-shattering speed of 231 mph.
1931 Campbell tops the world record once more with 245·733 mph.

the Daytona traps at 228·04 km/h (141·73 mph).

The popularity of board track racing during the 1920s drew attention from Speed Week. Except for amateur events the beach lay quiet until 1927, when a gallant Englishman, Major Henry Segrave, opened a bright new era. Land Speed Record attempts, stirring battles between drivers, manufacturers and nations, enjoyed no brighter chapter than the Segrave–Campbell contests.

When Wales' Pendine sands and the Fanoe Island beaches limited their efforts, Captain Malcolm Campbell turned to a dry lake bed in South Africa while Major Segrave shipped his twin-engine Sunbeam to Florida. Segrave scored first with a 326·608 km/h (203·792-mph) run in March of 1927, but Campbell's Napier came to Daytona and bettered Segrave's time the following February. Two months later Ray Keech returned LSR laurels to America for a short time when he reached 333·45 km/h (207·55 mph) in his giant 3-engine White.

Segrave pushed his Napier Special beyond 371·5 km (231 mph) in March of 1929 only to have Sir Malcolm register a 395·384 km/h (245·733 mph) in 1931. Although Campbell returned to Florida in 1935, when he posted a record 445·40 km/h (276·82 mph), Daytona Beach had reached its limits. September of 1935 saw Campbell's Bluebird II on the salt flats of Utah, where the next generation of record holders would more than double Sir Malcolm Campbell's initial 487·74-km/h (301·13-mph) Bonneville run.

Daytona continued holding an annual Speed Week, in 1936 staging a 388-km (241-mile) race over a rough three-mile combination of the beach and parallel highways. Won by Milt Marion's Ford, it marked Bill France's debut as a race organizer.

The enormous popularity of board track racing continued until the late 1920s. Other US racing, even Indianapolis, was overshadowed by the more than 20 sharply-banked 1·6-to-3·2-km (1-to-2-mile) wooden saucers that dotted the American landscape from coast-to-coast. The better drivers, especially those using supercharged Millers and Duesenbergs – such as Milton, Murphy, Lockhart, Harry Hartz, DePaolo and Billy Arnold – often notched up winning averages in the 210-km/h (130-mph) range, and in 1927 Lockhart recorded a 237·6-km/h (147·7-mph) lap on the Atlantic City boards.

But the big wood bowls were not to last. They were costly to maintain and they were dangerous. Several were destroyed by fire, as demonstrated by one newspaper report which read 'The Culver City Speedway burned to the ground last night with a great saving in lives.'

The American road racing renaissance

Road racing in America barely survived the 1920s and 1930s. The Elgin Trophy races were revived in 1933 when Fred Frame's Ford V8 won the stock car feature and Phil Shafer's Buick roadster took the Special Car race. There were scattered road races in the Los Angeles area, and in October 1936 Roosevelt Raceway, a 6·5-km (4-mile) road course with giant grandstands, opened at Old Westbury, Long Island. Planning to carry on the Vanderbilt tradition, Roosevelt's ambitious promoters arranged a dazzling opening event with a strong field of American and European stars. Scuderia Ferrari sent Nuvolari, Brivio and Farina in supercharged Alfa Romeos; Raymond Sommer and Jean-Pierre Wimille represented France; Earl Howe and Major 'Goldie' Gardner represented England; Pat Fairfield drove for South Africa. Three Indianapolis 500 winners, Wilbur Shaw, Mauri Rose and Bill Cummings, joined such other oval track aces as Rex Mays, Ted Horn and Billy Winn to complete the 45-car field.

Fastest of the Americans – in fact, faster than all the Europeans except for the works Alfa Romeos – was Billy Winn's short-wheelbase, high-riding Miller. Tazio Nuvolari captured the first Vanderbilt Trophy, but Winn held second place until his rear axle packed up near the finish.

For 1937, the promoters shortened and straightened the tight, relatively slow, 16-turn circuit. Not accustomed to road racing, spectators had been heard saying they had gone faster on their way to the track than Nuvolari's 106-km (66-mph) winning average.

Supported by the Nazis, the 1937 German entry of Mercedes-Benz W125S and type C Auto Unions were nearly invincible. Only Alfa drivers Nuvolari and Farina joined America's oval-track brigade in challenging the Germans.

Rudolf Caracciola and Dick Seaman drove supercharged 8-cylinder Mercedes while Rosemeyer and von Delius raced the 600-hp V16 rear-engined Auto Unions. Several Americans drove outdated Alfas, but Rosemeyer averaged 132·7 km/h (82·5 mph) to win with Seaman second, as Rex May's Alfa took third.

ARCA-SCCA

Used occasionally for local events, following World War Two, Roosevelt Raceway declined to become a shopping centre. One club to use the raceway was the ARCA, the Automobile Racing Club of America. Begun in 1929 by the three Collier brothers as the Overlook Automobile Club when they were teen-aged enthusiasts, Collier estate driveways were given such names as 'Members Straight' and 'Maison Blanche'.

Now known as the ARCA, its low-powered specials gave way to MGs. Miles and Sam Collier became MG Cars first American agents. Ford specials and a Freddy Dixon Riley appeared in members' hands and occasional Bugattis, Alfas and Maseratis began to grace ARCA meets. Significantly, George Rand, who had lived and raced in France, came home to become an active ARCA member. Annual 'races around the houses' were held at Alexander Bay, and the ARCA competed on public roads at Briarcliff, in suburban Westchester, New York, last raced on in 1908. As one member's family owned a major New York newspaper the ARCA received permission to race through the grounds of the New York World's Fair!

Still relished is the memory of the startled New Yorkers who saw George Rand leading a dozen roaring Grand Prix cars through the streets of Queens on their way to the Fair. The 6 October 1940 World's Fair Grand Prix was the ARCA's finest, and final, event. War was in the air, many members were in reserve units and two days after Pearl Harbor George Rand declared the ARCA inactive.

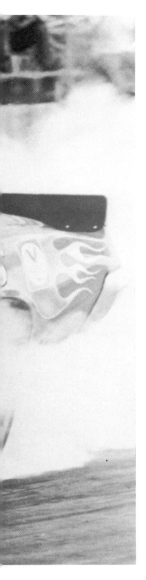

Although the ARCA may not have held more than 20 races, it would be former ARCA members, particularly Sam and Miles Collier and George Rand, who would play the key roles in turning the Sports Car Club of America into a racing-oriented organization.

Founded in 1944 by New England enthusiasts whose interest was largely that of collecting old sports cars, the SCCA avoided racing until October 1948, when Cameron Argetsinger, a law student at nearby Cornell, convinced the Watkins Glen village elders that staging a road race would bring fame – and fortune – to their hamlet. Former ARCA member Frank Griswold drove the winning Alfa coupé, while Briggs Cunningham's hybrid Buick-Mercedes and the Collier brothers' MGs filled four of the first five places in the first Watkins Glen race.

The picturesque lanes of Bridgehampton, Long Island, were raced on the following June; the Chicago region of the SCCA ran races through the resort village of Elkhart Lake, Wisconsin, and Cali-

Remington, were Muroc regulars as was Wally Parks, a young Los Angeles magazine editor, who led the hot rodders from the salt flats and outlaw dragging over deserted streets and highways to abandoned airfields and, beginning in 1948, to their own quarter-mile strips.

Evenly-matched AA-Fuel dragsters blasting off from a standing start, reaching 400 km/h (250 mph) and completing their quarter-mile runs in less than six seconds – that is what racing is all about for more than seven million US drag fans. From 'Funny Cars' – 320-km/h (200-mph) plus, plastic-bodied replicas of late-model sedans – to pick-up trucks and jalopies, drag racing created its own heroes.

Among the drag-strip stars, are 'Big Daddy' Garlits, three times national champion and first to exceed 290 km/h (180 mph), and designer-driver Mickey Thompson, whose rear-engined Buicks ran at Indianapolis in 1962. Currently a force in US racing is Hawaiian-born Danny Ongais, a former drag racer, as is Gary Gabelich, who set the present

Above left : Drag racer Micky Thompson establishes both ends of the national record on the Ontario Motor Speedway with 6·16 et and 233·76 mph.

Above right : Gary Gabelich in Blue Flame sets a new land speed record of 630 mph in 1976 on the salt flats of Utah.

Below left : Designer-driver Mickey Thompson is one of the top racers on the drag strip.

fornia believers soon had Pebble Beach, Santa Barbara and Torrey Pines. Alec Ulmann staged the first Sebring on 31 December 1950. The American road-racing renaissance was under way.

Poor crowd-control forced Watkins Glen, the Bridge, Elkhart Lake and Pebble Beach to build road courses on private land nearby. An unlikely benefactor, United States Air Force General Curtis Le May, ensured road racing's survival by making the nation's Strategic Air Command bases available to the SCCA.

Drag racing

In the early 1950s Dragsters and Stock Cars, types of racing machines unique to the American scene, came of age. Indianapolis remained the nation's racing capital, but southern California, with its salubrious climate and abundance of trained engineers, attracted a new generation of innovative race car constructors.

Hot rods – garish, chrome-encrusted, pop-art monstrosities, often housing the latest in fuel-injected engines and sophisticated suspensions – flourished in California. Before its conversion to a US air base the 10-mile-wide, 20-mile-long dry bed of Muroc Lake, 90 miles north of Los Angeles, was a rodder's dream. Washed mirror-smooth each year by melting mountain snows, Muroc had been used for record runs in the 1920s by such luminaries as Tommy Milton and Frank Lockhart.

Engine wizards Clay Smith and Ed Winfield, as well as two who were to play key roles in the Ford racing programme, Fran Hernandez and Phil

Land Speed Record with a 1,001·453-km/h (622·407-mph) two-way average at Bonneville in October 1970.

Shirley Muldowney, 37-year-old mother of a drag racing son, shattered the establishment by winning the 1977 National Hot Rod Association top championship. Matching her Chrysler-powered, 2,500-hp rail against several former title-holders, the attractive Mrs Muldowney set a 407·91-km/h (253·52-mph) record top speed and 5·71-second elapsed time en route to the championship.

A political solution

Following a driving career during stock car racing's gypsy days of uncertain purses and dangerous driving conditions, in 1947 Big Bill France founded NASCAR, the National Association of Stock Car Auto Racing. Snubbed by the AAA, America's national automobile club, who said that they prefered to concentrate on established Indianapolis cars, Bill France went on his own to build the most successful of auto racing's sanctioning organizations.

Because of the AAA's lack of foresight, newly formed clubs, such as NASCAR, the SCCA and NHRA went their separate ways. The Paris-based FIA continued working with the AAA until 1955, when the AAA used the Le Mans disaster as an excuse to disband their contest board and get out of racing. USAC, the United States Auto Club, was formed in 1956, with sanctioning responsibilities for Indianapolis and other events that had been a part of the AAA national championship.

American racing now lacked international representation as well as an organization that would

enable its various clubs to avoid schedule conflicts and driver exchange problems, so ACCUS, the Automobile Competition Committee for the United States-FIA was formed in 1957. Leading ACCUS since its beginnings have been Charles Moran, George Rand and Indianapolis businessman Tom Binford (formerly president of USAC and now chief steward for the 500) who work with representatives of NASCAR, USAC, IMSA, SCCA and NHRA on the ACCUS-FIA board.

Grass roots racing and the speedway
However, ACCUS member clubs are only the tip of the iceberg. Hundreds of regional racing organizations stage between 1,500 and 2,000 races on 1,000 or more quarter-to-half-mile dirt tracks – no one knows precisely how many – on every summer weekend. The small ovals are home to modified and supermodified cars, classes subject to a bewildering variety of definitions, many hiding soundly engineered chassis and the latest in fuel-injected engines under tatty bodies. Large followings are also enjoyed by sprint cars and the tiny but powerful midgets, roadsters sporting rugged roll cages.

It is at the small tracks, especially in the Midwest, with their family picnics and band concerts, that you find the grass roots of American racing. Broadsliding the kidney-jarring, dusty ovals is a perilous pastime, yet many drivers, including millionaire heroes like A. J. Foyt, the Unser brothers and Mario Andretti, say dirt track racing is what they most enjoy. USAC's flourishing Midget division alone runs a 50-race, or more, championship schedule, some of which events are held indoors. USAC also sanctions a busy sprint car championship and, compared with NASCAR, a limited stock car division.

USAC's strength lies in its national 'big car' championship, a 12-to-15-race series that is blessed with the Indianapolis 500 as its showpiece. Since

1970 Indianapolis purses have exceeded 1,000,000 dollars annually with 250,000 dollars or more as the winner's share. Some 300,000 spectators on race day, by far the largest crowd in the world of sport, plus two weekends of trials that attract an additional 600,000 to 700,000 spectators, enabled Tony Hulman, who died in November 1977, constantly to improve his giant racing plant.

Until 1961, when Jack Brabham triggered the rear-engine revolution at the Speedway by finishing ninth in John Cooper's diminutive, under-powered

Top and Above: All these cars competed in the 1977 *Los Angeles Times* 500 at Ontario Speedway, California. Holly Farms No 11 was driven by Cale Yarborough, who finished third. Hawaiian Tropic No 1 was driven by Donnie Allison. MC Matador No 12 was driven by Bobby Allison. No 95 was driven by Harry Jefferson.

Climax, qualifying times and winning averages had moved up in an orderly fashion.

Speedway results became less predictable after Colin Chapman brought his cars to Indianapolis. Jim Clark's Lotus, powered by Ford, was second in 1963, while Rodger Ward gave Ford another second in 1963, and yet another in 1964 with a Watson-built car. Clark won the 500 in 1965 with Ford's new 4-cam engine. Indianapolis' traditional front-engined roadster was now history, and even so devout an 'Offy' believer as A. J. Foyt joined the Ford rear-engined brigade.

Graham Hill's Lola-Ford was the winner in 1966; Foyt won his third 500 in 1967 and Bobby Unser broke the Ford streak in 1968, driving a rear-engined turbocharged Offenhauser built by Dan Gurney. Qualifying speeds soared to 275·474 km/h (171·208 mph) in 1968 when Joe Leonard earned the pole in one of Andy Granatelli's soon-to-be-outlawed turbines.

Foyt's 274·444 km/h (170·568 mph) was fastest in the 1969 trials, although Andretti won the race and Peter Revson pushed the 1971 qualifying time past 288 km/h (179 mph). Six years later Tom Sneva, a young high school principal driving for Roger Penske, broke the Speedway's 200-mph barrier. Foyt was to win the 1977 race, an unprecedented fourth 500, but Sneva finished second and went on to become the 1977 national champion.

For the past decade, USAC and the Speedway's elite – Foyt, Andretti, two-time winners Al and Bobby Unser and Johnny Rutherford – have appeared less insular. Obsessed with winning his fourth

the final seconds. Stock car racing's popularity is centred in the American Southeast, where it outdraws all other sports, although successful Grand Nationals are also held in California, Texas and Michigan. Its 'good ol' boys', the Richard Pettys, Cale Yarboroughs and David Pearsons, enjoy followings beyond those of America's football and baseball stars. The sedans they drive – Champion Yarborough's Chevy, David Pearson's Mercury, or six-time national champion Richard Petty's Dodge – are the safest race cars in the world.

Limited to current models and those of the two prior years, besides enjoying all normal racing safety features the driver is harnessed inside a cage of heavy steel tubing that extends into and reinforces his door panels. Starting life as an ordinary 6,000-dollar or 7,000-dollar Detroit sedan, the car can take another 25,000 or 30,000 dollars to make it competitive. Although a number of modifications are legal you may not alter the sedan's profile, but you may strengthen it, and add weight, the greatest of sins being to try to lighten your race car. Yarborough, who repeated as NASCAR champion in 1977, won nine of 30 races, finished in the top five 25 times and won 431,576 dollars. Richard Petty, who had, for him, a mediocre season, won five races and pocketed 330,000 dollars. Final 1977 manufacturer standings showed Chevrolet with 21 victories, Dodge with seven and Mercury with two.

On the stock car scene William Henry Getty France is an evangelist. He believed in racing automobiles that the public could identify with, and has seen 'win on Sunday, sell on Monday' become an

500, Foyt had little time for other forms of racing, although when he ran sports cars at Nassau, Daytona, Sebring and Le Mans he excelled. USAC ovals are holding VW-supported Super Vee races; a lady driver, Janet Guthrie, qualified for the 1977 500; many front-line Indy cars are using turbocharged Cosworth-Fords and Indianapolis cars raced at Brands Hatch and Silverstone in 1978.

Stock car racing

The most popular form of motor sport in the United States is stock car racing. NASCAR's 30-race Winston Cup Series for late model sedans attracts more spectators, pays larger purses and, in race after race, provides bumper-to-bumper competition down to

axiom. Stock cars, of sorts, were racing before the mid-1930s, when 'Big Bill' first became involved. But they travelled a poorly organized trail of rutted dust bowls, with shifty promoters who frequently departed with the cash box before the drivers finished racing.

Although stock car racing's beginnings were on dirt, by the early 1970s, all Grand Nationals were being staged on paved ovals. Darlington, the first of

Right : Three-time Indianapolis 500 winner, A. J. Foyt Jnr, wheels his Coyote racer onto the track. He and Andretti were the first drivers to top 200 mph in practice for the 500 in 1977.

NASCAR's super speedways, opened in 1950, and in 1959 Bill France realized his dream when Daytona International Speedway, a 4-km (2·5-mile) banked oval that now seats over 100,000 spectators, played host to Daytona Speed Week. Beyond the Winston Cup series for the late-model sedans, NASCAR also sanctions Modified (for intermediate and compact cars such as Camaro, Maverick, Mustang and Javelin) Baby Grand and Hobby divisions.

American successes overseas

As with so many of his generation, Phil Hill's first sports car was an MG. Three years later, in 1950, with Ritchie Ginther acting as his crew chief, Phil won the first Pebble Beach, driving an XK120 Jaguar. Moving up to racing both his own and patron's Ferraris, Phil compiled such an outstanding record that January 1956 saw him paired with Olivier Gendebien in a works Ferrari in the Argentine. The most successful sports car team of their time, Hill and Gendebien numbered three 24 Hours of Le Mans, including 1958, the first ever for an American, among their many victories.

When Phil Hill captured the Italian GP at Monza in 1960 it was the first GP for an American since 1921. Then, in 1961, Phil Hill became the first American to earn the world driving championship. But the triumph was a bitter-sweet one, as Wolfgang von Trips, his Ferrari team-mate, rival and friend, was killed at Monza during the event in which Phil clinched the championship.

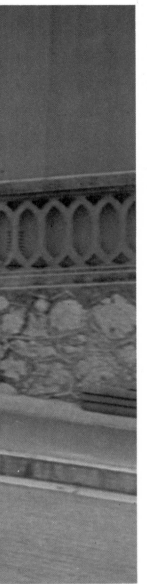

Phil Hill left Ferrari to join those Ferrari stalwarts who had shifted to ATS. When ATS failed to produce a competitive F1 machine Hill concentrated on sports cars. After winning the 1964 Daytona 2,000 km in a Ferrari, Phil piloted Jim Hall's Chevrolet-powered Chaparrals to earn a repeat win at the Nürburgring, then with Mike Spence he beat the favoured Jackie Stewart/Chris Amon Ferrari in the BOAC 6 Hours at Brands Hatch. One of his last victories came in the 1966 Can-Am at Laguna Seca, the course that replaced Pebble Beach, where, 16 years earlier, Phil Hill had seen his first chequered flag.

Dan Gurney may be the most versatile of American drivers. He joined Ferrari as a sports car driver in 1959 but was promoted to F1 in mid-season. One of Dan's better years was with Porsche, in 1961, when he earned second place in the drivers' championship, going on to give Porsche its only, and his first, Grand Prix victory in the French GP at Rouen the following year.

Driving for Brabham, Dan won the GPs of Mexico and France in 1964, his second win at Rouen being another first for a new marque. Gurney's career peaked in 1967, when he shared the winning Ford with A. J. Foyt at Le Mans and a week later drove his own Eagle to victory in the GP of Belgium at Spa – the first GP for an American car since 1921.

But Grand Prix was only a part of Gurney's racing life. In NASCAR, Dan's Mercury sedan won five major stock car races. And although he failed to win the 500 he was frequently a top contender, finishing second in 1968 and 1969.

When Gurney's Lola-Ford won the Bridgehampton Can-Am it became the only non-Chevrolet-powered winner during the Can-Am's first four years. By winning the 1967 Rex Mays 300 Indy car race at Riverside Dan completed a year of championship victories in Stock Car, Grand Prix, Can-Am and Championship cars.

In 1964 Dan and Carroll Shelby started AAR –

Gregory won the 1965 Le Mans – an event he entered a record 16 times – driving a Ferrari 250/275LM owned by three-time Le Mans winner Luigi Chinetti. Gregory was also one of a growing band of road racers to run at Indianapolis.

Ritchie Ginther first raced a Ford-engined MG-TC in California's Sandberg Hillclimb in 1951. After riding with Phil Hill in the 1953–4 Mexican road races and racing a variety of makes on the West Coast, the diminutive Ginther joined Ferrari as chief test driver and a member of their 1960 F1 team. Following Ferrari and three years with BRM, Ginther moved to Honda, where he won the 1967 Mexican GP for one of the Japanese manufacturer's two F1 victories.

American drivers at home

Until he was sidelined by a minor heart problem in 1960 Carroll Shelby's laconic drawl and gracious ways were a welcome part of American racing. Winner of a classic showdown against Gurney, Hansgen and Gregory at Riverside in 1957, Shelby and Roy Salvadori brought Aston Martin its long-sought Le Mans triumph in 1959. As a constructor, Shelby's Ford-powered Cobras ruled SCCA big-bore racing from 1963 until 1969, and in 1965 Cobra ousted Ferrari from the FIA-Manufacturer's Championship. Shelby also played a vital role in Ford's racing programme: all six victories enjoyed by Ford factory cars, including the 1966 and 1967 Le Mans, were won by teams under Carroll's direction.

Walt Hansgen earned four national titles, usually in Cunningham D types, then drove for Ford. He rarely put a wheel wrong while at home but was constantly in trouble at Le Mans and was to lose his life at the Sarthe circuit in 1966 during April practice.

English-born Ken Miles, who settled in California, and Pennsylvania's Bob Holbert had somewhat parallel careers. Both began in MGs, Ken's famed *Flying Shingle* was almost unbeatable in California and Holbert recorded an impressive 14 wins and nine seconds out of his 24 MG races. Both drivers moved up to Porsches (each modestly saying that the other was America's best Porsche pilot) and Holbert won four national SCCA titles.

Bob didn't enjoy his one trip to Le Mans in 1960 ('It was three days before I learned how to ask for a glass of water') but that didn't stop the Holbert/Gregory works Porsche from winning its class in record time and finishing fifth overall. Then Bob joined team Cobra, where Miles was Shelby's Man Friday. In 1963, alternating between his Porsche and Shelby's Cobra, depending on the course and conditions, Holbert captured the first US Road Racing Championship. Three years later Ken Miles died while testing Ford's new J car at Riverside.

Until 1963, when the SCCA first recognized professional racing, talented Americans who sought rewards more tangible than trophies either went overseas or found a sponsor. One of the better stay-at-home drivers who also excelled in selling himself was Roger Penske. Winning national titles in 1962–3 in a Birdcage Maserati, a Cooper Monaco and a controversial rebuilt F1 Cooper which he dubbed the 'Zerex Special' after a sponsor's product, Penske also drove a Jim Hall Chaparral before retiring from driving in 1964.

Now a successful businessman, Roger remains in racing as the owner of Michigan International Speedway and of cars that have won Indianapolis, the Can-Am and Trans-Am Championships, Grand Prix and Stock Car races.

Top : Phil Hill in his Ferrari at Monaco, 1961.

Left : In 1961 Phil Hill became the first American racing driver to win the World Champion title.

Above right : Dan Gurney in his Eagle won the Belgian Grand Prix in 1967 – first GP victory for an American car since 1921.

All American Racers – which Gurney would take over in 1967 and make into a major race car constructor. Dan also worked with England's Harry Weslake on his own engines and Gurney-Weslake heads. Bobby Unser won the 1968 500 in Dan's own machine, and Gurney-built Eagles are among the most popular of Indy cars. Versatile indeed.

Masten Gregory, Carroll Shelby and Ritchie Ginther were other Americans who did well overseas during the 1950s and '60s. After failing to complete the 1954 Argentine 1,000 km, Gregory bought the winning Ferrari and campaigned it in Europe. In 1957, his first full year in Formula 1, Masten completed every GP he started, finishing fourth in the drivers' championship. With Jochen Rindt

After buying an assortment of Europe's best sports cars, in 1963 Jim Hall tried a full season of Grand Prix racing in a BRP Lotus-BRM, a fifth at the Nürburgring being his best finish. He earned the 1964 US Road Racing Championship in his own plastic-bodied, automatic-transmission Chaparral, and with Hap Sharp won the 1965 Sebring 12 Hours. Introduced at the Bridgehampton Can-Am, Hall's winged Chaparral 2F, with its huge driver-controlled aerofoil, shocked the racing world. Overnight, it seemed, Indianapolis, F1, Stock Cars – everything on wheels – had sprouted wings!

With the introduction of prize money the SCCA soon sanctioned a varied series of 'pro' races. Its best, the Canadian American Challenge Cup, introduced in the autumn of 1966, was timed to catch the GP circus while it was in America for the US and Canadian GPs. Designed for Group 7, big unlimited-displacement-engined sports cars, the Can-Am produced spectacular racing. Watching the international stars battle the home troops in machines as fast as GP cars made the Can-Am an immediate success.

After John Surtees' Lola-Chevrolet won the 1966 Can-Am Championship Bruce McLaren and Denny Hulme took charge, alternating as Can-Am champions for the next four years. Team McLaren's routine of bringing over new models, then selling them to eager buyers at the season's end, was shattered in 1970 by Bruce McLaren's fatal crash at Goodwood. Nevertheless, Hulme was an easy winner that year.

The new men
A major Can-Am benefit was that it spotlighted America's good young drivers. As Mark Donohue said after becoming the 1967 US Road Racing champion, 'The USRRC was fine, but it's like playing tennis with your wife. When you run with these international guys and they smoke you off you really try harder.'

Peter Revson (with George Follmer and Donohue, the era's best American road racers) joined Team McLaren and became the 1971 Can-Am champion. Predictably, as Can-Am's prestige and purses grew Porsche investigated what it would take to upset the McLaren-Chevrolet.

The man Porsche talked to was Roger Penske. The result was Porsche's 900-hp turbocharged 917K. Penske driver George Follmer easily won the Can-Am title in 1972, and Donohue, who missed part of the 1972 season because of an injury, toyed with the McLarens to take the 1973 Can-Am crown.

Above left: Mark Donohue, winner of the 1972 Indianapolis 500, in his new Eagle.

Top centre: Phil Hill breaks another record, this time in his Chaparral – the first American car ever to win a race at Nürburgring.

Above centre: Phil Hill, driving a Chaparral with a stabilizer, takes first place in the 1966 Monterey Grand Prix.

After Jackie Stewart had demonstrated that Jim Hall's ground effects Chaparral 2J (two rear-mounted engines sucked air from under the car and gave it incredible road holding) was blindingly fast, though unreliable, Team McLaren succeeded in having the 2J declared illegal. Now they mounted a vigorous attack against the turbocharged Porsches. This time the FIA ruled against them, and McLaren withdrew from the Can-Am. The Can-Am had a new problem – where you could have been competitive in a 35,000-dollar McLaren-Chevrolet it now took a 125,000-dollar Turbo Porsche.

The Can-Am collapsed in 1974. F5000, which the SCCA pushed as its replacement, was a failure, although perennial F5000 champion Brian Redman did a good job in turning back the occasional challenge of such stalwarts as Al Unser and Mario Andretti. In 1977 the SCCA re-established the Can-Am as its premier series.

Club racing is the SCCA's strongest suit. Its annual runoffs at Road Atlanta attract over 500 divisional leaders, fiercely competing for national

Above right : Peter Revson at Watkins Glen, NY, the winner of the 1972 Can-Am championship.

Above, far right : World champion Jackie Stewart was running third in the Can-Am race, Watkins Glen, NY, until he was forced into the pits.

Right : Bruce McLaren wins the Can-Am Cup in 1967, John Surtees (right) wins the Stardust Trophy.

Above centre : Jochen Mass leading Vittorio Brambilla in the 1977 US GP West at Long Beach.

Above right : Hans Stuck in a Brabham Alfa-Romeo at Long Beach in1977.

Right : The V8 engine of 'Cyclone', a Rail dragster.

Left : 'Maverick', a Dodge pick-up with a special light fibreglass body, 'burning off' at the start of a race.

amateur honours in the club's 24 racing classes.

Both Mark Donohue and Peter Revson were products of SCCA training. Leaving McLaren after the 1973 season, in which he won the British and Canadian GPs, Peter Revson now drove for Shadow. At Kyalami for the 1974 South African GP – a circuit Revson knew well, having been a close second to Jackie Stewart in 1973 and a solid third the year before – handsome, debonair Revson was killed during practice a few days past his 35th birthday.

Coming out of retirement to drive Penske's new GP car, which he had helped to design, Mark Donohue crashed during an untimed practice session for the 1975 Austrian GP. Two days later, Donohue who had won Indianapolis and almost everything else in American racing, died in hospital. He was 38.

Until 1969 when John Bishop, former executive director of the SCCA, went on his own and founded IMSA, the International Motor Sports Association, the SCCA controlled almost all US road racing. Sanctioning professional racing only, IMSA's GT series, for the big turbocharged BMWs, Porsches and a few American makes, such as the Chevrolet Monza, is an outstanding success.

Many IMSA drivers also run in events sanctioned by rival organizations, particularly the SCCA's Trans-Am series. Former IMSA GT champion Peter Gregg is the 1977 Trans-Am title-holder.

At the age of 15 Mario Andretti and his twin brother Aldo settled in Nazareth, Pennsylvania, which happens to have a half-mile track. Beginning with typical dirt track modifieds, by 1964 Mario was racing Indy roadsters. Winning the first of his

four USAC National championships in 1965, Mario also captured the 1967 Daytona 500 Stock Car classic and in 1969 won the Indianapolis 500. At Watkins Glen for the 1968 US GP, driving a Chapman Lotus in his first F1 outing, Andretti set a lap record and earned pole position. 'After all', Mario said, 'Ascari was my first hero.' Yet, it would be 1976 before Andretti could give most of his time to GP racing. His 1977 GP season, in which he won the US GP West and the French, Spanish and Italian GPs, brought his total GP victories to six.

Then in 1978 Mario Andretti had his most successful Formula 1 season so far, winning six Grand Prix with Colin Chapman's Lotus-Ford 79 to take the drivers' world championship.

In 1976, with the running of the US GP West at Long Beach, California, the United States became the only nation holding two GPs. Modern GP racing came to America in December 1959 when Alec Ulmann staged the season's finale at Sebring and a young New Zealander, Bruce McLaren, garnered his first GP laurels.

A lack of spectators, with literally more people in the pits than the stands, prompted Ulmann to take the 1960 US GP to Riverside, where Stirling Moss won. The crowd in California was even smaller than that in Florida. Watkins Glen latched on to the US GP in 1961 and, 17 years later, shows no sign of letting go.

Despite the threat of fuel-shortage-induced restrictions and a spate of proposed anti-noise laws, US motor sport continues to thrive, although rising attendance figures and larger purses have not matched racing's soaring costs.

GRAND PRIX

Nowadays Grand Prix racing provides the setting for not one but two world championships – one for drivers, the other for the constructors of the cars and engines which they use. Compared with earlier times it is a highly commercialized sport involving huge sums of money.

Inevitably in a personality-orientated sport the drivers' contest produces the greater publicity. It is also the more senior of the two FIA-sponsored contests, dating back to 1950, when Dr Giuseppe Farina became motor racing's first official World Champion.

The championship has always been operated on a points basis, but from time to time the rules have been modified. For example, until 1960 a championship point was awarded to the driver making the fastest time – or shared if more than one driver recorded the fastest time.

Today points are awarded on the basis of nine, six, four, three, two and one for the first six places in the finishing order in each of the qualifying Grands Prix, of which there were 17 (the highest number so far) for the 1977 contest. Before calculating a driver's final points score for the year the qualifying races are divided into two parts. In the case of an odd number of races part one contains one more race than part two.

A driver is then allowed to count all but his worst score from each part of the season. In practice it is rare for a driver to score points in every qualifying race, but if this does happen he drops his lowest score from each part of the season. In the event of a points tie the championship, or any lesser place in the finishing order, would be awarded to the driver scoring the more first places, then second places, and so on down to sixth places. Should there still be a tie the tying drivers' two discarded scores would also be assessed, and if this still resulted in a tie the *Commission International de Sportive* is empowered to announce the finishing order in any manner it deems fit.

A driver can score points no matter how many changes of car or engine he may make during the course of a season.

The constructors' World Championship, known officially and rather ponderously as the International Cup for Formula One Manufacturers, is based on a rather different points scoring system. Here, although the allocation of points for each of the top six finishing positions is the same, only the best result achieved in each race with a combination of chassis and engine can be counted. Also the final points score is based on the results of all qualifying races (17 in 1977). Of all contemporary Formula One car constructors, only three – Ferrari, Renault and BRM – also manufacture their own engines. In all other cases the name of the engine has to be

Above left : Competitors in Grand Prix racing require a supply of two types of tyre, one for racing on wet surfaces, one for dry surfaces.

Above : James Hunt prior to the start of the 1978 British Grand Prix.

Top right : Villeneuve cornering in the 1978 British Grand Prix.

Above right : Princess Grace presenting the trophy to Patrick Depailler, winner of the 1978 Monaco Grand Prix.

Above far right : More of the organizational side of motor racing – tyres and a team headquarters.

Right : An impressive spray of water during the Race of Champions at Brands Hatch, 1976.

linked to that of the chassis for the purpose of scoring championship points (e.g., Lotus–Ford or Brabham–Alfa Romeo), and in the event of a chassis being fitted with more than one make of engine – once commonplace but now less so – the chassis-engine combinations must be listed separately in the championship table.

To qualify as a World Championship round a Grand Prix must be staged for Formula One cars, and must be run for a minimum distance of 250 km (155 miles), a maximum length of 322 km (200 miles) and a maximum duration of two hours. Should a race still be in progress at the end of that period the chequered flag must be shown to the race leader at the end of his current lap and the race ended.

Because of advances in tyre technology which have led to the supply of different tyres for wet and dry

track conditions a Grand Prix must be officially declared either a 'wet' or a 'dry' race before the start. A 'wet' race is allowed to run through non-stop, and should the track dry individual teams are left to decide when to bring their drivers to their pit for a change to 'dry' tyres. However, a 'dry' race may be halted prematurely by the Clerk of the Course if he feels that rain has made the track too hazardous for the race to continue without a change of tyres.

If the race has run less than one-third of its scheduled distance it will be restarted from scratch after a pause to enable all teams to change to 'wet' tyres. If the race has run between one-third and two-thirds of its scheduled distance it will be restarted to run for the remaining scheduled laps, the cars being lined up in the order of classification at the time the race was stopped rather than in their original grid positions based on practice times. If the race has run at least two-thirds of its scheduled distance at the time it is stopped it will be deemed to have been ended, the finishing order and the World Championship points being awarded on the basis of the running order at the end of that lap.

The rules of the game

In the interests of both competition and safety motor racing takes place according to the small print of rule books, the master of which carries the name of

the *Féderation Internationale de l'Automobile*, the world governing body of motor sport. The FIA appoints representative organizations in all affiliated countries (in the United Kingdom for example it is the Royal Automobile Club), who in turn produce rule books for the conduct of the sport within their own countries. Individual organizing clubs are also permitted to issue supplementary regulations for their own events, but these must comply with the ground rules laid down by their national club, just as national rules follow the guidelines of the FIA.

Grand Prix racing, the highest form of international motor racing, is conducted according to rules drawn up by the world governing body's sporting subcommittee, the *Commission Internationale de Sportive* and published annually in the *FIA Year Book of Automobile Sport* (published by Patrick Stephens Ltd). While national motor sporting clubs are responsible for the organization of Grands Prix in their own countries (although the responsibility can be delegated to an affiliated race-organizing club) the event must be conducted entirely by the rules laid down in the FIA rule book.

Motor racing categories are structured in terms of formulae which control the technical specification of competing cars, and those eligible to partici-

wheels to the leading edge of the rear wheels could not exceed 140 cm (55·1 in) and the maximum width of the rear wing was 110 cm (43·3 in). In addition, total front overhang was restricted to 120 cm (47·2 in) and total rear overhang to 80 cm (31·5 in) beyond the wheel centre lines. The overall maximum width of the car was fixed at 215 cm (84·6 in), and that of each wheel at 53·3 cm (21 in).

Stringent regulations also governed the specification of materials, the method of construction and the placement of such accident-vulnerable items as fuel cells, fuel, oil and ignition lines, all aimed at improving safety. In the interests of driver protection strict rules governed standards of impact resistance and roll-over protection. As well as rules specifically relating to Grand Prix cars, those conforming to Formula One rules also had to meet all the basic regulations controlling design and specification of all single-seater racing cars, no matter what their engine size or potential use. These cover such diverse requirements as a maximum height above the ground of 90 cm (35·4) for any bodywork, the use of recessed fuel-fillers, and a maximum height of 60 cm (23·6 in) for exhaust pipe outlets.

Even if, as seems likely, the current 3-litre formula remains in force for several more years it is likely to

pate in Grand Prix races have to conform to what is known as Formula One. In the past the base rules of Formula One have been amended every few years in an effort to promote closer, safer, sometimes faster, sometimes slower racing, but such has been the success of the current Formula One, introduced in 1966, that it has undergone only detail modifications and improvements, mainly in the interests of safety, ever since. These rules seem likely to continue as the basis for Grand Prix racing for many years to come. The basic requirements as operated for the 1978 Grand Prix races were as follows:

Engines were restricted to a cylinder capacity of 3,000 cc, 1,500 cc if fitted with a supercharger, and to a maximum of 12 cylinders. There was also the opportunity to use turbine engines in place of reciprocating-piston engines, their size being dictated by an equivalence formula.

The minimum weight of a Formula One car, without ballast, was 575 kg (1,267·3 lb), and all cars had to conform to a number of dimensional rules. For example, the overall width behind the front

be refined in detail so as to maintain the careful balance between performance, competitiveness and safety which has led to its success and long life.

Grand Prix engines

Without question the current Formula One regulations, restricting cars to engines of 3-litre displacement – or 1½ litres with supercharging – have proved the most successful in the history of Grand Prix racing. This has been largely due to equality of performance between rival cars, made possible through the universal availability of a competitive and – in Grand Prix terms – relatively inexpensive power unit, the Ford DFV V8, designed by Keith Duckworth, chief executive of the company which manufactures the engine, Cosworth Engineering Ltd, of Northampton. Their achievements have been marked by the RAC with the award of the coveted Diamond Jubilee trophy for 1976.

This engine has dominated Grand Prix since its debut in the 1967 Dutch Grand Prix. After an initial period of exclusive use by one team, Lotus, it has

Top : Jabouilles's Renault at the 1977 British Grand Prix.

Top right : The Ford-Cosworth DFV8 engine.

Above left : Cars being weighed in the presence of the scrutineers.

Above : A Brazilian flag marshal and his set of flags

Right : Power revealed – a Ferrari Boxer 3L engine.

become almost standard equipment among teams which do not manufacture their own racing engines.

With the eclipse of BRM the Ford DFV has only four serious rivals: Ferrari, whose flat-12 engine has proved the most successful challenger; Alfa Romeo, who came close to scoring their first Grand Prix success in 1977, having made their flat-12 unit available exclusively to the Brabham team from the beginning of 1976; Matra, whose V12 engine powers the Ligier car and gained its first Formula One victory in the 1977 Swedish Grand Prix; and Renault, whose turbocharged V6 unit, mounted in a Renault chassis on Michelin tyres – when everyone else has been using Goodyears – constituted the most interesting technical development of the 1977 season.

It took only 134 Grands Prix for the Ford DFV engine to feature in its 100th GP success, and significantly it had taken 67 appearances to score its 50th Grand Prix victory, a remarkable record of consistency and longevity. Of the remaining 34 races, Ferrari were victorious in 25, BRM in 4, Repco (in a Brabham chassis) in 3, and Honda (in their own

chassis) and Gurney Weslake (in an Eagle) in 1 race each.

Whereas the Ford DFV engine was producing only 408 bhp when it won its first race, its output had risen almost to 480 bhp by the time of its 100th Grand Prix success, and Cosworth Engineering had just launched a research and development programme with a series of experimental engines aimed at increasing the V8 engine's power output still further.

While its main rivals now enjoy more than 500 bhp their power advantage has been at least partly offset by greater fuel consumption and consequent extra weight as they drive on to the start line with full tanks. This factor convinces Keith Duckworth that his philosophy of producing a compact, lightweight and efficient V8 engine is the correct one for Grand Prix racing as presently constituted, and it is why any eventual successor to the DFV is likely to have a similar number of cylinders. Duckworth has recently suggested that future Grand Prix formulae should place limitations on fuel consumption. He feels that the research and development that would follow such restrictions would be of benefit to the automobile industry as a whole in the light of the world's need to conserve energy resources.

Renault are the first team to exploit the possibility of using a turbocharged 1½-litre engine under the current Grand Prix formula, but so seriously do rival manufacturers view this development that should the Renault out-perform the conventionally-powered engines by a significant margin other turbocharged units will appear very quickly in response. Ferrari announced as early as the summer of 1977 that they would develop such a Formula One engine, to be used, if required, during the 1978 racing season.

With Ford, Fiat (Ferrari), Chrysler (Matra), Alfa Romeo and Renault all either directly or indirectly involved on the engine side of Grand Prix racing the power game is in a healthy state of international competition. The rewards for success, in terms of publicity and prestige, are well known, but equally important to the motor industry is the advanced engineering knowledge to be derived from participation itself. There would be as widespread grief

within the industry as among spectators, therefore, in the event of any fundamental change in current Formula One engine regulations. After 12 seasons of racing they have made Grand Prix racing closer-fought than ever before and led to a much-needed element of financial stability in what must inevitably be an extremely expensive branch of motor sport.

The structure of a Grand Prix team

In an era of super-star adulation it is the Grand Prix driver who enjoys the publicity spotlight at a motor race. Yet his is only one part of a team effort which lies behind every race performance. If he loses, it could be through his own fault; if he wins the applause should be not for him alone but for the team as a whole, a team who have contributed to his success from the trackside or back at team head-quarters.

The structure of individual Grand Prix teams varies in much the same way as in the management of seemingly similar businesses. In some cases the team patron will also act as team manager. In others he will appoint a manager, giving him complete authority within a prescribed annual budget. In other cases patron and manager will work side-by-side at a race meeting, each assuming overall responsibility for the operation of one car and driver

throughout practice and race days.

Each Grand Prix team must be tailored to its resources and for the most efficient use of the available manpower and equipment. A typical team, involving two cars and drivers per race, might well comprise the following supporting personnel:

A chief executive, who doubles as team director at a race track and retains control of all contractual commitments – to sponsors, race organizers and publicity media – and of policy decisions such as whether to run a particular car in a race.

A team manager, who reports directly to the team director but is in overall charge of preparations for the team's race and spare cars and responsible for providing such necessary back-up facilities as pit-signalling and timing personnel and equipment, and for liaison with tyre and other component suppliers, both at the track and back at base.

A team administration manager who, as deputy team manager, is mainly responsible for paperwork arising from the team's movements – provision of travel schedules and documents, customs clearance, catering facilities, hotel accommodation and transportation for all members of the team. At a race circuit he may also be responsible for timing and pit-signalling information and/or the recording of such technical information, as changes in car specification

Above : Hunt in the 1976 Japanese Grand Prix. At this point, all the attention of the back-up team – and, of course, the media – is focused on the racing driver.

Above right : Team mechanics at work on engines.

Right : Lafitte receiving instructions and advice prior to the start of the 1977 Italian Grand Prix.

Far right : Colin Chapman, designer and builder of Lotus cars, whose career began in 1948 and has been marked by many Grand Prix successes.

made during the course of a meeting and their effect on performance.

A chief mechanic, who will not only oversee the work of all other mechanics but will act as the number one mechanic on the team leader's race and spare cars.

A deputy chief mechanic, who will also act as the number one mechanic on the second team driver's race and spare cars.

At least one other mechanic will be permanently allocated to each driver, and the team may also have specialist mechanics with particular expertise in all aspects of car preparation – tyres, brakes, electrics, transmission – and who may be called upon to work on either driver's cars.

Most teams have at least one giant transporter, usually with a smaller support vehicle, with a permanent driver who is also responsible for the inventory of cars, spares and tools transported from factory to race track and home again, and for their safe-keeping throughout a meeting. Deputy transporter drivers may be appointed from among the mechanics on a race-by-race basis, to spread the driving load.

These days no Grand Prix team seems complete without its own motorhome, which acts as a drivers' rest and changing room, a hospitality suite for sponsors and the media and team dining room. Having its permanent staff – often a husband-and-wife team – it relieves trackside racing staff of the catering function, which in the past was also theirs.

The well-equipped Grand Prix team, while it is away racing, will have left behind an equally talented collection of people concerned with the design, construction, maintenance and sometimes repair of cars and components, as well as with manning the team's administrative offices. The latter function can be a vital lifeline for a team, who may suddenly require replacement parts rushed to an airport.

Often a team's base service is managed, and even largely staffed, by former mechanics who have had their fill of the nomadic life or whose family responsibilities now make globe-trotting unattractive. Their trackside experience well qualifies them to provide an efficient support service at the team's factory.

The team's design office will normally comprise a chief designer and at least one design draughtsman, plus an assistant. Of these it is the chief designer who is the most regular visitor to race meetings, although he will be more in evidence during practice days than on race day itself, when his work will have been largely completed. He will try to be present at all the team's test sessions, however, for his main trackside function will be to evaluate modifications he has designed into cars and/or components, study driver and chassis performance, advise on further changes and collate data which may lead to further improvements in the team's cars or their eventual replacements.

At a race meeting the chief designer will also give rival cars close scrutiny comparing performance in as many areas as possible – straightline speed, cornering speeds, braking distances and, of course, lap times. He will also discreetly glance at instrument readings during pit stops. As every designer has a similar interest in his rivals' cars their surreptitious wanderings along the pit road can be a source of much trackside ribaldry!

It can be seen, then, that the Grand Prix driver can do little without the support of a small army of talented people. It is one of his duties to earn, by his driving performance and his personal relationships, their unstinted and dedicated backing from factory and pit road which is so essential to consistent success in this, the most highly competitive class of motor racing.

Grand Prix driving – a full-time job

A Grand Prix driver, unless he enters other forms of motor racing, actually races on fewer than 20 days each year, yet his performance on those occasions depends largely on how he has occupied himself on the other 345 days.

One reason why most successful Grand Prix drivers confine themselves to Formula One events is because to do the job properly is virtually a fulltime occupation for the true professional, who will engage in promotional activities for much of the time when he is not engaged in driving.

The greater part of his driving, in fact, is likely to take place not at race meetings, but in the lonelier atmosphere of otherwise deserted tracks which have been hired by his team for private testing. Sometimes 'group testing' takes place, and several teams will use facilities laid on by a tyre company to evaluate their latest products; but teams tend to confine serious development testing to private sessions, for obvious reasons.

In most teams the number one driver carries the double burden of being the team's principal race-winner as well as its chief car-tester, if only because of his assumed greater ability to drive his car

Above left: A huge transporter well stocked with racing tyres.

Above: This pit scene at the 1978 Spanish Grand Prix illustrates the purposeful, finely tuned team organization that prevails today; and also the assertive commercialism that sustains modern motor sport.

Above right : The graphic language of pit signals, designed for split-second comprehension.

Above : Team gear and a motor home, aspects of the nomadic life led by those closely involved in motor sport.

late accurately to engineers in the pit road, exactly how his car is behaving under various conditions.

He must also be able to drive consistently from the beginning to the end of a long testing session. The true effect of changes made to the car during a day will be camouflaged if his driving improves as the day progresses, or if he becomes tired and therefore slower.

Race-winning at Grand Prix level depends a great deal on the testing preceding it, and as an indication of the importance that leading teams attach to development testing, Jody Scheckter, who won the Argentine Grand Prix soon after joining the Walter Wolf Racing Team and who elsewhere describes how he drove round the Monaco street circuit on his way to the 100th Grand Prix victory with a Cosworth Ford DFV engine, took part in no fewer than 41 days of test driving in 1977, excluding all the days of official practice preceding the 17 Grands Prix and one non-championship race which comprised his Formula One season.

This meant that Scheckter drove on at least 95 days during the year in fulfilling his Formula One contract, and allowing for travelling time to and from race meetings and test sessions, plus occasional visits to team headquarters for cockpit fitting and business meetings, he was at the disposal of his team on some 150 days that year. In theory this left him with more than half the year for other activities, but so inflexible is a Grand Prix racing and testing programme that it can be extremely difficult for a Formula One driver to dovetail other racing into his schedule, even if the terms of his contract allow it. Grand Prix racing, therefore, is very much a full-time job – as indeed it should be for such a generous rate of payment.

consistently on or close to its limit. It is a burden which, in the main, he will carry gladly, for a heavy programme of car-testing will help him to sustain, and even sharpen, his edge on the driver who rarely climbs into a cockpit other than for official pre-race practice and qualification and the race itself.

While statistics show that there are relatively few consistent Grand Prix winners, most team managers and chief designers will tell you that there are even fewer really top-calibre test drivers with the ability to identify what a car may be doing in any instant, what it should be doing, why it is failing to do so and what should be done to enable it to do so. Thus a sound technical understanding of chassis behaviour is an essential requirement for a test driver, who at the very least must be able to identify, then trans-

The 1977 Monaco Grand Prix

Jody Scheckter, at the wheel of his Wolf-Ford, led throughout the 76 laps of the 1977 Monaco Grand Prix, chased for the first 44 of them by John Watson and his Brabham-Alfa Romeo and for the remaining 32 laps by Niki Lauda's Ferrari. By the end of the race the rest of the field, headed by Carlos Reutemann in the second Ferrari, were more than half a minute behind, and for the last 28 laps there had been not a single change of position among the first six cars and drivers.

A procession? Yes, but street circuits tend to produce races like that, if only because they offer so few places for overtaking between cars of closely similar performance. This is why at Monaco, more than anywhere else, the race really begins the moment the track is opened for the first of the official practice and qualification sessions, three days before the Grand Prix itself.

And when the list of practice times was published after the first training session the Brabhams were in front, Hans Stuck having been timed at 1 min 30·73 sec and John Watson at 1 min 30·86 sec. Niki Lauda, who had won the race the previous two years, could manage only the fourth fastest time that morning, and Carlos Reutemann was right behind him in the other Ferrari, at 1 min 31·33 sec, a bare one-hundredth of a second slower than his team leader. The surprise that morning, apart from the sudden pace of the Brabhams, was the marked improvement in competitiveness of the two six-wheeled Tyrrells, Monaco expert Ronnie Peterson being third fastest at 1 min 31·15 sec, and Patrick Depailler sixth quickest at 1 min 31·42 sec. Scheckter was only seventh quickest, ahead of Mario Andretti, the last of the drivers to be timed at under 1 min 32 sec.

Because of the tightness of the Monaco circuit only the fastest 20 of the 25 drivers out practising that morning would find their way on to the starting grid on the Sunday. Much of the first practice period is devoted to trimming cars to the circuit, and during the interval that followed there was much activity in the paddock as gear ratios, roll bars, springs and shock absorbers were changed in the hope of higher speeds for the afternoon session.

Unfortunately the weather, which had been threatening all day, broke during the interval and that afternoon only 15 of the 25 drivers ventured on to the streaming wet track, and with the fastest of them, Andretti, lapping at just over 2 minutes there could be no improvements in starting-grid positions. All now depended on the final session on the Saturday afternoon (there was to be no Formula One practice on the Friday).

This time John Watson was the pacemaker, his best time of 1 min 29·86 sec making him the only driver to lap in under the 1½-minute mark. He had given the Brabham-Alfa Romeo its first pole position. Stuck, meanwhile, had broken a valve spring, and although he tried the team's spare car he was unable to improve on his Thursday time, which turned out to be worth only fifth place on the grid. A late charge by Jody Scheckter, who earlier in the day had been busier than anyone when more rain had soaked the track during an untimed session, brought the Wolf-Ford right up to the front row alongside Watson, his time being 1 min 30·27 sec.

For once Lauda had to give best to Reutemann in practice times, the Argentinian's 1 min 30·44 sec lap earning him inside place on the second row of the grid, while Peterson continued his good form with the Tyrrell to finish fourth fastest at 1 min 30·72 sec, a bare hundredth of a second ahead of Stuck, who had Lauda alongside him at 1 min 30·76 sec. Then came James Hunt and Patrick Depailler; Jochen Mass and Mario Andretti; Alan Jones and Jean-Pierre Jarier; Gunnar Nilsson and Vittorio Brambilla; Riccardo Patrese (in his first Formula One drive) and Jacques Laffite; Jacky Ickx and Emerson Fittipaldi and, on the back row, Hans Binder and Rupert Keegan. Arturo Merzario, Boy Hayje, Harald Ertl, Alex Ribeiro and Ian Scheckter were the five failing to qualify, the last two after accidents.

Little things can mean the difference between success and failure in Grand Prix racing, and in John Watson's case it can be argued that he virtually lost the race in his choice of starting position. As fastest driver he was entitled to select either the left or right side of the front row. He chose the left side, for a straighter run towards the entry to Ste

Bottom left : Power unleashed – the start of the 1977 Grand Prix at Monte Carlo. In use since 1929, this Grand Prix circuit is a unique test of skill.

Bottom centre : Jody Scheckter, on what has become his 'home' circuit, leads John Watson. He went on to win the 1977 event.

Bottom right : This picture of Watson at Monte Carlo in 1977 shows the extent to which protective clothing for racing drivers has been developed.

Below right : Niki Lauda's Ferrari at speed.

Below far right : Lauda before the 1977 Monaco Grand Prix.

Right : Ronnie Peterson at Monte Carlo, 1977. This talented Swedish driver died from the injuries he received when he was involved in a crash soon after the start of the 1978 Italian Grand Prix at Monza.

Centre : Patrick Depailler competed at Monaco in 1977 and won the event the following year.

Far right : Emerson Fitti-paldi was forced to retire when the engine of his Copersucar failed after 37 laps.

Devote corner, little realizing that when he lined up his rear wheels would be over some new road markings.

When the race began he suddenly developed excessive wheelspin and saw Scheckter rocket away to his right to take the all-important lead before the first corner. In his efforts to regain his lost ground Watson ran into a brake problem, which sent him down the escape road at the chicane on lap 45. This dropped him to third behind Lauda, but four laps later he was out for good, his car stranded at Ste Devote, stalled and locked in gear. He walked back to the pits to join six earlier retirements.

Peterson's early challenge in fifth place ended when his Tyrrell developed a braking problem; Stuck had had to abandon his Brabham after 19 laps when an electrical short-circuit started a small fire while he was running fourth; Hunt had been running fifth in his McLaren when his engine blew up at the start of lap 26; Emerson Fittipaldi's Copersucar entry had failed with a broken engine after 37 laps; Hans Binder had parked his Surtees with fuel injection troubles after 41 laps; and Patrick Depailler's

Tyrrell was abandoned five laps later with a combination of braking and gearbox problems. The only other retirement was Gunnar Nilsson, whose John Player Special, built by Lotus, broke its gearbox after 51 laps.

By this time Scheckter and Lauda were making it a two-driver race, the Wolf comfortably ahead until Scheckter eased up during the closing laps, enabling Lauda to approach to less than a second of him as he acknowledged the chequered flag after 1 hour 57 min 52·77 sec of intense concentration. Scheckter had averaged 79·609 mph for his historic victory.

Reutemann had challenged hard during the early stages, but had run into a tyre problem, so he eased back once Lauda had passed him and gradually fell into the clutches of the race-long battle between Jochen Mass's McLaren and Mario Andretti's JPS Lotus, finishing just two seconds ahead of them. Mass held off Andretti's determined assault – at one point they went into Ste Devote side-by-side! – and took fourth place, Andretti was a second behind him, and Alan Jones made a strong late challenge with his Shadow to take sixth place a further second behind. Laffite's Ligier-Matra and

Brambilla's Surtees were the only other cars to complete the full 76 laps, but Patrese did well to finish eighth in his Shadow in his first GP, with 75 laps completed. He was ahead of Jacky Ickx, who stood in for Clay Regazzoni, the Swiss driver having vacated the Ensign cockpit in order to rush over to Indianapolis for a qualifying trial. The only other survivors were Jean-Pierre Jarier, who completed 74 laps with his ATS Penske for 11th place, and Rupert Keegan, who brought up the tail with his Hesketh, which covered 73 laps.

It had been a hard afternoon for the men and their machinery, but it would begin all over again a few days later as preparations began for the Belgian Grand Prix at Zolder, where Andretti would dominate practice, Nilsson would win the race (his first GP success) and Scheckter would fail to finish. One of the fascinations of Grand Prix racing is the uncertainty of it all.

Jody Scheckter talking about the Monaco Grand Prix

Sunday, 22 May 1977 was a significant milestone in the history of Grand Prix racing. It was the date of

Top : Riccardo Patrese cornering in the 1977 Monaco Grand Prix.

Above left : Jochen Mass at the wheel of a McLaren in 1976.

Above : Jacques Laffite in a Ligier-Matra JS.

Top right : Jean-Pierre Jarier leads Vittorio Brambilla and Laffite in the 1977 Monaco Grand Prix. This particular shot seems to confirm the 'processional' nature of the event about which critics sometimes complain.

Above right : Another view of Jarier's Penske ATS at Monaco.

Right : Jochen Mass, who came home 4th at Monte Carlo in 1977.

the Monaco Grand Prix, the race that brought the 100th GP victory by a car and driver using the Ford Cosworth DFV engine, a power unit whose debut in the Dutch Grand Prix a decade earlier, with the great Jim Clark, had also been its maiden victory.

The success around the two-mile Monte Carlo street circuit brought pleasure to many people, but to none more than Jody Scheckter. He had led all the way, which is the way any true professional racing driver likes to win his races. More than that, his victory – the second he had scored for Walter Wolf Racing in his first season with the team – was in sense a 'home' victory, for Scheckter, born in South Africa, had made Monaco his adopted home some months earlier and now lived a few hundred yards from the circuit. Besides, Monaco is considered to be one of the great challenges to a Grand Prix driver, a circuit needing the utmost respect and a driving skill and level of concentration of an unusually high order, as Jody Scheckter explains. . . .

Every race circuit presents a driver with a unique challenge, and it is through his ability first to

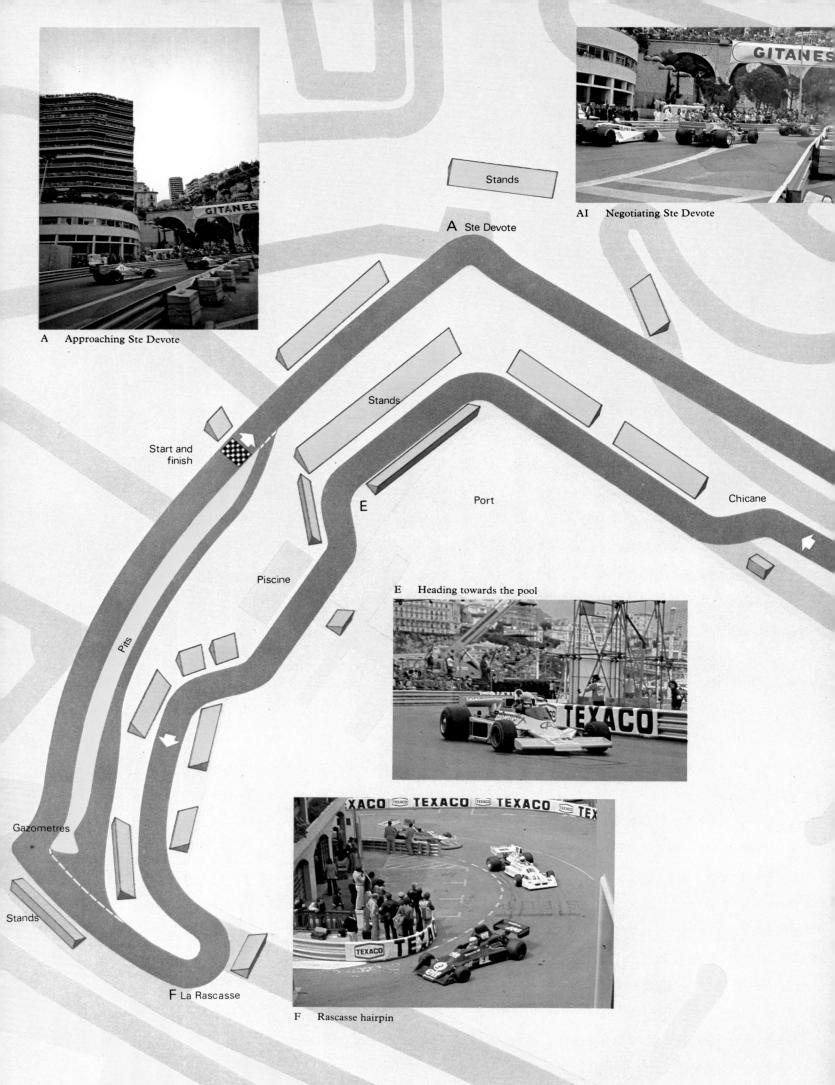

Stands

A   Ste Devote

AI   Negotiating Ste Devote

A   Approaching Ste Devote

Stands

Start and
finish

E

Port

Chicane

Piscine

E   Heading towards the pool

Pits

Gazometres

Stands

F La Rascasse

F   Rascasse hairpin

Casino Square

C   Ancienne Gare hairpin

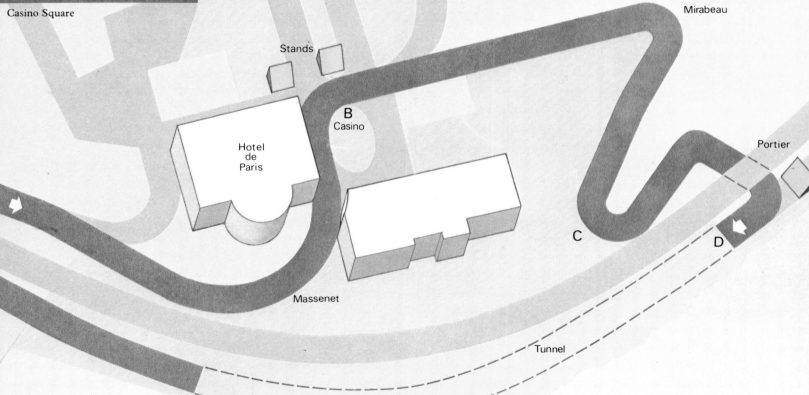

Stands

B

Casino

Hotel
de
Paris

Mirabeau

Portier

Massenet

C

D

Tunnel

CI   The harbour front after Portier

Into the tunnel

THE MONACO CIRCUIT

identify it, then cope with it, that he succeeds or fails. It is the variety, even among superficially similar circuits, that provides one of the fascinations of motor racing for the professional driver. We are highly competitive people by nature, we thrive on challenges, and the need to tackle the new problems presented by a different circuit every two weeks is in our lifeblood.

Today, of course, Monaco is unique among Grand Prix circuits in being the last remaining course run entirely over public roads. As such it presents problems not encountered anywhere else, not even at Long Beach, California, where city streets form only part of the course for the United States Grand Prix West. Some drivers seem to find difficulty in adjusting themselves psychologically to Monaco's demands, and so never seem to be at their best there. While I do not for a moment underestimate the challenge the circuit offers, I think I am stimulated by it, in particular by the need to sustain a rare level of concentration and driving accuracy throughout the length of a two-hour Grand Prix with scarcely a moment of relaxation along the way. It is probably the most tiring two hours of a Grand Prix driver's year, but it can also be the most satisfying. Let me take you for a flying lap round the circuit, a journey which should be completed in about 90 seconds and which, I might add, has to be repeated no fewer than 76 times in the course of a Grand Prix.

We will assume that I have already completed a

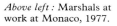

Above left : Marshals at work at Monaco, 1977.

Top right : Negotiating the hairpin at Loew's Hotel (formerly the station) in the 1977 Monaco Grand Prix.

Above right : Another view of the left-handed hairpin at Loew's Hotel.

Left : The right-hander in Casino Square on the Monaco circuit.

lap, so my Wolf-Ford will be in fifth gear as I cross the start/finish line on the Boulevard Albert 1er. At this point the road is curving gently to the right and I shall have moved over towards the right in preparation for a straight-line approach to the sharp right-hand corner, constructed artificially, at Ste Devote.

In the past this was a fast and potentially very dangerous corner, and after several multi-car pile-ups there it was decided to slow things down a bit. The first 'solution' was less than successful, but the latest arrangement of sloping ramps and islands is a considerable improvement, though it does call for a rather unnatural driving technique.

I go down through the gearbox, gear by gear, until I am in second, simultaneously being hard on the brakes until I am about half-way through the corner. Then I suddenly let go of the brakes, swing hard over and carefully adjust the accelerator so as to get maximum possible exit speed, but without brushing the guard rail, which always seems to be perilously close as you come out of the corner.

Next comes what must seem to spectators a simple job – a straight drive uphill. In fact it is not so simple as it seems. You have to leave Ste Devote as fast as possible, which means that you are on the limit at that point. Also, the hill is not as straight as it looks, and we have to drive extremely close to the kerbs to straighten it out as much as possible. I will be up into third, and then fourth, as I take the steepest part of the hill. Then, the gradient eases off.

'A nasty ridge'

This is a point where you have to concentrate very hard and be very accurate in your pedal control and car placement because there is a nasty ridge running across the road that tends to make the car very light, just when you need to be hard on the brakes again before the left-hander leading towards the Casino Square. You must be very careful to keep the car properly balanced over the ridge if you are to get the proper braking effect afterwards, especially as the left-hander tends to be pretty bumpy and can easily put your car into a violent oversteer. It is all too easy to touch a kerb there through being bumped off line.

For the right-hander at Casino Square I take the tight line on the right, easing the lock as I come out of the bend and simultaneously moving over to the left side of the track again. Having gone down into third through the left-hander, I hold it until I am leaving the Square and over another hump at the start of the short downhill straight that follows. Then it is back up to fourth again for a few seconds, followed by another hard application of the brakes and a change down to third, then second for the slippery right-handed Mirabeau corner.

The main problem here is understeer, which, if you are not careful, can take you nose-first into the guard rail as you emerge from the corner. To counter this I try to place my two inside wheels over the inside kerbing on the right, to give me maximum freedom for movement to my left. The twisty little drop down to the tight left-handed hairpin at what used to be the station and is now Loew's Hotel is simply a matter of straightening out your line as much as possible without hitting any kerbs, then hard on the brakes again and into first gear as you lock over to the left.

Even keeping the car well balanced you need all the road here, so inevitably you emerge from the corner on the right side of the track, then you immediately move over to the left, taking second as you drop downhill, so that you are best placed to take the right-hand corner as the track continues to take you downhill. Here again you have to be careful with understeer, or you can strike the kerb on the outside of the bend.

Next comes a somewhat gentler application of brakes as you line up for the right-hand bend that brings you on to the harbour front and the road

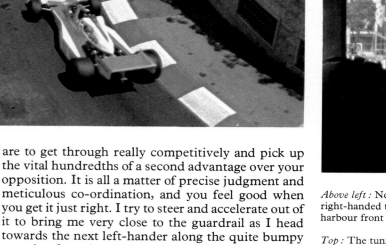

leading through the famous Monaco tunnel. Because this is such a fast section of the course it is imperative to get through that right-hander, still in second gear, as quickly as possible. It is this that turns an apparently simple corner into a difficult one.

'Heading for the chicane'

Racing through the tunnel is part of the Monaco aura, and it certainly takes some getting used to, even though these days the illumination is a lot better than in the past. Although the tunnel is curving right all the way it is very fast, and you are up into fifth gear long before the end of it. Then you are out into the daylight again and heading for the most crucial point on the circuit – the chicane.

Here there is quite a steep downhill approach which poses the first problem, because you need to be on the brakes while the car is still light, having crested the hump at the top of the slope. Sure and precise braking is essential here because you must judge your line through the left–right chicane with extreme accuracy. There are only tiny fractions of an inch of clearance, first on the left, then on the right at the apex, then on the left again at the exit, if you

are to get through really competitively and pick up the vital hundredths of a second advantage over your opposition. It is all a matter of precise judgment and meticulous co-ordination, and you feel good when you get it just right. I try to steer and accelerate out of it to bring me very close to the guardrail as I head towards the next left-hander along the quite bumpy stretch of track which tends to unsettle my car. Having come through the chicane in fourth gear – yes, it's fast as well as tricky! – I need third again for the left-hander, letting the car run wide on the exit so that I am well placed for left and right curves that follow as the track skirts the Monaco swimming pool.

The track is a lot faster than it seems at first through these two curves, but you need some sharp braking and a change down into second before taking the next right-hander and the left-hander which immediately follows it as you leave the pool behind you. The right-hander is a conventional slow corner, but I find I need to steer towards the outside of the left-hander to prevent the car sliding excessively on what is another very slippery part of the course. Then come quick changes up into third, then fourth,

Above left : Negotiating the right-handed turn onto the harbour front at Monaco.

Top : The tunnel, a famous feature of the Monaco circuit.

Above : The exit from the Monaco tunnel. The chicane is not far ahead at this point.

before another turn to the left and then the right-handed Rascasse hairpin.

The left turn is quite a tricky manoeuvre because you are simultaneously turning, slowing and dropping down through the box into first gear, and I find it is necessary to brake hard initially, then ease off the pedal to prevent the car from pivoting; another example of the need for good co-ordination.

'A clean exit'

Emerging from the hairpin you tend to run close to the guard rail on the left side, then there is just time to take second gear, then drop back into first, for the tight right-hand turn that brings you back on to the start/finish straight. There is quite a pronounced ridge half-way round this corner, just when you are accelerating hard, so the back end becomes light and the revs go up as you develop wheelspin. You must use good throttle control to contain this as much as possible, and must also watch your exit line because there is a high kerb and a pronounced gutter on the left, to be avoided at all costs. A good, clean exit line from the corner, of course, will also benefit you all the way to the start/finish line as you work your way back up through the box into fifth, accelerating hard

all the way.

That, then, is a lap of Monaco – 90 seconds' worth of sustained concentration and delicate car control. Of course, the actual driving is only part of the task of race winning. All the preparation beforehand, both in private testing on other circuits and during official practice at Monaco itself, contributes considerably to your performance on race day, or should do so if you have done your work properly. I don't intend to give away any trade secrets about how to set-up a Grand Prix car for Monaco – winning there is difficult enough as it is! – but I will say this: I like to have a car there which I can swing around, one which has good traction, and above all one which handles consistently, so that I can have every confidence in what it is doing or about to do. After all, with all those guardrails around – not to mention the large immovable objects behind them, like the Hotel de Paris and the Casino – there is precious little margin for error, as so many have found out to their cost.

Above right : The right-hander onto the harbour front at Monaco.

Right : Watson negotiating the Loew's Hotel hairpin.

THE GRAND PRIX WORLD CHAMPIONSHIP WINNERS 1950-78

Year	Champion and Runner Up	Constructors' Champion
1950	Giuseppe Farina (*Alfa Romeo*) Juan Fangio (*Alfa Romeo*)	Alfa Romeo
1951	Juan Fangio (*Alfa Romeo*) Alberto Ascari (*Ferrari*)	Alfa Romeo
1952	Alberto Ascari (*Ferrari*) Giuseppe Farina (*Ferrari*)	Ferrari
1953	Alberto Ascari (*Ferrari*) Juan Fangio (*Maserati*)	Ferrari
1954	Juan Fangio (*Maserati and Mercedes*) Froilan Gonzalez (*Ferrari*)	Mercedes-Benz
1955	Juan Fangio (*Mercedes-Benz*) Stirling Moss (*Mercedes-Benz*)	Mercedes-Benz
1956	Juan Fangio (*Ferrari*) Stirling Moss (*Maserati*)	Ferrari
1957	Juan Fangio (*Maserati*) Stirling Moss (*Vanwall*)	Maserati
1958	Mike Hawthorn (*Ferrari*) Stirling Moss (*Vanwall*)	Vanwall
1959	Jack Brabham (*Cooper-Climax*) Tony Brooks (*Ferrari*)	Cooper-Climax
1960	Jack Brabham (*Cooper-Climax*) Bruce McLaren (*Cooper-Climax*)	Cooper-Climax
1961	Phil Hill (*Ferrari*) Wolfgang von Trips (*Ferrari*)★	Ferrari
1962	Graham Hill (*BRM*) Jim Clark (*Lotus-Climax*)	BRM
1963	Jim Clark (*Lotus-Climax*) Graham Hill (*BRM*)	Lotus-Climax
1964	John Surtees (*Ferrari*) Graham Hill (*BRM*)	Ferrari
1965	Jim Clark (*Lotus-Climax*) Graham Hill (*BRM*)	Lotus-Climax
1966	Jack Brabham (*Repco Brabham*) John Surtees (*Ferrari and Cooper-Maserati*)	Repco Brabham
1967	Denny Hulme (*Repco Brabham*) Jack Brabham (*Repco Brabham*)	Repco Brabham
1968	Graham Hill (*Lotus-Cosworth*) Jackie Stewart (*Matra-Cosworth*)	Lotus-Cosworth
1969	Jackie Stewart (*Matra-Cosworth*) Jacky Ickx (*Brabham-Cosworth*)	Matra-Cosworth
1970	Jochen Rindt (*Lotus-Cosworth*)★ Jacky Ickx (*Ferrari*)	Lotus-Cosworth
1971	Jackie Stewart (*Tyrrell-Cosworth*) Ronnie Peterson (*March-Cosworth*)	Tyrrell-Cosworth
1972	Emerson Fittipaldi (*Lotus-Cosworth*) Jackie Stewart (*Tyrrell-Cosworth*)	Lotus-Cosworth
1973	Jackie Stewart (*Tyrrell-Cosworth*) Emerson Fittipaldi (*Lotus-Cosworth*)	Lotus-Cosworth
1974	Emerson Fittipaldi (*McLaren-Cosworth*) Clay Regazzoni (*Ferrari*)	McLaren-Cosworth
1975	Niki Lauda (*Ferrari*) Emerson Fittipaldi (*McLaren-Cosworth*)	Ferrari
1976	James Hunt (*McLaren-Cosworth*) Niki Lauda (*Ferrari*)	Ferrari
1977	Niki Lauda (*Ferrari*) Jody Scheckter (*Wolf-Cosworth*)	Ferrari
1978	Mario Andretti (*Lotus-Cosworth*) Ronnie Peterson (*Lotus-Cosworth*)★	Lotus

★ Title awarded posthumously.

Niki Lauda in his Ferrari at the Casino corner, Monaco, 1977.

CUSTOM CARS

The word 'customizing' is derived from 'custom building', and has come to mean 'personalizing a car'. Ways of doing so are many and various.

In the beginning those who could afford to buy a motor car did so by a circuitous route – they bought a rolling chassis with an engine from one source and then had the body of their choice built on it by a coachbuilder.

This system survived well enough until Henry Ford developed mass-production and suddenly everybody had a car. The few still continued to go to specialist coachbuilders to have cars custom-built. But the heyday of the great styling houses of the twenties and thirties is gone.

However, the yearning for a unique and individual car continues to this day. An entire industry has sprung up based on this fact, offering a complete range of aftermarket extras, or 'bolt-on-goodies' as they are popularly known. This is supported by both young and old, but it is the young who began and have continued the craze for modifying their own cars.

It started in post-war USA with a cult born of a lust for pure, unadulterated power: dragging. At its crudest level, dragging means hurling a car down a straight quarter-mile in an attempt to achieve the highest possible terminal speed and elapsed time. First, engine modifications were made in an effort to gain more power and speed. Following on this came the body modifications to reduce weight and lower wind resistance. Today's motoring laws make it impossible to run the same car on the street and the strip; but in the beginning that was exactly the way it was.

The young would take their street cars to the strip, race them and then go home in them. Some didn't bother to find a strip – they settled for a stretch of deserted road. This highly illegal practice of street racing still has a large following today, although it is discouraged now as hard as it was then. To avoid detection, the racers began to disguise their cars and a new facet to customizing was born.

Most dragsters have a noticeable 'big'n little' effect where the rear wheels are very much larger than the front ones. This 'hiked' appearance is common to nearly every customized car, or rod (as it is known), seen on the street today; drag racing is solely responsible for this fact.

The street racer also began to remove the large wheels they used in competition, replacing them with smaller wheels with legal tyres. Thus the Low-rider was born. Now a cult in its own right, the car almost scrapes the ground as it drives along; sometimes it is necessary to fix castors under the boywork.

By the end of the 1950s, racing was becoming secondary and the focus was turned on the car itself. Power was still a major factor but the car also had to look good and be legally roadworthy. 'Street is neat' became the current phrase.

As the cult developed, it naturally divided along certain paths, each with its devotees. These divisions fall into three broad categories – the rodders, the vanners and the restoration purists.

Restoration may seem a strange word to use in such a modern context, but its co-existence with rodding has caused many a bitter argument between supporters of the two camps. The reason for this is simple. The original rodders could only afford to buy the older cars of the thirties. The habit has stuck and earlier cars are also in demand. By definition street rods now belong to a period when the flat windscreen was still in common use. Curved screens

were not mass produced until the fifties and here occurs the first split. A car with a flat screen (a pre-1950 model) is generally termed a rod, and with a curved screen (post-1950) is a custom.

So a large selection of the custom world concentrates on early cars and it is here that they come into conflict with the purists who believe solely in restoration to original trim. The shortage of vehicles from this period and the recent improvement in GRP (glass-reinforced-plastic) moulding processes has meant that the thirties' cars can be reproduced in great numbers to a high standard of accuracy.

The biggest selling glassfibre replica is that of the Model T Ford. Ironically the car that signalled the deathknell of the private coachbuilder is now the mainstay of the customizing scene. In all of its forms – pick-up, centre-door, open 'bucket', C-cab delivery van – the ubiquitous T is still with us.

In its open, T-bucket form, Henry Ford's people's car has produced some of the wildest, most radical cars ever. Huge chrome engines sporting equally huge and equally chromed blowers (superchargers) and flowing chromed headers (exhaust manifolds) present a fearsomely attractive view to the passer-by.

Aside from chromework there are other forms of decoration that are more or less *de rigueur*. Front axles are nearly all of the drop tube type – an effect known as channelling – which lowers the front aspect of the car by several inches, placing the lower edge of the radiator shell below the line of the chassis. Roof chops are almost obligatory as well, lowering the roof line by a few inches all round. The technical complexities involved in this are immense, including the need to cut down window glass

Back axles are painted and chromed and the type of axle selected is important. Most rods have inde-

Overleaf: This 1948 Oldsmobile 4-door coupé from Belgium has been dramatically roof-chopped and shows the popular flame design.

Above left: This highly decorated Jeep variant comes from the Philippines.

Above right : 'Pinball Wizard', a Ford Pop in one of the many paint schemes it has appeared in over the years. The Pop is the most common street rod in the UK. This one has a 383-ci Chrysler V8 and Jaguar IRS.

Centre right : This 1924 Daimler tanker in a beer-can disguise shows that the concept of advertising products on wheels is not a modern one.

Below right : This fibreglass beach buggy is based on a VW chassis.

pendent rear suspension (IRS) with coil-over-shock springing which gives good performance and has cosmetic value. The heavy duty IRS units from the big Jaguars have long been established favourites. Regrettably the Jaguar IRS is not as common in America as it is in Britain, and the enormous demand is making them gradually scarcer in the scrapyards – traditionally the source of many parts for the enthusiast.

Rear-end units are becoming more sophisticated with many cars wearing combinations of home-brew – or custom-made – and Formula One hubs, drive shafts and differentials.

Sophisticated use of airbrush techniques has given rise to the art of muralling where beautifully executed scenes appear on the boot, bonnet and sides of the car. From this has sprung the theme car, in which the whole concept of the vehicles is decided on long before the work commences and the bodywork, colour scheme and mural scenes are all of a style.

Paint finishes with mysterious-sounding names like Flip-flop, Candy Apple, Pearl, Glowable and Mirraflake abound, and are often used in conjunction with each other as overlays and pin-striping. When the decoration is complete, the paintwork is finished off with several coats of clear lacquer. Vans are particularly popular with mural artists – the larger space available, together with the absence of body moulding lines, makes life very much easier for them.

The majority of rodders choose a name for their cars which has either a jokey meaning or one which refers to the style of the body or murals.

The customizing trend is growing all the time. The European scene is dominated by Britain and Scandinavia, although customizing is not as widespread there as it is in the USA.

Above left : 'California Dreamin', a 1950 Ford Pilot with the original V8 flathead engine.

Left : Perhaps the best-looking British car yet, 'Small Fry' is a 1938 Austin Ruby. Running a supercharged 3·5 Rover V8 engine, the rear axle detail features a mixture of parts from Jaguar, Hesketh F1 and the specialist manufacturer, Baldacchinno.

Top right : A 1932 Ford Model B roadster with a 327-ci V8 engine.

Centre right : Another 1932 Ford Model B roadster. This one is a glassfibre replica of the five-window coupé made by the Jago workshops.

Bottom right : Two examples of the Model T: a Chrysler Hemi-powered T-bucket (left) and a 1924 pick-up with a 350-ci Chevy Corvette motor (right).

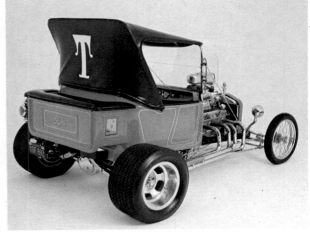

Top left : 'Jam Roller' – a 1936 Austin 10 using 3·5 V8 Rover power.

Left centre and bottom : 'All Shook Up', a Junior Comp(etition) Altered dragster – a 1934 Jago Model B replica in Highboy form. It runs the 4·5-litre version of the Daimler Hemi engine. Open headers (i.e. no silencers) shown in the engine detail would not be legal in the UK.

Above right : 'Andromeda' – a supercharged Chrysler Hemi propels this Model T built in 1977

Right : The Model B again. Another 1932, in cabriolet trim, with a 283-ci Chevy motor. Visible at the front is the non-standard drop axle which lowers the car several inches.

Above left : Restoration and rodding are not *too* far divided, as this lovely 1931 Duesenberg convertible shows.

Left : Ford V8 shows loving attention to detail. There is probably more chrome on this engine than there is on the total area of the average modern saloon.

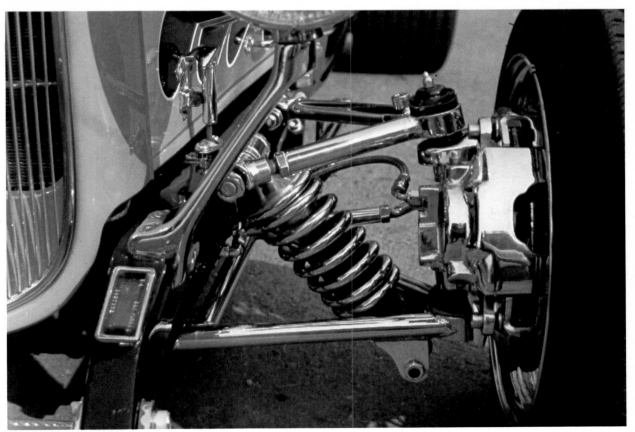

Right : The chrome engine of the Jago Model B (above) and a detail of the chromework and painting on the front independent suspension (below).

Top left: A 1969 Impala Lowrider. Adjustable hydraulic or gas suspension makes it possible to choose the amount of ground clearance.

Centre left: A mural on a Rover 100 (left) by Ray Mumford, who also did the Parisian scene on the 'French Connection' 351-ci-engined Mustang.

Bottom left: Another Mumford mural – 'Bullitt', a 1967 289-ci fastback Mustang.

Above right : 'Old Henry's Ford Keeps on Truckin'' is the legend on the side of this hybrid 1946 Ford pick-up.

Right : This is a 140-mph Chevy V8 powered milk float, one of the more radical customs on the British scene.

Above left : A hand-painted mural by Kolor Me Kustom on a 1975 Dodge van.

Left : Interior detail from the same van which appears in long shot on facing page (bottom left).

Top right : A 1975 Datsun, again by Kolor Me Kustom, shows the growing fondness for pick-ups.

Centre : Rear-end mural on a Chevy pick-up and (bottom right) the front view.

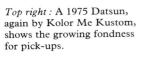

Above left : Australian treatment of the Ford 100E. A 1956 model with a 202 Holden motor.

Left : Furry interior shot of 'Dedication' – a car decorated in memory of Elvis.

Above right : Supercharged 1971 Chevrolet Corvette – the classic American sports car.

Bottom right : Boot mural of 'Dedication' (left). Two trikes, tenuously connected with the motorcycle, pictured at Daytona (right).

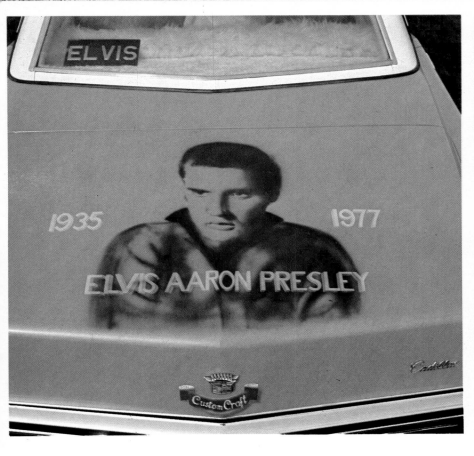

Top left : Another Chevy Lowrider – a 1952 Bel Air from California.

Centre : An estate conversion gives this Corvette a unique flavour without robbing it of its usual aggressive appearance.

Left : 'What's Hot', a tasteful 3-litre Capri.

Above right : The Pontiac GTO, last of the big muscle cars to be produced before America discovered pollution and invented the emission-controlled engine. Its immense 400-ci motor put a staggering 375-bhp on the road.

Right : A radio disk-jockey runs this 302 RHD Mustang. Apart from the red Candy Apple and Flip-flop paint job, it's a close copy of the one he runs on the strip.

100 GREAT CARS

BENZ

Germany
cylinders: 1; capacity: 577 cc; hp: $\frac{3}{4}$; speed 16 km/h (10 mph).

This vehicle is generally regarded as the first passenger motorcar, certainly the first to run successfully and to lead to commercially built models a few years later. Karl Benz was a partner in a small firm making coal-gas stationary engines, and in 1885 he built a light three-wheeler to house the single-cylinder engine he had already designed. This engine had the modern feature of electric ignition by battery and coil, and drove the large rear wheels by a combination of belts and chains. Like many early car designers, Benz employed a single front wheel as he did not know of the Ackermann steering system whereby the wheels can be turned without the axle turning as well. A swivelling front axle, though used on some early cars, was clumsy and unstable. The Benz had a large horizontal flywheel below the engine which also served as a starter, the procedure being to grab one of the spokes of the flywheel and give a hard pull. This practice continued on the production Benz cars of the early 1890s.

Built in 1885 and patented and tested the following year, the Benz Dreiradwagen was followed in 1887 by a similar machine with a more powerful engine and wooden spoked wheels. Supported by two financial backers, Julius Ganss and Friedrich von Fischer, Benz began to make similar cars for sale in 1888, and in that year sold a manufacturing licence to Emile Roger of Paris who made three-wheelers at first, followed by four-wheelers. Benz himself turned to four wheels in 1893, and for the next six years he was Europe's leading car maker, thanks to the simplicity and comparative reliability of his products.

PANHARD-LEVASSOR

France
cylinders: 2; capacity: 1,060 cc; hp: 4; speed: 19 km/h (12 mph).

The Panhard has often been called the

ancestor of the modern motorcar, for its layout of front-mounted engine, driving through sliding pinion gears to the rear wheels became adopted as the standard practice, only to be partially abandoned after the Second World War with the widespread adoption of rear engines and front wheel drive.

The first cars built by the partnership of René Panhard and Emile Levassor (financier and designer respectively) had centrally mounted engines, but in 1891 the front-engined model was introduced. It had a 4-hp V-twin engine, four speed gear system (it could not be called a gearbox until 1895, when the gear wheels were enclosed in a box to protect them from mud and dust) and rear wheels driven by chains and sprockets bolted to the spokes.

In 1894 the Daimler-licensed V-twin engine was replaced by a Maybach-designed vertical-twin called the Phoenix. In this engine the surface carburettor was replaced by a Maybach float-feed version. Both these improvements were offered on the Panhards sold to the public in 1895, the year in which Emile Levassor led the 1,340 km (832 mile) race from Paris to Bordeaux and back. However, Levassor was denied official victory because of a formula in the regulations giving a big advantage to four-seater cars, while his car had only two.

Panhard cars sold steadily in the later 1890s, gaining four-cylinder engines and steering wheels in place of tillers in 1896. They had a well-deserved reputation for longevity, and a number of them survived in use up to the outbreak of the First World War.

DURYEA

United States of America
cylinders: 1; capacity: 1,302 cc; hp: 4; speed: 16 km/h (10 mph).

The Duryea brothers, Charles and Frank, were bicycle makers who became pioneers

of the car industry in America. In 1892 Charles designed an engine and purchased a horse-drawn Phaeton for $70 in which to mount it. However his cycle business claimed too much of his time and it was left to Frank to redesign the engine and improve the chassis, so that it was not until 21 September 1893 that the car first took to the streets of Springfield, Massachusetts.

It had a single-cylinder two-stroke engine with electric ignition and a spray carburettor. Final drive was by chain to the nearside rear wheel, and there were two forward speeds. Although on its first trials, in the inventor's words 'It ran no faster than an old man could walk' it was soon improved, and with a new two-cylinder four-stroke engine the Duryea went into production in 1895. The Duryea Motor Wagon Company was the first in America to be formed expressly for the purpose of making petrol motorcars. It was also the first American make to enter competitions, winning the *Chicago Times Herald* race from Chicago to Evanston and back in November 1895. Frank drove while Charles followed behind in a horse-drawn sleigh in case of a breakdown. Two Duryeas took part in the 1896 London to Brighton Emancipation Run. After 1898 production was transferred to Peoria, Illinois, where Charles had his cycle factory, and three-wheelers were made for several years.

PEUGEOT

France
cylinders: 2; capacity: 1,282 cc; hp: $3\frac{3}{4}$; transmission: four speeds; speed: 19 km/h (12 mph).

Peugeot has the honour of being the oldest motor manufacturer in the world still in the hands of the same family. Armand Peugeot's first two cars were steamers designed by Léon Serpollet but in 1891 he built a petrol-engined car with which he followed the Paris–Brest race of that year.

Edward VII. The King's first car was a Daimler, acquired in 1900 while he was still Prince of Wales, and as a result of his satisfaction with the make, Daimlers remained the official cars of the British Royal Family until the 1950s.

PACKARD

United States of America
cylinders: 1; capacity: 3,035 cc; hp: 12; speed: 32 km/h (20 mph).
The story has often been told of how James Ward Packard, owner of a troublesome Winton car, took it back to the factory with some suggestions, only to be told by Alexander Winton 'If you're so smart Mr Packard, why don't you make a car yourself?' James Packard was an engineering graduate of Lehigh University and so the challenge did not seem as ridiculous as it might have done to most men. Within a year Packard and his brother had hired two of Winton's men and begun building a car in their electrical plant at Warren, Ohio. Their product, known as the Model A, was a light, buggy-type vehicle powered by a single-cylinder horizontal engine mounted under the seat. With its tiller

Left, above and below : 1898 Benz with engine detail.
Above : 1899 Panhard-Levassor.
Right : 1897 Coventry Daimler.

This used a V-twin Daimler-type engine made under licence from the German company, and so was a cousin of the Panhard which had the same engine and sliding pinion gearbox. Peugeot's engine, however, was mounted in the rear, while, in the absence of a radiator, the water was cooled by being circulated through the tubular chassis. By the end of 1891 five cars had already been sold, and three years later sales had exceeded 100, which was better than any other car maker in the world with the exception of Benz. One of the recognized extras in 1894 was a whip with which to chase away dogs. Already four body styles were available, a two-seater, a four-seater victoria, a four-seater vis-à-vis, and a five-seater brake in which the rear seats were arranged transversely so that the passengers faced each other. By 1895 a five-seater omnibus and a delivery van had been added to the range.

Peugeot were early in the competition field, fielding no fewer than five cars in the 1894 Paris–Rouen Trial, in which they finished second and third. Peugeots ran in the main event of 1895, the Paris–Bordeaux–Paris Race, in which an interesting entry was that of André Michelin's pneumatic-tyred car.

DAIMLER

Great Britain
cylinders: 2; hp: 4; speed: 29 km/h (18 mph).
The Daimler Motor Syndicate was formed in 1893 by F. R. Simms to exploit the Daimler patents in England, but a factory was not set up until 1896. Despite the name and the fact that Gottlieb Daimler was on the board of the British company, the designs of British and German Daimlers could hardly have been more different.

While the German cars were rear engined, with belt transmission and spur gear drive, the British Daimlers were on Panhard lines with front mounted vertical twin engines, sliding pinion gearboxes and double chain drive. The original ones had hot tube ignition and tiller steering; wheel steering replaced the tiller in 1897, but the hot tube was retained as a standby to the magneto until well into the 20th century. A variety of body styles was offered on the early Daimlers including two- and four-seaters with forward facing seats, open wagonettes with side facing seats for passengers and as a closed 'station bus'. The cars were solidly built and lasted a long time, which led to a number of garages going into business as Daimler improvers, bringing the old cars up to date by fitting wheel steering, increasing engine base and sometimes wheelbase, and improving the bodies. Foremost among these was Frank Morriss of Kings Lynn, official car repairer to King

steering and wire wheels it was little different from hundreds of prototypes which the fledgling American car industry was turning out, although its three-speed gearbox was an improvement on the two-speed epicyclic transmission favoured by many of its rivals. The Packard's first major public showing was at the Madison Square Garden Automobile Exhibition in New York in 1900, when the three cars demonstrated proved so popular that they were all bought on the spot. Particularly impressed was William Rockefeller, who purchased two of them.

The Model A was followed by the Models B and C, the latter with wheel steering, and in 1903 by the Model L. On one of these, Tom Fetch and Marius Krarup drove from San Francisco to New York in 61 days. In 1904 Packard design took a completely new direction with the adoption of a front-mounted vertical four-cylinder engine.

RENAULT

France
cylinders: 1; capacity: 273 cc; hp: 1¾; transmission: three speeds; speed: 35 km/h (22 mph).

The first production car to use a propeller shaft to transmit power to the rear wheels, in place of chains or belts, the 1899 Renault was one of the most reliable cars of its day. This was convincingly demonstrated when two Renaults made their competition debut in the 1899 Paris–Trouville voiturette race. Much smaller and lighter than their competitors, the 3½-hp voiturettes looked too fragile to survive the rugged race. In those days unpaved roads and gaping potholes frequently broke the axles of cars, but nevertheless the first two to cross the line were Renaults, the winner being constructor Louis Renault himself.

The prototype had been built in 1898 and had a minute engine which developed only 1¾ hp. Sceptics dismissed it as hopelessly underpowered, but it weighed only 448 lb, so performance was reasonable. From this very first example he used a propeller shaft, and never used any other

Above and below right : 1900 Locomobile Steamer with detail of engine in the rear.
Left : 1900 De Dion Bouton – a tiller-steered vis-à-vis.
Right : 1903 'Curved Dash' Oldsmobile.

form of final drive on his cars, not even on the monster racers of the 1904 to 1907 era. A small shop was set up on the family estate at Billancourt, and there the 1899 Renault was born. It differed from the 1898 prototype in having a larger, squarer bonnet, and in using tiller steering in place of a wheel, an apparently retrograde step which Louis reversed the following year. By the end of 1899, 100 workers were on the payroll, and 71 cars had been delivered. Most were open two-seaters, but at least one tiny pillbox coupé was made, almost as tall as it was long. The larger engine (500 cc and 3½ hp) used in the Paris–Trouville racing cars was employed in the regular production cars of 1900, a very common practice at this time, when it could be said with reasonable truth that the racing car of today was the touring car

of tomorrow. The engines, still made by De Dion-Bouton, were now water-cooled, and the cars had radiators at each side of the bonnet. This layout was changed in 1904 when the radiator was moved to a position behind the engine which was covered by what came to be called a 'coalscuttle' bonnet.

de DION BOUTON vis-à-vis

France
cylinders: 1; capacity: 402 cc; hp: 4; transmission: two speeds; speed: 40 km/h (25 mph).

As with Rolls-Royce, the De Dion-Bouton company was formed through the collaboration of a wealthy aristocratic enthusiast (the Comte Albert de Dion) and a talented engineer (Georges Bouton). The

latter's most important contribution to early car development was the introduction of the high-speed engine, turning at up to 1,500 rpm compared to the 500 or so of the Benz. People said that Bouton's engine would shake itself to pieces in no time but Bouton found that the maximum speed for vibration was around 900 rpm, after which it was reduced. This engine, developed in 1895, was first used in tricycles, and was put into a small car in 1899. This was of the vis-à-vis seating pattern, in which two passengers sat facing the driver and other passenger, thus travelling with their backs to the direction in which the car was going. The single cylinder engine was located under the rear seat from which it drove by a simple two-speed system with separate clutches for high and low gear, operated by turning a wheel on the steering column. A turn anti-clockwise expanded the low speed clutch to move the car away from rest, and a turn in the opposite direction released the low speed clutch and actuated the high speed one. Another feature of the car, known as the De Dion axle, although it was designed by Bouton, was the final drive system, in which power was transmitted via half shafts independently of the fixed 'dead' axle. This system was revived on some racing cars of the 1950s.

The De Dion-Bouton voiturette was simple and reliable as well as being reasonably priced (though it must be remembered that the £175 asked for it in 1900 represents well over £2,000 in today's money). In 1902 the engine was moved to the front under a bonnet and the single-cylinder De Dion was made for a further ten years, though supplemented by larger models with two-, four- and eight-cylinder engines.

LOCOMOBILE Steamer

**United States of America
cylinders: 2; capacity: 558 cc; hp:
10; transmission: single speed; speed:
40 km/h (25 mph).**

The steam car played a much more prominent role in early motoring in the United States of America than in Europe, and one of the most popular makes was the Locomobile. First sold in 1899, it was a simple design with a two-cylinder horizontal engine driving the rear axle by a single chain, a bicycle-type tubular frame, full elliptic springs to all four wheels, and tiller steering. Once it was running, the steam car had several advantages over its petrol engined rival, being quieter and free from the vibration which was a serious problem in early petrol cars, and above all, having no gearbox which caused such trouble to inexperienced drivers. Against these assets had to be set the lengthy starting procedure, which took up to 45 minutes, and involved 20 separate steps. Another drawback was that steam had to be used carefully, otherwise the car would have to stop at the foot of a hill for several minutes in order to build up enough steam to accomplish the climb. Nevertheless the little Locomobile sold well at the modest price of $600, and in 1901 and 1902 they were the leading sellers among American passenger cars. In 1901 they outsold their nearest petrol-engined rival, Oldsmobile, by more than three to one. The four-storey factory at Bridgeport, Connecticut, was said to be the largest of its kind in the world. In 1903 Locomobile sold their steam car rights back to the Stanley brothers from whom they had purchased them in 1899 and turned to the manufacture of petrol engined cars. Total production of steamers was 5,400.

MERCEDES

**Germany
cylinders: 4; capacity: 5,900 cc; hp:
35; transmission: four speeds; speed:
86 km/h (53 mph).**

The first Mercedes car, like the Panhard, is often called the ancestor of the modern motor car, as it included all the Panhard's classic features, together with improvements such as a honeycomb radiator, pressed steel frame and gate-type gearchange. Above all, the Mercedes *looked* much more modern than its contemporaries, thanks to its longer and lower build, the sharply raked steering column, and the mounting of the radiator in front of the bonnet instead of below it between the front springs as in most older designs. The engine of the first Mercedes car (which was made by the German Daimler company and named after the daughter of Emil Jellinek, the unofficial agent for the make in the South of France) was a four-cylinder unit of 5·9 litres capacity which developed about 35 hp. The inlet valves were mechanically operated with variable lift, which gave a more flexible engine which ran as smoothly at low speeds as at its maximum of 1,000 rpm. The gate change enabled the driver to change from, say, top to second gear, instead of having to pass through third as in the progressive system.

The new car made its first public appearance at the Grand Prix de Pau on 17 February 1901, but it was insufficiently tested, and broke down soon after the start. However, at the Nice Speed Week a short time later the Mercedes redeemed itself, winning two out of the three main events, and thereafter the make never looked back, either in racing successes or in sales to the public.

OLDSMOBILE Curved Dash

**United States of America
cylinders: 1; capacity: 1,565 cc; hp:
5; transmission: two speeds; speed:
32 km/h (20 mph).**

This is an example of the famous 'Curved Dash' Oldsmobile, the first design of Ransome Eli Olds to see production. Despite a disastrous factory fire in March 1901 which destroyed all the blueprints and from which only one prototype car escaped, the car was soon in production, and by the end of the year over 400 had been made. This figure rose to 2,500 the following year, 4,000 in 1903, 5,508 in 1904 and 6,500 in 1905, making it the largest produced American car before the advent of the Model T Ford in 1908. The Oldsmobile was a simple design, with a large single-cylinder engine and an angle steel frame with two long springs on either side,

which ran the whole length of the car, the centre part serving to strengthen the frame. The gear change was a two-speed epicyclic system, as with many of the smaller American cars of the period. Olds entered his cars in several long distance journeys, including New York City to Portland, Oregon, 7,064 km (4,400 miles) covered in 44 days. In 1901 Roy D. Chapin, a 21-year-old apprentice who later became sales manager for Olds and in 1909 founded the Hudson Motor Car Company, drove a Curved Dash from the Detroit factory to New York Automobile Show, an unusual event at a time when practically all show cars were delivered by rail. The Oldsmobile sold well in Great Britain and the Scandinavian countries, and was built under licence in Germany as the Polymobil. Production ended in 1905, and although Oldsmobiles are still made today, now as a Division of General Motors, they have never quite had the fame that was earned by the Curved Dash Runabout.

LANCHESTER

Great Britain
**cylinders: 2; capacity: 3,900 cc; hp:
22; transmission: three speeds; speed:
77 km/h (48 mph).**

The Lanchester was one of the most individual designs of its era, for Fred Lanchester worked from first principles and borrowed hardly at all from the work of others. The first prototype had a single-cylinder engine, but the production cars of 1900 onwards were twins, with the cylinders horizontally opposed, each with its own crankshaft, which gave unusual smoothness of running for the period. An epicyclic gearbox gave three forward speeds and one reverse. Both gear changing and braking were controlled by levers, the only pedal being the accelerator. The cantilever springs were especially designed so that their frequency of bounce was similar to the motion of a man walking. Steering was by side lever, a system which Lanchester continued to offer until 1910, long after all other makers had gone over to wheel steering. Water cooling was offered as an option from 1902 onwards, and gave slightly more power from the same size engine owing to the absence of the large fans which blew air over the cylinder

Above: 1911 Rolls-Royce Silver Ghost.
Right: 1904 Lanchester.
Far right, above and below: 1904 Franklin with detail of 1·7-litre, 4-cylinder, air-cooled, transversely mounted engine.

heads in the air-cooled engines. An advanced feature offered by Lanchester for a few years from 1905 was a disc brake on the transmission, in an extension of the clutch box. Two models of two-cylinder Lanchesters were offered in 1903, the 16 and 18 hp and these were replaced in 1904 with the company's first four-cylinder car, rated at 20 hp, and with a conventional vertical in-line engine. The appearance was still characteristically Lanchester, though, as the engine was mounted between driver and passenger, so there was no bonnet.

FRANKLIN

United States of America
**cylinders: 4; capacity: 1,800 cc; hp:
7; transmission: two speeds; speed:
48 km/h (30 mph).**

Of all the companies which made use of air-cooled engines, Franklin is the best known because they employed this system up to the end of car production in 1934, and never made a water-cooled car. Until 1925

they were all designed by John Wilkinson, and made in a factory at Syracuse, NY, which H. H. Franklin had founded for the manufacture of die castings. Franklin and Wilkinson were brought together by the Brown and Lipe company who later made transmissions for many makes of assembled car. The first cars were offered for sale in 1902; they were light, spidery looking two-seaters, but were unusual amongst small cars in having four-cylinder engines. These were mounted transversely at the front of the car, as in the modern Mini, but drove the rear wheels via a two-speed planetary gearbox. The engine had overhead valves, an advanced feature for its day. The frame was wooden, a feature not unusual in 1902, but Franklin persisted with it until 1927. Production was modest to start with, only 13 cars being made in the first year, but 1903 saw 184 Franklins leave the factory, and in 1904 the figure was 712. Cars of this year were not greatly different from the first models, though the wheelbase was lengthened to carry a four-seater tonneau body, and the wire wheels of the original were replaced by wooden artillery types. In 1904 a Franklin broke the San Francisco–New York record when L. L. Whitman and C. S. Carris set a figure of 32 days 23 hours 20 minutes, the previous record (by a water-cooled car) being 61 days.

ROLLS-ROYCE Silver Ghost

Great Britain
cylinders: 6; capacity: 7,036 cc; hp: 48; transmission: four speeds; speed: 101 km/h (63 mph).

The first six-cylinder Rolls-Royce was the 30-hp model which had been introduced in 1905. This was one of the least satisfactory designs of Henry Royce, in contrast to the excellent four-cylinder 20-hp which was being made at the same time. The 30-hp was under-powered for its weight, and the long crankshaft set up severe vibration. In addition it was an ungainly vehicle, the radiator too far ahead of the front axle to be aesthetically satisfying. All these faults were rectified in the 40/50-hp model which Royce worked on during 1906, and which was finished just in time to be shown at the London Motor Show in December. The crankshaft vibration was eliminated by increasing the size of the pins and journals making the shaft a much more solid unit, while increased engine size and improved valve layout raised power from an unsatisfactory 30 hp to a more creditable 48 hp. The cylinders were cast in two blocks of three, and pressure lubrication was adopted in place of the drip and splash system of the earlier car. A larger wheelbase enabled even the lengthy 40/50 engine to be accommodated without projecting too far forward. The thirteenth 40/50 chassis, which left the factory in February 1907, was equipped with silverplated fittings and given the individual name *The Silver Ghost*. This was not unusual at a time when many cars were given such names (other Rolls-Royces were *The Rogue* and *The Dragonfly*) and it was not until many years later that the name Silver Ghost came to be applied to all 40/50s made between 1907 and 1925. The Silver Ghost was submitted to a 3,220 km (2,000 mile) RAC observed trial, and then to a 24,150 km (15,000 mile) trial. After the car had emerged from these trials with flying colours, production started of the 40/50 in the spring of 1907. This was the car which earned Rolls-Royce the accolade 'The Best Car in the World' which all subsequent models have been fortunate to enjoy.

BUICK

United States of America
cylinders: 4; capacity: 2,720 cc; hp: 22; transmission: two speeds; speed: 48 km/h (30 mph).

Famous today as the upper middle priced car in the General Motors range, the Buick was made in a variety of models in the early years of the century. In 1909 the range consisted of seven models, of which the Model 10 shown was the cheapest, at $1,000 for a rumble seat roadster. This was the smallest four-cylinder Buick, and was actually cheaper than the two two-cylinder Models F and G which were hangovers from an earlier era. It had been introduced the previous year, and soon outsold all other Buicks, helping the make to become the second largest producer in the United States, after Ford. It has justly been called 'the car that made Buick'. Like practically all Buicks from the first, it had an overhead valve engine, and a two-speed epicyclic gearbox with the high speed lever at the driver's side. Initially it was available in only one body style, a rumble-seat roadster, and in only one colour, Buick grey, but by 1909 tourers with or without rear doors were made and other colours such as blue were listed. The Model 10

was widely used in competitions, sharing honours with the big specially-built racing Buicks such as *The Bug* which Bob Burman and Louis Chevrolet raced all over the country. The Model 10 was dropped in 1911 as Buick management had decided to concentrate on larger, higher priced cars, but although the company survived, sales took a serious plunge for several years.

RENAULT AX

France
cylinders: 2; capacity: 1,060 cc; hp: 10; transmission: three speeds; speed: 64 km/h (40 mph).

Throughout his lifetime, Louis Renault followed the example he set at the beginning of his career, by including a well-made small car at the bottom of his range. The best known example in pre-1914 days was the AX, made in many forms from 1905 to 1914. It had a vertical twin engine of 1,060 cc (Renault abandoned De Dion-Bouton engines to make his own in 1903) with thermo-syphon cooling using the large dashboard radiator which was to be a feature of Renault cars until 1928. It was designed to carry a two-seater body, when it could cruise at 56 km/h (35 mph), but as with so many cars, customers asked for

four seats, and even closed coachwork, which overloaded it. The engine was slightly enlarged to 1,260 cc for the AG model, this being widely used as a taxicab from 1908 onwards. There were more Renault taxis in London than any other make prior to 1914, and some were still in use when over 20 years old. The little two-cylinder Renaults were in production for ten years and many are still in existence today, in veteran car clubs all over the world.

FORD Model T

United States of America
cylinders: 4; capacity: 2,894 cc; hp: 20; transmission: two speeds; speed: 64 km/h (40 mph).

Today the Ford Model T is acclaimed as 'The Car that put the World on Wheels', 'the Universal Car', and so on, but at its birth in 1908 there was little to indicate the fame that it was to achieve. It was a logical development of the Model S, using the same water-cooled, side valve, four-cylinder engine, and planetary two-speed gearbox. An important difference was that the T's engine had a detachable cylinder head, which greatly helped owner maintenance. The T was the first Ford to have left-hand drive, which was only just becoming popular on American cars, although it had always been the rule of the road to drive on the right. Henry Ford priced his new model at $850 for a four-seater tourer, and it was this more than any other factor which made the Model T a best-seller from the start. Ford's profit margin must have been very small, but like Morris in England a decade and a half later, he

Far left: 1913 Cadillac – the first car to adopt electric starting and lighting (1912).
Left: 1912 Model T Ford convertible.
Above: 1904 Stanley Steamer
Below: 1909 Renault AX with 1,060-cc vertical twin engine.

realized that if a low price boosted sales, a small profit on each car soon built up a very healthy financial position. In the first year of production, October 1908 to October 1909, Ford sold 17,771 Model Ts, and within four years the factory was turning out ten times this figure. As sales increased, so prices could be reduced, and by 1916 the Model T tourer cost only $360 (the rock bottom price was $260 for a two-seater in 1923, £52 at the prevailing rate of exchange). The T's planetary transmission, with separate pedals for forward and reverse and no gear lever, made driving such a different technique that some states in America issued two separate licences, for Fords and for other cars. The story is told of the man who, on learning of the Model T's impending demise in 1927, bought three – enough to last his lifetime – because he knew that he could never learn to drive any other car.

STANLEY Steamer

**United States of America
cylinders: 2.**

By 1910 the mass popularity of the steam car was long past, and the breed was already becoming a specialist vehicle. Steam car owners still fiercely championed their machines, but there were fewer and fewer of them. The 'industry' was down to two makes, Stanley and White, and the latter would defect to the ranks of internal combustion within 12 months. The Stanley was a relatively simple design, with a horizontal two-cylinder engine mounted just ahead of the rear axle, which it drove directly, and a firetube boiler under the rounded bonnet. This did not generate

steam as rapidly as the flash boiler of the White, but it provided plenty of reserves of steam for sudden bursts of speed. Because of this, Stanleys were popular competition cars, and for a time were unbeatable in hill climbs by any petrol-engined cars. Like all steam cars, its main drawback was the time required for starting from cold, which could be up to 30 minutes. A pilot light burning all night reduced this, but used up precious fuel and was unpopular with insurance companies. An unusual feature for the date was the wooden frame, as nearly all other car makers had gone over to pressed steel which Stanley did not adopt until 1915. There were three models in the 1910 range, of 10, 20 and 30 hp.

CADILLAC

**United States of America
cylinders: 4; capacity: 6,012 cc; hp: 50; transmission: three speeds; speed: 97 km/h (60 mph).**

The 1912 Cadillac was the world's first car to be fitted with an electric self-starter,

possibly the most important single invention in the popularization of the motor car. Prior to this a few cars had been equipped with compressed air and even clockwork spring starters, but nearly all still relied on muscle power and the handcrank. The Cadillac's starter was the work of Charles F. Kettering, of Dayton, Ohio, who had developed a small electric motor to replace the hand crank on cash registers. Though rivals scoffed that such a small motor could never work, Kettering found that it could work very well indeed for short periods, which was all a starter motor should be called upon to do. The 1912 Cadillac not only employed an electric starter, but also Kettering's coil ignition, and electric lighting for both the headlights and the interior of the closed models. Thus in one model, the long established features of hand crank, magneto ignition and acetylene lighting were all done away with. The electric starter was soon made available to other car makers, first of all those within the General Motors empire such as Buick and Oakland, then to other companies including overseas ones such as Lanchester in England.

In other ways the 1912 Cadillac was a conventional machine with a four-cylinder, side valve engine, though this was to be replaced two years later by America's first V-8 power unit.

HISPANO-SUIZA Alfonso

Spain
cylinders: 4; capacity: 3,620 cc; hp: 64; transmission: four speeds; speed: 129 km/h (80 mph).

Like the Prince Henry Vauxhall, the Alfonso model Hispano-Suiza was one of the first sports cars, made in an era before the term came into use, yet admirably filling the criteria of a car with above average performance and handling, built for enjoyment rather than utility motoring. The name Hispano-Suiza (literally Spanish-Swiss) came from the fact that the Swiss designer, Marc Birkigt, was the designer of the cars built at Barcelona (and also in France at Bois-Colombes). The 15T or Alfonso XIII model was derived from the series of long-stroke four-cylinder racing cars which the company had made in 1910, and earned its name from the fact that one of the first customers was Spain's king, probably the greatest enthusiast for motoring among European royalty, then or at any time since. It was put on the market in 1911 and remained in production until about 1916, though as most of Europe was involved in the Great War from 1914 onwards, the last models were confined to the Spanish market and little is known about them. The Alfonso was made in two wheel base lengths, 270 cm (8 ft 8 in) and 295 cm (9 ft 10 in), the shorter one carrying two-seater coachwork, the longer tourer or even saloon bodies. The comparatively large engine gave it an effortless and unfussy top gear performance, and many owners including the King found it untiring even for journeys of several hundred miles.

MERCER 35 Raceabout

United States of America
cylinders: 4; capacity: 4,910 cc; hp: 60; transmission: four speeds; speed: 120 km/h (75 mph).

The Mercer Type 35 Raceabout, together with the Stutz Bearcat, was the archetypal American sporting car which was made by many firms, and might appear under the names runabout, raceabout, roadster or speedster. They differed from their contemporaries in Europe in that, although rakish and sporting in appearance, they had perfectly stock, slow turning engines as used in the maker's touring cars. The

Above: 1913 Vauxhall Prince Henry
Below left: 1912 Hispano-Suiza Alfonso
Right, above and below: 1912 Mercer 35 Raceabout with detail of the driving controls – the archetypal US sporting car.

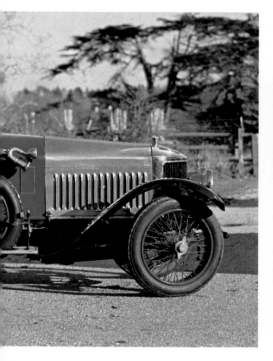

Mercer was designed by Finlay Robertson Porter, and used a four-cylinder T-head engine which developed 60 bhp, and gave the Raceabout a top speed of 120 km/h (75 mph) thanks to high gearing and low weight. Of bodywork there was little, save two bucket seats, a bolster fuel tank and a small tool box. There was no windscreen, though some cars were fitted with a monocle screen for the driver. This has become indelibly associated with the Mercer Raceabout, but it must have given very little protection at any speed, and was less effective than a pair of goggles. Brakes were not the Raceabout's strong point, and it was said that by the time the car had stopped the emergency was 20 yards behind, but their precise steering endeared them to sporting motorists who had the necessary $2,250 to $2,600 to spare. The Raceabout was made from 1911 to 1914 inclusive, and can be dated from the letter suffix, the Type 35R being the 1911, the 35C the 1912 and 35J the 1913–14 models.

VAUXHALL Prince Henry

Great Britain
cylinders: 4; capacity: 3,964 cc; bhp: 75; transmission: four speeds; speed: 120 km/h (75 mph).

Up to 1908 the Vauxhall had been one of the staider British cars, with no competition career, but in that year the designer, Laurence Pomeroy, went to work on the engine of the 20-hp model, and by 1910 he had succeeded in extracting 60 bhp from the three-litre unit. This was installed in the three team cars entered for the 1910 Prince Henry of Prussia tour. They had light, doorless four-seater bodies and sharply pointed radiators. The model was offered for sale from 1911 onwards, under the name 'Prince Henry'. The first production cars were also doorless, but soon small doors reaching about halfway down the body sides were offered, in deference to those who might wish occasionally to carry lady passengers. Though it was still not a car for the elderly, in years or frame of mind, the Prince Henry established an excellent reputation for smooth running as

well as sensitive handling, flexible top gear performance and a respectable maximum speed of 120 km/h (75 mph). It was one of the first of the breed which came to be known as sports cars, although the term was not used at this time. In 1913 a larger engine of 3,964 cc was introduced, giving greater power at a lower engine speed, and it is significant that most of the surviving Prince Henrys are of this type. Heavier touring bodies were now fitted, and even the occasional closed coupé. A two-seater is on show at Britain's National Motor Museum at Beaulieu.

PEUGEOT Bébé

France
cylinders: 4; capacity: 856 cc; hp: 10; transmission: two speeds; speed: 56 km/h (35 mph).

The Bébé Peugeot was made from 1912 to 1916 and was out of the ordinary run of

Peugeot cars in several ways. For a start, the design was the work of an outsider, Ettore Bugatti in fact, and was originally planned to be manufactured and sold under the Bugatti name. Then it had a much smaller engine than any contemporary Peugeot and a most unusual transmission system. This consisted of two concentric propeller shafts one revolving inside the other, and continuously driving bevels, the selection of speeds being by means of a sliding dog clutch at the front end of the shaft. Reverse was obtained by a separate gear lever and remote control linkage to the rear axle. Another unusual feature was the rear suspension by reversed quarter elliptic springs which became standard Bugatti practice.

The Bébé was made mostly in open two-seater form, but a few pill-box like closed coupés were built and racing versions competed in events such as the Cyclecar Grands Prix at Amiens and Le Mans in 1913.

Above: 1917 Morris Cowley
Left: 1919 Hispano-Suiza H6
Above right: 1915 Dodge with British body.

been replaced by a more conventional bi-bloc unit with cast iron blocks. This was necessitated because of problems in keeping the steel cylinder sleeves aligned in the aluminium block, and must have been more satisfactory as it was used until 1928. A little-known role that the Model 34 played in British industry was the acquisition and close study of one by J. D. Siddeley in 1918 which led to some aspects of the first Armstrong Siddeley of 1919 being close to Howard Marmon's ideas.

MARMON

United States of America
cylinders: 6; capacity: 5,529 cc; bhp: 74; transmission: three speeds; speed: 113 km/h (70 mph).

The Marmon from Indianapolis was a respected make which included among its laurels victory in the first Indianapolis 500 Mile Race, held in 1911. In 1916 the Model 34 was introduced, which was to become the most important design of Marmon's 30-year history. Designed by Howard Marmon, Fred Moscovics and Alanson P. Brush, it was the first car to make widespread use of aluminium. This light metal was employed in the cylinder block and

crankcase which were an integral casting, sump, pistons, water pump and engine mounts, indeed the only steel parts of the engine were the head and cylinder sleeves. Differential housing, radiator shell and the entire body were also of aluminium. The result was a handsome car which weighed only 1,496 kg (3,295 lb) or about three-quarters of contemporaries of the same size. It was called the Model 34 from its rated horsepower (actually 33·75), though the engine developed a good 74 bhp.

In 1916 a Model 34 set a new record for the New York to San Francisco run, four drivers covering the distance in five days and further records followed in the 1920s, by which time the aluminium engine had

DODGE

United States of America
cylinders: 4; capacity: 3,478 cc; hp: 25; transmission: three speeds; speed: 72 km/h (45 mph).

The rise of Dodge was one of the most remarkable success stories of the American motor industry, for it came at a time when most of the other leading companies, such as Ford and Willys, had been in business for a number of years. In 1914 the brothers John and Horace Dodge, who had previously manufactured engines for Ford, set up in business to make conventional touring cars in a higher price range than Ford but not so high as to be beyond the reach of a mass market. Only a handful were made in 1914, by 482 workers, but in 1915 a total of 45,000 cars were made, bringing Dodge into third place in the pro-

United States of America
cylinders: 4; capacity: 2,952 cc; bhp:
55; transmission: three speeds; speed:
97 km/h (60 mph).

The Essex was launched in January 1919 as a cheaper companion line to the Hudson, to enable the company to penetrate the market of the Ford Model T and Chevrolet 490. It had a four-cylinder engine with inlet-over-exhaust valves which gave considerably more power than Ford or Chevrolet, though it was very little larger. Sales in the first year were nearly 22,000, although the prices were higher than the makers had intended, because of the high cost of raw materials in the immediate post war years. In 1920 the US Post Office bought a large fleet of Essex tourers for delivery of rural mail and to publicize this they entered one for the San Francisco–New York record attempt, setting a new record with a time of four days 14 hours. In 1922 Essex broke new ground with the introduction of their coach, a two-door sedan which sold for only $1,195, undercutting the equivalent Chevrolet model and putting the company early in the trend towards closed cars which swept America in the 1920s. It is said that the name 'Essex' was chosen after a study of a map of England: company executives had almost decided on Kent, but switched to Essex as they thought it implied a six-cylinder engine, which the car did not in fact have until the 1925 season.

HISPANO-SUIZA H6

France
cylinders: 6; capacity: 6,597 cc; bhp:
135; transmission: three speeds;
speed: 153 km/h (95 mph).

Although Spanish in origin, the Hispano-Suiza became much better known as a French car in the 1920s, as the products of the French factory at Bois-Colombes, near Paris, were generally more expensive and glamorous than their Spanish cousins from Barcelona. This reputation was established by the H6 which was the star of the 1919 Paris Motor Show. During the war the Hispano-Suiza company had worked on aero engines, and this was reflected in the design of the new six-cylinder engine which was in fact half of a projected V-12 aero engine. It had a single overhead camshaft, and an immensely strong seven-bearing crankshaft which was machined from a solid billet of forged steel. It also had four wheel brakes operated by a mechanical servo, and it immediately made the rear-wheel-braked Rolls-Royce Silver Ghost seem old fashioned.

Though the H6 was intended to carry touring or town car coachwork, its power and brakes made it ideal for development as a sports car and in 1921 the aperitif millionaire, André Dubonnet, entered his standard four-seater tourer in the Georges Boillot Cup and won it. This led to a team of cars being built for the 1922 Boillot Cup, with larger engines of 7,982 cc and shorter wheelbases. They won in 1922 and 1923, and the larger engine was offered as an alternative in Hispano touring cars from 1924. The big sixes were made until 1934.

duction league table, and they have been at least in the top ten ever since. At first only open tourers were made, but in 1916 came the innovation of an all steel sedan body. General Pershing used Dodges as staff cars in his Mexican campaigns and they also saw service on the Western Front after the United States had entered the Great War in 1917. The 25-bhp four-cylinder Dodge engine was used with practically no change until sixes were introduced in 1927.

MORRIS Cowley

Great Britain
cylinders: 4; capacity: 1,496 cc; bhp:
20; speed: 80 km/h (50 mph).

William Morris was a former racing cyclist and bicycle maker who began the manufacture of cars in his native Oxford in the spring of 1913. From the start Morris used a high proportion of bought-out components, for he was not ashamed of the title car assembler and realized that this was the way to turn cars out rapidly without heavy capital expenditure. His first Morris Oxfords, powered by the British White and Poppe engine were two-seaters, and when he decided to cater for the four-seater market he 'shopped around' for a suitable engine and found one made by the Continental Motor Manufacturing Company of Detroit. This one-and-a-half-litre, four-cylinder engine had been developed by Continental in anticipation of a light car boom in America which never materialized, so they were happy to dispose of them to Morris at the bargain price of £18 each. His gearboxes and rear axles he also bought in America, from the Detroit Gear Machine Company, so that the Cowley which was launched in 1915 was in some respects an American car. It was originally made as a two- or four-seater tourer, but á coupé was offered for 1916. Few of these were made because of the war, and in fact total production of the Continental-engined Cowley was not more than 1,450 as Morris turned to Hotchkiss of Coventry for his engines after 1920. Nevertheless it is important as an example of how Morris went about his business and as a successful assembled car.

CHEVROLET 490

United States of America
cylinders: 4; capacity: 2,801 cc; bhp:
30; transmission: three speeds; speed:
80 km/h (50 mph).

The Chevrolet 490 was introduced in 1915 by William C. Durant as an answer to Ford's Model T. Indeed, it was called the 490 because the price of a 1915 Model T tourer was $490 and Durant intended to match Ford as closely as he could. Before he could get his car onto the market, though, Ford cut his price to $440, and Durant could never get as low as this. Nevertheless the buyer did get more of a car for his money, with an overhead valve engine which gave 10 bhp more than Ford's side valve unit, though the capacity was very similar, a conventional three-speed gearbox and maximum speed of 50 mph. The 490 soon put Chevrolet into the ranks of the mass producers, sales rising from 13,292 in 1915 to nearly 63,000 in 1916 and 110,000 in 1917. Post war prices were inevitably higher, running from $735 for the tourer to $1,375 for a two-door sedan but sales continued to prosper, reaching over 150,000 in 1920. Though larger Chevrolets were made at this time, the 490 was the steady seller which kept the balance sheet healthy and saved the company from the potential disaster of two unsuccessful models, the V-8 of 1917 and the air cooled car of 1922. It was replaced for 1923 by the Superior which used the same engine but had lower and more modern lines.

KISSEL Gold Bug

United States of America
cylinders: 6; capacity: 4,654 cc; bhp: 61; transmission: three speeds; speed: 113 km/h (70 mph).

The Kissel from Hartford, Wisconsin, was for most of its life (1906–31) a conventional touring car assembled from well-known components. Its claim to fame rests on the small number of speedsters, nicknamed 'Gold Bugs' which were made from 1919 to 1925. These did not differ from the touring cars mechanically, but they carried very striking bodies built by Kissel but designed by Conover T. Silver, the New York agent for the make. These were in the tradition of the American speedster which was intended as a second car for fair-weather motoring, so had little in the way of weather protection or luggage accommodation. The first Silver Special was made in 1917, and it was the 1919 show model, painted pure chrome yellow all over, which earned the name Gold Bug. This was never an official name, and was in fact suggested by a reader of the *Milwaukee Journal* whose automotive editor ran a competition for the most suitable name for the yellow-painted car he had been driving around the roads of Wisconsin that summer. Although many were subsequently painted in the traditional yellow, the name was used for all Kissel speedsters, whatever their colour.

Kissels were not widely used for competitions, though at the 1923 Ascot Road Races a modified Gold Bug with shortened wheelbase and stronger valve springs was lying third behind two real racing cars before it was slowed down by two collisions.

BUGATTI Brescia

1922; France
cylinders: 4; capacity: 1,368 cc; bhp: 40; transmission: four speeds.

The so-called 'Brescia' Bugatti had its origins in the Type 13 small competition car first made in 1910. This was put into production again after the First World War, being Bugatti's only model until the introduction of the straight-8 Type 30 in 1922. It had a four-cylinder overhead camshaft engine with Bugatti's characteristic design of curved tappets operating the valves, the post war models having four valves per cylinder. Three wheelbases were available, 196 cm (6 ft 6½ in), Type 13; 236 cm (7 ft 10½ in), Type 22; and 251 cm (8 ft 4½ in), Type 23. The Type 13 was purely a competition car whose successes included taking the first four places in the 1921 Italian Voiturette Grand Prix at Brescia, from which the model derived its name. Strictly speaking the racing cars were called 'Full Brescia', while the longer touring models were 'Brescias Modifiés'. One of the best-known British campaigners of the Brescia was Raymond Mays whose *Cordon Bleu* and *Cordon Rouge* (sponsored

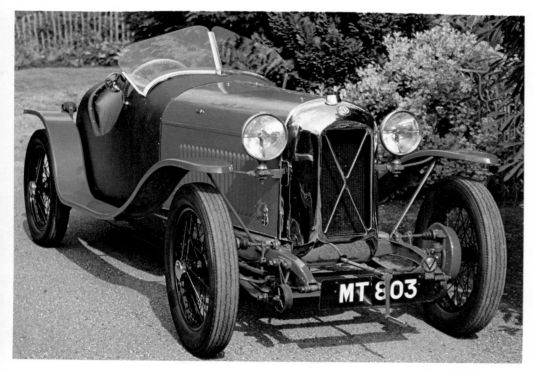

Left: 1926 Bentley 3-litre – one of the best-known
British sports touring cars.
Below left: 1922 Bugatti Brescia
Above: 1928 Salmson
Below right: 1922 Fiat 501

by the champagne firm of G. H. Mumm)
took many first places in sprints and hill
climbs between 1921 and 1924. Mays fitted
front wheel brakes to *Cordon Bleu*, a practice followed by other users of the faster
Brescias. The more staid Brescias Modifiés
were fitted with a wide variety of touring
coachwork, usually open, though there
were a few four-door saloons.

The Brescia was the only Bugatti to be
made under licence outside France, by
Crossley in England, Diatto in Italy and
Rabag in Germany. Not more than 25
were made in each country so the royalties
cannot have enriched Bugatti greatly. The
Brescia was phased out during 1926, by
which time some 2,000 had been made.

FIAT 501

Italy
**cylinders: 4; capacity: 1,460 cc; bhp:
23; transmission: four speeds; speed:
80 km/h (50 mph).**
The first mass-produced Italian car, the
Fiat 501, was designed by Carlo Cavalli
during the First World War and put into
production in 1919. It was a conventional
four-cylinder touring car with monobloc
side valve engine with detachable head,
full electric lighting and all braking on the
rear wheels. Although the latter was a step
forward in Fiat practice, at least one road
tester preferred the transmission brake of
the earlier Tipo Zero. As originally made,
the 501 had squared-off military type mudguards but these gave way to the conventional rounded type in the summer of 1922
and those sold in England, even before
1922, usually had rounded types supplied
by the British coachbuilders. The factory
supplied open tourers and two-seaters and
an angular saloon, but numerous coachbuilders went to work on the 501 chassis.
Although not especially cheap on the
British market it sold well because of its

sturdiness, while in Italy it benefited from
the fact that it had no direct rivals, most
other Italian cars being in the more sporting and expensive class. Some sporting
models of the 501 were made, such as the
501S with 26·5 bhp and 100 km/h (60 mph)
and the racing 501SS with twin overhead
camshaft engine which gave 30 bhp and
took the first four places in the 1922 Italian
Voiturette Grand Prix. There was also a
Colonial model with wider track and the
longer wheel base Tipo 502 made from
1923 onwards. Production of the 501/502
ceased in 1926, by which time about 80,000
had been made.

SALMSON

France
**cylinders: 4; capacity: 1,087 cc; bhp:
16; transmission: four speeds; speed:
72 km/h (45 mph).**
The Salmson company came to prominence as makers of aero engines during the
First World War and their entry into car
manufacture was by building the British
GN cyclecar under licence, which they did
from 1919 to 1921. The first car to bear
the Salmson name was designed by Emile
Petit and appeared in 1921. Though the
frame was of flimsy, cyclecar type construction, it had a proper four-cylinder
engine and shaft drive, though without a
differential. The engine was an overhead
valve unit and had the unusual feature of
pushrods which operated the inlet valves
as *pull* rods. This unit developed 16 bhp
and was adequate to propel a light two-
seater at up to 72 km/h (45 mph), with a
fuel consumption of 45 mpg. It was not
at that time a sports car, but a special car
was built for the 1921 Cyclecar Grand
Prix, equipped with a twin overhead camshaft engine and this was installed in the
1923 production 1·2-litre sports and in the
1925 1,100-cc sports. By this time the
Salmson was established as one of France's
leading small sports car makers (the other
was Amilcar) and sold well in England
where there was no native equivalent.
Front wheel brakes appeared on the racing

versions in 1922 and on the road-going cars
in 1926, while differentials finally arrived
on the 1927 models.

BENTLEY 3-litre

Great Britain
**cylinders: 4; capacity: 2,996 cc; bhp:
90; transmission: four speeds; speed:
129 km/h (80 mph).**
Bentley is the name which comes most
readily to mind when the phrase 'vintage
sports car' is mentioned.

The three-litre Bentley was announced
in the motoring press in May 1919 but it
was not until Christmas that a car was
actually running and the first delivery to a
customer took place in September 1921.
With many cars this delay would have been
fatal but the public's appetite had been so
whetted by the specifications that interest
remained high. The Bentley had a four-
cylinder engine with a capacity of just
under three-litres (it was the first British
car to be described in litres rather than
horsepower and there were many enquiries
about the meaning of the term), and a
single overhead camshaft operating four
valves per cylinder. The cylinder head was
non-detachable and there were only brakes
on the rear wheels, so it was far from being
a revolutionary design, but the promise of
fast, comfortable touring and the price of
£750 made it stand out among other cars
of the time. In fact, by the time the cars
reached the public, the chassis price had
risen to £1,150, or £1,350 with four-seater
tourer body, but orders came in steadily
and 141 cars were made in 1922, 204 in
1923 and 402 in 1924. The circle of potential buyers of a car like the Bentley was
small but close-knit, so that news of a good
new model quickly spread around. Racing
successes began in May 1921 when a works
car driven by Frank Clement won a race at
Brooklands and Bentleys competed at
Indianapolis and the Tourist Trophy in
1922, in events mainly contested by out
and out racing cars. Their first Le Mans
victory came in 1924 and the greatest in
1927 when a car involved in a multiple
pile-up was straightened out and went on
to win.

Above left : 1923 Citroën 5CV with 'clover-leaf'
bodywork.
Left : 1924 Lancia Lambda tourer
Above : 1927 Austin Seven/Swallow

LANCIA LAMBDA

Italy
**cylinders: 4; capacity: 2,121 cc; bhp:
50; transmission: four speeds; speed:
113 km/h (70 mph).**

The Lancia Lambda was one of the few
cars to combine great technical originality
with immediate commercial success. Its
two most radical features were the frame
made of hollow steel pressings which
served not only as a chassis but as the
lower part of the body and independent
front suspension by sliding pillars and
vertical coils. While neither of these ideas
was entirely new (Vauxhall had used a
similar body/frame in 1904, and the suspension had been employed by Morgan
since 1910) it was the first time they had
been combined in one car. The engine was
a narrow angle V-4, the angle between the
two 'banks' being only 22° so that it was
possible to make a monobloc casting. The
Lambda had a very modern appearance

for its day, being lower than any other car
of its size, and had a very respectable performance aided by good road holding.
Nevertheless it was never thought of as a
sports car in its native Italy and its length
made it unsuitable for racing. Saloons
were made as well as tourers and from 1927
onwards a separate chassis frame was
available for those who wanted a coach-
built body. About 13,000 Lambdas were
made between 1923 and 1931.

CITROËN 5CV

France
**cylinders: 4; capacity: 856 cc; bhp:
11; transmission: three speeds; speed:
61 km/h (38 mph).**

André Citroën had made a fortune in the
manufacture of gears and ammunitions
before he turned to car making in 1919.
His first product was a 10-hp tourer, which
he supplemented in 1922 with a 7-hp two-
seater known in France as the 5CV (French

units of horsepower were larger than
British). It was a light car in the Austin
Seven idiom, with a four-cylinder side
valve engine and shaft drive, though
Citroën did not provide front wheel brakes.
However these were available from various
proprietory firms, as were overhead valve
conversions. Originally offered solely as a
two seater with pointed tail, the 5CV range
was supplemented by a three-seater 'clover-
leaf' in which the third passenger sat in
the centre of the car behind the front seats,
and also a cabriolet. Several colours were
available, but a favourite was yellow, which
led to the cars being nicknamed 'Demi-
Citron' (half a lemon, the 5CV power
rating being half that of the original 10CV
Citroën). About 80,000 were made in five
years, and the Citroën was copied by the
German Opel company for their Laubfrosch which was also made in large
numbers. Citroën won the case they had
introduced against Opel who had virtually
blueprinted their car, but Adam Opel,
who had expected Citroën's reaction is
reported to have said that this cost him
much less than having to pay a competent
designer and all the development costs for
a car of equivalent appeal, as would otherwise have been the case.

AUSTIN Seven

Great Britain
**cylinders: 4; capacity: 747 cc; bhp:
15; transmission: three speeds; speed:
51 km/h (44 mph).**

The Austin Seven was one of the most
important cars to be made in Britain, for it
gave the motoring public the attributes of
a full-size car, four cylinders, four seats,
four wheel brakes and shaft drive, at a
price no higher than was asked for the
crude, two-cylinder cycle cars. It was said
to have been designed by Herbert Austin
on the billard table of his Warwickshire
home and was launched in 1922. With a

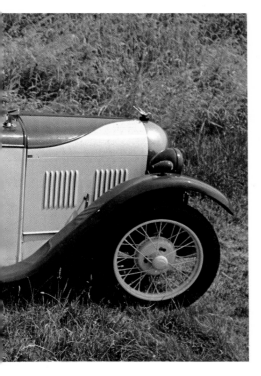

wheelbase of only 187 cm (6 ft 3 in) and overall length of 260 cm (8 ft 8 in), it nevertheless accommodated four people and its 698-cc engine could propel the car at 61 km/h (38 mph). The chassis was a simple A frame, with quarter elliptic springs attached to the two arms at the rear, while suspension at the front was looked after by a single transverse semi-elliptic spring. Although there were four wheel brakes, they were not coupled until 1930; before that the hand brake worked on the front wheels and the pedal on the rear.

Engine capacity was increased to 747 cc in 1924, and remained at this size until the Seven was discontinued in 1939. Although on paper the Seven seemed unsuited to competitition work, it competed at Shelsley hill climb in 1922 and was being raced at Brooklands by March 1923 when Capt A. C. Waite won a handicap race and a month later the same car won the Italian Cyclecar Grand Prix at a speed of 89·89 km/h (55·86 mph). Later E. C. Gordon England tuned the Seven to a remarkable degree, taking countless records at Brooklands and Montlhéry, and in its final supercharged form from 1936, the little engine was giving 116 bhp. However, it is as a versatile passenger car that the Austin Seven will be chiefly remembered.

CHRYSLER 70

United States of America
cylinders: 6; capacity 3,267 cc; bhp: 68; transmission: three speeds; speed: 121 km/h (75 mph).
The Chrysler was the last major native make to appear on the American market and to gain a permanent foothold there. Not that Walter P. Chrysler was without experience, for he had worked for Buick and Willys before acquiring the Maxwell Motor Company in 1923. While he continued the four-cylinder Maxwell for a further two seasons, he introduced alongside it a new six-cylinder car with several advanced features. These included a seven-bearing crankshaft, the first in America on

a medium-sized car, hydraulic brakes on all four wheels, and balloon tyres. At a price of $1,645 for a sedan, the Chrysler 70 was an immediate success, and sold 32,000 units in its first season. The usual open and closed body styles were offered, and one of the most popular was the rumble seat roadster. Chrysler had no intention of entering the competition field, merely wanting to give the middle income market the best possible car for their money but the Chrysler's performance soon attracted the sporting motorist. In July 1924 Ralph DePalma broke both the stock car and racing car records for the 15·28 km (9½) mile Mount Wilson (California) climb, while in England Malcolm Campbell drove a streamlined Chrysler at Brooklands in 1925. The make also ran at Le Mans in 1925, 1928 (finishing 3rd), 1929 and 1931.

LORRAINE-DIETRICH

France
cylinders: 6; capacity: 3,445 cc; bhp: 90; transmission: three speeds; speed: 145 km/h (90 mph).
The sporting Lorraine-Dietrich was in many ways the French equivalent of the three-litre Bentley, of which it was a close rival in the Le Mans 24 Hour Race. It was derived from a rather pedestrian tourer, the 15CV, which had a number of American features such as a three-speed gearbox with central change and coil ignition. The sporting model, announced in 1924, had many modifications including larger valves, twin horizontal Zenith carburettors, dual ignition with two separate distributors and front wheel brakes. There was also a special oil-cooling system with twin coolers mounted in the radiator. Other differences included Rudge knock-on wire wheels in place of artilleries and Dewandre Servo assisted brakes. Four speeds were standardized on all models from 1926. With a lightweight four-seater body, these cars were capable of 145 km/h (90 mph), compared with 97 km/h (60 mph) for the standard 15CV. In 1924 they finished second and third at Le Mans, winning the race in 1925 and 1926 when Lorraines were also third and second respectively. The works did not enter for Le Mans after this, but private entrants ran cars as late as 1935, by which time they were at least eight years old. Jean-Pierre Wimille, who was later to win fame as a racing driver, finished second in the 1931 Monte Carlo Rally, driving a secondhand Lorraine-Dietrich sports saloon.

PACKARD Single Eight

United States of America
cylinders: 8; capacity: 5,875 cc; bhp: 84; transmission: three speeds; speed: 121 km/h (75 mph).
Packard was perhaps the most consistently respected American make of car, holding the position enjoyed by Daimler in Britain from the early 1900s until after the Second World War. In 1923 they introduced their straight-eight, known as the Single Eight to distinguish it from the Twin Six, a twelve-cylinder car which it replaced. It had four wheel brakes as standard, being only the second production American car

to have them. The 1925 models were known as the Second Series and were generally similar to the first but with the refinement of Bijur chassis lubrication, by which one pull of a plunger on the dashboard greased 32 chassis parts. Also new was the Bendix three-shoe internal expanding braking system. Balloon tyres and detachable disc wheels were standard. Unlike many European quality car makers, Packards were sold complete, although the Super Eight was also available just as a chassis and the work of many well-known American and European coachbuilders was seen on this chassis. The Third Series of 1927 incorporated a hypoid rear axle giving the car lower lines – three years ahead of Rolls-Royce – while on the same model engine capacity was increased to 6·3 litres (384 cu in). The practice of naming models by series instead of making annual model changes was continued on the Packard Eights up to 1942 with the 22nd Series. Among owners of Packards in this era were the Kings of Belgium and Norway, Joseph Stalin and four American Presidents (Harding, Coolidge, Hoover and Roosevelt).

TATRA Type 11

Czechoslovakia
cylinders: 2; capacity: 1,056 cc; bhp: 12; transmission: four speeds; speed: 51 km/h (44 mph).
Although not the biggest Czech car manufacturing company, Tatra was the best-known abroad because of the originality of its designs. The company had its origins before the First World War, when its products were called Nesselsdorf after the town where they were made, which was then in the Austro-Hungarian Empire. After 1918 the town was renamed Koprivnice, and the cars were given the easier to pronounce name of Tatra, after the nearby range of mountains. The first Tatras were large cars carried over from the Nesselsdorf range, but in 1923 the talented designer, Hans Ledwinka, produced a completely new design of light car using a tubular backbone frame in place of the conventional chassis, with the body supported on outriggers from the central tube. The car had independently sprung wheels at the rear and a transverse leaf spring with a rigid front axle at the front. The engine was an air-cooled flat twin which lived under a coal-scuttle bonnet similar to that of the Renault though there was, of course, no dashboard radiator. The Tatra Type 11, as it was called, was an immediate success for it was much cheaper than other Czech cars at that time, but thanks to the swing axle suspension it could cope with the country's poor roads better than many large cars. The tubular backbone was rigid and allowed for lighter body work, and as well as the original open four seater, the Type 11 was made in saloon, coupé and cabriolet form, and as a light truck. The flat twin was abandoned in 1934 after 11,070 had been made, but the frame and suspension principles were continued in four- and six-cylinder cars made throughout the 1930s, when independent suspension was also adopted for the front wheels.

ALFA ROMEO 1750

Italy
**cylinders: 6; capacity: 1,752 cc; bhp:
85; transmission: four speeds; speed:
145 km/h (90 mph).**
The sports Alfa Romeos were as different from the Mercedes Benz as could be imagined, gaining their performance through lightness and agility rather than brute force. During the early 1920s the company had made a series of three-litre six-cylinders designed by Giuseppe Merosi, but when Vittorio Jano took over as chief designer in 1926 he introduced a new series of overhead camshaft six-cylinder cars, starting with the 1500. This was an attractive little touring car with a creditable top speed of 109 km/h (68 mph). A short chassis version was made for sporting work, but the series did not really blossom into a sports car until 1928 when the twin-overhead camshaft Gran Sport with Roots-type supercharger appeared. This won numerous races including the 1928 Mille Miglia, Belgian 24 Hour Race, Coupe Boillot and Circuit des Routes Pavées. In 1929 the capacity was increased to 1752 cc, making the famous 6C 1750 model. This was available in three forms, the single-overhead camshaft Turismo with 305 cm (10 ft 2 in) wheelbase and a top speed of 113 km/h (70 mph), the twin-overhead camshaft Gran Turismo 270 cm or 285 cm (9 ft or 9 ft 6 in., 129 km/h [80 mph]), and the Gran Sport which was the same car with a supercharger and top speed of 153 km/h (95 mph). The best looking of the 1750s were the short chassis cars with Zagato two-seater coachwork. Innumerable racing successes came to this model, including the 1929 and 1930 Mille Miglia and Belgian 24 Hour Races and the 1930 Tourist Trophy. The 1750 was made until 1934 when it was replaced by a larger model of which the six-cylinder engine was made in 1920 cc and 2·3-litre forms. Total production of it and the previous 1500 was 3,656, of which about 500 were two-seaters.

ISOTTA-FRASCHINI Tipo 8A

Italy
**cylinders: 8; capacity: 7,370 cc; bhp:
120; transmission: three speeds;
speed: 129 km/h (80 mph).**
In the inter-war period, the Isotta-Fraschini was the leading make of luxury car in Italy, occupying the same position as Rolls-Royce in Britain and Hispano-Suiza in France. Although they had made a variety of chassis in pre-war days, they concentrated on one model from 1919 onwards, the straight-eight Tipo 8. This was the first straight-eight car to go into production anywhere in the world and had a nine-bearing overhead valve six-litre engine with aluminium block and pistons. It had a three-speed gearbox in unit with the engine, with a central gear lever, and four wheel brakes, though without any kind of servo assistance as the Hispano-Suiza had. This was rectified on the Tipo 8A introduced in 1925, which also had a larger engine. This was intended to lure away some of Hispano's customers by providing better performance and more

silence. This it undoubtedly did, but it still lagged behind its French rival, particularly in the latter's 45-bhp eight-litre form. However, the Isotta established a niche for itself in the USA. A New York showroom was opened in 1924 and customers included Rudolf Valentino (who had two), Jack Dempsey, Clara Bow and William Randolph Hearst. In 1926 a sporting model called the Tipo 8A SS (Super Spinto) was introduced which, with 150 bhp at its disposal, was claimed to reach 161 km/h (100 mph). However, buyers did not on the whole associate Isotta-Fraschini with speed and few of these were sold. The final version of the straight-eight Isotta was the Tipo 8B, made from 1931 to 1935, which used the 150-bhp engine in a heavier chassis.

RENAULT 45

France
**cylinders: 6; capacity: 9,120 cc; bhp:
125; transmission: three speeds;
speed: 145 km/h (90 mph).**
One of the largest cars made in the 1920s, the Renault 45 was in many ways an archaic survivor from Edwardian days. It was descended from the 40-bhp six-cylinder car made from 1913 to 1921 and had its cylinder cast in two pairs of three, fixed head and wooden wheels. As originally introduced in 1921 its brakes were only on the rear wheels, which led to the comment that 'it stopped imperceptibly, in the manner of an ocean liner.' Even after the addition of front wheel brakes, it was never renowned for stopping power and consequently was never seen on the racing circuits. A special streamlined saloon version did, however, become the first car to average more than 161 km/h (100 mph) for 24 hours, a feat performed at Montlhéry in 1926. The 45 came in two wheelbase lengths, 375 cm (12 ft 6 in) and 393 cm (13 ft 1 in), the latter usually carrying formal limousine or coupé de ville coachwork, while on the shorter wheelbase a number of attractive sporting tourers were built. Perhaps the handsomest of these was the 'Scaphandrier', a tourer with a minute hood which covered the rear seats only. The 45 was made from 1921 to 1929 when it was replaced by the straight-eight Reinastella.

DUESENBERG Model J

United States of America
**cylinders: 8; capacity: 6,882 cc; bhp:
265; transmission: three speeds.**
The Duesenberg company of Indianapolis had been formed in 1912 to manufacture racing cars, which they followed with a touring car, the Model A, in 1920. It was an advanced machine, with single-overhead camshaft straight-eight engine and hydraulic four-wheel brakes, but the company did not really spring to prominence until eight years later, when the dynamic Errett Lobban Cord, who had already revitalized the Auburn company, proceeded to do the same with Duesenberg. He gave Fred Duesenberg *carte blanche* to design a car which would out-perform anything else on American roads, with price very much a secondary con-

sideration. The result was the Model J which made its appearance in December 1928. It had an engine which was not only large at nearly 6·9 litres, but also very advanced in that its valves were operated by twin overhead camshafts, hitherto the preserve of small, specialist competition cars from Europe. This dramatic engine, with its four valves per cylinder and aluminium pistons, developed 265 bhp, more than twice the power of any other American car. With a light tourer body, a top speed of 187 km/h (116 mph) was claimed, with 141 km/h (89 mph) in second gear. Even with a heavy limousine body, any Model J could exceed 161 km/h (100 mph). Naturally, such a car could not be cheap, and the chassis alone cost $8,500 at a time when a complete Packard seven-passenger limousine was priced at under $6,000, and even the vast Locomobile 90 was only $7,500 for a complete seven-passenger car. With coachwork by such firms as Murphy, Le Baron or Derham, the price of a complete Model J could be anywhere between $12,000 and $20,000. With the Wall Street Stock Market crash occurring less than twelve months after the car's introduction, it is surprising that it remained in production at all, but it soldiered on until 1937, by which time approximately 470 had been made.

FORD Model A

United States of America
**cylinders: 4; capacity: 3,285 cc; bhp:
40; transmission: three speeds; speed:
97 km/h (60 mph).**
By 1927 practically everyone at Fords realized that the nineteen-year-old Model T was long overdue for replacement. Bringing out a new model was a traumatic experience for all concerned, for a whole generation of workers, salesmen and customers had grown up with the T. The Ford factories closed down for nearly five months and meanwhile dealers showed their faith in the company by ordering 375,000 examples of a car whose specifica-

tions remained secret. When it appeared the Model A was seen to be a conventional car, rather short and high by 1927 standards, but endowed with a 20 cu in (3·3 litre) 40-bhp engine which combined with light weight, gave it a very satisfactory performance. The two-speed epicyclic transmission of the T was replaced by a conventional three-speed box with central change, but the transverse spring front and near suspension was retained, and indeed this lasted throughout the early part of the Ford V-8 era, up to 1948. Model A prices started at $460 for the 2-seater roadster and went up to $1,200 for a town car, of which few were sold. In 1929 Ford extended the range to include the world's first production station wagon, by which time there were also van, pick-up and taxi Model As, as well as the longer wheelbase AA truck. In 1932 the A went into production in the Soviet Union as the GAZ-A, being the first quantity-produced car in that country and was made up to 1936. In USA, the A was succeeded by the V-8 which used the same chassis, in 1932, after some 4½ million had been made.

MERCEDES-BENZ SSK

Germany
cylinders: 6; capacity: 7,020 cc; bhp: 225 (with supercharger); transmission: four speeds; speed: 185 km/h (115 mph).
The large Mercedes-Benz sports cars of the 1920s are among the most famous German cars, typifying their country and era in the same way that the three-litre Bentley did in Britain. The line began with the K, or 24/100/140PS six-cylinder model designed by the great Ferdinand Porsche in 1925. This was made in both open and closed form but was not widely seen as a

sports car. In 1927 it was followed by the S, a lower car with larger engine and better brakes which was quite widely used in competitions, and this in turn was developed into the SS of 1928. This had a still larger engine in the same chassis, and a slightly higher radiator. Very handsome touring and coupé bodies were built on this chassis and it was also used for competition work. Probably its best known success was Rudolf Caracciola's victory in the 1929 Tourist Trophy. A true competition model soon appeared, known as the SSK, with a wheelbase 45 cm (18 in) shorter than the S. This won numerous races, including the 1930 Irish Grand Prix and 1931 German Grand Prix.

A feature of the whole series of Mercedes Benz sports cars was the supercharger which, unlike many of its kind, was not permanently engaged but could be activated by a sharp pressure on the accelerator pedal. This produced a banshee-like wail and a sudden surge of power. Production of these big cars ceased in 1933, by which time 146 of the Type S, 112 of the SS and 33 of the SSK had been made.

Above right : 1931 Alfa Romeo 1750
Right : 1931 Model A Ford
Below left : 1932 Duesenberg Model J
Below right : 1929 Mercedes-Benz SSK with 7·1-litre, 6-cylinder engine.

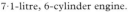

CADILLAC Model 452

United States of America
cylinders: 16; capacity: 7,420 cc; bhp: 165; transmission: three speeds; speed: 145 km/h (90 mph).

Cadillac had pioneered the V-8 engine in America in 1914 and in 1930 they again broke new ground by introducing the world's first production car with a 16-cylinder engine. This was in effect two straight-eight engines mounted at an angle of 45° and sharing a common crankshaft. Each bank of cylinders had its own ignition and fuel systems, though the overhead valves were operated by a common camshaft lying in the V between the banks. The design incorporated hydraulic valve adjusters which gave exceptionally silent running. It was said that the critical listening test for the V-16 specified that, at idling speed, nothing more than the spark of the contact points should be heard.

Unlike many luxury cars, the V-16, or Model 452 as it was called by the company, was listed with a complete range of bodies which were the work of General Motors' director of design, Harley Earl, and were built by the Fleetwood Metal Body Com-

Above : 1933 Morgan Aero – the best-known of the three-wheelers.
Below left : 1931 Cadillac Model 452.
Above right : 1934 Bugatti Type 57.

pany which by that time was a General Motors-owned concern. Fifteen different body styles were offered, from a two-passenger roadster to a town brougham at $9,500. Sales of the Model 452 were remarkably good for the Depression era, starting at 3,250 for the first two years, though they later dropped to around 500 per year. The model was made until 1937 when it was replaced by a new design of V-16 with shorter stroke engine which ran until 1940.

MORGAN three-wheeler

Great Britain
cylinders: 2; capacity: 980 cc; bhp: 45; transmission: three speeds; speed: 113 km/h (70 mph).
The Morgan was the best known make of three-wheeler, not only in Britain but throughout the world, and one of the few which had a successful and lengthy competition career. Throughout the 1920s the Aero model with its big V-twin Blackburne engine was a familiar sight in trials such as

the ACU Six Days, the Scottish Six Days and the London-Edinburgh. Morgans raced at Brooklands, but from 1924 to 1928 only in motorcycle events. Three wheelers had an anomalous position in Britain and, for example, were always exhibited at motorcycle shows at Olympia. By 1933 the fiercest of the Morgans was called the Super Sports Aero and had just been given a three-speed gearbox, previous models making do with two. Other refinements only recently introduced included an electric starter and a plate clutch and although there were brakes on the front wheels, they were not coupled with that on the rear wheel, nor were they on any Morgan three-wheeler. The air-cooled V-twin JAP engine was mounted ahead of the bonnet, fully exposed to the air. A year later this model gave way to a less sporting version with a water-cooled Matchless engine, and in 1934 came the first Morgan with a four-cylinder engine, a 1,122 cc Coventry Climax.

PONTIAC straight-eight

United States of America
cylinders: 8, sv; capacity: 3,660 cc; bhp: 75; transmission: three speeds, synchromesh; speed: 124 km/h (78 mph).
One rung up the GM ladder from the best-selling Chevrolet, the Pontiac was a young make, launched in 1926 to boost the flagging sales of the Corporation's Oakland division. At first a conventional 187 cu in (three-litre) six was marketed, but with the demise of the Oakland line at the end of 1931 Pontiac inherited their unsuccessful V-8. A year later this and the six were dropped in favour of a new 223 cu in (3·7 litre) straight-eight by G. T. Christopher. Engineering was typical of the period, with side valves, mechanical pump feed and three-speed synchromesh gearbox; the wire wheels, vee grille and no draught ventilation were common to all contemporary GM products. Less conventional was a list price of less than $600, the first time an inline eight had been offered for as little. Four years earlier, indeed, Marmon had created a sensation with their Roosevelt, which retailed at fractionally under the $1,000 mark. On

75 bhp the Pontiac attained nearly 130 km/h (80 mph) and a wide variety of body styles included coupés and a convertible roadster. Despite the bleak economic climate, sales rose from 51,000 to around 89,000, giving Pontiac fifth place on the home market. Though the company would remain loyal to straight-eights longer than almost anyone else (the last ones were made in 1954), Christopher soon moved on to Packard, for whom he masterminded the cutprice 120, one of the sensations of 1935.

BUGATTI Type 57

France
cylinders: 8, twin ohc; capacity; 3,257 cc; bhp: 135; transmission: four speeds; speed: 152 km/h (95 mph).
France bred some of the finest fast touring cars of the 1930s, thanks to her excellent roads. Cars like Delahaye's 135, the 20CV Grand Sport Hotchkiss, the four-litre Lago Talbot and the Type 57 Bugatti offered excellent road holding, top speeds of 145–150 km/h (90–100 mph), and easy cruising at around the 130 km/h (80 mph) mark, though the custom bodies they wore were often splendidly claustrophobic and impractical. Bugatti's 1934 contribution, the last of his cars to see series production, was a serious attempt to build a vehicle suitable for everyday use, with a performance superior to that of the earlier sohc eights, Types 44 and 49. As always, the traditional reversed quarter elliptic rear suspension featured, synchromesh was deemed an unnecessary luxury, and hydraulic brakes would not replace mechanicals until 1938. The 3·3-litre dohc straight-eight engine gave 135 bhp in standard form, raised to 160 with the aid of a supercharger on the 57C version, the fastest stock saloon purchasable in 1939. An example of this model put 179 km (112 miles) into the hour at Montlhéry autodrome, while the 57S and 57SC with shorter, lower frames were even faster. After the fall of the franc in 1936, the 57 became a real bargain in England, selling for less than £900. All told some 700 57s were built: attempts to revive the model after the War under the Type 101 designation came to nothing.

CITROËN 7CV Traction Avant

France
cylinders: 4, ohv; capacity: 1,628 cc; bhp: 36; transmission: three speeds, synchromesh; speed: 114 km/h (65 mph).

During the model's run of 23 years nearly 760,000 Tractions were built, 708,339 of these with the four-cylinder engine. The car bankrupted Citroën (Michelin had to mount a rescue operation), but it set new standards in structural strength and road-holding: cruising speed, if unspectacular, could be maintained without regard to weather or surface. If ohv and hydraulic brakes were unfamiliar to Citroën owners, the rest was new to the world – a full unitary structure build up on a flat floor backbone. To this a U-shaped wheel-barrow was attached to take the engine and

Above : 1938 BMW 328.
Below left : 1936 Fiat 500 Topolino.
Above right : 1936 Citroën Traction Avant.

front wheel drive unit. Suspension was by torsion bars, independent at the front, and in the prevailing 'streamline' craze the Citroën's lines were both restrained and modern. Faults were an awkward dashboard gearchange, tricky maintenance, and a susceptibility to rust. Few of the elegant roadsters have survived and this type was not reinstated after the Second World War. Further, the first 7CVs with their 1·3-litre engines were underpowered and capacity was hurriedly raised to 1·6 litres. The definitive four-cylinder Traction was, of course, the 1,911-cc 11CV, which was giving 60 bhp by the end of its run in 1957 and propelling the car at 129 km/h (75 mph). This engine – or at any rate its

bottom end – also featured in the original D series of 1956 and in a line of fwd light vans from 1939 onwards.

FIAT 500

Italy
cylinders: 4, sv; capacity: 569 cc; bhp: 13; transmission: four speeds, synchromesh; speed: 83 km/h (52 mph).
The first all-new baby car since the Austin Seven of 1922 was Dante Giacosa's Fiat 500 (Topolino, or Mickey Mouse), announced in 1936. His creation was a true big model in miniature, innocent of cyclecar influences, with four-speed synchromesh gearbox, hydraulic brakes, and independently sprung front wheels. Mounting the power unit over the front axle ahead of the radiator gave plenty of leg room, while the 500 was strictly a two-seater. Four-seater versions (with the exception of the shortlived 1939 English export variant) did not appear until 1949, when a switch to ohv boosted output from 13 to 16·5 bhp. The original Topolino was the perfect shopping car, with viceless handling, a length of only 3·26 metres (128½ in), a weight of 535 kg (1,176 lb), and a turning circle of 8·5 metres (28 ft). It cruised at around 70 km/h (45 mph), and fuel consumption averaged 5·5 lit/100 (50 mpg). The gravity fuel feed with its three way plumbing on the floor was a trifle crude, the price of generous body width was an awkward sliding window mechanism, and the two bearing crankshaft disliked more than 4,000 rpm, but rolltop convertible coachwork was a bonus on so cheap a car. Over 122,000 of the original type were followed by another 400,000 of the later B and C series, production of which ended early in 1955. 500s were also made in France as the Simca-5 and in Germany by NSU of Heilbronn.

BMW 328

Germany
cylinders: 6, ohv; capacity: 1,971 cc; bhp: 80; transmission: four speeds, synchromesh; speed: 152 km/h (95 mph).
First seen in the German Eifelrennen in the summer of 1936, the 328 broke new ground in sports car design, escaping from the traditions of uncivilized bodywork, high noise levels and hard suspension. It was also the outstanding all-rounder of its time. Though its racing successes included victory in the 1940 Mille Miglia, it also distinguished itself in rallies and even in British reliability trials and was an entirely practical road car, capable of 160 km/h (100 mph) in favourable circumstances. In 1937 S. C. H. Davis put 167·57 km (102·23 miles) into the hour at Brooklands on a stock 328. The simple twin tube frame derived from the earlier 315 and 319 sixes, but new were hydraulic brakes and a special cylinder head with hemispherical combustion chambers which helped extract 80 bhp from the triple carburettor two-litre engine. The streamlined roadster body was handsome and comfortable, a bonnet strap distinguishing the car from lesser sporting BMWs such as the 327, a two-seater cabriolet available with the 80 bhp unit. Though only 462 328s were made, the model was still competitive after the Second World War, Ernst Loof developing the theme on his handbuilt Veritas two-seaters using secondhand 328 components. The classic 328 was marketed in Britain as the Frazer-Nash-BMW. The engine design was taken up in England by Bristol, who used it in their own cars, and also supplied it to A.C., Cooper, Frazer Nash and Lister. It was not until 1961 that the Bristol unit was withdrawn from production.

CORD 810

United States of America
cylinders: 8 Vee, sv; capacity: 4,730 cc; bhp: 125; transmission: four-speed preselector; speed: 145 km/h (90 mph).
Chosen by New York's Museum of Modern Art as an outstanding example of industrial design, the 1936 Cord was almost the last American attempt to break with the national stereotype. True, Gordon Buehrig's inspired shape with its alligator bonnet and simple wraparound grille showed evidence of penny pinching; the use of two dies for four doors was an economy; and the interior hardware consisted largely of leftovers. But if the Lycoming-built sv V-8 engine broke no rules, arranging it to drive the front wheels was heresy, as was the ingenious four-speed gearbox with overdrive top and electric preselection of the ratios. The headlamps retracted manually into the

Right : 1936 Cord 810.
Far right, above : 1946 Volvo PV444.
Far right, below : 1938 Lancia Aprilia.

front wings, there were no running boards, and other features included hydraulic brakes and independent front suspension. Straight line performance was good rather than spectacular though the supercharged 812 of 1937 attained 180 km/h (112 mph). The Cord was a driver's car which cornered fast and invited liberal use of the gears. Teething troubles were inevitable: gears jumped out and engines overheated, while the money ran out after a mere 3,000 Cords had been built. The factory closed in August, 1937, though attempts were subsequently made to adapt the body dies to a conventionally engineered Hupmobile. The 1960s saw several Cord revivals. The most promising of these was the 8/10 of 1964, a convertible scaled down to 8/10ths size with a synchromesh gearbox and Chevrolet Corvair aircooled flat six engine.

LANCIA Aprilia

Italy
cylinders: 4, Vee, ohc; capacity: 1,352 cc; bhp: 46; transmission: four speeds; speed: 125 km/h (77 mph).
The last of Vincenzo Lancia's own creations – he only just lived to see it enter production – the Aprilia was not cheap: its home market price was a good third higher than the norm for its class. The gearbox lacked synchromesh and the unitary hull was rustprone. Where it scored was in an unparalleled combination of roomy body, surefooted handling, good aerodynamic shape, fast and easy gearchange, hydraulic brakes, and a short stroke engine capable of sustained high revs. Front and rear wheels were independently sprung, with Lancia's familiar coils

and sliding pillars at the front, while adequate body space was assured by the use of a compact, narrow angle V4 engine. The Aprilia was never intended as a sports car – like the old Lambda it served as a taxi in its native land – but on a twisting road it was hard to catch. As always, Lancia offered a platform type chassis for specialist coachbuilders, and before the Second World War the model was assembled in France as the Lancia Ardennes. From 1939 capacity went up to 1·5-litres with an output of 50 bhp, and in that year a scaled down, and cheaper, version with beam rear axle and 903-cc engine, the Ardea, was introduced. Production was resumed in 1945, and the last of 31,000 Aprilias came off the lines towards the end of 1949.

LINCOLN Continental

United States of America
cylinders: 12, Vee, sv; capacity: 4,786 cc; bhp: 120; transmission: three speeds, synchromesh; speed: 145 km/h (90 mph).
Commissioned for his personal use by Edsel Ford, Henry's son, and styled by E. T. Gregorie, the Continental showed outstanding elegance in a stereotyped era. Low built, with a simple grille, no running boards, and an exposed spare wheel mounted vertically at the rear, the car was for many years the only post Second World War model manufactured to be accorded full Classic status. Admittedly, beauty was skin deep: beneath the surface lay the chassis of the Lincoln Zephyr, a cheap V12 introduced in 1936 to boost the flagging sales of Ford's prestige division. The weaknesses of the old transverse leaf suspension were offset by a long wheelbase, and the Zephyr had a modest thirst of 14 lit/100 (20 mpg) but the Lincoln label dictated a 12-cylinder engine that was difficult to service. By 1940 Zephyrs (and Continentals) had hydraulic brakes and

column change, but the new model cost nearly twice as much as a regular Zephyr and Lincoln still lost money on the operation. Nor could the stylists leave well alone: 1942 and later cars had ugly box front wings which spoilt the lines. Not even power seats and windows, and the power hoods of the convertibles could keep sales going, and the last of 5,324 Continentals was delivered in 1948. The name, however, lived on in the spare wheel kits marketed by accessory makers, and the styling (if not the V12 engine) would be revived on the 1955 Continental Mk II.

VOLVO PV 444

Sweden
cylinders: 4, ohv; capacity: 1,414 cc; bhp: 40; transmission: three speeds, synchromesh; speed: 118 km/h (74 mph).
The first Swedish car to sell abroad in significant quantities, the PV 444 was developed during the Second World War, though deliveries did not begin until 1947. In the 1930s, the company had concentrated on big, American-type sv sixes, but the fuel shortage and the narrowness of Sweden's roads called for something smaller. Thus Erik Jern's new creation was essentially an American car in miniature, albeit the unitary structure was based on the German Hanomag of 1939. Carburettors and electrical equipment were imported from the USA; Detroit influence was reflected also in the three-speed gearbox and the box front wings inspired by the 1942 Ford. Also American in concept was the coil and wishbone independent front suspension, and brakes were hydraulic. The capacity of the four-cylinder ohv engine was a modest 1·4 litres, weight was 968 kg (2,128 lb) and top speed was around 115 km/h (70 mph). The cars were selling modestly in the Low Countries by 1950, and six years later Sweden's motor exports were running at 16,000 a year. Also in 1956, Volvo made their first incursion into the American market. Though the saloon's ugly fastback styling changed little, later versions of the 444 were impressive, with 90 bhp, 1,588 cc engines, and top speeds close to 160 km/h (100 mph). The last of these improved 544s did not leave Göteborg until October 1955, by which time production of the family had run to over 330,000 units.

MG TC

1946; Great Britain
cylinders: 4, ohv; capacity: 1,250 cc;
bhp: 54; transmission: four speeds,
synchromesh; speed: 125 km/h (77
mph).

The TC typified the small British sports car of the 1930s. Its simple frame rode on four semi-elliptic springs and styling derived directly from an earlier Midget, 1933's J2: long bonnet, traditional radiator with octagon badge, exposed headlamps, large diameter instruments, fold flat screen, centre lock 45 cm (18 in) wire wheels, and a large unstreamlined tank at the rear holding 63 litres (13½ gallons) of fuel. The sole concessions to modernity were the synchromesh gearbox and hydraulic brakes ('heresies' first seen on the 1936 TA), and a 1,250-cc edition of the short stroke ohv Morris engine already used in the TB announced on the eve of the Second World War. This unit would attain 5,400 rpm. Admittedly, full flow wings with running boards were fitted instead of the old J2's cycle type, but these had been standard on MGs since 1934. Yet the TC introduced a generation of Americans to the joys of open air motoring. Left-hand drive was never available, and only 2,001 of the 10,000 cars built between 1945 and 1949 crossed the Atlantic, but among those to cut their teeth on the TC was future World Champion Phil Hill. Coil spring independent front suspension and left-hand steering eventually arrived in 1950 on the TD,

Right: 1946 MG TC.
Far right, above: 1959 Citroën 2CV (*left*),
1959 Renault 4CV (*right*).
Far right: 1949 Morris Minor.

which sold like wildfire in America (10,621 of the 11,560 made in the peak year of 1952 were exported) and the family survived into 1955 with the TF, a facelift which achieved more popularity in old age as a collector's item than it had ever enjoyed when current.

CITROËN 2CV

France
cylinders: 2, horizontally opposed,
ohv; capacity: 375 cc; bhp: 9; trans-
mission: four speeds, synchromesh;
speed: 64 km/h (40 mph).

The five millionth 2CV was delivered during 1976, vindication of a formula which few people took seriously when it first appeared at the Paris Salon 28 years previously. Despite some sophisticated features – all independent suspension with the wheels on each side interconnected, front wheel drive, hydraulic brakes, and unitary construction, the Citroën was conceived as a French variation on the Model-T theme, a hack for the farmer or small businessman with economy and ease of maintenance as the prime objectives. Thus the little 375-cc flat twin engine was given square dimensions (62 × 62 mm) to make for long life and air cooling to render it frostproof. Flexible suspension allowed the body to be lifted clear of the wheels, doors and bonnet lifted off and the seats could be removed to increase load space. For indivisible loads, one simply furled the rolltop roof. The overdrive fourth gear was a further insurance against excessive engine wear. For the rest, lines were angular, the corrugated panels were finished in a uniform grey and extras were the responsibility of the accessory merchants. The Citroën set its own tempo, cruising at 55 km/h (35 mph), but the ingenious suspension was undaunted by farm tracks and fuel consumptions of 5·5 lit/100 (over 50 mpg) were commonplace. Spare parts were cheap: in 1953 £7.60

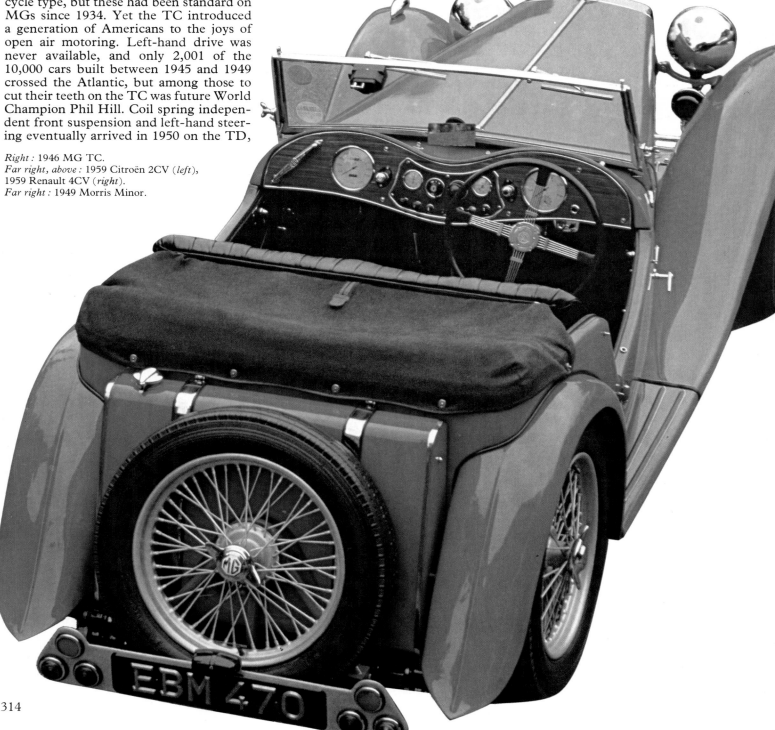

was quoted for a set of pistons, rings and cylinders, and £4.70 for all four wings. In 1977, the 2CV could be had with 435-cc or 602-cc engines and was being manufactured or assembled in six foreign countries.

RENAULT 4CV

France
cylinders: 4, ohv; capacity: 760 cc; bhp: 19; transmission: three speeds, synchromesh; speed: 91 km/h (57 mph).
Developed secretly during the German occupation, the 4CV was selected by Pierre Lefaucheux, Renault's first state-appointed Director-General, as the company's post-war staple. The model broke with the accepted front engine/rear drive formula, the use of a rear engine permitting four-door saloon bodywork on a car of only 2·1 metres (82 in) wheelbase. Further, the 760-cc ohv engine put the car in the French 4-hp taxation class and on the modest output the oversteer endemic to such a layout mattered little. A worse fault was the woolly linkage of the three-speed gearbox, but the tiny three bearing engine was tough and the hydraulic brakes coped adequately with a weight of only 590 kg (1,260 lb). All four wheels were independently sprung and the 4CV's potential was soon recognized by tuners, specials based on the car doing battle with the air-cooled Dyna Panhards at Le Mans and elsewhere. By 1950, capacity was down to 747 cc, to bring the car into the 750-cc competition category and numerous small makers used the 4CV floor pan as their starting point, best known of these being the Alpine first seen in 1955. The factory also offered their own sports saloons with five forward speeds, outputs of over 40 bhp, and speeds of 130 km/h (80 mph), a far cry from the 19 bhp of the original. Also built under licence in Japan by Hino, the 4CV stayed in production with little change until 1961. During this period, over a million found buyers.

MORRIS Minor

Great Britain
cylinders: 4, sv; capacity: 918 cc; bhp: 27·5; transmission: four speeds, synchromesh; speed: 100 km/h (62 mph).
Up to 1939, Britain's baby cars had been roomy, economical, cheap and well suited to the smooth and tortuous roads of their homeland. They had, however, little appeal abroad. All this changed in 1948, with the advent of the Morris Minor, brainchild of Alec Issigonis and Jack Daniels. Full unitary construction was utilized and the combination of good aerodynamic shape, wide track, torsion bar independent front suspension and rack and pinion steering made for handling to the best European standards. Previous small Morrises already had four forward speeds and hydraulic brakes, but for economic reasons a flat-four engine had to be abandoned. Instead, Morris made do with the faithful 918-cc sc 8-hp engine, current since 1935, and hardly up to the new model's potential. Top speed was a laboured 100 km/h (62 mph), and even through the gears it took nearly half a minute to reach 80 km/h (50 mph). Enthusiasts circumvented these shortcomings with superchargers, special cylinder heads, and even heart transplants (Austin A40, ohc Coventry-Climax). With the Austin-Morris merger of 1952 came a worthier engine, the 803-cc ohv Austin A30, and with this new lease of life the Minor continued, to become Britain's first million seller in 1961. Even then the car had another ten years to go: it was only discontinued at the end of 1970 to make room for the uninspired Marina on the Oxford assembly lines. Total production ran to 1,582,302 units.

FERRARI 166

Italy

cylinders: 12, twin ohc; capacity: 1,995 cc; bhp: 110; transmission: five speeds; speed: 180 km/h (112 mph).

Ferrari of Maranello are indelibly associated with competition cars: during a quarter of a century the marque has never been out of the running in Formula 1, has been victorious in eight of eleven post war Mille Miglia and won nine times at Le Mans. Until the advent of the 250GT in 1956, true roadgoing Ferraris were rare and produced only in batches of five or six. The breed's importance lay in its mystique. It assumed the mantle of the French Bugatti. They were complex mechanics to master with plenty of temperament: early gearboxes were tricky and handling not improved by a tendency to increase outputs without bringing the chassis up to date. Against this, the V-12 engines were flexible, giving smooth acceleration from 15 km/h (10 mph) even in the overdrive fifth gear. Early models, the work of Ing. G. Colombo, appeared in a diversity of

forms but the basic specification embraced a 60-degree V-12 with one chain-driven overhead camshaft per block, a seven bearing crankshaft machined from the solid, coil ignition, a five-speed gearbox without suspension synchromesh, a robust box section frame, wishbone and transverse leaf independent front, hydraulic brakes working in alloy drums and centre lock wire wheels. The first model to be sold commercially was the 166 (Ferrari type designations signify the capacity of a single cylinder) available in a variety of tunes from the Inter (one dual choke carburettor, 110 bhp) up to the Mille Miglia, a true sports racer with dual magneto ignition, three carburettors and 150 bhp.

JAGUAR XK 120

Great Britain

cylinders: 6, twin ohc; capacity: 3,442 cc; bhp: 160; transmission: four speeds, synchromesh; speed: 192 km/h (120 mph).

In 1936, Fritz Fiedler of BMW had proved that a sports car need be neither noisy or

harsh. Twelve years later W. M. Heynes's Jaguar design team took matters a step further by offering still more sophistication at an unprecedentedly low price. The car's streamlined roadster body was a show stopper and it cost £1,263 only but the specification was staggering: torsion bar independent front suspension giving an excellent ride, a four-speed close ratio gearbox and a twin ohc seven bearing six cylinder engine offering 160 bhp from 3·5 litres, (more than contemporary V-8s from across the Atlantic). Further, this engine was not temperamental and could run 300,000 km (over 200,000 miles) between major overhauls: below 5,000

rpm it was commendably quiet. In 1949 an XK 120 showed its mettle by covering the flying mile at Jabbeke at 213·4 km/h (132·4 mph), and though the standard article was flat out at 192 km/h (120 mph) this was way ahead of all but the fastest specialist models available in 1939. Americans nurtured on the MG TC took readily to the new Jaguar and only a sixth of the 12,000-odd produced during a six year run were equipped with right hand steering. Further, the twin cam engine was very much alive in 1977 with five Le Mans wins to its credit. It must also rate as one of the most versatile power units of all times, having been used not only in sports and sports racing models, but also in saloons (from Mk VII to XJ6), limousines (the Vanden Plas Daimler), ambulances (Dennis), racing hydroplanes, and armoured cars.

VOLKSWAGEN Beetle

Germany
cylinders: 4, horizontally opposed, ohv; capacity: 1,131 cc; bhp: 25; transmission: four speeds; speed: 100 km/h (62 mph).
With over nineteen million units delivered, the Volkswagen Beetle was phased out of production in Europe at the end of 1977. What started as the impossible dream of Adolf Hitler ended up as the most truly universal car since the Model T Ford's demise. What is more, it had broken the

Ford's sales record as long ago as 1972. The promised 1939 price of under £70 may have been hopelessly unrealistic but the VW was tailormade as the people's transport. The square-dimensioned, air-cooled engine developed its modest output at a low 3,300 rpm; thus maximum speed, only 100 km/h (62 mph) in 1950, was also cruising speed and VW owners did not have to lift their feet on the autobahn. The all independent torsion bar suspension gave an excellent ride and the use of a separate platform chassis minimized problems of corrosion. Ferdinand Porsche's teardrop shape made for low wind resistance and in 1950 (or even in 1939) the VW was not vastly different from its 1977 counterpart, the immediate identification being the divided rear window of older cars. Cylinder capacity was of course smaller (1,131 cc as against 1,192 cc on later basic models), the four-speed gearbox was innocent of synchromesh and hydraulic brakes had only just made their appearance in 1950 on *de luxe* variants.

NASH Rambler

United States of America
cylinders: 6, sv; capacity: 2,830 cc; bhp: 82; transmission: three speeds, synchromesh; speed: 128 km/h (80 mph).
Nineteen sixty is generally regarded as the year of the compacts but the story began ten years earlier with Ted Ulrich's Ram-

bler, a model important enough to achieve make status in 1958 – not to mention the dropping of the Nash name. The Rambler's third place in 1959's home sales must have made the Big Three thankful that their answer was on the way! Though small American independents often lacked the cash to exploit good ideas, Nash managed to ride out a shaky initial reception: only 11,428 of 192,000 cars sold in 1950 were the new type. While the vehicle was designed around the standard US formula of lazy six-cylinder sv engine, three-speed gearbox, column shift and coil spring independent front suspension, the Rambler was a good half metre (20 in) shorter than a Chevrolet; with a capacity of 172·6 cu in (2,830 cc) as against the Chevrolet's 235·5 (3·8 litres). Wheelbase was 2·54 metres (100 in) as against 2·9 metres (114 in) for the Ford and 2.92 (115 in) for the Chevrolet. Further, Ulrich deviated from the norm with full unitary construction, already featured on bigger Nashes, while the original Rambler was a German-style convertible with fixed roof rails giving the necessary structural strength. Sedans, hardtops and station wagons came later. Nor was the car cheap: the list price of $1,808 ($300–400 above the Big Three's levels) was justified by such inclusive equipment as heater, demister, radio and clock. The fully enclosed wheels impeded both servicing and manoeuvrability and had gone by 1955, but a thirst of only 11·5 lit/100 (25 mpg) had its attractions.

Above left: 1948 Ferrari 166, racing version.
Below left: 1953 Volkswagen Beetle.
Above: 1950 Jaguar XK 120.

CHRYSLER New Yorker

United States of America
cylinders: 8, Vee, ohv; capacity: 5,440 cc; bhp: 180; transmission: four speeds, semi-automatic; speed: 163 km/h (102 mph).

The short stroke V-8 engine with overhead valves was not a Chrysler innovation: two years earlier such designs had been standardized by two GM divisions, Cadillac and Oldsmobile. The Chrysler's importance lay in its advanced cylinder head design with hemispherical combustion chambers which offered 180 bhp (20 bhp more than the opposition), from 331 cu in (5·4 litres), and this without loss of reliability, though more complicated engineering ('two of everything to Cadillac's one') increased servicing charges. The Chrysler proved susceptible to tuning: by 1954 stock engines gave 235 bhp and a special for the Indianapolis 500 as much as 404 bhp. By this time Detroit was committed to the horsepower race that would engage manufacturers' attentions for twenty years. Cadillac and Lincoln edged ahead in 1953 and again (briefly) in 1955, when mid-season changes handed the lead, first to Packard and then back to Chrysler, with 355 bhp from 354 cu in (5·8 litres) on their fastest car, the first of the 300 series of hardtop coupés. In other respects the 1951 New Yorker was orthodox American, apart from such Chrysler idiosyncracies as the transmission handbrake and a reluctance to espouse fully automatic transmissions until 1953. Power steering was, however, already an option. Unfortunately for the Corporation, its President, K. T. Keller, had no use for stylists and sales fell steadily until the belated advent of Virgil Exner's Flight Sweep models in 1955.

PEGASO Z102

Spain
cylinders: 8, Vee, 4 ohc; capacity: 2,810 cc; bhp: 170; transmission: five speeds; speed: 200 km/h (124 mph).

Truck manufacturers often produce exotic cars – the Leyland Eight of 1921 is a classic example – and the Spanish Pegaso was no exception. Made in the former Hispano-Suiza works to the design of Wilfredo Ricart, it was certainly the most complicated sports model then on the market. The aluminium alloy V-8 engine featured twin gear driven overhead camshafts per block and dry sump lubrication. It delivered its maximum power at 6,500 rpm. The five-speed constant mesh gearbox was mounted in unit with the De Dion rear axle and limited slip differential, the rear brakes were inboard and front suspension was independent by double wishbones and torsion bars. This handbuilt masterpiece cost £3,000 even in its homeland, and the exotic bodies were the work of Touring of Milan and Saoutchik of Paris. Pegasos were available in 2·5-litre form with or without supercharger, or as unblown 2·8-litres. By 1954 there was also a twin supercharged 3·2-litre version from which 285 bhp and 300 km/h (185 mph) were claimed. Even the mildest Z102s had a top speed of 200 km/h (125 mph), and roadholding was

superb. Failings were a fearsome appetite for sparking plugs and a high noise level. Prices as much as $30,000 were quoted in the USA, hence exports were low: most of the hundred odd Z102s built stayed in Spain. The simpler 4·7-litre pushrod Z103 of 1956 was made in tiny numbers only and three years later the company decided to concentrate exclusively on trucks.

BENTLEY Continental

Great Britain
cylinders: 6; capacity: 4,566 cc; bhp: (not disclosed); transmission: four speeds, synchromesh; speed: 195 km/h (120 mph).

The fastest four-seater closed car of its era, the Bentley Continental represented the ultimate in GTs for those with £7,000 to spend – a great deal of money by 1953 standards. For this outlay the buyer got not only an elegant fastback body, but also a top speed of 195 km/h (120 mph), a cruising speed in the 150–160 km/h (95–100 mph) bracket, and fuel consumption of 14 lit/100 (20 mpg), thanks to a low wind resistance which made the car entirely habitable at such velocities. Mechanically, the new Bentley reflected contemporary Rolls-Royce thinking, with 4·6-litre six-cylinder engine, and a four-speed synchromesh gearbox with the magnificently precise right-hand change, a combination used on the company's products since 1932. The legendary servo brakes were given hydro mechanical actuation (Rolls-Royce were reluctant to rely exclusively on hydraulics!) and India designed special tyres to cope with this unprecedented performance. Though some special bodies – including a convertible by Park Ward – were produced, the commonest and most felicitous style was H. J. Mulliner's original fastback, found on most of the 207 R series Continentals built. Later examples featured the 4·9-litre engine standardized from mid 1955 on the S series saloons, but though an automatic gearbox was fitted to these latter, the S Continental could still be had with manual as late as 1957. Four hundred

Above: 1953 Pegaso Z102 – only 125 were built over seven years.
Above right: 1953 Bentley Continental.
Below right: 1953 Lancia Aurelia B20 GT.

and thirty one S cars were built but though there would be Continental versions of the eight cylinder S2 and S3 (1960–5) in later years the model lost its individuality.

LANCIA Aurelia GT

Italy
cylinders: 6, Vee, ohv; capacity: 2,451 cc; bhp: 118; transmission: four speeds, synchromesh; speed: 180 km/h (113 mph).

The term *Gran Turismo* had been coined by Alfa Romeo in 1931 for their supercharged long chassis saloons but the car that started the modern GT fashion was Vittorio Jano's Lancia Aurelia coupé. Essentially the GT theme embraced a closed 2/4-seater designed to travel fast and far; within a decade it would have superseded the traditional open sports model. True, the Lancia's rear seats were very occasional but it derived from an excellent saloon, the 1950 Aurelia, successor to the well proven V-4 Aprilia. Full width styling permitted a wider angle V-engine, now a 1,754-cc six with pushrod operated ohv in place of the ohc of earlier models. Unitary construction and coil spring independent front suspension were retained, but the four-speed synchromesh gearbox was mounted in unit with the independently sprung rear end, and the rear brakes were inboard. On 55 bhp, early Aurelias were not spectacular performers but for his first coupé of 1951 Jano used a twin carburettor two-litre engine and a shorter wheelbase, the result attaining 160 km/h (100 mph). Two years later capacity was increased to 2·5 litres and in definitive 1954 form the car featured a De Dion rear axle. Floor change was now available as an alternative to the column shift with its complex linkages and top speed was 180 km/h (over 110 mph) with an easy cruising gait of 145 km/h (90 mph). The model's run continued into 1958 and its rally record included wins in the Liège-Rome-Liège and Monte Carlo events.

FORD Thunderbird

United States of America
cylinders: 8, Vee, ohv; capacity: 4,785 cc; bhp: 193; transmission: three-speed, synchromesh with overdrive; speed: 180 km/h (113 mph).

Though often regarded as Ford's answer to the Chevrolet Corvette, the Thunderbird, creation of Lewis Crusoe, was promoted as a 'personal' rather than as a sports car. Hence came its success, for it never competed against the foreign imports. The idea was a luxury package for the man or woman who wanted something different: power brakes, steering, seats and windows and a detachable hardtop were standard equipment on this two-seater, styling was an individual interpretation of the basic 1955 theme and the 292 cu in (4·8-litre) V-8 engine was exclusive to the Thunderbird, though admittedly available on the more expensive Mercury line. A wheelbase of 2·59 metres (102 in) made for compact overall dimensions, and at 4·454 metres (175½ in) the new Ford was actually shorter than 1960's much publicized compact sedans. Most cars used either a three-

speed automatic or a three-speed synchromesh gearbox with overdrive. Also available was the Continental-type spare wheel mounted vertically at the rear: this feature was not in fact standardized until 1956. Chassis engineering followed regular American lines with hydraulic drum brakes and Ford's ball joint independent front suspension. Over 16,000 cars were sold in 1955 (Corvette sales were a miserable 674), and even with their new V-8, Chevrolet's two-seater still lagged well behind in 1956. Regrettably, Ford management elected to discard the handsome two-seater in 1958 in favour of a bulbous six-seater convertible lacking in elegance and individuality alike and subsequent T-birds were merely expensive cars.

MERCEDES-BENZ 300SL

Germany
cylinders: 6, ohc; capacity: 2,996 cc; bhp: 240; transmission: four speeds, all synchromesh; speed: 230 km/h (144 mph).

First seen as the spearhead of a works racing revival, prototypes of the 300SL

won at Berne and Le Mans in 1952, subsequently adding the tough Carrera Panamericana to their score. Production, however, did not get under way until 1955. The new coupé was the company's first true sports car since the demise of the vast blown SS in the early 1930s and though only 1,400 of the original gullwings were built, these had assumed collector status almost before deliveries ceased. The swing up doors with their high sills, hallmark of the breed, were dictated by the tubular space frame structure, this also necessitating the inclined engine mounting and rendering rhd versions impossible. The seven-bearing six-cylinder power unit was a development of the touring 300 of 1951, though in SL form it ran to Bosch fuel injection (prototypes had had three carburettors) and dry sump lubrication. The hydraulic servo brakes worked in finned drums and like most Mercedes since 1932 the car featured all independent springing with swing axles at the rear. The 300SL was costly to maintain and called for a skilled hand at the wheel but even in standard form 230 km/h (144 mph) were available and with a 3·25:1 rear axle the factory claimed 260 km/h (about 160 mph). In 1957 the gullwing gave way to an open roadster, a reversal of prevailing fashions: the last cars delivered in 1961 had disc brakes. The gullwing, however, remains as the archetype of what is now termed a Milestone sports car.

FIAT 600

Italy
cylinders: 4, ohv; capacity: 633 cc; bhp: 21·5; transmission: four speeds, synchromesh; speed: 95 km/h (60 mph).

Finding a successor for the immortal Topolino posed a problem for Fiat's Dante Giacosa and almost every possible configuration was tested before the definitive design appeared. The 600 was a master-

piece of shoehorning rivalled only by BMC's Mini – four people and their luggage were crammed into a machine which was actually shorter, if a little wider and heavier, than the two-seater 500C. What is more, capacity of the engine went up only 64 cc to 633 cc, while the new unit took up less room, being mounted at the rear, alongside its radiator. Unlike the 500, the 600 featured full unitary construction: the transverse leaf independent front suspension was a Topolino legacy, but at the rear an independent layout replaced semi-elliptics. On early 600s the handbrake worked on the transmission. The modestly rated ohv engine had three main bearings and top speed was 95 km/h (60 mph), raised to over 100 km/h (65 mph) with the bigger 767-cc unit of 1960s D series. Inevitably the modifiers and tuners stepped in, developments ranging from *elaborazioni* (lightly customized saloons) up to true specials like Abarth and Moretti, which utilized only the floor pan, suspension and cylinder block of the original Fiat. Sales were destined to top the two million mark. Although the last cars left Turin in 1970, the SEAT factory at Barcelona continued to turn out 600s (still Spain's national best seller in 1974) for several years. Fiat 600 derivatives were offered in 1977 by Fiat's Argentinian and Yugoslav affiliates.

CITROËN DS19

France
cylinders: 4, ohv; capacity: 1,911 cc; bhp: 75; transmission: four speeds, synchromesh; speed; 133 km/h (83 mph).
A new Citroën is usually a sensation, as witness the original Traction (1934) and the 2CV (1948). On the DS19 the company broke new ground with a revolutionary self-levelling suspension, already tried at the rear of the superseded 15CV six. This hydropneumatic system relied on gas in

compression as the springing medium. Only a sudden humpback bridge could catch it unawares, though since power derived from the engine, the car would sink on its haunches within seconds of the ignition being switched off. Hydraulic power was also applied to the brakes (inboard discs were used at the front), clutch, gear change and steering, while it jacked the car for wheel changes. Two pedal drive was combined with full manual control of the four-speed gearbox with its overdrive top. Front wheel drive was retained, but the unitary hull, of futuristic appearance, had a glassfibre roof and offered superb all round vision. A solitary legacy of the past was the 2-litre longstroke four-cylinder engine, but even this was given a new top end with hemispherical combustion chambers. The car was both complicated and expensive, so for 1957 Citroën offered the simplified ID on which the hydropneumatics were confined to the suspension. Nearly one and a half million Ds would find buyers before the range was dropped in 1975, later developments including short stroke engines, swivelling headlamps, and more sophisticated gearboxes – an automatic and a five-speed manual.

MORRIS Mini-Minor

Great Britain
cylinders: 4, ohv; capacity: 848 cc; bhp: 34; transmission: four speeds, synchromesh; speed: 110 km/h (69 mph).
If the Austin Seven set the pattern for baby cars between the wars, Alec Issigonis's Mini was the undisputed basis for the thinking of the 1960s. The combination of front wheel drive and east-west engine would be adopted by five major European groups, not to mention two from Japan.

Far left: 1957 Mercedes-Benz 300SL.
Above left: 1959 Citroën DS19.
Right, above and below: 1957 Ford Thunderbird with detail of the driving controls.

Few of these, however, rivalled the compactness of the original Mini, a four seater 3·05 metres (120 in) long, 1·41 metres (55½ in) wide and 1.346 metres (53 in) high. The gearbox was located in the sump of the 848-cc four-cylinder engine, driving the front wheels by spur gear, all four wheels were independently sprung by rubber in compression and the 25 cm (10 in) wheels were a novelty outside the bubble car class. The sliding windows and unsynchronized bottom gear were crudities but the Mini possessed incredible adhesion and was unbeatable in city traffic. Britain's best selling model of all time (over four million by 1977), it bred almost as many specialist derivatives as the Fiat 600. By 1961 the makers had broken away from the utilitarian concept with the rally winning Cooper series, the 1,275-cc S of 1965 attaining 160 km/h (almost 100 mph) and taking less than eight seconds to reach 80 km/h (50 mph). Though the Mini would become a make in its own right in 1970 it was initially marketed with Austin and Morris labels. The differences were in colour and in grille pattern – wavy bars on Austins and straight ones on Morrises.

LOTUS Elite

Great Britain
cylinders: 4, ohc; capacity: 1,216 cc; bhp: 71; transmission: four speeds, all synchromesh; speed: 180 km/h (113 mph).

Glassfibre bodywork had been used on specialist sports cars since the early 1950s but Colin Chapman's Lotus Elite, unveiled in 1957, was the first production model on which the new medium was applied to a unitary hull. The only metal structural member was a tubular reinforcing hoop at windscreen level. Glassfibre lent itself to inexpensive accident repairs; a damaged piece was simply cut out and a new section 'knitted' in. The Elite was the first true roadgoing machine from the company, previous models being aimed at the club racing fraternity and usually sold as kits of parts for the home builder. The new coupé could in fact be had in kit form, an arrangement which saved the handyman some £700. Rated one of the best handling cars of its era, the Elite featured all independent springing, with Chapman struts at the rear. Steering was by rack and pinion. Lotus, like Jaguar, favoured all disc brakes (inboard at the rear) and there was synchromesh on all forward gears. The centre lock wheels were shod with radial ply tyres and the sohc Coventry-Climax engine was standardized with outputs of up to 83 bhp from 1·2 litres. A high noise level was the principal failing, but this compact little machine weighing only 686 kg (1,513 lb) would return 10·8 lit/100 (26 mpg) at a steady 160 km/h (100 mph). Only 988 Elites were made between 1958 and 1964.

FACEL Vega 1960

France
cylinders: 8, Vee, ohv; capacity: 6,276 cc; bhp: 360; transmission: four speeds, all synchromesh; speed: 230 km/h (140 mph).

The combination of a big, lazy American engine and European bodywork had been tried in the 1930s on inexpensive fast tourers like the British Railton. Jean Daninos's 1954 Facel Vega represented a different approach, for the V-8 Chrysler unit was adopted, not to save money, but in default of any suitable French engine. The Facel, in fact, paved the way for a new generation of Euro-Americans (Gordon-Keeble, Jensen, Iso) for fast luxury travel. Only the engine and the optional automatic transmission were imported: Facel themselves built the robust frame with its coil spring independent front suspension, manual gearboxes being the work of Pont-à-Mousson. The Brasseur-styled coupés featured wrapround screens and rear windows and vertical headlamp clusters, while the aircraft-style facia pioneered the floor mounted console for extra instruments. Engine capacity went up steadily from 4·6 to 6·3 litres, with output doubling, from 180 to 360 bhp. For a big car, the Facel handled well, and power steering (initially with automatic only) was available in 1957 but stopping 1,650 kg (around 3,600 lb) of car from 230 km/h (140 mph) was too much for the regular drum brakes and discs were not standardized until 1960. Disastrous attempts to widen the range with an all French small sports car hastened the company's demise but in any case the V-8 was too expensive: in the free Swiss market it cost more than a Jensen, Aston Martin, Maserati or even Ferrari.

JAGUAR E-Type

Great Britain
cylinders: 6, twin ohc; capacity: 3,781 cc; bhp: 265; transmission: four speeds, synchromesh; speed: 240 km/h (150 mph).

The XK family's successor, the E-type. appeared in 1961: the fourth of a series of show stoppers using the twin ohc six-cylinder engine. Previous ones had been the XK 120 (1948), the Mk VII saloon (1950), and the 2·4 litre, first of the unitary Jaguars, in 1955. Few of the E-type's ingredients were new: all disc brakes had made their début in 1952 on the C-type sports racer, reaching the roadgoing range five years later on the XK 150. The unitary hull was a heritage of the compact saloons and the 265 bhp 3·8 litre power unit had been regular equipment on the XK 150S. Independent rear suspension might be a novelty in the catalogue but it had already been tested in Briggs Cunningham's experimental Le Mans car of 1960. The E-type combined all these features, plus twin electric fans to assist cooling. Available as a roadster or two seater fixed head coupé, it possessed an electrifying performance: 240 km/h (150 mph) and 187 km/h (116 mph) on the two highest gears, an 0–160 km/h (0–100 mph) acceleration time of under 16 seconds, and an 0–200 km/h time of half a minute. More important, the car cost £2,200 at a time when £5,700 was asked for a 300SL Mercedes-Benz and over £6,000 for the simplest Ferrari. The E-type survived into 1975, with a bigger 4·2 litre engine from 1964. Seven years later came the first V-12, of 5·3 litres' capacity. Like the first XK six, it was tried in a sports car before being offered in saloons. Of 72,584 E-types of all series, 49,032 were sold in the USA.

PORSCHE 356C

Germany
cylinders: 4, horizontally opposed, four ohc; capacity: 1,966 cc; bhp: 130; transmission: four speeds, all synchromesh; speed: 200 km/h (125 mph).

Very much an acquired taste, the 356 Porsche was probably the fastest method of tackling a winding road. Essentially the configuration was Volkswagen, as on the

184 HYL

Above left : 1964 Jaguar E-Type, 3·8-litre, fixed
head coupé.
Above : 1960 Facel Vega HK500.
Right : 1962 Lotus Elite.
Below right : 1963 Porsche 356C Carrera.

first prototype of 1948 – a platform frame
with air-cooled flat four engine at the rear,
and all independent suspension by torsion
bars – but gone were the days when VW
components were used. Nothing was now
interchangeable. The superb four-speed
gearbox had synchromesh on all forward
ratios. From 1956 onwards the range was
graduated, though bodies were common.
At the bottom of the 1962 lineup was the
so-called ladies' model with 1·6-litre pushrod engine giving 60 hp. It was good for
160 km/h (100 mph), and in optional 90
bhp form would do 180 km/h (120 mph).
For the last six years, however, Porsche
had offered their Carrera, using a detuned
four ohc racing engine with dual ignition
and dry sump lubrication. Even in original
guise (1,500 cc, 100 bhp), it could attain
200 km/h (125 mph), and now it ran to two
litres, 130 bhp, and (for the first time) all-
disc brakes. Advertised maximum speed
was not much higher, but the car accelerated to 100 km/h (60 mph) in 9 seconds,
and was for advanced students only.
During its currency (1961–63), Porsche
were turning out between 8,000 and 9,000
356s a year, but only 310 of these 26,000
cars were two-litre Carreras.

CHEVROLET Corvette Stingray

United States of America
cylinders: 8, Vee, ohv; capacity: 5,346 cc; bhp: 360; transmission: four speeds, all synchromesh; speed: 233 km/h (147 mph).

To Americans, even in the early 1960s, a sports car was synonymous with a foreign import and it stands to the Corvette's credit that it was responsible for the destruction of this image, carrying on the good work where Auburn, Cord and Stutz had left off in the 1930s. The model's formative years, however, were far from auspicious. Launched in 1953, the Corvette was the world's first series production car with glassfibre bodywork, but although the lines were pleasing, the specification was not. The lightly tuned ohv Chevrolet six lacked sufficient urge and there was no alternative to a two-speed automatic gearbox until 1955. It was not until the new ohv V-8 became available in 1956 that the Corvette made any impression and even then the brakes were not up to the car's 200 km/h (125 mph) potential. Outputs built up steadily, from 255 bhp in 1956 to 380 bhp (with the optional fuel injection) in 1962, and sales also showed an upturn, passing the 10,000 mark for the first time in 1960. The Stingray, however, boosted deliveries to over 21,000 in its initial season. It was an entirely new creation on a short, 2·489 metre (98 in) wheelbase with all independent suspension. Once again the two-seater roadster and coupé bodies were constructed of glassfibre, and a wider range of options included power steering, limited slip differentials, and three gearboxes (three- and four-speed manual, or automatic). Engine outputs ran as high as 375 bhp, and the specification given above is a typical one for export.

ASTON MARTIN DB5

Great Britain
cylinders: 6, dohc; capacity: 3,995 cc; hp: 282; transmission: five speeds, all synchromesh; speed: 240 km/h (150 mph).

The DB4 of 1958 was the British answer to the Ferrari, and had almost as distinguished a competition career, although Aston Martin did not win the sports car Constructors' Championship until 1959. Here was the GT theme developed to a high level in a car which accelerated from a standstill to 160 km/h (100 mph) and back in 30 seconds. Aston Martin had been using twin ohc sixes since 1950, when W. O. Bentley's 2·6-litre Lagonda, designed for David Brown's other car firm, was adapted to the DB2 coupé. The DB4's new seven bearing motor of square (92 × 92 mm) dimensions gave 240 bhp as against the 162 of later DB2/4s, and on 1964's DB5 series still more urge (282 bhp) was combined with greater refinement. The all coil suspension (independent at the front) derived from earlier cars, and race bred features included power disc brakes and rack and pinion steering. There was now synchromesh on all forward gears, and on the DB5 a fifth ratio was added, as well as a twin plate clutch. The body, styled by Touring of Milan, used that company's constructional medium of aluminium panels over a framework of small diameter steel tubes. Other refinements were electric windows, and, on later DB5s, electrically controlled rear dampers. For those who found the car's impressive performance – 240 km/h (150 mph) with 180 km/h (110 mph) in fourth – inadequate, there was a 314 bhp Vantage engine option with three carburettors. Production was modest – 1,150 units in two seasons – and for 1966 the model gave way to the DB6 with improved aerodynamics.

LANCIA Fulvia

Italy
cylinders: 4, Vee, twin ohc; capacity: 1,091 cc; bhp: 60; transmission: four speeds, all synchromesh; speed: 138 km/h (86 mph).

Lancia enjoy the reputation of never having built a bad car, though by 1964 there were few links with the old Lancia and Jano designs. The new fwd models, however, were as outstanding as their predecessors. First of these, the Flavia of 1961, was a flat four designed by Franco Fessia and based on the abortive Cemsa-Caproni of 1947. Features were unitary construction, hypoid final drive, all disc brakes, and transverse leaf independent front suspension, although on his second Lancia, the Fulvia, Fessia reverted to the traditional V4 unit. Intended to replace the old Appia saloon, the Fulvia had a twin ohc engine giving 60 bhp from 1,100 cc, and propelling the standard version at 135 km/h (85 mph). In 1965 came the first sporting variant, a 1,216-cc coupé with floor instead of column change and a 71 bhp twin carburettor engine. Subsequent evolution bred a generation of rally cars, Kallström and Häggbom winning the RAC event twice in succession (1969 and 1970). By 1971 even standard Fulvias had servo brakes, five forward speeds and 1·3-litre power units; 160 km/h (100 mph) were within their compass, but the 1600 HF coupé, virtually a rally replica, was considerably faster. When Fiat acquired the Lancia interests, the old types were phased out: the saloons disappeared during 1974, though the coupés had a couple more years to run. Curiously, it would be the flat four designs that would survive and not the V-4s, the former reappearing in the big Gamma of 1976.

FORD Mustang

United States of America
cylinders: 8, vee, ohv; capacity: 4,727 cc; bhp: 271; transmission: four speeds, all synchromesh; speed: 186 km/h (116 mph).

A sale of 400,000 units in the first twelve months is remarkable for a new model and Ford set the fashion for 'pony' cars with their 1964 Mustang. It took Chevrolet more than two years to catch up. Market research had suggested a coming demand for a 'young' automobile, and the gamble

paid off. The Mustang was sporty in appearance and only 4·61 metres (181 in) long. And it could be all things to all men, from a frugal 260-cu in (3·3 litre) six up to 271 bhp V-8s giving speeds of 190 km/h (120 mph). Two four-seater bodies were offered – a coupé and a convertible; otherwise specification depended on the customer's tastes. Automatic was available as well as three- and four-speed synchromesh gearboxes and the extras list offered power brakes and steering and air conditioning. The car was based on the compact Falcon and featured the same combination of ball joint independent front suspension and semi elliptics at the rear. Front disc brakes did not appear until the 1965 season and even then they were only an option. During the remaining years of the horsepower race the Mustang was progressively developed, reaching its zenith in 1968 with a seven-litre edition good for over 210 km/h (130 mph), while for those in quest of more there were Carroll Shelby's sports cars. Like all the 'pony' cars, the Mustang was the victim of safety, emission and economy campaigns and the fastest of its 1977 namesakes disposed of a meagre 139 bhp.

Top left : 1966 Ford Mustang.
Top right : 1963 Chevrolet Corvette Stingray.
Above : 1972 Lancia Fulvia.

LAMBORGHINI Miura

Italy
cylinders: 12, four ohc; capacity: 3,929 cc; bhp: 350; transmission: five speeds, all synchromesh; speed: 275 km/h (170 mph).

Few super cars can have less likely origins than the Lamborghini: its makers were originally in the farm tractor business, hence possibly the bull emblem which rivalled Ferrari's prancing horse. Lamborghini never raced but the early front engined 3·5 and four-litre V-12s created by Gian Paolo Dallara from 1963 onward had been impressive enough and the Miura was the most sensational of a new generation of rear-engined sports cars. Significantly it was a coupé (the open bodied version was not built in series), and its four cam V-12 engine was mounted transversely at the rear of a monocoque structure based on a box section frame. In unit with the motor was a five-speed transaxle, an unusual feature of which was synchromesh on reverse, while the engine room was separated from the crew by a plexiglass division. The Miura was all independently sprung, by coils and wishbones, and brakes were dual circuit discs. With six dualchoke carburettors, twin electric fans, and dry sump lubrication, output ran to 350 bhp, sufficient to propel the car at 275 km/h (170 mph). By 1971 three triple choke carburettors were being used and on 385 bhp the Miura attained 290 km/h (180 mph). Weight was a modest 1,245 kg. (2,736 lb). The last of 900 Miuras was

delivered in 1973 though Lamborghini replaced the car with the even more spectacular Countach.

PONTIAC GTO

United States of America
cylinders: 8, Vee, ohv; capacity: 6,374 cc; bhp: 335; transmission: four speeds, all synchromesh; speed: 193 km/h (120 mph).

The GTO was an improbable offering by Pontiac's regular standards. These were stolid and middle class, the plated silver streaks on the bonnet being necessary to distinguish the cars from Oldsmobiles. Improved handling, however, came with 1959's wide track models, and in 1961 heresy struck, in the shape of the compact Tempest with its ohc engine and transaxle. Neither feature lasted long, but one of the offshoots of the family was the GTO, first of the muscle cars aimed at those who liked the Ford Mustang image but wanted something bigger. Wheelbase was 2·92 metres (115 in) and the car came as a coupé or a convertible, the latter with a cruciform braced frame to give extra stiffness. Engineering was orthodox, apart from the lowered and reinforced suspension, but buyers got such 'sports' features as separate bucket seats with belts and a four-speed gearbox with floor change. (Automatic was, however, optional.) The standard 1966 engine was a 389-cu in (6·4-litre) ohv V-8 giving 335 bhp with a single quadrajet carburettor but the triple carburettor option gave an extra 25 bhp and speeds of

200 km/h (125 mph). Disc front brakes were an extra and would remain so until 1968. Increasing emphasis on safety led to the intrusion of gimmicks, these including a mock Duesenberg grille (and SJ designation!) and even flower power decals on the bonnet top. By 1973 the GTO was dead.

FERRARI Dino 206

Italy
cylinders: 6, Vee, 4 ohc; capacity: 1,987 cc; bhp: 180; transmission: five speeds, all synchromesh; speed: 235 km/h (146 mph).

By 1961, Grand Prix Ferraris had rear engines, followed soon afterwards by their sports racing machinery as typified by the 250LM. Competition thinking, however, took some time to penetrate the company's road car programme and the Dino was a

Above left : 1966 Pontiac GTO convertible.
Left : 1969 Ferrari Dino 206.
Top right : 1970 Ford Capri – England's answer to the Mustang.
Above : 1974 N.S.U. Ro80.

by-product of Fiat's growing financial involvement at Maranello. Its four ohc V-6 engine was built by Fiat to Ferrari designs and was shared by a conventionally engineered sports Fiat. Strictly, the Dino was mid- rather than rear-engined, a layout which offers not only better weight distribution but space for luggage behind the transversely mounted power pack. As a result, the car's handling had few peers. Features of the design were an all synchromesh gearbox with visible gate in the vintage manner, a tubular frame, all independent springing, dual circuit servo disc brakes, and an aerodynamic two seater coupé body styled by Pininfarina. Weight was 1,110 kg and the Dino would exceed 225 km/h (140 mph), with 187 km/h (116 mph) coming up in fourth. In 1969, the

alloy cylinder blocks of the first cars gave way to cast iron on a more powerful 2·4-litre edition, this also featuring transistorized ignition. By 1975 the six-cylinder Dinos had been replaced by the 308 with a 2·9-litre engine, a bigger car with room for four people. From 1971 the Dino range included a Sport model of semi open type in Porsche's established Targa idiom.

N.S.U. Ro80

Germany
engine: twin rotor; capacity: 995 cc; bhp: 114; transmission: three speeds, automatic; speed: 180 km/h (113 mph).
This was the first family saloon to feature Felix Wankel's revolutionary rotary piston engine, already offered since 1963 in N.S.U.'s two-seater Spyder; it anticipated a parallel programme by Mazda of Japan. The twin carburettor, twin rotor power unit was compact and light (weight was

120 kg/265 lb), but despite a capacity equivalent to only one litre, it developed 113·5 bhp. This engine drove the front wheels via a three-speed torque converter transmission giving two pedal control and full manual override. All four wheels were independently sprung by McPherson struts, both disc brakes and steering were power assisted, and the unitary structure incorporated such safety features as a fuel tank set ahead of the rear wheels, hazard warning lights, and a padded dash. The Wankel would run up to 7,000 rpm without vibration – or indeed without any sensation of excessive revs – but problems of rotor sealing and troubles with the automatic clutch beset early owners, and the Ro80 was a thirsty car (14 litre/100 km or 20 mpg). After Volkswagen took over, N.S.U.'s cheap rear-engined models were dropped, and sales fell dramatically, from nearly 59,000 in 1972 to 1,286 in 1974, when the Ro80 was the staple offering. The last of some 37,000 cars left the works in March, 1977. Ironically, the model's main heritage was the K70, an alternative version with conventional four cylinder engine which was never marketed under the N.S.U. label. It did, however, appear as a VW, and led in 1977 to the abandonment of rear engines and air cooling at Wolfsburg.

FORD Capri

Great Britain, Germany
cylinders: 4, ohc; capacity: 1,598 cc; bhp: 75; transmission: four speeds, all synchromesh; speed: 148 km/h (92 mph).
The Anglo-German Capri was an instant success comparable with the earlier American Mustang, of which it was the European equivalent. Once again, the theme was a sporting occasional four-seater coupé available with an infinite variety of engines, tune and equipment. 'Different' styling was, however, matched by conventional Ford mechanical elements: a unitary structure riding on McPherson struts at the front and semi elliptics at the rear, rack and pinion steering, and disc front brakes. The three door hatchback version would not appear until 1973. Into this chassis-body combination went anything from a modest 1·3-litre four (inline in Britain, Vee in Germany) up to a three-litre V-6 (German versions were slightly smaller), disposing of 144 bhp and propelling the Capri at 165 km/h (105 mph). On 1,600-cc and bigger cars a brake servo was standard. These models were offered with an automatic option and there was a wide selection of factory extras. Success is reflected in sales of a million between early 1969 and August 1973, while the German Capri was distributed in America by Lincoln-Mercury dealers, doing well until the parent concern launched their parallel Pinto, itself using engines of European origin. The 1977 English and German ranges ran parallel, the only basic difference between the two being in the two-litre class, where Dagenham preferred a sohc four and Cologne a V-6. The cheapest English Capri then cost £2,662. The specification given is that of the Dagenham-built 1969 1600.

DATSUN 240Z

Japan
cylinders: 6, ohc; capacity: 2,392 cc; bhp: 161; transmission: four speeds, all synchromesh; speed: 205 km/h (127 mph).

Japan has never been sports car country, though a sporty version of the old 860-cc sv Datsun was available in 1952, and in 1963 their 1·5-litre Fairlady roadster enjoyed a modest success in some export markets. The 240Z coupé, however, won a Car of the Year award in America as well as having numerous racing wins to its credit, while the company would go on to sell 450,000 units in six years, an all time record for any sports model. (An interesting comparison is furnished by the four-cylinder TR Triumphs, with deliveries of 152,298 units between 1953 and 1967). Though twin-cam engines were fitted to some home market Datsuns, the standard power unit was a seven bearing sohc six on orthodox lines, with two Hitachi carburettors and an output of 161 bhp. This was usually mated to a four-speed all synchromesh gearbox, though there were five-speed and automatic versions. The

Datsun followed European unitary techniques with a 'wheelbarrow' mounting for the engine. All four wheels were independently sprung by McPherson struts at front and rear. Brakes (disc at the front) were servo assisted. Unlike many of its European competitors, the Datsun was strictly a two-seater. In 1973 a 240Z won the taxing East African Safari. In 1974 came the 260Z with 2·6-litre engine and a 2+2 version was added. Two years later a more powerful 2·8 litre fuel injected version was offered for the American market.

CITROËN SM

France
cylinders: 6, vee, four ohc; capacity: 2,670 cc; bhp: 180; transmission: five speeds, all synchromesh; speed: 220 km/h (137 mph).

Though specialist makers (D.B. in France, Cooper in England) had made use of Citroën suspensions and transmissions, the factory itself had never marketed a sports car before 1970. Acquisition of the Maserati interests had, however, given Citroën opportunity to obtain an exciting

four-cam V-6 engine, and the marriage of Italian expertise with the French firm's advanced engineering – hydropneumatic suspension, variable rate power steering, and dual circuit disc brakes – resulted in the SM. Suspension was firmer than on the D saloons, and by raising the steering ratio Citroën compensated for the lack of feel endemic in power assisted systems. Swivelling headlamps, already a feature of the D, were incorporated, the outer pair of a bank of six behind a transparent cover being arranged to move. Also shared with later Ds was the five-speed all synchromesh gearbox, though on SMs the lever was floor mounted. The car was the most sophisticated grand tourer of its period, and in standard form it attained over 220 km/h (135 mph) on 180 bhp. From 1972, fuel injection was adopted, and automatic transmission was available on 1974 models. Unfortunately the SM became a victim of the energy crisis – and of Citroën's shaky finances – after only 12,920 had been built. A four-door saloon exhibited in 1975 was stillborn, and later that year the two-door models disappeared as well. When Maserati were reconstituted under de Tomaso control, their new four-door car

Braking

Good distant road observation will give the driver all the time needed for smooth, controlled actions. This is essential when braking, especially from speed, when the foot should alight on the brake pedal like a butterfly settling on a leaf. You can then press firmly and in normal circumstances the wheels will not lock.

Weight will always be transferred forward when a car is being braked. It is essential to remember this as maximum adhesion and balance are always at a premium where safety is concerned.

As an instance, take a front-engined car weighing 1,000 kg and assume that it weighs 600 kg (1,350 lb) at the front and 400 kg (900 lb) at the rear. Under firm braking, the weight transferred could alter this ratio to 700/300. This would give effective braking on the straight but if applied when turning the added weight on the outside front wheel, combined with lightness at the rear, could produce a pivot on which the car could spin.

To keep the car well balanced there are three simple rules to obey for maximum safety, though commonsense must prevail and these do not necessarily apply at slow speeds in traffic.

1. By good distant observation ensure that firm braking is carried out while travelling straight.
2. Watch for variations in the road

Above : Traffic in the rush hour is allowed to flow by means of huge ten-lane freeways in Los Angeles.
Right : The problem of congestion has led to restricted access to main streets in many cities.

surface and vary brake pressure accordingly.
3. Before going steeply downhill select a lower gear to assist retardation. Brake firmly on the straight and, if necessary, lightly in the bends. Do not be inhibited about this as the car will gain momentum from the descent and must be restrained, to avoid entering each succeeding section at a faster speed.

Using a lower gear to assist braking on long downhill sections is extremely helpful in avoiding the phenomenon known as 'brake fade'. This is a gradual reduction in braking efficiency brought about by long periods of heavy braking in which the friction material of the brakes loses efficiency through overheating.

Brake fade can be recognized when further pressure on the brake pedal fails to improve deceleration, and to the driver the action of the brake pedal feels spongy. It is more likely to be experienced with drum brakes than with discs, and then only under somewhat extreme conditions, but it underlines the wisdom of planning braking in sections so that heat can be released and air passes over to cool the system.

At times, through inattention or the actions of others, emergency braking is called for. Response to situations like this must be fast, but the vehicle must be kept under full control.

Keep both hands on the steering wheel, brake firmly with the foot brake, do not declutch until the last moment and leave the handbrake alone.

Wheels decelerating rapidly will stop more quickly than wheels that are locked and sliding. Moreover, while the wheels are turning steering can be effectively applied, but once the wheels skid the vehicle cannot be steered. Try not to stall the engine; the situation may change and you may need to accelerate out of danger.

Passenger comfort can be greatly increased if normal stopping is smooth. Often the car will come to a halt with a jerk which could be avoided with a little thought. Remember that the weight transferred forward under braking will remain there until the vehicle stops, when it will

quickly move back to normal. By good planning aim to lose all unwanted speed a few feet earlier than usual. Then, without taking your foot from the brake pedal, let it rise. You will see the front of the car rise with it. Now reapply the brakes lightly and the car will stop on an even keel. If this technique is new to you it would be best to practise it in a quiet area until you achieve complete accuracy in judging distance.

Another technique, very useful on snow and ice, is cadence braking, or pump braking. This involves applying the brakes with a smooth, not-too-fast pumping action to ensure that the wheels never reach the point of locking as might be expected on treacherous surfaces. Here, again, braking distances will be longer and this must be allowed for.

Advantage should be taken of such opportunities as red traffic lights and traffic hold-ups to apply the handbrake, put the gear in neutral and relax.

Acceleration

When firm acceleration is applied to a vehicle weight is transferred backward. This is why passengers are pinned back into their seats as the bodywork of a car settles on to the rear wheels.

This characteristic can be used to increase stability when cornering, as the movement of weight on to the rear wheels will offset the car's tendency to roll outward on the suspension when driving through bends.

Obviously to try to apply firm acceleration in some corners while in top gear would be dangerous, as the speed would be far too high. In these circumstances, a lower gear must be selected before entering the turn so that acceleration can be applied without increasing the chosen speed.

The accelerator is also a decelerator, and if the driver's observation and anticipation are well developed it can be used to vary the speed of the car as needed, often without resorting to braking. This is 'acceleration sense'. Very few drivers have it. It is a difficult technique to learn, requiring much patient practice, but once mastered is never forgotten.

A driver with acceleration sense, coming

up behind a slow-moving lorry on a steep uphill, will get into the right position for overtaking by gradual deceleration and progressive reductions in gear. The car will then be held exactly in place, neither gaining nor losing speed, until the opportunity arises to overtake, and the overtaking will be carried out under firm acceleration.

Acceleration sense has other advantages. Always to be either accelerating or braking without passing through the deceleration stage wastes petrol, and as more use is made of firm braking the shoes or pads get unnecessary wear. More petrol is needed to regain momentum. This method of driving is wasteful, it gradually saps the energy of the driver and it is most uncomfortable for the passengers.

Overtaking and passing
The decision to overtake a moving vehicle is voluntary, and the responsibility for its safe and accurate execution is the overtaking driver's.

The manoeuvre is in two categories – one, when progress will be uninterrupted, and the other when one must wait until it is safe to pass. The principles to be adopted are the same in both cases.

Uninterrupted overtaking
From as far away as possible the driver should take up a position on the road which gives a view up to and well ahead of the vehicle to be overtaken so that it can be established that:
  (a) There are no road works, vehicles, cyclists or pedestrians that will cause the driver ahead to deviate.
  (b) There are no side or cross roads from which other traffic could emerge.
  (c) There are no obstructions to the driver's view which could hide an oncoming vehicle until the driver is committed to overtaking.
  (d) There is a gap into which the driver can put the car after passing.

Having checked the mirrors and seen that conditions are safe to the rear as well as ahead, and also that position, speed and gear are right, it remains only to ensure that the driver ahead knows he is about to be passed.

This is particularly important on a narrow road. One can never be sure that the other driver will not choose that moment to light a cigarette or swerve to avoid a pothole.

If you intend to sound the horn do so far enough away to enable the driver ahead to react. In many cases it is better to flash the headlights, as the horn note may not be heard.

Waiting to pass
That you will have to wait for a safe opportunity to pass is usually apparent from afar, but this is no reason for abandoning the drill used on the approach to an uninterrupted overtake.

From behind a slow-moving vehicle the view ahead will be obstructed by the vehicle itself, so information obtained beforehand will be invaluable in assessing the new situation.

The driver now has to draw a fine balance as to the positioning of the car in relation to the vehicle ahead. From a long

way back the view will be good, but it takes time to catch up and pass, during which the situation may change. Too close and the view will be poor. Here, too, time will also be wasted in overcoming the inertia of the car and steering out to pass.

Unfortunately, one cannot measure the correct position, as it depends on many factors, such as the speed of the vehicles, the power of the overtaking vehicle, the choice of gear and rate of acceleration and, not least, the load the overtaking vehicle may be carrying.

The ideal position would be where the driver sits in line with the offside of the vehicle to be overtaken, and with a clear view ahead. The car would be sufficiently far back to enable the driver to move out to the full passing position and go past in a straight line. The gear selected should be one that will carry the vehicle up to and past without having to be changed and, at the same time, keeping the time of exposure to danger to a minimum.

When the opportunity to pass arises, ensure you are in the right gear, check the mirrors to make sure a faster vehicle is not passing you both, signal, move out, make a last check that there is a gap ahead for you to move into, then accelerate smoothly and rapidly.

Moving out early is important, as everyone concerned then knows how much room you need, in wet weather the risk of skidding is reduced, and the view ahead is always improving.

Many overtaking accidents occur through poor judgement of speed and distance. You can test yourself and practise on a quiet road by waiting until a vehicle comes towards you. When you are still well apart, select some point, such as a telegraph post or a gateway, where you estimate you will meet. If, without changing speed, you get there first, you are on the safe side. If he is first you are not. If you consistently meet as you have expected your judgement is good.

Too many drivers go wrong when they follow with no intention of overtaking and do not leave enough room for faster vehicles to occupy the gap in between before making further progress. This causes slow-

moving traffic queues and a great deal of frustration.

Cornering
When a car is driven round a bend centrifugal force will act on the side of it and try to push it outward. When turning left the thrust is to the right; when turning right it is to the left. If the force becomes greater than the grip of the tyres on the road, the car will skid. This will happen earlier if the tyres are badly worn.

The outward thrust is such that the metal part of the wheel is allowed to move sideways by the flexible tyre wall while the point of contact of the tyre remains in place. The result is that each succeeding piece of tyre meeting the road will be out of line with the piece before, so when cornering there is always a difference between where the wheel is pointing and where the car is actually going.

The angle formed by this difference is known as the 'slip angle'. If the slip angle at the front is greater than that at the rear the car will understeer, that is, it will run dangerously wide out of the corner. If the slip angle at the rear is the greater the car will oversteer, that is, it will describe a tighter arc than is intended.

It must be rememberd that centrifugal force will be modified in three ways – by weight, speed and the tightness of the turn. The greater the speed and tightness of turn, the greater the force becomes. The heavier the vehicle, the heavier is the force acting on it.

It will be seen that if the car goes wider and wider out of the corner the application of more steering will only accentuate the problem, for further tightening of the turn will increase the side force.

Under acceleration through a corner, weight is thrown backward on to the rear wheels, resisting the side force that is trying to make the bodywork lean outward on the suspension. Any error of judgement will cause the driver to accelerate or brake in an attempt to rectify the situation. Either will make matters worse.

Deceleration will allow the weight to rise off the rear wheels, the outward roll of the bodywork will be increased and a skid

will ensue. Braking would transfer weight forward, the back of the car would lift and with increased body-lean would put excessive weight on the outside front wheel which would act as a pivot round which the car would spin.

As weight is affected by centrifugal force it will generally be found that rear-engined cars will oversteer and front-engined cars will understeer.

All of these problems can be avoided by a strict method of driving, that is by:

(a) Looking well ahead and accurately assessing the sharpness of the bend.
(b) Positioning the car in the correct place on the road.
(c) Adjusting the speed and, if necessary, the gear.
(d) Taking the car through the corner under drive.
(e) Not applying firm acceleration until the vehicle is straight.

Once the accurate speed for the bend has been established, do not make the error of accelerating into it. Put on sufficient drive to maintain the chosen speed and no more. It is unwise to spoil a well-conceived plan by over acceleration.

Adverse weather conditions

Fog and mist. A basic principle of safe driving is 'see and be seen'. Obviously in fog it is difficult for a driver to see and for others to see him, so the vehicle must be equipped so as to overcome the problem before the fog season arrives.

Lighting. Never drive in fog on parking lights alone. At the very least use dipped headlights. However, although headlights make the vehicle visible to others, they do not give the best illumination to the driver. The light source is high and illuminates the fog at the driver's eye-level, producing a dazzling glare. Fog lamps fitted low will overcome this as their beams are at ground level and one tends to look over them and see obstructions earlier.

There would be greater safety to front and rear if all vehicles had high-intensity rear lights. Whatever may be said, the preceding rear lights may be all that can be seen, and drivers will follow them. As high-intensity lights can be seen more clearly they encourage a longer following distance, more comforting for all concerned.

Inside the car. A great deal can be done by the driver to maintain the view ahead.

(a) Do not lean forward and peer into the fog. Your view will not be lengthened and you will strain your eyes.
(b) Keep the driver's window open a little, as you will often hear danger before you see it.
(c) Keep the windscreen demister working fully.
(d) Use the windscreen wipers and washers at regular intervals to prevent the build-up of dirty globules of water on the windscreen.
(e) If you wear spectacles, keep them clean.
(f) Clean all lights whenever the opportunity presents itself.
(g) In daytime fog, and when there is street lighting, it is more restful to the eyes to equalize the incoming light by using the sun visor to prevent overhead light striking in at the top of the windscreen.
(h) White lighting is more penetrating than yellow, whose colour is in sympathy with fog and leads the driver wrongly to believe that he can see more. For the same reason, do not wear fog glasses.

Far left: Motorways are designed to keep traffic flowing freely, with separate lanes for overtaking and slow-moving vehicles.

Above and left: Drivers are helped by warning signs, particularly in bad weather conditions. Snow and ice on the road increase the risk of skidding. When driving in hazy conditions, fog lamps are best as they are fitted low and do not create a glare.

The driver. When meeting fog, the fringe area is usually thin but do not make the basic mistake of assuming it will continue at that density. Brake early and enough to allow for the worst.

Light up before reaching the fog and, if there is time, clean the windscreen. If there is no time to clean the windscreen before reaching the fog, it may be better to stop.

In town fog it is safest to follow a known route, where the hazards are familiar. When turning across traffic at junctions choose those controlled by traffic lights if possible. If that cannot be done stop, turn the window down fully, listen as well as looking for oncoming traffic and sound the horn before moving off. When you do decide to make the turn, be sure you are in the correct gear so that the time of exposure to danger is minimized.

Snow and ice. Most drivers are inhibited when driving on snow or ice, knowing the possibility of skidding if required to stop unexpectedly.

The fact that a light initial application of the brakes is essential adds to the problem, as the foot goes hesitantly on to the pedal, making for even longer braking distances.

Remember that excessive speed for the conditions and coarse use of the controls causes skids. Speed should be kept within the capability of the individual driver, which will encourage the delicate touch required for stability.

Driving along. When moving away from the stationary keep the steering wheels straight and turn them only when on the move.

When possible, use one gear higher than normal to reduce the amount of torque – turning force – going to the driving wheels which if excessive will produce wheelspin.

Torque going through the differential gear to the driving wheels will, like water, take the line of least resistance. So if one wheel has a solid grip and the other is on an ice patch, it is to the latter wheel that the power will go, the wheel will spin while the car remains stationary.

It may sometimes be found that a car will move backward more easily than forward. It is always worth trying, but never apply more than minimal power, and if necessary slip the clutch. If the car does not move slip quickly into forward gear, but do not be carried away and accelerate hard or you will be back where you started.

Once on the move remember that stopping distances are at least trebled on surfaces like these, and never forget that the time and distance required to deal with a hazard are also trebled.

Do not attempt to drive uphill if the traffic ahead is stopped or in difficulties. It is far better to stop in a suitable place on the approach until the way is clear. Try to ensure a clear run up and maintain the same gear throughout, even though it means going slowly.

Stopping. When stopping use the brakes. Do not try to slow down by progressively changing down through the gearbox, as some skill is needed to change gear without some snatch at the driving wheels and this could cause the skid you wish to avoid.

By using the brakes retardation starts immediately. When changing gear the car is still moving into the hazard and could cause the driver to resort to a late application of the brakes. This could be disastrous.

If the car does not respond as it should when driving away, make sure that the handbrake has not frozen on. If possible, when parking for the night, leave the handbrake in the off position.

Do not drive on parking lights in falling snow. Use dipped headlights or, far better, fog lamps. Headlights at night light up the flakes like a lace curtain, reducing visibility badly. The low beams from fog lamps light up the road surface with almost no reflected glare.

In soft snow it is cosier to follow in tracks made by other vehicles. Avoid doing so if the surface is frozen, as it can be difficult to get out of them without upsetting the car's stability.

When the road is wet at night, take care, especially on open bends where wind may have frozen the water. Black ice is almost impossible to detect, but an aid to detection is to keep a window open and listen to the swish of the tyres through the water. If it suddenly stops you are almost certainly on ice.

Equipment. Especially in isolated areas, never go into extremes of weather conditions unprepared, and do not carry your emergency equipment in the boot. The lid may freeze or you may not be able to get out of the car to reach it.

Carry a good car rug, a spade, some coarse matting to put under the wheels should the car get bogged down, a plastic windscreen scraper, a small bag of grit and a tow-rope.

In some areas chains on the wheels are essential if progress is to be made at all. If it seems likely that they will have to be used and you are not expert in fitting them, practise putting them on during the summer. The first snowfall is no time to discover the problems involved.

Tyres. Never go into winter with tyres worn almost to a minimum. No matter what the conditions may be, always run them at the recommended pressures.

An expert driver can keep going in the worst conditions, any driver should consider whether the journey is absolutely necessary and if it should be attempted at all.

Rain. Before windscreen wipers were improved and washers became universal drivers kept a good distance from the vehicle ahead or suffered a windscreen covered in mud. Now that it is easy to wash the screen, many people drive far too closely for reduced visibility and poor surfaces – and are unable to stop in an emergency. The rule must be 'keep your distance'.

At 96 km/h (60 mph) in medium heavy rain a tyre will disperse $4\frac{1}{2}$ litres (8 pints) of water every second through the cuts in the tread pattern. This amount of water is going to be thrown up and will come backward in a swirling jet if mud flaps are not fitted. If they are fitted the tendency is for the jet to atomize into four sprays. Whichever occurs, the result for the following driver is the same as clawing through a heavy mist.

In the reduced visibility caused by rain use headlights by day and night to ensure that you are seen in the mirror of the driver ahead and by oncoming traffic. Do not attempt to overtake unless absolutely sure it is safe.

In heavy rain worn tyres will be incapable of channelling away the surface water to enable them to cling to the road surface. This causes a build-up of water ahead of the point of contact, and it is possible at speeds as low as 80 km/h (50 mph) for the wheels to ride up on this water and lose adhesion completely. This is known as aquaplaning, and in this condition one can neither brake nor steer until speed is lost and adhesion regained. It is a rare occurrence but reason

enough never to run on tyres which can no longer cope with such conditions.

Always maintain wiper blades in good condition, and when washing the windscreen wash the wiper blades too. Otherwise the dirt and grease that has collected on them will be spread over the windscreen when you switch the wipers on. Equally important is to use an additive in the windscreen washer bottle to remove traffic film thrown up from the road.

Emergencies
Power steering failure. Faults can arise through breakage of the pump driving belt, but more commonly through leakage from oil seals. Do not stress the system by applying heavy steering while stationary.

If the system fails steering will not be lost but will become heavy and spongy. Take a firm grip on the steering wheel, brake smoothly and stop, preferably off the road. Do not drive on, even slowly, if there is any wander on the steering. It is an offence to drive with defective steering.

Call a well-equipped garage; the vehicle may have to be lifted to a workshop if repairs cannot be carried out on the spot.

Burst tyre. A burst or rapidly deflating tyre need not necessarily lead to loss of control provided the driver keeps both hands on the wheel and stays calm.

Rear. Keep a firm grip on the steering wheel and decelerate immediately. The car may wander, so brake smoothly when it is straight, which will tend to lift the back of the car as the weight moves forward, keeping it stable.

Front. This is far more dangerous than a rear-tyre deflation. The steering will be difficult to keep straight so some steering effort may be needed. Decelerate at once and as speed is lost very lightly apply the brakes and get the car off the road.

When stopping bear in mind that you have to change a wheel and try to select a place that will not put you at the mercy of passing traffic. On occasions like this a warning triangle is helpful, to warn others of the obstruction.

Shattered windscreen (or windshield). Every driver should know what type of windscreen is fitted to his car so that when the unexpected occurs it can be dealt with expeditiously.

If a shattered windscreen becomes opaque practically nothing will be seen through it. Keep calm, try to remember what the situation around you looks like and do not brake fiercely or you may be struck from the rear.

Punching firmly straight ahead with the fist so that the wrist and forearm are protected, knock a hole in the screen. Signal, draw over to the side of the road and stop.

If the windscreen is laminated or zone-toughened it may not be necessary to break it.

Laminated windscreens struck hard enough to shatter an ordinary one will only crack and will not become opaque. Zone-toughened screens will become opaque except for an area in front of the driver which will remain large and relatively clear and will give enough view ahead for a safe stop, though not enough

Above : In rain keep your distance to avoid spray on your windscreen caused by other cars.
Right : In snowy conditions always use dipped headlights.

for the journey to be completed.

It is possible to drive without a windscreen, but before doing so knock all the glass outward, first covering the vents on the fascia. Do not leave the pieces of glass on the road.

Close all the windows before moving off and drive slowly. The build-up of air pressure is often enough for reasonable comfort over short distances. Do not go too fast; the rear window may pop out.

Brake failure. Total failure of the foot brake system is extremely rare. In fact many cars have a dual system so that if the front brakes fail, the rear ones will still work and *vice versa*.

Remember that the handbrake is mechanically operated. It will not fail for the same reasons as the foot brake and is most unlikely to fail at the same time.

If the brakes fail take the foot from the accelerator, pull the handbrake on smoothly and leave it on. Change down progressively through the gears, letting the clutch up with very few engine revolutions to provide more retardation. Take care, if the road is slippery, as this method of changing down can create enough drag on the rear wheels to cause a skid. If necessary, when most of the speed has been lost move in to the kerb and scrub the wheels against it. Do not do this when travelling quickly or steering control will be lost.

Do not attempt to switch off the engine or in your haste you may operate the steering lock and lose control.

If a collision is inevitable, try to pick something soft to hit, such as a hedge. Whatever happens, try not to hit a solid object head on. Try to hit it at an angle so that you do not come to a dead stop.

Even the possibility of brake failure is argument enough always to wear a seat belt.

Skid control

It has been said with some justification that a car driven correctly will never skid. In practice, this may not be so. A patch of black ice on a bend, a spillage of slippery material on the road surface after an accident can catch the best driver unawares.

A skid will occur when the force of momentum acting on the car becomes greater

than the grip of the tyres on the road. Thus, when travelling straight ahead, heavy braking on a poor surface will lock the wheels and create a straight sliding motion. When turning at excessive speed for the contour or road condition side force will break the grip of the tyres at front or rear – or of all four tyres – and cause the vehicle to move outward from the curve through which the driver intended to pass.

Although skids can be caused by other means there is one basic cause – excessive speed for the prevailing road or traffic conditions. Should anything untoward occur in these circumstances the driver's reaction will be fast and hard, resulting in coarse steering, harsh braking and sometimes, in taking avoiding action, rough acceleration – all excellent ways of breaking the grip of the tyres on the road. Hence the skid.

There are three types of skid: four-wheel, front-wheel and rear-wheel. To correct a skid as quickly as possible it is essential to recognize instantly the sensation produced by each one.

Four-wheel skid. A sensation of gaining speed though the brakes are hard on. The car will go straight on but may gradually slide sideways if the road has a heavy camber. The steering will be completely ineffective in this type of skid.

Method of correction : Momentarily remove the braking to allow the road wheels to roll, then reapply smoothly and firmly. Repeat the process, if necessary, with a

controlled pumping action. You may be running out of safety distance by this time but try to keep cool so that your braking does not become coarse and re-establish the skid.

Front-wheel skid. A sensation of the front of the car sliding smoothly away from you. It usually occurs when turning, and the application of more steering will have no effect as the tyre's point of contact is already slipping.

Method of correction : Remove the foot from the accelerator immediately. Do not brake or declutch. If practicable, quickly straighten the steering wheel and reapply steering smoothly. Regrettably this is often a counsel of perfection, as any attempt to straighten the steering may take the vehicle on to the other side or off the road even more quickly. In such cases, it is best to keep steering into the corner and rely on the reduction of speed to re-establish control.

Only practical experience will help the driver to make an instant decision one way or the other, which is why this skid is so dangerous.

Rear-wheel skid. A sensation of the car trying to spin on its vertical axis. It occurs when turning and can be controlled with the steering.

Method of correction : Remove the foot from the accelerator immediately and at the same time steer in the direction in which the back of the car is moving. Do not brake or declutch. Wait until the skid diminishes, and as it does gradually remove the corrective steering. Most important – do not reapply acceleration until all four wheels are in line, and then only lightly. If you accelerate while corrective steering is still applied a secondary skid in the other direction can be caused. This is when the car goes out of control.

In right bends, the back of the car will move to the left, and to the right in left-hand bends.

To sum up – in poor conditions slow down to a speed within your capability as a driver. A driver well versed and trained in skid-control will, by developing road observation to a high degree, see the possibility of a skid well in advance and will take steps to avoid the situation.

REFERENCE

BIOGRAPHIES

AGNELLI

GIOVANNI, b. Villar Perosa, nr. Turin, Italy, 1866. d. 1945.
GIANNI, b. Turin, 1921.
Italy's greatest car firm, Fabbrica Italiana Automobili Torino (F.I.A.T.) or 'Find It All There' according to early advertisements, was founded in 1899 by Giovanni Agnelli, a 33-year-old former cavalry officer turned amateur engineer, and a group of prominent Turin citizens. Since

Gianni Agnelli

then, the fortunes of the firm (which now embraces Lancia and Ferrari) have always been guided by an Agnelli. Edoardo followed his father and grandson, Gianni, heads the organization today. Agnelli the elder was a rich man with socialist tendencies. He believed in providing work, he was a pioneer of industrial welfare and in contributions to charity he did not lag behind the British car manufacturer, Lord Nuffield. His grandson served in the Italian Army during World War II, winning the War Cross for Military Valour and afterwards fighting alongside Allied troops in the Italian Liberation Army. He became Managing Director of Fiat in 1964 and Chairman in 1966. He continues the traditions begun by his grandfather and Fiat are noted for the welfare care of their employees (although like other car manufacturers they are not immune to strikes). Amongst Agnelli's interests is football and his money has been behind many of the big transfers

of international stars to Italian clubs. Since 1945, he has been Mayor of Villar Perosa, the little town some 48 kilometres (30 miles) from Turin, where the Agnelli family originated.

ANDRETTI, Mario

b. Montona, Italy, 1940.
Few people are aware that Mario is a twin and that at one time his brother Aldo showed as much promise behind the wheel as he until a bad crash lessened his enthusiasm. The Andretti family were displaced by the wartime frontier troubles near their native village of Montona and escaped to the surroundings of Leghorn. In 1959, Mario's father decided to take the family to USA and they settled in Nazareth, Pennsylvania. Mario raced modified stock cars, sprints and midgets and 'arrived' in 1965 when he won the National Championship. It was the start of a remarkable run. He won the title again in 1966, was runner-up in 1967 and 1968 and won for the third time in 1969. This was also the year when he won the classic 500

Mario Andretti

Miles Race at Indianapolis. Small and wiry, the Italian-American is one of the very few stars of the American circuits to acquit himself with merit in Grands Prix—Dan Gurney is probably the best of the rest in modern times. Andretti won the South African Grand Prix in 1971 but did not become established as a top line Grand Prix racer until the seasons of 1976 and 1977. He won the Japanese Grand Prix at the end of '76 and the following year, with Jody Scheckter, of South Africa, provided the only serious challenge to World Champion Niki Lauda. Andretti clinched the 1978 World Championship after being placed sixth in the Italian Grand Prix.

Art Arfons and *Green Monster*

ARFONS

WALTER, b. Akron, Ohio, USA, 1917.
ARTHUR (ART), b. nr. Akron, Ohio, USA, 1926.
Two brothers who played a major role in the history of the World Land Speed Record in the sixties. They are, in fact, half-brothers, son and stepson of a miller. Despite the ten years difference in their ages, they formed a successful racing partnership and for many years were top stars in US drag-racing. However, they fell out; Walter had to retire from driving due to heart-trouble; and the partnership split up. Yet—not speaking to each other despite having neighbouring workshops in Akron, Ohio – the Arfons brothers were still to make a mark on the world record. Walter, backed by the Goodyear Tyre Company, was first to succeed when his *Wingfoot Express*, driven by Tom Green, did 664·8 km/h (413·2 mph), beating both Donald Campbell's 608·5 km/h (403·1 mph) and Craig Breedlove's three-wheeler mark of 655·6 km/h (407·45 mph). Art Arfons, backed by the rival Firestone Company, then took the record in his *Green Monster*, lost it to Breedlove, who raised it yet again before Art came once more into the picture. In 1965, the duel was resumed with Breedlove, Art Arfons and then Breedlove again holding the record. That marked the end of the Arfons Brothers as far as the world record was concerned. At 40, said Art 'old lions have to turn away from the young ones.'

ASCARI

ANTONIO, b. Bonferraro di Sorga, Verona, Italy, 1888. d. 1925.
ALBERTO, b. Milan, Italy, 1918. d. 1955.
Two of Italy's greatest racing drivers, father and son. Both died at the age of 36 after mysterious crashes and both were killed on the 26th day of the month. Antonio began as works driver for de Vecchi,

AUSTIN, Sir Herbert

b. Gt. Missenden, Bucks., England, 1866. d. 1941.

Worked for the Wolseley Sheep Shearing Company in Australia. Returned to England in 1895 and when the company toyed with the idea of entering the motor-car business, Austin designed a tri-car, based very much upon the designs of Léon Bollée. In 1897, however, he evolved a very much improved design. In 1899, he designed the four-wheeled Wolseley voiturette. In 1905 he had a disagreement with the company on future policy and set up on his own. His first cars were based on Clement and Gladiator designs and by 1914, the Austin Company was Britain's largest motor firm. Austin had to struggle to keep the firm going in the aftermath of war but saved himself by creating the Austin Seven, known world-wide as the 'Baby Austin' in 1922. The little family car became one of the most successful and

turous bent (it was the New York Herald which sent Stanley to find Livingstone). He felt that motor racing had a great future and donated a trophy and prize for which motor clubs from all over the world could compete. The French Automobile Club, the world's first, was asked to supervise and conduct the event. The French accepted and duly won the race themselves in 1900 and again in 1901. England (S. F. Edge) were the victors in 1902 and Germany (represented by the Belgian Camille Jenatzy) in 1903 before the race again went to France in 1904 and 1905. The French wanted to alter the rules – they felt that as the biggest manufacturers they were entitled to more entries – and as the other countries would not agree, the French organized the French Grand Prix, forerunner of the world's present day major Grand Prix series. Bennett, fed up with all the bickering turned to ballooning and other interests and so was lost to the cause of motoring.

Sir Herbert Austin

Where the **Austin** *"Twenty" is made.*

taking part in the 1911 Modena Six Days, an endurance event. He joined Alfa as a test driver but then came the Great War. Afterwards he bought a Fiat 5-litre Indianapolis model and won the two great Italian hill climbs of the period before being put out of action for two years after crashing in the Targa Florio. His comeback was so effective that he was signed as Alfa Romeo works driver. Ill-luck dogged him. In his first race outside Italy, he was leading the French GP when his engine failed with two laps to go; in the Targa Florio he was 50 yards from victory when his engine seized.

Antonio Ascari

But he won the Italian GP at Monza and began the 1925 season by winning the European GP at Spa. He was leading the French GP when he crashed and died in the ambulance on the way to hospital. His son Alberto won his first car race at Modena in 1947, became a works driver for Ferrari in 1949, Champion of Italy and World Champion in 1952 and 1953. He went to Lancia, won the Mille Miglia in 1954 and gained the firm's first F1 victories at Turin and Naples. He crashed into the harbour at Monaco but four days later took a Ferrari out at Monza, overturned, and like his father before him, died on the way to hospital.

best-known machines of its time. Perhaps surprisingly, in racing form, it also achieved successes both on the track and in the sphere of record-breaking. Austin did not live to see his company become part of the giant British Leyland organization along with the company created by his arch-rival, William Morris (Lord Nuffield), a situation with similarities to the merger of the Benz and Daimler concerns. Outside motoring his interests were in politics and he was Unionist Member of Parliament for the Kings' Norton Division of Birmingham from 1918 to 1924.

BENNETT, James Gordon

b. New York, USA, 1841. d. 1918.

Son of the owner of the New York Herald, Bennett went to Europe and established a European edition of the newspaper with headquarters in Paris. A serious looking man with a high forehead and the obligatory moustache of his day, he was of adven-

BENTLEY, Walter Owen

b. London, England, 1888. d. 1971.

'W.O.' as everyone called him, left college to become a railway apprentice and at the same time acquired his first motor-cycle. Winning a gold medal in the 1907 London to Edinburgh Reliability Trial persuaded him that his future did not lie with trains and on completing his apprenticeship he joined the National Motor Cab Company. With his brother, 'H.M.', he then went into business on his own with the British concession for three French motor-cars, the Buchet, La Licorne and DFP. Bentley began racing and record-breaking with a DFP but the Great War intervened. Bentley served in the Royal Naval Air Service but was given scope to develop his talents and designed the Bentley Rotary aero-engine. After the war he formed the Bentley car company which, with a string of successes at Le Mans, upheld the prestige of Britain in international motor racing in the twenties and thirties, the 'Bentley Boys' becoming a legend in their own time. Like many other men in the history of the automobile, Bentley's business acumen was not the equal of his great design and engineering talent and eventually his firm was taken over by Rolls-Royce. They, however, formed a new company, Bentley Motors (1931) Ltd., which continued to make quality cars for many years. Before he retired, Bentley designed the V-Twelve Lagonda and the post-war 2½ litre 6-cylinder engines used in Lagonda and Aston Martin cars.

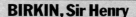

W. O. Bentley

BENZ, Karl

b. Pfaffenrot, Black Forest, Germany, 1844. d. 1929.
Marcus may or may not have invented the automobile, but Benz certainly was father of the motor industry. The son of a village blacksmith who became one of the early

Karl Benz

locomotive drivers and died in a rail crash, Benz studied engineering, worked in a factory and then set up his own business at Mannheim, manufacturing small gas en-

gines. His first machine was a motor cycle which proved a failure but in 1885 his first car was ready for trial. It was a three wheeler with the engine behind the seat. Benz successfully drove it around the dirt track surrounding his factory. This vehicle, and a subsequent one, attracted large crowds but they did not run very well. Consequently, Benz conducted further trials late at night until the automobile ran to his satisfaction. The Benz was the forerunner of most modern cars in that it was water cooled and had a differential gear and electrical ignition. Benz himself failed to move with the times and left his company in 1903. After the first World War, the Benz firm was merged with Daimler to produce the famous Mercedes Benz.

BIRKIGT, Marc

b. Geneva, Switzerland, 1878. d. 1953.
A Swiss who loved Spain, he was the designer and constructor of Hispano-Suiza cars, manufactured in France and Spain between 1904 and 1939; and also of the Hispano-Suiza aero-engines used in Allied military aircraft in both world wars. His native country has never been pro-automobile and so, like other famous men, Birkigt departed for Spain. There he worked for La Caudra, an engineer major in the Spanish Army, and a manufacturer of batteries and electric vehicles. Birkigt and others persuaded the Major to switch to internal-combustion engines but the firm failed, was revived and failed again. Then, in 1904, the Hispano-Suiza firm emerged from the wreckage with Birkigt as chief designer. The Swiss was not totally immersed in cars, he also produced a best-selling line in lorries. King Alfonso, a keen motorist, was attracted to the Hispano-Suiza and under his patronage, other Royal customers came along. Between 1909 and 1912, the cars had great success in races, including the Catalan Cup. The magnificent car which came to be known as the 'Alfonso' was followed by the Hispano-Suiza H6 and V12 models which increased the company's prestige still further. In the Second World War, Birkigt, who refused to cooperate with the Nazis or the Vichy Government, left his factories in France to

return to Spain. After the war, new management moved in and started the Pegaso cars. Birkigt went back to France again but found himself out of sympathy with the climate of early post-war France. Honoured with decorations from both France and Switzerland he retired to his estate near Geneva.

BIRKIN, Sir Henry

b. Nottingham, England, 1896. d. 1933.
Always known as 'Tim', this small, shy man with a stutter, was in the tradition of the great amateur drivers. With his white helmet, blue open-necked jersey, white trousers and blue and white polka dot scarf streaming out behind him, he represented an age long gone. Yet, almost alone, he upheld British racing prestige in the years between the Grand Prix successes of Segrave and the advent of Dick Seaman. He will always be associated with the 'Bentley Boys', that fabulous team gathered together by millionaire Woolf Barnato, which included jockey George Duller, theatrical impresario Jack Dunfee, journalist Sammy Davis and medical specialist Dr. Benjafield. For years they monopolized the famous Le Mans 24-Hour Race and in 1929, Birkin scored his first big win there,

Birkin at the wheel, Le Mans, 1928

in partnership with Barnato. Birkin loved driving at the limit and the finest performance of his career came in the 1930 French Grand Prix when he pitted a four-seater open Bentley against the sleek Grand Prix Bugattis and Delages. They laughed at him . . . but it was Birkin who laughed at the end of the 247-mile race for only the Bugatti of Etancelin finished in front of the Bentley and Birkin was gaining rapidly at the finish. He died three weeks after finishing third in the 1933 Tripoli Grand Prix. He burned his arm on the exhaust-pipe and the wound turned septic.

BOILLOT, George

b. France, 1885. d. 1916.
Boillot, a flamboyant, theatrical character, was the unofficial motor racing champion of France pre-1914 and the idol of his countrymen. A skilled mechanic and designer, he was employed by Peugeot and made his name in a small racing car called the Lion-Peugeot. His outstanding ach-

evement was in the French Grand Prix of 912. It was held over the Dieppe circuit out instead of one race of 770 km (478 miles) it consisted of two such races on consecutive days. The big Fiats, twice the size of the Peugeots, were favourites but in the sequel both races resolved into a duel between the Fiat driver, American Bruce-Brown, and Boillot, from which the Frenchman emerged triumphant. The following year, the strong, tough Georges, with his bristling handlebar moustache, went on to more victories in the Coupe de l'Auto and again in the French Grand Prix, this time on the Amiens circuit. A few days before the 1914 French GP, Archduke Ferdinand was assassinated in Serbia and tension was in the air. The German

Jack Brabham

Mercedes team was greeted by the French crowd in silence. But they won. After another great drive by Boillot his car broke down 64 km (40 miles) from the finish when he was in the lead and the German cars filled the first three places. It was the last race for the gallant Frenchman. He was killed in action in the war which broke out a week later, being shot down in an aerial battle over Verdun on 21 May, 1916.

BOLLÉE

AMÉDÉE Père: b. Le Mans, France, d. 1916.
AMÉDÉE fils: b. 1867. d. 1926.
LÉON, b. 1870. d. 1913.

The father designed and built private team vehicles which had such innovations as independent front suspension, a differential gear for the back axle, and engines, front, rear and amidships. His elder son made petrol cars from 1896 to 1914, including a streamlined racing machine in 1898. The younger son is best remembered for his three-wheeled tandem of 1895 but from 1903 he manufactured conventional motor-cars. His tricycle was a sensation at the time. It appealed to the cyclists who were looking towards the new motorization and it was widely-publicized by the French newspaper, *Le Petit Journal*. Three cars were sent across the Channel to take part in the original Emancipation Day Run of 1896 and Bollée tricycles have featured in

most of the Runs since up to the present day. After selling the manufacturing rights in a four-wheeler to Darracq, Léon set up on his own account and contravened agreements with his father and brother whereby Amédée was to build the heavier cars and Léon light carriages. Léon's cars continued in demand until his comparatively early death and stayed in production for some twenty years afterwards – until 1933.

BRABHAM, John Arthur (Jack)

b. Sydney, Australia, 1926.
Reared on midgets and dirt-tracks in his native Australia, 'Black Jack' went to Europe in 1955, signed with the Cooper team in 1956, became Formula Two champion in 1958 and World Champion for the first time the following year. The tall, dark, solemn-faced Australian went out and did it again, winning five Grands Prix in a row on his way to a second title. By 1962, Jack, a quiet man off the track, was building his own cars and in 1966 by winning the French Grand Prix he became the first driver to win a Grand Prix in a car bearing his own name, a feat emulated two years later by Jack's former team-mate, the New Zealander, Bruce McLaren; 1966 also saw Brabham win his third World Championship, the only driver ever to do so driving his own car, and his Repco-Brabham also took the World Manufacturers Championship. Jack sold out his British interests and retired in 1970 to the relief of his wife, Betty, and the family returned to Australia. One of their sons, Geoffrey, took up racing with a degree of success.

BREEDLOVE, Craig

b. Costa Mesa, California, USA, 1937.
A former fireman who became the fastest man on wheels, the slightly-built Breedlove met more than his share of misfortunes away from the salt flats where he gained his fame. Three marriages broke up and Breedlove's business interests lurched from one disaster to another. Yet his niche in the history of record-breaking is secure as the man who first broke the 600 mph

(965·4 km/h) barrier on wheels. On the Bonneville Salt Flats on November 15th, 1965, Breedlove piloted his jet-powered *Spirit of America* through the official stretch at 966·371 km/h (600·604 mph), a record which was to stand for a number of years until Gary Gabelich succeeded to Breedlove's title in a car which Breedlove himself had refused to drive because of dissatisfaction with the terms offered. But Breedlove's accomplishments speak for themselves. In 1963, he passed Cobb's 400 mph (643·6 km/h) mark then he wrecked his three-wheel car in breaking the 500 mph barrier (804·5 km/h) and finally went on to beat 600 mph in a four-wheeled car. For good measure, his second wife, Lee, claimed the women's world speed record at 496·47 km/h (308·56 mph).

BUGATTI, Ettore

b. Milan, Italy, 1881. d. 1947.
France's most famous manufacturer was the son of an Italian artist and himself remained an Italian citizen until shortly before his death. In 1898 he purchased a petrol-engined tricycle and with his interest in mechanical engineering aroused he apprenticed himself to a Milan machine-shop. A year later he built a two-engined tricycle and won eight out of ten races. Offered a position by De Dietrich in 1902 he left Italy for Alsace, then German territory, and spent most of the rest of his life there. He rented a large property at Molsheim and began to make Bugatti cars. A Bugatti finished second in the 1911 French Grand Prix and the marque enjoyed fantastic success until the outbreak of the Second World War. In 1925 and '26, for example, Bugattis won 1,045 events; in 1927, 806 races and hill-climbs; five Targa Florios in succession. Ettore also built luxury cars and designed the Bébé Peugeot ten years before the Austin Seven. The Peugeot is regarded by many as the forerunner of today's popular small cars. 'Le Patron' had aviaries, kennels, stableyards, museums, a boatyard and a hotel at his factory. He loved horses and the Bugatti radiator is based on a horseshoe although some claim that it was based on the arch of Molsheim's

Ettore Bugatti

tower. He had personal tragedy: his son, Jean, died testing a car; his father and his wife died during the Second World War; and after the war he had to go to court to get his factory back. He won the case, went to bed that night – and never rose again.

BUICK, David Dunbar

b. Arbroath, Scotland, 1855. d. 1929.

Buick, who gave his name to the car on which the giant General Motors empire was founded, was only two when his family went to the New World and settled in Detroit. Trained as a machinist, he became an innovator in the design of plumbing for indoor bathrooms, did very well and at the age of 47 sold out for 100,000 dollars. With his son, Tom, he tinkered happily in a workshop at the back of his Detroit home. First he built an engine and then installed it in a car, the first Buick appearing in 1903, the first production model the following year. But Buick's co-investors had run out of money and William Crapo Durant took over financial control. Buick found his share of the company becoming less and less until he was only an employee and a nominal member of the board. So in 1908 he left the company, never to return. Eventually he died almost destitute but he left behind him a memorial, a car which remained in the forefront of American automotive engineering through the succeeding decades and became famous all over the world. In the 70s, General Motors expressed confidence in their Buick Division by building a new headquarters at Flint, Michigan, USA, nicknamed 'The Taj Mahal'.

CAMPBELL

SIR MALCOLM, b. Chislehurst, Kent, England, 1885. d. 1949.
DONALD, b. Kingston Hill, Surrey, England, 1921. d. 1967.

Malcolm Campbell was only a schoolboy when he was fined for dangerous driving – on a bicycle. He went on to break the World Land Speed Record nine times and in doing so became the first man past the 300

Donald Campbell and *Bluebird* (above), Sir Malcolm Campbell (right)

mph (482·7 km/h) mark. His record cars were named *Bluebird* after Maeterlinck's famous story and his son, Donald, continued the nomenclature when he followed in father's footsteps after the Second World War. The father gave up land attempts after breaking the 300 mph barrier in 1935 and turned his attention to the water. Later Donald was to raise the water record to nearly the speed of his father's last land record. In Australia in 1964, Donald raised the land record to 403·10 mph, a figure subsequently beaten by Bob Summers in *Goldenrod*, these two records representing the best achievements of cars with direct-drive to the wheels. They could not match the tremendous speeds of the new race of jets. Father and son both had tumultous domestic lives, both won the Segrave Trophy (Malcolm twice, Donald a record four times) and looked very much alike. But the father died in bed while Donald was killed 180 metres (200 yards) from breaking the 300 mph mark on water when his boat somersaulted and crashed into the dark waters of Lake Coniston in northern England.

CARACCIOLA, Rudolf

b. Remagen, Rhine, Germany, 1901. d. 1959.

Although he died a Swiss national, Caratsch as he was known – dark, dapper and good-looking – is probably the German racing driver best remembered by his compatriots and by racing followers all over the world. Experts have said that his countrymen Rosemeyer, von Brauchitsch, Lang and more recently, 'Taffy' von Trips, could drive faster. That may be but none achieved the success of Caratsch. For fourteen years from 1926 to 1939 he was a top liner and won four European Championships, one of them for sports cars. He won the first German GP in 1926, the 1929 Tourist Trophy at Ards, Northern Ireland, and the 1931 Mille Miglia, the Swiss GP in 1935, 1937 and 1938, the Italian GP in 1934 and 1937, the 1935 French and Belgian Grands Prix, the 1935 Tripoli GP and the 1936 Monaco GP. The German GP he won no less than six times. He drove his last race in 1952 and throughout his career drove for Daimler-

Rudolf Caracciola

Benz except for the 1932 season when the German team did not race and he was permitted to sign for Alfa Romeo and a brief foray in a Thorne Special at Indianapolis. His crash at 'The Brickyard' in 1946 sidelined him for six years. The secret of his success was that he never overstrained his cars, never wore the tyres to ribbons and was seldom involved in accidents. In other words, Caratsch was a driver with a rare sensitivity for his machine. He was a recognized master in the rain, one of his greatest wins being at Monaco in 1936 when it rained incessantly. His life was not without tragedy. His first wife Charly was killed in an avalanche whilst skiing and he himself died of a liver complaint at a comparatively early age.

CARLSSON, Erik

b. Trollhättan, Sweden, 1929.
Big, burly and friendly, Carlsson was perhaps the first man to establish rally stars as personalities known to the general public. He made his name by winning the RAC International Rally three years in succession from 1960 to 1963, which made him a favourite with the British public, a popularity endorsed when he married Britain's leading woman rally driver, Pat Moss, sister of Stirling. Carlsson's first major event after completing military service was the 1953 Swedish Rally and his subsequent successes in minor events brought him a works offer from SAAB, by whom he is still employed. That year he won the Finnish 1000 Lakes; in 1959, the Swedish and German Rallies; and then during his RAC hat-trick, the Acropolis and the Monte Carlo. In 1963 he won the Monte for the second year in a row and the following year celebrated his marriage by winning the San Remo and a Cup in the Alpine Rally.

CHAPMAN, Anthony Colin Bruce

b. Richmond, Surrey, England, 1928.
Designer and constructor of Lotus competition cars and production sports cars. Son of a publican, Chapman began dabbling in the second hand car business while studying engineering. When a petrol shortage hit the car business, Chapman turned his attention to motor sport and began converting a 1930 Austin Seven into a trials special. The rebuilt car was registered as a

Lotus, the first of its line. After service with the RAF, Chapman joined the British Aluminium Company, built Lotus No. 2 and started racing. In 1952 the Lotus Engineering Company came into being in a stable at the back of Chapman's father's public house. Team Lotus was formed to handle racing activities leaving the Engineering Company to concentrate on selling cars. Great successes followed, the highlight perhaps being 1965 when the No. 1 works driver, Jim Clark, won the World Championship for the second time; Lotus the Constructors Championship, also for the second time; and the combination took the chequered flag in the Indianapolis 500. The car manufacturing side, after years with the emphasis on 'do-it-yourself' kits now builds de-luxe sports cars at a modern plant near Norwich in Norfolk.

CHEVROLET, Louis

b. La Chaux de Fonds, Switzerland, 1878. d. 1941.
Son of a Swiss watchmaker who moved to France, Louis Chevrolet emigrated to Canada with his brother Arthur in 1900. He had worked for Mors and De Dion Bouton in France and finding nothing in Canada went to work for the New York branch of De Dion. From there he went to a firm of Fiat importers, scoring his first racing success with one of the Italian cars at the Morris Park race track. He attracted the attention of William Crapo Durant, then forming his General Motors organization, and both brothers were signed for the Buick racing team. Louis became one of America's most famous racing drivers and soon the first Chevrolet car was on the market. But Louis had a row with Durant and in 1912 left the company which bore his name. Two years later he formed the Frontenac Motor Company, building four and eight cylinder racing cars. They competed at Indianapolis but Louis himself never won there and it was left to his younger brother Gaston to take the 500 Mile classic in 1920, winning by over six minutes without even stopping to change a tyre. Gaston was killed in a race crash a few months later and although Louis gave up driving, his modified Frontenac-Fords dominated the dirt tracks in the 1920s. The Depression, the death of his son, the loss of his designs and drawings in a fire and finally an incurable illness, clouded his later years. He was buried beside his brother Gaston at Indianapolis.

CHIRON, Louis

b. Monaco, 1899.
Chiron saw Great War service as a volunteer with the French Army. In 1923, he bought a Bugatti and took part in a number of hill-climbs and the following year drove professionally. By 1925 he had done well enough to be signed for the Bugatti works team. Volatile and enthusiastic, his name became associated with the Targa Florio although, in fact, he never won it: twice finishing second, once third and once fourth. He became France's most popular racing driver after winning the 1928 Italian Grand Prix in a Bugatti. He also had bad luck in his native Monaco GP since al-

though he won in 1931, on three other occasions he finished second and once he was third. But he scored many other major victories including the Italian, Belgian, German, French, Spanish and Czechoslovakian Grands Prix. After finishing third in the Autumn Cup at Montlhéry in 1956 there were to be no more laurels but it was not until he was sixty that Chiron finally gave up racing. Indeed, he was 56 when he took part in his last Grand Prix, driving a Lancia to sixth place at Monaco. During his driving career Chiron also took part in eleven Monte Carlo Rallies. He won in 1954 and thus became the only man to

Louis Chiron

win both the Monaco classics. When he gave up competing Prince Rainier persuaded him to accept a post as Clerk of the Course of the Monte Carlo races and the Rally, a post in which he became almost as well-known to later generations as he had been to their fathers on the race circuits.

CHRISTIE, J. Walter

b. USA, 1886. d. 1944.
In 1904, Christie became the first man to patent a front wheel drive car. He demonstrated it in January of that year and then proceeded to produce a new model every year until 1909. In 1906 he drove one of his own cars in the Vanderbilt Cup and was doing well until hit by Lancia's FIAT. The following year he went to Europe and took part in the French GP but failed to finish. However his cars were successful in sporting events, being driven on many occasions by the top American drivers of the time, George Robertson and Barney Oldfield. The first fwd car ever to win a race was a Christie which won a 250 Mile event at Daytona Beach in 1907. In 1916, Oldfield, driving a Christie, set a one mile dirt track record with a time of 47 seconds. Christie, a man with a very inventive turn of mind, set up a taxicab business in New York in 1909 and also sold passenger cars.

The taxis were closed coupes of great elegance and style but proved too good for the job in hand and the business was of short-lived duration. Christie continued inventing and in 1937 produced a tank which at that time was the fastest vehicle to run on tracks. It is also noteworthy because its unique suspension, with independently sprung road wheels, was to be utilized in British as well as Russian tanks before it appeared on American production tanks. But Christie is assured of his niche in motoring history as a pioneer of front wheel drive.

CHRYSLER, Walter Percy

b. Ellis, Kansas, USA, 1875. d. 1940.
The story of Chrysler is the story of the American dream – the farm-boy from Kansas who rose to be one of the world's outstanding industrialists. Unlike so many other pioneer automobile manufacturers,

Walter P. Chrysler

Chrysler left his company in good shape when he retired. His passion for engineering began in childhood for his hometown was the site of workshops for the Union Pacific Railroad and the future auto tycoon began his working life as a railway locomotive cleaner. Cars attracted his attention at the beginning of the twentieth century and, a married man with just 700 dollars in the bank, he bought a 5,000 dollar Locomobile. In his mid-thirties, Chrysler was plant manager of the American Locomotive Company works, which had a car manufacturing subsidy. At this time he met the bankers who were rescuing the ailing General Motors and he joined that company in 1912. By 1916 he was General Manager of the Buick Division at an annual salary of a half-million dollars and by the end of the Great War he had established himself as one of America's top twelve industrialists. Later Chrysler revived the Maxwell firm and used it as a basis to build a car bearing his own name, a prototype appearing in 1924. In 1925, Chrysler killed off the Maxwell and Chalmers marques and formed the Chrysler Corporation which was to grow into a world-wide organization.

CITROËN, André

b. Paris, France, 1878. d. 1935.
A French national of Dutch extraction, this remarkable man, sometimes called 'The French Ford', reconverted his company which had made gears and ammunitions during World War I, to produce motor cars and created a car empire which was to outshine all the pioneer French firms. He played a pioneering role, first in introducing American mass production methods to Europe, then in introducing the all-steel body (1925) and monocoque construction (1934). The tooling and development costs of his monocoque, front-wheel driven and torsion bar sprung car, launched in 1934, brought bankruptcy to his company which passed under the control of the Michelin tyre company, but after its numerous teething troubles were solved, the car became a tremendous success and remained in production for 22 years. Citroën cars had another more doubtful claim to fame: they were extremely popular with French stick-up men – *traction avant* bandits. After the take over by Michelin, André Citroën was forced to resign and he died little more than a year later.

Jim Clark with Colin Chapman, world champions, 1963

when most of the major works teams favoured Scandinavian drivers. Starting in local rallies with the man who remained his regular co-driver, Jim Porter, he became East Midlands champion in 1961 but it was not until 1963 that he gained his first works drive with the short-lived Reliant team. As a Ford private entrant he won the Welsh, Scottish and Gulf London Rallies the following year but it was Rover who signed him in 1965 and not Ford. He repaid their confidence by winning the Group One category of the classic Monte Carlo Rally. Ford were finally won over and he has since scored a string of international victories for them, starting with the Scottish and the Canadian Shell 4000 and then breaking the long run of Scandinavian domination of the RAC International of Great Britain. His many triumphs include the Circuit of Ireland (more than once), the Scottish, Acropolis and Tulip Rallies. The seal on Clark's right to the title of England's best rally driver came in 1976 with the award of the Segrave Trophy, which had never before been awarded for rallying.

André Citroën (above left) welcomes the driver of the Citroën car after a non-stop tour of France and Belgium, 1934
John Cobb's Railton Mobil Special

CLARK, James (Jim)

b. Kilmany, Fife, Scotland, 1936. d. 1968.

A Scottish farmer's son, Clark began his illustrious motor sport career in local rallies and sprints and graduated through sports cars to single-seaters. His breakthrough came in 1960 when after trials he was signed by Aston Martin for F1 and Lotus for F2 and Formula Junior. It was to be the Lotus tie-up which was significant because Astons withdrew from Grand Prix racing. In December, 1961, Clark scored three victories in 17 days, in the South African, Natal and Rand Grands Prix. In 1962, he narrowly missed the world title, winning the Belgian, British, United States and Mexican GPs. But in 1963, Clark made no mistake and took the championship with three races still to go. In 1964, he was awarded the Order of the British Empire in the Queen's Birthday Honours; 1965 was better still with Clark again winning the championship and also the Indianapolis 500, during which he led for 190 of the 200 laps. The dark, introverted Scotsman had proved himself the best race-driver in the world. Yet it was typical of the man that he was most touched by being made a Freeman of the village of Duns, the Border community near his home. Although he was still to win many races he never again took the championship for in 1968 at Hockenheim – 'a stupid race on a stupid circuit' – he crashed due to a tyre failure and died. Clark had been a difficult man to know yet the world mourned him for his undeniable brilliance as a driver.

CLARK, Roger

b. Narborough, Leicestershire, England, 1939.

Universally recognized as England's top rally driver, Clark had a hard struggle to the top, his career coinciding with a period

COBB, John Rhodes

b. Esher, Surrey, England, 1899. d. 1952.

Cobb three times broke the World Land Speed Record in his twin-Napier-engined four-wheel drive Railton Special, the last piston-engined car to hold the title at 634·26 km/h (394·12 mph), with a speed in one direction of 649·5 km/h (403 mph). That was at Utah in 1947 and it was to be seventeen years before Donald Campbell beat it in a gas-turbine car nearly twice as powerful as Cobb's. Cobb, a giant, thin-haired man, in business-life a fur broker, was singularly ignored by King and country and did not receive the honours showered on other British record-breakers

such as Segrave and Campbell. He first broke the record in 1938, exceeding 350 mph (563·15 km/h), increased by nearly 20 mph the following year and came back after the Second World War to become the first man past the 400 mph (643·6 km/h) barrier. During the war the Railton Special had been stripped down and the parts stored in dispersed places. It was truly remarkable that afterwards it could be reassembled and perform so magnificently. Cobb, alas, like Segrave before him and Donald Campbell afterwards, was subsequently killed in attempting the World Water Speed Record. The location was Loch Ness in Scotland, and Cobb was travelling through the water at 200 mph (321.8 km/h) when the craft exploded.

CORD, Erret Lobban

b. Warrensburg, Missouri, USA, 1894. d. 1974.

Cord has been called many things – supersalesman, entrepreneur, empire-builder and so on – but no one has ever called him a brilliant engineer. Yet one only has to look at the cars with which he was associated in his career – Auburn, Cord and Duesenberg, each one regarded today as a Classic – to realize that the man deserves more credit than posterity has given him. He began his career by rebuilding broken-down Model T Fords and was said to have made and lost three fortunes by the time he was twenty-one. In 1924, he joined Auburn as general manager with a share in the company and brought about a revival in their flagging fortunes. He employed talented men, designer Gordon M. Buehrig was one of them, and produced wonderful cars including the first American front wheel drive car to gain popular approval. In this he was aided by the design genius of Harry Miller, who had patented his solution to the problem of front wheel drive in 1929. In the twenties, Cord, like Stutz and Mercer, was offering cars with a guaranteed speed of 160 km/h (100 mph). Cord's empire was, however, affected by the financial problems of most car manufacturers in the thirties. Cord took his family to England at one stage but returned to the States in time to preside over the last rites of the Cord Company in 1937.

DAIMLER, Gottlieb

b. Schorndorf, Germany, 1834. d. 1900.
Son of a baker, Daimler was apprenticed to a gunsmith but after learning the trade he worked for various engineering firms and with the help of Wilhelm Maybach designed the first practicable four-stroke internal combustion engine. He set up in business with Maybach and patented (in 1883) the first 'high-speed' petrol engine with tube ignition, forerunner of the modern car engine. Two years later, they produced a motor cycle powered by this engine and in 1886 ran a four wheeled vehicle, a year after Benz had run a three-wheeler. Daimler was more far seeing than Benz and the rights to manufacture to Daimler patents and specifications were sold to Panhard et Levassor in France, Austro-Daimler in Austria and the Daimler Motor Co. in England. This last agreement was signed in December, 1896, just after Daimler had visited England to take part in the first Emancipation Day Run from London to Brighton. But the success of Daimler cars had been assured much earlier when in the 1894 Paris to Rouen run, Daimler-powered cars finished first, second and third. Contrary to some stories Daimler and Benz never met and the com-

Gottlieb Daimler

panies were amalgamated long after Daimler's death in 1900. Both played major roles in the story of the motor car but there is a strong case for saying that the bald and bearded Daimler was the most important of all the pioneers.

DAVIS, Sydney Charles (Sammy)

b. London, England, 1887. d. –
An engineering draughtsman and accomplished artist who became motor-racing correspondent and sports editor of *Autocar*,

the English motoring magazine, 'Sammy' was one of the outstanding drivers between the wars. In 1922 he set ten world and twenty-two class records with Aston Martin and in 1926 joined the Bentley team to become one of the most famous of 'The Bentley Boys'. Partnered by Dr Benjafield, he scored a notable victory in the 1927 Le Mans 24-Hour Race. Later he raced with Alvis and Riley and in 1930 won the British Racing Driver's Club Gold Star. He was also a regular competitor in rallies. In beret, beard and spectacles, looking more French than British, he was still a prominent and active figure in motor sport circles at the age of eighty.

DePALMA, Ralph

b. Italy, 1883. d. 1956.
In 27 years of racing, DePalma won, it is claimed, more than 2,000 of the 2,800 events he entered. Leaving his native Italy at nine years of age, he grew up in Brooklyn, New York, and like so many auto racers began his competition career on a motor cycle. He saw his first motor race, the Vanderbilt Cup, in 1904, when he himself was 21 but it was not until he was 25 that he took part in his first four wheel

Ralph DePalma

event, driving an Allen-Kingston in the Fort George hill climb. From an undistinguished beginning he went on to twice win the Vanderbilt Cup and to take the chequered flag in the 1915 Indianapolis 500. In 1919, he broke the World Land Speed Record in a Packard at 241·15 km/h (149·875 mph), a record accepted only in the States due to the American authorities not being internationally recognized at the time. DePalma's versatility was demonstrated when he crossed the Atlantic to finish second in the French GP of 1921. His great rival, Barney Oldfield, retired at 40 but the Italian-American kept on. When he finished seventh at Indianapolis in 1925 many thought he too would retire but less than two months later he won the main

event at Rockingham Park, New Hampshire, and in 1929, at the age of 46, he won the Canadian Championship. He eventually retired in the 1930s.

DIESEL, Rudolph

b. Paris, France, 1858. d. 1913.
Born in France of German parentage, Diesel was 12 when the Franco-Prussian War led to the expulsion of German nationals and the Diesel family went to

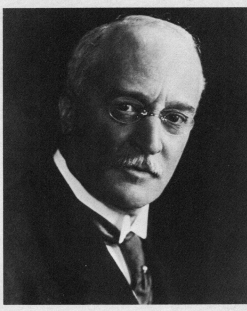

Rudolf Diesel

England. Soon afterwards Rudolph was despatched to an uncle in Augsburg and later went to technical school in Munich. He became a refrigeration engineer but he was obsessed with the idea of 'declaring war on the steam engine' and registered his first patent for a rational internal combustion engine in 1892. He had backing from two big firms, Krupps and Maschinenfabrik Augsburg. Other firms took out licences, ships were fitted with his engines and before the First World War, Diesel locomotives made their appearance on the railways, some travelling at more than 100 km/h (62 mph). It was, however, to be many years before the motor industry fully explored the possibilities of his engines and Diesel himself did not live to see it. Beset by difficulties, real and imaginary, this melancholy man, hailed in some quarters as an inventor on a par with Marconi and Edison, climbed over a ship's rails one night and disappeared for ever in the cold, grey waters of the North Sea. His engines remain all over the world.

DODGE

JOHN, b. Niles, Michigan, USA, 1864. d. 1920.
HORACE, b. Niles, Michigan, USA, 1868. d. 1920.
The Dodge brothers were in the bicycle business and were regarded as good machinists. Their company prospered to the extent that a Canadian firm made a successful take-over bid. The brothers moved to Detroit where they opened a machine-shop and became sub-contractors to the Olds Motor Works. Their engines were good and no one realized it more than

Henry Ford. He offered them shares in his company at a nominal value providing they would build engines for him. Against all advice they accepted the offer and once again they prospered. When Henry Ford decided that he wanted them out of his company, the price he paid was sufficient to enable them to found the Dodge Motor Company. However, the brothers were not so percipient in the matter which led to their break with Ford. Henry saw expansion at a tremendous rate and bought a site near Dearborn on the River Rouge for a new plant. The Dodge brothers strongly disagreed and led a band of rebel stockholders. Ford bought them out and the rest of the Ford story is history. However, so successful was their new company that the Dodge brothers had little time for regrets.

DUCKWORTH, Keith

b. Blackburn, Lancashire, England, 1933.

One of the most remarkable engine-designers in the history of the automobile is a quiet-spoken Englishman with a wry sense of humour and a turn of phrase which has made him one of the more quotable of motor racing's backroom boys. Keith Duckworth, Chairman of the Cosworth Engineering Company of Northampton, may well have carved for himself a place in history which will never be matched. In 1967, an engine which he had designed for the Lotus team, powered Jim Clark to victory in the Dutch Grand Prix. In 1977, South Africa's Jody Scheckter won the Monaco Grand Prix in a Wolf car powered by the same engine. In between the DFV 3-litre V-8 engine designed by Duckworth and backed by Ford had won 98 other major Grand Prix races, the most remarkable statistic in racing history. The engine has also been a winner on hillclimbs and in the 24 Hours of Le Mans. Another engine, derived from it, has been successful at Indianapolis and in other United States AC races. Duckworth's

achievement in winning 100 Grand Prix races was marked by the Royal Automobile Club with its premier award, the Diamond Jubilee Trophy. Duckworth's comment: 'My approach to design is very fundamental – faced with a problem I attempt to analyse the requirement.'

DUESENBERG

FRED, b. Lippe, Germany, 1876. d. 1932.
AUGUST, b. Lippe, Germany, 1879. d. 1955.

Fred Duesenberg was born in Germany and taken to the USA in 1885 when he was eight years old. He and his younger

Fred Duesenberg

brother, Augie, began working with cars at the turn of the century. Fred was a self-taught engineer. He left school at 17 and started a bicycle business. He also raced bikes and at one time held two world records. In 1901 he opened a garage in his adopted town of Des Moines, Iowa, and in 1903 built his first racing-car. Later he was financed by a local lawyer, one of the first recorded cases of what is now termed sponsorship, and firstly under the name Mason, the Duesenberg became a very

successful racing car. Drivers who drove Duesenberg included great names like Oldfield, Rickenbacker, DePaolo, Murphy, Hartz and Milton. The cars were placed in 24 of 27 major races entered and won at Indianapolis in 1924, 1925 and 1927. Murphy drove one to victory in the French

Augie Duesenberg

Grand Prix of 1921, the first time an American won a European GP. At one time or another, Duesenbergs held records ranging from the standing kilometre to 24 hours. Augie showed great ability as a designer and over a period of sixteen years, three passenger models were produced, claimed by admirers to be the most luxurious truly *fast* cars ever built. Fred died of injuries sustained in an accident in 1932; Augie lived on to launch an unsuccessful comeback by Duesenberg cars in 1947.

Duesenberg 3 litre 1921

DURANT, William Crapo (Billy)

b. Boston, Mass., USA, 1861. d. 1947.
Durant was one of the great entrepreneurs of the automotive industry and founder of the giant General Motors Corporation. The idea behind General Motors was to form a vigorous combine controlling its own suppliers and building a car to suit every purse. The basis for the combine was Buick, with its volume sales, and Oakland was another constituent company. Then Durant captured Henry Leland's

Keith Duckworth

353

Cadillac organization for his empire, a move that saved General Motors when Buick hit financial difficulties. Later Durant ran into difficulties he could not solve and it was left to Alfred Sloan to reform General Motors into the powerful organization it remains today. Durant, like most of his kind, was never down for long and he set up another motor-manufacturing combine embracing Durant, Star, Locomobile and Flint but this too collapsed and in 1932, Durant, who was nothing if not far-seeing, went into the infant supermarket business. He died a comparatively poor man when one considers that the empire he founded is now one of the richest organizations in the world and its chief executive the highest-paid man in the United States, if not in the world.

DURYEA

CHARLES, b. Canton, Illinois, USA, 1861. d. 1938.
FRANK, b. Linn, Illinois, USA, 1869. d. 1967.
The Duryea brothers have the best claim to have produced the first basically sound United States four wheel automobile, although within the family it has been disputed which brother made the major contribution. Charles was the older and like so many of the early car manufacturers started with a bicycle business. When he turned to cars he enlisted his brother's help and it is generally believed that the first Duryea car was running on the streets of Springfield, Mass., in 1892, two years before Elwood Haynes produced a car and three in advance of Ford. A second Duryea model appeared in 1894. The first road race run in America with more than two cars competing was the Chicago to Evanston and back Thanksgiving Day Race of 1895. It was won by a Duryea. The first automobile patent issued to an American manufacturer went to Charles Duryea and, in 1896, the name of Duryea crossed the Atlantic when Duryea cars took part in the Emancipation Day Run in England. All in all, the place of these two brothers in American automotive history is assured. Frank, the younger, lived to see the industry grow into the giant it is today and for posterity, contemporary journals have recorded that both brothers 'were excellent workmen', an epitaph which would satisfy many.

EDGE, Selwyn Francis

b. Sydney, NSW, Australia, 1868. d. 1940.
Edge is best-known as one of the outstanding early British racing drivers and record-breakers – he won the 1902 Gordon Bennett Race amongst others – but he was also very active in the infant motor industry, the driving force behind at least one successful marque and, probably, the archetype car salesman. In 1898, he took his Panhard to Montague Napier's engineering works for the tiller steering to be converted to a wheel. Later Napier made an improved engine for the car and in 1899 Edge set up a selling organization and contracted to take the whole output of Napier cars. It was with a Napier that he achieved

S. F. Edge in a Napier

his Gordon Bennett success and the cars also did well in events such as the Tourist Trophy. At the new Brooklands track, Edge and Napier proved a record-breaking combination and during these years of glory, Napier could fairly claim to be Britain's leading manufacturer. Edge remained a prominent figure in the industry long after his own racing career was over. He headed the British end of the French De Dion Bouton firm, one of the most prolific of early manufacturers, and in the 1920s was Managing-Director of the successful AC Car Company.

EYSTON, Captain George

b. Oxford, England, 1897.
In 1923 George Edward Thomas Eyston launched upon a record breaking career surpassing even that of America's legendary Ab Jenkins. Most of his early records were set at Brooklands in England and Montlhéry in France – on the latter track he became the first man to reach 100 mph (160·9 km/h) in a baby 750 cc car. Record after record fell to him, culminating in 1937 with the World Land Speed Record at Bonneville, USA, the seven ton *Thunderbird* clocking 502 km/h (312 mph). He held more records with different types of car than any other driver, before or since, and in 1948 was awarded the Order of the British Empire. Perhaps his most remarkable achievement however was to break records in darkness at Montlhéry when uncompleted track repairs had left a gaping hole in the banking. His record feats tended to obscure his undoubted ability as a racing driver, one of his best performances being the class win at record speed, partnering Count Johnny Lurani, in the 1933 Mille Miglia in an MG Magnette.

FAGIOLI, Luigi

b. Abruzzi, Italy, 1898. d. 1952.
Fagioli was short, stocky, swarthy, with broad shoulders and muscular, hairy arms. He knew only one style of driving – flat out – and provided his car lasted the distance he was rarely out of the first three or four places. Like so many drivers before and since, Fagioli was not exactly young when he first began winning races. This was in 1930 when at the wheel of a Maserati he won three races. He stayed with Maserati

until 1933 when he joined Enzo Ferrari in the Alfa team the latter was running on behalf of the factory. He won three major races, including the Italian Grand Prix,

Luigi Fagioli

and was second to Louis Chiron in three more, thus gaining enough points to become Champion of Italy. As a result, the German Mercedes team, making a comeback to racing, engaged him as a support driver to Caracciola. Team orders were that the German should win whenever possible but Fagioli won the Spanish, Italian and Monaco Grands Prix, the former by ignoring signals from his pit. The situation could not continue and after the 1936 season, Fagioli was signed by Auto-Union. In 1938 he retired but came back in 1950 in an Alfa team with Fangio and Farina and was placed in six major Grands Prix. Driving a Lancia in practice at Monaco Grand Prix of 1952 (a sports car race that year) he crashed in the tunnel and died.

FANGIO, Juan Manuel

b. Balcarce, Buenos Aires, Argentina, 1911.

If Nuvolari was the outstanding racing driver between the wars, there are many

George Eyston in an MG Magic Magnette, 1934

who would argue that Fangio was the greatest of post-war drivers. His career in World Championship Grand Prix racing was fairly brief yet between 1949 and 1957 he won the world title no less than five times. Perhaps even more remarkable is that he came to Grand Prix racing even later than Nuvolari – at the age of thirty-eight. Fangio learned to race in the rough and tumble of saloon car events on the dirt roads of Argentina where finesse was the last thing required. Most of his early victories were in South American races during the years of the Second World War. In 1939, he won the Argentine 1,000 Km and he continued in this vein until a brief foray to Europe in 1948, during which he started in one race and retired. But in 1949, driving first a Maserati and then a Ferrari, Fangio won his first four races in Europe and was placed six times out of ten starts. So impressed were Alfa Romeo that they signed him for 1950 and

he narrowly missed the World Championship, winning three championship races and seven other major races. He took the title in 1951. In 1952 and 1953, the years of a Formula Two World Championship, Fangio drove for Maserati and did well without gaining premier honours. But in 1954 he was back as No. 1, still with Maserati, and in 1955, heading the all-conquering Mercedes team, took the title again. Driving a Lancia Ferrari he was champion yet again in 1956 and took the title for the fifth and last time in 1957, once again with Maserati. He retired the following year after winning his native Buenos Aires Grand Prix and subsequently became a successful businessman. The humble housepainter's son had gone places fast. Fangio was an amazingly safe driver. He had only two accidents: one at Monza where he started when on the brink of physical exhaustion; and another in 1953 when he returned after his first accident.

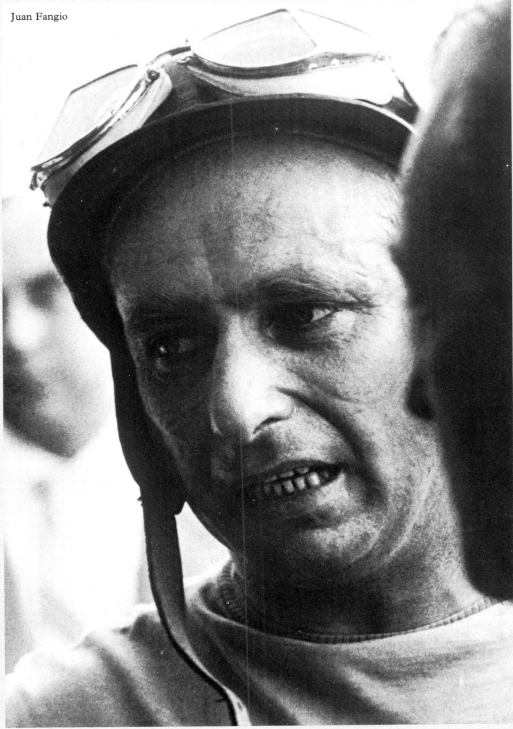

Juan Fangio

FARINA, Giuseppe

b. Turin, Italy, 1906. d. 1966.
'Nino', a doctor of law, was a member of the Farina family famous as coach-builders and designers and perhaps not surprisingly learned to drive when he was only nine years old. Despite a crash in his first event which landed him in hospital with a broken shoulder and damaged skull he was taken under the wing of the great Nuvolari. He became Italian Champion in 1938 and Number One driver to the Alfa Romeo team the following year. A veteran when he returned to racing after the war, Nino enjoyed an Indian summer as one of the Alfa 'Three F's' team of Fangio, Farina and Fagioli. Winning the British, Italian and Swiss Grands Prix, he became the 1950 World Champion, the first under the rules that more or less are still in force. Two years later he joined Ascari and Villoresi in the Ferrari team and as late as

Second World War he was building 150 bodies a month on the Lancia Augusta and Aprilia and the small Fiats. At the same time he created luxury bodies on the Lancia Astura and other cars, combining the best features of American and European design. The modern GT concept had at least some of its beginnings in the streamlined shells he created. After the war Farina designed the Cisitalia coupé which was to become the trend setter for all future GT cars. He also was first in realizing that the coach-building industry could survive only if it passed from the artisanal to the industrial stage. By 1948 Pinin Farina was a world figure, an arbiter of automotive design until he retired from the stage in 1959. Amongst his later successful designs were the Lancia Aurelia GT and the Lancia Flaminia. By 1953, the Italians, according to a contemporary, 'had complete ascendancy in body design' and Farina's ideals, classical purity and func-

Enzo Ferrari

Giuseppe Farina in a Maserati, 1951

1955 he was placed in the Argentine and Belgian Grands Prix. He suffered many appalling crashes on the circuits, in some of which others were killed, but he remained, as always, a man of steel. He died in a road crash in France, in circumstances which were never fully explained.

FARINA 'Pinin'

b. Turin, Italy, 1895. d. 1966.
Joined his brother's carriage repairing business at eleven and established his own design firm in 1932. By the outbreak of the

tionalism, had created the situation for scores of car designers to express their ideas. Car manufacturers flocked to him, amongst them Fiat, Austin and Peugeot. Later came the Ferrari. There is little doubt that Farina played a major role in inspiring many other first-class Italian automotive designers to emerge after the Second World War. Before his death, Pinin Farina had his surname changed to Pininfarina, and this has become the name of the company he founded, now headed by his son Sergio Pininfarina and his son-in-law Renzo Carli.

FERRARI, Enzo

b. Todena, Emilia-Romagna, Italy, 1898.
A fair racing-driver who became an outstanding team manager and entrant. Scuderia Ferrari was established in 1929 and in 1931 concluded an agreement with Alfa Romeo to manage that firm's racing activities. In 1940, Ferrari produced his first car and set up as a constructor after World War Two. 1949 saw the first of many Ferrari victories at Le Mans and in 1957 he won the world constructors' title, the first occasion on which it was awarded. He was materially supported by Fiat from the sixties and eventually the Italian giant took a majority shareholding after an abortive Ford bid to take over Ferrari. The agreement with Fiat was conditional upon Ferrari remaining boss. Over the years, Il Commendatore, as he is known, has suffered many tragedies as well as triumphs, including the death of his son Dino and several Ferrari works drivers. He has always shown great ability in picking drivers, some of them unknowns, for his team. It is debatable if some World Champions would have won the title without the shrewd backing of Ferrari. His stable of title-holders has included the late Alberto Ascari, Juan Manuel Fangio and Niki Lauda, men generally recognized as amongst the greatest of all time. Fangio did win the Championship on other occasions in other cars but perhaps Ferrari was the vital factor when Mike Hawthorn (England) won the title in 1958; Phil Hill (United States) in 1961; and John Surtees

(England) in 1964. The silver hair and dark glasses of Enzo Ferrari are familiar to readers of the motor sport magazines but few have actually seen him. He no longer goes to see his cars race.

FITTIPALDI, Emerson

b. São Paulo, Brazil, 1946.

With a father, Wilson, a racing motor-cyclist and journalist and a brother, Wilson Jnr., a racing driver, Emerson Fittipaldi was almost certain to become a racer himself. And so it proved. After winning kart, saloon and Formula Vee championships in his native Brazil, he came to England and speedily attracted attention. He had his F1 debut in 1970 as third driver in the Lotus team and broke through with a victory in the United States Grand Prix. In 1972, still driving for Lotus, he won the World Championship, beating Jackie Stewart by sixteen points. In 1973, the positions were reversed but the following year, Fittipaldi, now driving for the McLaren team, was World Champion again. In 1975 he was runner-up to the Austrian, Lauda, to complete a remarkable sequence of being twice champion and twice runner-up in only six years of Grand Prix racing. Fittipaldi then left McLaren to join his brother in the new Brazilian team, Copersucar, a move which may have been patriotic but certainly killed his World Championship chances in 1976 and 1977. There is no doubt that Fittipaldi, with the right car, is still young enough to be once more a championship contender. He came second in the 1978 Brazilian Grand Prix.

FORD, Henry

b. Springwells Township, nr. Detroit (now Greenfield Village, Dearborn), Michigan, USA, 1863. d. 1947.

William Ford left Ireland in 1847 at the height of the Great Famine and settled in Michigan. He worked first on the Michigan Centre Railway and then on the farm of a fellow Irishman where he married Mary, the farmer's foster daughter. He bought his own farm and it was here that his first son, Henry, was born. Hard work on the farm for small return, a fall from a horse and his first sight of a traction engine 'took me into automotive transportation' he was to say later. He built his first crude but successful quadricycle in 1896 and three years later became works manager of the Detroit Automobile Company. He and the company soon parted, the company being renamed Cadillac, another name which was to become famous. Ford built

Emerson Fittipaldi

a racer and at the old Grosse Pointe Track won the 'World Championship' defeating the great Alex Winton and a Pittsburgh millionaire, William Murray. Victory gained him financial backing for the Henry Ford Company, founded in 1901, but this was soon disbanded and Ford turned again to racing, building two monsters, 'Arrow' and '999'. Barney Oldfield drove '999' to victory in the Manufacturers Challenge Cup and on the back of that success the Ford Motor Company as it exists today was founded in 1903. Models

A, B and C were followed by Model F and the company flourished. Model N sold nearly 10,000 cars and Ford dreamed of a light four cylinder touring car of not less than 20 horsepower, capable of carrying five people. The Model T was an over-night sensation. Ford ordered production to be concentrated on the new car and it continued unchanged, a year after, 'any colour you like so long as it's black' said Ford. It was the greatest success story in the history of the motor car. It is often overlooked that the Model T not only made a fortune for Ford but also for many other manufacturers. The car was stark and devoid of trimmings, other than a very

Henry Ford

good tool kit. For years accessory manu-facturers were to get rich on providing 'extras' for the Model T. What is not often realized is that Ford, although not the first to introduce left-hand steering, was the first manufacturer of any con-sequence to do so. With the Model T he announced that the steering wheel had been moved to the left-hand side, the logical side for American roads. Critics argued that it would cause more accidents but left-hand drive was here to stay. The Ford Company remains one of the world's major manufacturers today and, harking back to Henry's time, has always been active in motor sport, not least in backing the World Championship Cosworth Grand Prix engine. Henry Ford was a man of great vision: he established the eight-hour working day; guaranteed a minimum wage; and brought motoring to the masses. The Ford Foundation still gives help and encouragement to scholars.

FOYT, Anthony Joseph Jnr

b. Houston, Texas, USA, 1935.

'AJ' as he is known has good claim to being the American race driver of modern times and one of the most versatile drivers in the world. A burly Texan, outspoken and tough, he began in motor sport in 1953 and seven years later became US National Champion for the first time. The following year – 1961 – he scored the first of his victories in the Indianapolis 500 and became the only man to win the 500 as National Champion and then go on to defend his title. The National Championship fell to him time and again – he chalked up yet another record after winning it five times – and so did the 500. By 1970 he had driven in 187 USAC championship events, emerging the victor forty-two times, as well as being placed on thirty-six occasions. These results also demonstrate his expert mechanical ability for he has done the major part of the engine work on his own championship cars since 1967. His all-round ability has been shown not only at

A. J. Foyt

Indianapolis but also on the dirt-tracks and in sprint and stock-cars. Moreover, he has been the victor in Europe's Le Mans 24-Hours Race and in the stock car classic, the Daytona 500.

GABELICH, Garry

b. San Pedro, California, USA, 1940.
Gabelich would be a man out of space to the record-breakers of the twenties and thirties who might not appreciate the long hair and hippy ways. Gabelich was nearly a man *in* outer space since, until 1968, he trained as an astronaut. He became the American Power Boat Association fuel-hydro champion and then drove a drag-boat at the hitherto unheard-of speed of 324 km/h (200·44 mph). At the age of 30 he drove *Blue Flame* in an attempt on Craig Breedlove's world land speed record. After 39 days of ups and downs, mostly downs, on the morning of Friday, 23 October, 1970, Gabelich took the record at a fantastic 1002 km/h (622·407 mph). Gabelich wore his lucky canary-coloured T-shirt, Levi's and a black stocking cap. Around his neck he had 28 strands of beads, a hair-clip from his girl friend, a St. Christopher medal, various Indian good-luck pieces, a Mexican peso, several key-chains and four letters which had been carried by John Cobb in his record-breaking 400 mph run. But Gaby's luck ran out soon afterwards when he received multiple injuries in a drag-racing accident.

GRÉGOIRE, Jean-Albert

b. Paris, France, 1899.
Garage owner who speedily made a name for himself driving in hill climbs and rallies. He had an inventive turn of mind and became very interested in the subject of front wheel drive then in the doldrums. In 1899, the Latil & Riancey car had front wheel drive but by 1925, the only French car of the type was the Bucciali which, although exhibited annually at the French Motor Show, was never delivered to any customers as far as is known. In the United States, Miller built front wheel drive racing cars for Indianapolis and in Britain a fwd competition Alvis appeared in 1925. Grégoire obtained backing and designed and built the Tracta car which made its racing debut at Le Mans in 1927 being one of seven finishers out of 29 starters. Grégoire and his associates designed a special enclosed constant velocity joint to deal with the steering problems encountered with front wheel drive and the Tracta joint, as it was subsequently known, was used all over the world on cars, lorries, cross country vehicles, coaches, submarines, helicopters and agricultural machines. During the war years, Jean-Albert designed the aluminium Français Grégoire from which the Dyna Panhard was derived. After the war he was associated with the production model Hotchkiss Grégoire and one of the early turbine cars, the Socéma Grégoire, in 1954.

HAWTHORN, John Michael (Mike)

b. Mexborough, W. Riding, Yorkshire, England, 1929. d. 1959.
Big, blond, bow-tied extrovert Mike Hawthorn was the type of man who brought life, colour and laughter to everything he attempted. He made his name in one magic day at Goodwood. Driving a F2 Cooper-

Bristol before a crowd of 50,000, he won the first two races he had ever competed in in a proper single-seater racing car. Then, in the main event, the Richmond Trophy, he held second place behind the burly Argentinian Froilan Gonzalez in the 4½-litre Ferrari Thinwall Special and held off all the other F1 cars. Britain had no cars with Grand Prix pretensions at the time so Hawthorn signed for the Italian Ferrari team and in one of the most thrilling races of all time snatched victory in the 1953 French Grand Prix after a wheel-to-wheel duel with Fangio in a Maserati. In 1954 he crashed in flames at Syracuse and was badly burnt about the legs. After a brief spell with Vanwall he returned to Ferrari in 1955 but was then involved, driving a works Jaguar, in the terrible Le Mans disaster when Levegh's Mercedes ploughed into the crowd. With BRM in 1956, he again returned to Ferrari and in 1958 took the World Driver's Championship. But his great friend, Peter Collins, was killed and Hawthorn retired. The following January his Jaguar saloon crashed into a tree on the Guildford by-pass and Hawthorn was killed instantly.

HEALEY, Donald Mitchell

b. Perranporth, Cornwall, England, 1898.
The man who possibly did more for the prestige of British sports cars than any other began with a small garage business in his native Cornwall. In 1930, he joined the sporting car manufacturers, Invicta, at their Cobham, Surrey, works and drove Invictas very successfully in rallies. In three successive Alpine Rallies he won the coveted Coupe des Alpes and hit the headlines with a dashing win in the 1931 Monte Carlo Rally. When Invicta went into liquidation, Healey joined the Triumph firm where he became chief designer. He

continued to compete and was third in the 1934 Monte with a Triumph Gloria. After the Second World War, Healey decided to set up on his own and evolved the Healey which soon tasted success, Count Lurani winning his class in one in the 1948 Mille Miglia and Tommy Wisdom breaking the hour class record at Montlhéry. The brilliance of Healey's 1952 design led to a deal with Austin and the Austin-Healey became a mass-production car. Healey later designed another winning car, the Jensen-Healey.

HILL, Graham Norman

b. Hampstead, London, 1929. d. 1975.
One of motor sport's greatest personalities, the moustachioed, wise-cracking Londoner was mourned all over the world

when the plane in which he was flying his team back from a Continental practice session crashed into the fog-shrouded trees near his Hertfordshire, England, home. Hill could not drive until he was in his twenties and took up racing much later than most men who become stars of the Grand Prix circus. But he soon made up for lost time and in seven seasons for BRM and five for Lotus, he won Monaco a record five times, the United States Grand Prix three times and the Dutch, German, Italian, Spanish, Mexican and South African races. For good measure he went to the States and won the Indianapolis 500 as a 'rookie' in 1966. He was World Champion in 1962, driving for BRM, and repeated the feat in 1968 with Lotus. In 1969 he crashed badly in the United States GP, breaking both legs. Instead of retiring

he overcame his disability and although never the same force in GP racing, scored a victory in the Le Mans 24-Hour Race. Later he formed his own racing team with a promising driver, Tony Brize, who, alas, died with him on that foggy night.

HUNT, James

b. Epsom, Surrey, 1947.
Son of a successful City of London businessman, he was christened 'Hunt the Shunt' in his F3 days but nevertheless went on to become World Champion in 1976. The Austrian driver and reigning champion Niki Lauda was leading the title race until the German Grand Prix when he crashed and was badly burned. Hunt's troubles were off the track. It appeared that some officials had only to see him to snap,

Graham Hill, victor in the Goodwood 100, 1962 (left), and on his victory lap at Monaco, 1969 (top) Mike Hawthorn (far left) in a Maserati

359

Sir Alec Issigonis

'Disqualified'. Despite Lauda's brave return to action six weeks later, Hunt took the title by one point through finishing third in the final race of the season, the Japanese GP, the track being awash. Both Hunt and Lauda were at one time with the British March team, the head of which, Max Mosley, gave Hunt his nickname. Hunt broke into F1 with the team privately backed by Lord Hesketh and scored his first F1 win with them. But it was with the McLaren team that he finally reached the top. The blond 'Master James' Hunt has star quality, a manner alternating between charm and aggravation and a penchant for

James Hunt

making the headlines. His following amongst the young aficionados is formidable. He makes his home at Marbella, Spain; is managed by his brother Peter; and was briefly married to the current wife of actor Richard Burton.

ISSIGONIS, Sir Alec

b. Smyrna, Turkey, 1906.
Son of a Greek who became a naturalized Briton, Sir Alexander Arnold Constantine Issigonis, CBE, is one of the most colourful automobile designers of modern times, responsible for the long-running Morris Minor, which made its bow in 1948, and what is generally regarded as the outstanding small car of all time, the transverse-engined, front-wheel drive Austin and Morris Minis which have remained in production ever since their introduction in 1959. His birthplace, Smyrna, was predominantly Greek when Alec was born and the child lived the sort of life appropriate to the grandson of a wealthy engineering

Camille Jenatzy

manufacturer. Alec's father, however, was educated in England and liked the country so much that he became naturalized before returning to Turkey to carry on the family business. When war came they were all interned and then in the Greco-Turk war which followed, they were evacuated by the Royal Navy to Malta. Alec was seventeen when, in 1923, his mother brought him from Malta to study at the Battersea Polytechnic in London. His first job was in a drawing-office working on a semi-automatic transmission. The job entailed visits to the Midlands, centre of the English car industry and he was invited to join the Humber Company. He took part in speed trials and hill climbs, built his own special and joined Morris. War work halted thoughts on car design but afterwards Issigonis began serious design studies for a small car. The Minor and the Mini followed. He was knighted in 1969.

JANO, Vittorio

b. San Giorgio Canavese, nr. Turin, Italy, 1891. d. 1965.
Italian who designed for Fiat, Alfa Romeo and Lancia, his most famous creations including the Alfa Romeo P2 and P3 Monopostos, the Lancia D50 GP cars, and the Alfa Romeo 1500, 1750, 2300 and 2900, and the Lancia Aurelia sports cars. He obtained his first job at the Rapid Works in Turin at the age of eighteen and two years later transferred to Fiat, where his ability was recognized and he was placed in the design department. He became senior draughtsman and was also concerned with the works racing teams. He was then persuaded by Enzo Ferrari to join Alfa Romeo and in a few months produced the famous P2 which, on its first appearance, with Antonio Ascari driving, won the 200-Mile Circuit of Cremona. Then, in the 1924 European Grand Prix at Lyons, Campari became the first man ever to win a Grand Prix on a make of car that was entirely new to that form of racing. The following year Jano's cars brought Alfa the World Championship. Many other successes followed but eventually in a reorganization, Jano left Alfa and joined Lancia in 1938. Although never so happy as he had been at Alfa, Jano nevertheless produced some outstanding cars. He died tragically at seventy-four – shooting himself because he was convinced he was suffering from cancer.

JENATZY, Camille

b. Brussels, Belgium, 1868. d. 1913.
A cycle racer in his youth, the bearded Jenatzy qualified as a civil engineer then went to Paris in 1897 where he set up as manufacturer of electric carriages. The following year a magazine organized a hill climb competition at Chanteloup which Jenatzy entered to gain publicity for his electric carriages. He averaged over 25·75 km/h (16 mph) and won conclusively despite the presence of a twin-engined Léon Bollée tri-car which was thought to be the fastest machine of the time. Another competition, this time from a standing start, led to a series of challenges between the Marquis de Chasseloup-Laubat and Jen-

atzy, both in electric cars, and eventually to the Belgian building the very first specialized record breaking car, *La Jamais Contente,* in English 'Never Satisfied', a verbal arrow aimed at his wife by the driver. On 12 April 1899, Jenatzy covered the kilometre in 34 seconds, the first man to exceed a speed of more than 100 kilometres per hour. His success fired Jenatzy's enthusiasm for motor racing and he became known on the circuits as 'The Red Devil'. His major triumph in this field came in 1903 when he won the Gordon Bennett Trophy, the World Championship of its time, run that year in Ireland. He had a tragic end – accidentally shot by a friend while taking part in a wild boar hunt in the Ardennes.

JENKINS, David Abbot (Ab)

b. Salt Lake City, Utah, USA, 1883. d. 1956.

Mormon Ab Jenkins emblazoned his racing car transporter with the words 'Ab Jenkins, the World's Safest Driver' and he

Ab Jenkins

backed his claim by stating that over a fifteen-year period, he had averaged 85,000 miles per year without accident. Tall, dark and handsome, Ab was preaching 'Don't drink and drive' in the twenties and thirties but his place in motoring history is secured by the many records he broke in his 'Mormon Meteor'. Between 1936 and 1951 he held records at almost every distance from the standing-start 50 kms to 10,000 kms, with the 50 miles, 100 mile and 24-hour records thrown in. These records were set on the Bonneville Salt Flats in Utah and it was because of Jenkins' pioneering that first Sir Malcolm Campbell and later other world land speed record breakers used the Flats for later attempts. These early records led also to the Flats becoming the headquarters of drag-racing. A freak of nature, the flats are in fact the bed of a large salt lake, covered in water during the winter months. In the summer under the fierce glare of the sun – 110 degrees in the shade, if any shade can be found – the water evaporates, leaving a hard and relatively flat surface.

LAMBERT, John William

b. Mechanicsburg, Ohio, USA, 1860. d. 1952.

Most history books give the Duryea brothers as builders of the first American automobile. Some give the name of Elwood Haynes. Very few mention Lambert. Yet, the evidence is strong that Lambert, a mechanical genius who invented the first automatic corn planter, was driving a gasoline-powered automobile on the main street of Ohio City, Ohio, in 1891, a year before the Duryea brothers built their first successful automobile. Lambert failed to secure customers for his car and when a friend, Elwood Haynes, asked permission to advertise the Haynes as the first American car, Lambert agreed. He stayed out of the controversy in after years as to who was first, although he later formed two car-manufacturing companies himself, the Union Automobile Company and the Buckeye Manufacturing Company. By 1909, Lambert had 1,000 employees and was producing 3,000 cars and trucks a year. The firm left the automobile business during the First World War but Lambert Incorporated, under the direction of John's grandson, still manufactures automotive parts and other industrial products. Lambert patented more than 600 inventions, most of them of an automotive nature. Amongst them was a gearless friction-drive automobile which he began manufacturing in 1900.

LANCHESTER, Frederick William

b. London, England, 1868. d. 1946.

Dr. Frederick Lanchester was far ahead of his time. To give but one example, he designed a form of disc brake decades before such things became a viable proposition as demonstrated by the Jaguar cars at Le Mans. Son of an architect and surveyor, he began his working life as a draughtsman and then went to a gas engine company near Birmingham. He rented a workshop from his employer and made his own small petrol engines with a vapourizer which was to be used on all Lanchester cars until 1914. He also invented a flame impulse starter which solved the problem of starting gas engines – up to then a procedure involving hauling on the flywheel. After a visit to the States, dabbling in aeroplanes and producing a great variety of workable inventions, Lanchester, with his brothers Frank and George, turned to motor cars. As a result, Britain's first four wheeled petrol car of wholly native design took its trial run early in 1896. Three years later, Lanchester was awarded a special Gold Medal by the Automobile Club for 'excellence of design'. In 1904, the Lanchester firm despite the undoubted excellence of their cars, went bankrupt. The company was saved but Lanchester himself was now only a paid designer. Lanchesters continued as cars of quality until the crisis of 1930–1 when they were taken over by Daimler.

LANCIA, Vincenzo

b. Fobello, Upper Valsesia, Italy, 1881. d. 1937.

Lancia's name is perpetuated in the modern World Championship-winning rally cars. Like other manufacturers he began his career as a mechanic and then a racing driver. A giant of a man, forever bellowing with laughter and with a well-developed flair for the spotlight, he was a mechanic with Ceirano when their company became F.I.A.T. in 1899. He displayed talent as a driver and in 1904 won the Coppa Florio for the marque. At the Vanderbilt Cup in 1905 he astonished the crowd by drinking

Vincenzo Lancia

a bottle of champagne before the start – but at the end of the fourth lap he was twenty minutes ahead of the field. On the eighth he pulled out of the pits right in front of Walter Christie and the American's car was wrecked. The crowd who had been cheering Lancia now wanted to lynch him. It took an hour to fix Lancia's Fiat and it cost him the race – he came in fourth. Undaunted, he was back in the States the following year to finish second in the same race. In 1906, he also won the Coppa d'Oro. Lancia founded his own firm in November, 1906, but continued to race for Fiat until 1908. Lancia cars subsequently earned a fine reputation for performance and quality.

LAUDA, Niki

b. Vienna, Austria, 1949.
Grand Prix driver Niki Lauda survived the most terrible crash in the German Grand Prix of 1976 but suffered terrible burns, the signs of which are painfully evident on his face. Nevertheless, Lauda showed courage of the highest order in returning to the tracks in very short order when many men would have retired. Son of a wealthy paper-processing plant owner, Lauda began racing in Minis then bought his way into a higher class of racing on the 'rent-a-driver' principle which has bedevilled the sport's economics in modern times. Lauda, however, turned out to have talent as well as cash and made very quick progress, being awarded the accolade of a Ferrari works contract in 1974. He nearly won the world title that year, succeeded in taking it in 1975, narrowly lost it to Hunt in 1976 and regained it in 1977, four remarkable years by any standards. At the

close of the 1977 season, Lauda announced that he would drive for Ferrari no more and went to the Brabham team instead.

LAUTENSCHLAGER, Christian

b. Magstadt, nr. Stuttgart, Germany, 1877. d. 1954.
A bull-necked daredevil with a bushy handlebar moustache, Lautenschlager is often thought to be the best racing driver of the pre-1914 era. He began work as an apprentice locksmith at the age of 14, worked in Switzerland for a time, returned to Germany to work in a bicycle factory then went back to his native Stuttgart where he became a mechanic at the works of Gottlieb Daimler. He eventually became foreman in the driving department, responsible for the inspection and running-in of new cars. He had his first race in 1906, finishing ninth in the Circuit of the Ardennes. Two years later, he won the French Grand Prix at Dieppe, his fine physical condition playing a major role since his car was a giant 120 hp Mercedes and the race was over a distance of 770 km (478 miles). Lautenschlager won by almost nine minutes from the Frenchman, Hémery, in his Benz. He did not race again until 1913. His major triumph came the following year when, in the last big race before the Great War, he was first in a 1-2-3 Mercedes success.

LAWSON, Harry J

b. London, England, 1852. d. date unknown.
History has dealt hardly with Lawson, a far-seeing entrepreneur who, alas, skated close to the realms of fraud and paid the penalty, his eventual end being wrapped in mystery. Nevertheless, he was one of the

Christian Lautenschlager

first Englishmen to see the potential of the motorcar and in 1895 formed the British Motor Syndicate. He tried to buy every patent available and then, like Selden in the States, demand a royalty from every other manufacturer. He formed the Motor Club and in 1896 organized an 'Emancipation Day' Run from London to Brighton to celebrate the repeal of the act which insisted that cars be preceded by a man on foot to give warning of their approach. One of Lawson's guests on this occasion was the great Gottlieb Daimler who sold the British manufacturing rights of his patents to Lawson. He formed the British Daimler Motor Co. and had he concentrated on that might have become a respected manufacturer. But many of his other companies were bubbles which speedily burst and even members of the Motor Club, headed by Frederick Simms, broke away to form the Automobile Club of Great Britain and Ireland (later the RAC). Like Selden, Lawson too failed to establish a monopoly and little was heard of him after 1903.

LEDWINKA, Hans

b. Klosterneuburg, nr. Vienna, Austria, 1878. d. 1967.

An Austrian who became Czechoslovakia's top designer, he worked for most of his career with the Tatra firm. He was raised by and apprenticed to an uncle who was a machinist. Thus he developed a consuming interest not only in cars but heavy trucks and steam locomotives. He brought many innovations into his designs but unlike others famed in automotive history, Ledwinka never claimed to have invented his innovations. He was especially talented in designing cars for people of modest means – 'better than the VW people's car' said Tatra supporters – but, alas, the Nazis settled the argument by invading Czechoslovakia and stopping production of Ledwinka's brain-child. Nevertheless, his work was recognized over the years by Gold Medals, Government Orders and – in 1944 – an honorary Doctorate from his native Vienna. Although he worked mainly in Czechoslovakia and, to a lesser extent, in Germany, he remained an Austrian citizen. When the Communists took over the country, Ledwinka was jailed for six years on a charge of building trucks for the German Army. He was released in 1951 but left Czechoslovakia for Germany where he resumed designing.

LELAND, Henry Martin

b. Barton, Vermont, USA, 1843. d. 1932.

A precision-engineer and machine tool designer who became involved with motorcars in late middle age. He was with Cadillac from 1902 until 1917 and became famous for the Cadillac V-8 of 1914. Later he designed the 1920 Lincoln V-8. He was not only an engineer and a designer but also a giant of the developing motor industry and known to his colleagues as 'The Grand Old Man of Detroit'. Even men like Alfred P. Sloan, of General Motors, and Henry Ford, regarded him with respect. Sloan said of Leland, 'Quality was his God.' A man of puritanical beliefs, he felt that there were only two ways to tackle a job – a right way and a wrong. It has been said that because of men like Henry Leland, the United States became the most powerful industrial nation in the world. Leland's first engineering opportunities came during the Civil War when, rejected as underage for the Army, he worked on lathes for the Springfield Armory. From there, he went via the Colt Revolver works to become a tool maker in Providence, Rhode Island, and played an important part in producing the first universal grinder. In 1890 he went into business for himself in Detroit and in 1896 began making internal combustion engines. He became adviser and engine supplier to Olds; then director and technical adviser to Cadillac and next founded the Lincoln Motor Company. Many of Leland's ideas subsequently appeared in both General Motors and Ford cars.

LEVASSOR, Emile

b. Paris, France, 1844. d. 1897.

In a brief decade, Levassor made a remarkable impact on the history of the automobile. He was in partnership with René Panhard in Paris, making woodwork machinery, when he was commissioned by Edouard Sarazin, the French licensee, to make Daimler engines. Shortly afterwards Sarazin died and his widow, to whom the Daimler licence passed, married Levassor in 1890. By 1891, Levassor had evolved the classic design with which his name is associated and the firm of Panhard et Levassor became one of the most famous in the motor industry. As a racing driver, Levassor earned undying fame by an epic drive in the 1895 Paris to Bordeaux to Paris race in which he was first home. He was thrown from his car during the Paris–Marseilles race of 1896 and died the following year although historians differ as to the precise cause of death, some saying that it was a direct result of the 1896 mishap although it is more likely that his crash was nothing to do with it. Either way, France and the motor industry lost a brilliant man.

LOEWY, Raymond

b. Paris, 1893.

Known primarily as a Studebaker designer, Loewy's revolutionary concepts in 1946–7, derided by some at the time, set new standards of car design. He was amongst the first to design cars with large luggage compartments, extended rear vision and streamlining back and front. He was in every sense a new breed of designer for his background was not in the motor industry at all but in the general field of industrial design. He was responsible for the Aga cooker, the Coldspot refrigerator and the famous train, the Pittsburgh Flyer, having established an industrial design consultancy in New York as far back as 1928. In 1934 his 421 Hupmobiles had curved windscreens, some of the first examples in the States. After the Second World War, he did the work which made him famous as a car designer. His 1953 Studebaker Commander Coupe featured backward-sloping rear pillars which in due

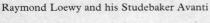

Raymond Loewy and his Studebaker Avanti

time became popular but he is best known for his Studebaker Avanti. He was also said to have advised Rootes, the British manufacturers (later part of the Chrysler empire) on the design of the 1948 Hillman Minx and Humber Hawk.

LYONS, Sir William

b. Blackpool, Lancashire, England, 1901.

Silver-haired and distinguished, there are no outward signs of his humble beginnings, although Sir William is still known as 'Bill' to his intimates. He began in a modest workshop at Blackpool before the Second World War, building a motor-cycle sidecar called the Swallow which achieved sufficient success to encourage him to go into the car business. He produced a long-bonneted racy-looking car which he called the SS. Lyons himself drove one to victory at Donington in 1938 with his director of engineering third in the same race. 'This is the first recorded instance of Lyons having an affair with a Swallow and producing a Jaguar,' said one motoring correspondent when the SS gave way to the Jaguar after the war. The new range of cars became firmly established with successes at Le Mans where they won in 1951, 3, 5, 6 and 7, the last three years proving a practical demonstration of disc brakes. Jaguar Cars later became part of the giant British Leyland organization. Sir William has remained one of the industry's leading statesmen.

MAKINEN, Timo

b. Helsinki, Finland, 1938.

'The Flying Finn' is one of the few rally drivers in the world to catch the public imagination in the same way as the stars of the Grand Prix racing circuits. His father operates a newspaper transport fleet and Timo learned to drive on one of his father's

Timo Makinen

trucks. Even then he was a fast driver, as a long list of summonses for speeding prove. He began ice racing and rallying, worked for the British Motor Corporation in Helsinki and was recruited by the parent company for their rally team in 1962. Driving Mini Cooper and Healey 3000 only class

wins came his way at first but in 1964 with the Cooper S he won the Tulip Rally outright. The following year he took the Monte Carlo Rally with what has been described as the most incredible display of driving in adverse conditions ever seen. He also won the Thousand Lakes in his native Finland and went on to win it three years in succession. Year after year he was among the leaders in the RAC Rally but misfortune dogged him and it was not until BMC withdrew from rallying and Mäkinen signed for the Ford team that he finally gained a victory in the British international event which was not only deserved but also extremely popular. Later he joined the Fiat team. Mäkinen is also an accomplished powerboat racer, amongst his victories being the 1969 Round Britain Race.

MARCUS, Siegfried

b. Malchin, Mecklenburg, Germany, 1831. d. 1899.

Claimed by Austria to be 'Inventor of the Automobile', he designed and built an internal combustion engine, utilizing benzine as fuel. He originally intended it to power an airship but decided on a horseless carriage instead and installed the engine in a four wheeled handcart which had its first run at Schmelz Cemetery in 1865. The vehicle ran for only a couple of hundred yards before expiring. He produced a modified design in 1868 but his attention was distracted by many other inventions including a safety valve for steam engines and a quickly solidifying compound for filling teeth – dentistry being another of his many interests. His automobile was put on show at the Vienna Exhibition of 1873 although still to make a successful run. In 1875, his machine is claimed to have covered an eight mile route on the outskirts of Vienna. It is believed that Marcus automobiles were produced, one of which is on display at the Vienna Technical Museum, and is occasionally driven by the curator.

MARMON, Howard

b. Richmond, Indiana, USA, 1876. d. 1943.

A young man with a flair for engineering, Marmon built his first car around 1902 and two years later set up on his own as a manufacturer. Like so many automotive pioneers, his business acumen did not match his genius in design and he turned to racing to publicize his cars. Marmons did well on the race tracks and among their successes was the Cobe Trophy at Indianapolis in 1910, Ray Harroun being the driver, and the Kane County Trophy at the Elgin Road Races the same year. The turning-point came, however, in 1911 when a Marmon Wasp, driven by Harroun, won the first 500-Mile Race at Indianapolis in six hours and forty-two minutes. Eighty-thousand people watched the victory of the narrow-bodied, pointed-tail machine which, because it did not have room for a riding-mechanic, carried a rear-view mirror, the first known use of what was to become standard equipment on all cars. Marmon would also have had second place but Dawson's car suffered radiator

damage on the last lap. Marmon carried on designing road cars which like their racing counterparts were usually ahead of their time (one Marmon speed record survived for twenty years) but in the twenties he suffered the troubles of most United States manufacturers of the time. Thomas J. Little left Lincoln Cars to head a Marmon revival in 1927 but the firm finally expired in 1933.

MAYS, Raymond

b. Bourne, Lincolnshire, England, 1899.

A talented, tall and gentlemanly British driver who, despite hundreds of wins in hill climbs and on the racing circuits of

Brooklands and Crystal Palace, is likely to be best remembered as the man who tried to keep the British flag flying in motor racing with (before the Second World War) the ERA (English Racing Automobile) and after, the BRM (British Racing Motor). In many ways he was more successful with the ERA. Although this little car could not compete against the Grand Prix giants of the time, it was wonderfully successful in international voiturette or light-car racing and drivers such as 'B. Bira', Bob Gerard, Humphrey Cook and Mays himself performed valiantly. After the war, Mays launched the BRM project and endeavoured to get national support for it. He persevered against all odds but it was to be a long time before the breakthrough he had worked so hard for came along and a BRM took the chequered flag in a Grand Prix race. Years later, the BRM team, by then no longer under the direction of Raymond Mays, dropped to the back of the grids and lost what lustre Mays and his colleagues had given the name. Through much of his career, Mays worked in close association with two friends, both clever designers, Amherst Villiers and Peter Berthon.

McLAREN, Bruce

b. Auckland, New Zealand, 1937. d. 1970.

A small, quiet but friendly man who became a first class racing driver and a manufacturer of renown. He came to Europe in 1958 under the New Zealand 'Driver to Europe' scheme and signed for Cooper. He became a Grand Prix regular and won the United States, Argentine, Monaco and Rheims GPs. In 1966, he shared the wheel of the winning Ford at Le Mans with

Raymond Mays in a Talbot

fellow New Zealander, Chris Amon, and the same year built the first McLaren F1 car. In 1968, McLaren won the Race of Champions and the Belgian Grand Prix and from 1967 to 1970, Group Seven McLarens won the Can-Am series four times in a row, Bruce himself taking the title in 1967 and 1969. His Can-Am achievements won him the coveted Segrave Trophy but before it could be presented to him he was killed testing a Can-Am McLaren at Goodwood. Under the direction of Teddy Mayer, the McLaren team continued active after its founder's death and today has many Grand Prix and other successes to its credit.

MILLER, Harry Armenius

b. Menomonie, Wisconsin, USA, 1875. d. 1943.

Miller was America's most successful racing-car designer between the wars. Engines based upon his designs were still being used at Indianapolis in the 1970s.

Bruce McLaren

Harry Miller

Miller came from a poor background and lacked formal education. As it was, he made several fortunes and lost them. A small man, dark-haired, blue eyes and ruddy complexion with a Paul Whiteman moustache, he was typical of the Roaring Twenties in his light grey suits and expensive Fedoras. His associate, Fred Offenhauser, also became a name famous in American racing history, the Offy engines, on which both men had worked, being manufactured long after Miller had gone bankrupt in 1932. Miller's last years were clouded ones. He designed and built

many cars but none retrieved his fortunes. He ended his days disfigured by cancer of the face, running a small machine-shop in Detroit. The only memorial to Harry Miller was in the illustrious records of the great racing drivers who rode to victory in his cars or in cars powered by his engines. There was Jimmy Murphy, whose Miller-engined Duesenberg won the 500 first time out; Dave Lewis and Benny Hill, who finished second in the 500 when the front-wheel drive Miller made its first appearance at Indianapolis; Leon Duray, who set Indianapolis lap records and a closed-course world record; Frank Lockhart, who used two Miller power plants in his record-breaking Stutz Black Hawk; and a legion more.

MITCHELL, William L (Bill)

b. Cleveland, Ohio, USA, 1912.

Balding, jovial Bill Mitchell retired from General Motors in the 1970s. For almost twenty years he had been head of styling with the world's biggest motor corporation and regarded as an outstanding man in his field. He left behind him at GM a coupé called the Phantom, a car designed in his final months with the firm and left behind as reminder to design staff of what can be accomplished in the automotive world. Mitchell set out in life as an art student in New York in the thirties and throughout his career never made a secret of his great love for the classic cars of the twenties and thirties. He was undoubtedly also influenced at times by some of the great French designers. As a stylist he probably had more influence on the shape of cars in the sixties than any other man in the world. His critics sometimes accused him of over-decorating his production cars but it seems fairly certain that posterity will regard Bill Mitchell as one of the greats in automobile design and styling. Certainly there is nothing fussy about the beautiful styling model, the Panther, which he left behind him at General Motors.

MORRIS, William (Lord Nuffield)

b. Oxford, England, 1877. d. 1963.
Forced by his father's illness to give up ideas of being a surgeon, Morris left school at 15 and set up with a capital of £4 as a bicycle repairer in the back room of his family's home in Oxford High Street. He moved on to repairing motor-cycles and cars and opened a garage at Cowley, near Oxford. Here he designed and built his first car, the famous Bullnose Morris. A shrewd and determined business-man he swiftly became one of Britain's leading manufacturers and in 1934, became the first motor manufacturer to be raised to the peerage. In 1952 his company merged with the Austin Motor Company to form the British Motor Corporation. Morris himself led a quiet life and was something of a hypochondriac. It was his obsession with illness that led him to become one of medicine's biggest benefactors and between 1926 and his death in 1963, he gave away more than £30 million to charities, many of them for the cause of medical research. The centenary of his birth was celebrated in Oxford in 1977 and an engraved glass panel was unveiled at the entrance to Morris's original bicycle shop.

MOSS, Stirling

b. London, England, 1929.
It was inevitable that Stirling Moss would become a driver of fast cars. His father, Alfred, a London dentist, was one of the few British drivers to race at Indianapolis between the wars; and his mother, Aileen, was a fine driver and rally competitor. Moss and his sister, Pat, were brought up on sport. Both were keen horse-riders and Pat made the British show-jumping team. Stirling was also a keen boxer. When he took up motor racing, the sport in Britain was just recovering from the Second World War and it was in little 500 cc machines that Moss first attracted attention. He graduated to light cars, or voiturettes as they used to be known, with the HWM team and then became a name in Grand Prix racing. Stirling's preference for British cars often meant that he was handicapped since at the time, British manufacturers had still to attain their later dominance of the sport. Yet Moss was so good that the German Mercedes team finally tempted him to join them. His biggest successes came, however, as leader of the Vanwall team, the team which really made British Grand Prix cars a force to be reckoned with. Moss never won the World Championship – being contemporary with the great Juan Manuel Fangio – but he is undoubtedly the greatest driver not to do

Stirling Moss after winning the Italian Grand Prix, 1957

so. He was four times runner up, from 1955 to 1958. He was immensely skilled and possessed great determination. But his career was ended prematurely by a serious crash at Goodwood in 1962.

NAZZARO, Felice

b. Italy, 1881. d. 1940.
Nazzaro was an overnight sensation when, in 1907, driving for Fiat, he won the Targa Florio in Sicily; the Kaiserpreis in Germany; and the major race of the time, the French Grand Prix. The following year he won the Coppa Florio in Bologna for Fiat but in 1911 left the firm to manufacture a car under his own name with which he won the Targa Florio in 1913 and the Coppa Florio in 1914. After the war, Nazzaro returned to Fiat and, although over forty, won the 1922 French Grand Prix at Strasbourg. A broken oil-pipe on the last lap cost him the European Grand Prix and he drove his last Grand Prix in 1924 when his car failed him. Unlike so many stars of the race circuits, Nazzaro survived his many tussles on the track and remained with the Fiat firm almost up to the time of his death in 1940. He is still regarded as one of the finest drivers ever, who would have been great in any age.

NEUBAUER, Alfred

b. Northern Bohemia, Austro-Hungary, 1891.

After serving in the Imperial Austro-Hungarian Army, Neubauer became a test and race-driver, first for Austro-Daimler and then for Mercedes. He had some modest successes but would certainly not have earned a niche in motor racing's hall of fame had it not been that in 1926 he gave up driving to become team manager, a post he was to hold until 1955. He brought a new approach to the art of running a professional motor-racing team and his burly figure, complete with a necklace of stop-watches, and sergeant-major bark, became a familiar sight on the race circuits of the world. From 1934 to 1939, the Mercedes team won 34 Grands Prix; in 1954–55, Mercedes were once again all-conquering in Grand Prix racing and also won the World Sports Car Championship. The drivers he discovered and encouraged are legion: Hermann Lang, Dick Seaman, Juan Manuel Fangio, Stirling Moss, Peter Collins, and many more. When Neubauer was around there was only one boss. Mercedes withdrew from racing after 1955 and Neubauer went into retirement, a man who was a legend in his lifetime.

NORDHOFF, Heinz

b. Hildesheim, Germany, 1899. d. 1968.

Son of a bank clerk, Nordhoff found himself at the end of the Second World War in 1945 a homeless, jobless refugee. The future looked bleak for a middle aged engineer, wounded in the first war and ruined in the second. But the British were looking for a man to rebuild the Volkswagen factories and in the American-trained Nordhoff, an Opel executive before the war and head of that company's Brandenburg lorry factory during hostilities, the British thought they had the man. Brandenburg had been the largest lorry factory in Europe, producing four thousand units per month and Volkswagen needed a man who could handle that sort of production problem. Nordhoff took over in 1948 and the measure of his success lies in the giant factory at Wolfsburg, the other major German plants in Kassel, Hanover, Brunswick and Emden and VW factories all over the world. Under his direction, 'The Beetle', Hitler's original People's Car, became the largest-selling single motor car in the world, with an estimated quarter of a million persons earning their living directly, or indirectly, from Volkswagen. The Nordhoff family commitment was total: one of his daughters became a VW public relations executive in the United States; the other married a grandson of the VW designer, Ferdinand Porsche.

Heinz Nordhoff and VW employees

sers, his slight, short figure dominated the circuits in the twenties and thirties. Only the brawny, hairy arms, the lean, tanned face and outjutting jaw gave a clue that this was the man whom many regarded as the Devil himself once behind a wheel. Like many other racers, he began as a motor-cyclist and won more than 300 races in Italy and abroad. He was 35 before he began motor racing in earnest. That year of 1927 he was fifth in the Mille Miglia and won the Rome Royal Prix. He never looked back. In 1930 he won the Mille Miglia, the first man to do so at a speed of more than 100 kph (62 mph), and took it again in 1933. His second victory reputedly came after he drove many miles in darkness without headlights to persuade the leader, Achille Varzi, that there was no car immediately behind him. In 1948, at the age of 56, Nuvolari nearly won the Mille Miglia again. Between 1934 and 1936, the Man-

tuan won 14 GPs and was placed in nine, his nearest rival, Caracciola, winning nine and being placed in four. Tazio's greatest victory was in the German Grand Prix of 1935 when his Alfa was victorious against the bigger and faster Mercedes and Auto-Unions. In 1936, he went to the United States and won the Vanderbilt Cup in a field which included Indianapolis 'greats' Wilbur Shaw and Mauri Rose. Years of exhaust fumes finally got to him; he won his last race in 1950; had an operation in 1951; and died two years later.

OLDFIELD, Berna Eli (Barney)

b. Wauseon, Ohio, USA, 1877. d. 1946.

The ebullient, cigar-smoking Oldfield, peaked cap reversed on his head, goggles across his brow, was the idol of early American motor-racing crowds. He was one of the early drivers to use Daytona Beach for record attempts and he barnstormed his way around America, creating news and sensations everywhere he went. Some of the cars that Oldfield drove in his career were as sensational as their pilot. The giant Blitzen-Benz was always a centre of attraction. At the Sheepshead Bay and Brighton Beach tracks, both in Brooklyn, New York, and the Elgin Road

Neubauer, right, with the Mercedes team, 1955

Tazio Nuvolari, 1932

NUVOLARI, Tazio Giorgio

b. Castel d'Ario, Mantua, Italy, 1892. d. 1953.

'The Flying Mantuan' or 'Il Maestro' as he later became known was arguably the world's greatest racing driver. Dressed in yellow turtle-neck sweater and blue trou-

design. Boardroom differences led to Olds leaving the Oldsmobile Company but undeterred he set up another, this time making Reo cars, the name being derived from his own initials. He thus enjoyed the distinction of having two cars in production named for him. The Reo firm continued until 1936 and Olds himself, much respected for his religious work and philanthropic deeds, lived on to the ripe old age of eighty-six. Olds has another claim to fame: his house in Lansing, Michigan, is believed to be one of the first in the world to have a garage attached. Certainly pictures exist of the garage (with an experimental Oldsmobile standing in front) as early as 1898.

Volkswagen. Son of a tinsmith, Porsche trained as an electrical engineer and the first car he built was a petrol-electric carriage, the System Lohner-Porsche. With a racing version of this machine, Porsche broke many hill-climb records. Five years later he was Managing Director of Austro-Daimler. The designs and inventions which poured from his fertile brain, the brilliant cars which were built: all this would – and has – filled a book. Alas, at the end of the Second World War, Porsche, nearing seventy, was arrested by the Allies and held in custody for two years. After his release, he lived to see his seventy-fifth birthday celebrated by a rally to the works by Porsche owners from all over the

Oldfield (above), Porsche (right)

Races in Chicago, the crowds flocked to see Oldfield and his exciting machines. 'He is always a great attraction at any race', said one contemporary newspaper account. On the board tracks of Sheepshead, Ralph DePalma beat Oldfield in a match race. Oldfield was driving the 'Golden Submarine', a pioneer aerodynamic coupé, created by that engineering genius, Harry Miller. DePalma had the Indian sign on Barney. In the 1914 Vanderbilt Cup, DePalma signalled his pits for a tyre change. Oldfield fell for it and pulled in to change *his* tyres. DePalma did not stop but roared on to win the race. That year the French dominated Indianapolis but Oldfield finished fifth in a Stutz, the first American car across the line. Barney's accolade was a Broadway musical, 'The Vanderbilt Cup', in which he appeared. Nevertheless, his name will always be associated with Henry Ford's 999 in which he won the Manufacturers Cup at Grosse Point in his first race. 'Ford and his 999 made me – and I made them.'

OLDS, Ransom Eli

b. Geneva, Ohio, USA, 1864. d. 1950.
Olds experimented with both electric and steam vehicles (he built a steam tri-car in 1893) before deciding that there was more potential in gasoline-powered machines. In 1901 he began series production, not the first American manufacturer to do so, but for a time, the largest. His Curved Dash Oldsmobile became so famous that it was the subject of a song hit of the day, 'In My Merry Oldsmobile'. It was easy to drive, had good ground clearance and a very flexible engine (made first by the Dodge Brothers and later by Leland and Faulconer). Thus it was a machine very suitable to the rough dirt roads which abounded in USA at the time. To meet the demand, Olds had to introduce a form of mass production and smaller manufacturers all over America copied his basic

PORSCHE, Ferdinand

b. Maffersdorf, Bohemia, Austro-Hungary, 1875. d. 1951.
Described by some as the most versatile automobile engineer in history, Porsche was designer for Steyr, Austro-Daimler, Daimler-Benz (Mercedes S-type), Auto Union (GP racing car), Volkswagen, Cisitalia (GP racing car) and Porsche, as well as of successful aero-engines in both world wars, not to mention the Tiger tank of World War II. A tough, outspoken, uncompromising man, he was also a top rally driver of his day. Yet, despite the fact that the cars which bear his name still flourish today he is probably remembered by most people because of his association with the

world. Shortly afterwards, Porsche suffered a stroke and died. With his son, Ferry, behind them Porsche cars later enjoyed success in competitions, starting with a class win at Le Mans in 1953.

RAILTON, Reid Anthony

b. Alderley Edge, Cheshire, England, 1895. d. 1977.
Railton was an outstanding designer in the 30s, his major achievement being the Railton Special in which John Cobb became the first man to travel at more than 400 mph (643·6 km/h) on land. An engineer, trained at Manchester University, Railton became an expert in streamlining and advised on the design of the various Blue-

birds in which Sir Malcolm Campbell broke the World Land Speed Record five times between 1931 and 1935. Railton passenger cars were also marketed from 1933 to 1939. But record breakers seem to have been Railton's first love. He was the brains behind the MG Special in which Captain Goldie Gardner broke many small car records while the car he designed for Cobb was described at the time as 'the strangest piece of machinery ever constructed for human speed.' It had a detachable aluminium skin which lifted off for Cobb to reach his seat and which enclosed the S-shaped girder which did duty as a chassis, the two aero engines and the wheels. In the Railton, Cobb took the record in 1938 and again in 1939 and came back in 1947 to travel at more than 400 mph in one direction. By that time Railton had long been resident in the United States. He died at Berkeley, California.

RENAULT

FERNAND, b. Paris, France, 1865. d. 1909.
MARCEL, b. Paris, France, 1872. d. 1903.
LOUIS, b. Paris, France, 1877. d. 1944.
The French firm of Renault has been a great name almost throughout the entire story of motoring. Louis built his first car in the garden shed of the family home at Billancourt, near Paris, and in 1899 Fernand and Marcel joined forces with him to set up Renault Frères. Between 1899 and 1903, Marcel and Louis were outstanding racing drivers, Louis scoring seven major victories in three years. After the Paris–Vienna Race of 1902, Marcel did not race again until the ill-fated Paris–Madrid. It was reported that he was reluctant to start and he may have had a premonition because he was killed in what became notorious as 'The Race of Death'. Louis, declared winner of the light car category, never raced again. The Renault firm became one of the world's major manufacturers and remains so today, although now under the control of the French Government. Tragedy stalked the Renault family to the last. During the German occupation of France during the Second World War many Frenchmen fell out with each other and there were accusations and counter-accusations. When the war ended Louis Renault was imprisoned, maltreated and died in hospital.

RICKENBACKER, Captain E. V.

b. Columbus, Ohio, USA, 1890. d. 1973.
Good-looking Eddie Rickenbacker was a star of the American race circuits when the United States entered the First World War on the side of the Allies. At Indianapolis in 1914, Rickenbacker drove a

Eddie Rickenbacker

Duesenberg into tenth place in a race in which the first four places were scooped by the French. Two years later, Rickenbacker had a comfortable lead when the steering knuckle of his Maxwell broke. He took over a team-mate's car and still managed to finish sixth. Described as 'a competitive stern man, ambitious and proud, a hard winner and a poor loser', Rickenbacker was just the sort of man the American flying corps needed. He survived the war a hero and America's top air ace. He went back into motoring, had a brief flurry at trying to market a car of his own make and became President of the Indianapolis Speedway Corporation. He once said: 'Approximately seventy per cent of all the mechanical improvements that went into the private automobile were originated on the Indianapolis Speedway, or at least perfected there.' The last part of his statement is more correct than the first – the rear-view mirror was certainly brought to public attention at Indianapolis but developments like balloon tyres, four-wheel brakes, the straight-eight engine and so on, came from Europe in the first place. Prior to World War II he held senior positions with airline companies.

RINDT, Karl Jochen

b. Mainz, Germany, 1942. d. 1970.
Born in Germany of Austrian and German parentage, Rindt was brought up in Austria by grandparents after his father and mother had been killed in an air raid. An idol of the crowds, Rindt had an all too short but glorious period as one of the world's greatest racing drivers. An unknown when he burst upon the racing world in 1964 by winning at Crystal Palace, England, in a privately entered F2 Brabham, Rindt was soon signed to a three year contract by the Cooper team. Cooper's fortunes were waning and when his contract expired, Rindt had a season with Brabham. His fortunes changed in 1969 when he joined Lotus and gained his first F1 success in the United States GP. It opened the flood gate. In 1970 he racked up five more victories – Monaco, Dutch, British, French and German – but was killed during practice for the Italian GP. His lead for the title was so unassailable

that the sport's rulers declared him the first posthumous World Champion. The young Austro-German also had a win at Le Mans to his credit (in partnership with the American driver Masten Gregory).

ROBERTSON, George

b. USA, 1884. d. 1955.

Known as 'Big George', Robertson was the first American driver to defeat the top European makes in an international event driving an American car. He made his big time racing debut in a Christie but it was not until 1908 that the burly ace really hit the headlines. In that year, driving a Simplex with Lescault, he won the 24 Hour Race at New York's Coney Island; won the 195 mile Founders Day Cup at the Fairmount Park Course in Philadelphia in a Locomobile; and climaxed it with victory in the Vanderbilt Cup, again driving a Locomobile, when he defeated an assortment of Renaults, Mercedes, Isotta Fraschini, Methesons and Chadwicks. The following year was almost a repeat. Driving a Simplex with Al Poole he won the 24 Hour Brighton Beach Race and solo took Simplex cars to victory in the Lowell Road Race and the Second Founders Day Cup. In 1910 he set several speed records at Daytona Beach but was giving a reporter a run before the Vanderbilt Cup when the reporter panicked, grabbed the steering wheel and the car crashed. Robertson was badly injured and never raced again but he stayed in motor sport. In 1921 he managed the Duesenberg team which won the French Grand Prix and in 1936 became manager of the new Roosevelt Speedway. A year before his death he drove his Vanderbilt winner 'Old Number 16' in a run to celebrate the fiftieth anniversary of the Vanderbilt Cup.

ROLLS, Hon. Charles Stewart

b. Hendre, Monmouthshire, England, 1877. d. 1910.

C. S. Rolls, third son of the First Baron Llangattock, was a cyclist, an automobile racer and a free balloonist. He bought his first car, a Peugeot, in 1894 and put up the best performance in the 1900 Thousand Miles Trial, the event which first brought motoring to prominence before the British public. In partnership with Claude Johnson, Secretary of the Automobile Club of Great Britain and Ireland (later the RAC), he set up an agency in London selling Belgian Minerva and French Panhard et Levassor cars. Royce was contemptuous of their wares, demonstrated his own car – and made two converts. Rolls and Royce signed their first agreement on 23 December, 1904. The next few years were heady ones for Rolls and his colleagues. In 1906 he was first in the Tourist Trophy, broke the record at New York's Empire City track and set a road record from London to Monte Carlo. The famed 'Silver Ghost' ran from London to Edinburgh and back, locked in third gear, and was then run day and night for a further 15,000 miles. In 1910, the year Royce collapsed from overwork, Rolls was killed flying his own Wright aeroplane and it was left to Claude Johnson to carry the Rolls-Royce burden.

C. S. Rolls (above), Rosemeyer (above right)

ROSEMEYER, Bernd

b. Lingen, Lower Saxony, Germany, 1910. d. 1938.

Three short, dazzling seasons were enough to make fair-haired Rosemeyer a motor racing legend. A talented motorcyclist he was given a trial by Auto Union and handled the revolutionary 16-cylinder giants so well that he was signed on the spot. He became Number Three to Hans Stuck and Achille Varzi and with a 'no holds barred' blistering style rapidly became an idol of the crowds. In 1935, he won the Czech GP; in 1936, the German, Italian and Swiss Grands Prix plus the Coppa Acerbo and the Eifelrennen. In 1937, he took the Eifelrennen and Coppa Acerbo again, the Vanderbilt Cup and the Donington Grand Prix. On 28 January, 1938, he was trying to beat Class Speed Records on the Frankfurt-Darmstadt Autobahn. A strong wind was blowing. It caught the Auto-Union, flung it into a bridge abutment. They found Rosemeyer unmarked, but dead. A simple stone marks the place and his widow, famous airwoman Elly Beinhorn, his son Bernd and many others long attended an annual memorial service.

ROSIER, Louis

b. Puy de Dôme district, Auvergne, France, 1905. d. 1956.

Garage-owner Rosier raced first on motorcycles and then took part in hill-climbs but the Second World War broke out before he could make a mark in motor racing. Amazingly, after the war and at the age of 42, he began a career which for a few years made him one of Europe's top drivers and he did it by sustained consistency rather than high-speed heroics. Piloting the rugged and reliable 4½-litre Lago-Talbot he finished in the first four in five major Grands Prix in 1948, having won the Albi Grand Prix in 1947 in a 4½-litre Talbot. In 1949, he scored a great victory in the Belgian Grand Prix at Spa and became Champion of France, a title he was to win four years in succession. Subsequently he won the Dutch GP, the Albi GP (for the second time) and in 1950, with his son Jean-Louis acting as relief for only two laps, the 24 Hours of Le Mans. He took the Albi GP again in 1952 and 1953, this time driving a Ferrari; and his last major success came in 1956 when with Jean Behra he won the Paris 1,000 Kilometres Race at Montlhéry. His first crash was his last one. In October that year, again in pouring rain at Montlhéry, Rosier's Ferrari spun, hit a bank and overturned, Rosier suffering head injuries. He died three weeks later, aged 51, and was posthumously awarded the French Order of the Nation in recognition of his motor racing achievements.

ROYCE, Sir Henry

b. nr. Peterborough, England, 1863. d. 1933.

Frederick Henry Royce was the son of a miller but he became obsessed with engineering. In 1903 he built a two-cylinder car and followed up with a three-cylinder and then a four. In 1904, he met Charles Stewart Rolls and so Rolls-Royce, probably the most famous name in motoring, came into being. Royce was a strange man in many ways and lived only for his work. He begrudged the time it took to have meals and was baffled by any employee who was not prepared to work day and night and through the week-end. In 1910

Sir Henry Royce

he collapsed, perhaps not surprisingly, from overwork and never again visited the Rolls-Royce factories. Instead, he directed operations by mail from his house near Le Canadel in France and senior men would be summoned across the Channel when necessary. He also had a home at West Wittering, Sussex, England. Royce's memorial is in the reputation his cars earned for quality of workmanship and reliability. He once said, 'It is impossible for us to make a bad car. The doorman wouldn't let it go out.'

SEAMAN, Richard

b. nr. Chichester, Sussex, 1913. d. 1939.

Son of very wealthy parents, Richard Seaman took part in reliability trials and hillclimbs with a Riley even before going to Cambridge University. He continued with motor sport at Cambridge, where he met the American millionaire, Whitney Straight, who was also an enthusiast. Seaman then bought a Bugatti which he raced at Brooklands and Donington. Straight decided there was a future in professional motor racing and Seaman followed him. Driving an MG he won the Prix de Berne, was fifth in the Czech GP and second in the Nuffield Trophy at Donington. He then borrowed a works MG and flew to Africa to take part in the East London GP. Straight won in a Maserati with Seaman fifth. His mother then bought him one of the new 1½-litre ERAs with which he set up his own team. For 1936, he acquired an outdated Delage from Lord Howe and rebuilt it. He won five races with the old car and added the British Empire Trophy in a

borrowed Maserati for good measure. An invitation to try out with the Mercedes Grand Prix team followed and Seaman seized his chance. He did well from the beginning with his best performance in 1937 reserved for the USA where he was second in the Vanderbilt Cup. He married a German girl – against his mother's wishes – and in 1938, as a fully-fledged member of the Mercedes team, won the German Grand Prix. He was also second in the Swiss GP and third in the Donington GP. In 1939, he was leading the Belgian Grand Prix when he crashed into a tree, the car caught fire and Seaman died from his injuries. Yet again, a career full of promise had been tragically ended.

SEGRAVE, Sir Henry O'Neal de Hane

b. Baltimore, USA, 1896. d. 1930.

Segrave, son of an Irish-domiciled father and an American mother, left Eton to become an infantry officer when the Great War broke out. Later he joined the Royal Flying Corps, was shot down and invalided out with several silver plates in his foot. Driving for Sunbeam, he became the first and only British driver to win an international Grand Prix between the wars, driving a British car. He won the French Grand Prix in 1923 and the Spanish in 1924. In 1927, having won 31 races out of 49, he devoted his time to speed records, having enjoyed a brief taste of triumph the previous year when with a V-12 4-litre Sunbeam he had held – for six weeks – the World Land Speed Record. In March, 1927, at Daytona Beach, Florida, again in a Sunbeam, he took the record at 327·75 km/h (203·70 mph). Two years later he regained the record at a speed of 372·26 km/h (231·36 mph) in a Napier-Lion-

engined *Golden Arrow* and ten days later, in a Napier-engined racing boat, *Miss England*, he beat Gar Wood's *Miss America V* for the Fischer Cup at Biscayne, Miami. He was knighted and went on from success to success. Then he built a new boat, *Miss England II* to attack the World Water Speed Record. He took the record at 158·90 km/h (98·76 mph) but on a third run the boat hit an obstruction and sank. Segrave died 2½ hours after being taken from the water.

SELDEN, George Baldwin

b. Clarkson, N.Y., USA, 1846. d. 1932.

Selden was a shrewd lawyer who in 1877 applied for a patent for a carriage driven by a two-stroke gas engine. He could not see a good commercial opening for the machine and delayed the final grant of the patent until 1896, some months after Charles Duryea had been granted a patent for his automobile. In 1899, Selden sold manufacturing rights in his patent to a financial syndicate and efforts were made, successful in many cases, to extract royalties from manufacturers for using the Selden patent. Many legal battles followed and due to the perseverance of Henry Ford and his company, Selden's claimed 'invention' of the automobile was discredited in 1911. During the litigation, a car was built in accordance with the Selden specification with the date '1877' painted on the side. Put to a practical test, it managed to struggle along for about 450 metres (1400 feet) before expiring. The Court was not impressed. The verdict was handed down that Selden had 'not made a basic contribution' to the invention and manufacture of the automobile. The controversy has been raised at intervals ever since.

Sir Henry Segrave in a Talbot, 1924

SHAW, Wilbur

b. Shelbyville, Indiana, USA, 1903. d. 1954.

One of the greatest American drivers, Shaw was also the man who saved Indianapolis from sharing the fate of Brooklands after the Second World War and for the last nine years of his life, until his death in an aeroplane crash, he was President and General Manager of the Speedway. As a driver he three times won the Indianapolis 500 and was the first to win in successive years. Child of divorced parents and a drop-out from school, Shaw worked for Stutz and then Imperial Motors before breaking into racing on half-mile dirt tracks. Several failures at Indianapolis, the loss of his wife in childbirth and suspension by the American Automobile Association seemed to have finished Shaw almost before he had begun. But a new romance rekindled ambition and he came back to win six of the first seven 100-mile dirt-track events for which he was eligible. He crashed over the wall at Indianapolis in 1931 – a dramatic scene subsequently featured in many movies – but was unhurt. He was a fatalist and shrugged off such happenings. Second in the 500 in 1933 and again in 1935, he finally scored the first of his three triumphs in 1937 – beating Ralph Hepburn by 2·16 seconds. After the Second World War, Indianapolis was neglected and derelict. Shaw launched a one-man crusade to save the track and found financial support from a young, aggressive and civic-minded industrialist named Tony Hulman. American and world motor racing owes them both a debt. Hulman died in October, 1977.

STEWART, John Young (Jackie)

b. Dumbuck, Dumbarton, Scotland, 1939.

Younger brother of a top sports-car racer and himself a champion clay pigeon shooter, Jackie Stewart, quick-talking extrovert with a more than agile mind, was destined to be a world champion from the day he first sat behind the wheel of a single-seater. And having achieved the pinnacle of

Jackie Stewart and team-mate François Cevert after finishing first and second in the Belgian Grand Prix, 1973

his profession, he quit the sport and turned his attention with equal success to being consultant and public relations man for a variety of tyre, oil and other firms, jetting around the world with a briefcase just as he had done with a racing car. 'Discovered' by Surrey timber merchant, Ken Tyrrell, Stewart held an overwhelming margin of victory in the world championship of 1969 and completed a hat-trick of successes in 1971 and 1973 before hanging up his helmet to concentrate on his business interests. At Spa, in Belgium, on 12 June, 1966,

it nearly all came to an end. The race had started in the dry but four miles away on the other side of the circuit, the track was awash. Car after car went off and it was Graham Hill who found Stewart, half-conscious, trapped in his car which had hit a post sideways, fracturing the fuel tank and soaking the driver with petrol. Stewart survived to become three times champion and one of the sport's greatest ambassadors.

THOMAS, John Godfrey Parry

b. Wrexham, Wales, 1887. d. 1927.

Thomas was the idol of the crowds at Britain's Brooklands race track in the twenties but he was more than a magnificent driver – he was a brilliant designer and technician and a first-class engineer. Before the Great War he designed an electrically-driven airship, an armoured road-train, petrol-electric trams and trains, rail cars and electric transmissions. During the war he designed aero engines for Leylands and afterwards designed and produced the Leyland Eight Touring Car, intended for the luxury market. His racing career began in 1922 and after many victories, Parry Thomas tackled the world land speed record in a 27-litre Liberty aero-engined, chain-driven Higham Special, *Babs*. He became the world record holder in April, 1926, with a speed of 275·17 km/h (171·02 mph) on Pendine Sands. Campbell then broke Thomas's record and on March 3rd, 1927, the Welshman attempted to regain the honour. After two fast runs he was told the timing appara-

Parry Thomas

tus had failed. On a third run, travelling at more than 270 km/h, the offside driving-chain broke, flailed into the cockpit and killed the driver. *Babs* was buried in the sands but has since been dug up and restored to running order.

VANDERBILT, William Kissam Jnr

b. Staten Island, USA, 1880. d. 1944
Dark, moustachioed and good looking, Vanderbilt was one of the wealthiest men on earth. Having travelled widely through Europe he recognized the major role the automobile was to play. He also realized that France and Germany were far ahead of the United States in car design and reliability. Road racing, he felt, could bring a great many benefits to the American automobile industry and so he donated the Vanderbilt Cup. One of the rules was that the race be open to European entries, so giving the Americans a chance to compare performance and construction. The first race was a success and the series continued until 1916 (with a gap of two years after the first three races) terminating with the US entry into the First World War. The series was briefly revived in the

William K. Vanderbilt Jnr and son William

thirties at the instigation of George Vanderbilt and known as the Vanderbilt Trophy. Vanderbilt did not confine his activities to giving the Cup. At one time he held the World Land Speed Record and he was also American Champion. He fought in the law courts to prevent motor racing being stopped in the States, actively interested himself in the construction of roads and was referee for his own Vanderbilt Cup. Certainly, the attention that Vanderbilt focused on the infant US auto industry cannot be overrated.

VANDERVELL, Guy Anthony (Tony)

b. Westbourne Park, London, England, 1898. d. 1967.
Son of the man who founded the famous electrical firm, CAV (the initials of C. A. Vandervell), Tony built his own business empire based upon engine bearings. In his younger days he had been a racing motor-

cyclist and driver and he deplored the slump in British motor racing after the Second World War. From experiments with a Ferrari which became the Thinwall Special, he developed his own Vanwall Grand Prix team and after a disappointing start in two glorious seasons Vanwall put Britain back in the Grand Prix picture. In 1957, Vanwalls won three races to Maserati's four and the No. 1 Vanwall driver, Moss, was runner-up to Maserati's Fangio. The following year Vanwall swept to the World Manufacturers Championship with six victories against only two apiece for Ferrari and Coventry-Climax. Moss was runner-up again, edged out by one point by Ferrari's Mike Hawthorn. The other Vanwall driver, Tony Brooks, finished third in the title race.

VARZI, Achille

b. Novara, Italy, 1904. d. 1948.
Of the outstanding Italian drivers between the wars, Varzi was the closest rival of the inimitable Nuvolari, his order and style contrasting with the impetuosity of the Mantuan. He bought an Alfa from Campari and, at 24, finished second in the European Grand Prix at Monza, a performance which led to Alfa signing him for the works team in 1929. The move paid off with Varzi winning three races, including the Rome and Monza Grands Prix. There was no room in the Alfa team for both Nuvolari and Varzi and the latter switched to Maserati, becoming Champion of Italy for the second time. He then had three years with Bugatti during which he won the Monaco Grand Prix in a wheel-to-wheel duel with Nuvolari, the Tripoli GP and (twice) the Tunis GP. When Alfa Romeo officially withdrew from racing Varzi joined Ferrari, who had taken over Alfa Romeo racing operations, winning the Mille Miglia, the Targa Florio and the Tripoli Grand Prix to once again become Champion of Italy. He drove for Auto-Union in the following two seasons with varying fortune but his health declined due to drugs. He returned to the circuits in 1946 and once again joined Alfa Romeo. He raced for them in Europe and South America, had wins in the Turin and Bari Grands Prix and a string of seconds in the Buenos Aires, Swiss, Belgian and Italian Grands Prix. On 30 June, 1948, he was killed in an accident on the rain-soaked Swiss Bremgarten circuit, ironically only the second accident of his career. Christian Kautz and Omobono Tenni were killed at the same meeting.

VOISIN, Gabriel

b. Belleville-sur-Sâone, France, 1880. d. 1973.
Voisin is almost unique amongst car designers with a reputation as a dashing man about town, a lover of ladies, host at parties in which guests were frequently pushed into swimming pools – and host too for presidents and crowned heads on his yacht. Unique too in the fact that he began his career as a pioneer aeroplane designer and constructor and did not switch to car manufacture and design until after the Great War. His cars became noted for

imaginative and spectacular bodywork which owed much to Voisin's early days with aircraft, and met with almost instantaneous success. Celebrities like Rudolph Valentino, Maurice Chevalier, Josephine Baker and the authors Anatole France and H. G. Wells all drove Voisins. They were fast cars and rapidly made a reputation in competitions: in 1960, Voisin at the age of 80, drove a 30 year old Voisin 17-CV from

Gabriel Voisin

Paris to Nice, a distance of nearly 1,000 km (600 miles) in 14 hours. He was not such a genius with finance as design. He temporarily lost control of his factory in 1931, regained it and finally lost it in 1937. Yet the most remarkable aspect of the man is that if he had died at 40 he would still have had an international reputation in aeronautics; and at 70 when his car factory was taken from him, he turned to the design and manufacture of the Biscooter, a two seater minicar, manufactured in Spain from 1951 to 1958.

WAKEFIELD, Charles Cheers

b. Liverpool, England, 1859. d. 1941.
The decision of a Liverpool Customs Officer to allow his younger son, Charles, to go into oil brokerage instead of the Civil Service, had a major effect on the motor industry and on the world land, air and water speed records. At 32, the agent for a leading American oil company, he was still under 40 when he launched out on his own. In 1909, seeing the possibilities of the motorcar, he placed on the market a new blend of oil called Castrol designed to lubricate the engines of these new machines. It became, and remains, one of the most famous lubricants in the world. Wakefield backed many of the great speed attempts between the wars, and also spent much of his leisure time in social work, notably with orphanages. A knighthood was followed in 1915 by his election as Lord Mayor of London and in 1930, at the age of 71, he was raised to the Peerage as Baron Wakefield of Hythe, the first leader of the motor industry to receive this distinction from the King. He remained in active control of his company until his death early in the Second World War.

MUSEUMS & COLLECTIONS

ARGENTINA
Museo del Automóvil del Complejo Museográfico 'Enrique Udanondo' de Luján,
Provincia de Buenos Aires.
Over 150 historic cars are displayed including Alfa Romeo, Anasgasti, Brasier, Bugatti, Ferrari, Jaguar and Rolls-Royce. Veteran vehicles include a Daimler (1892), a Benz (1897) and a Holzman (1898). The collection also displays a complete history of the automobile in Argentina, including a Yruam model built about 1927/8.

AUSTRALIA
NEW SOUTH WALES
Brock's Motor Museum,
17 Military Road, Watson's Bay, Sydney, New South Wales.
E. R. Hardmans Garage,
Beardy Street, Armidale, New South Wales.
Green's Motorcade Museum Park, R.M.B.,
56 Hume Highway, Cross Roads, New South Wales 2170.

1914 Hispano, Green's Motorcade Museum

The museum is set in 14 acres and houses both cars and motorcycles. Among the vehicles is a four-cylinder De Dion Bouton (1905). A number of Rolls-Royces (a Silver Ghost (1911), a Saloon (1914) and a Tourer (1912)). Two interesting Vauxhall cars are shown, a Prince Henry (1914) and 30/98 model (1926). Other vehicles on display include, a Crossley 15 hp Boat Tail (1913), a Hispano (1914) and two Fords — a Model 'T' (1911) and an 'A' Two-door (1928). The museum also has a fully operational garage of the 1920's and a fire station dated 1915, which was salvaged from a Sydney suburb.
Vintage Car Museum,
Toby Street, Forster, New South Wales.
NORTHERN TERRITORY
Stuart Antique Auto Collection Car Museum,
19 Leichhardt Terrace, Alice Springs, Northern Territory.
Contains both veteran and vintage cars that helped pioneer the interior of the

country. In addition, motorcycles and steam engines are on show.
QUEENSLAND
Boyd's Antiquatorium,
295 Bourbong Street, Bundaberg, Queensland.
The display features vintage cars, motorcycles, early locally made machinery and fire engines.
Gilltrap's Yesteryear World,
PO Box 131, Coolangatta 4225, Queensland.

Austin 1800 (top) and a Ferrari racing car (above) from Gilltrap's Yesteryear World

This collection contains the world's best known veteran car *Genevieve* – the 1904 Darracq – which starred in the film of the same name. Australian vehicles are represented by the prototype Australian Six (1918), Holdens and Caldwells. Others shown include a De Dion Bouton (1899), a Scottish-built Albion (1902), an Isotta Fraschini (1923) and an Austin Taxi (1935). As well as cars the museum also contains motorcycles, commercial vehicles and aircraft engines and locomotives.
Laidley Pioneer Village,
Drayton Street, Laidley, Queensland.
Suncoast Pioneer Village,
David Low Highway, Bli Bli, Queensland.
A collection of items from the pioneering days. Featured are a large number of historical cars including a De Dion Bouton (1904), trucks, fire engines and buses.
SOUTH AUSTRALIA
Birwood Mill Museum,
Birwood, 5234 South Australia.

TASMANIA
Bridge Inn Antique Autos,
Bridge Street, Richmond, Tasmania.
A display featuring veteran and vintage cars and associated equipment. Of special interest is Tasmania's largest collection of early Ford vehicles dating from 1911. The associated equipment display includes a collection of 15 antique petrol bowsers.
Military Museum,
22 Bass Highway, Deloraine, Tasmania.
A display of military vehicles and equipment, including trucks, jeeps, scout cars and bren-gun carriers of the Second World War, also featured is a four wheel drive truck from the First World War.
Morley's Motor Museum,
Midland Highway, Brighton, Tasmania.
The museum's collection includes veteran, vintage and post vintage cars ranging from an Alldays and Onions (1906) to a Triumph Renown (1951). The display of over 30 vehicles also features fire engines, taxis, trucks, hearses and motorcycles.
Tasman Antique Auto Museum,
57 Blair Street, New Norfolk, Tasmania.
Vehicles on display include several Essex roadsters, a Whippet (1930) and Hudsons ranging from 1921 to 1940. The museum claims to have the biggest range of Hudsons in Australia.
VICTORIA
Alambee Auto and Folk Museum,
Warren Street, Echuca, Victoria.
Victoria's largest display of fully restored vehicles, including a Crossley (1920), also a large range of Model 'T' Fords. A Mac truck (1919) and vintage Packards and Studebakers.
Antique Car & Folk Museum,
20–24 Princes Highway, Lakes Entrance 3909, Victoria.
Lakes Entrance Antique Car and Folk Museum,
20–24 Princes Highway, Lakes Entrance, Victoria 3909.
The collection comprises cars, motorcycles, trucks, fire engines and tractors. Oldest car on display is the 14 hp IHC motor buggy (1909). Other makes shown include a Morris Cowley Tourer and a Panhard et Levassor, both built in 1924. An English-made Crossley Coupé de Ville (1926), a Falcon Knight (1928), a Horch Sports Car (1930) and a Hillman *Wizard* (1932). There are also many motorcycles, ranging from 1901 to 1950.
Lance Dixon's World of Cars,
603 Doncaster Road, Doncaster, Victoria.
Specializes in sports racing cars and luxury touring cars.
Science Museum of Victoria,
304–328 Swanston Street, Melbourne, Victoria.
The car exhibits include a Ford Quadricycle (1896), a replica of Henry Ford's first motor car, a Hertel (1897), this was the first car imported into Australia. A Thomson Steam Car (1898), the first car to be built in the country. Two other interesting models are an Australian-built Hartnet (1949) and a Holden (1950).
WESTERN AUSTRALIA
Wanneroo Vintage Car Museum,
Wanneroo Road and Karoborup Road, Wanneroo, Western Australia.
This museum currently being formed is due to open in December 1979.

Western Australian Museum,

Francis Street, Perth, Western Australia 6000.

An early Star (1898/9), a Benz (1900) and an Oldsmobile (1902), one of the first cars to be used in Western Australia, are among the 30 vehicles permanently on show. There are a number of Rolls-Royces dating between 1911 and 1937, as well as a Detroit Electric (1914), which has 5-forward and 5-reverse speeds. Two new vehicles acquired by the museum are a Holden 48/215 Sedan (1951) and a Flying Standard 14 hp Saloon believed to be a 1946 model.

AUSTRIA
Heeresgeschichtliches Museum,
Arsenal, Vienna 1030.

The main exhibit of interest is the Gräf and Stift touring car in which the Archduke Franz Ferdinand was assassinated at Sarajevo on June 28th 1914, which heralded the start of the First World War.
Sammlung-Brandstetter,
St Pölten, Niederösterreich, Brunngasse 23.

The collection contains racing cars and motor cycles of Austrian drivers and riders who raced between 1922 and 1939.
Technisches Museum für Industrie und Gewerbe,
Mariahilferstrasse 212, Vienna 1140.

One of the most important exhibits in this Austria's National Technical museum is the claimed ancestor of all petrol driven vehicles, the Marcus (1875). Two electric driven Lohner-Porsche both built in 1900. Other Austrian built vehicles include a Nesselsdorfer (1899), a Braun-Voiturette (1900), a Gräf and Stift (1911). Examples of Steyrs and Austro-Daimlers as well as German-built Benz, Daimlers and a Piccolo (1903) are displayed.

BELGIUM
Provinciaal Automuseum Houthalen,
Domein Kerlkerhoef, 2550 Houthalen.

The museum was opened in July 1970 and has combined a large number of its exhibits with the former Mahy collection. There are a large number of cars on display and those manufactured in Belgium are well represented and include a Belga Rise Type BR8 (1938), eight models produced by the F.N. Company from a Type 4CV (1901) to a Prince Baudouin (1934). Also displayed are Fondu, Imperia, Minerva, Nagant, Piedboeuf and Vivinus models. Among the foreign exhibits are 18 Fords built between 1906 and 1938, seven Packards from the USA, Bentleys, Daimlers and Rolls-Royces from England. There is a very comprehensive library.

BRAZIL
Museu Paulista de Antiquidades Mechanicas,
Rua San Antonio 611, Terreo, San Paulo.

CANADA
Autos of Yesteryear Museum,
Edmundston, New Brunswick.
Canadian Automotive Museum,
99 Simcoe Street South, Oshawa, Ontario, L1H 4G7.
Car Life Museum,
45 Oak Avenue, Charlottetown, Prince Edward Island.

Craven Foundation Museum,
760 Laurence Avenue West, Toronto, Ontario, M6A 1B8.

The Foundation's collection consists of some 70-vehicles ranging from a US Long Distance Runabout (1901) to a Rolls-Royce Continental Coupé (1933). Also displayed are 23 miniature model cars, formerly owned by Francis Mortanni of Montmorency, France. Other vehicles on display include a Tudhope-McIntyre Motor Buggy and a Sears Highwheeler Auto Buggy, both built in 1906. A Brewster Town Car, a Metz Roadster and a Simplex Touring, all 1914 models, as well as the sleek Bentleys, Cadillacs and Duesenbergs of the 1930s.

Heaman's Antique Autorama,
Highway 3, PO Box 105, Carmen, Manitoba ROG 0J0.
Manitoba Automobile Museum,
PO Box 235, Elkhorn, Manitoba, RPM 0N0.

Oldest vehicle in the museum is a Reo (1908), the unusual name originated from the initials of its designer, Ransom E. Olds. Two other interesting models a Case (1913), and a Briscoe (1914) – nicknamed *The Cyclops* because of its single headlight mounted in the centre of the radiator. The cars, all donated by the late Mr Clarkson of Manitoba, also include a rare Metz (1909), and a McLaughlin Model 8 (1909). In addition to the cars there are early carriages and farm machinery.

Musée Automobile 6,
PO Box 6000, Fredericton, New Brunswick.
Reynolds Museum,
PO Box 728, Wetaskiwin, Alberta, T9A 1X7.

Over 1,600 cars, trucks, fire engines, airplanes, tractors and horsedrawn vehicles make up this very large collection. A rare exhibit is the Scottish-built Innes (1899), which has a wooden frame, tiller steering, and wagon type wheels with solid rubber tyres. Among the steam driven cars is a Mason and a Milwaukee, both dated 1900. A White Touring (1908), a Stanley (1922) and a Brooks (1924). Electric driven vehicles include a Baker (1908), a Hupp Yeats (1911) and Milburn Coupés of 1914 and 1915. Other makes displayed in addition are Abbott, Buick, Cadillac, Ford, Hupmobile, Overland, Reo, International and many more.

CHANNEL ISLANDS
Jersey Motor Museum,
St Peter's Village, Jersey.

1942 VW Kubelwagen, Jersey Motor Museum

The museum established in 1973 is dedicated to preserving historic motor vehicles of all types and, particularly, transport and photographic records relating to the Island

of Jersey. Exhibits include an Austin Seven *Chummy* (1926) and a Talbot 4CT (1912). Also featured are Allied and Nazi German military vehicles, a Daimler Armoured Scout Car (1943), Ford Jeep (1942), VW Kubelwagen (1942) and a 125 cc DKW motorcycle (1939) used by the German occupiers, 1940–5.

CZECHOSLOVAKIA
National Technical Museum,
Kosteini 42, Prague 7.

The collection covers all forms of transport including a number of interesting cars. Featured is the original Nesselsdorf *President* (1897), the first product of the present Tatra works. A racing car produced by the same manufacturers dated about 1899. Also shown is a Bugatti (1912), and a Grand Prix Mercedes-Benz (1938). There is also a model of Josef Bozek's steam-car (1815).

Tatra Technicke Museum,
Koprivnice.

The Tatra works museum contains over 30 vehicles manufactured by the company including cars, trucks and racing cars. There are also many engines on display.

DENMARK
Aalholm Automobil Museum,
5880 Nysted, near Nykobing F. Lolland.

Founded in 1964 by Baron J. O. Raben-Levetzau there are some 200 cars exhibited at Aalholm Castle, including a De Dion tricycle (1897), a rare La Croix de Laville (1898) and a Delaugère-Clayette (1904). Also a large selection of nearly 100 American cars with Fords, Lincolns and Cadillacs well represented. A number of Renaults are shown including a 40 CV model and six Rolls-Royces including a Silver Ghost of 1908.

Danmarks Tekniske Museum,
Ole Romers Vej, Helsingor.

A Danish-built Hammel built about 1886

1912 Swift, Danmarks Tekniske Museum

is the oldest vehicle on show, and is still in full working order. Also featured is a Delaunay-Belleville (1906), this was the Danish Royal family's first car. Other interesting exhibits include a Szawe (1922) and a car built by H. C. Christiansen in 1899. On show is the first dynamo, built by Zenobe Gramme, and the first motor-driven aeroplane built by the Dane, Ellehammer in 1906. Danish-built motor cycles are also represented.

Det Jyske Automobil Museum,
8883 Gjern, near Silkeborg.

The museum consists of about 80 vehicles, with over 40 different makes represented including a Renault (1912), an Adler (1913) and a V12 Cadillac (1913). It also has many pre-1937 American-built cars.

Egeskov Veteranmuseum,
5772 Egeskov, near Odense.
Founded in 1967 the collection shows some 30 cars and about 40 motorcycles. In addition there are some ten aeroplanes and 30 odd horse-drawn carriages. Among the vehicles is a famous veteran from the First World War a *Marne-Taxi*. There is also a Nimbus motorcycle (1921), manufactured by Fisker and Nielsen of Copenhagen.

FRANCE
Autobiographie Renault,
53 Avenue des Champs-Elysées, 75008 Paris.
Tracing the history of the Renault company from the single cylinder Voiturette (1898) through the Torpedo models of the 1920s the Dauphines of the 1950s to the up to date models.
Automobiles M. Berliet,
Venissieux, Rhône 69200.
The museum is situated at the Berliet works and is confined to the company's own vehicles, numbering about 20, they include the first one-cylinder model produced in 1894. A Voiturette (1895). A racing car (1906), which participated in the 1908 Targa-Bologna run and completed the 426 km in 4 hours, and a 1938 4-cylinder model.
Automobiles Peugeot,
75 Avenue de la Grande Armée, Paris 16e.
Peugeot cars have a number of their very

1939 Peugeot 402 B N5 (top) and a 1908 Peugeot *Torpedo* Type II6 (above) from Automobiles Peugeot

early models including three built in 1892, one from 1894 and another from 1895. In addition there are a number of *Torpedo* models, a Type 81B (1906), a Type 116 (1908) and a Type 163 (1920). Also, a Cabriolet 172 BC (1924) and a Limousine 402 B N5 (1939).

Musée Automobile de Bretagne,
RN 12, Rennes, Ille-et-Vilaine.
The collection contains about 70 vehicles including a number of rare cars including a Hurtu (1898), a Barré (1905), a Suère (1912) and an Amilcar (1938).
Musée Automobile de l'Abbatiale,
Le Bec-Hellouin 27, 27800 Brionne (Eure). Has a large collection of sports and racing cars including a Bugatti *Brescia* (1920) and a Bugatti 40 (1930). Also a Barquette Simca-Gordini (1937), an MG TF (1955), the Ferrari Berlinette-Tour de France (1961). Racing cars include former world champion Jack Brabham's Brabham-Repco BT 19 (1966) and a Martini-Holbay Mk 12, Formula 3, driven by French champion Jacques Laffite.
Musée Automobile de Provence,
RN 7, Orgon, Bouches-du-Rhône 13660.
Musée Automobile de Vendée,
Route des Sables d'Olonne (D949) 85440 Talmont St Hilaire.
Over 100 vehicles built between 1885 and 1940 with the oldest being a De Dion Bouton (1885). Also shown is a Hugot (1898), a Peugeot single cylinder (1907) and a Chenard et Walcker (1912). In addition other makes represented include Rochet Schneider, Brasier, Hispano-Suiza, Delahaye and Bugatti.
Musée Automobile Raffaelli,
Circuit Paul Ricard, RN 8, Le Beausset 83330.

Features over 50 racing cars and motorcycles from Bugatti to Matra, all on permanent display at the racing circuit.
Musée d'Automobiles de Normandie,
Clères près Rouen, Seine Maritime 76690. Some very interesting early vehicles are on display and include a Panhard-Levassor (1894), a Delage (1906) and a Grégoire (1910). There are a number of racing cars a Delahaye (1936), a Le Mans type Talbot-Lago (1955) and a Grand Prix Maserati (1956). In addition there are many other rare makes such as Suère, Lafitte and Bignan.
Musée d'Automobiles du Forez,
Sury-le-Comtal 42450, Loire.
The 50 cars exhibited in the collection include several rare models. A La Coix de Laville (1903), also a Motobloc (1907) and a 50 CV Delaunay-Belleville (1914), only a very limited number of this model were

Delahaye, Musée d'Automobiles du Forez

manufactured. In addition there is a De Dion Bouton Tricycle (1898), a Clément (1906) and a Peugeot Lion (1907). A Delage and an American Hotchkiss both built in 1922 and a Voisin (1932).
Musée de l'Automobile,
RN 20, Vatan, Indre 36150.
Musée de l'Automobile de Chatellerault,
3 rue Clément Creps, Chatellerault, Vienne 86100.
Musée de l'Automobile du Mans,
Le Mans, Sarthe 72040.
Musée de l'Automobile Francais,
Nancy-Velaine-en-Haye 54840.
Musée de l'Automobile Francais,
Route de St-Dizier, Villiers-en-Lieu 52100.
Musée du Conservatoire National des Arts et Métiers,
292 Rue St-Martin, Paris 75003.
This museum has a collection containing a number of unique early propelled vehicles including Cugnot's steam tractor built in 1771. Amédée Bollée's *L'Obeissante* steam-wagon of 1873. A Peugeot quadricycle (1893). Two other steam vehicles are on show, the De Dion (1885) and the Serpollet (1888).
Musée du Lys Chantilly,
Rond Point de la Reine, RN 16, Le Lys par Lamorlaye 60260.
Musée Français de l'Automobile,
Château de Rochetaillée-sur-Saone, Rhône.
Owned by Monsieur Henri Malartre, has over 150 cars. Models unique to the collection include two early steamers, a Secretand (1891) and a Scotte (1892) also a Rochet-Schnider (1895) an Audibert et Lavirotte (1898) and an Ours (1907). Racing cars are also shown and include a Rolland Pilain 9 (1923) and two 6-cylinder Gordinis of 1952 and 1954.
Musée de la Roue,
3 bis, Route de Nimes, Uzes, Gard 30700.
This collection is devoted to all forms of land transport, some 35 cars are featured including a Peugeot (1897) and an Alcyon (1907). Other makes include Bentley, Bugatti and De Dion.
Musée National de la Voiture et du Tourisme,
Compiègne, le Château de Compiègne, Oise.

Contains many important early cars including Amédée Bollée's steamer, *La Mancelle* (1878), and also his *Diligence à Vapeur* (1885). Two of the first cars built by Panhard et Levassor in 1891. Jenatzy's electric car *Jamais Contente* (1895) as well as many other historic vehicles.

GERMAN DEMOCRATIC REPUBLIC
Verkehrsmuseum,
Augustusstrasse 1, 801 Dresden.
Wartburg Automobilmuseum,
59 Eisenach, Wartburg Allee.

GERMAN FEDERAL REPUBLIC
Adam Opel AG,
6090 Rüsselsheim.

1913/14 Opel racing car 260 PS (above) and a 1912 5/12 HP two-seater (below) from the Opel collection

The company's collection includes some 35 cars, motor cycles and bicycles, from the one-cylinder Opel Patent (1898), through the Opel racing car 260 PS (1913/14) to the Kadett, two door special sedan (1938). Also featured are some 'specials', such as the Diesel world record car and the Opel safety vehicle OSV40.

Automobilmuseum der Daimler-Benz AG,
Stuttgart-Unterürkheim.
Situated at the company's works the collection is confined to the Daimler, Mercedes and Benz vehicles, including their car, aircraft and boat engines. Both the first Benz and the first Daimler are shown, the former is a replica, as well as a complete record of the company's remarkable activities in the motor racing field, including the famous S-type Mercedes-Benz and Grand Prix cars of the 1930s. There are also the great 540K model and the Grosser Mercedes-Benz, as well as the rear engined 130H and 170H types produced after the amalgamation of Daimler and Benz in 1926.

Auto Motorrad Museum,
Weserstrasse 225, 497 Bad Oeynhausen 13.
Over 100 vehicles are on show including a Seck (1898), many examples of both Bugatti and Mercedes as well as such models as a Porsche RSK (1958), the 907 model (1968) and the 917 (1971). There are also single-seater racing cars of Lotus and BMW formula 2s and Cooper F3 models.
Auto Museum Hillers,
Kurt Schumacher Allee 42, 2000 Hamburg 1.
Automuseum Nettelstedt,
Rietkampstrasse 415, Nettelstedt 4991.
BMW Museum,
Petuelring 130, 8 Munchen 40.
The museum attached to the company's headquarters has a fully electronic display and as well as featuring racing and road cars, includes motorcycles and also BMW's early aircraft engines. Panoramic screens, giant slide and film projectors are another feature of this unique building.
Deutsches Automuseum,
Schloss Langenburg, 7183 Langenburg.
There are a large number of interesting exhibits including a Dixi (1928), this car was in fact an Austin 7 made under licence. A curious three-wheel *Phänomobil* (1908). Other less well known German built vehicles include Neander, Hanomay, Stoewar and Lloyd. Racing and sports cars include a Bugatti type 37 (1925), an NSU Rennwagen (1926) and an Opel Rak 2 (1928).
Deutsches Museum,
8000 Munchen 26.
Contains over 100 vehicles and includes many early examples of Benz, including the original one built in 1886. Porsche, BMW and Opel are also well represented as are Grand Prix cars produced by Auto-Union and Mercedes-Benz in this very important collection.
Oldtimergasse,
Hamburger Str 195, 2000 Hamburg.
Poddig Automobil Museum,
Sophie Charlotten Strasse, 41–43, 1000 Berlin 19.
Verkehrsmuseum Karlsruhe,
Werderstrasse 63, 7500 Karlsruhe.
Veteranen- Automobil- und Motor-rad-Museum,
Bächinger Strasse 68, 8883 Grundel-Fingen/Donau.

Many rare cars are featured in the collection including a two seater open tourer Hispano-Suiza (1908), a Delage type D8 (1933), a 4-cylinder Grégoire Speedster (1919), a Salmson S4DA (1935) and a 12-cylinder Ferrari Export Ghia (1952).

HOLLAND
Lips Autotron,
Drunen.
The collection, opened in 1972, houses about 220 vehicles, with over 109 different makes represented. There are seven Dutch built Spykers (the Spyker became widely known as a result of its co-starring role in the film *Genevieve*) including one built in 1904. Steam cars include four Stanley Steamers. Other interesting exhibits include a Swiss built Millot (1901) and the French built Sultane (1906). Also shown are Rolls-Royces, Lagondas, Alvis, Mercedes and two American built cars a Pierce Arrow Motorette (1902) and a Holsman of the same year.
Nationaal Automobiel Museum,
Veursestraatweg 280 Leidschendam.
Contains many interesting models. The Dutch built Spykers are represented by a 7 hp open two-seater (1909), a four-cylinder truck-chassis (1918) and a 13/30 (1919). Other rare vehicles include two early 3½ hp Benz (1899), an electric Hedag (1905) and an open three wheeled Cyklon (1912). American cars include seven examples of the American Dodge, built between 1914 and 1935 and an unusual Franklin 11B sedan (1927). In addition there are many motorcycles, fire engines and horse drawn carriages to be seen.

HUNGARY
Automuzeum Haris Testverek,
Moricz Zsigmond Korter 12, Budapest Xl, 1117.
Contains a large selection of early Hungarian built cars including Aurores of 1898, 1900 and 1904, and a Ganz-De Dion tricycle (1897). On exhibition as well in this museum are a number of locally built motor cycles, including a Csonka-J, and a Ganz.

IRELAND
Veteran Car Museum,
Blarney Castle, County Cork.

ITALY
Centro Storico Fiat,
Via Chiabrera 20, Turin 10126.
Based at the Fiat works the museum traces the complete history of the company since 1899 to the modern day. Apart from the cars, Fiat agricultural vehicles, trains and engines are on show. There is also a very comprehensive photographic and reference library.
Lancia S.P.A.,
Via Vincenzo Lancia 27, 10141 Turin.
Covers the history of Lancia from the first model, the Alpha (1908), through the very successful Lambda (1922–30), to the Flavia and Fulvia models of the 1960s. Also featured are the Company's military vehicles of both the First and Second World Wars. The sports and racing cars include the V8 Formula 1 D50, driven by Ascari, Villoresi and Castellotti in the early 1950s.

Museo Alfa Romeo, Arese

Museo Alfa Romeo,
Arese.
The Alfa museum contains a complete history of the company from the Torpedo 24 hp built by Castagna in 1910, followed a year later by the 15 hp model. The racing history began in 1913 with the 40/60 hp model, which reached a speed of 130 km/h (80 mph); other racing models include Nino Farina's 1950, and Fangio's 1951 Grand Prix cars. Also the Daytona (1968), and the Le Mans (1970). As well as these all the company's production models to the present day are exhibited.

Museo Dell' Automobile,
S. Martino en Rio 42018.

Museo dell' Automobile Carlo Biscaretti de Ruffia,
Corso Unita d'Italia 40, Turin 10126.
Named after one of Italy's leading motor pioneers the museum was opened in 1960. It contains the world's most important collection of Italian cars, beginning with the Bordino steam coach (1854). Two other early makes are a Pecori steamer (1891) and a Bernardi (1896). Exhibits include a selection of Alfa Romeos, Ferraris, Fiats, Lancias and Maseratis, as well as the less well known names such as Legnano, Nazzaro and San Giusto. There are a number of foreign cars including a Peugeot (1894), and a Léon Bollée (1896).

Museo Nationale della Scienza e della Technica Leonardo da Vinci,
Via S. Vittore 21, 20123 Milan.
The transport section of the museum contains about a dozen vehicles and includes a Bianchi (1903), two Isotta-Fraschinis of 1930 and 1947 and a Fiat experimental gas turbine car of 1954.

Padiglione Automobile D'Epoca,
Autodrome di Monza, 13054 Monza.
Pininfarina, PO Box 295, 10100 Turin.
The models housed in the collection are

1969 Ferrari 512/S Berlinetta special (top) and a 1967 Ferrari Dino Berlinetta prototype (above) at Pininfarina, Turin

those styled by Pininfarina and include Alfas, Fiats, Ferraris, Lancias, a Sigma Grand Prix car and a Studio CR25.

NEW ZEALAND
Museum of Transport and Technology,
Western Springs, Auckland 2.
Opened in 1965 the exhibits are planned to show all forms of transport on land, sea and air. The vehicles on show include a Renault Charabanc (1911), the only known vehicle of its type in the world. An International Auto Buggy (1908), a six-cylinder Essex (1929). Also displayed is an English built Duo Cycle Car (1912); the gearing on this model is achieved by expanding pulleys and a moveable back section, again it is the only known surviving model. Incorporated at the museum is a display commemorating the achievements of New Zealand's most famous racing driver, the late Bruce McLaren.

Queenstown Motor Museum,
Queenstown.
Southward Museum Trust,
Main Road North, Paraparaumu.
The collection will be open to the public in 1979 and will contain over 200 vehicles, including, bicycles, cars, farm machinery, fire engines and motorcycles. A number of interesting vehicles have been acquired, the oldest being a Benz (1895). There is also a Luxwerke (1897), an International High Wheeler (1909) and a Stutz Indian-

apolis Race Car (1915). Two 1922 models are an Essex four-cylinder Tourer and a Rover Coventry Tourer. There are a number of cars from the 1950s including an Alvis TD 21 Saloon, Mercedes-Benz, Studebakers and Ferrari. Other makes represented include Daimler, Ford and Rolls-Royce, a Russian built ZIM (1950) and a Hungarian Tatra Saloon (1928).

NORWAY
Norsk Teknisk Museum,
Fyrstikkalleen 1-Oslo 6.
The automobile section contains about 20 cars including a Bjering (1920) which was designed for Norway's very narrow roads by H. C. Bjering. Also on show are the first recorded car in Norway, a Benz Victoria (1895), a Cadillac (1912), which was King Olav V's first car, a Minerva (1913), also owned by the country's Royal family and an Austrian built Lohner-Porsche (1902). Two American rarities are a Milburn electric (1917) and a Daniels (1918).

POLAND
Technical Museum of Palace of Culture and Science,
Palac Kultury Inauki, Warsaw 00901.

PORTUGAL
Museu do Automóvel,
Caramulo.
Portugal's only automobile museum comprising of over 40 vehicles, many of which were owned by the founder Dr João Lacerda. The oldest car on show is a Peugeot 5 hp (1898), other models include a 16 hp Fiat (1909), an American Hotchkiss (1910) and a Chenard & Walcker (1925). Rolls-Royce are represented by two early Silver Ghost models of 1911 and 1913. Two other interesting exhibits are the Delahaye fire engine (1913) and a Spanish built Abadal (1914).

ROMANIA
Musée Technique Prof D. Leonida,
Candiano Popesco 2, Parcullibertati, Bucharest.

SOUTH AFRICA
James Hall Museum of Transport,
Wemmes Pan, Johannesburg, Transvaal.

SOVIET UNION
Polytechnical Museum,
Novaya Ploshad, 3/4, Moscow.

SPAIN
Colección de Automóviles de Salvador Claret,
Sils, Gerona.
The only collection, at the time of writing, open to the public, it contains many interesting exhibits, including a number of Hispana-Suizas, the earliest dated 1907. A Salamanca (1904) is shown, as are an Alba and a Salvador, both built in 1916. Also featured are Bugattis and Rolls-Royces, including a six-cyclinder, 47 hp model built in 1918.

SWEDEN
AB Volvo,
Car Division, S-40508 Göteborg.
The exhibits trace the history of Volvo since its first model launched in April 1927. This was the four-cylinder Jakob, this car had an open body and was not suited to Nordic climate, so a covered version, the PV4, was introduced a few months later. The PV4 entered the 1928 Moscow–Leningrad–Moscow speed and economy trial and won its class. The company's 121/122S model, launched in 1956, was the car that put the Volvo name on the world markets, and this was followed in 1961 by the P1800, which Roger Moore, alias *The Saint*, alias Simon Templar, drove throughout the early series of the popular TV series. The collection includes the most up-to-date models, among them the 240, 264 and 343.

Fredriksdal Open-Air Museum,
Sodra Storgatem 31, 252 23 Helsingborg.
The museum was established to illustrate Swedish rural life. The Carriage Hall contains many different types of vehicles including one of the town's oldest cars constructed in 1898 by the manufacturer C. Jönsson.

Gamla Bilsalongen,
P1 7718, Skellefta.

Gillstads Bilmuseum,
Gillstad.

Industrihistorika,
Gotaplatsen, 41253 Goteborg.

Klostermuseum Ystad,
Ystad.
The main feature of the museum is the oldest surviving Swedish built vehicle, the Cederholm steamer (1892).

Landskrona Museum,
Adolf Fredriks Kasern, 26131, Landskrona.
The museum is established in the town where the Swedish aeroplane constructor and pilot, Enoch Thulin was born and lived. In 1920 the company began the construction of cars and two of these on show, the first a 20 hp built in 1921 and the other manufactured in 1925 is a 15 hp air-cooled engine, the vehicle was designed for use in snow and runs on a sleigh. The sleigh is made of iron-plate and the four runners are made of wood.

Saab-Scania,
Scania Museet, 15187 Södertälje.
The Scania museum in its present form became a reality in 1969 when a special building was made available at the company's headquarters. The collection includes two firsts, the first Vabis car (1887), and the first series produced Scania car (1903). Also on show is the last car made by the Scania-Vabis company in 1929. Featured as well are engines, ambulances, tankers and buses built by the company between 1907 and 1934. There are also a large number of engines and components as well as photographs and drawings.

Skokloster Motormuseum,
Skokloster.
Oldest car featured is a two-cylinder, rear-engined Benz Comfortable (1898). Other early models include two French built vehicles, an air-cooled Renault (1899) and a 16 hp Motobloc (1909), this is one of the few remaining examples of this make. Swedish vehicles are represented by Scania-Vabis, Volvo, Thulin and a Tidaholm fire engine (1929). Two interesting British vehicles on display are an Austin 23 hp (1911) and a Ford Junior (1932), this car was the first English designed Ford car.

Söderström Kollektion,
Förenade Bil Import AB, Box 6005, 200 11 Malmö.
The collection consists of over 50 cars including a number of Bentleys from a 4½-litre (1929) model to the Flying Spur model (1958). There are also nine Bugattis built between 1910 and 1938, six BMWs, a Spanish built Diaz y Grillo (1916), an American Hupmobile (1911), a Lorraine-Dietrich (1930), as well as the better-known makes such as Mercedes, M.G. Riley and Rolls-Royce.

Tekniska Museet,
Museivägen 7, N. Djurgården, 115 27 Stockholm.
The collection consists of some 40 cars, with a great number of Swedish cars and lorries, including a Vabis (1897), Scanias of 1902 and 1903, an Åtvidaberg (1910), based on the American Holsman, and a Thulin (1923). Also featured are a Léon Bollée tricycle (1896) and De Dion Boutons of 1897, 1898 and 1899. There are also some 20 motorcycles built between 1895 and 1935.

Scania truck (above), 1913 Scania car (right)

1897 Scania Vabis

Vattebygdens Automobil Museum,
Motell Vallerleden E4, Huskvarna-Granna.

SWITZERLAND
Collection Strinati,
35 Chemin du Pré-Longard, 1223 Cologny.
The collection consists of mainly sports and grand touring cars built between 1936 and 1956 and includes an Aston Martin DB2, an Alfa Romeo 8C 2900, BMW models, 328 and 507, a Jaguar SS100, Mercedes-Benz 540K and 300SL models. Talbots are represented by a T150C, a 150C-SS and a Lago Grand Sport Model.

Talbot TI50C-SS (above) from the
Collection Strinati, Cologny
1934 Mercedes-Benz GP racing car Type
M25 (left) from the Verkehrshaus der
Schweiz, Lucerne

Musée De l'Automobile,
Château de Grandson, Lake Neuchâtel, Vaud.
Situated in the largest, fortified medieval dwelling still to be inhabited in Switzerland it includes a strong contingent of Swiss built vehicles including an Egg (1895), a Dumont (1901) and a two-cylinder Turricum (1909). Also featured is a Rolls-Royce Phantom 1 (1927), and a Type 22 Bugatti (1926).

Musée d'Histoire des Sciences,
128 rue de Lausanne, 1202 Genève.
As the title implies the museum covers all aspects of scientific advancement, the automobile is represented by the steam tricycle constructed by René Thury in Geneva in 1878.

Verkehrshaus der Schweiz,
Lidostrasse 5, 6006 Lucerne.
The Swiss Transport Museum has over 50 vehicles on show. It contains a unique collection of Swiss built vehicles including a Popp (1898), a Berna (1902), a Weber of the same year, a Dufaux racing car (1905), a Turicum (1907), an Ajax (1908) and a Fischer and Martini, both built in 1913, also a Pic-Pic (1919). Also on display is a Mercedes-Benz Grand Prix car, model M25 (1934). Commercial vehicles include two Swiss built machines, an Orion lorry chassis (1903) and a Saurer fire engine (1913).

UNITED KINGDOM
Autoworld
Blackpool Pleasure Beach, South Shore, Blackpool, Lancashire.
Vehicles range from 1886 to 1970, and include a Léon Bollée 3 hp Voiturette (1896), and a Siddeley 6 hp (1904), the first model to bear the Siddeley name. A 48 hp Daimler Roi de Belge Tourer (1908) is the only known surviving model and a Porsche 917 (1970) featured in the film Le Mans.

Birmingham Museum of Science and Industry,
Newhall Street, Birmingham B3 1RZ.
Founded in 1950, the exhibits include John Cobb's Railton Mobil Special – the land speed record holder from 1947 to 1964. A Léon Bollée (1897), a Star (1898), also an example of F. W. Lanchester's prototype petrol electric car, with a wooden body and suspension.

Bradford Industrial Museum,
Moorside Mills, Moorside Road, Bradford BD2 3HP, Yorkshire.
The Transport Gallery houses a range of locally built Jowett cars built between 1910 and 1953. Featured as well is an American Foster steam car (1901).

Caister Castle Motor Museum,
Caister Castle, Norfolk.
Contains over 50 Veteran and Vintage cars including a unique White 15 hp steam car (1904). A Montague-Napier (1902) racing car, built for racing-driver Charles Jarrot, and 10 hp Morris Oxford (1913).

Campden Car Collection (Incorporated with Woolstaplers Hall Museum),
High Street, Chipping Campden, Gloucestershire.
Included in the collection is an eight-cylinder Alfa Romeo Le Mans, built between 1931 and 1934. A Bugatti type 44 (1928) and a type 46 (1930). Jaguar models are represented by a C type (1951), an XK120 (1954), the famous D type (1955), which won Le Mans in 1955, 1956 and 1957, and an E type 3·8 engined car.

Cheddar Motor and Transport Museum,
Cheddar Gorge, Cheddar, Somerset, BS27 3QR.
Owned and operated by the South-West section of the Veteran Car Club, the exhibits include a White Steam Car (1903), lesser known makes such as Swift and Turner.

City of Coventry Herbert Art Gallery and Museum,
Jordan Well, Coventry, West Midlands.
Situated in the home of the British motor industry the collection includes many locally built vehicles including an English

Daimler car (1897), a Payne and Bates (1901), a Riley Tri-car (1904), this is a regular competitor in the RAC's London to Brighton Run. A Hillman (1908), a Maudslay (1910). In addition there is the gas-turbine Rover-BRM (1965), driven by the late Graham Hill and Jackie Stewart in the 1965 Le Mans 24-hour race and also a single seater Techcraft-BRM (1967). There are many bicycles and motor cycles also on show.

The C. M. Booth Collection of Historic Vehicles,
Falstaff Antiques, 63 High Street, Rolvenden, Kent.
The main feature is the unique collection of Morgan three-wheel cars including a Runabout (1913), Grand Prix (1922), Aero and Family both 1927 and a Super Sports (1935). Also the only known surviving Humber Olympia Tricar (1904).

Donington Collection with Leyland Historic Vehicles,
Castle Donington, Derby, DE7 5RP.
The Donington Collection is the largest of single seater racing cars in the world, and has recently been joined by Leyland Historic Vehicles, which traces over 80 years of British automobile history, from vehicles such as the Coventry Lever Tricycle (1876), the first Wolseley (1895), the Thornycroft 10 hp twin-cylinder car (1903), through to the modern Jaguars, Range Rover, Minis and Triumphs. Also displayed is the 1961 prototype Rover T4 gas turbine car.

Doune Motor Museum,
Carse of Cambus, Doune, Perthshire, Scotland.
Lord Moray's unique collection of vintage and post-vintage thoroughbreds featuring Hispano-Suizas, Alfa Romeos, Aston Martins, Bugattis, Maseratis, MGs and Rolls-Royces.

Hull Transport Collection,
36 High Street, Kingston upon Hull, Humberside.
Featured is a Panhard et Levassor Motor Wagonette (1897) – similar to the model which won the Paris–Marseilles race of 1896; an English Daimler (1899) and a Coventry Motette Motor Tandem Tricycle (1898), both built in Coventry. Another British built vehicle, the Sturmey-Voiturette, was designed by Henry Sturmey, who also invented the Sturmey-Archer gear still widely used on bicycles. The collection includes horse-drawn vehicles, as well as bicycles and motor cycles.

Museum of Transport,
25 Albert Drive, Glasgow, C41 2PE, Scotland.
Opened in 1964 the cars include the finest collection of Scottish built vehicles anywhere: Argylls of 1900, 1907, 1910 and 1927, Albions of 1900, 1904 and 1910, Arrol-Johnsons from 1910 and examples of both the Beardmore and Galloway. In addition to the cars there are many bicycles, horse-drawn vehicles, trams and railway locomotives.

Myreton Motor Museum,
Aberlady, Lothian, Scotland.
Opened in 1966 it features over 80 vehicles, including a Renault 8·3 hp (1923), a Buick Regent (1923), a 13·9 hp Morris (1925). There are Lanchesters, Lagondas, Austins and Fords. Cycles, horse-drawn, farm and military vehicles are also displayed.

The National Motor Museum,

Beaulieu, Hampshire, SO4 7ZN.
Founded in 1952 by Lord Montagu, the exhibits tell the story of motoring from 1895. Early British models include J. H. Knight's single cylinder (1895), probably Britain's first petrol-driven car. A Coventry build Pennington three-wheeler (1896), Herbert Austin's 3·5 hp Wolseley (1899) and a 2·5 hp Simms of the same year. Record breaking cars feature the Sunbeam 350 hp (1920), the Sunbeam 1,000 hp (1927), the *Golden Arrow* (1929) and the late Donald Campbell's *Bluebird* (1961). There are Racing and Sports Car sections and also commercial vehicles. Motorcycles are featured in the Graham Walker gallery. The Reference and Photographic Libraries are among the world's finest reference sources on motoring and road transport history.

Royal Scottish Museum,

Chambers Street, Edinburgh, EH1 1JF, Lothian, Scotland.
Road transport exhibits include three early petrol-engine cars, a Léon Bollée (1896), an Arnold Benz (1897) and one of the earliest examples of a Scottish built car the 8 hp Albion (1900), also a Locomobile Steamer (1900). There are many aeronautical, locomotive and shipping exhibits on permanent display.

Science Museum,

Exhibition Road, South Kensington, London, SW1 2DD.
The road transport section includes a Benz (1888) – believed to be the oldest car in Britain. Also featured are a Lanchester (1896), a Rolls-Royce (1904), and the world's first gas-turbine car the Rover *JET 1* (1959). Sectioned cars and engines provide detailed exhibits that help to explain the development of the motor car to modern days.

Stanford Hall Museum,

Lutterworth, Leicestershire, LE17 6DH.
Considered to be the most important collection of historic motorcycles in the world. The car section also contains a number of very important exhibits, including a Wilson-Pilcher (1904), the manufacturers of this model producing the first preselector gearbox. A French made Hurtu (1898) and an air-cooled Carden (1921) are also on show.

Stratford Motor Museum,

1 Shakespeare Street, Stratford-upon-Avon, Warwickshire.
A collection of exotic touring cars including a Rolls-Royce Silver Ghost and Phantoms I and II, a Mercedes 38/250SS, Hispano-Suizas, Bugattis, Lagondas and Jaguars. Featured is an authentic recreation of a 1920s garage, complete with signs, equipment and tools, and a superb picture gallery containing many original Gordon Crosby pictures.

Totnes Motor Museum,

Totnes, Devon.
The museum specializes in vintage sports and racing cars and covers a span of some 50 years. Vehicles range from an Austin 7 to such exotic machines as the 4·5-litre Talbot-Lago and the Alfa Romeo Tipo racing car (1972).

Ulster Folk Museum,

Cultra Manor, Holywood, Co. Down, Northern Ireland.
The motor section features two Belfast built vehicles a 14–20 hp Fergus (1915) and an O.D. car built about 1918. Foreign cars include a Swiss Martini 4·5-litre (1904) and an Italian Lancia 2·1-litre (1924).

World of Motoring,

Syon Park, Brentford, Middlesex, TW8 8JF.
Contains a number of unique models including a Beeston Quad (1889), a rare Ford Model 'T' Estate (1912), a Stellite (1914), which is one of only four known to exist. Sporting exhibits include a Fiat 501 (1921), Sima-Violet (1924), Bugatti (1925) and a Wolseley straight-8 (1928). Horse-drawn and military vehicles and motorcycles are also featured. Adjacent to the collection is the London Transport Collection which traces the history of public transport in the capital from 1829 to the present day.

UNITED STATES OF AMERICA
ARKANSAS
Museum of Automobiles,

Route 3, Morrilton, Arkansas 72110.
The museum displays privately owned veteran, vintage and classic cars for collectors throughout the State. Annual Automobile Fairs, Concours d'Elegance and Driving Events all make up this living museum.

CALIFORNIA
Briggs Cunningham Automotive Museum,

250 Baker Street, Costa Mesa, California 92626.
Cars raced by Briggs Cunningham at Le Mans during the 1950s and 1960s are displayed including the Frick-Tappet modified Cadillac V8 50/61 engine and chassis nicknamed *Le Monstre* by the French. Also the C-1 and C-4R models. Apart from these machines the oldest car on display is a De Dion Bouton (1898). There is also an American *Traveller* (1910) – this car designed by Harry Stutz was generally referred to as *Underslung* because the frame went under the axles. The Bentley name is represented by seven models all built between 1926 and 1952. Jaguars include an SS100 (1938) and a 'C' Type sports racing (1953) – this car was the actual one that won the Le Mans 24-hour race in 1953, driven by Tony Rolt and Duncan Hamilton. Maserati, Mercedes, Ferrari and Duesenberg cars are also included. Another feature of the museum is a permanent exhibition of paintings and drawings, entitled *Automobiles in Art*, it contains work by artists such as Peter Helck, Walter Gotschke, John Burgess and the late F. Gordon Crosby.

Jack Passey Jr Collection,

2025 Freedom Boulevard, Freedom, California 95019.

Los Angeles County Museum of Natural History,

900 Exposition Boulevard, Los Angeles, California 90007.
The museum's automobile section consists of 48 vehicles and includes a replica of the Anthony Electric Roadster (1897). There are also a number of locally built cars such as the Breer *Steam Stanhope* (1900), a Tourist rear entrance tonneau (1902) and a Roadster (1903), also a Durocar Tourer (1909) and a Moreland truck (1913). The 1950s have a number of representatives – an Allard Roadster K-3 (1953), a BMW Sport Coupe 507 (1957) and a Jaguar XK120 (1954).

Movie World,

6920 Orangethorpe Avenue, Buena Park, California 90620.
As the title suggests many of the cars were either owned by movie stars or used in films or on television. Exhibits include a Lincoln Tourer (1928), owned by Cecil B. DeMille, a Rolls-Royce Phantom I (1929) owned by Charlie Chaplin, and a Bentley built for the Beatles. Also shown is a Ford 'A' two-door Phaeton (1931) used in the TV series *Nanny and the Professor* and a Lincoln Convertible (1948) used in the film *Whatever Happened to Baby Jane*.

COLORADO
Buckskin Joe's Antique Auto Museum,

Canon City, Colorado.

1933 Pierce Silver Arrow at Movie World, Buena Park

Museums and Collections

Rippey's Veteran Car Museum,
2030 South Cherokee Street, Denver, Colorado 80202.
Several British luxury vehicles feature in this collection including a Lagonda (1913), Rolls-Royces, Daimlers and Bentleys. American exhibits include a model FC Peerless (1903), a Detroit Electric (1916), a Chrysler Custom Imperial (1933) and a model 62 Cadillac (1941).

Forney Transportation Museum,
1416 Platte Street, Valley Highway and Speer Boulevard, Denver, Colorado 80202.
Two interesting exhibits are Amelia Earhart's Goldbug Kissel Kar (1922) and a 25-foot wheelbase, six-wheeled Hispano-Suiza (1923). Other vehicles include a Marmon, a Pierce, a Vauxhall limousine (1912), a Renault Opera Coupe of the same year, and a seven passenger Lincoln limousine (1926).

DISTRICT OF COLUMBIA

Museum of History and Technology,
Smithsonian Institution, Washington, DC 20560.
The Vehicle Hall contains a number of highly significant models, with an emphasis on the development of cars in the United States. Notable are numerous pioneer motor vehicles including the Roper steam velocipede (1869), the Long steam tricycle (1880), the Haynes (1894) and the Balzer quadricycle (1894). Early production cars include Autocar, Olds, Riker, White and Franklin. There are two early racing cars made by Alexander Winton, *Bullet 2* (1902), driven by Barney Oldfield, and the 1903 model, which was the first car to be driven coast to coast. Also displayed are carriages, bicycles and commercial vehicles.

FLORIDA

Early American Museum,
Silver Springs, PO Box 188, Florida 32688.

Elliott Museum,
Hutchinson Island, Jensen Beach, Florida 33451.

Martin County Historical Society,
888 N. E. MacArthur Boulevard, Florida 33494.

GEORGIA

Stone Mountain Antique Auto Museum,
2042 Young Road, Stone Mountain, Georgia 30083.

HAWAII

Automotive Museum of the Pacific,
197 Sand Island Road, Honolulu, Hawaii 96819.

ILLINOIS

Chicago Historical Antique Automobile Museum,
3200 Skokie Valley Road, Highland Park, Illinois 60035.
Has a fine collection of Classic cars including a Packard Dual Cowl Phaeton (1929), formerly owned by Chicago Mayor William 'Big Bill' Thompson.

Fagan's Antique and Classic Automobile Museum,
162nd and Claremont Avenue, Markham 12043, Illinois.

Museum of Science and Industry,
Jackson Park, Chicago, Illinois.
The oldest vehicle housed in the museum is an Italian built one-cyclinder Bernardi (1893). There is a large number of interesting American built models including a

Stoddard-Dayton (1907), a Kansas built Gleason (1909), a Sears Motor Buggy (1910), a Simplex (1911), (only two examples of this model are known to still exist). Two other early models are a National (1913) and a Brewster (1914). Craig Breedlove's land speed record breaker *Spirit of America* which broke the 500 mph record in 1964 and the 600 mph record in the following year is also on show.

INDIANA

Early Wheels Museum,
817 Wabash Avenue, Terre Haute, Indiana 47808.

Elwood Haynes Museum,
1915 South Webster Street, Kokomo, Indiana 46901.
The museum was developed as a memorial to Elwood Haynes, who besides building the first successful commercial automobiles in America, was also the inventor of stainless steel and Stellite, an alloy still widely used in both science and industry. The Haynes cars on display are the 1905 model, a Blue Ribbon Special (1923) and an Apperson Jack Rabbit also built in 1923.

Goodwin Museum,
South Main at Walnut Street, Frankfort, Indiana 46041.
Has a number of rare vehicles on display including Duesenbergs of 1929, 1932 and 1934. Also there is a Gatts two seater (1905), only four of which are still known to exist, and a unique Frisbie (1900), believed to be the only one ever produced. Also displayed are Cord, Auburn and Briscoe models.

Henry H. Blommel Historical Auto Collection,
Route 5, Coonersville, Indiana.

KANSAS

Abilene Auto Museum,
Abilene Centre, Abilene, Kansas.

Kansas State Historical Society,
Memorial Building, 10th and Jackson Street, Topeka, Kansas.
The museum has two interesting vehicles on display, the first is the locally built Great Smith (1908), which is the only known survivor of its type. Smith cars were built between 1902 and 1910. The other model is the Thomas Town Car (1909); this landaulet model 'R' has a four-cylinder engine.

KENTUCKY

Calvert Auto Museum,
PO Box 245, Calvern City, Kentucky 42029.

1927 Mercedes-Benz SS at Historic Car and Caravan, Virginia

MASSACHUSSETTS

Museum of Transportation,
Larz Anderson Park, Brookline, Massachussetts 02146.
Headquarters of the Veteran Motor Car Club of America, the museum has almost 70 vehicles in its collection, they include Wintons of 1899 and 1901, a CGV touring car (1905), two important electric vehicles, an Electramobile (1905) and a Bailey (1908). Two 1929 vehicles are the Ford Model 'A' Town car and a Pierce-Arrow Coupe. There are a number of cars from the 1950s including a Kaiser-Darrin (1953), a Ferrari 315 Grand Prix car (1956) and an unusual Rolls-Royce shooting brake (1959).

Sturbridge Auto Museum,
Old Sturbridge Village, Route 20, Sturbridge, PO Box 486, Massachussetts 01566.

MICHIGAN

Detroit Historical Museum,
5401 Woodward Avenue, Kirby, Detroit, Michigan 48202.

Gilmore Car Museum,
5272 Sheffield Road, Hickory Corners, Michigan 49060.
A collection of 50 antique and classic cars including a Fordmobile, a Stevens Duryea and a White Steamer, all built in 1903. A Packard (1908), a Holsman (1909) and a Marmon (1911).

Henry Ford Museum,
Dearborn, Michigan 48121.
Founded by the motor magnate in the mid-1920s the display contains over 200 cars, beginning with the oldest operating vehicle in America a Sylvester Roper coal-burning carriage (1863). Electric vehicles are represented by Riker, Columbia, Baker, Bailey and Waverly, as well as Thomas A. Edison's 1895 car built to test his new alkaline-nickel-iron battery. The collection as well as featuring many Fords presents an all-round exhibit of American manufacturers including models produced by Duryea, Franklin, Buick and Packard. Classic models such as Rolls-Royce, Bugatti, Lincoln and Duesenberg are also on show. The library is comprehensive.

Sloan Panorama of Transportation,
1221 E. Kearsley Street, Flint, Michigan 48503.

Woodland Cars of Yesteryear,
6504 28th Street, S.E. Grand Rapids, Michigan.

MINNESOTA
Hemp Old Vehicle Museum,
PO Box 851, Country Club Road, Rochester, Minnesota 55901.
MISSOURI
Autos of Yesteryear,
Highway 63, North Rolla, Missouri 65401.
Kelsey's Antique Cars,
Highway 54, PO Box 564, Camdenton, Missouri 65020.
Among the cars displayed is a Maxwell Roadster (1909), a Stutz Bearcat (1914) and a Packard 120 Convertible (1942).
National Museum of Transport,
3013 Barrets Station Road, St Louis, Missouri 63122.
NEBRASKA
Hastings Museum,
Highway 281 and 14th Street, Hastings, Nebraska 68901.
Sawyer's Sandhills Museum,
440 Valentine Street, Valentine, Nebraska 69201.
Contains many unusual models including a Flanders (1910), a Jeffery (1914), a Patterson (1916) and a Flint (1924).
NEVADA
Harrah's Automobile Collection,
PO Box 10, Reno, Nevada 89504.

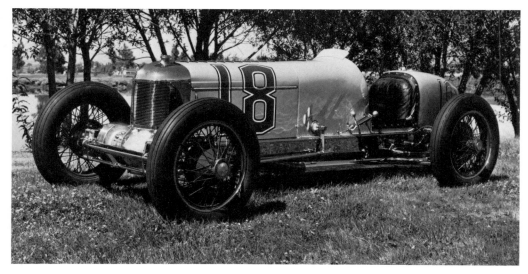

Reputed to be the world's largest automobile collection, consisting of over 1,100 vehicles on display, it was founded by William Harrah in 1948 with the acquisition of a Maxwell (1911). Complete lines of Franklins, Fords, Packards and 18 Duesenbergs are on display, as well as two Bugatti Royales – only six still exist from the original seven that were built. A feature is the original Thomas Flyer (1907) that won the New York-to-Paris Race in 1908. It has been fully restored to the condition it was in when it arrived in Paris at the end of the race. The collection also has one of the most complete research libraries of its kind in the world.
NEW JERSEY
Roaring 20s Autos,
RD1, Box 178-G Wall, New Jersey 07719.
NEW YORK
Golden Age Auto Museum,
30 Shultze Street, Canojoharie, New York 13317.
Long Island Automotive Museum,
Meadow Spring, Glencore, New York 11542.
Upstate Auto Museum,
Route 20, Bridgewater, New York 13313.

OHIO
Frederick C. Crawford Auto-Aviation Museum,
10825 East Boulevard, University Circle, Cleveland, Ohio.
Has a large selection of vehicles ranging from a Benz *Comfortable* (1897), a four-cylinder Winton Racing Car (1902), this car achieved 111 km/h (69 mph) on Daytona Beach on March 28th 1903. A one-cylinder Orient (1904), an Isotta-Fraschini Brougham (1927) and an American Motors AMX Sports Car Prototype (1966) are also on show.
OKLAHOMA
Horseless Carriage Unlimited,
PO Box 1887, Muskogee, Oklahoma 74401.
PENNSYLVANIA
Boyertown Museum of Historic Vehicles,
Warwick Street, Boyertown, Pennsylvania 19512.
Features many locally built models including a Duryea. Other local makes include the Boss Steam Car (1902), the Sternberg-Graham-Vantine (1912) and Dile Sport Roadster (1914). Additional makes displayed are Daniels, Dodge, Plymouth and La Salle.

1929 Miller racing car from Hurrah's Automobile Collection, Reno

Pollock Auto Showcase,
PO Box 248, Downingtown, Pennsylvania 19335.
Swigart Museum,
Museum Park, Route 22 East, Huntingdon, Pennsylvania 16652.
Reputed to be the oldest car museum in America being established in the early 1920s. A Studebaker Electric (1908) which used to operate in the tunnel between the Senate building and the Capitol in Washington DC, and a Carroll (1920) – believed to be the only remaining example of the make – are just two interesting exhibits. Also included is a Scripps-Booth (1916).
Gene Zimmermann's Automobil-rama,
Holiday West, Route 15, Harrisburg, PO Box 1855, Pennsylvania 17015.
SOUTH DAKOTA
Horseless Carriage Museum,
Keystone Route, PO Box 255, Rapid City, South Dakota 57701.
Pioneer Auto Museum,
Highway 16 and 83, Murdo, South Dakota 57550.

TENNESSEE
Cox's Car Museum,
PO Box 253, Gatlinburg, Tennessee 37730.
Dixie Gun Works Inc.,
Gunpowder Lane, Union City, Tennessee 38261.
The collection comprises some 30 cars such as an International (1908) and a Maxwell (1909). There are 16 Fords on display all built between 1914 and 1941, as well as other American makes including Studebaker, Packard and Cadillac.
Smoky Mountain Car Museum,
Highway 441, Pigeon Forge, Tennessee 37863.
The museum has over 30 fully restored vehicles of all ages including one of the first shaft driven cars a Hupmobile 20 (1909), a Cadillac 4 (1911), a Haynes Model 34 (1916), a Cord L-29 (1930) and a four-cylinder Allstate (1953). Two added attractions are James Bond's customized Aston-Martin DB5, which featured in the movies *Goldfinger* and *Thunderball* (the car has its own ejector-seat, bullet shield, retractable machine guns, etc.) also a special built for singer Hank Williams jnr estimated to be worth over $22,000.
TEXAS
Classic Car Showcase,
PO Box 22592, Houston, Texas 77027.
Pate Museum of Transportation,
US Highway 377, between Fort Worth and Cresson, Texas.
The museum houses not only cars but aircraft, boats and a large reference library. Among the interesting cars on display are a Schacht (1904), a Premier (1917). This latter is a rare seven passenger model and has an unusual tilted steering wheel and push-button transmission. Also shown is a Russian built ZIM (1950). In addition there are Fords, Cadillacs, Studebakers and Buicks and even an Austin London Taxi built in 1955.
VERMONT
Steamtown USA,
Bellows Falls, Vermont.
VIRGINIA
Historic Car and Caravan,
PO Box 748, Luray Caravans, Virginia 22835.
Among the 70 odd exhibits is an Ohio built, two-cylinder Schacht (1906) and one of the finest sports and road racing cars ever produced, a Mercedes-Benz SS (1927). Other models include Cord, Lincoln and Pierce Arrow.
Roaring Twenties Antique Car Museum,
Route 230, Hood, Virginia 22723.
WISCONSIN
Berman's Auto and Antique Museum,
Highway 14, Oregon, Wisconsin.
Brooks Stevens Automotive Museum,
10325 N. Port, Washington Road, 13-W Mequon, Wisconsin 53092.
Four Wheel Drive Museum and Historical Building,
FWD Corporation, Clintonville, Wisconsin.
Sunflower Museum of Antique Cars,
Sunflowers Lodge, Lake Tomahawk, Wisconsin.

VENEZUELA
Museo del Transporte,
Caracas.

MOTORING ORGANIZATIONS

Since the days motor cars first began to appear on the roads, there has been a need for motor clubs. Many were founded – only to founder a little later. But at the turn of the century some clubs, such as those in France and Great Britain, were steered through their first faltering steps and became established, sometimes with royal support.

The initial demand, though, was for social purposes – a meeting place for automobilists as they were then called – for organized tours and racing. As there was a lack of signposts, requests were made through the clubs for local guides. Later came the need for road assistance.

The motor clubs then became motoring organizations and many introduced special membership for those who only wanted road assistance and touring facilities. Between the wars similar associations were started and as more cars appeared on the roads so more organizations sprang up to aid drivers. More cars also caused more rules, regulations and restrictions to be introduced and this led to the organizations extending their services to include legal advice and insurance.

Today the role of most of the world's motoring associations is one of service rather than social.

ALGERIA
Automobile Club National d'Algérie
99 bd Bouakouir, Alger. Correspondence: BP 67 – Alger Gare (Algérie).
Tel No. 64-97-71
Touring Club d'Algérie
1 rue Al-Idrissi, Alger BP 550, Alger–Gare.
Tel No. 64-08-37 – 63-58-10

ANDORRA
Automobil Club d'Andorra
Babot Camp, 4. Andorra la Vella
Tel No. 20. 8. 90
The club provides maps, guides and general information for tourists.

ARGENTINE
Automovil Club Argentino
Avenida del Libertador 1850 1461
Buenos Aires.
Tel No. 821-6061, 83.0091, 83.6061
For road assistance phone:
821-6081 83-4403 83-7711
84-0624 83-3755
Touring Club Argentino
Esmeralda 605, Tucuman 781
Ser. piso Buenos Aires.
Tel No. 392-7994 392-8170
392-3917 392-6742 392-6817
392-6947

AUSTRALIA
Australian Automobile Association (AAA)
Phoenix House, 88 Northbourne Ave., PO B 1555, Canberra City
A.C.T. 2601.
Tel No. 47 7311
Affiliated Clubs are:
National Roads and Motorist Association,
151 Clarence St., Sydney, NSW 2000.
Tel No. 290 0123
Royal Automobile Club of Victoria,
123 Queen St., Melbourne 3000.
Tel No. 60 02 51
Royal Automobile Association of

South Australia,
41 Hindmarsh Square,
Adelaide 5000.
Tel No. 223 45 55
Royal Automobile Club of Queensland,
Cnr. Ann and Boundary Sts., Brisbane 4000, PO Box 339.
Tel No. 21 15 11
Royal Automobile Club of Western Australia,
228 Adelaide Terrace, Perth 6000,
Box C 140 GPO.
Tel No. 25 05 51
Royal Automobile Club of Tasmania,
Cnr. Murray and Patrick Sts., Hobart 7001.
Tel No. 34 66 11
Cost of membership varies from Club to Club and averages around 10 dollars. Most also offer special caravan membership for between three and four dollars, while the RAC of Tasmania has social and country membership. The road rescue service with some clubs covers the vehicle no matter who is driving it and others cover the person whatever car they may be driving. The service operates on a reciprocal basis and visitors from other states may obtain service on production of their current membership card. All give a 24 hour service except the RAASA and some impose restrictions on time and distance. Patrols in radio linked vans attend breakdowns and also act as pilots through main towns and cities. General touring information is available and in addition to route maps, a number of guides can be obtained on such topics as boating, snow slopes, golf courses, picnic grounds, places of interest, and inspection of wineries.
Confederation of Australian Motor Sport (CAMS)
382 Burke Rd., Camberwell, Victoria 3124, PO Box 441, Camberwell, Vic 3124.
Tel No. 29 2327 (3 lines)

AUSTRIA
Österreichischer Automobil-, Motorrad- und Touring Club (ÖAMTC)
Schubertring 1–3, 1010 Vienna.
Tel No. 0222/72 99 0
The Club operates breakdown and technical assistance services on all major roads covering some three quarters of the country's road network. On some roads the services work on a 24 hour basis while on others it is available either during the day or evening hours only.

The organization began as a touring club in 1896. Two years later a motor club was formed and the two merged in 1946. At present it has over 80 roadside offices.

Stranded motorists should phone the nearest office and a patrol will be directed to their assistance. If he is unable to get the car going again within a reasonable time, the vehicle will be towed to a repair workshop. A charge can be made to non-members.

The Club offers a tourist service and maps can be obtained. Insurance and legal assistance can be arranged for members.

BANGLADESH
Automobile Association of Bangladesh (A.A.B.)
3/B Outer Circular Rd., Dacca 17.
Tel No. 243444 – 250541

BARBADOS (West Indies)
Barbados Automobile Association (B.A.A.)
Room 406, Plantations Building, Broad St., Bridgetown B.W.
Tel No. 6 46 40

BELGIUM
Royal Automobile Club de Belgique
Rue d'Arlon, 53 B-1040 Brussels.
Tel No. 2/230 08 10
One of the oldest motoring organizations in the world, having started in 1896. The Club operates a 24 hour breakdown service with patrols on motorways and in main cities. Assistance can be obtained any time by phoning the Club. The service is also free to visitors provided they are members of a foreign motoring club. The Club offers touring information and will recommend hotels, restaurants, garages, repair workshops and camp sites. Insurance facilities are available to members and legal assistance can be arranged.
Touring Club Royal de Belgique (T.C.B.)
rue de la Loi 44, B-1040 Brussels.
Tel No. 02 513 82 40

BOLIVIA
Automovil Club Boliviano
avenida 6 de Agosto 2993 – San Jorge Casilla 602, La Paz.
Tel Nos. 51667 42998 42074 22065

BRAZIL
Automovel Club do Brasil
90 rua do Passeio ZC-06, Rio de Janeiro.
Tel No. 52 4055
Touring Club do Brasil
Praça Mauasln – Estação Maritima de Passageiros, Berilo Neves

Rio de Janeiro.
Tel No. 223-1762
Information bureau Tel No. 243-6578
Confederação Brasileira de Automobilismo
Rue Alvaro Alvim 31 – Sobreloja, ZC 06, Rio de Janeiro 20 000 RJ.
Tel No.: (021) 231.08.18 (021) 221.67.46

BRUNEI
Brunei Automobile Club (B.A.M.C.)
Weights and Measure Office, Bandar Seri Begawan, Brunei.
Tel No. 4659 87-288.

BULGARIA
Union des Automobilistes Bulgares
6 rue Sveta Sofia, Sofia C. PO Box 563.
Tel No. 87. 88. 01 02. 88. 00. 02
A breakdown service operates from early morning to late at night on the E5 International road, but for much shorter periods on other roads – mainly during daylight hours.

There are over 80 patrol cars covering some 4,000 km and assistance can be obtained by phoning Sofia 146. The service is free to members of foreign clubs providing the on-the-spot repairs can be completed within an hour.

The organization offers information to tourists on a wide range of items including road conditions, routes, camp sites, hotels, workshops and places of interest to visit.

CANADA
Canadian Automobile Association (C.A.A.)
150 Gloucester St., Ottawa K2P OA6 (Ontario).
Tel No. 610-562-1902 613-237-2105 (General Manager)
The CAA operates in a similar way to the American Automobile Association.
Affiliated clubs are:
British Columbia Automobile Association
VANCOUVER
999 West Broadway; Box 9900.
Tel No. 610-922-5060
CHILLIWACK
Southgate Shopping Centre.
KAMLOOPS
Thompson Park Shopping Centre.
NANAIMO
2115 Departure Bay Rd., Northbrook Shopping Mall.
NELSON
556 Baker St.
NEW WESTMINSTER
775 Sixth St.
PENTICTON
339 Martin St.
PRINCE GEORGE
609 Central St., Spruceland Shopping Centre.
VICTORIA
1075 Pandora Ave.
Alberta Motor Association
EDMONTON
109th St., & Kingsway Ave.
Tel No. 610-831-1926
CAMROSE
4807 Fiftieth St.
GRANDE PRAIRIE
10828–100th St.
LLOYDMINSTER

4900–50th Ave.
CALGARY
905–11th Ave., South West
LETHBRIDGE
608–5th Ave., South.
MEDICINE HAT
414–6th Ave., South East.
RED DEER
5913 Gaetz Ave.
FORT McMURRAY
10116A Hardin St.
BANFF
Bear St.
Saskatchewan Motor Club
REGINA
200 Albert St., North.
Tel No. 610-721-1212
ESTEVAN
329–12th Ave.
MOOSE JAW
80 Caribou St., West.
NORTH BATTLEFORD
2002–100th St.
PRINCE ALBERT
68–13th St., West.
SASKATOON
321–4th Ave., North.
SWIFT CURRENT
300 Begg St., West.
YORKTON
50 Broadway East.
Manitoba Motor League
WINNIPEG
870 Empress St.
Tel No. 204-786-5411
BRANDON
940 Princess Ave.
Touring Club Montreal
MONTREAL
1401 McGill College Ave., Quebec.
Tel No. 514-288-7111
Quebec Automobile Club
QUEBEC
2600 Boulevard Laurier, Box 5600.
Tel No. 418-688-3578
TROIS RIVIERES
1300 rue Notre Dame
LEVIS
300 Côte du Passage
Maritime Automobile Association (New Brunswick)
ST JOHN
Haymarket Square Shopping Centre, City Rd.
Tel No. 506-657-3470
MONCTON
K-Mart Plaza.
MAA – Newfoundland
ST. JOHN'S
333 Duckworth St.
MAA – Nova Scotia
HALIFAX
1872 Brunswick St.
GLACE BAY
3 Newton St.
Ontario Motor League
TORONTO
160 Bloor St., East.
Tel No. 416-924-8793
Hamilton Automobile Club
HAMILTON
393 Main St., East.
Tel No. 416-525-1210
BRANTFORD
431 St. Paul Ave.
OAKVILLE
125 Navy St.
OML – Essex County Automobile Club
WINDSOR
1215 Ouellette Ave.
Tel No. 610-362-0224
CHATHAM
OML-Kent Branch, 810 Richmond St.
OWEN SOUND

OML – Blue Water Club,
187–10th St., West.
SARNIA
OML – Lamoton Club, 889
London Rd.
OML – Toronto Club
TORONTO
2 Carlton St.
Tel No. 416-964-3111
BARRIE
OML – Toronto Club, 153
Dunlop St., East.
BRAMPTON
239 Queen St., East.
OSHAWA
OML – Oshawa Office, 348 King
St., West.
SAULT SAINT-MARIE
OML – Algoma Division, 224
Queen St., East.
OML – Eastern Ontario Club
KINGSTON
2300 Princess St.
Tel No. 613-546-2679
BELLEVILLE
162 Front St.
OML – Tri County Club
KITCHENER
2958 King St., East.
Tel No. 519-576-1020
GUELPH
94 Gordon St.
OML – London Motor Club
LONDON
479 Highbury Ave.
Tel No. 519-453-3140
WOODSTOCK
Ontario, 656 Dundas St.
STRATHROY
87 Colborne St.
OML – Ottawa Club
OTTAWA
150 Gloucester St.
Tel No. 613-238-1311
OML – Peterborough Club
PETERBOROUGH
238 Lansdowne St., East.
Tel No. 705-745-5747
OML – Niagara Peninsula Club
ST. CATHARINES
76 Lake St.
Tel No. 416-688-0321
OML – Elgin Norfolk Club
ST. THOMAS
1091 Talbot St.
Tel No. 519-631-6490
SIMCOE
46 Peel St.
OML – Nickel Belt Club
SUDBURY
353 Lorne St.
Tel No. 705-674-6496
NORTH BAY
190 McIntyre St.
OML – Northwestern Ontario Club
THUNDER BAY
585 Memorial Ave.
Tel No. 807-345-1261
Canadian Automobile Sport Clubs Inc.
5385 Yonge St., Suite 28,
Willowdale, Ontario M2N 5R7.
Tel No. 416 22-5411 222-5458

CENTRAL AFRICAN REPUBLIC
Association Internationale Auxiliaire des Touring Clubs de l'Afrique Centrale (TOURAC)
40 rue de la Loi, Brussels, Belgium.

CHILE
Automovil Club de Chile
Avda Pedro de Valdivia No. 195 –

Casilla 16695 Correo 9, Santiago, Chile.
Tel No. 74 95 16
Federación Chilena de Automovilismo Deportivo (F.A.D.E.C.H.)
Echaurren 75 – Santiago, Chile.
Tel No. 94989 92137

COLOMBIA
Touring y Automovil Club de Colombia
Avda, Caracas No. 46–64/72
Bogota.
Tel No. 327580

COSTA RICA
Automovil-Touring Club de Costa Rica
Apartado 4646, San José.
Tel No. 3570

CYPRUS
Cyprus Automobile Association
30 Homer Ave., PO Box 2279,
Nicosia.
Tel No. 021 73883

CUBA
Automovil y Aero Club de Cuba
Malecon 217, Bajos, Havana.
Tel No. 61-2551

CZECHOSLOVAKIA
Ustredni Automotoklub CSSR
Opletalova 29, 116 31,
Prague 1.
Tel No. 223544–7
Affiliated club:
Automotoklub SSR
Bratislava, Rooseveltovo nam. 1.
Tel No. 34026

DENMARK
Royal Danish Automobile Club
Frederiksberg Allé 41, 1820
Copenhagen V.
Tel No. 01-21-11-01
Federation of Danish Motorists
Blegdamsvej 124, 2100
Copenhagen OE.
Tel No. 01-13-21-12
Founded 1909
F.D.M. has 43 branches.

EAST AFRICA – Kenya, Tanzania, Uganda
Automobile Association of Kenya (A.A.E.A.)
Kenya AA House, Westlands,
Nairobi. PO Box 40087.
Tel Nos. Nairobi 46826/9, 46820,
45084

ECUADOR
Automovil Club del Ecuador (ANETA)
Quito, Avenida Eloy Alfaro y
Berlin, Apartado Postal 2830 –
Quito.
Tel No. 237779 527408 540355

EGYPT
Automobile and Touring Club of Egypt
10 Kasr El Nil, Cairo.
Tel No. 977241 977242 977243

EL SALVADOR
Automovil Club de El Salvador (A.C.E.S.)
Alameda Roosevelt y 41 Av.
Sur No. 2173, PO Box (06) 1177 –
San Salvador.
Tel No. 23 – 8077

ETHIOPIA
Automobile Club Eritreo
Via Giustino de Jacobis n 4–6–8,
P.O. Box 1187, Asmara.
Tel No. 11615

FINLAND
Autoliitto (Automobile and Touring Club of Finland)
Fabianinkatu 14, 00100, Helsinki
10.
Tel No. Helsinki 650 022
Road assistance is given on a voluntary basis through members who have the necessary equipment and will help if they see a road user in difficulties at the roadside.

Otherwise it is mainly a touring club with categories of membership for town and country, family and overseas.

Founded in 1919, the Club changed its name in 1972 and now has over 30,000 members.

FRANCE
Automobile Club de France
Place de la Concorde, 6–8, 75008
Paris.
Tel No. 265-34-70
Founded 1895
Operates through a number of affiliated clubs some of whom offer road services. In some cases it is free of charge, while others make a small charge.
Fédération Française des Clubs Automobiles
61–67 rue Haxo, 75020 Paris.
Tel No. 797-43-29
Fédération Française du Sport Automobile
136 rue de Longchamp, F-75116
Paris.
Tel No. 553-20-89 727-97-39
Touring Club de France
65 Av. de la Grande Armée,
F-75782 Paris Cedex 16.
Tel No. 502 1400
The Club has 32 regional offices located in main towns.

GERMANY
Allgemeiner Deutscher Automobil-Club e.V. (ADAC)
Postfach 700.080, Baumgartner-strasse 53, D 8000 Munich 70.
Tel No. 089 76 76 1
Founded in 1903, and with a membership of over 2 million, the Club has some 140 roadside offices with 730 patrols and 639 vehicles. The ADAC Road Assistance Service uses 68 vehicles to cover 3,500 km of federal motorways and roads daily from 8 am–8 pm. Hours can differ in wintertime. Telephone booths are located every 2 km along motorways and in the event of a breakdown drivers should call for 'Strassenwacht-Lilfe' (road patrol breakdown service). Meanwhile in towns, there is an urban ADAC breakdown service which operates on a 24 hr basis, especially those in large towns – e.g. Frankfurt, Hamburg, Munich.

The Club also has 17 frontier offices which offer assistance, provide Carnets, Customs documents, sell guides and maps, and act as exchange offices.

Information is available from all the offices on hotels, garages, repair workshops and camping sites but not on restaurants. A guide of recommended establishments is published by ADAC.

Other services offered include insurance, which is arranged through a company, and legal assistance through lawyers chosen by the Club.

Automobilclub von Deutschlande V. (AVD)
Postfach 71 0166, Lyoner Strasse 16, D-6000 Frankfurt a.M. 71.
Tel No. (0611) 66 06 1
Although the elder of the two clubs – being founded in 1899 – it has no roadside offices and only one frontier office. Road assistance covers 3,500 km and 48 patrols operate on motorways.

The Club offers a touring service with information on routes, road conditions, hotels, restaurants, camping sites etc., and will recommend touring establishments. It has an agreement with an insurance company and does offer insurance facilities to its members in cases of accidents and luggage thefts etc. Legal assistance is available through lawyers recommended by the Club and at cost price.

Deutscher Touring Automobil-Club (DTC)
8 Munich 65, Postfach 140.
Tel No. 8 11 1048   8 11 1212

Deutscher Camping Club e.V (DCC)
8 Munchen 40, Postfach 400428.
Tel No. 33 40 21

Deutscher Kanu-Verband e.V (D.K.V.)
D-41 Duisburg 1, Berta-Allee 8.
Tel No. 77 39 66

Deutscher Segler-Verband (D.S.V.)
D-2000 Hamburg 76, Adolfstr 56.
Tel No. 040 220 51 37.

GHANA
The Automobile Association of Ghana
Fanum House, (No. 4, 3rd Otswe St.) South Labadi Rd. Extension, Accra or PO Box 7047, Accra.
Tel No. 75983 23953

GREECE
Automobile et Touring Club de Grèce (ELPA)
2–4 rue Messogion – GR 610 Athens.
Tel No 77.91.615
A rescue service is available every day and is extended in the summer to cover a much larger area. It operates through patrols who can be called by phone. Breakdowns in certain mountainous regions are towed to the nearest repair workshop.

The Club, founded in 1924, offers information relating to itineraries, road conditions, and places of interest to visit. Lists of hotels, restaurants and camping sites are available but these are compiled by the National Tourist Organization of Greece. Although the Club does not issue its own maps, it does have copies of the Tourist Guide of Greece and these can be obtained from its office.

Touring Club Hellénique
12 rue Polytechniou, Athens 103.
Tel No. 5240 872 5240.854 5248.600/601/602

GUATEMALA
Club de Automovilismo y Turismo de Guatemala (Catgua)
4a, avenida 2–07, Zona 9, Ciudad de Guatemala.
Tel No. Office – 64882 Agency – 64883

HONG KONG
Hong Kong Automobile Association
Hennessy Rd. Post Office, Wanchay. PO Box 20045.
Tel No. 5-767949 5-737474

HUNGARY
Magyar Autoklub (M.A.K.)
11 Romer Floris u. 4/a, 1277 Budapest.
Tel No. 355-921 351-374 154-001
28 branches.

ICELAND
Icelandic Automobile Association
Skulagata 51, PO Box 311, Reykjavik.
Tel No. 2-99-99

INDIA
Federation of Indian Automobile Associations
1st Floor, Churchgate Reclamation, Vir Nariman Rd., Bombay 400 020
Tel No. 29 10 85 (5 lines)
Automobile Association of Eastern India
13 Promothesh Barua Sarani, West Bengal, Calcutta 19.
Tel No. 47-9012, 47-5131-3, 47-4455
Founded in 1904, the Automobile Association of Eastern India has branch offices at:
ASANSOL
Apcar Gardens.
Tel No. 7440
BARAUNI
PO Barauni Oil Refinery, Begusarai.
CUTTACK
PO Box 7.
Tel No. 947
DARJEELING
Happy Valley T.E.
Tel No. 163
DHANBAD
Dhanbad Automobiles Pvt Ltd., Bank Rd.
Tel No. 2426.
DOOARS
PO Binnaguri.
Banarhat 2
DURGAPUR
City Centre, Priyadarshini Indira Rajpath, 9.
Tel No. 3148
JAMSHEDPUR
c/o Tisco Hotel, 7B, Rd.
Tel No. 2620
PATNA
Varma Rd. Tel No. 22454/22493
RANCHI
Auto Agency Fairyalai Chowk, Ranchi 1.
Tel No. 22220
ROURKELA
Hirakud Automobile, Ring Rd.
Tel No. 2271 2272
SILIGURI
Bagdogra Auto Supply, Dist. Darjeeling.
SHILLONG
c/o Shillong Club Ltd.
Tel No. 40505

Automobile Association of Upper India
14-F Connaught Place, New Delhi, PO Box 28.
Tel No. 42063 40419 44312
The Federation of Motor Sport Clubs of India PVT Ltd.
c/o Alpha Motor Co., Liberty Buildg, 2nd Floor Marine Lines, Bombay 400 020.
Tel No. 293899

INDONESIA
Ikatan Motor Indonesia
Gedung KONI Pusat, Senayan, Jakarta or Kotakpos 609 – Jakarta Kota.
Tel No. 581102

IRAN
Tsuring et Automobile Club d'Iran
Khiaban Varzeche, 37. or
BP 1294 – Teheran.
Tel No. 319040 319041 319042 319043 319044 319045

IRAQ
The Iraq Automobile and Touring Association
All Mansor, Baghdad.
Tel No. 35 862 36 001

REPUBLIC OF IRELAND
Royal Irish Automobile Club
34 Dawson St., Dublin C.2.
Tel No. Dublin 775141/3
Automobile Association
23 Suffolk St., Dublin 2.
Tel No. Dublin 779481

ISRAEL
Automobile and Touring Club of Israel
19 Petah Tikva Rd., PO Box 36144, Tel Aviv, 66183.
Tel No. 622961/2

ITALY
Automobile Club D'Italia
Via Marsala, 8 – 00185 Roma or Casella Postale 2389 – 00100 Roma.
Tel No. 4998
Rescue service operates on a 24-hour basis every day including public holidays and covers the whole country. Service can be obtained from patrols on motorways or by means of telephones located alongside motorways.

During the summer season (June 1–Sept 30) there is a reinforced service called 'Holiday Assistance' to help motorists stranded on motorways. Service can be obtained by the one telephone number: 116. Full information is available on itineraries, road conditions, hotels, shops and places of interest. Two types of touring assistance are offered – Normal and Extra – and maps of the country (dealt with in 4 parts) and certain districts can be obtained together with descriptions on some Italian towns. Visitors can buy petrol at reduced prices, and special terms are granted for repairs carried out in some garages.

IVORY COAST
Ministry of State for Tourism
BP 20. 949 Abidjan.
Tel No. 325197
F.I.S.A. (Fédération Ivoirienne de Sport Automobile)
BP 20 973 – Abidjan.

JAMAICA
Jamaica Motoring Club
Kingston 10, Jamaica. PO Box 49.
The Jamaica Automobile Association
16 Lady Masgrave Road, Kingston
Tel No. 92-77096 92-77571

JAPAN
Japan Automobile Federation
Shiba – Koen, 3-5-8, Minato-Ku, Tokyo 105.
Tel No. 436 2811
Touring Club of Japan
Yayoi Building 5F, 10–20, Jiyugaoka 2-chome Meguroku, Tokyo 153. PO Box 5, Ebara, Tokyo 142-91.
Tel No. (03) Tokyo 783 4561 786 8559 723 0311

JORDAN
Royal Automobile Club of Jordan
PO Box 920, Amman.
Tel No. 44261 22467

KENYA
The Automobile Association of Kenya
AA House – Westlands, PO Box 40087, Nairobi.
Tel No. 46826

SOUTH KOREA
Korea Automobile Association
94 Dabsipri-Dong, Dongdaemun-Ku, or CPO Box 2008 – Seoul.
Tel No. 95 7219

KUWAIT
Kuwait International Touring and Automobile Club
Khaldiah, Airport Rd., PO Box 2100, Kuwait.
Tel No. 812539 815192

LAOS
Royal Automobile Club du Laos
Vientiane.

LEBANON
Automobile et Touring Club du Liban
Immeuble Fattai, Rue du Port, Beirut. BP 3545.
Tel No. 221698 221699 229222

LIBYA
Automobile and Touring Club of Libya
Al Fath Boulevard, Maidan al-Ghazala, PO Box 3566, Tripoli L.A.R.

LIECHTENSTEIN
Automobil-Club des Furstentums Leichtenstein (ACFL)
Bannholzstrasse 10 – 9490 Vaduz.
Tel No. (075) 2-60-66

LUXEMBOURG
Automobile Club de Grand-Duché de Luxembourg
13 route de Longwy, L – Helfenterbruck/Bertrange.
Tel No. 31-10-31

MADAGASCAR
Automobile Club de Madagascar
Rue Ravoninahitriniarivo Alarobia, Tananarive BP 571.
Tel No. 420 30

MALAYSIA
Automobile Association of Malaysia
3 Jalan 8/1D, PO Box 34, Petaling Jaya, Selangor.
Tel No. 54646 54647

MALTA
Malta Automobile Federation
c/o Dar Il-Kenn, St. Mark St., St. Julians.

MAURITIUS
The Automobile Association of Mauritius (A.A.M.)
Labama Building, 35 rue Sir William Newton, Port Louis.
Tel No. 2-4173 (3 lines)

MEXICO
Asociación Mexicana Automovilística, A.C.
Av. Chapultepec No. 276 Colonia Roma – Apartado Postal 24-486, Mexico, 7 D.F.
Tel No. 511-10-84
Asociación Nacional Automovilística
Edificio ANA, Calle Miguel E Schultz. 140, BP 1720 Z.P.1 Mexico 4 DF.
Tel No. 546-50-89 546-02-67 546-99-65
Asociación Mexicana de Turismo
Liverpool No. 10 Mexico 6 D.F.
Tel No. 566-52-84 546-70-24 535-43-28

MONACO
Automobile Club de Monaco
23 boulevard Albert 1er, MC-Monaco. B.P. 314.
Tel No. 30-30-72 30-32-20 30-27-72

MOROCCO
Royal Automobile Club Marocain
3 rue Lemercier, Boite Postale 94, Casablanca.
Tel No. 25.00.30 25.05.62
Founded 1913.
Touring Club du Maroc (T.C.M.)
3 avenue de l'Armée Royale, Casablanca.
Tel No. 713-04 757-30 652-31 792-88

NEPAL
Automobile Association of Nepal (A.A.N.)
728 Exhibition Rd., Kathmandu.
Tel No. 11999

NETHERLANDS
Koninklijke Nederlandsche Automobiel Club
Sophialaan 4, NL 2005 - The Hague.
Tel No. 070 -46-92-80 (12 lines)
KNAC does have a road rescue service which operates on a 24 hour basis and covers the whole country. Assistance is obtained by phoning the Club. On-the-spot repairs are carried out if it is not a major breakdown, otherwise the vehicle is towed to a garage. It has no legal assistance service, but it can be arranged through an agreement with an insurance company. KNAC have a number of centres where vehicle inspections can be carried out, and and they also give tuition on anti-skid methods in a number of schools.

Over 3,000 people take the courses each year.
The Club offers the usual touring services, which include the necessary documentation for travel abroad. They will plan a journey and make reservations for hotels and flats, and obtain rail, boat and air tickets. Maps of the country, but not other countries, and itineraries are available.
Koninklijke Nederlandse Toeristenbond ANWB
P.O. Box 2200, Wassenaarseweg 220, The Hague.
Tel No. (070) 26 44 26
Operates through branch offices located in :
ALKMAAR
Koelmalaan 16.
AMERSFOORT
Arnhemseweg 16-18.
AMSTELVEEN
Kostverlorenhof 5.
AMSTERDAM
Museumplein 5 – Surinameplein 33.
APELDOORN
Loolaan 31.
ARNHEM
Bergstraat 2, Het Dorp
Dorpsbrink 1.
ASSEN
Kloekhorststraat 44.
BREDA
Wilhelminapark 25.
DORDRECHT
Nic. Maessingel 200.
EINDHOVEN
Elzentlaan 139-141.
EMMEN
De Weiert 84.
ENSCHEDE
De Klanderij 130.
GRONINGEN
Ubbo Emmiussingel 27.
HAARLEM
Stationsplein 70.
THE HAGUE
Wassenaarseweg 220–De Savornin Lohmanplein 10.
HEERLEN
Apollolaan 146.
's-HERTOGENBOSCH
Burg. Loeffplein 13.
HILVERSUM
Noordse Bosje 1.
HOOGVLIET
Binnenban 6.
LEEUWARDEN
Lange Marktstraat 22.
LEIDEN
Breestraat 142-144.
MAASTRICHT
Koningsplein 60.
MIDDELBURG
Plein 1940, No. 6.
NIJMEGEN
Berg en Dalseweg 22.
ROTTERDAM
Westblaak 210.
SCHIEDAM
Parkweg 216.
TERNEUZEN
Kersstraat 3.
TILBURG
Spoorlaan 396.
UTRECHT
Van Vollenhovenlaan 277-279.
IJMUIDEN
Lange Nieuwstraat 422.
ZAANDAM
Peperstraat 146.
ZWOLLE
Tesselschadestraat 155.

NEW ZEALAND
The New Zealand Automobile Association Inc.
92–100 Lambton Quay, Wellington, PO Box 1794, Wellington.
Tel No. 735-484.
Motorsport Association New Zealand
9 Tinakori Rd., Thorndon, Wellington, PO Box 3793.
Tel No. 723-520 723-521

NORWAY
Kongelig Norsk Automobilklub
Parkveien 68, N – Oslo 2.
Tel No. Bureaux, Club and Hotel, 56 – 26 – 90
Much of the Club's efforts are directed towards providing general information on touring services. It supplies the necessary documentation for tourists and recommends hotels and camping sites – a list of which are published in the Club's review. Letters of credit are issued and these are acceptable for repair costs, hotel bills, car hire, petrol and spare parts.
The Club publishes maps of Norway, but not of other countries, and guides. It also owns about 50 cabins along the coast from Oslo to Kristiansand and in the mountains. On the general motoring front, they do not provide road rescue services, but do have facilities for vehicle inspections and will arrange legal assistance for members.
Norges Automobil-Forbund
Storgt. 2 N – Oslo 1.
Tel No. 33 70 80

PAKISTAN
The Automobile Association of West Pakistan
8 Multan Rd. (Samanabad Turn), PO Box 76, Lahore.
Tel No. 414854
Founded 1928.
The Karachi Automobile Association
Standard Insurance House, I.I. Chundriger Rd., Karachi 0226.
Tel No. 23 21 73

PARAGUAY
Touring y Automovil Club Paraguayo
25 de Mayo y Brasil, Asunción, Casilla de Correo no. 1 204.
Tel No. 26-075 21-706 21-801 20-014 (Touring) 23-987 24-366 (Assistance)

PERU
Touring y Automovil Club del Peru
César Vallejo 699 (Lince) Lima, 14, PO Box 2219, Lima.
Tel No. 40-3270 22-5957
Founded 1924.

PHILIPPINES
Philippine Motor Association
4071 R. Magsaysay Blvd., PO Box 999, Manila, Philippines 2806.
Tel No. 60-97-02 60-93-60
Founded 1931.

POLAND
Polski Zwiazek Motorowy
02-518 Warszawa, ul. Kazimier-zowska 66.
Tel No. 49-93-61 49-41-38
Backed by over 30 local clubs, PZM has no roadside offices, but does

run a number of frontier posts which are open 24 hours a day throughout the year. Currency can be exchanged at these posts and full and detailed information concerning Poland and PZM can be obtained. Brochures, folders, road maps, camping maps and traffic rules are available free of charge and maps of Poland, guides, atlases, town plans and other touring publications are on sale.
A road rescue service covers much of the country, especially national roads carrying heavy traffic, and is available by phone between 7 am–10 pm in provincial towns and 7 am–7 pm in other districts.

PORTUGAL
Automóvel Club de Portugal
Rua Rosa Aranjo, 24-26 BP 2594, Lisbon – 2.
Tel No. 563931 (10 lines)

PUERTO RICO
Federación de Automovilismo de Puerto Rico
PO Box 153, Hato Rey, Puerto Rico 00919.
Tel No. 761-0680

QATAR
Automobile et Touring Club de Qatar
Al-Bida St., PO Box 18, Doha.
Tel No. 22-734 23-415

RUMANIA
Automobil Clubul Roman (A.C.R.)
Str. Nikos Beloianis, 27 – Bucuresti 22. B.P. 3107.
Tel No. 14.99.27 13.42.60 15.41.85
Patrols, equipped to give roadside assistance, cover much of the country and can be called by phone. Minor repairs taking less than 30 minutes to complete are carried out free of charge, while there is a tariff for other breakdowns according to the time taken. The Club has its own legal section. A full touring service is also available.

SENEGAL
Automobile Club du Sénégal
Immeuble Chambre de Commerce, place de l'Indépendance, BP 295, Dakar.
Tel No. 226-04
Founded 1926.
Touring Club du Sénégal
c/o La Délégation générale au Tourisme, place de l'Indépendance BP 1412.
Tel No. 230-61

SINGAPORE
Automobile Association of Singapore
AA House, 336 River Valley Rd., PO Box 85, Killiney Rd., Singapore 9.
Tel No. 37 24 44

SOUTH AFRICA
The Automobile Association of South Africa (A.A.S.A.)
AA House, 42 de Villiers St., PO Box 596, Johannesburg 2000.
Tel No. 28 1400
Branches
BEAUFORT WEST
1st Floor, Trust Bank Building, Donkin St., PO Box 131.

Motoring Organizations

BELLVILLE
4c Anstey Centre, Teddington St.,
PO Box 418.
BENONI
Lorna Court, Rothsay St.,
PO Box 148.
BETHLEHEM
30a Oxford St., PO Box 152.
BLOEMFONTEIN
AA House, 56 Church St.,
PO Box 547.
BOKSBURG
4 Pretoria St., PO Box 278.
BRAKPAN
641 Voortrekker Rd., PO Box 166.
CAPE TOWN
AA House, 7 Martin Hammer-
schlag Way, Foreshore, PO Box 70.
CARLETONVILLE
87 Annan Rd., PO Box 269.
DURBAN
AA House, 537 Smith St.,
PO Box 242.
EAST LONDON
AA House, 3a Terminus St.,
PO Box 253.
ERMELO
9 Trust Bank Arcade, Joubert St.,
PO Box 642.
FLORIDA
Henshell House, 10 Goldman St.,
PO Box 19.
GEORGE
Millwood Building, Cnr. York &
Victoria Sts., PO Box 130.
GERMISTON
Academy Centre, 181 Meyer St.,
PO Box 484.
KEMPTON PARK
West Street Arcade, 37 West St.,
PO Box 178.
KIMBERLEY
3 Stockdale St., PO Box 397.
KLERKSDORP
Clarasan Chambers, Cnr. Boom &
Emily Hobhouse Sts., PO Box 821.
KROONSTAD
17 Fairweather Heights, 25 Brand
St., PO Box 92.
KRUGERSDORP
3 President Building, Monument
St., PO Box 537.
LADYSMITH
174 Murchison St., PO Box 17.
NELSPRUIT
56 Brown St., PO Box 186.
NEWCASTLE
104 Old Mutual Centre,
Cnr. Scott & Voortrekker Sts.,
PO Box 2258.
NYLSTROOM
Rentmeester Building, Arcade,
88 Potgieter St., PO Box 258.
PAARL
Arcade, Backmin Centre, 39 Lady
Grey St., PO Box 382.
PIETERMARITZBURG
NAU Building, Cnr. Buchanan &
Carbineer Sts., PO Box 88.
PIETERSBURG
Talmot Building, Schoeman St.,
PO Box 7.
PORT ELIZABETH
AA House, 2 Rink St., PO Box 19.
PORT SHEPSTONE
35A Wooley St., PO Box 172.
POTCHEFSTROOM
Johan Dreyer Building, Cnr. Kerk
& Potgieter Sts., PO Box 397.
PRETORIA
AA House, 395 Schoeman St.,
PO Box 477.
QUEENSTOWN
6 Robinson Rd., PO Box 109.
RANDBURG
79 Crossroads Shopping Centre,

Hendrik Verwoerd Drive,
Private Bag X 3030.
RUSTENBURG
146 Smit St., PO Box 1088.
SASOLBURG
102 Munchner Haus, Civic Centre,
PO Box 639.
SKUKUZA
Skukuza Camp, Kruger National
Park, PO Box 13.
SPRINGS
Wima Court (Ground Floor)
Cnr. Fourth St. & Fifth Ave.,
PO Box 940.
STELLENBOSCH
Standard Bank Building, Bird St.,
PO Box 369.
UITENHAGE
AA Mutual Centre, Rich St.,
PO Box 44.
UPINGTON
Joe Kowen Building, 46 Scott St.,
PO Box 83.
VANDERBIJLPARK
UBS Building, Eric Louw St.,
PO Box 480.
VEREENIGING: 1a Leslie St.,
PO Box 833.
WELKOM
AA House, 327 Stateway,
PO Box 741.
WINDHOEK
Carl List Haus (Ground Floor),
Cnr. Kaiser & Peter Muller Sts.,
PO Box 61.
WITBANK
Westra Building, Cnr. Haig and
Paul Kruger Sts., PO Box 339.
WORCESTER
10 Quenets Arcade, High St., PO
Box 135.

SPAIN
**Real Automovil Club de
España**
10 General Sanjurjo, Madrid – 3.
Tel No. 447. 32. 00
An assistance service introduced
by the Central Traffic Department
is in operation covering a wide area
and will ultimately be extended to
all roads. An S.O.S. telephone network has been set up and motorists
in need of help should ask the
telephone operator for 'auxilio en
carretera'. This service also includes
an ambulance network with special
vehicles connected by radio to
hospitals participating in the
scheme. Where an S.O.S. telephone
is not available, assistance should
be sought from the nearest Guardia
Civil Station.
RACE offers touring information
but does not issue touring publications such as maps and guides.

SRI LANKA (CEYLON)
Ceylon Motor Sports Club
4 Hunupitiya Rd., Colombo 2.
PO Box 196 – Columbo.
Tel No. 26558
**Automobile Association of
Ceylon**
40 Sir M.M.M. Mawatha,
Colombo 3. PO Box 338.
Tel No. 21 528   21 529   28 979

SWEDEN
**Kungl. Automobil Klubben
(Automobile Club Royale de
Suède)**
Södra Blasieholmshamnen 6, Fack,
S-103 20 Stockholm 16.
Tel No. 08/23-88-00
Information on most aspects of

touring are given by KAK and it
does offer touring assistance mainly
through travel agents. Similarly it
will make hotel reservations and
book rail, plane and boat tickets.
For tourists there are maps of
Sweden, motel guides available free
of charge, and KAK road atlas for
which there is a fee. Members can
obtain legal assistance, but KAK
does not provide a road rescue
service.
**Svenska Bilsportförbundet
(Fédération Suèdoise du Sport
Automobile)**
Storforsplan 44-Box 4 – 123
21 Farsta.
Tel No. 08-930500
Motormännens Riksförbund
Sturegatan 32, S-Stockholm
Fack, 102 40 Stockholm.
Tel No. 6705 80
Branch offices are at :
ESKILSTUNA
Kungsgatan 48–50.
Tel No. (016) 13 70 90, PO Box
524, 63107
GÖTEBORG
Södra vägen 3.
Tel No. (031) 1771 30, Box
53197, 400 15
HELSINGBORG
Stortorget 16.
Tel No. (042) 110255, Box 1374,
25102
JÖNKÖPING
Ostra Storgatan 55.
Tel No. (036) 16 02 60, Box 2115
55 002
LULEÅ
Stationsgatan 26.
Tel No. (0920) 203 00, Box
107,951 22
MALMÖ
Tullhuset, Skeppsbron 2.
Tel No. (040) 380 15. AP Box 17,
201 20
NORRKÖPING
Bräddgatan 15.
Tel No. (001) 12 95 35, Box 664,
60105
ÖREBRO
Kungsgatan 23.
Tel No. (019) 13 06 50, Box 483,
70106
ÖSTERSUND
Prästgatan 25.
Tel No. (063) 12 75 45, Box 621,
83101
SKÖVDE
Storgatan 26.
Tel No. (0500) 180 60, Box 1
54101
SUNDSVALL
Nybrogatan 24.
Tel No. (060) 15 44 15. Box 304,
85105
UPPSALA
Dragarbrunnsgatan 24.
Tel No. (018) 13 76 70, Box 337,
75105
VÄSTERÅS
Munkgatan 9–11.
Tel No. (021) 18 03 50, AP –
Munkgatan 9–11 722 12 Västerås
Swedish Touring Club
Stureplan 2, S. Stockholm.
AP Fack, 103 80 Stockholm.
Tel No. 08/22 7200

SWITZERLAND
Automobile Club de Suisse
2 Laupenstrasse, 3001 Berne.
Tel No. 25 08 44
The Club has seven categories of
membership, active, honorary,

juniors, veterans, on leave, ladies,
and guests, and the fees vary accordingly. Information on all aspects of
travel, at home and abroad, are
available, and members can make
use of a comprehensive touring
assistance service. Maps of Switzerland and guides listing recommended hotels, restaurants, and
garages, both at home and overseas,
can be obtained. Insurance can be
arranged to cover accidents, legal
protection and luggage, and a special
policy is available for legal protection abroad. The Club operates a
legal assistance service and through
the Touring Club de Suisse offers
a rescue service covering the whole
country.
Touring Club de Suisse
9 rue Pierre-Fatio, CH-1211
Geneva 3.
Tel No. 35 76 11

SYRIA
Automobile Club de Syrie
Youssef El-Azme Square,
Damascus, BP 3364.
Tel No. 220277
Touring Club de Syrie
rue Baron, Imm. Jésuites, Aleppo,
BP 28.
Tel No. 15210 – 45 847

THAILAND
**The Royal Automobile
Association of Thailand**
1174 Paholyothin Rd., Bangkok 9.
Tel No. 5790430 5790431

**TRINIDAD AND TOBAGO
(West Indies)**
**Trinidad and Tobago
Automobile Association**
56 Frederick St., Port of Spain.
Tel No. 62-34445

TUNISIA
**National Automobile Club
de Tunisie**
29 Avenue Habib Bourguiba –
Tunis.
Tel No. 241.176 – 243, 921
Touring Club de Tunisie
15 rue d'Allemagne, Tunis.
Tel No. 24 31 82 24   31 14

TURKEY
**Türkiye Turing ve Otomobil
Kurumu**
364 Sisli Meydani, Istanbul.
Tel No. 46-70-90 (4 lines)
A rescue service operates every day
from 9 am to 5 pm, except Saturday
afternoons and Sundays, within a
radius of 150 km around Istanbul.
It works on a patrol basis and can be
obtained by phoning the Club's
headquarters in the capital, or the
information bureau at entry to the
City. The service is free to members
if the repair can be completed
within 15 minutes, otherwise a
charge is made – normally half the
normal garage tarriff. This also
applies to visitors who are members
of foreign motoring organizations.
The Club's office at entry to
Istanbul is open everyday from
mid-April to mid-October from
9 am to 7 pm (Tel No. Z: 21. 65.88).
Under the Club's touring services,
hotels and restaurants are recommended and a list of these are in the
guide 'Istanbul and Ankara, a Hand-
book for tourists'.

UNITED ARAB EMIRATES
Automobile and Touring Club for United Arab Emirates
PO Box 1 183, Sharjah U.A.E.
Tel No. 23183

UNITED KINGDOM
The Royal Automobile Club
Pall Mall, London, SW1Y 5HW.
Tel. No. 01-839 7050
Touring Services: Tel No. 01-686 2525
Motor Sport: Tel No. 01-235 8601
Auto-Cycle Union: Tel No. 01-235 7636
Speedway Control Board: Tel No. 01-235-8601
Britain's senior motoring organization, the RAC offers a comprehensive road rescue service operating on a 24-hour basis (closes Christmas Day only) and covers the whole of England, Scotland, Wales and Northern Ireland. For an additional fee members can use the Club's Recovery Service which ensures they get home, or to their destination, whichever they choose, in the event of a breakdown or accident. Membership also covers husband or wife of member for no extra charge.

The Club also offers a comprehensive touring service for home and abroad, and will make all the necessary bookings. It has its own legal department and in certain cases will represent a member in court free of charge. Finance facilities for buying a car can also be arranged and the Club's insurance department can provide cover with a wide range of policies.

The RAC is also the controlling body for motor sport in Britain and organizes the round Britain international rally, the British Grand Prix and the annual London to Brighton Run for veteran cars.
Area offices are:
BELFAST
65 Chichester St.
Tel No. 33944
BIRMINGHAM
93–95 Hagley Rd.
Tel. No. 021-455 8451
BOURNEMOUTH
9 Poole Rd.
Tel No. 765328
BRISTOL
4–6 Whiteladies Rd.
Tel No. 32201
CARDIFF
202 Newport Rd.
Tel No. 35544
CROYDON
PO Box 8, RAC House, Lansdowne Rd.
Tel. 01-681 3611
EDINBURGH
17 Rutland Square.
Tel. No. 031-229 3555
GLASGOW
242 West George St.
Tel. 041-248 4444
LEEDS
34 Regent St.
Tel. No. 448556
LIVERPOOL
Queen's Building, James St.
Tel. No. 051-227 3421
MANCHESTER
135 Dickenson Rd.
Tel. 061-225 9700
NEWCASTLE UPON TYNE
2 Granville Rd.
Tel No. 814271

NORWICH
Norvic House, Chapel Field Rd.
Tel No. 28255
NOTTINGHAM
21 Gregory Boulevard.
Tel No. Nottingham 623331
OXFORD
226 Banbury Rd.
Tel No. 53333
PLYMOUTH
RAC House, 15–17 Union St.
Tel No. 69301
WATFORD
130 St Albans Rd.
Tel No. 33555

The Automobile Association
Fanum House, Basing View, Basingstoke, Hants.
Tel No. Basingstoke 20123
Specially trained patrols operate throughout the country and are equipped to carry out minor roadside repairs. They cover an area under radio control and members needing assistance can telephone for aid. Assistance is given free of charge on production of membership card. In addition to the normal breakdown service, the AA also operates a Relay Service to a member's home or destination. The association's technical service includes garage and vehicle inspections, and there is a full touring service for members at home and travelling abroad. The AA bookshops display a large selection of maps, touring guides, and other publications covering a variety of subjects. Free legal representation is provided and a wide range of insurance services can be obtained. Members can also take advantage of a personal loan scheme.
Regional offices:
SOUTH-EAST REGION
Fanum House, 7 High St., Teddington, Middlesex TW11 8EQ.
Tel No. 01-977 3200
MIDLANDS REGION
Fanum House, Dogkennel Lane, Halesowen, W. Midlands B63 3BT.
Tel No. 021-550 4721
NORTH REGION
Fanum House, Station Rd., Cheadle Hulme, Cheadle, Cheshire, SK8 7BS.
Tel No. 061-485 6188
WEST AND WALES REGION
Fanum House, Park Row, Bristol, BS1 5LY.
Tel No. Bristol 297272
SCOTLAND AND NORTHERN IRELAND REGION
Fanum House, Erskine Harbour, Erskine, Renfrewshire, PA8 6AT.
Tel No. 041-812 0144

Royal Scottish Automobile Club
Blythswood Square, Glasgow.
Tel. 041-221 3850

UNITED STATES OF AMERICA
American Automobile Association (AAA)
8111 Gatehouse Rd., Falls Church, Va 22042.
Tel No. 703: 222-6000
Over 200 clubs are affiliated to the AAA and membership is interlocking and reciprocal. Motorists can join their home clubs at any AAA office, and membership can be

transferred from one club to another at no cost, although the original club is billed for emergency road service until the current membership ends. Exception to this rule is if the member transfers within 30 days of joining the association. Cost of membership varies not only in the annual subscriptions and entrance fees, but also according to one or two car families, and the number of drivers covered by the membership. General touring information is available at all the clubs but not all of them offer a world wide travel service.
Clubs affiliated are:
ALABAMA
Alabama Motorists Association, 2305 Fifth Ave., Birmingham.
Tel No. 205: 323-4491
ARIZONA
Arizona Automobile Association, 748 E. McDowell Rd., Phoenix, Box 5235, Zip No. 85010.
Tel No. 602: 252-7751
ARKANSAS
Arkansas Auto. Club, 201 Chester St., Little Rock, Box 3797, Zip No. 72203.
Tel No. 501: 376-3016
CALIFORNIA
Auto. Club of S. California, 2601 S. Figueroa St., Los Angeles, Terminal Annex, Box 2890.
Tel No. 213: 746-3111
California State Auto. Assn., 150 Van Ness Ave., San Francisco, Box 1860.
Tel No. 415: 565-2012
CANAL ZONE
Panama and Canal Zone Auto. Club,
5275 Morrison St., Diablo Heights, Box 5004, Balboa.
Tel No. 52-6102
COLORADO
Rocky Mountain Motorists, 4100 E. Arkansas Ave., Denver.
Tel No. 303: 756-8811
CONNECTICUT
Connecticut Motor Club, 2276 Whitney Ave., Hamden.
Tel No. 203: 288-7441
Auto. Club of Hartford, 815 Farmington Ave., West Hartford.
Tel No. 203: 236-2511
DELAWARE
Delaware Motor Club, 911 Tatnall St., Wilmington.
Tel No. 302: 655-7511
COLUMBIA
Dist. of Col. Div. AAA, 8111 Gatehouse Rd., Falls Church, District of Columbia.
Tel No. 703: AAA-6666
FLORIDA
East Florida Division, AAA 4300 Biscayne Blvd., Miami.
Tel No. 305: 573-5611
St. Petersburg Motor Club, 1211 1st Ave., Box 13,368, Zip No. 33733.
Tel No. 813: 895-1611
Peninsula Motor Club, 1515 No. Westshore Blvd., Tampa, Box 22087.
Tel No. 813: 872-7711
GEORGIA
Georgia Motor Club, 1100 Spring St., N.W., Atlanta.
Tel No. 404: 875-7171
Savannah Motor Club, 12 Bishops Court, Trustees' Garden, Box 9512.

Tel No. 912: 234-2516
HAWAII
Auto Club of Hawaii, Outrigger East Hotel, 150 Kaiulani Ave., Honolulu.
Tel No. 808: 923-7345
IDAHO
Idaho State Auto. Assn., 414 Main St., Boise, Box 917.
Tel No. 208: 342-9391
ILLINOIS
Chicago Motor Club, 66 E. So. Water St., Chicago.
Tel No. 312 Franklin 2-1818
INDIANA
Auto. Club of Southern Indiana, Evansville.
Tel. No. 812: 425-2288
Hoosier Motor Club, 40 W. 40th St., Indianapolis.
Tel No. 317: 923-3311
IOWA
Motor Club of Iowa, 1049 State St., Bettendorf, Box 4290, Davenport.
Tel No. 319: 355-5331
Dubuque Auto. Club, 1497 Central Ave., Dubuque, Box 416.
Tel No. 319: 582-7219
Sioux City Auto. Club, 1315 Zenith Drive.
Tel No. 712: 252-4261
KANSAS
Auto. Club of Kansas 4020 W. 6th St., Topeka, Box 1067, Zip No. 66601.
Tel. No. 913 Crestwood 2-6360
KENTUCKY
Blue Grass Auto. Club, 155 Walnut St., Lexington, Box 1581, Zip 40501.
Tel No. 606: 254-7731
Louisville Auto. Club, 435 E. Broadway, Box 1113.
Tel No. 502: 582-3311
LOUISIANA
Central Gulf Div., AAA, 3445 No. Causeway Blvd., Metairie, Box 7345.
Tel No. 504: 837-1080
MAINE
Maine Auto. Assn., AAA Bldg., Marginal Way, Portland, Box 3544.
Tel No. 207: 774-6377
MARYLAND
Auto. Club of Maryland, 1401 Mt. Royal Ave., Baltimore.
Tel No. 301: 462-4000
MASSACHUSETTS
Massachusetts Division, AAA, 1280 Boylston St., Chestnut Hill.
Tel No. 617: 738-6900
Tri-County Auto. Club, 1515 Northampton St., Holyoke, Box 1099.
Tel No. 413: 539-9881
Auto. Club of Merrimack Valley, 155 Parker St., Lawrence, Box 39.
Tel No. 617: 686-9541
Auto. Club of Berkshire County, 196 South St., Pittsfield, Box 1018.
Tel No. 413: 445-5635
Auto. Club of Springfield, 110 Ft. Pleasant Ave., Springfield, Box 5.
Tel No. 413: 785-1381
Bancroft Auto. Club, 290 Park Ave., Worcester.
Tel No. 617: 791-5531
MICHIGAN
Auto. Club of Michigan, Auto Club Drive, Dearborn.
Tel No. 313: 336-1234

389

Motoring Organizations

MINNESOTA
Minnesota State Auto. Assn.,
7 Travelers Trail, Burnsville,
Zip No. 55337.
Tel No. 612: 890-2500
Austin Auto. Club,
500 E. Oakland Ave., Austin.
Tel No. 507: 437-4514
Duluth Auto. Club,
738 E. Superior St., Duluth.
Tel No. 218: 728-4227
Auto. Club of Minneapolis,
LaSalle at 13th St., Minneapolis.
Tel No. 612: 332-0255
Auto. Club of St. Paul,
170 E. Seventh St., S.L. St Paul.
Tel No. 612: 222-5041

MISSISSIPPI
Mississippi Region of Central Gulf
Division, AAA,
199 Hwy. 80W, Jackson, Box
1506, Zip 39205.
Tel No. 601: 352-8841

MISSOURI
The Automobile Club,
1301 Village Drive, St. Joseph.
Tel No. 816: 233-1377
Auto. Club of Missouri,
3917 Lindell Blvd., St. Louis.
Tel No. 314: 533-2233

MONTANA
Montana Auto. Assn.,
607 N. Lamborn St., Helena,
Box 1703.
Tel No. 406: 442-5920

NEBRASKA
Cornhusker Motor Club,
5011 Capitol Ave., Omaha.
Tel No. 402: 558-1010

NEVADA
California State Auto. Assn.,
Nevada Division, 601 W. First St.,
Reno, Box 2497, Zip No. 89505.
Tel No. 702: 322-9401

NEW HAMPSHIRE
New Hampshire Division, AAA,
70 Queen City Ave., Manchester,
Box 179, Zip No. 03105.
Tel No. 603: 669-0101

NEW JERSEY
Auto. Club of Southern New
Jersey,
201 Kings Highway, Cherry Hill.
Tel No. 609: 428-9000
New Jersey Auto Club,
1 Hanover Rd., Florham Park.
Tel No. 201: 377-7200
Shore Motor Club of South Jersey,
901 Tilton Rd., Northfield.
Tel No. 609: 646-6000
North Jersey Auto. Club,
419 Broadway, Paterson.
Tel. No. 201: 279-2500
West Jersey Motor Club,
Memorial Pkwy at Firth St.,
Phillipsburg, Box 110.
Tel No. 201: 859-2177
Auto. Club of Central New Jersey,
321 W. State St., Trenton, Box
2001.
Tel No. 609: 396-2551

NEW MEXICO
New Mexico Division, AAA,
2201 San Pedro, N.E.,
Albuquerque, Box 8736.
Tel No. 505: 265-7611

NEW YORK
New York State Auto. Assn.,
828 Washington Ave., Albany.
Tel No. 518: 482-6787
Albany Auto. Club,
828 Washington Ave., Albany.
Tel No. 518: 482-3321
Cayuga County Auto. Club,
7 Court St., Auburn, Box 416.
Tel No. 315: 253-8661

Southern New York Auto. Club,
21 Washington St., Binghamton,
Box 987, Zip No. 13902.
Tel No. 607: RAymond 2-7255
Auto. Club of Western New York,
976 Delaware Ave., Buffalo, Box
68, Zip No. 14240.
Tel No. 716: 882-5400
Chautauqua County Auto. Club,
19 Lake Shore, Dunkirk, Box 251.
Tel No. 716: 366-4850
Finger Lakes Auto. Club,
328 No. Meadow St., Ithaca.
Tel No. 607: 273-6727
Jamestown Auto. Club,
111 W. 5th St., Jamestown, Box
279.
Tel No. 716: 488-1981
Auto. Club of Fulton County,
338 No. Comrie Ave., Johnstown.
Tel No. 518: 762-4619
Niagara-Orleans Auto Club,
7135 Rochester Rd., Lockport.
Tel No. 716: 434-2865
Auto. Club of New York,
28 E. 78th St., New York.
Tel No. 212: 586-1166
Tri County Motor Club,
5 W. Main St., Norwich.
Tel No. 607: 334-9269
St. Lawrence County Auto. Club,
201 State St., Ogdensburg.
Tel No. 315: 393-4280
Cattaraugus-Allegany Auto Club,
East State Rd., Olean, Box 387.
Tel No. 716: 372-3511
Auto. Club of Rochester,
777 Clinton Ave., So. Rochester.
Tel No. 716: 461-4660
Schenectady Auto. Club,
112 Railroad St., Schenectady.
Tel No. 518: 393-3656
Seneca Auto. Club,
73 Fall St., Seneca Falls, Box 419.
Tel No. 315: 568-8742
Sherrill Auto. Club,
Rt. 5 and Sherrill Rd., Sherrill.
Tel. No. 315: 363-4580
Auto. Club of Syracuse,
514 W. Onondaga St., Syracuse.
Tel. No. 315: 478-4163
Troy Auto. Club,
206 Broadway, Troy.
Tel No. 518: 272-3650
Auto. Club of Utica and Central
N.Y.,
409 Court St., Utica.
Tel No. 315: 797-5000

NORTH CAROLINA
Carolina Motor Club,
701 S. Tryon St., Charlotte, Box
60, Zip No. 28201.
Tel No. 704: 376-7511
Winston-Salem Auto. Club,
611 Coliseum Drive, Winston-
Salem.
Tel No. 919: 725-1921

NORTH DAKOTA
North Dakota Auto. Club,
Jct. I–29 & I–94, Fargo, Box 3147.
Tel No. 701: 282-6222

OHIO
Ohio AAA Assn.,
6155 Huntley Rd., Columbus.
Tel No. 614: 846-9400
Akron Auto. Club,
111 W. Center St., Akron.
Tel No. 216: 762-0631
Alliance Auto. Club,
2322 S. Union Ave., Alliance.
Tel No. 216: 823-9820
Ashland County Auto. Club,
502 Claremont Ave., Ashland.
Tel No. 419: 322-1171
Ashtabula Auto. Club,
842 Center St., Ashtabula.

Tel No. 216: 997-5586
Barberton Auto. Club,
139 E. Tuscarawas Ave.,
Barberton.
Tel No. 216: 753-7779
Logan County Auto. Club,
141 E. Columbus Ave.,
Bellefontaine.
Tel No. 513: 592-1836
Brewster Auto. Club,
221 S. Wabash Ave., Brewster.
Tel No. 216: 767-4012
Belmont County Auto. Club,
983 National Rd., Bridgeport.
Tel No. 614: 635-2050
Crawford County Auto. Club,
314 S. Sandusky Ave., Bucyrus.
Tel No. 419: 562-3891
Guernsey County Auto. Club,
834 Wheeling Ave., Cambridge.
Tel No. 614: 432-7343
Canton Auto. Club,
2722 Fulton Drive, N.W., Canton,
Box 8499, Zip No. 44711.
Tel No. 216: 455-6761
Mercer County Auto. Club,
105 N. Walnut St., Celina.
Tel No. 419: 586-2460
Ross-Highland Auto. Club,
83 W. Main St., Chillicothe,
Box 510.
Tel No. 614: 774-2424
Cincinnati Auto. Club,
Central Parkway at Race St.,
Cincinnati.
Tel No. 513: 762-3100
Cleveland Auto. Club,
6000 So. Marginal Rd., Cleveland.
Tel No. 216: 579-6000
Columbus Auto. Club,
15 E. Main St., Columbus.
Tel No. 614: 221-6641
Conneaut Auto. Club,
191 Main St., Conneaut.
Tel No. 216: 593-3800
Coschocton County Motor Club,
Div. Ohio AAA Assn.,
416 Main St., Coshocton.
Tel No. 614: 622-2910
Crestline Auto. Club,
224 New Seltzer St., Crestline.
Tel No. 419: 683-3053
Dayton Auto. Club,
825 S. Ludlow St., Dayton.
Tel No. 513: 222-2801
Columbiana County Motor Club,
213 E. Fourth St., East Liverpool.
Tel No. 216: 385-2020
Findlay Auto. Club,
124 E. Main Cross St., Findlay.
Tel No. 419: 422-4961
Fostoria Auto. Club,
105 Perry St., Fostoria, Box 925.
Tel No. 419: 435-3125
Sandusky County Auto. Club,
624 W. State St., Fremont, Box 69.
Tel No. 419: 332-9949
Galion Auto. Club,
212 Harding Way West, Galion.
Tel No. 419: 468-3571
Darke County Auto. Club,
302 S. Broadway, Greenville,
Box 38.
Tel No. 513: 548-2230
Butler County Auto. Club,
829 High St., Hamilton, Box 414,
Zip No. 45012.
Tel No. 513: 863-3200
Hardin County Auto. Club,
220 E. Franklin St., Kenton.
Tel No. 419: 673-4249
Fairfield County Auto. Club,
714 N. Memorial Drive, Lancaster.
Tel No. 614: 653-0912
Lima Auto. Club,
635 W. Spring St., Lima,

Box 1192.
Tel No. 419: 228-1022
Lodi Auto. Club,
645 Wooster St., Lodi.
Tel No. 216: 948-1449
Richland County Auto. Club,
34 Sturges Ave., Mansfield, Box
273.
Tel No. 419: 522-0141
Washington County Auto. Club,
308 Front St., Marietta, Box 755.
Tel No. 614: 374-6821
Marion Auto. Club,
171 E. Center St., Marion, Box
583.
Tel No. 614: 382-7012
Massillon Auto. Club,
1972 Wales Rd., N.E. Massillon.
Tel No. 216: 833-1084
Knox County Auto. Club, Div.
Ohio AAA Assn.,
1 Public Square, Mt. Vernon.
Tel No. 614: 397-2091
Newark Auto. Club, Div. Ohio
AAA Assn.,
130–132 W. Main St., Newark.
Tel No. 614: 345-4018
Tuscarawas County Auto. Club,
1112 4th St., N.W. New Phila-
delphia, Box 605.
Tel No. 216: 343-4481
Huron County Auto. Club,
275 Benedict Ave., Norwalk,
Box 320.
Tel No. 419: 668-1622
Oberlin Auto. Club,
27 E. College St., Oberlin.
Tel No. 216: 774-6971
Miami County Auto. Club,
601 W. High St., Piqua.
Tel No. 513: 773-3753
Auto. Club of Southern Ohio,
710 Waller St., Portsmouth, Box
240.
Tel No. 614: 354-5614
Erie County Auto. Club,
1437 Sycamore Line, Sandusky.
Tel No. 419: 625-5831
Shelby County Motor Club,
122 S. Main, Sidney.
Tel No. 513: 492-3167
Springfield Auto. Club,
Bechtle Ave., & Commerce Rd.,
Springfield, Box 1268, Zip 45504.
Tel. No. 513: 323-8661
Steubenville Auto. Club,
149 North 3rd St., Steubenville,
Box 1407.
Tel No. 614: 283-3307
Tiffin Auto. Club,
59 E. Market St., Tiffin.
Tel No. 419: 447-0551
Toledo Auto. Club,
2271 Ashland Ave., Toledo.
Tel No. 419: 241-4141
Wyandot County Auto. Club,
235 N. Sandusky Ave., Upper
Sandusky.
Tel No. 419: 294-2315
Champaign County Auto. Club,
106 Scioto St., Urbana.
Tel No. 513: 653-3633
Wadsworth Auto. Club,
133 W. Boyer St., Wadsworth.
Tel No. 216: 335-1566
Warren Auto. Club,
660 N. Park Ave., Warren.
Tel No. 216: 399-7553
Fayette County Auto. Club,
209 E. Market St., Washington
Court House.
Tel No. 614: 335-3950
Wooster Auto. Club,
377 W. Liberty St., Wooster,
Box 777.
Tel No. 216: 264-9899

Greene County Auto. Club,
657 Home Ave., Xenia, Box 'A'.
Tel No. 513: 372-8004
Youngstown Auto. Club,
116 E. Front St., Youngstown.
Tel No. 216: 744-8461
Muskingum Motor Club,
1120 Maple Ave., Zanesville,
Box 2187.
Tel No. 614: 454-1234
OKLAHOMA
Oklahoma Division, AAA,
3525 Northwest 23rd St.,
Oklahoma City, Box 75022.
Tel No. 405: 946-5411
Auto. Club of Oklahoma,
2121 E. 15th St., Tulsa.
Tel No. 918: 936-2121
OREGON
Auto. Club of Oregon,
600 S.W. Market St., Portland.
Tel No. 503: 227-7777
PENNSYLVANIA
Pennsylvania AAA Federation,
600 N. Third St., Harrisburg,
Box 2865.
Tel No. 717: 238-7192
Lehigh Valley Motor Club,
1020 Hamilton St., Allentown,
Box 1910.
Tel No. 215: 434-5141
Blair County Motor Club,
1101 13th Ave., Box 271, Altoona.
Tel No. 814: 946-1277
Bedford County Motor Club,
144 E. Pitt St., Bedford, Box 678.
Tel No. 814: 623-5196
McKean County Motor Club,
93 Congress St., Bradford, Box
371.
Tel No. 814: 368-3113
Auto. Club of Butler County,
422 N. Main St., Butler, Box 1948.
Tel No. 412: 287-2713
South Penn Motor Club,
230 Lincoln Way East, Chambersburg, Box 340.
Tel No. 717: 264-4191
Clearfield County Motor Club,
8 E. Market St., Clearfield, Box
589.
Tel No. 814: 765-4971
Potter County Motor Club,
209 N. Main St., Coudersport,
Box 509.
Tel No. 814: 274-8470
Northampton County Motor Club,
Hecktown & Country Club Rds.,
Easton.
Tel No. 215: 258-2371
Erie County Motor Club,
420 W. 6th St., Erie.
Tel No. 814: 454-0123
Westmoreland County Motor Club,
Otterman & Maple, Greensburg.
Tel No. 412: 834-8300
Mercer County Motor Club,
311 Main St., Greenville, Box 614.
Tel No. 412: 588-4300
AAA Central Penn Auto. Club,
2023 Market St., Harrisburg, Box
3261, Zip No. 17105.
Tel No. 717: 236-4021
Anthracite Motor Club,
9 No. Church St., Hazleton.
Tel No. 717: 454-6658
Huntingdon County Motor Club,
212–4th St., Huntingdon, Box 397.
Tel No. 814: 643-1030
Auto. Club of Indiana Co.,
714 Church St., Indiana.
Tel No. 412: 349-4193
Johnstown Motor Club,
437 Vine St., Johnstown, Box 186.
Tel No. 814: 535-8585
Valley Auto. Club,

303 Market St., Kingston, Box B.
Tel No. 717: 824-2444
Lancaster Auto. Club,
34 N. Prince St., Lancaster,
Box 1507.
Tel No. 717: 397-6135
Lewistown Motor Club,
131 W. Market St., Lewistown.
Tel No. 717: 248-9601
Nittany Motor Club,
7 W. Church St., Lock Haven,
Box 706.
Tel No. 717: 748-2405
McKeesport Auto. Club,
622 Market St., McKeesport.
Tel No. 412: 673-9791
Allegheny Automobile Association,
830 Park Avenue, Meadville,
Box 830.
Tel No. 814: 724-2247
Keystone Auto. Club,
2040 Market St., Philadelphia.
Tel No. 215: 864-5000
Knights of Columbus Auto. Club,
157 N. 15th St., Philadelphia.
Tel No. 215: LOcust 3-9424
West Penn Motor Club,
202 Penn Circle West, Pittsburgh.
Tel No. 412: 362-3300
Pottstown Auto. Club,
135 High St., Pottstown.
Tel No. 215: 323-6300
Schuylkill County Motor Club,
340 S. Centre St., Pottsville.
Tel No. 717: 622-4991
Beaver County Motor Club,
300 Adams St., Rochester.
Tel No. 412: 775-8000
Elk-Cameron Motor Club,
50 So. St. Marys St., St. Marys,
Box 226.
Tel No. 814: 834-7838
Motor Club of N.E. Penn.,
1035 N. Washington Ave.,
Scranton.
Tel No. 717: 344-9661
N. Central Motor Club,
One East 6th Ave., South
Williamsport, Box 418.
Tel No. 717: 323-8431
Susquehanna Valley Auto. Club,
17 N. Fourth St., Sunbury, Box
788.
Tel No. 717: 286-4507
Uniontown Motor Club,
111 W. Main St., Uniontown.
Tel No. 412: 438-8575
Warren County Motor Club,
201 Penna. Ave., Warren, Box 925.
Tel No. 814: 723-6660
Washington County Motor Club,
196 Murtland Ave., Washington,
Box 717.
Tel No. 412: 222-3800
Auto. Club of Chester County,
129 E. Gay St., West Chester.
Tel No. 215: 696-4830
Reading-Berks Auto. Club,
920 Van Reed Rd.,
Wyomissing,
Box 1696.
Tel No. 215: 374-4531
White Rose Motor Club,
118 E. Market St., York, Box
1669.
Tel No. 717: 845-7676
RHODE ISLAND
Auto. Club of Rhode Island,
1035 Reservoir Ave., Cranston.
Tel No. 401: 944-7300
SOUTH CAROLINA
South Carolina Branch of Carolina
Motor Club,
Middleburg Office Mall-Suite,
104 Forest Drive, Columbia.
Tel No. 803: 256-7485

SOUTH DAKOTA
South Dakota Auto. Club,
1300 Industrial Ave., Sioux Falls.
Tel No. 605: 336-3690
TENNESSEE
Chattanooga Auto. Club,
816 Chestnut St., Chattanooga.
Tel No. 615: 265-1034
East Tennessee Auto. Club,
100 W. Fifth Ave., Knoxville,
Box 1107.
Tel No. 615: 637-1910
Mid-South Auto. Club,
1121 Church St., Nashville.
Tel No. 615: 244-8889
TEXAS
Panhandle Plains Auto. Club,
1171 South Polk, Amarillo, Box
2724, Zip No. 79105.
Tel No. 806: 376-5821
Southwest Motor Club,
4425 N. Central Expwy, Dallas.
Tel No. 214: 526-7911
Texas Division, AAA,
3000 Southwest Freeway, Houston,
Box 1986.
Tel No. 713: 524-1851
UTAH
Auto. Club of Utah,
560 E. 5th South, Salt Lake City,
Box 178, Zip No. 84110.
Tel No. 801: 364-5615
VERMONT
Auto. Club of Vermont,
97 State St., Montpelier, Box 458.
Tel No. 802: 223-6373
VIRGINIA
Tidewater Auto. Assn.,
739 Boush St., Norfolk.
Tel No. 804: 622-5634
Auto. Club of Virginia,
2617 W. Broad St., Richmond.
Tel No. 804: 353-6611
WASHINGTON
Auto. Club of Washington,
330–6th Ave., Seattle.
Tel No. 206: 682-0707
Inland Auto. Assn.,
West 1717 Fourth Avenue,
Spokane.
Tel No. 509: 455-3400
WEST VIRGINIA
Bluefield Auto. Club,
622 Commerce St., Bluefield,
Box 90.
Tel No. 304: 327-8187
Southern West Virginia Auto.
Club,
4000 MacCorkle Ave., Charleston.
Tel No. 304: 925-6681
Central West Virginia Auto. Club,
Court St., and Washington Ave.,
Clarksburg, Box 2189.
Tel No. 304: 624-6481
Marion County Motor Club,
315 Fairmont Ave., Fairmont.
Box 672.
Tel No. 304: 363-2600
Huntingdon Auto. Club,
612 Ninth St., Huntingdon,
Box 1638, Zip No. 25717.
Tel No. 304: 523-6423
Northern West Virginia Auto.
Club,
1431 University Ave., Morgantown, Box 988.
Tel No. 304: 292-3395
Parkersburg Auto. Club,
312–7th St., Parkersburg, Box 66.
Tel No. 304: 485-7451
Weirton Auto. Club,
3126 West St., Weirton.
Tel No. 304: 748-1616
Wheeling Auto. Club,
496 National Rd., Wheeling,
Box 1061.

Tel No. 304: 233-1810
WISCONSIN
Wisconsin Division AAA,
433 W. Washington Ave.,
Madison, Box 33, Zip No. 53701.
Tel No. 608: 257-0711
WYOMING
Wyoming Division AAA,
1609 West Lincolnway, Cheyenne,
Box 1228.
Tel No. 307: 634-7769
**American Automobile Touring
Alliance (AATA)**
2040 Market St., Philadelphia,
Pa 19103.
Tel No. 864-5000
Affiliated clubs are:
ALA Auto. & Travel Club,
888 Worcester St., Wellesley,
Massachusetts.
Keystone Automobile Club,
2040 Market St., Philadelphia.
National Automobile Association,
1730 Northeast Expressway,
Atlanta, Georgia.
National Automobile Club,
65 Battery St., San Francisco,
California.
**American Automobile Competition Committee for the
United States, FIA, Inc.**
Suite 302, 1725 K St., N.W.
Washington, D.C. 20006.
Tel No. 202: 833-9133

URUGUAY
Automovil Club del Uruguay
Avenida Agraciada, 1532,
Casilla Correo 387 – Montevideo.
Tel No. 98.58.71 91.78.39
98.47.10 88.4.15
**Centro Automovilista del
Uruguay**
Bulevar Artigas 1773, esq Dante,
Montevideo.
Tel No. 42091/92 412528/29
There are branches in many major
towns.
Touring Club Uruguayo
Ave. Uruguay 2009 al 2015,
Montevideo.
Tel No. 4 48 75 4 61 93 4 78 09

U.S.S.R.
Intourist
16 avenue Marx, Moscow K-9.
Tel No. 292 22 60
There are agencies at more than 30
cities, including Kiev, Leningrad,
Odessa, Tbilisi and Kharkov.
**Federacia Automobilnogo
Sporta S.S.S.R. (Federation
de sport automobile de
l'URSS)**
BP 395 – Moscou D-362.
Tel No. 491-86-61

VENEZUELA
**Touring y Automovil Club
de Venezuela**
Plaza Sur de Altamira – Edif.
Autocomercial Locaux 2 et 4;
Apartado 68102 Altamira,
Caracas.
Tel No. 324 108-09

YUGOSLAVIA
Auto-Moto Savez Jugoslavije
Ruzveltova 18, BP 66, YU – 11000
Belgrade.
Road assistance operates every day
from 5 am to 11 pm in towns, and
from 8 am to 8 pm elsewhere. Many
vehicles used for rescue are equipped
for towing. Assistance can be obtained by phoning 987.

INDEX

ACKNOWLEDGMENTS

The publishers would like to thank the following organizations and individuals for their kind permission to reproduce the photographs in this book:

All-Sport 252 left, 252–253 centre, (Werner Deisenroth) 257 above, (Tony Duffy) 248–249, 258, 259 centre left, above centre and below right, 260 centre left, 260–261 centre, 261 centre, 264–265 above, 264 below, 265 above and below, 266, 267 centre and below; Australian Information Service, London 218–220; The Bettmann Archive 35 below right, 38 below, 39 above left, 98–99 above, 233; Rodney Bond 99 above and below; Brown Brothers 226–227 below, 228 below, 228–229, 231 above, 232 centre; Camera Press Ltd. 103 below, (Julian Calder) 337 below, (Norman Sklartwitz) 337 above; Castrol Ltd. 236–237 (P. Myers); Colorsport 204–205 above, 204 below, 210 below left and below right, 217 below right; Gerry Cranham 255 below right, 259 above left and centre right, 262 below right, 263 above left; Custom Car 270–271, 274–275 above, 274 below, 275 centre, below left and below right, 276 above, centre and below, 278 below, 279 above, 280 centre left, centre right and below, 280–281 above, 282–283, 282 below, 283 centre, below left and below right, 284 above and below, 285 above and below left, 286 centre and below; Daily Telegraph Colour Library 216 centre; Daimler-Benz 14–15 above, 16, 54 above, 88 below; The Detroit Public Library, National Automotive History Collection 35 above, 58–59 centre, 59 right, 226, 226–227 above, 227 below; Diffusion Photos de Presse Internationale 250 left, 251 centre right, 252–253 below, 256 left, 258–259 below, 262 above left, 263 below left; (Studebaker Historic Vehicle Collection), Discovery Hall Museum, South Bend, Indiana 73 above, centre and below, 81 above; Phil Drackett 344 centre, 353 below left, 358 left, 362 above right inset, 364 left, 369 below; Drake Well Museum 98 below left and below right; Robert Estall 98–99 below; Mary Evans Picture Library 10–11 above and centre, 10, 11, 12 above and centre, 167, 169 above and below, 173 below, 179 above, 362 below inset; Fiat 58–59 below, 88 above, 88–89 above, 160–161, 160 below, 161 below; Ford Motor Company Ltd. 34, 35 below left (P. Myers), 148–151, 155–157, 158–159 above, 158 below, 159 below, 199 right and below; General Motors 38 above, 39 above right and below, 78–79, 95 centre, 158 centre, 162; Museum of Transport, Glasgow 30 above; Geoffrey Goddard 47 below, 178, 179 above, 180–181 centre left, 181 centre right, 182 left, 184 above, 187 below centre, 192–193 above and below, 193 above right, 196, 196–197 above, 198, 212–213 below, 242–243, 263 above right, 354, 356 left, 372 below; The Goodyear Tyre & Rubber Co. Ltd. (Bernard Cahier) 243; Jeanne Griffiths 169 centre right, 251 below; Simon G. Griffith 89 left; Angelo Hornak 176 below; The Illustrated London News 74–75 above, 345 right; Indianapolis Motor Speedway 232 below, 234, 234–235 above and below; Japan Information Centre, London 92–93 below; Keystone 70 right, 198–199 above and below, 209 below, 344 left, 346 below left, 348 above, 350–351, 352 below, 358–359, 360 above, 365 above, 367 above, 369 above, 371 left, 372 above; Mark Lawrence endpapers, 96–97, 104–105, 273 above, 276–277 above, 281 below, 287 below; Keith Lee 224–225; Leyland Historic Vehicles Ltd. 79; London Art Technical Drawings Ltd. 29, 204–205 above, 205, 206–207 below, 216 above, 217 above and below left, 246–247 above, 247 below, 251 centre left, 252–253 above left, 253 above right, 254–255 below, 260–261 above, 261 above, 262 above right, 262 centre and below left, 263 below right, 266–267 above and centre, 268–269, 307 below; Alexander Low 232–233; Mansell Collection 357 right; Leo Mason 197 right, 200–201, 208–209, 250 right, 251 above, 257 below, 259 above right; The Monitor Group 106–107 below; Andrew Morland 285 centre right and below right; P. Myers 31 left and right, 40 left and right, 228 above; National Motor Museum 9 centre and right, 20 below right, 22–23 centre, 46 below, 47 above, 48 below, 49, 50 below, 51–52, 54–55 below, 55 right, 58, 59 above, 62 centre and below, 63 above, 66 above and below, 67 above and below, 70 left, 70–71, 72 above, 74 above and below, 75 below, 82–83, 86–87, 90 centre and below, 94–95 above and below, 95 above and below, 106–107 above, 173 above, 202–203 above, 212–213 above, 235 right, 240–241 above and below, 241 above left and above right, 315 below, 347 below, 353 above left and right, 353 below right, 361 right, 365 below, 368 left, 373 right; Phipps Photographic 204 above, 207 above right and below; Photo Researchers, Inc. (Tom Burnside) 164–165; John Player & Sons 256–257; Popperfoto 14 below, 27 above, 62 below, 78 below, 188, 189 above, 189 below centre, 194, 194–195 above, 222, 223 below right, 344–345 above, 346 above left and right, 347 below, 348 below, 349 left, 350 right, 351, 352 right, 355 right, 356–357, 357 centre, 359 above and below inset, 362 above left, 363, 366, 366–367, 370 right; Porsche 7 inset; Cyril Posthumus 10–11 below, 13 below left, 17 centre, 17 below left, centre and right, 19 centre and below, 46–47 above, 50–51 above, 50 centre, 54 below, 54–55 above, 90 above, 91, 166–167 above, 170–171, 172 below right, 174 above and below, 177, 179 centre left and centre right, 181 below, 182–183 above and centre, 183 above and below, 184–186, 187 above, above centre and below, 189 above centre, below left and right, 190–191 above, 190 below, 191 above and below, 192, 193 below, 194–195 below, 195 above right, 202 left, 212, 213 right, 214 above and below, 214–215 above and below, 222–223 below, 230 above, 238 below, 239, 344–345 above, 345 left, 346 above left, 349 right, 355 above left, 361 below, 364–365, 367 below, 371 right; Radio Times Hulton Picture Library 13 above and below right, 15 above left and right, 16–17 above, 19 above, 22 below left, 23, 26, 28–29 below, 172 below left, 180–181 above, 223 above left and right, 230–231 above and below, 345 right, 350 left, 352 centre, 354–355 below, 360 below right, 370 left, 373 right; Red Saunders/Sunday Times, London 342–343; Renault Ltd. 28–29 above; Rex Features Ltd. 246, 247 below, 338, (M. Madow) 339 below; Peter Roberts 8, 9 left, 15 below, 18, 20 above, 20 below left, 21, 24–25, 27 below, 30 below, 33 below, 36–37, 44–45, 60–61, 68, 69, 76–77, 84, 85, 92–93 above, 154 below, 158 above; Royal Automobile Club 22 above, 173 centre, (P. Myers) Paintings by F. G. Crosby 168–169, 172–173 above, 176–177, 180; Roger Scruton 255; Shell 368 right; Jasper Spencer-Smith 65 below, 72 below, 80 above, 298–299 above, 304–305, 308–309, 316 below, 320 left, 323 above and below, 333 above; Peter Stubberfield 326 below; Syndication International Ltd. 261 below; Colin Taylor 216 below; Derek Tye Collection 374–383; United Press International 230 below, 238–239, 241 below, 244–245; G. Usher 93 right; Mireille Vautier (De Nanxe) 103 above; Roger-Viollet 12 below, 42 above, 43 below, 166 below, 174–175, (Boyer) 42 below, (Harlingue) 43 above; Volvo Concessionaires Ltd. 161 above, 162–163 above and below, 163 above and below; Nicky Wright 1, 2–3, 4–5, 6–7, 32–33 above, 32 below, 33 above, 41 above and below, 48–49 above, 53, 56, 57 above and below, 64, 64–65 above and centre, 65 right, 240–241 above and below, 241 above left and above right, 275 above, 277 below, 278–279 above, 279 below, 280 above, 283 above, 286 above, 286–287 above, 290–298, 299–303, 304 above and below, 306–307, 307 above and centre, 308–314, 315 above left and above right, 316 above, 316–317, 318–319, 320–321, 321 centre and below, 322, 322–323, 324, 325 above, 324–325, 326 above, 327–329, 330 above, 331–332, 333 below; Zefa (F. Damm) 339 above left and above right, 341 above, (K. Goebel) 89 right, (Gerolf Kalt) 196–197 below, 206–207 above, (W. L. Hamilton) 273 below, (Orion Press) 92, 272–273, (J. Pfaff) 334–335, 341 above, (J. Pugh) 273 centre, (A. Thill) 254–255 above, (Til) 197 below.

Illustration by Terry Collins and Chris Baker

Cars by kind permission of:

Anca Motors Ltd.; Auburn-Cord-Duesenburg Museum; J. Austin; R. Barnard; G. Batt; C. Bendorn; L. Botton; Briggs Cunningham Auto Museum/G. Brown; M. Butler; P. Diamond; E. Dridge; I. Easedale; B. Ennals; H. Fitterling; B. Friedman; V. Gabb; L. B. Goldsmith; R. Goode; J. Gordon; A. Gortway; B. Haig; C. W. P. Hampton; B. R. Hearn; F. Hobbs; B. Hodges (Yesterday's Wheels); R. Hutchings; A. E. K. Kabslake; P. Kunkel; S. Langton; D. Leach; R. Middleton; S. F. Mitchell; R. Mudd; W. Oates; Onslow Motors; H. Posner; Rolls Royce Motors Ltd; J. Savage; G. Scott; R. A. Scott; E. D. Sharman; R. Staadt; Stroud Motors; B. Terry; W. Vaux Yeovil; A. Warner; G. Weightman; G. Wilde.